REGULATORY FINANCE:

UTILITIES' COST OF CAPITAL

Roger A. Morin, PhD

in collaboration with
Lisa Todd Hillman

1994
PUBLIC UTILITIES REPORTS, INC.
Arlington, Virginia

TABLE OF CONTENTS

Page

LIST OF TABLES

LIST OF FIGURES

PREFACE

The purpose of this book is to provide a complete, accurate, and easily understandable explanation of the contribution of financial theory toward solving the problem of estimating a company's cost of capital, particularly that of a regulated utility. Not only is modern financial theory transforming traditional approaches to cost of capital and capital structure determination, but a profound transformation is occurring within the utility industry itself. This book explains the evolution, meaning, and practical significance of modern financial theory for utility regulation.

The occasionally formidable mathematics are replaced by verbal intuitive explanations and easily understood diagrams and practical applications. Technical definitions and equations are kept to a minimum. Derivations and equations are relegated to appendices and footnotes whenever possible for the convenience of readers interested in such details. For the average reader, however, technical matters are reduced to a minimum, and no special knowledge or educational level is assumed. A rudimentary knowledge of basic accounting, algebra, and time value of money concepts is all that is necessary. Additional familiarity with statistics and economics and a first course in finance are helpful in certain portions of the book, although not requisite. The result is an accurate, yet easily understood presentation of the subject matter.

The book is directed at anyone professionally involved in corporate finance, cost of capital, and capital structure issues, particularly in the case of regulated utilities. The book is targeted at two broad groups of people - those who are involved in the regulatory process and those who counsel and provide services to regulatory commissions and to regulated utilities. The knowledge of regulatory finance theory gained here should be helpful to public service commission staffs, utility attorneys, investors, accountants, utility economists, cost of capital witnesses, utility financial analysts, academicians interested in rate of return regulation, and corporate staffs involved in Treasury, revenue requirements, and regulatory functions.

Although the content of this book is addressed primarily to the specific regulatory finance concerns of public utilities, it has a broader interest. The alternative theories and models of security valuation and the cost of capital are analyzed at a level sufficiently broad so as to be valid for all industries. The book is intended to give cost of capital professionals in the unregulated arena as well as in the regulated arena a better understanding of financial theory. Moreover, the knowledge gained here should prove helpful to several professional groups outside the regulated arena. For example, the materials contained in this book are certainly applicable to the fields of cable television industry regulation, ad valorem tax adjudication, and perhaps the regulation of the health care industry.

The emphasis throughout the book is application rather than theoretical elegance. Finance models are surveyed and evaluated on the basis of their conceptual consistency, applicability, and difficulty of implementation. The assumptions underlying the various theories are carefully spelled out. Numerous practical solutions to circumvent obstacles are offered, and the emphasis is clearly on pragmatism. A multitude of case studies and examples drawn from actual regulatory proceedings illustrates the text material. Several recurring controversies encountered in regulatory proceedings are elucidated.

The techniques and concepts described in the book are sufficiently broad as to apply to all types of investor-owned and publicly-owned regulated utilities, whether they be gas, electric, water, telecommunications, or others. The numerous examples and case studies are drawn from a wide spectrum of utilities and capture to some extent the institutional differences between utilities.

The first chapter provides the conceptual and institutional background. The rudiments of rate of return regulation are reviewed and the central role of cost of capital is highlighted. The relationship between risk and return, crucial to cost of capital estimation, is thoroughly explained in Chapters 2 and 3. Careful attention is paid to risk estimation in practical terms.

The cost of equity capital, which is by far the most difficult and controversial element in cost of capital determination, occupies the majority of the remaining chapters. Five chapters are devoted to Discounted Cash Flow techniques. The first chapter in the sequence provides the necessary conceptual background, as well as the major extensions and applications of the theory, and the next four chapters deal solely with practical issues, including the proper design of comparable groups, variations of the standard Discounted Cash Flow model, and flotation cost controversies. Chapter 9 offers personal reflections on cost of capital methodology, preparing the groundwork for the contemporary techniques discussed in subsequent chapters. Techniques based on Market-to-Book ratios, including Q-ratios and econometric cost of capital models are the subject of Chapter 10. Contemporary techniques, including Risk Premium approaches, the Capital Asset Pricing Model, and Arbitrage Pricing Model are the subject of subsequent chapters. Extensions and a myriad applications of the modern theory of finance are presented, culminating with Chapter 14, which deals with techniques designed to estimate the divisional cost of capital for an individual entity such as a regulated subsidiary, operating company, non-traded asset, or segment of a holding company. The venerable Comparable Earnings approach is discussed in Chapter 16.

The broader questions of composite cost of capital and capital structure are treated in Chapters 17 to 20. The effect of capital structure on cost of capital, and the practical implications of the theory are explained. Interrelationships between rate base and invested capital, and the treatment of various components of the capital structure is analyzed. The related issues of intercorporate ownership and double leverage are raised.

The book concludes with an overview of alternatives to rate of return regulation, including incentive plans, price caps, and sharing mechanisms. The growing presence of alternative regulatory frameworks in the utility industry does not nullify the role of rate of return in regulation. The various parameters of alternative regulatory frameworks, for example price cap indices, are inexorably linked to rate of return as a reasonableness check. Rate of return continues to play a role in assessing the validity and adequacy of the parameters inherent in any alternative regulatory framework.

Dramatic fundamental and structural transformations have occurred in capital markets, financial theories and models, and the utility industry's operating environment since the publication of my *Utilities' Cost of Capital* book in 1984. Volatile capital markets, refined theories, and increased competition triggered by national policies have revolutionized the determination of a utility's cost of capital. The divestiture of AT&T, the FERC's restructuring Order 636, the National Energy Policy Act, and the Safe Drinking Water Act, accounting rule changes, represcription of capital recovery rates, changes in customer attitudes regarding utility services, the evolution of alternative energy and information sources, massive deregulation, and mergers-acquisitions are transforming utilities in ways vastly different from the assumptions of simple financial theories and models. Mergers and acquisitions, asset restructurings, diversification activities, asset redeployments, deregulation of certain assets, and corporate takeovers are the order of the day. These structural changes are changing investor expectations and risk perceptions. On the academic front, new data sources have emerged, extensions and refinements of standard financial theories have flourished, and an arsenal of empirical findings have been published.

Thus, what began as a routine revision of my 1984 *Utilities' Cost of Capital* book mushroomed into a full-fledged rewrite and incorporation of substantive new material. The scale of the revision was such that a new broader and more apt title evolved. Thus, *Regulatory Finance,* came into being.

Regulatory Finance differs in two significant ways from Utilities' Cost of Capital. First, the coverage has been vastly expanded. For example, the topical question of a utility's optimal capital structure is fully addressed in separate new chapters. A capital structure simulation model is presented to address this issue. With the fundamental restructuring of corporate America in general and utilities in particular, the proliferation of diversification activities, asset deregulation, changing corporate structures, and increased scarcity of utility pure-plays, the issue of divisional cost of capital surfaces. Thus, an entirely new chapter is devoted to the theory and practice of divisional cost of capital estimation. A wide array of methodologies is presented and illustrated. A voluminous new chapter is devoted to the analysis of alternative regulatory frameworks. Separate chapters dealing with the technical issues of flotation cost and alternative functional forms of the DCF model are included.

The second major change has to do with updating the coverage. Besides adding several new chapters, the discussions in most of the chapters have been expanded. Expanded material on risk measurement and risk assessment is presented. A variety of applications, examples, and case studies are drawn from more recent and current testimonies reflecting the new utility environment. Modern financial theory applications in line with new research findings are found in several chapters. Expanded coverage of the double leverage issue is included.

This book is the culmination of a continuing series of national cost of capital seminars offered on an ongoing basis to the utility industry since 1980, sponsored jointly by The Management Exchange Inc., now EXNET, and Public Utilities Reports Inc. I would like to express my deep appreciation to Tish Bliss of EXNET and to James M. McInnis, former President of Public Utilities Reports, who believed, supported, and implemented the idea of such seminars, and inspired me to undertake the writing of this book. I am also indebted to Victor L. Andrews, friend, colleague and ex-chairman of the Department of Finance at Georgia State University, for his intellectual leadership throughout the duration of the cost of capital seminars that we jointly taught and from which this book culminated. He is responsible for several sections of this book, and his contributions are generously acknowledged throughout the text.

Many people have provided me with assistance in preparing this book, and I would like to acknowledge their help. My special thanks to Public Utilities Reports Inc. publisher Susan Johnson for her leadership role, constant prodding, and patience in making this book become reality. My thanks to Anne Brown Rodgers for her indefatigable editing scrutiny and support of this effort. My gratitude extends to Donna M. Watson for improving and assembling the components of the book into final form.

I extend special gratefulness to Lisa Todd Hillman who collaborated diligently and patiently throughout this entire venture and was responsible for much of the surgical analysis and editing of the initial manuscript. Her help was invaluable at various stages in preparing this book for publication, including the computerized spreadsheet files that accompany this book.

Where views and opinions are expressed in the book, they are my own and do not necessarily reflect the views of Public Utilities Reports or Georgia State University. I assume responsibility for any errors found in an undertaking of this type.

Readers wishing to address comments, criticisms, inquiries, and suggestions beneficial in future editions are encouraged to do so. Of course, they will be acknowledged. Every effort will be made to reply to such letters. Correspondence should be addressed to:

Professor Roger A. Morin
Center for the Study of Regulated Industry
Georgia State University
College of Business Administration
University Plaza
Atlanta, Ga. 30303
(404) 651-2674

Chapter 1
Rate of Return Regulation

1.1 The Rationale of Regulation

While this book is not intended to cover all facets of rate of return regulation, but rather to cover the application of finance in regulatory rate hearings, it is nevertheless appropriate to preface the book with some brief comments on the general setting. More complete discussions are available in regulatory texts such as Phillips (1993), Bonbright (1966), Kahn (1970), and Howe and Rasmussen (1982).

The capitalistic free-market system, which normally sets prices, output levels, and general terms of trade in society, is generally unworkable in the case of some services provided by public utilities because utilities act as monopolies. That is, they do not experience serious competition in a particular market area. As a result, public utility regulation replaces the free market system by establishing allowable prices for the rendering of public services.

The purpose of regulation is to replicate the results that the competitive market system would achieve in the way of reasonable prices and profits. This view was eloquently expressed by Bonbright:

> Regulation, it is said, is a substitute for competition. Hence its objective should be to compel a regulated enterprise, despite its possession of complete or partial monopoly, to charge rates approximating those which it would charge if free from regulation but subject to the market forces of competition. In short, regulation should be not only a substitute for competition, but a closely imitative substitute.[1]

Regulation provides a correcting mechanism for market failure due to the presence of natural monopoly. The latter occurs when it is less costly to have a single provider of a service than to have multiple or competing providers. Public utilities can operate at substantially lower costs under monopolistic conditions than under competition by eliminating the duplication of costly plant facilities and distribution networks, or by facilitating the realization of optimal plant sizes. Economies of demand diversity that result from serving an entire market rather than serving a smaller fragmented market will also emerge under a regime of regulated monopoly.

---

[1] See Bonbright (1966), 93.

The recent socio-political trend toward the free market and away from economic regulation has not escaped public utilities. Recent years have brought growing competition and deregulation in vast areas of telecommunications, power generation, and energy transmission. In the electric utility industry for example, competition from cogenerators, independent power producers, self-generators, and from other utilities in bulk power markets has intensified markedly. Economies of scale are becoming increasingly difficult to locate in several public utility markets, with some markets even exhibiting increasing costs to scale. The natural monopoly argument for the existence of regulation, although necessary, is no longer sufficient to fully justify the institution of regulated monopoly.

Since public utilities are suppliers of essential and indispensable services to society and industry, they are clearly affected by the public interest. Closely allied with the bedrock industries of communication, transportation, and distribution, they constitute the essential infrastructure of the economy and the motor of economic growth. Moreover, public utilities are typically under legal obligation to serve all customers in their market area at reasonable rates and without undue discrimination. The institution of regulated monopoly facilitates the fulfillment of these legal obligations. Regulation has been used to pursue a myriad of other goals, typically social objectives, to implement notions of fairness or equity, and to redress the distributions of income. The subsidization of telephone rates or power rates is but one example. The use of regulation as an instrument of social policy is controversial in that other tools, such as selective taxes and subsidies, are far more suitable and more efficient.

To protect consumers from monopolistic prices and to preserve the public interest, the instrument of regulated monopoly has generally been adopted as a substitute for competition in markets served by public utilities, such as the production and distribution of gas and electricity, telecommunications, water, and cable television. Regulation achieves its aims by regulating output prices through the determination of a fair and reasonable rate of return that it allows utilities to earn. The output prices determined by the regulator will dictate the utility's profits. Given the amount of capital employed by the utility, the prices charged will in turn determine a rate of return. In determining the overall level of prices for the utility's products, the regulator must determine the rate of return on capital that should be earned. It is through the regulation of prices that the limitation on profit is achieved.

In a normally competitive industry, the forces of competition hold prices down to the costs of production, including a requisite expected return on invested capital. This expected rate of return is an average long-run concept and is not necessarily guaranteed at all times. Over the long-run, it will reflect the risks of the industry. The greater the risks confronted by the industry, the greater is the expected rate of return. The principal objective of regulation is to determine an allowed rate of return in such a way as to emulate the returns for industries in the competitive market. Regulatory commissions act as a substitute for the market place, setting allowed rates of return so as to satisfy consumer demand at non-monopolistic prices and ensure good performance. By controlling not only prices but also entry and service standards, the regulatory commission is the guarantor of acceptable performance.

In the next four sections, a brief overview of the regulatory process and of the issues generally involved is presented for the uninitiated, with special emphasis on the allowed rate of return.[2]

1.2 Overview of the Regulatory Process

The regulation of output prices involves two major tasks, as described in Kahn (1970). The first is to set the proper level of rates in the aggregate, and the second is to develop the structure of rates. The level of rates, taken as a whole, ensures that total revenues will cover all operating expenses, including a fair return on the capital invested. The structure of rates, or "rate design" as it is commonly referred to, determines the apportionment of total costs among different customer classes and categories of service. Rate design is not discussed in this book, as it lies largely outside the province of finance.

In a nutshell, the determination of rates is implemented by defining a total "revenue requirement," also referred to as the total "cost of service," then by adjusting the rates so as to achieve these totals. More specifically, the rates set by the regulators should be sufficient to cover the utility's costs, including taxes and depreciation, plus an adequate dollar return on the capital invested. The expected return in dollars, or profit, is obtained by multiplying the allowed rate of return set by the regulator by the "rate base." The rate base is essentially the net book value of the utility's plant that is considered used and useful in dispensing service, plus some reasonable allowance for working capital requirements. It may also include any new investment to be undertaken by the utility. An estimate of revenue requirements is derived from a thorough scrutiny of total company costs during a "test year," adjusted for known changes between the test year and the period for which the rates will be in effect.

---

[2] For a comprehensive overview of the regulatory process and of the issues involved, see Howe and Rasmussen (1982), Chapter 4. Classic treatments of the same subject are also found in Garfield and Lovejoy (1964), Phillips (1993), and Kahn (1970).

The test year can be historical, current, or forward. In the past, most utility commissions have employed a historical test year. In the 1970s, during periods of rapid cost inflation, the use of a current or forward test year became more prevalent, in an attempt to temper the eroding effects of inflation on earnings and to offset to some extent the attrition of earnings due to regulatory lag.[3] Those who favor the use of a historical test year contend that ratemaking should be based on verifiable actual costs, rather than on arbitrary and speculative estimates. Moreover, in times of inflationary adversity, the use of the historical test year constitutes an incentive for efficiency in utility operations. Those who favor a forward test year point to the deleterious effects of regulatory lag during inflationary periods, exacerbated by adherence to a historical test period. More frequent rate filings, deterioration of financial condition, down-grading of bonds, and difficulty in attracting capital are the inevitable consequences of reliance on antiquated historical data.

The process of determining revenue requirements can be encapsulated by the following equation:

Revenue Requirements = Cost of Service

$$R = O + D + T + kB \qquad (1\text{-}1)$$

where
R = revenue requirements
O = operating expenses
D = depreciation allowance
T = taxes
k = a fair rate of return
B = rate base

In words, revenue requirements must be sufficient to cover the costs of service, which are comprised of operating expenses, taxes, depreciation, and a fair return on the net plant employed by the utility. The average revenue per unit of output, or product price, is in turn obtained by dividing the revenue requirements by the quantity of output demanded, denoted by the letter Q:

$$\text{Price} = \frac{\text{Revenue Requirement}}{\text{Quantity Demanded}}$$

$$= R/Q$$

---

[3] For an analysis of regulatory lag and possible remedies, see Kolb, Morin, and Gay (1983).

Two simplified numerical examples will illustrate the calculation of revenue requirements and highlight the issues involved.

EXAMPLE 1-1

North American Utility has a rate base B of $10 million, and expects to produce and sell 1 million units Q. These can be kilowatt-hours, cubic feet of gas, number of residential telephones, etc. The rate of return k allowed by the public service commission is 12%. The operating expenses O of production are expected to be $6 million, and depreciation and taxes $D + T$ will amount to $2.8 million.

The price per unit of output can be derived by dividing the revenue requirement by the quantity of output as follows:

$$\text{Price Per Unit} = \frac{\text{Revenue Requirement}}{\text{Output}}$$

$$= (O + D + T + kB)/Q$$
$$= [\$6 + \$2.8 + 0.12\,(\$10)] / 1{,}000{,}000$$
$$= \$10{,}000{,}000 / 1{,}000{,}000$$
$$= \$10.00 \text{ per unit}$$

The regulator sets a price of $10.00 per unit so as to enable the utility to earn a 12% return on its capital. This return is only an expectation however, and is not guaranteed by the regulator. The actual return earned may very well deviate from what was anticipated, due perhaps to a shortfall in demand or to an understatement of costs. Or perhaps, as is likely, the regulator does not react instantaneously to the deviations from expected revenues and costs, and will only reset the prices after a lag period. This delayed reaction to outcomes that differ from expectations is referred to as "regulatory lag." The issue of regulatory lag is treated more fully in Chapter 2, which deals with investment risk.

In the absence of regulatory lag, if the utility's revenues exceed the sum of operating costs and 12% of the rate base, product prices are reduced until the return is decreased to 12%. On the other hand, if the utility's investments yield less than 12%, and the utility's investments are considered prudent by the regulator, product prices are increased until the return reaches 12%.

To anticipate the material of subsequent chapters, the $1.2 million of dollar returns generated by the revenues in excess of operating expenses will serve to service the $10 million of capital supplied by investors, including both

FIGURE 1-1
CALCULATIONS TO DETERMINE TOTAL REVENUE
REQUIREMENTS

			%
Assume:	Debt	$540,000,000	60%
	Equity	360,000,000	40%
	Total Capital	$900,000,000	100%

Fair Return on Equity (17% x 360,000,000)	$ 61,200,000
+ Income Taxes (50% of Profit Before Taxes)	$ 61,200,000
Required Profit Before Taxes	$122,400,000
+ Interest (10% x 540,000,000)	$ 54,000,000
Required Profit Before Interest and Taxes	$176,400,000
+ Operating Expenses (including depreciation, assumed)	$350,000,000
= Total Required Revenue	$526,400,000

Note: Cost Rate to Service Capital and Taxes = Required Profit
Before Interest and Taxes/Capital Base

Cost of Capital Including Tax = 176,400,000/900,000,000

= 19.6%

Source: Adapted from Robichek (1978)

bondholders and shareholders. These investors as a group have certain return requirements, in our example 12%, in much the same way that suppliers of materials or labor services expect a certain wage based on supply and demand conditions in those markets. The return required by investors is set in capital markets by the forces of competition. This required return is the cost of capital or the opportunity cost of the total funds employed by the utility.

The next example is slightly more complex and realistic and places more emphasis on the actual determination of the allowed rate of return.

EXAMPLE 1-2

The upper portion of Figure 1-1 shows North American Utility's total assets of $900 million, financed 60% by debt and 40% by equity capital. The lower portion of Figure 1-1 depicts the process used to compute revenue requirements. Operating expenses, including depreciation, are assumed to be $350 million. Figure 1-2 sketches the method of computing the allowed return.

The first and pivotal step is to determine the dollars necessary to service the capital invested. As shown in Figure 1-2, earnings of $115.2 million are required to service both the debt and equity capital of the company. This latter figure is arrived at by multiplying the allowed rate of return of 12.8% by the rate base of $900 million. To develop the allowed rate of return of 12.8%, the regulator determines the fair and reasonable return to debt capital and to equity capital, in our example 10% and 17%, respectively. These rates are in turn multiplied, or weighted, by the relative proportions of debt and equity in the firm, here 60% and 40%, respectively, to produce the 12.8% allowed return as follows:

Type of Capital	Amount of Capital	Allowed Return	% Proportion	Weighted Return
Debt	$540	10%	.60	6.0%
Equity	$360	17%	.40	6.8%
		Allowed Return		12.8%

The overall allowed return of 12.8% is the weighted average return on the pool of funds assembled by the utility in the proportions assumed.

In the second step, the revenue requirements are calculated, following a procedure that has evolved in practice, and is often referred to as the "embedded cost

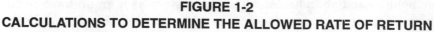

FIGURE 1-2
CALCULATIONS TO DETERMINE THE ALLOWED RATE OF RETURN

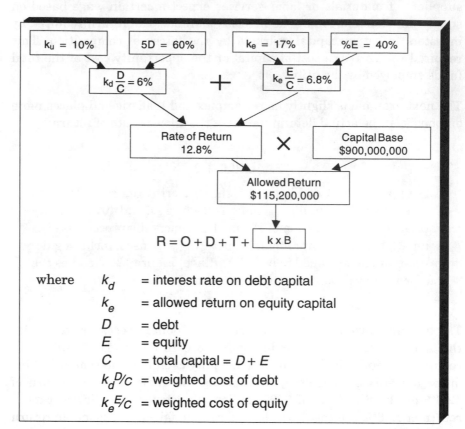

where k_d = interest rate on debt capital

k_e = allowed return on equity capital

D = debt

E = equity

C = total capital = $D + E$

$k_d D/C$ = weighted cost of debt

$k_e E/C$ = weighted cost of equity

approach." The computation is shown in the lower portion of Figure 1-1, based on the information from Figure 1-2. The method of calculation follows directly from the fundamental ratemaking formula in Equation 1-1:

$$
\begin{aligned}
B &= \$900 && \text{(Given)}\\
k &= 12.8\% && \text{(Fig. 1-2)}\\
O + D &= \$350 && \text{(Given)}\\
T &= \$61.2 && \text{(Fig. 1-1)}\\
R &= O + D + T + kB\\
&= 350 + 61.2 + 0.128 \times 900\\
&= \$526.4
\end{aligned}
$$

A sum of $61.2 million is required to service the requirements of common stockholders. But in order to provide one dollar of return to the stockholders, the utility must earn two dollars on a pre-tax basis, if the tax rate is 50%. As seen from Figure 1-1, to provide $61.2 million to equity owners, the regulator must allow twice that amount, or $122.4 of before-tax profits. An additional sum of $54 million is necessary to service the requirements of bondholders. But since interest payments are deductible before computing taxable income, only one dollar of revenue is required to service one dollar of interest money. The total amount of revenues required to service total capital and the attendant taxes is the required profit before interest and taxes of $176.4 million shown on Figure 1-1, which is 19.6% of the total capital. Based on a rate base of $900 million and an allowed return of 19.6% including taxes, the expected earnings of the utility will be $176.4 million (i.e., 0.196 x $900), sufficient to pay the company's contractual obligation to its bondholders of $54 million (0.10 x $540), and to service the after-tax requirements to shareholders of $61.2 million (0.17 x $360), or $122.4 million before taxes. Adding the operating expenses of $350 million to the amount of $176.4 million required to service capital, total revenue requirements of $526.4 million are obtained.

As the two examples make abundantly clear, the utility's allowed rate of return occupies a central role determining utility rates.

1.3 The Allowed Rate of Return

The heart of utility regulation is the setting of just and reasonable rates by way of a fair and reasonable return. How then does a regulatory commission determine a rate of return that is fair and reasonable? Although there are no hard-and-fast rules, no mathematical formula or scientific panacea that can be mechanically applied, two landmark Supreme Court cases define the legal principles underlying the regulation of a public utility's rate of return and provide the foundations for the notion of a fair return:

1. *Bluefield Water Works & Improvement Co. v. Public Service Commission of West Virginia* (262 U.S. 679, 1923).

2. *Federal Power Commission v. Hope Natural Gas Company (320 U.S. 391. 1944).*

The *Bluefield* case set the standard against which just and reasonable rates are measured:

> A public utility is entitled to such rates as will permit it to earn a return on the value of the property which it employs for the convenience of the public equal to that generally being made at the same time and in the same general part of the country on investments in other business undertakings which are attended by corresponding risks and uncertainties . . . . The return should be reasonable, sufficient to *assure confidence* in the financial soundness of the utility, and should be adequate,

under efficient and economical management, to *maintain and support its credit and enable it to raise money* necessary for the proper discharge of its public duties.[4]

The *Hope* case expanded on the guidelines to be used to assess the reasonableness of the allowed return. The Court reemphasized its statements in the *Bluefield* case and recognized that revenues must also cover "capital costs." The Court stated:

> From the investor or company point of view it is important that there be enough revenue not only for operating expenses but also for the capital costs of the business. These include service on the debt and dividends on the stock . . . . By that standard the return to the equity owner should be *commensurate with returns on investments in other enterprises having corresponding risks.* That return, moreover, should be sufficient to assure confidence in the financial integrity of the enterprise, so as to *maintain its credit and attract capital.*

The statements of the Court in the *Hope* and *Bluefield* cases established the following standards of fairness and reasonableness of the allowed rate of return for a public utility:

1. A standard of capital attraction

2. A standard of comparable earnings

3. Financial integrity

The economic logic underlying these standards is straightforward. There is an opportunity cost associated with the funds that capital suppliers provide a public utility. That cost is the expected return foregone by not investing in other enterprises of corresponding risks. Thus, the expected rate of return on a public utility's debt and equity capital should equal the expected rate of return on the debt and equity of other firms having comparable risks. Moreover, a utility is entitled to a return that will allow it to maintain its credit so that it continues to have access to the capital markets to raise the funds required for investment. The allowed return should therefore be sufficient to assure confidence in its financial health so it is able to maintain its credit and continue to attract funds on reasonable terms.

The U.S. Supreme Court reiterated the criteria set forth in *Hope* in the *Federal Power Commission v. Memphis Light, Gas & Water Division* (411

---

[4] Emphasis in the quotations throughout the book is provided by the author, unless otherwise stated.

U.S. 458, 1973), and *Permian Basin Rate Cases* (390 U.S. 747, 1968) cases. In the latter case, the U.S. Supreme Court endorsed the standards of *Bluefield* and the end-result standard of *Hope,* and stressed that a regulatory agency's rate of return order should

> . . . reasonably be expected to maintain financial integrity, attract necessary capital, and fairly compensate investors for the risks they have assumed . . . .

In the *Duquesne Light Company et al. v. David M. Barasch et al.* (488 U.S. 299, 1989) decision, the Court not only reasserted the standards of *Hope* and *Bluefield*, but also rendered a number of important new guidelines in setting rates for regulated utilities. The Court established regulatory risk, which is defined as the risk of a particular regime in a given jurisdiction, as a distinct risk to be recognized by regulators in setting a fair rate of return.

The notion of financial integrity permeates the aforementioned landmark cases. There are many dimensions and factors that determine a utility's financial integrity. The return on equity should certainly be designed at a minimum to keep the stock price at or slightly above book value on average. If replacement costs are taken into account, the return should be high enough to produce a Q-ratio equal to that of comparable risk companies if regulation is to emulate the competitive result. The return should also be high enough to produce coverages consistent with an optimal bond rating. The optimal bond rating for a regulated utility from ratepayers' point of view is discussed in Chapter 19.

Similar standards as those contained in *Hope* and *Bluefield* were promulgated by the high courts in other nations. For example, the concept or standard of just and reasonable rates of return are clearly evident in Canadian regulatory policy. In the setting of rates, it was argued in *Northwestern Utilities v. City of Edmonton* (2 D.L.R. 4, p. 8, 1929) that rate levels should be *just* and *reasonable* to the consumer as well as to the utility and in the latter case, the earnings should yield a *fair* rate of return on money invested. Clearly, if rates are to be just and reasonable to the utility and yield a fair return, the allowable return on common equity should be commensurate with returns on investments in other firms having corresponding risks, and sufficient to assure confidence in the financial integrity of the firm. Otherwise, the utility will be unable to maintain creditworthiness and attract capital on reasonable terms. The concepts of justice, fairness, and reasonableness are intimately related to comparability of returns, financial integrity, and creditworthiness.

As was the case in *Hope* and *Bluefield*, *Northwestern* makes frequent references to returns on investments in other firms. For example, the Court stated:

> By a fair return is meant that the company will be allowed as large a return on the capital invested in its enterprise as it would receive if it were investing the same amount in other securities possessing an attractiveness, stability and certainty equal to that of the company's enterprise.

The principle of capital attraction was enunciated in *British Columbia Electric Railway v. Public Utilities Commission of British Columbia, et al.,* (25 D.L.R. (2d)689, pp. 697-698,1961), where it was stated that "earnings should be sufficient. . . .to enable [the utility] to . . . attract capital either by the sale of shares or securities." Clearly, if earnings are to be sufficient for a firm to attract capital on reasonable terms, the firm must offer a return that is comparable to that offered by competing investments. One interpretation of the latter is that a utility must provide returns achieved on its past investments comparable to those achieved in enterprises of comparable risk.

It is clear from the *Hope-Bluefield* and *Northwestern-British Columbia Railway* pronouncements that among the factors to be considered in determining a fair return are (1) the earnings necessary to assure confidence in the financial integrity of the utility and to maintain its credit standing, (2) the payment of dividends and interest, and (3) the amount of risk.

It must be understood that both capital attraction and financial integrity standards must be fulfilled in determining a fair rate of return. Despite a deterioration in credit standing, a utility may be able to attract capital temporarily, but at prohibitive costs and under unfavorable terms. Eventually, the utility will face hard funds rationing and/or the costs of financing will become prohibitive, and the utility can no longer attract capital at a reasonable price.

1.4 Implementing the Concept of Fair Return

In contrast to the transparency of the legal and economic concepts of a fair return, the actual implementation of the concept is more controversial. The fair return to the equity holder of a public utility's common stock has been typically derived from four main approaches:

1. Comparable Earnings

2. Discounted Cash Flow (DCF) Techniques

3. Risk Premium

4. Capital Asset Pricing Model (CAPM)

These approaches are treated extensively in subsequent chapters. Briefly, the Comparable Earnings standard uses as the measure of fair return the returns earned on book equity investments in firms having comparable risks. In application, the rates of earnings on common equity experienced by firms comparable in risk to the utility in question are considered. The attraction of capital standard, which focuses on investors' return requirements, is applied through the DCF or market value method. This test defines fair return as the return investors anticipate when they purchase equity shares of comparable risk companies in the financial marketplace; this is a market-based rate of return, defined in terms of anticipated dividends and capital gains relative to stock prices.

Modern developments in financial theory have given considerable impetus to the determination of fair return based on formal risk-return models. Risk Premium approaches, which make use of information on the relative risk premium between stocks and bonds, are applied to estimate a fair return. More refined market-based techniques, such as the Capital Asset Pricing Model (CAPM) and the Arbitrage Pricing Model (APM) have appeared in the regulatory process. These techniques are analyzed in subsequent chapters as well.

The *Hope* case was also responsible for the so-called "end result" doctrine, suggesting that the regulatory methods employed are immaterial so long as the end result is reasonable to the consumer and investor. In other words, a regulator is not bound to use any single formula in determining rates. It is the result reached and the impact of the rate order rather than the method or the theory employed that is controlling. Potential infirmities inherent in the methods used are of secondary importance, according to this doctrine. This is a reassuring assertion, given the stringency and surrealism of the assumptions that frequently characterize the models and theories employed in the determination of a fair return. The end-result doctrine is reminiscent of the philosophy of economic positivism, which states that the value of a model or theory should not be assessed by the severity or realism of its assumptions, but rather by its ability to explain or predict economic phenomena.

1.5 Regulatory Issues

There are numerous issues, points of contention, and controversies in regulatory proceedings.[5] Discussion of these issues can best be structured on a

---

[5] It is obviously impossible to do justice to all aspects of regulation in such a limited space; only a brief outline of the issues that play a role of particular importance when financial theory is introduced into regulatory proceedings is reported. See Howe and Rasmussen (1982), Chapter 4, and Kahn (1970) for a more comprehensive treatment of regulatory issues.

sequential term-by-term analysis of the fundamental cost of service formula:

$$R = O + D + T + kB \qquad (1\text{-}2)$$

The allowed rate of return k, or cost of capital, can be expressed as the weighted sum of debt cost k_d and equity cost k_e with the ratios of debt D and equity E to the total capital C serving as weights:

$$k = k_d\, D/C + k_e\, E/C \qquad (1\text{-}3)$$

Substituting Equation 1-3 into Equation 1-2, an expanded cost of service formula is obtained:

$$R = O + D + T + (k_d\, D/C + k_e\, E/C)\, B \qquad (1\text{-}4)$$

Following each term of Equation 1-4, the dominant regulatory issues arising in practice are as follows:

The Appropriate Level of Operating Expenses

Operating costs, acceptable for ratemaking, are monitored and subject to scrutiny by the regulator. Regulators make judgments with respect to which cost items are authorized for inclusion in the cost of service computation. Controversies over the disallowance of certain expense categories are frequent, for example, advertising expenses, charitable donations, and executive salaries.

The distinction between outlays to be charged directly as operating expenses and outlays to be capitalized, that is, entered into revenue requirements in the form of annual depreciation charges, is also scrutinized closely.

It is interesting to note that while the operating expenses and capital outlays of public utilities constitute the major component of revenue requirements, and directly involve the efficiency with which society's resources are used, regulators devote relatively less attention to these items in sharp contrast to the major attention given to controlling the rate of return. Perhaps this is not so surprising, given the political visibility of profit levels and the administrative infeasibility of monitoring company expenses.

The Method of Depreciating Capital Outlays

Several options are available for depreciating utility plant, including straight-line, double-declining, and sum-of-the-digits methods. Tax savings are generated if a utility is allowed a more rapid rate of depreciation in the early years of an asset's life for tax purposes than for ratemaking purposes. Tax savings also occur if investment tax credits are available to the utility. Some regulatory commissions require that these savings be "flowed-through" to customers in the years in which they are earned, thereby reducing revenue requirements in those years relative to what it would otherwise be. Other regulatory commissions require that these savings be "normalized," and that the rate base be reduced each year by the amount of the reduction in the normalization reserve for that year. This issue is explored in more detail in Chapter 3, insofar as it influences the quality of the utility's earnings, its riskiness, and hence its cost of capital.

The Appropriate Level of the Capital Base

The choice of what should be included or excluded from the rate base, the test period to use, and the valuation basis are controversial issues.

With regard to the proper inclusions and exclusions, traditional practice is to include all assets that are "used and useful." This is notably ambiguous in the case of construction work in progress (CWIP). Can CWIP be classified as used and useful, and is it not essential for continuing service for current ratepayers and for the going concern value of the enterprise? The issue of CWIP and the attendant allowance for funds used during construction (AFUDC) are addressed in Chapter 3, insofar as they affect the quality of earnings, cash flows, risk, and the utility's cost of capital.[6]

Two general concepts of rate base valuation prevail: *original cost* and *fair value*. Reproduction cost or current cost concepts are variants of the fair value concept. All three concepts attempt to measure changes in the value of utility plant and facilities since their original inception. Because of its administrative tractability and verifiability, the original (historical or book) cost approach is preferred in practice by a majority of commissions.[7]

Valuation of the rate base was highly controversial before the landmark *Hope* decision in 1944. The *Smith v. Ames* (U.S. 467, 1898) judgment by the Supreme Court in 1898 had set the stage for fair value, embroiling regulators and courts in endless battles over the definition and measurement of fair value and sunk capital. In *Smith v. Ames* the Court stated:

---

[6] See Morin (1986A) and Morin (1986B) for an analysis of the financial, revenue requirements, and economic aspects of CWIP.

[7] For a complete discussion of capital recovery issues, see Morin and Ramirez (1988).

> What the company is entitled to ask is a fair return upon the
> value of that which it employs for the public convenience . . . .
> And, in order to ascertain that value . . . the amount and
> market value of its bonds and stock . . . are to be given such
> weight as may be just and right in each case.

In the *Hope* decision, the Court eliminated the necessity for regulatory
commissions to rely on reproduction cost exclusively in determining rates.
The "end-result" doctrine was promulgated, and as long as investors are
fairly treated and as long as rates are fair to consumers, the Court would
not dictate any particular rate base. In the *Hope* decision, the Court dealt
a major blow to the notion of a fair value rate base. The inherent circularity of a fair value rate base, whereby rates are made to depend upon fair
value when fair value of the utility itself depends on earnings under
whatever rates are anticipated, was recognized by the Court.

Attention then shifted from the rate base to the fair rate of return,
although controversy over the rate base still remains.

It should be mentioned that there are welfare implications depending on
the rate base valuation method used. Gordon (1977) has shown that the
risk and thus shareholders' required rate of return is higher under the
replacement than under the historical cost method. Moreover, the risk to
ratepayers is higher with a replacement cost rate base because any unanticipated changes in costs of production are reflected immediately in the
rates. On the other hand, when using a historical rate base, the rates are
adjusted only when the physical plant and facilities are actually replaced.

The most controversial step in the determination of revenue requirements, and the principal concern of this text, is the determination of a fair
rate of return. As can be seen from Equation 1-3, both the specific return
on each type of capital, debt and equity, and the relative mix of debt and
equity employed, must be addressed.

Return on Debt Capital

The return on debt is the least controversial element. Payments on bonds
and on preferred stock are embedded costs, clearly stated on the bond and
preferred stock certificate. The embedded cost of debt and preferred stock
is simply the total interest payments divided by the book value of the
outstanding debt, and preferred dividends divided by the amount of preferred outstanding, respectively. If future interest rates are expected to
differ from the interest rates on the existing debt, and the utility is
expected to issue fixed-cost financing in the near future, such known and

measurable costs should be incorporated into the embedded cost calculation to the extent possible.

In practice, the calculation of the embedded cost of debt should also account for issuance costs, premium or discounts at the time of issue, and should recognize sinking fund and call provisions. This is because premiums or discounts and flotation costs influence the effective yield to the investor and cost to the utility and are typically allowed to be recovered by regulators. Embedded cost rates of debt and preferred stock can be calculated by either the "yield-to-maturity" or the "simple-interest" (also called "amortization") methods. These routine mechanical methods are described and illustrated in Bowring (1985) and also in Parcell (1992).

Return on Common Equity Capital

The cost of common equity capital is controversial, and a major share of regulatory proceedings is devoted to the determination of a fair rate of return on common equity. A large portion of this text is in fact aimed at estimating the allowed return on common equity.

Unlike the fixed and known contractual payments on bonds, earnings on common stock are residual in nature, available only after prior legitimate claims on earnings have been met. It is difficult to specify what these residual earnings will be in advance. Application of the standards laid down in the *Bluefield* and *Hope* decisions presents a number of problems, which this text will attempt to elucidate. One major roadblock in applying the comparable risk standard of *Hope* is the measurement of risk, so that comparable risk investments can be used as a guide in establishing a fair return. The basic questions of how the return to the equity owner is to be measured, whether it should be on the basis of book or market value, and over what time period present problems as well.

Before the mid-1960s, regulators placed almost exclusive reliance on the Comparable Earnings approach. Because of several problems encountered in implementing that approach, the Discounted Cash Flow (DCF) approach has supplanted Comparable Earnings in popularity. In the early 1990s, the DCF approach experienced several frontal attacks as to the realism of its assumptions and the difficulty of implementing the model given current capital market conditions. Following major theoretical developments in finance, the Capital Asset Pricing Theory (CAPM) has achieved some notoriety in regulatory proceedings. More recently, contemporary advances in finance and economics have spawned the Q-ratio, the Arbitrage Pricing Theory (APT), and more elaborate Risk Premium approaches, all of which are gaining prominence in regulatory proceedings. The return on equity is inevitably determined by judgment, enlightened by the implementation of a vast arsenal of techniques, models, and theories, each with its own set of assumptions, simplifications, premises, and problems. These methodologies will be surveyed and analyzed in later chapters.

Capital Structure

The existence of an optimal proportion of debt and equity capital is occasionally a contentious issue. Sometimes, the regulator will impute debt/equity proportions other than those actually employed by the utility, if the capital structure is deemed non-optimal by the regulator. The correct mix of debt and equity capital is particularly relevant for ratepayers, since equity capital costs substantially more than debt capital owing in part to the tax deductibility of interest payments on debt. Another issue in determining the capital structure is whether book value weights or market value weights should be employed in computing the weighted average cost of capital. These topics will be covered in Chapters 17 and 18.

1.6 Limitations of Rate of Return Regulation

In this text, the framework of rate of return regulation is taken as a given, along with the existing legal and procedural context, although it may not necessarily be the best. Nevertheless, some caveats and reservations are worthy of mention. Chapter 21 offers a critical assessment of rate of return regulation and discusses alternative regulatory frameworks.[8] Even if the rate base and the allowed rate of return can be correctly identified, rate of return regulation as an institution has potential shortcomings.

With the spirit and spur of competition removed, what incentives does the utility have to be efficient and produce at least cost? Under the umbrella of rate of return regulation,where ideally the allowed return is continuously adjusted downward if the utility becomes more cost efficient, and upwards otherwise, will the firm strive for efficiency?

Some incentives for efficiency within the framework of rate of return regulation have been proposed and some implemented. Allowing a range of permissible returns instead of a specific number, within which the utility's return could fluctuate, reaping some reward for success, and penalty for failure, could provide utility management some incentive for

---

[8] A critique of public utility regulation is available in Howe and Rasmussen (1982), Chapter 6. See also Gordon (1977), Averch and Johnson (1962), Myers (1972), and Kahn (1970).

efficiency. Price cap regulation, sometimes referred to as "social contract" regulation, is said to afford similar incentives.

An allowance over and above the cost of capital has been proposed to provide the same incentives to management that competition provides in the unregulated sector of the economy. But as Averch and Johnson (1962) have shown, there is an incentive to overcapitalize when the allowed return exceeds the cost of capital, and the stock price increases with the quantity of capital employed by the utility; investment projects that would not be accepted by a profit maximizing firm may be acceptable to a regulated utility due to the associated increase in the rate base. Myers (1972) has advocated the conscious use of regulatory lag as an incentive device. However, regulatory lag is a double-edged sword. What serves as an incentive today may become a disincentive next year. The utility must determine whether the benefits obtained with such a scheme are sufficient to offset the resulting increase in the risk of the return to be realized.

Control over the allowed return may not be sufficient to protect the consumer against monopoly pricing for a utility operating in more than one market. A utility with two markets for example, where demand is more price elastic in one market, is motivated to lower the price in that market below cost in order to increase demand. Not only may an increase in capacity be required, but losses in that market fall on the consumer, and the price in the other market is raised toward the monopoly price.

Finally, non-price dimensions of utility products may be ignored by strict adherence to the limitation of profits. Quality of service, reliability, and safety of service may be compromised according to this argument. But the fact that utilities are greatly exposed to public criticism for inadequate service tempers this argument. If anything, there is an inclination to expand the rate base and improve service in rate-of-return regulation. Besides, additional costs of improving service can always be included in the cost of service. A thorough reading of the literature leaves one with the feeling that in spite of its failings, rate of return regulation has served society well. Regardless of regulatory framework, rate of return will continue to play a role if for no other reason than to assess the merits of alternative regimes. For example, the validity and reasonableness of various indices in a Price Cap regime of regulation are assessed on their ability to deliver a fair and reasonable return to investors.

1.7 The Concept of Cost of Capital

As discussed in previous sections, the revenues generated when the allowed rate of return is applied to the rate base are used to service the capital supplied by investors to the utility. The aggregate return required by these investors is called "cost of capital." The cost of capital is the opportunity cost, expressed in percentage terms, of the total pool of capital employed by the utility. It is the composite weighted cost of the various classes of capital (bonds, preferred stock, common stock) used by the utility, with the weights reflecting the proportions of the total that each class of capital represents.

While utilities enjoy varying degrees of monopoly in the sale of public utility services, they must compete with every one else in the free open market for the input factors of production, whether it be labor, materials, machines, or capital. The prices of these inputs are set in the competitive marketplace by supply and demand, and it is these input prices that are incorporated in the cost of service computation. This is just as true for capital as for any other factor of production. Since utilities must go to the open capital market and sell their securities in competition with every other issuer, there is obviously a market price to pay for the capital they require, for example, the interest on debt capital, or the expected return on equity.

The cost of capital is the compensation required by investors for postponing consumption and exposing capital to risk. While the market price of labor, materials, and machines is easily verifiable, the price of the capital input is more complex to determine. When investors supply funds to a utility by buying its stocks or bonds, not only are they postponing consumption, giving up the alternative of spending their dollars in some other way, but they are also exposing their funds to risk. Investors are willing to incur this double penalty only if they are adequately compensated. The compensation they require is the price of capital. If there are differences in the risk of the investments, competition among firms for a limited supply of capital will bring different prices. These differences in risk are translated into price differences by the capital markets in much the same way that commodities that differ in characteristics will trade at different prices.

The important point is that the prices of debt capital and equity capital are set by supply and demand, and both are influenced by the relationship between the risk and return expected for those securities and the risks expected from the overall menu of available securities.

The graph shown in Figure 1-3 illustrates the alternative investments available to investors, along with their risks and returns. One can think of the graph as a pricing schedule for capital, with the prices shown on the vertical axis and the commodities of varying risks on the horizontal. The numbers are illustrative only. Referring to the graph, long-term Treasury bonds are considered risk-free, and offer investors a 7% return, followed by prime commercial paper yielding 8%. Next on the risk spectrum would be corporate and utility bonds rated Aaa, offering 9%. Next in line on the quality spectrum would be corporate bonds rated AA and A, yielding progressively higher returns because of higher risks. Next would be bonds rated Baa, yielding 10%. High-quality stocks, such as public utility stocks, are next yielding 12%, followed by average quality stocks yielding 13%, followed in turn by deep discount bonds yielding 14%.

FIGURE 1-3
PRICING SCHEDULE FOR CAPITAL
(RISK-RETURN MENU)

RISK-RETURN RELATIONSHIPS FOR A RANGE OF SECURITIES

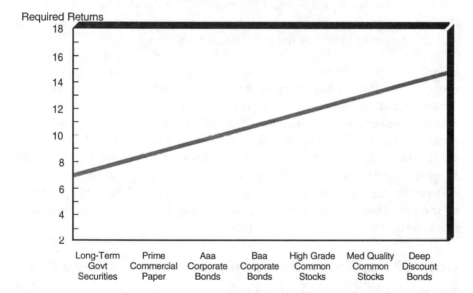

The Price of Capital and Opportunity Cost

The concept of cost of capital is firmly anchored in the opportunity cost notion of economics. The cost of a specific source of capital is basically determined by the riskiness of that investment in light of alternate opportunities and equals the investor's current opportunity cost of investing in the securities of that utility. A rational investor is maximizing the performance of his or her portfolio only if returns expected on investments of comparable risk are the same. If not, the investor will switch out of those investments yielding low returns at a given risk level in favor of those investments offering higher returns for the same degree of risk. This implies that a utility will be unable to attract capital unless it can offer returns to capital suppliers comparable to those achieved on alternate competing investments of similar risk.

The price of capital is expressed as a percentage rate per dollar of capital supplied, referred to as the investor's "required rate of return." Cost of capital is synonymous with required return (market yield). The duality between cost and return can be demonstrated as follows. A utility issues a financial security to investors, and receives an immediate inflow of cash, to be followed by periodic cash outflows required to service the security issued. The initial cash inflow to the utility corresponds to an equivalent cash outflow for the investors who purchase the security. The sequence of periodic cash outflows servicing the security corresponds to a sequence of cash receipts for the investors. The cash flows from the utility's point of view and from that of investors are exact counterparts, mirror images of one another. In the case of a bond for example, the compensation received by bondholders is the expected stream of coupon payments over the life of the bond plus the expected proceeds from either the sale or redemption of the bond. In the case of common stock, it is the stream of future dividends and the expected proceeds upon resale at some future date.

Based on orthodox time value of money concepts, the investor's return is the rate of return that makes the present value of the expected cash receipts equal to the current price or outflow. The cost of the funds raised to the utility is the rate that makes the present value of the cash outflows required to service the security equal to the cash received initially. But since the cash flow stream to the investor is identical to that of the utility, these two rates must be identical.[9] In other words, the cost of capital to the utility is synonymous with the investor's return, and the cost of capital is the earnings that must be generated by the investment of that capital in order to pay its price, that is, in order to meet the investor's required rate of return.

Cost of Capital and Rational Investment Behavior

The concept of cost of capital can be approached not only by reference to the fundamental economic concept of opportunity cost, which pertains to the supply side of capital markets, but also by reference to the demand side of the capital markets.

The demand side viewpoint recognizes that regulated utilities are private corporations with shareholders-owners, and that management's principal responsibility is to maximize their well-being, as measured by stock price. Thus, only those investment decisions that maximize the price of the stock

---

[9] This statement abstracts from the effects of flotation costs. In fact, costs to the issuer exceed the return required by investors to the extent that flotation costs decrease the net amount of funds actually available to the issuer. This is discussed further in Chapter 6.

should be undertaken. A utility will continue to invest in real physical assets if the return on these investments exceeds or equals its cost of capital. The cost of capital is the minimum rate of return that must be earned on assets to justify their acquisition, and the regulator must set the allowed return so that optimal investment rates are obtained, and that no other investment rate would result in a higher share price.

In this context, the cost of capital is the expected earnings on the utility's investments that are required in order for the value of the previously invested capital to remain unchanged. If new capital does not earn its price or required rate of return, the value of existing equity has to make up the difference. If the new capital earns a return greater than its price, existing shareholders will participate in the difference. If earnings on the investment of capital meet the required rate of return, existing shareholders will neither gain nor lose.

$$\text{Cost of Capital} = \text{Required Rate of Return}$$
$$= \text{Required Earnings/ Capital Invested}$$

1.8 The Allowed Rate of Return and Cost of Capital

The regulator should set the allowed rate of return equal to the cost of capital so that the utility can achieve the optimal rate of investment at the minimum price to the ratepayers. This can be demonstrated as follows.

In Example 1-2 shown earlier, a utility with a rate base of $900 million was considered, financed 60% by debt and 40% by equity. The cost of capital was estimated at 12.8%. Now, suppose the regulator sets the allowed return at 10% instead. To service the claims of both the bondholders and shareholders, earnings over costs should amount to $115.2 million, that is, 12.8% x $900 million.

If the utility is allowed a return of only 10% on a rate base of $900 million, earnings of only $90 million are produced. While the earnings are sufficient to cover the interest payments of $54 million ($900 x .60 x 10%) to the bondholders who have a prior claim on earnings, they are not enough to cover the claims of shareholders in the amount of $61.2 million. The stock price has to fall to a level such that an investor who purchases the stock after the price reduction will just obtain his opportunity cost. If the utility nevertheless undertakes mandatory capital investments that are allowed to earn 10%, while the cost of the funds is 12.8%, the inevitable result is a reduction in stock price and a wealth transfer from shareholders to ratepayers.

Conversely, if the allowed rate of return is greater than the cost of capital, capital investments are undertaken and investors' opportunity costs are more than achieved. Any excess earnings over and above those required to service debt capital accrue to the equity holders, and the stock price increases. In this case, the wealth transfer occurs from ratepayers to shareholders.

Investments are undertaken by the utility with no wealth transfer between ratepayers and shareholders only if the allowed rate of return is set equal to the cost of capital. In this case, the expected earnings generated from investments are just sufficient to service the claims of the debt and equity holders, no more no less. Setting the allowed return equal to the cost of capital is the only policy that will produce optimal investment rates at the minimum price to the ratepayer.

1.9 Determining the Cost of Capital

The standard procedure that has evolved for determining the allowed rate of return is now described. As demonstrated in an earlier section, the allowed return should be set so that the opportunity costs of bondholders and stockholders are covered. The general procedure is schematically depicted in Figure 1-4. The cost of debt and common equity are first determined separately, then weighted by the proportions of debt and equity in the capital structure to arrive at the weighted average cost of capital, which is finally translated into an overall allowed rate of return.

As an example, Table 1-1 below illustrates the computation of the overall rate of return requested from the Pennsylvania Public Service Commission by Hope Gas Company in a 1993 filing for rate relief.[10] The overall return of 10.06% is obtained by multiplying the embedded cost of debt, both long-term and short-term, by its respective proportion in the capital structure, and adding to this the product of the cost of common equity and the proportion of equity in the capital structure.

---

[10] See Morin (1992) for a full discussion of this case.

FIGURE 1-4
SCHEMATIC REPRESENTATION OF COST OF CAPITAL
DETERMINATION

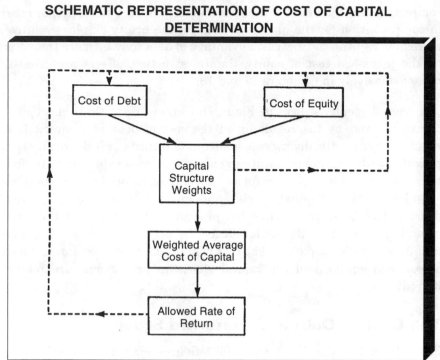

TABLE 1-1
HOPE GAS, INC.
COMPOSITE COST OF CAPITAL
DECEMBER 31, 1992

Type of Capital	Amount	Capitalization	Annual Cost of Capital	Components
(1)	(2)	(3)	(4)	(5)
Common Equity	$2,132,838,000	58.48%	12.30%	7.19%
Long-Term Debt	$1,122,119,000	30.77%	7.91%	2.43%
Short-Term Debt	$ 92,000,000	10.75%	4.02%	0.43%
Total Capitalization	$3,646,957,000	100.00%		10.05%

Source: Morin (1992)

Two feedback effects on the cost of capital are shown in Figure 1-4. The mix of debt and equity employed in computing the weighted average cost of capital influences the return required by debt and equity capital suppliers. For example, increasing the proportion of low-cost debt financing lowers the overall cost of capital but increases the financial risk of the company to the detriment of the shareholders who require a higher return in compensation for the increased risk. As the utility employs relatively more debt capital, the low cost advantage of debt may be more than offset by the increased cost of equity. Capital structure effects are discussed more extensively in Chapters 17 and 18.

The second feedback loop in Figure 1-4 stems from the impact of the return allowed by the regulator on the cost of debt and equity. If the regulator systematically awards inadequate returns or if the utility is not provided with a fair opportunity to earn its allowed rate of return, investors will demand higher returns in compensation for the increased "regulatory" risk. Regulatory risk and its impact on cost of capital is discussed in Chapter 2. While the procedure for computing the cost of capital is clear from the table above, the origin of the required input numbers is not so apparent. The cost of debt and preferred stock, the cost of common equity, and the capital structure proportions are required ingredients.

The Cost of Debt and Preferred Stock

From Table 1-1, the 7.91% and 4.02% figures for the costs of long- and short-term debt are "embedded" cost figures. Under standard regulatory practices, which use book value rate bases, the embedded cost of debt is the actual interest obligation, including amortization of discount, premium, and expense, of the utility's embedded debt outstanding related to the principal amount outstanding as of a particular date, expressed as a percent.

Similarly, the cost of preferred stock is the actual dividend obligation of the stock outstanding, related to the net proceeds from the sale of that stock. Frequently, the utility is allowed to include the amount of interest or dividend forecast for an impending debt or preferred stock issue. While the inclusion of the embedded cost of debt and preferred cost in the overall cost of capital assures that the actual costs associated with the current amounts outstanding are taken into account in the computation of revenue requirements, the company's current borrowing rate can be much higher or lower than its embedded rate.

It is sometimes proposed that the current rather than the embedded cost of debt and preferred should be used. The use of incremental, or current, yields would reflect more adequately the opportunity cost of the funds invested in the utility and the returns foregone by investors. Moreover, the cost of capital number utilized routinely in capital expenditures analysis requires the use of current market yields.

The counter-argument is that the application of current yields to their respective book values would not provide bondholders and preferred stockholders with their opportunity cost. They receive the same interest and dividend payments, irrespective of the utility's earnings. The difference between the embedded and the current yields would accrue to common shareholders, conferring upon them a windfall gain or loss over and above their return requirement that is already being covered. In other words, it is impossible to flow the difference between embedded and current yields to bondholders and preferred shareholders without altering the common stockholder's return.

Moreover, why should regulation exonerate bondholders and preferred stockholders from the risk of mistaken expectations? When the investor initially purchased the security, the risk of interest rate changes and the risk of inflation were incorporated into the investor's required return. Should regulation exempt investors from the risk of erroneous anticipations? Finally, the use of book value regulation preempts the use of current yield instead of embedded yield. Since the time the investor purchased the securities, changes in interest rates are reflected in changes in the market value of the securities, not in the book value. Only when the securities were initially purchased did book value represent opportunity cost. After that, it is market price that captures opportunity cost, not book value. If the use of current yield is advocated as an alternative to embedded yield, consistency and logic require the use of market value weights.

Capital Structure Weights

The numbers listed under "% proportions" in Table 1-1 refer to the proportions of long- and short-term debt and common equity actually employed, and not to the proportions to be employed in the future. Moreover, the weights are book value and not market value weights. The pros and cons and implications of book versus market weights are explored in Chapter 17.

The Cost of Equity Capital

The percentage cost of equity is arrived at by judgment, supported by a wide array of models, concepts, and methodologies that make up the remainder of this book. Broadly speaking, the techniques for estimating the cost of common equity fall into two general families: accounting-based and market-based techniques. Accounting-based techniques are associated with the Comparable Earnings standard, while market-based approaches, such as DCF, Capital Asset Pricing Model, and Arbitrage Pricing Model, are directly consistent with the market-based standards of a fair return enunciated in the *Bluefield* and *Hope* cases. Some of the techniques treat risk explicitly and directly as a separate variable in the model; others treat risk implicitly and indirectly as somehow subsumed in security prices. These techniques are summarized below in Figure 1-5.

FIGURE 1-5
COST OF EQUITY MEASUREMENT

	Techniques	
	Accounting	Comparable Earnings
Direct	Market	Discounted cash flow
	Market	Market-to-book, Q
	Market	Risk premium
Indirect	Market	CAPM
	Market	APM

1.10 The Use of Multiple Methods in Cost of Equity Determination

The court cases discussed previously indicated that there are no specific rules or models for determining a fair rate of return. It is dangerous and inappropriate to rely on only one methodology in determining the cost of equity. For instance, by relying solely on the DCF model at a time when the fundamental assumptions underlying the DCF model are tenuous, a regulatory body greatly limits its flexibility and increases the risk of authorizing unreasonable rates of return. The results from only one method are likely to contain a high degree of measurement error. The regulator's hands should not be bound to one methodology of estimating equity costs, nor should the regulator ignore relevant evidence and back itself into a corner.

There are four generic methodologies available to measure the cost of equity: DCF, Risk Premium, and CAPM, which are market-oriented, and Comparable Earnings, which is accounting-oriented. Each generic market-based methodology in turn contains several variants.

When measuring equity costs, which essentially deals with the measurement of investor expectations, no one single methodology provides a foolproof panacea. Each methodology requires the exercise of considerable judgment on the reasonableness of the assumptions underlying the methodology and on the reasonableness of the proxies used to validate the theory. It follows that more than one methodology should be employed in arriving at a judgment on the cost of equity and that these methodologies should be applied across a series of comparable risk companies.

Each methodology possesses its own way of examining investor behavior, its own premises, and its own set of simplifications of reality. Each method proceeds from different fundamental premises that cannot be validated empirically. Investors do not necessarily subscribe to any one method, nor does the stock price reflect the application of any one single method by the price-setting investor. There is no monopoly as to which method is used by investors. In the absence of any hard evidence as to which method outdoes the other, all relevant evidence should be used and weighted equally, in order to minimize judgmental error, measurement error, and conceptual infirmities. A regulatory body should rely on the results of a variety of methods applied to a variety of comparable groups, and not on one particular method. There is no guarantee that a single DCF result is necessarily the ideal predictor of the stock price and of the cost of equity reflected in that price, just as there is no guarantee that a single CAPM or Risk Premium result constitutes the perfect explanation of that stock price.

No one individual method provides an exclusive foolproof formula for determining a fair return, but each method provides useful evidence so as to facilitate the exercise of an informed judgment. Reliance on any single method or preset formula is inappropriate when dealing with investor expectations. Moreover, the advantage of using several different approaches is that the results of each one can be used to check the others.

The concept of cost of capital described in this chapter can be succinctly summarized as follows: A regulated utility should be entitled to a return that allows it to raise the necessary capital to meet service demand without cost to existing shareholders. This return is the weighted average of the embedded cost of debt and preferred capital, and a return on the common equity capital equal to the currently required return on equity. The two principal problems in implementing the approach are the determination of the appropriate set of capital structure weights and the estimation of the required return on equity. The optimal capital structure issue is treated in Chapter 17.

This book focuses on the rate of return component of regulation. The first few chapters establish the conceptual foundations of rate of return and cost of capital. In Chapter 2, the factors that impinge upon the required return are identified. Since all such factors can be subsumed under the broad heading of "risk," the concept of risk and its measurement are examined. The relationship between return and risk, which underlies the cost of capital concept, is emphasized. The next several chapters survey the techniques available to estimate the cost of equity capital, pointing out the assumptions, strengths and weaknesses, and applicability of each technique. The last few chapters discuss the composite cost of capital and the related capital structure effects.

References

Averch, H.A. and Johnson, L. Behavior of the Firm Under Regulatory Constraint. *American Economic Review* , June 1962, 1053-1069.

Bonbright, J.C. *Principles of Public Utility Rates,* New York: Columbia University Press, 1966.

Bowring, J. "The Calculation of Debt Cost For A Regulated Utility." *Electric Potential* , September 1985.

Garfield, P.J. and Lovejoy, W. *Public Utility Economics,* Englewood Cliffs NJ: Prentice-Hall, 1964.

Gordon, M.J. "Rate of Return Regulation in the Current Economic Environment." In *Adapting Regulation to Shortages, Curtailments and Inflation,* edited by J.L. O'Donnell, 15-28. East Lansing MI: Michigan State University, 1977.

Howe, K.M. and Rasmussen, E.F. *Public Utility Economics and Finance,* Englewood Cliffs NJ: Prentice-Hall, 1982.

Kahn, A.E. *The Economics of Regulation: Principles and Institutions,* New York: Wiley and Sons, 1970.

Kolb, R.W., Morin, R.A., and Gay, G.D. "Hedging Regulatory Lag with Futures Contracts." *Journal of Finance,* May 1983.

Morin, R.A. "An Empirical Study of the Effect of CWIP on Cost of Capital and Revenue Requirements, Part I." *Public Utilities Fortnightly,* July 10, 1986A, 21-27.

Morin, R.A. "An Empirical Study of the Effect of CWIP on Cost of Capital and Revenue Requirements, Part II." *Public Utilities Fortnightly,* July 24, 1986B, 24-28.

Morin, R.A. Hope Gas Inc., Prepared Testimony, Public Service Commission of West Virginia, Case No. 91-025-G-42T, 1992.

Morin, R.A. and Ramirez, G. "Valuation and Capital Recovery: A Theoretical Model." Working Paper, Center for the Study of Regulated Industry, Georgia State University, 1988.

Myers, S.C. "The Application of Finance Theory to Public Utility Rate Case." Bell Journal of Economics and Management Science, Spring 1972, 58-97.

Parcell, D. *The Cost of Capital: A Practitioners Guide*. National Society of Rate of Return Analysts, Certified Rate of Return Analyst Program, 1992.

Phillips, C.F. *The Regulation of Public Utilities: Theory and Practice,* Arlington, VA: Public Utilities Reports Inc., 1993.

Robichek, A.A. "Regulation and Modern Finance Theory." *Journal of Finance,* June 1978, 693-705.

Additional References

Bonbright, J.C., Danielsen, A.L., and Kamerschen, D.R. *Principles of Public Utility Rates,* Arlington, VA: Public Utilities Reports Inc., 1988.

Carleton, W.T. "Rate of Return, Rate Base, and Regulatory Lag Under Conditions of Changing Capital Costs." *Land Economics,* May 1974, 145-151.

Morin, R.A. *Utilities' Cost of Capital,* Arlington, VA: Public Utilities Reports, Inc., 1984.

Chapter 2
Risk and Return

Regulated public utilities are entitled to recover through the rates charged to their customers all costs of providing service, including a fair return on capital. The landmark *Bluefield* and *Hope* cases established the criterion that the fair return be commensurate with those available on alternate investments of comparable risk. Implementation of this criterion requires a firm and comprehensive conceptualization of the relationship between return and risk. The previous chapter established the direct linkage between the allowed rate of return and the cost of capital. This chapter links the cost of capital to risk. The determinants of required return under the general heading of risk are described in the first section, and the nature and measurement of risk are explored from two distinct conceptual frameworks in the second section. Chapter 3 discusses the practical aspects of risk measurement.

2.1 The Determinants of Required Return

As an aid to understanding the investor's required rate of return, it is useful to conceptualize the required return on any security, such as a share of common stock, as the sum of the riskless rate of interest and a risk premium as follows:

Required Return = Risk-free Rate + Risk Premium

$$k = R_F + R_P \qquad\qquad (2\text{-}1)$$

where
k = required return
R_F = risk-free rate
R_P = risk premium

The risk-free rate is the price of time, that is, the reward for postponing consumption and for not exposing funds to risk. The risk premium is the additional return compensation for assuming risk. This concept is illustrated in the example below:

EXAMPLE 2-1

GTE Northwest has long-term corporate bonds that mature in 2010. Based on the current market price of these bonds, it can be determined that the investor's expected return from those bonds is 9%. At the same time, the yield on long-term U.S. Treasury bonds is about 7%.

Therefore, GTE Northwest bondholders are requiring a risk premium of 2%. From the above equation:

Required Return = Risk-Free Rate + Risk Premium
$$k = 7\% + 2\%$$
$$= 9\%$$

To gain additional insight into the meaning of cost of capital, it is useful to disaggregate further the factors that cause the cost of capital of a firm to be high or low. This is shown schematically in Figure 2-1.

FIGURE 2-1
THE DETERMINANTS OF REQUIRED RETURN

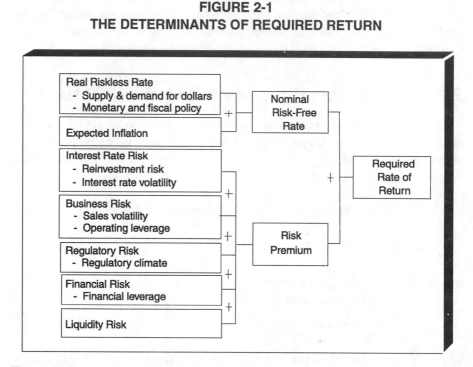

The risk-free rate, R_F, can be disaggregated into a "real" risk-free rate of interest, r, and an inflation premium, π. The risk premium, R_P, can in turn be decomposed into a subset of four elements: interest-rate risk, business risk, financial risk, and liquidity risk, denoted by the symbols i, b, f, and l, respectively. Hence, the required return is the sum of the following six elements, each of which exerts an influence on its magnitude:

$$k = r + \pi + i + b + f + l \qquad (2\text{-}2)$$

Of course, all the components of risk are fluid and change dynamically over time. It is quite plausible that an increase in business and financial risk over time is offset by a decrease in one or the other of the components, such as the real rate or the inflation component, so that the cost of equity capital remains constant. For example, increases in business risk, caused by more intense competition and/or deregulation, are frequently offset by corresponding reductions in financial risk, that is, more conservative capital structures. Each risk component of required return (cost of capital), as displayed in Figure 2-1, is now discussed separately.

Real Risk-free Rate of Return (r)

The real risk-free rate is the return that would be required by investors in the absence of inflation and risk. The amount and timing of all the cash flows generated by the risk-free security are known with certainty and are unaffected by inflation. Hence, the real risk-free rate reflects the pure time value of money to an investor, which can be regarded as the price of postponing consumption by one year, and is determined by the supply and demand for funds in the economy. The supply of funds reflects the time preference of individuals for consumption of income, and the basic thriftiness and saving propensity of the population, and is influenced by the relative ease or tightness of the government's monetary policy. The demand for funds is largely dictated by the availability of investment opportunities in the economy and by the government's fiscal policies.

Inflation Premium (π)

To the real risk-free interest rate is added a premium equal to the rate of inflation expected by investors. Lenders seek compensation for the expected erosion in the purchasing power of their investment holdings. If, for example, investors require a real return of 4%, but expect the purchasing power of the interest or dividend payment flows to decline by 6% per year in the future, then they will demand an additional compensation of 6%. If they do not include an 6% inflation premium, the return they receive in real terms will be -2%. By raising the required return to 10% to include an inflation protection premium of 6%, investors actually receive 4% in real terms. Of course, investors will only receive compensation for expected inflation, and not for unanticipated inflation. If the actual inflation deviates from the expected rate, the real return will be correspondingly higher or lower than 4%. The sum of the real rate of interest and the inflation premium is known as the "nominal" risk-free rate, and is readily observable in the market for government securities. The risk-free rate can be specified for a given holding period as the yield on a U.S. government bond of comparable maturity.

Interest Rate Risk (i)

To the nominal rate is added a risk premium to compensate investors for uncertainty about future real rates of return and inflation rates. Interest-rate risk refers to the variability in return caused by subsequent changes in the level of interest rates. It stems from two sources. The first source is the uncertainty regarding the rate at which interest or dividend receipts can be reinvested. In the case of a bond, for example, the holding period return will be largely dictated by the rate at which the periodic interest coupons can be reinvested, and the greater the uncertainty of future interest rates, the greater is the reinvestment risk.

The second source of interest rate risk stems from the negative relation-ship between interest rates and value. When interest rates rise, a previously issued bond paying a fixed contractual return will become a less desirable investment, falling in price. This is because any change in the bond's required return can only be accomplished through a capital loss, since the bond's contractually fixed interest payments do not vary over its life. If an investor decides to sell the bond before maturity, the price that someone else is willing to pay will depend on prevailing interest rates at that time. If, for example, prevailing interest rates are at 12%, a bond yielding 10% on its face value will be worth less than the 12% bonds currently available in the market. The entire process works in reverse as well. Fixed income contracts increase in value as interest rates decline. Stock prices, particularly those of high-yielding public utilities, are also influenced by fluctuations in prevailing interest rates on alternative competing investments, since the dividends derived from ownership of stocks compete with the coupon interest payments from bonds.

The first three components of required return discussed thus far reflect broad economic forces outside a firm's control and systematically affect all firms. The remaining components of risk are specific to a particular company.

Business Risk (b)

The fourth component of return is the business risk perceived by investors. Business risk encompasses all the operating factors that collectively increase the probability that expected future income flows accruing to investors may not be realized, because of the fundamental nature of the firm's business.

Business risk is due to sales volatility and operating leverage. Sales volatility, also referred to as demand risk, refers to the uncertainty in the demand for the firm's products due in part to external non-controllable factors, such as the basic cyclicality of the firm's products, the products income and price elasticity, the amount of competition, the availability of product substitutes, the risk of technological obsolescence, the degree of regulation, and the conditions of the labor and raw materials markets.

Sales volatility is also related to internal or controllable factors. The reaction of a firm's management to the business environment, such as the adoption of a particular cost structure, are important dimensions of business risk. If all production costs are variable, then operating income varies proportionately to sales variability. If, as is the case for utilities, a large portion of costs are fixed, then operating income will be far more volatile than sales. This magnification effect of fixed costs on the variability of operating income is referred to as "operating leverage."

The business risk of utilities is assessed by examining the strength of long-term demand for utility products and services. Many factors have an impact on business risk, including the size and growth rate of the market, the diversity of customer base and its economic solidity, the availability of substitutes and degree of competition, and the utility's relative competitive standing in its major markets, including residential, industrial, and commercial markets.

The regional economics of a utility's service territory exert a strong influence on the company's risk. The proportion of total revenues as between industrial, commercial, and residential customers measures a utility's dependence on any given class of customers. Within a given class, such as industrial, the concentration of revenues from the top five, ten, or twenty business customers is an additional measure of a company's vulnerability and exposure.

Diversification and flexibility in the fuel mix, and the dependability of fuel deliveries are examples of internal risk factors for electric utilities. Operating efficiency from the standpoint of cost and quality of service is another factor that may influence a utility's competitive risk exposure. Other examples of internal risk factors include the degree of diversification in the firm's asset structure, managerial efficiency, growth strategy, research and development policies, and competitive posture.

The impact of inflation on a specific company's sales, costs, profits, cash flows, prices, and the firm's response to such inflationary conditions are also part of the firm's business risk. The size of a utility's construction program is also a source of business risk, to the extent that new construction is to meet projected demand. In addition, projected demand is more difficult to forecast than existing demand, and this forecasting risk is compounded by regulatory lag and attrition. Construction factors also impinge on financial risk, as discussed below.

A regulated utility is also subject to forecasting risk to the extent that budgeted forecasts are made one to two years before regulatory determination of its rates. Potential deviations from expected profitability can occur because of unanticipated increases in costs (interest, O&M, etc.) and/or unanticipated decreases in revenues. Any factor that complicates the investor's ability to assess future prospects will accentuate business risk.

Business risk manifests itself not only through demand uncertainties but also through supply uncertainties. An illustrative case in point is the supply risks of local gas distribution companies (LDCs) that followed the 1986 deregulation of natural gas prices. These companies became responsible for making decisions regarding prices, contract differentiation, and supply portfolio composition. The provision of gas supplies to its customers was therefore subject to greater risk of approval by the regulators. The uncertain and evolving roles of LDCs in providing gas supplies to various customer groups who have several supply alternatives in a deregulated market complicated the decision process. Moreover, deregulation brought with it greater ability for producers and other natural gas marketers to sell within the service area of LDCs, creating great uncertainty as to the size of market to be supplied. This risk and the reliance upon other parties for the security of supply and supply planning created a radically different supply risk for LDCs under deregulation.

Short- v. Long-Term Business Risk. A further distinction is frequently made between short-term and long-term business risks. Short-term business risks involve short-term uncertainties and volatilities that are expected to occur within one year. They are usually business-cycle related. Long-term business risks are longer-term uncertainties over and above short-term risks that involve changes in the structural and chronic supply/demand forces in a given industry. Examples of the latter include the gradual penetration of competitive forces and/or deregulation in a given industry, the emergence of technology-based growth opportunities in an industry, impending environmental legislation and its impact, and the gradual transition to different modes of regulation.

Regulatory Risk. Regulation for public utilities is a major component of business risk because of its impact on revenues and earnings. Decisions of state regulators and federal regulatory agencies, such as the Environmental Protection Agency, the Nuclear Regulatory Commission, the Energy Planning Board, and others, have a direct impact on utility finances. Regulation can increase business risk if it does not provide adequate returns and/or if it does not provide the utility with the opportunity to earn a fair rate of return.

The Supreme Court's recent opinion in *Duquesne Light Co. et al. v. Barasch et al.* (109 S. Ct. 609, 1989) addressed a number of issues relating to regulatory practices and established that regulatory risk is a special class of risk that must be recognized by regulators when setting the allowed rate of return.[1]

Regulatory risk generally refers to the quality and consistency of regulation applied to a given regulated utility, and specifically to the fairness and reasonableness of rate awards. Regulatory jurisdictions are evaluated on the basis of three major factors: earnable return on equity, regulatory quality, and regulatory technique. In assessing these three factors, several issues must be examined, including the length of regulatory lag, the inclusion or exclusion of construction work in process (CWIP), the type of test year employed (whether historical or forward), the normalization of tax timing differences versus flow-through techniques, the proportion of earnings represented by the allowance for funds used during construction (AFUDC), environmental issues, and judicial and legislative mandates.

Regulation can compound the business risk premium if it is unpredictable in reacting to rate hike requests both in terms of the time lag of its response and its magnitude. For example, the absence of a purchased gas adjustment mechanism injects regulatory lag. More generally, if the regulatory response to rising operating costs and higher capital costs because of high unanticipated inflation is inadequate or untimely, or if the utility is not given the opportunity to cover higher costs because of political factors or inadequate regulation (rate base exclusions, disallowances), the business risk premium rises further, along with capital costs.

Regulation can also diminish business risk. Bonded rate increases, adoption of forward test years, the use of deferral and normalization accounts and automatic adjustment mechanisms, such as fuel adjustment clauses, are examples of attempts to lower regulatory risk.

Unreasonable rate treatment for any utility can not only raise the cost of capital and, hence, ratepayer burden, but may also have serious public policy implications and repercussions for the entire business or economic region. When adhering to questionable implementations of a given methodology, or when ignoring relevant evidence, a regulatory body runs the risk of ignoring the policy implications of a recommendation. For example, the quality of regulation and the reasonableness of rate of return awards clearly have implications for regulatory climate, economic development, and job creation in a given territory. Fair and reasonable regulation must be consistent with the economic well-being of the area served.

---

[1]   See Kolbe and Tye (1992) for a further discussion of this issue.

Regulatory lag is an important determinant of regulatory risk. Its presence makes it difficult to earn a reasonable rate of return, especially in an inflationary environment. Moreover, regulatory lag limits the pricing flexibility of the utility, and the company may be unable to respond to competitive pressures. It also creates mismatches between regulatory rates and supply-demand costs so that prices are either too high or too low. Inefficient resource allocation and distorted consumer pricing signals may result.

Incentives to innovate and to introduce new services may be dampened due to regulatory lag to the extent that the utility is unable to capture the cost savings of its innovations. Frequently, the payoff of its innovations and efficiency gains are asymmetric; cost savings from successful innovations are passed on to ratepayers, while unsuccessful ventures are disallowed and absorbed by investors. The net result is that utilities may use capital/labor ratios that are not cost-minimizing.

Several environmental issues increase regulatory risks and create the need for non-revenue producing investments. For example, in the 1990s, the financial effects of the Clean Air Act on coal-fired generation plants is a source of cost and availability uncertainty for electric utilities with fossil electric generating units. Consumer resistance to distribution/transmission site noise level, appearance, and the spectre of electro-magnetic fields (EMF) result in increased costs and construction delays. Another example is the uncertain final financial effects of the Safe Drinking Water Act on water utilities. Water utility companies will need to upgrade their facilities to comply with evolving environmental standards. Because the standards are still evolving and are yet to be determined, there are uncertainties related to upgrading and compliance costs. Future water quality regulations will increase retail water utility fixed costs and capital investment. This will in turn increase operating and financial leverage, thus increasing risk and required rate of return.[2]

Financial Risk (f)

Financial risk stems from the method used by the firm to finance its investments and is reflected in its capital structure. It refers to the additional variability imparted to income available to common shareholders by the employment of fixed-cost financing, that is, debt and preferred

---

[2] For a complete study of how changes in the operating environment of water utilities have increased their investment risk and their cost of capital, both in absolute terms and in relation to other utilities, and how increased capital and operating costs of complying with new and evolving water quality standards have an impact on their risk and required rate of return, see Morin (1992).

stock capital. Although the use of fixed-cost capital can offer financial advantages through the possibility of leverage of earnings (financial leverage), it creates additional risk due to the fixed contractual obligations associated with such capital. Debt and preferred stock carry fixed charge burdens that must be supported by the company's earnings before any return can be made available to the common shareholder. The greater the

EXAMPLE 2–2

One of the most important ideas in finance is that financial risk increases with leverage and that the greater the leverage, the greater the cost of equity. For example, consider a company with a total capitalization of $600,000. The company can be either financed entirely through common equity contributed by the shareholders, or by issuing $300,000 of debt at a 10% rate of interest and having an equity investment of just $300,000. The expected earnings before interest and taxes (EBIT) are $100,000. The financial results obtained for the two alternative capital structures are shown in Table 2-1 below for three assumed levels of EBIT, $80,000, $100,000, and $120,000.

TABLE 2-1
DEMONSTRATION OF THE IMPACT OF
LEVERAGE ON EQUITY RETURNS

	All Equity ($000)			50% Debt ($000)		
EBIT	$80	$100	$120	$80	$100	$120
Interest	0	0	0	30	30	30
Profit before Taxes	80	100	120	50	70	90
Taxes (50%)	40	50	60	25	35	45
Profit after Taxes	40	50	60	25	35	45
Return on Equity	40/600	50/600	60/600	25/300	35/300	45/300
	6.7%	8.3%	10%	8.3%	11.7%	15%

At an EBIT level of $100,000, the use of debt financing has increased the return on equity from 8.3% to 11.7%. The shareholders' gain is the result of raising funds on the debt market at an after-tax cost of 5% and investing these funds to yield a return well in excess of that cost. But the risk to the shareholders is increased. The earnings available to common shareholders become more volatile, as the relative amount of debt used becomes greater. Leverage is a double-edged sword. Just as shareholders' gains are magnified in the case of favorable operating results, potential losses are also magnified in the case of unfavorable results. In this example, the consequences to the shareholders of a 20% variation in Earnings Before Interest and Taxes in either direction are calculated. The return on equity figures of Table 2-1 can be summarized as follows:

Operating Results	Equity Financing	50% Debt Financing
$ 80,00	6.7%	8.3%
$100,000	8.3% 1	1.7%
$120,000	10.0%	15.0%

It is clear from these results that variations in operating earnings cause magnified variations in equity returns when debt financing is used. The spread in equity returns is wider in the case of debt financing, and the greater the leverage, the greater the spread and the greater the cost of common equity.

percentage of fixed charges to the total income of the company, the greater the financial risk. The use of fixed cost financing introduces additional variability into the pattern of net earnings over and above that already conferred by business risk, and may even introduce the possibility of default and bankruptcy in unusual cases.

Prudent management requires that lower financial risks should be used to offset high business risks. Industries with significant variability in revenues (durables, auto, capital goods) generally have low debt ratios to offset the higher business risk. The converse is also true.

More generally, a financial risk premium is required by both bondholders and common shareholders. Common equity holders require compensation for the additional magnification induced in their future earnings, while bondholders require compensation for the greater risk of default. A formal analytical expression for the required return on levered common equity is derived in Chapter 17, showing the profound effect of the variability introduced to the firm's income stream by senior fixed charges on the market valuation of common stock. The expression linking equity returns and capital structure is as follows:

$$r = [R + (R - K_d)D/E](1 - t) \qquad (2\text{-}3)$$

where
r = rate of return on common equity
R = rate of return on total assets
K_d = interest rate on debt
D/E = debt to common equity proportion
t = income tax rate

In words, this expression states that the return on the book value of equity is directly proportional to the rate of return on assets, plus a risk premium equal to the excess of the asset rate over the debt rate levered by the debt/equity ratio in book value terms. A given variation in R due to business risk is magnified into a larger variation in the return on equity, r; the greater the relative proportion of debt, D/E, the greater is the magnification effect.

Although financial risk is unique to a specific firm and is distinct from the firm's business risk, business and financial risk are interrelated. The overall risk to the common stock investor is a composite of the business and financial risk. The overall risk of two firms may be similar when a high business risk firm has assumed less financial risk while a low business risk firm has assumed greater financial risk. In general, unregulated companies have greater business risk than regulated utilities, and because of these differences in business risk, utilities have adopted a correspondingly higher amount of financial risk in their capital structures.

Finally, it should be noted that financial risk can arise not only because of variations in capital structure, but also because of the use of financing methods that impart some unpredictability to future earnings. The presence of convertible bonds or convertible preferred shares, or the presence of securities issued with warrants attached create uncertainty as to the exact time at which the rights of those securities will be exercised and as to the impending dilution in earnings per share.

Construction Risk. Construction risk is an important component of financial risk. If a company has a large construction budget in relation to its size, that company requires substantial external financing in the immediate future. It is imperative that the company has access to needed capital funds on reasonable terms and conditions. A regulated utility is even more susceptible to construction risk than an unregulated company. An unregulated company has more discretion and latitude in scheduling and deferring capital projects. A utility, because of its mandated obligation to serve, does not possess the same flexibility. The problem is compounded for a regulated company that must secure funds from capital markets in order to fund new construction commitments, irrespective of capital market conditions, interest rates conditions, and quality consciousness of market participants.

On debt markets, construction is one of several key determinants of credit quality and, hence, of capital costs. A company's future construction plans are scrutinized by bond rating agencies before assessing credit quality. The construction budget in relation to internal cash generation is a key quantitative determinant of credit quality, along with construction expenditures as a proportion of capitalization. CWIP to capitalization and common equity ratios are also analyzed by investors and become key determinants of capital costs and funds availability.

Moreover, if a utility has an impending large construction program, rate relief requirements and regulatory treatment uncertainty will increase regulatory risks as well, lowering credit quality. Regulatory risks stemming from a substantial construction program include approval risks, lags and delays, potential rate base exclusions, and potential disallowances.

Liquidity Risk (l)

The ability to buy or sell an investment quickly and without a substantial price concession is referred to as liquidity. Liquidity risk represents the possibility of sustaining a loss from current value when converting an asset into cash. Securities listed on the New York Stock Exchange are highly liquid, whereas the shares of over-the-counter companies are less marketable. Closely-held securities possess very little liquidity.

Size Effect. Liquidity risk is likely to be size-related. Investment risk increases as company size diminishes, all else remaining constant. The size phenomenon is well documented in the finance literature. The size effect is most likely the result of a liquidity premium, whereby investors in small stocks demand greater returns as compensation for lack of marketability and liquidity. Investors prefer high to low liquidity and demand higher returns from less liquid investments, holding other factors constant. The size effect is discussed further in Chapter 13.

In summary, required return on investment is determined by the nominal risk-free rate and a risk premium. The risk-free rate is driven by expected inflation and by variations in the real rate of interest. The latter is determined by investors' time preference for consumption, by the availability of investment opportunities in the economy, and by the demand and supply for funds, largely influenced by fiscal and monetary policy.

These factors are systematic in that they affect all securities. The risk premium is affected by business, financial, and liquidity risk. The role of regulatory risk is in turn crucial in determining the level of business risk. Construction risk also influences the degree of financial risk.

2.2   The Concept of Risk

The *Hope* case strongly suggested that a fair return should be commensurate with the returns earned by other firms with corresponding risks. Hence, the proper measure(s) of risk to be used in regulatory proceedings is crucial in setting a fair return for public utilities. The previous section identified the various risk components that determine the required return on a security. This section addresses the actual measurement of risk by investors.

The appropriate measure of risk in regulatory proceedings depends on the framework in which investors view risk. There are two general frameworks within which the measurement of risk can be approached:

1.   Firm-specific risk

2.   Portfolio risk

The firm-specific viewpoint considers the risk of a security as if that security were viewed in isolation by the investor and envisages risk as the total variability of its returns. In contrast, the portfolio viewpoint considers the risk of a security in the context of a diversified portfolio and envisages risk as only that portion of the security's total risk that cannot be diversified away by the investor. Which is the predominant viewpoint is an empirical question.

In a comprehensive study of individual investors' behavior, Blume and Friend (1978) found that when purchasing stock, 82% of all stockholders evaluate both the risk involved and the potential return. The three most commonly used measures of risk by these investors are price volatility (standard deviation), earnings volatility, and published beta coefficients. The first two measures of risk are consistent with the total variability (firm-specific) framework, and the third measure is consistent with the portfolio framework. In a survey of 210 investment bankers regarding methods employed by them to assess utility risk, Chandrasekaran and Dukes (1981) found that beta was the most popular, followed by standard deviation, coefficient of variation, and skewness. In a study of 165 public utility firms and public utility commissions, Dukes and Chandy (1983) found that beta was the risk measure most used by 65% of the utilities and 82% of the commissions. The standard deviation was used by 14% of the utilities and 42% of the commissions. Both frameworks are thus relevant.

The next section approaches risk from the total variability viewpoint, and the subsequent section from the portfolio viewpoint.

Firm-Specific Risk

The objective of any investor is to realize a given rate of return on the funds he or she manages. The realization of this return is not guaranteed in advance, however. The realized return, in the form of income and capital gains from holding a particular security, may differ from the expected return. The risk of an investment is therefore related to the potential variability of its return. Measuring risk is thus equivalent to measuring variability of market returns.[3] The classic measure of variability employed by statisticians is variance, σ^2, or more commonly its square root: the standard deviation, σ. Both of these measures are essentially measures of dispersion around an average.

Variance is simply the average deviation from the mean and is calculated by estimating the squared deviation of the realized return from its average value, summing the squared deviations and dividing by the number of observations. The variance is written as:

$$\sigma^2 = \sum_{t=1}^{n} \frac{(R_{it} - \overline{R})^2}{n} \qquad (2\text{-}4)$$

where n is the number of observations, $\overline{R}$ is the average realized return for security i, and R_{it} are the individual period returns. The standard deviation is obtained by taking the square root of the variance. The average realized return, $\overline{R}$, is calculated by summing the realized returns and dividing by the number of observations, that is,

$$\overline{R} = \sum_{t=1}^{n} \frac{R_{it}}{n} \qquad (2\text{-}5)$$

The individual security returns for a given period, R_{it}, include not only the dividend or interest income from the security but also any appreciation in

---

[3] The most widely used measure of variability is the standard deviation of return. The quantification of risk in the standard deviation framework owes its origins to Markowitz (1952), and can be found in any corporate finance or investments textbook. See for example, Brealey and Myers (1991), Brigham and Gapenski (1991), and Reilly (1994).

the value of the security during the period in question. More formally, the return for a given period can be written as:

$$R_{it} = \frac{D_t + (P_t - P_{t-1})}{P_t}$$

(2-6)

where
R_{it} = return of security i during period t

D_t = dividends received during period t

P_t = price of security i at the end of the period

P_{t-1} = price of security i at the beginning of the period

Table 2-2 below illustrates the computation of standard deviation. Column 2 shows the four quarterly returns of the security in the last year. The average return per period is 4%, and the variance is 242 / 4 = 60.5, and the standard deviation is the square root of 60.5, or 7.78%. In other words, the average realized return for the security over the four quarters was 4%, with an average deviation of 7.78% around this mean return. Basically, the standard deviation measures the size and frequency of the deviations of the realized returns from the average, and places a heavy weight on large deviations, since it is computed by squaring all the deviations. The standard deviation of the security's returns over the one-year interval can be assessed in a similar manner from the past observations of 52 weekly returns or 12 monthly returns, instead of four quarterly returns.

TABLE 2–2
CALCULATION OF STANDARD DEVIATION

Period	Return	$R - \bar{R}$	$(R - \bar{R})^2$
Quarter 1	+ 8%	4%	16
Quarter 2	+13%	9%	81
Quarter 3	+ 3%	- 1%	1
Quarter 4	- 8%	- 12%	144
	$\bar{R} = 4\%$		242

R = return per sub-period

$\bar{R}$ = average return for the overall period

Figure 2-2 shows the probability distribution of returns for the company in the example of Table 2-2.

Probability distributions depict the distribution of possible return outcomes with an indication of the subjective or objective probability of each

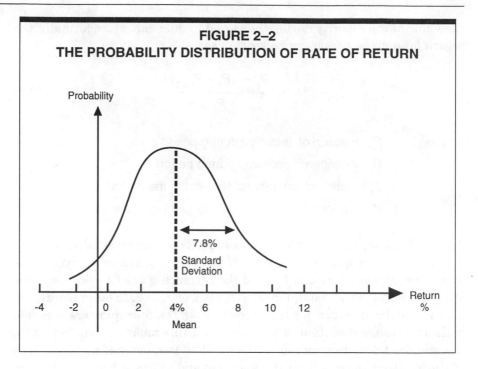

FIGURE 2–2
THE PROBABILITY DISTRIBUTION OF RATE OF RETURN

occurrence. Empirical research has shown these distributions to be normally (bell-shaped) distributed. These distributions are essential for investors who want to know the average return they can expect from each potential investment and the risk associated with that investment.

Of course, the investor is interested in future variability and not in historical variability per se. The variability of realized returns is only a surrogate for the future variability and is valid only if the historical standard deviation remains reasonably stable over time. The next chapter will elaborate on this point.

In summary, for the investor who views a security in isolation, a good estimate of its risk is a sample standard deviation of realized rates of return.

Risk from a Portfolio Viewpoint

Before recent theoretical development, it was generally believed that the correct measure of a security's risk was the standard deviation of realized rates of return. Progress in portfolio theory has provided the theoretical basis for measuring investor risk on a share in a new light. What portfolio theory has made clear is that the only risk of concern to an investor is the risk that he cannot diversify away by holding a large number of shares directly or indirectly through investment in a mutual fund or other financial institution. For investors who hold only the securities of one firm, the total risk of that security, as measured by the standard deviation, is most relevant. But for investors who diversify by investing in several other securities, it is the contribution of a security to the risk of the portfolio as a whole rather than the security's own total risk that is relevant.

To illustrate this point intuitively, consider two equity investments in isolation, both of which have a large standard deviation of return. One investment is in gold mining, a highly volatile but counter-cyclical sector, and the other is in heavy capital equipment, a volatile cyclical sector. If when the first stock goes up the other one goes down, and conversely, then the return on a combination of these two securities is relatively stable. The price movements in the gold stock are offset by equal but opposite price movements in the cyclical stock. Accordingly, the portfolio is almost risk free, although its component securities have very risky returns. This example suggests that the measurement of risk should be more appropriately directed at measuring the extent to which an individual security contributes to the overall risk of a portfolio.

It can be shown that the risk of a security is proportional to the covariance of its returns with the portfolio's overall return. Let R_p represent the return on a portfolio of securities, σ_p^2, the variance of R_p, and X_i the proportion of funds allocated to each security in the portfolio. Then the portfolio's return is the weighted sum of the returns of its component securities, and the portfolio's risk is the weighted sum of the individual securities' risks and pairwise covariances:

$$R_p = \sum_{i=1}^{n} X_i \, R_i \qquad (2\text{-}7)$$

$$\sigma_p^2 = \sum_{i=1}^{n} \sum_{j=1}^{n} X_i \, X_j \, \sigma_{ij} \qquad (2\text{-}8)$$

where σ_{ij} is the covariance between R_i and R_j and $\sigma_{ii} = \sigma_i^2$. For a portfolio that consists of only one security, then clearly the relevant risk of security i is simply σ_i. To analyze the contribution of security i to portfolio risk, σ_{ip}, take the first derivative of Equation 2-8 with respect to x_j :

$$\frac{d\sigma_p^2}{dX_i} = 2X_i \sigma_i^{\,2} + 2\sum_{k \neq 1}^{n} X_k \sigma_{ik} = 2\sum_{k=1}^{n} X_k \sigma_{ik} = 2\sigma_{ip}$$

Thus, the risk of security i is proportional to its covariance with the portfolio's return, R_p. This is shown in Myers (1972).

The fundamental idea underlying the modern view of risk is that security price fluctuations are attributable to both the general influence of the market and to factors specific to the company, such as new products, mergers, rate hearings, financing practices, and reorganizations. The general market movement in turn reflects economic events that affect all firms, such as inflation, politics, interest rates, and monetary and fiscal policy. The partitioning of total variability into a market-related component and a company-specific component can be conceptualized graphically, as in Figure 2-3. The individual security's returns are shown on the vertical axis and the corresponding returns on the overall market on the horizontal axis. To each past time period corresponds a point on the graph: the security's observed return for the period and the market's corresponding return observed for the same period. The observations are seen to scatter around a straight line. The linear relationship can be expressed as follows:

$$R_{it} + \alpha_i + \beta_i R_{Mt} + \varepsilon_{it} \qquad (2\text{-}9)$$

where $\quad R_{it}$ = return of security i for a given period t

$\qquad R_{Mt}$ = return on a market index during period t

$\qquad \beta_i$ = beta, or slope of the line indicating the relationship between the security's price fluctuations and those of the general market

$\qquad \alpha_i$ = alpha, or intercept of the line, indicating the expected value of R_{it} when R_{Mt} is zero

$\qquad \varepsilon_{it}$ = residual error term

This relationship hypothesizes that the return on a security is related to a market return component, $\beta_i R_{Mt}$, and to a firm specific component, $\alpha_i + \varepsilon_{it}$. By taking the variance on both sides of Equation 2-9, it can be demonstrated that the variance of the rate of return on a security can be partitioned into a risk component due to the general variability in the overall market and a risk component due to factors peculiar to the company:[4]

---

4 Total risk as measured by the variance of returns, may be partitioned into the market and company-specific component as follows:

$\sigma^2 (R_i)$ = total risk of security i

$\quad = \sigma^2 (\alpha_i + \beta_i R_M + \varepsilon_i)$ $\qquad\qquad\qquad$ substituting (2-9)

$\quad = \beta_i^2 \sigma_M^2 + \sigma^2 (\varepsilon_i)$ $\qquad\qquad\qquad\qquad$ since $\sigma^2 (\alpha) = 0$

$\quad$ = MARKET RISK + SPECIFIC RISK

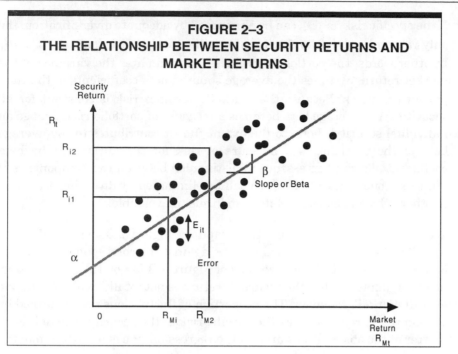

FIGURE 2–3
**THE RELATIONSHIP BETWEEN SECURITY RETURNS AND
MARKET RETURNS**

TOTAL RISK = MARKET RISK + SPECIFIC RISK

$$\sigma_i^2 = \beta_i^2 \, \sigma_M^2 + \sigma^2 \, (\varepsilon i) \qquad\qquad (2\text{-}10)$$

where σ_i^2 = total risk of a security measured by its variance

σ_M^2 = variance of return of the market index

$\beta_i{}^2$ = beta of the security, measuring the sensitivity of R_{it} to R_{Mt}

$\sigma^2 \, (\varepsilon_i)$ = portion of total risk attributable to specific factors

The first element of risk is the systematic component, $\beta_i \sigma_M^2$, and is related to the variance of the overall market, σ_M^2. The second element is the specific, or diversifiable risk, $\sigma^2 \, (\varepsilon_i)$.

Since investors are risk averse, they will diversify their portfolios by purchasing a large number of shares directly or through a mutual fund. The diversification efforts of investors will reduce in importance the specific risk component, and as a result, the risk of the stock will be proportional to its beta. As long as the firm-specific factors are uncorrelated with one another they can be eliminated by diversification by virtue of the law of large numbers; the ups and downs of one firm are offset by that of another.

If the specific risk, $\sigma^2(\varepsilon_i)$, can be eliminated by adequate diversification, the only relevant risk left to the investor is the market risk component, $\beta_i\sigma_M^2$. In other words, the portfolio's total risk approximates the variance of the market return, σ_M^2 times the average squared beta coefficients of the component securities. Because the market's variance risk is constant for all securities, the average beta becomes a measure of portfolio risk. And so an individual security's beta, to the extent that it contributes to the average beta of the portfolio, is a measure of risk for that security. The beta coefficient allows us in essence to distinguish between two components of total risk: one component, which can be eliminated by diversification, and another, which is market-related, and thus unavoidable.

This can also be seen from the graph of Figure 2-3, which plots an individual security's historical returns against the corresponding returns on the market. Not all observations of Figure 2-3 fall on the straight line, however, implying that the security's return is not totally explained by the overall market's behavior. The proportion of fluctuations not explained by the market is referred to as the specific risk of the security. The degree of scatter of the observations around the regression line is a reflection of the security's specific risk, $\sigma^2(\varepsilon_i)$.

Modern theory of investment behavior rests on the notion that the specific risk component not explained by the market can be diversified away by the investor. As the portfolio becomes progressively more diversified by the addition of securities, the specific risk component declines sharply. This is shown in Figure 2-4 adapted from Brigham and Gapenski (1991)

Thus, for a diversified investor, the relevant risk of a security is reduced to its market risk, or beta, the risk that cannot be eliminated by diversification.[5]

The calculation of systematic or market risk proceeds directly from Equation 2-9, which is a standard linear regression equation. Market risk, or beta, is the slope of that regression line. Securities with slope (beta) values of less than 1.00 are said to be less risky than the market, and stocks with beta values greater than 1.00 are said to be riskier than the market. Beta can be thought of as the sensitivity of a given security to the market as a whole or as a measure of the extent to which the return on the security tracks the trend of the market. Beta is a widely disseminated

---

[5] As the number of securities in a portfolio increases, R_p becomes progressively more correlated with R_M, the return on the market. This suggests that σ_{iM} is the only relevant measure of risk of security i. σ_{iM} is proportional to the coefficient β_i in the linear regression equation of Equation 2-9 since β_i is given by σ_{iM}/σ_M^2.

FIGURE 2–4
PORTFOLIO RISK AND DIVERSIFICATION

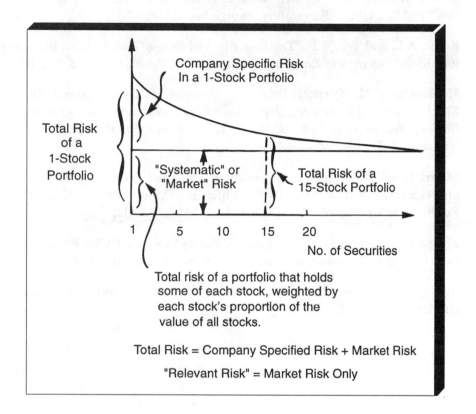

risk measure, and beta estimates are published regularly by such firms as Value Line, Merrill Lynch, and Barr Rosenberg & Associates.

References

Blume, M.E. and Friend, I. *The Changing Role of the Individual Investor.* Twentieth Century Report. New York: Wiley and Sons, 1978.

Brealey, R. and Myers, S. *Principles of Corporate Finance,* 4th ed. New York: McGraw-Hill, 1991A.

Brealey, R. and Myers, S. *Principles of Corporate Finance,* Instructors' Manual, Appendix C. New York: McGraw-Hill, 1991B.

Brigham, E.F. and Gapenski, L.C. *Financial Management: Theory and Practice,* 6th ed., Hinsdale IL: Dryden Press, 1991.

Chandrasekaran, P.R. and Dukes, W.P. "Risk Variables Affecting Rate of Return of Public Utilities." *Public Utilities Fortnightly,* February 26, 1981, 32.

Dukes, W.P. and Chandy, P.R. "Rate of Return and Risk for Public Utilities." *Public Utilities Fortnightly,* September 1, 1983, 35-41.

Kolbe, A.L. and Tye, W.B. "The Fair Allowed Rate of Return with Regulatory Risk." *Research in Law and Economics,* JAI Press Inc., 1992, 129-169.

Markowitz, H.M. "Portfolio Selection." *Journal of Finance,* March 1952, 77-91. Reprinted in *Modern Developments in Investment Management: A Book of Readings,* 2nd ed., edited by Lorie, J. and Brealey, R., 310-324. Hinsdale IL:Dryden Press, 1978.

Morin, R.A. California Water Association, Prepared Testimony, "Financial and Operational Risk Analysis of California Water Utilities," California Public Utilities Commission, Docket No. 90-11-033,1992.

Myers, S.C. "The Application of Finance Theory to Public Utility Rate Case." *Bell Journal of Economics and Management Science,* Spring 1972, 58-97.

Reilly, F.K. *Investment Analysis and Portfolio Management.* Hinsdale IL: Dryden Press, 1989.

Chapter 3
Risk Estimation in Practice

A plethora of empirical evidence supports the notion that investors expect—and realize—higher returns, on average, for assuming higher risks. This result holds true across bond quality differences, between corporate bonds and stocks, and across differences in stocks' standard deviations. The positive relationship between return and both standard deviation and beta is well documented in both the academic and trade financial literature. Summaries of the empirical evidence compiled by academic researchers are available in numerous investment textbooks, such as Reilly (1994), Sharpe and Alexander (1990), and Elton and Gruber (1991). The comprehensive study of historical returns on stocks and bonds published annually by Ibbotson & Associates supports the conclusion that, on average, stocks are riskier than bonds in terms of standard deviations. Dukes and Chandy (1983) surveyed the usage of various risk measures by utilities and regulatory commissions and concluded that beta and standard deviation were the most popular risk measures, confirming the results of an earlier study by Chandrasekaran and Dukes (1981). In a comprehensive study of risk measurement, Rosenberg (1986) found that both measures of risk are correlated with returns.

In the previous chapter, two fundamental objective scientific measures of risk were identified: the standard deviation of the rate of return to investors and the beta coefficient. Both measures aim at assessing the volatility of a security's return, but each in a different context. For undiversified investors, the standard deviation is the relevant measure of risk while for large diversified portfolios, the portfolio's volatility is more closely related to the beta coefficient of the constituent stocks than to their standard deviations. This chapter discusses the practical and conceptual difficulties encountered in measuring and applying risk measures. Sections 3.1 and 3.2 concentrate on the standard deviation and beta risk measures. Section 3.3 explores the relationship between these risk measures and company fundamentals, and Section 3.4 reviews other quantitative and qualitative risk measures used by investors. Section 3.5 presents an example of a risk filter designed to identify companies of comparable risk. Finally, Section 3.6 describes a risk estimation technique based on call option pricing concepts.

None of the risk measures discussed in this chapter measures risk in a pure absolute sense. All are proxies for future risks based mostly on historical data. Future risk is something that lies in the minds of investors, and there is no infallible method to ascertain it. Nevertheless, historical risk measures are relevant to the extent that they are used by investors to assess the future and to formulate their anticipations.

3.1 Standard Deviation as a Risk Measure

Variability of market return as measured by the standard deviation of realized market returns over some given time period is a widely used measure of risk by investors. All that is required for its computation is a time series of market prices and dividends at regular intervals over a given period, from which holding period returns can be computed. The calculation of the mean return and standard deviation can easily be calculated, as shown in Table 3-1, from the return data using the formulas supplied in Equations 2-4 and 2-5.

TABLE 3–1
CALCULATION OF STANDARD DEVIATION

Period	Return	$R - \overline{R}$	$(R - \overline{R})^2$
Quarter 1	+ 8%	4%	16
Quarter 2	+13%	9%	81
Quarter 3	+ 3%	- 1%	1
Quarter 4	- 8%	- 12%	144
	$\overline{R} = 4\%$		242

$$S^2 = \frac{242}{4} = 60.5$$

$$S = \sqrt{60.5} = 7.78\%$$

$R =$ Return per sub-period $S^2 =$ Variance

$\overline{R} =$ Average return for the overall period $S =$ Standard Deviation

The standard deviation of realized returns and its relationship to the mean return can be illustrated using a probability distribution of rate of return. In the probability distribution shown in Figure 3-1, the dispersion or scatter around the mean return of 4% is measured by the standard deviation of those returns at 7.8%.

Standard deviation can also be computed directly from the return data by using the standard deviation function available on most business electronic calculators. Alternately, commercial financial data bases supply historical standard deviation data. Raw monthly and daily market return data from 1928 to the most recent year are available for over 1,300 stocks listed on the NYSE from the University of Chicago's Center for Research in Security Prices (CRISP) computerized data bases. Standard deviations and betas can be readily computed from these data sources over any desired period. Earnings, dividends, volume data, and extensive information on market indices are also available. Value Line Investment Service provides direct estimates of standard deviation for over 1,600 stocks on the Value Line Data Base. Value Line computes the standard deviation

FIGURE 3-1
PROBABILITY DISTRIBUTION OF RATE OF RETURN

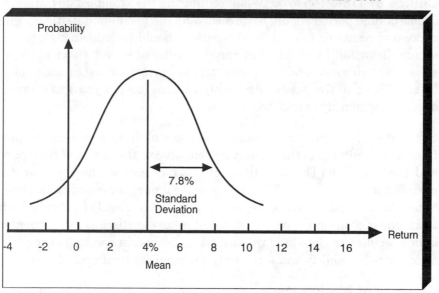

using weekly market returns over the most recent five-year period. Merrill Lynch's *Security Risk Evaluation* monthly publication also provides estimates of standard deviation on a monthly basis.

Andrews (1990) provided an interesting application of the standard deviation as a risk measure. To assess the relative risk of local distribution gas companies, the volatility of stock prices is estimated using the so-called "high-low-close estimator." This estimator is essentially the standard deviation of stock returns. Specifically, the high-low-close estimator is obtained by first calculating the variance of stock returns from the following equation:

$$\sigma^2 = 0.5 \ln (H_t / L_t)^2 - .39 \ln (C_t / C_{t-1})^2 \qquad (3\text{-}1)$$

where
σ^2 = variance of stock returns
ln = natural log
H_t = weekly high of stock prices
L_t = weekly low of stock prices
C_t = weekly close of stock prices
C_{t-1} = previous week's close of stock prices

and then annualizing the standard deviation of stock returns by taking the product of the square root of the mean variance over weekly intervals for 26 weeks from the above equation times the square root of 52.

Practical and Conceptual Issues

Choice of Time Period. When computing the standard deviation, the choice of time period should be governed by the need for statistical significance and economic relevance. The period should be long enough to avoid undue distortion by short-term random influences, yet short enough to encompass current conditions relevant for investors' assessment of the future. Three to five years of monthly returns, or ten years of quarterly data are frequently employed.

Stability. One potential limitation of the standard deviation computed from historical data is that it may be sensitive to the choice of time period and time interval. The sensitivity of the measure to the choice of time period, and the stability of the measure for a particular utility relative to other utilities and to other unregulated industrials should be checked. This is an unavoidable problem encountered in any statistical estimation and is not peculiar to the standard deviation. No risk measure is completely immune to instability and sensitivity to computational procedures.

Absence of Market Data. Frequently, there is no public market for the utility's common stock, as in the case of a subsidiary of a diversified parent, a wholly-owned subsidiary of a utility holding company, or a privately-held company. Or sometimes, one wishes to compare the relative riskiness of a constellation of subsidiaries, both regulated and unregulated. The standard deviation of market return cannot be estimated under these circumstances and substitute measures of risk must be computed. Several accounting-based risk measures correlated with the standard deviation of market returns are discussed in Section 3.4 of this chapter. For example, the volatility of earnings per share around historical trend, the average absolute percentage change in earnings per share over time, and the historical standard deviation of book returns on equity are suitable risk estimators.

Lack of Comparability. A frequent criticism voiced at standard deviation is that when it is used as a device to screen firms of comparable risk, the end result is usually a list of companies quite dissimilar to utilities in terms of the nature of their business. It should be emphasized that the definition of a comparable risk class of companies does not entail similarity of operation, product lines, or environmental conditions, but rather similarity of experienced business risk and financial risk. When the standard deviation is used as a screening device, the selected reference group of companies includes companies with similar business and financial risk, rather than companies with similar output or operations. Investors do make such risk comparisons as between industrial and utility stocks.

Total risk may be similar even though the business risk component of the reference companies is different. As discussed in Chapter 2, Section 2.2, a firm with low business risk can assume larger financial risks by a greater reliance on debt capital, while a volatile cyclical business can attenuate its total risk by a lower financial risk using less debt capital.

Downside Risk.   Objection to the standard deviation is sometimes voiced on the grounds that investors are much more concerned with losing money than with total variability of return. If risk is defined as the probability of loss, it appears more logical to measure risk as the probability of achieving a return that is below the expected return. Figure 3-2 shows three frequency distribution of returns, one symmetrical, one skewed left, and one skewed right.

If the probability distribution is symmetrical, specialized measures of downside risk are unnecessary, since a normal symmetrical distribution has no skewness;[1] the areas on either side of the mean expected return are mirror images of one another. Empirical studies of historical return distributions of industrial stocks indicate that they are not significantly skewed, and as a practical expedient, measures of downside risk, such as the "semivariance," are highly correlated with traditional measures of risk, such as the standard deviation.

Brigham and Crum (1977) suggest that the distribution of security returns for regulated utilities is more likely to resemble the negatively skewed distribution displayed in the middle of Figure 3-2. The process of regulation, by restricting the upward potential for returns and responding sluggishly on the downward side, may impart some asymmetry to the distribution of returns, and is more likely to result in utilities earning less, rather than more, than their cost of capital. Hence, the standard deviation is likely to provide a downward biased estimate of the risk of public utilities in relation to that of unregulated firms. The effect of skewness on security returns is revisited further in Chapter 13.

Coefficient of Variation.   The Dukes and Chandy (1983) survey of risk measures found wide support for the coefficient of variation (CV) as a measure of risk, particularly by regulators. The CV is defined as the standard deviation divided by the mean, and it measures the amount of risk per unit of return incurred by investors. The CV can be a useful measure of relative risk when two series of numbers are expressed in the

---

[1]   For a detailed analysis of the effect of skewness on security returns, see Francis (1975), Friend, Westerfield, and Granito (1978), Kraus and Litzenberger (1976), and Morin (1980).

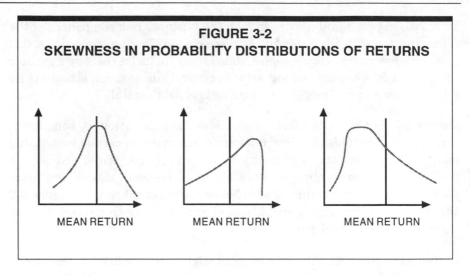

FIGURE 3-2
SKEWNESS IN PROBABILITY DISTRIBUTIONS OF RETURNS

MEAN RETURN   MEAN RETURN   MEAN RETURN

same units but are of different magnitudes. For example, if Company A has a standard deviation of earnings per share of $0.50 relative to a mean of $2.00 and Company B has a standard deviation of earnings per share of $0.50 relative to a mean of $20.00, it follows that Company A has a far more variable earnings history. Yet, both standard deviations are the same at $0.50; but CV is 0.25 for the earnings per share series of Company A, and 0.025 for Company B.

In computing the CV, care should be taken to measure relative peak to trough variability so as not to distort the relative risk of the variable in question. Further, the CV can assume infinitely large values when dividing the standard deviation by the mean, if the mean is very small or approaches zero. Moreover, if the mean is negative, the CV implies negative risk, an implausible result.

When dealing with percentages as in the case of security returns, it is sometimes alleged that the CV is redundant, since a percentage is already a scaled measure, by definition. The CV remains a useful measure of relative risk even when dealing with security returns, however. Equally risky investments as measured by the standard deviation does not imply equally attractive investments to investors. For example, Company A with a standard deviation of return of 10% relative to a mean of 16% is a far more attractive investment than Company B with a standard deviation of return of 10% relative to a mean of 8%. Although both standard deviations are the same at 10%, investors find Company A more attractive. This is because Company A's CV is only 0.625 versus 1.250 for Company B.

The CV of accounting book return (CVROE) can also be employed as a measure of comparative risk and as a proxy for the standard deviation of market return, $\sigma(R_m)$. It can easily be shown that $\sigma(R_m)$ is a linear function of CVROE. Intuitively, this is because there is a direct linkage between CVROE and $\sigma(R_m)$ as the latter is itself a scaled measure of risk.[2] This linkage can be seen by noting that market return, R_m, is defined as the ratio between the end-of-period stock price P_1 and the beginning-of-period stock price P_0:

$$R_m = P_1/P_0 \tag{3-2}$$

Taking the standard deviation of both sides of the equation:

$$\sigma(R_m) = \sigma(P_1/P_0) = \sigma(P_1)/P_0$$

Thus, $\sigma(R_m)$ is itself a scaled measure of risk with equity appearing in the denominator and is a linear function of CVROE.

It is also interesting to note that beta is a linear function of CV rather than σ, lending further credibility to the use of CV as a valid measure of risk.[3]

Divergence of Opinion as a Risk Measure. One useful indicator of risk is the degree of divergence of opinion among analysts about future earnings. The greater the variation in analysts' earnings or growth forecasts, the greater investor uncertainty on future prospects. Institutional Brokers Estimate System (IBES) compiles individual analysts' earnings forecasts for publicly-traded companies, along with long-term earnings growth. The variation in growth forecasts as measured by the standard deviation of individual forecasts, also provided by IBES, provides a measure of risk. Malkiel (1990) provided empirical evidence on the usefulness

---

[2] For a formal analysis of the relationship between the coefficient of variation and standard deviation, see Patterson (1989).

[3] Beta is defined as the covariance between a security's cash flows and that of the aggregate market as follows:

$$\beta = \frac{S_m\ \sigma(x_i)\ \rho_{im}}{S_i\ \sigma(x_m)}$$

where S_m refers to the market value of the aggregate index, S_i refers to the company's market value, $\sigma(x_m)$ refers to the standard deviation of aggregate cash flows, and $\sigma(x_i)$ refers to the standard deviation of company cash flows. The above expression is a scaled measure of $\sigma(x_i)/S_i$, the coefficient of variation, with the price-earnings ratio S_m/x_m as the scalar. This is shown in Patterson (1989).

of this risk measure. McShane (1993) provided a practical illustration of this risk indicator in an actual testimony regarding cost of capital.

Multiple Risk Measures. Another commonly voiced objection to the standard deviation as a measure of risk is that it is insufficient. When dealing with the complex and multi-faceted notion of risk, one should not depend on the results of a single estimate of risk. Additional measures of risk, based on different frameworks, are required to lend further reliability and credence to the results obtained from the standard deviation.

In a large diversified portfolio, the volatility of the portfolio's return is much more closely related to the beta coefficients of the constituent stocks than to their standard deviations. Most institutional stock, such as the stock of most utilities, is held in large diversified portfolios. A significant fraction of individuals' holdings is also invested in diversified portfolios. For undiversified portfolios, however, and even for reasonably diversified portfolios, there is evidence suggesting that investors' risk assessments depend also on the standard deviation of return. The probability distributions of return for two different stocks with the same mean return are illustrated in Figure 3-3.

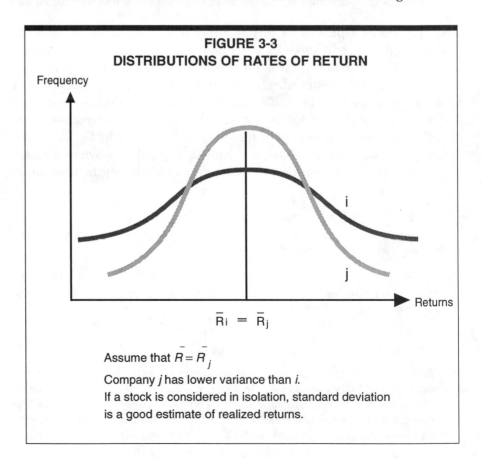

FIGURE 3-3
DISTRIBUTIONS OF RATES OF RETURN

Frequency

i

j

Returns

$$\bar{R}_i = \bar{R}_j$$

Assume that $\bar{R} = \bar{R}_j$

Company j has lower variance than i.
If a stock is considered in isolation, standard deviation
is a good estimate of realized returns.

The probability distribution of returns for Company j is clearly less dispersed around the mean than the distribution of Company i. In other words, Company j has a lower variance than Company i. Therefore, if a stock is considered in isolation, standard deviation is a good estimate of realized returns. Friend, Westerfield, and Granito (1978) and Morin (1980) summarized a myriad of evidence and supplied evidence of their own that both beta and standard deviation are positively related to returns. Hence, both the standard deviation and beta should be considered.

3.2 Beta as a Risk Measure

The empirical evidence that beta is an important determinant of return is overwhelming. Most, if not all, college-level finance textbooks discuss the pervasive and positive influence of beta on return when discussing the empirical validity of the Capital Asset Pricing Model. See for example Brealey and Myers (1991), Brigham and Gapenski (1991), and Ross, Westerfield, and Jaffee (1993).

Before discussing the practical usefulness of beta, it should be pointed out that the use of beta as a risk measure is not equivalent to unequivocal acceptance of the Capital Asset Pricing Model (CAPM). The CAPM is a formal theory of how beta risk affects security prices, and is treated extensively in Chapter 12. In this chapter, beta is used purely as one of several reasonable measures of risk to identify companies of comparable risk, and its use is not predicated on any formal security pricing theory.

Beta measures a security's volatility in relation to that of the market, and is generally computed from a linear regression analysis based on past realized returns over some past time period, as shown in Figure 3-4.

The dependent variable is the security's realized return over a certain time interval, and the independent variable is the corresponding return on some suitable market index, such as the Standard & Poor's 500 Industrial Index.

As discussed in Chapter 2 (see Equation 2-9), an estimate of the beta coefficient of a stock is obtained through an ordinary least-squares (OLS) regression of the monthly rates of return on the stock, R_{it}, on the monthly return of an aggregate market index, R_{Mt}, typically from the previous 60 months of return data. The relationship between security returns and market returns is depicted in Figure 3-5.

FIGURE 3-4
GRAPH OF THE STANDARD REGRESSION MODEL USED TO ESTIMATE BETA

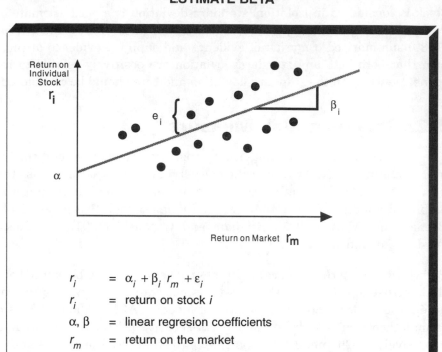

$$r_i = \alpha_i + \beta_i \, r_m + \varepsilon_i$$

r_i = return on stock i

α, β = linear regresion coefficients

r_m = return on the market

FIGURE 3-5
THE RELATIONSHIP BETWEEN SECURITY RETURNS AND MARKET RETURNS

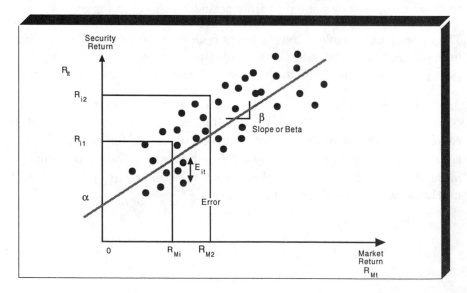

Beta is simply the estimated slope of the OLS regression line, which has the form:

$$R_{it} = \alpha_1 + \beta_i R_{Mt} + \varepsilon_{it} \qquad (3\text{-}3)$$

Value Line betas are widely available and well-known to investors. Beta estimates are available from several commercial sources including:

1. Value Line Investment Survey

2. Merrill Lynch *Security Risk Evaluation*

3. Goldman, Sachs. *Risk, Return and Equity Valuation*

4. Wells Fargo Bank *Security Market Plane Report*

5. Standard & Poor's

Value Line is the largest and most widely circulated independent investment advisory service, and exerts influence on a large number of institutional and individual investors and on the expectations of these investors. The Value Line data are conveniently made available to investors for a modest fee on computer diskettes updated on a monthly basis. Value Line beta is derived from a least-squares regression analysis between weekly percent changes in the price of a stock and weekly percent changes in the New York Stock Exchange Average over a period of 5 years. In the case of shorter price histories, a smaller time period is used, but 2 years is the minimum. In addition, Value Line betas are computed on a theoretically sound basis using a broadly-based market index, and they are adjusted for the regression tendency of betas to converge to 1.00. This necessary adjustment to raw beta factors is further discussed in the following section.

Practical and Conceptual Difficulties

Computational Issues.   Absolute estimates of beta may vary over a wide range when different computational methods are used. The return data, the time period used, its duration, the choice of market index, and whether annual, monthly, or weekly return figures are used will influence the final result.

Ideally, the returns should be total returns, that is, dividends and capital gains. In practice, beta estimates are relatively unaffected if dividends are excluded. Theoretically, market returns should be expressed in terms of total returns on a portfolio of all risky assets. In practice, a broadly-based value-weighted market index is used. For example, Merrill Lynch betas use the Standard & Poor's 500 market index, while Value Line betas use the New York Stock Exchange Composite market index. In theory, unless the market index used is the true market index, fully diversified to include all securities in their proportion outstanding, the beta estimate obtained is potentially distorted. Failure to include bonds, Treasury bills, real estate, etc., could lead to a biased beta estimate. But if beta is used as a relative risk ranking device, choice of the market index may not alter the relative rankings of security risk significantly.

To enhance statistical significance, beta should be calculated with return data going as far back as possible. But the company's risk may have changed if the historical period is too long. Weighting the data for this tendency is one possible remedy, but this presupposes some knowledge of how risk changes. A frequent compromise is to use a 5-year period with either weekly or monthly returns. Value Line betas are computed based on weekly returns over a 5-year period, whereas Merrill Lynch betas are computed with monthly returns over a 5-year period. In an empirical study of utility betas, Melicher (1979) found that while the beta estimating process differs between Merrill Lynch and Value Line, the beta estimates are reasonably comparable in absolute magnitude. Statman (1981) found a small but significant difference in these estimates of beta. He estimated the following relationship between the two beta estimates:

$$M.L.\ Beta = 0.127 + 0.879\ V.L.\ Beta$$

The results are not consistent with equality. Both regression coefficients were significant, and R^2 was 0.55. But for betas close to 1.00, the differences were very small. Harrington (1983) examined the betas provided by different investment services and found that, in terms of predicting ensuing betas, the Value Line forecasts exhibited the lowest mean square errors for a sample of utility stocks.

Reilly and Wright (1988) confirmed the difference in beta found by Statman. The difference was attributed to the alternative time intervals, that is, weekly versus monthly returns. The size and direction of the effect was a function of a security's market value. In other words, the size of the firm is an important consideration when estimating beta or using a published source. For large utility companies, the bias is small, and for practical purposes, far less than any inherent standard error of estimate or measurement error. Placing utilities into groups (industry estimates) palliates the problem.

It should be pointed out that when the objective of estimating beta is to ascertain the relative values of beta for different firms, it is reasonable to suppose that the relative ranking of the betas are less sensitive to the time period, length of return interval, and duration of time period, than are the absolute values of beta. For example, the ranking of all stocks based on

Value Line betas, which is calculated using weekly returns, may not differ substantially from the ranking obtained using the Merrill Lynch beta, which is calculated using monthly returns.

In addition to time period, duration and market index, measurement error is also a concern. Individual company betas are measured with error. To lessen the significance of measurement errors in estimating betas, proxy groups of companies and/or industry estimates can be used. The empirical finance literature shows that the standard error of estimate of betas is considerably smaller for portfolios than for individual company observations. Betas for groups of securities are more stable and more accurate than betas for individual securities.

Raw Beta Versus Adjusted Beta.   The regression tendency of betas to converge to 1.0 over time is very well known and widely discussed in the financial literature. Because of this regressive tendency, a company's raw unadjusted beta is not the appropriate measure of market risk to use. Current stock prices reflect expected risk, that is, expected beta, rather than historical risk or historical beta. Historical betas, whether raw or adjusted, are only surrogates for expected beta. The best of the two surrogates is adjusted beta.

Numerous studies have considered the question of beta measurement and generally reached similar conclusions. Betas have tended to regress toward the mean; high-beta portfolios have tended to decline over time toward unity, while low-beta portfolios have tended to increase over time toward unity. True betas not only vary over time but have a tendency to move back toward average levels. A company whose operations or financing make the risk of its stock divergent from other companies is more likely to move back toward the average than away from it.

Such changes in beta values are due to real economic phenomena, not simply to an artifact of overly simple statistical procedures.

From a Bayesian framework, and without any information at all on true beta, one would presume a stock's beta in relation to the market to be 1.00. Given a chance to see how the stock moved in relation to the market over some historical period, a modification of this "prior" estimate would seem appropriate. But a sensible "posterior" estimate would likely lie between the two values.

Statistically, betas are estimated with error.[4] Therefore, high-estimated betas will tend to have positive error (overestimated) and low-estimated

---

[4]   This section draws from Perry (1991).

betas will tend to have negative error (underestimated). Therefore, it is necessary to squash the estimated betas in toward 1.00. One way to do this is by measuring the extent to which estimated betas tend to regress toward the mean over time. As a result of this beta drift, several commercial beta producers adjust their forecasted betas toward 1.00 in effort to improve their forecasts. This adjustment, which is commonly performed by investment services such as Value Line and Merrill Lynch, uses the formula:

$$\text{adjusted } \beta = 1.00 + K \ (\text{raw } \beta - 1.00)$$

where K is an estimate from past data of the extent to which estimated betas regress toward the mean. Merrill Lynch obtains its adjusted beta values by giving approximately 66% weight K to the measured beta and approximately 34% weight to the prior value of 1.0 for each stock. These adjustments are modified slightly from time to time. Value Line betas are also periodically adjusted for their long-term tendency to regress toward 1.00 using a similar procedure. Another advantage of the beta adjustment technique, besides adjusting for regression bias, is that it also adjusts for any underlying tendency of the true betas to move toward 1.00.[5]

Several authors have investigated the regression tendency of beta. For example, Blume (1971) examined the stability of beta for all common stocks listed on the NYSE, and found a tendency for a regression of the betas toward 1.00. He demonstrated that the Value Line adjustment procedure anticipates differences between past and future betas. Chen (1981) also analyzed the variability of beta and suggested the Bayesian adjustment approach used by beta producers to estimate time-varying betas. A comprehensive study of beta measurement methodology by Kryzanowski and Jalilvand (1983) concludes that raw unadjusted beta (OLS beta) is one of the poorest beta predictors, and is outperformed by the Merrill Lynch-style Bayesian beta approach. Gombola and Kahl (1990) examined the time-series properties of utility betas and found strong support for the application of adjustment procedures such as the Value Line and Merrill Lynch procedures. Well-known college-level finance textbooks routinely discuss the use of adjusted betas.[6]

---

[5] For a thorough discussion of the method used for estimating Merrill Lynch betas, see *Security Risk Evaluation Service,* Merrill Lynch, New York, June 1984.

[6] See, for example, Chapter 9 of the best-selling corporate finance textbook by Brealey and Myers (1991) and the well-known investment textbook by Sharpe and Alexander (1990), Chapter 15, Section 8.1, "Adjusting Beta.

Beta Stability. Several empirical studies of beta coefficients, notably by Blume (1975) and Levy (1971), have revealed the marked instability of betas over time. Both authors noted a pronounced tendency of betas to regress toward unity, that is for high betas to decline over time and for low betas to increase. As discussed previously, many commercially available beta services such as Value Line and Merrill Lynch adjust for this regression tendency, so that the historical beta figures will more closely reflect the true beta. Even with this adjustment, betas may still exhibit substantial instability. If betas are going to be applied to determine the cost of capital through the CAPM, stability of beta is crucial. If betas are not stable, any assessment of cost of capital based on historical beta estimates may not hold true for the future period during which the new allowed rates of return will be in effect. But if beta is going to be used to provide an estimate of the relative risk of various securities, the relative relationships between the betas are likely to be less sensitive to instability than are the absolute values of beta. There is some scant evidence by Melicher (1979) that beta estimates for utilities were more stable than the betas of industrial companies at least in the 1976-1979 period. Grouping utilities (industry estimates) palliates the problem, as the beta of a portfolio exhibits far more stability than the beta of an individual security.

Historical versus True Beta. The true beta of a security can never be observed. Historically-estimated betas serve only as proxies for the true beta. The future may well differ from the past. Current changes in the fundamentals of a company's operations and risk posture may not be fully reflected in the historically-estimated beta. By construction, backward-looking betas are sluggish in detecting fundamental changes in a company's risk. For example, if a utility increased its debt to equity ratio, one would expect an increase in beta. However, if 60 months of return data are used to estimate beta, only one of the 60 data points reflects the new information, one month after the utility increased its leverage. Thus, the change in leverage has only a minor effect on the historical beta. Even one year later, only 12 of the 60 return points reflect the event.

Another example is shown graphically in Figure 3-6 where the true underlying beta of a utility is gradually increasing because of recently added risk factors, such as vast increases in plant construction costs, and increasing levels of competition. Yet, the historical beta measured over a 5-year estimation period lies midway between the true beginning-of-period beta and the current end-of-period beta, seriously underestimating the current beta.

This type of bias certainly applied to electric utilities in the 1970s and early 1980s. The fundamental risks of electric utilities fluctuated markedly during that period. Environmental problems, demand uncertainties, inflation-related problems, deterioration in the quality of earnings, price decontrol,

FIGURE 3-6
BIAS IN ESTIMATING BETA FROM HISTORICAL DATA

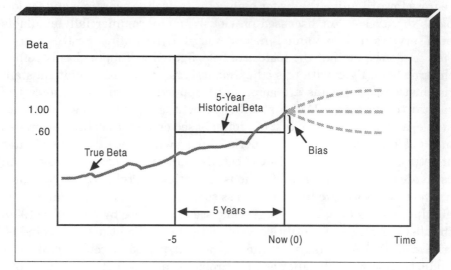

antitrust suits, and nuclear uncertainties contributed in raising the risk level of utilities in that era. A similar situation prevailed in the mid-1980s following the divestiture of AT&T and the emergence of broad-based competition. The telecommunication utilities were experiencing structural and fundamental shifts in risk that were not fully reflected in historically measured betas. This type of bias applies to water utilities in the 1990s, with their fundamental risks changing rapidly as a result of environmental problems, demand-supply uncertainties, stringent water quality regulations, and the uncertainties of environmental compliance costs.

These structural shifts in risk are not fully reflected in the measured beta and standard deviation of utility stocks, since such estimates are calculated using 5 years of past data using pre- and post-structural shift observations. So, any measured risk difference between utility stocks and stocks in general is misleading, and likely to be lower than that implied by a simple comparison of beta and standard deviation alone. The converse is also true, of course.

Hence, in these situations, backward-looking statistical analysis will only provide limited evidence that the risk and the cost of capital to these utilities have increased. Instead, a forward-looking conceptual analysis buttressed by empirical information and simulation modeling must be developed. This is discussed more fully in Chapter 11. Fisher and Kamin

(1985) suggested more efficient beta estimators that allow for betas changing over time and that give more weight to more recent information.

For utilities with listed call options, Section 3.6 proposes a tool designed to track short-run risk changes and to detect possible biases in historical beta.

Brigham and Crum (1977) analyzed the effects of risk non-stationarity in measured betas, hence on cost of capital, and concluded that a random shock that changes the true beta cannot be immediately measured by an estimated beta. For example, they contend that rising investor risk perceptions cause a decline in stock prices, which in turn produces low betas. The Brigham and Crum article generated voluminous discussion and controversy, which was reported in a special issue of *Financial Management* (Autumn 1978) devoted to the use of beta in utility regulation. The various comments offered by several noted financial scholars in that issue generally supported the view that betas could be biased, and that projecting beta from historical data could be dangerous.

While beta is a sensible and objective risk measure, firmly anchored in modern portfolio theory, it should be used cautiously.

Relevance of Beta.   According to both financial theory and empirical evidence, betas are critical and sufficient measures of risk. For diversified investors, beta is the only relevant measure of risk. Financial theory has shown that beta is a sufficient risk measure for diversified investors and the empirical literature has confirmed its importance in determining expected return. But the basic issue of the relevance of beta as the only measure of risk remains controversial. Several studies have found that investors receive incremental return for incurring risk that could be diversified.[7] Both beta risk and standard deviation risk appear relevant to investors, based on the evidence cited in Section 3.1. Rosenberg (1986), for example, concluded that while beta may be important to diversified investors, the use of additional measures of risk and return in ratemaking is justified.

Throughout its tumultuous history, the death of beta has been periodically announced over the years, but has inevitably been followed by its rebirth. The Fama and French (1992) study is a case in point. Fama and French found that differences in beta failed to explain the return performance of different stocks. But here again the autopsy of beta was premature, and reports of beta's death were greatly exaggerated. For one thing, financial theory is concerned with the relationship between *expected* returns and

---

[7]   See for example Sharpe and Cooper (1972), Levy (1980), Friend, Westerfield, and Granito (1978), and Morin (1980).

beta, whereas Fama and French employed *realized* returns. Moreover, in a subsequent research paper, Kothari, Shanken, and Sloan (1993) found significant return compensation for beta risk with little relation to market-to-book (M/B) ratios, unlike Fama and French. They also found that market risk premiums are much larger when betas are estimated using annual rather than monthly data. Other prominent financial economists have tackled the Fama and French findings head on and rehabilitated beta by finding that beta did in fact explain differences in share returns.[8]

Beta and Thin Trading. For securities for which there is only periodic trading, beta estimates are downward biased. This is because observed returns contain stale information about past period returns rather than current period returns. Intuitively, suppose the stock market index surges forward but an individual company stock price remains unchanged due to lack of trading, the estimated beta is imparted a downward bias. The stock is unable to catch up to market-wide movements and appears to be a lower beta stock.

Two approaches that consider the impact of thin trading are available, named after their founders: the Dimson (1979) adjustment and the Scholes and Williams (1977) adjustment. The Dimson beta is estimated by running a multiple OLS regression of stock returns on both the contemporaneous market return, R_{Mt}, and the lagged market return, R_{Mt-1}, and then adding up the two slope coefficients, β_{i1} and β_{i2}2:

$$R_{it} = \alpha_i + \beta_{i1} R_{Mt} + \beta_{i2} R_{Mt-1} + \varepsilon_{it} \qquad (3-4)$$

$$\beta = \beta_{i1} + \beta_{i2} \qquad (3-5)$$

In the Scholes and Williams approach, three separate OLS regressions are run between the stock returns and contemporaneous market return, R_{Mt}, the lagged market return, R_{Mt-1}, and the lead market return, R_{Mt+1}, respectively. The corrected beta is obtained by adding up the three separate slope coefficients and dividing it by $(1 + 2\rho)$ where ρ is the autocorrelation coefficient of the market returns over the time period:

$$R_{it} = \alpha_i + \beta_{i1} R_{Mt} + \varepsilon_{it} \qquad (3-6)$$

---

[8] See, for example, Roll and Ross (1993), and Chan and Lakonishok (1992).

$$R_{it} = \alpha_i + \beta_{i2} R_{Mt-1} + \varepsilon_{it} \qquad (3\text{-}7)$$

$$R_{it} = \alpha_i + \beta_{i3} R_{Mt+1} + \varepsilon_{it} \qquad (3\text{-}8)$$

$$\beta = \frac{\beta_{i1} + \beta_{i2} + \beta_{i3}}{(1 + 2\rho)} \qquad (3\text{-}9)$$

Absence of Market Data. In certain situations the usual beta cannot be computed. These include situations in which the utility's stock is not publicly traded, as in the case of wholly-owned subsidiaries of holding companies, or no market data are available, or the relative risks of the regulated with unregulated subsidiaries of a parent company are being compared. Several alternate measures of beta risk based on company fundamentals and accounting data can be used in such situations. The next section elaborates on the use of company fundamental data for risk estimation.

3.3 Risk and Company Fundamentals

Earnings Beta

One attempt to circumvent the absence of market data problem is to compute an "earnings beta." Since beta is a measure of the interrelationship between the returns of an individual company and those of the overall market, and since such interrelationship is to a large extent determined by the interrelationship of a company's earnings and corporate earnings in the overall economy, an "earnings beta" can be computed. A time series of a company's, subsidiary's, or division's quarterly earnings can be regressed on the corresponding index of aggregate quarterly corporate earnings published by the Commerce Department over the last ten years, and the slope coefficient from such a relationship is the "earnings beta." Since stock prices respond to earnings, the earnings beta and the usual stock beta should be highly correlated. The earnings beta is basically a measure of earnings cyclicality, that is, the extent to which fluctuations in a company's earnings mirror the fluctuations in aggregate earnings of all firms, and is well correlated with market beta. A similar measure of covariability risk can be constructed using accounting returns (ROEs) instead of earnings.

Gordon and Halpern (1974), for example, estimated the beta of a company division by assuming that the unobservable beta of the division is highly correlated with the slope coefficient from a regression of changes in divisional earnings on changes in total U.S. corporate profits. Growth in earnings per share and growth in after-tax cash flow per share are likely to be related to market return as well, and could be used instead of divisional earnings.

EXAMPLE 3-1

Based on a large sample of publicly-traded companies, let us say that stock market beta is statistically related to the earnings per share (EPS) beta as follows:

$$\text{Stock Market Beta} = 0564 + 0.251 \text{ EPS Beta}$$

If the earnings beta of a utility subsidiary is 0.90 based on a historical correlation of its earnings with the aggregate earnings on the Standard & Poor's 500 Index over the past 10 years, then its stock market beta is given by:

$$\text{Stock Market Beta} = 0564 + 0.251 \times 0.90 = 0.79$$

Pure-Play Beta

Another approach to develop a beta for a non-publicly traded firm is the "pure-play" beta. This method attempts to identify firms with publicly traded securities whose operations are as similar as possible to the division or subsidiary in question. Once a sample of pure-play firms is identified, the average beta of the sample is used as a surrogate for the non-traded company's beta. Methods of identifying valid proxy firms are discussed in Chapter 14, including Cluster Analysis and Spanning Portfolios. Fuller and Kerr (1981) provide empirical support for using the pure-play technique. The issue of determining the cost of capital for non-publicly traded subsidiaries is discussed further in Chapter 14. The search for pure-plays in the case of utility operations is relatively simple in most cases.

One difficulty with the pure-play approach is that although the reference companies may have the same business risk, they may have different capital structures. Observed betas reflect both business risk and financial risk. Hence, when a group of companies is considered comparable in every way except for financial structure, their betas are not directly comparable. Fortunately, there is a technique for adjusting betas for capital structure differences based on CAPM theory. This technique is discussed and illustrated in Chapter 14, which covers divisional cost of capital.

Accounting Beta

Given that accounting data capture the same events and information that influence market prices, and given that accounting data constitute an important source of information to investors in setting security prices, it stands to reason that accounting variables and market risk are related. Beaver, Kettler, and Scholes (1970) were among the first to examine the relationship between accounting measures of risk and beta. They examined the statistical relationship between beta and seven "financial statement" variables: dividend payout, asset growth, leverage, liquidity, asset size, earnings variability, and earnings beta. Their results were consistent with what one would expect from financial theory. Large, highly liquid firms with high dividend payout, low growth rates, low leverage, and stable earnings streams have lower risks.

The effects of company fundamentals on betas are usually estimated by relating beta to several fundamental variables by way of multiple regression techniques. An equation of the following form is typically estimated:

$$\beta = a_0 + a_1 X_1 + a_2 X_2 + a_3 X_3 + ... + a_n X_n + \varepsilon$$

(3-10)

where each X variable is one of the variables assumed to influence beta, and ε is the residual error term. The estimated historical relationship between accounting variables and beta can then be used to forecast the beta of a company. Following the Beaver, Kettler, and Scholes study, several studies summarized in Myers (1977), attempted to identify the accounting variables that are highly correlated with beta. These studies generally found that four accounting variables contribute most significantly to betas:

1. Earnings Cyclicality: beta depends on the interrelationship between swings in the firm's earnings and swings in earnings in the economy generally.

2. Earnings Variability: beta is strongly related to the volatility of earnings.

3. Financial Leverage: beta is highly related to financial risk.

4. Growth: beta is positively related to growth, given the traditional association between rapid growth and high business risk.

The advantage of the accounting beta is that it responds more quickly to a change in a company's fundamentals compared to historical beta. However, the weakness of the methodology is that the accounting betas are computed under the assumption that all companies respond in a similar manner to a change in fundamentals, that is, the regression coefficients in

Equation 3-10 are equally applicable to all companies. The example below conveys the main idea of the approach, which is to relate beta to an appropriate set of fundamental accounting variables.

Accounting-based approaches are useful tools to estimate the risks of a company for which no market data exist. An excellent example of using accounting data to infer the beta of companies without traded stock is contained in Pogue (1979). To infer the beta of unlisted oil pipeline companies, Pogue estimated the standard deviation in book rates of return for oil pipelines and for 18 reference industries for which market data were available. A beta prediction equation was developed from the 18 benchmark industry betas by relating the standard deviations of book returns for the 18 industries to their respective betas using simple linear regression. By inserting the standard deviations for oil pipelines into the fitted beta estimation equation, he obtained beta estimates of oil pipelines. Pogue was careful in accounting for different debt ratios among the reference companies by working with unlevered betas.[9] Using the derived betas, Pogue estimated the cost of equity capital for the oil pipelines with the Capital Asset Pricing Model.

EXAMPLE 3-2

A predicted value for U.S. Tel's beta is developed based upon a detailed analysis of a predictive model that takes into account a number of market and accounting variables. The specifics of this "back to the future" approach are as follows:[10]

First, the 5-year betas of each sample firm over the 1989-1993 "future period" are calculated. Second, the relationship between these betas and a set of accounting variables calculated using data from the 1984-1988 period is estimated by multiple regression techniques, as in Equation 3-10. Third, the estimated relationship and the corresponding accounting variables for U.S. Tel calculated using data for the 1989-1993 period are used to predict U.S. Tel's beta for the future.

Based on the empirical finance literature cited above, the accounting variables selected as having an impact on the firm's future beta are: earnings beta $X1$, growth in total assets $X2$, book value to

---

[9] See Chapter 14 for the technique and examples for purging the estimated beta of its financial risk component. The resulting unlevered beta can then be relevered by applying the desired capital structure.

[10] This example is adapted from Litzenberger (1979).

market price $X3$, debt ratio $X4$, historical beta $X5$, historical standard deviation $X6$, variation in cash flow $X7$, current dividend yield $X8$, and a dummy variable $X9$ for dividend cuts in the previous 5 years. The estimated relationship between future betas in the 1989-1993 period and the accounting variables over the 1984-1988 period is:

$$Future\ Beta = 0.326 - 0.015(X1) + .357(X2) + .125(X3) - 0.329(X4)$$
$$+ .334(X5) + 3.69(X6) + .04(X7) + .201(X8)$$

Inserting the following current values of the accounting variables for U.S. Tel in the above equation:

$$X1 = 0.5798 \quad X2 = 0.08771 \quad X3 = 1.217 \quad X4 = 0.3657 \quad X5 = 0.4632$$
$$X6 = 0.02509 \quad X7 = 0.1805 \quad X8 = 0.09394 \quad X9 = 0.00$$

The predicted future beta for U.S. Tel is 0.65.

Fundamental Beta

The fundamental beta combines the techniques of historical betas and accounting betas into one system. Barr Rosenberg,[11] who pioneered its development, found that fundamental beta is more accurate in predicting future beta than either historically derived estimates or accounting-based estimates alone.

Fundamental betas are developed through "relative response coefficients," defined as the ratio of the expected response of a security to the expected response of the market if both the security and the market are affected by the same event, for example, inflation or changes in energy costs. Those securities that react to an economic event in the same manner as the market will have high response coefficients, and vice-versa. The security's fundamental beta is determined by the relative response of security returns to economic events and by the relative contributions of various types of economic events to market variance. The fundamental beta of a security is the weighted average of its relative response coefficients, each weighted by the proportion of total variance in market returns due to that specific event. To compute fundamental beta, it is necessary to consider the sources of economic events,

---

[11] For an analytical description of fundamental betas, see Rosenberg and McKibben (1973), and Rosenberg and Guy (1976). Elton and Gruber (1991), Chapter 5, and Hagin (1979), Chapter 33, provide non-technical summaries of fundamental betas.

to project the reaction of the security to such moves, and to assign probabilities to the likelihood of each possible type of economic event.

To forecast fundamental betas, Rosenberg uses a multiple regression equation similar to Equation 3-10, but with considerably more variables. A vast array of variables on market variability, earnings variability, financial risk, size, growth, and a multitude of company and industry characteristics is used to capture differences between the betas of various companies and industries. Fundamental betas, which are commercially available from the firm of BARRA, are of the form:

$$\beta = a_0 + a_1 \ Factor_1 + a_2 \ Factor_2 + a_3 \ Factor_3 + ...etc. \qquad (3\text{-}11)$$

The weightings are based on historical estimates. The advantage of the approach is that it uses fundamental company data that are related to risk. The disadvantage is that the final regression equation (Equation 3-11) is arbitrary.

Rather than rely on historical measures, a model linking beta to its fundamental economic determinants can be derived and employed to quantify the impact of risk factors on beta and therefore on cost of capital. Chapter 14 fully discusses this approach, where it is shown that utilities are exposed to a number of significant risks that are likely to have an impact on their beta and, hence, on their cost of equity capital. These risks can be conveniently catalogued under the following headings:

Beta = Demand Risk x Operating Leverage x Financial Leverage

1. Demand risk: unanticipated variability in demand and prices, caused by macroeconomic conditions, regulation, competition, and supply imbalances.

2. Cost risk: unanticipated variability in operating and financing costs caused by macroeconomic conditions, regulation, competition, and technological change.

3. Leverage: the extent to which these demand and cost uncertainties are magnified by the operating cost and financial cost structures of the company.

3.4 Other Risk Measures

In the absence of market data, or as an adjunct to the beta and standard deviation measures of risk, several quantitative accounting-based proxies for risk and qualitative risk indicators are available.

Quantitative Accounting Risk Measures

As a proxy for beta and standard deviation, the volatility of the firm's earnings stream or the volatility of its book return on common equity can be computed using several common statistical measures.

The average deviation around growth trend of earnings per share over some past period, or the standard deviation of changes in earnings per share over time are plausible measures of risk. The "smoothness" of earnings, dividends, or sales, can be measured as well, using the mean absolute deviation of the actual values from their time trend; a perfectly smooth series will have a smoothness measure of zero.

The volatility of the book rate of return on common equity (ROE) is also an indicator of risk. The standard deviation, the mean absolute year-to-year percentage change, or the mean deviation around time trend of a time series of annual ROEs serve as risk proxies. The reader is referred to Pogue (1979) for a practical application of accounting risk proxies in an actual rate case. While it is sensible to infer that firms with volatile earnings will have volatile stock prices, this argument is relevant only to the extent that total risk is relevant to investors, rather than beta risk. In practice, beta and standard deviation are highly correlated for public utilities, and high total risk generally implies high market risk.

Several specialized risk measures have been developed by practitioners, investment bankers, commercial bankers, regulators, bond rating agencies, and utilities. Chandrasekaran and Dukes (1981) found that the most important variables used by investment bankers to evaluate the risk of public utilities were the times interest earned (Earnings before Tax and Interest/Interest) and overall cash-flow coverage ratios. Regulatory lag and high interest rates were considered significant for the risk in utility firms. In a study of the importance of variables related to risk, Dukes and Chandy (1983) found that the majority of both utility firms and commissions considered the interest coverage variable the most important. High levels of importance were also ascribed to internal cash generated as a percent of construction expenditures, market-to-book ratio, and internal generation of funds. A large proportion of AFUDC in relation to earnings available to common shareholders was also considered a crucial risk variable by utility firms and commissions.

Qualitative Risk Measures: Stock Ratings

Quality ratings published by several investment analysis services, such as Value Line, Fitch, and Standard & Poor's, provide subjective assessments of risk that influence the formation of investors' assessment of future risk.

For common stocks, useful risk analysis tools include the Standard & Poor's Quality Rating,[12] which is based principally on growth and stability of earnings and dividends over a 10-year period, and the Value Line Safety Rating. The latter is based 80% on the stability of the stock price adjusted for trend, measured by the standard deviation of weekly percent changes in the stock's market prices over a 5-year period, and 20% on subjective factors. The subjective factors include company size, financial leverage, earnings quality, balance sheet condition, and market penetration. Other useful risk indicators published by Value Line include the Price Stability Index, Financial Strength Rating, and Earnings Predictability Index.

Qualitative Risk Measures: Bond Ratings

Bond ratings by Moody's, Standard & Poor's, Duff & Phelps, Dominion Bond Rating Service, and Canadian Bond Rating Service are useful risk analysis tools. Bondholders are concerned with the risk of default on debt obligations and stockholders are concerned with the possibility of corporate bankruptcy. For a utility, this bond rating, or credit risk, results not only from the extent of internal financing, but also from a multi-dimensional blend of factors, including the nature of the service territory, business risks, financial risks, new construction risks, coverage ratios, and regulatory risks.

The specific criteria for determining bond ratings are discussed in most investments textbooks. Standard & Poor's *Credit Overview: Corporate and International Ratings* (1982) outlines the procedures for determining bond ratings for various industry groups, including utilities. Briefly, bond ratings vary directly with profitability, size, and interest coverage, while they move inversely with financial leverage and earnings stability. Interest coverage is one of the principal tests used by rating agencies to establish bond ratings. Dukes and Chandy (1983) also found that the most important variable used to evaluate riskiness was the interest coverage ratio. Coverage represents the protection of assets or the number of times earnings are greater than fixed contractual charges or interest costs. Maintaining a consistent earnings level sufficient to provide a minimum post-tax interest coverage of a certain amount is considered necessary to retain a given current bond rating. The relationship between the allowed return on common equity and the resulting interest coverage ratio is discussed in Chapter 10.

---

[12] Wagner and Lau (1971) found a significant relationship between beta and Standard & Poor's Stock Quality Rating. Stocks with high quality ratings had low betas, and vice versa. The ratings and the average beta for each quality group were as follows: A+ 0.74, A 0.80, A- 0.89, B+ 0.87, B 1.24, B- and C 1.23.

It is impossible to state the exact impact of an increase in any given financial ratio, such as coverage or dividend payout, on the company's bond rating. To answer this question would be to imply that a single benchmark determines bond rating, and that positive (or negative) achievement of one single benchmark automatically triggers an upgrading (or downgrading). Bond rating agencies examine a number of qualitative and quantitative factors, including equity ratio, coverage ratios, and internal cash generation, before rendering a rating decision. These factors are considered both individually and collectively, and the ability to satisfy a single benchmark is not necessarily a guarantor of a given credit rating.

The equity ratio and coverage ratios are the most important quantitative determinants of bond ratings, followed by internal cash generation. Thus, all else remaining constant, the higher the level of internal cash flow generation through retained earnings, the higher the credit quality. This is true for regulated as well as unregulated firms.

The ratings assigned to bond issues are important in terms of the marketability and effective cost to the ratepayer. The top four letter ratings, AAA down to BBB, are considered to be investment grade securities, meaning that financial institutions are potential purchasers of such bonds without violating the laws of prudent investment. Not only is an investment grade bond rating crucial for a utility to maintain continued access to capital, but the rating determines the cost and terms of the issue. Corporate bonds are discounted at progressively higher discount rates as their ratings deteriorate.

Investors rely greatly on agency bond ratings as a source of information on default risk because agency bond ratings reflect the risk of default and are closely tied to risk premiums. Concrete evidence supporting the relationship between bond ratings and the quality of a security is abundant. The empirical evidence gathered by Hickman (1958) supports the notion of a tradeoff between bond ratings or risk premiums, which in turn reflects default risk and expected return. The strong association between bond rating and equity risk premiums is well documented in a study by Brigham and Shome (1982). In studies by Schwendiman and Pinches (1975) and Melicher (1974), increasing beta values were consistently associated with deteriorating bond ratings.

Bond ratings and the risk of common stock investment are closely related. Many important financial risks common to both debt and equity holders originate in price stability and revenue variability. However, the priority of debt claims on operating cash flows, relative cost rates, and the proportions of debt to equity in the capital structure change the location and shape of the probability distribution of returns to each of the major classes of financing. Therefore, the risks between bonds and stock are not the same, although they are highly correlated. Companies with low bond ratings tend to be associated with high equity risks.

Bond ratings and stock ratings can be used as risk screening devices to identify companies of comparable risk. If a utility's bonds are rated BBB, for example, a reasonable risk filter would eliminate all companies with a rating other than BBB.

Two inadequacies of bond ratings are noteworthy. First, they are sluggish in changing to new conditions, due perhaps to inertia and slow reaction time by the ratings agencies. Typically, other barometers of risk will have changed well before the bond rating is altered by the agency. Evidence gathered by Wakeman (1982) and Weinstein (1978) showed that changes in bond ratings are not treated as new information by investors. Changes in bond ratings usually occur several months after investors have already reacted to the fundamental change in the bond's quality. Nevertheless, bond ratings are useful and valuable in that they provide unbiased estimates of bond risk.

Second, one has to go beyond the mere examination of ratings in evaluating the risk and potential return of a company. Companies with the same bond rating do not necessarily require the same expected growth. A given bond rating class is broad, and an investor is still left with an enormous range of issues from which to select. There are many more finer sub-classifications within a given bond rating category (Baa1, Baa2, Baa3, for example). Four investment-grade ratings categories is not a very discriminating classification system when 90% of all rated bonds are included in that system.

It should also be pointed out that bond rating and company size are generally negatively related. Morin (1992) contrasted the S&P bond rating and stock rating of small versus large capitalization stocks. For bond ratings, the first quintile of companies ranked in descending order of their market value of equity was ranked A- on average, versus CC for the bottom quintile. For stock ratings, the first quintile of companies was ranked A- to B+, versus C for the bottom quintile.

Market Reaction Measure of Risk

An alternative to the use of market and accounting data to measure risk is to examine how investors react to risk. The behavior of a utility's price-to-earnings ratio in relation to that of the market as as whole, or a comparison of relative market-to-book ratios can reveal investors' reactions to risk, assuming that all other things are the same.

Quality of Earnings

A major factor influencing quality of earnings, particularly in the electric utility industry, is the accounting for construction work in progress (CWIP). When the latter is included in the rate base, the current construction financing costs are realized in cash. When CWIP is not included in the rate base, an allowance for funds used during construction (AFUDC) is estimated and added to income. This lets public utilities capitalize the costs of debt and equity funds used in building new facilities.

Utility profits are composed of both AFUDC and operating income from sales of services. Since AFUDC does not generate cash, an increasing proportion of reported utility profits is unavailable for capital expenditures and dividend payments. When AFUDC is capitalized, increased uncertainty is injected into the reported income stream since it may never be realized in cash. The cost of capital is affected through this increase in risk. Empirical research by Fitzpatrick and Stitzel (1978), Lerner and Breen (1981), Brigham (1979), and Westmoreland (1979) has shown that firms that capitalize AFUDC are riskier because of increased fluctuations in operating incomes and cash flows over the construction cycle, augmenting business risk. The financial risk premium is increased as well, because of negative effects on cash coverage ratios, bond indenture clauses, and more frequent financing. Regulatory risk is also enhanced because the cash realization of AFUDC depends on prompt and reasonable rate relief over the life of the construction assets. Therefore, the higher the percentage of AFUDC in reported income, the greater the risks borne by shareholders resulting in reduction in market-to-book ratios.

Whether the tax savings attributable to accelerated depreciation and the investment tax credit are "normalized" or are used to reduce taxes for regulatory purposes ("flow through") can also exert a perceptible effect on risk and cost of capital. Relative to companies that normalize tax savings, flow through companies generate less cash flow per dollar of earnings and interest coverage ratios per dollar of interest expense are lower, thereby increasing risk and capital costs. This is shown in detail in Hyman (1982).

The results of empirical studies by Berndt (1979) and Morris (1980) indicate that companies operating under flow through experience an increase in cost of debt of the order of 25 to 35 basis points in relation to firms operating under tax normalization. The question of whether utilities should be required to flow through the tax benefits of accelerated depreciation and investment tax credits remains controversial, although the current tax laws have made the debate largely academic because such tax benefits cannot be obtained if they are flowed through.

Regulatory Climate Ranking

Regulation itself poses inherent risks for which investors require compensation. The U.S. Supreme Court's *Duquesne* decision asserted that regulators must consider regulatory risk in determining a fair rate of return. Regulatory risk, that is, perceived uncertainty about regulation, can be assessed by means of ratings assigned to regulatory bodies by investment firms. Several investment and research firms, including Argus Research, Value Line, Merrill Lynch, Salomon Brothers, Goldman Sachs, and Duff & Phelps, rate individual state public utility commissions based on the stringency with which they regulate rates. States where the regulatory climate is rated as "very favorable" are typically characterized by a relatively higher allowed rate of return on equity, minimal regulatory lag, forward test year, inclusion of CWIP in rate base, normalization of tax benefits, uncertainties over environmental compliance costs, exposure to prudence reviews, and automatic fuel adjusted clauses. States where the regulatory climate is rated as "unfavorable" are typically characterized by low allowed returns, substantial regulatory lag with no interim rate relief, flow through treatment of tax benefits, historical test year, and AFUDC treatment of CWIP. As documented by Navarro (1983), the allowed rate of return on equity and the inclusion of CWIP in the rate base are particularly significant to investors in measuring the regulatory climate for public utilities.

Several empirical studies have documented the regulatory climate's impact on utility cost of capital.[13]

Not surprisingly, the preponderance of the empirical evidence supports the notion that a favorable regulatory climate decreases a utility's risk and capital costs. Studies by Trout (1979), Archer (1981), Fitzpatrick and Stitzel (1978), Dubin and Navarro (1983), Hadaway, Heidebrecht, and Nash (1982), Navarro (1983), Davidson and Chandy (1983) and Fairchild and MacKenzie (1989) have established that utility capital costs are strongly related to regulatory climate ratings. High ratings result in low capital costs and low ratings in high capital costs. Fairchild and MacKenzie (1989) examined the relationship between regulatory climate for 100 electric utilities and six proxies for capital costs for each of 12 years in the 1977-1988 period. Regulatory climate was measured using Salomon Brothers' Regulatory Rankings. Proxies for capital costs included bond ratings, market-to-book ratios, and stock quality ratings. By correlating the regulatory quality rankings with the measures of capital costs, Fairchild and MacKenzie

---

[13] See for example Gapenski (1989), Buck and Groth (1986), Dubin and Navarro (1983), Archer (1981), Trout (1979), Fairchild and MacKenzie (1989), and Fanara and Gorman (1986).

concluded that regulatory climate continues to be an important determinant of public utilities' risk and capital costs when the relationship is examined using a consistent data set and testing methodology. In a cost-benefit analysis of utility bond ratings, Hadaway, Heidebrecht, and Nash concluded that electric utilities with high bond quality ratings on average provide lower cost services than financially weaker, lower-rated companies.

3.5 Risk Filter: Illustrations

An example of a risk filter employing several of the risk measures discussed in this chapter is shown in Table 3-2. The object of the risk filter was to identify companies comparable in risk to US West in a 1989 rate case.[14]

TABLE 3-2
MARKET RETURN AND MEASURES OF RISK: HIGH-QUALITY INDUSTRIALS
(Historical Growth)

Company Name	Beta	Financial Strength	Safety Rank	Price Stability	S&P Stock Rating
1 Amer. Home Prds	0.95	A+	1	95%	7
2 Amoco Corp.	0.85	A+	1	90%	8
3 Betz Labs	0.90	A+	1	90%	8
4 Coca-Cola Co.	1.00	A++	1	90%	7
5 Consol. Papers	0.90	A+	1	85%	8
6 Exxon Corp.	0.80	A++	1	95%	8
7 First Va Bank	1.00	A+	1	80%	7
8 First Wachovia	0.85	A+	1	95%	8
9 Gen'l Mills	1.00	A+	1	85%	8
10 Gen'l Re Corp.	1.00	A++	1	80%	9
11 Int'l Bus Mach	0.90	A++	1	95%	7
12 Kellogg	1.00	A+	1	85%	7
13 Kimberly-Clark	1.00	A+	1	85%	7
14 Longs Drug Stores	1.00	A+	1	85%	8
15 McDonald's Corp	1.00	A+	1	85%	7
16 Merck & Co	0.95	A++	1	90%	7
17 Moore Corp.	1.00	A++	1	85%	9
18 Procter & Gamble	0.95	A++	1	95%	8
19 Quaker Oats	0.95	A+	1	80%	7
20 Ralston Purina	0.90	A+	1	95%	7
21 Raytheon Co.	0.85	A+	1	95%	7
22 Vulcan Mat'ls	0.85	A+	1	95%	9
23 Wallace Comp Sv	0.95	A+	1	85%	7
24 Weis Markets	0.90	A++	1	80%	7
Averages	0.94	A+	1.0	88.33%	7.58

Source: Morin (1989)

---

[14] See Morin (1989).

The group of companies was constructed with the Value Line Screen Plus software program according to strict quality, or risk, criteria. The companies had to be industrials listed on the New York Stock Exchange to ensure comparable liquidity. In addition, they had to have Value Line's Financial Strength Rating of at least A+, the highest Safety Rating of 1, a beta between 0.75 and 1.00, and a Price Stability coefficient of at least 80%. The screening process excluded all utilities to circumvent the problem of circular logic, all non-dividend paying stocks, and all stocks with an S & P stock rating lower than A-. High-growth stocks were also eliminated because utility stocks are typically moderate in growth. There were a total of 24 stocks that met all these very stringent quality criteria, and for which corporate financial data were included in Value Line and in IBES. The average beta for the group served as a proxy for the US West beta. Cost of capital estimation techniques were then applied to the group as a proxy for US West.

Another example of a risk filter is shown in Table 3-3. The object of the risk filter was to identify companies comparable in risk to Bell Canada in a 1992 Canadian rate case. A sample of comparable Canadian industrials and public utilities was developed using four risk measures as guides. The first two risk measures were market oriented while the other two were accounting oriented. The first risk measure was beta. Because there are investors who are less than perfectly diversified, both market risk and company-specific risk were relevant. For this reason, the second measure of risk was company-related risk. This was measured by the variance of the return that remained, once the effect of the market had been removed from a security's total return. This type of risk is frequently referred to as "unsystematic" risk, or "residual" risk.

The third and fourth risk measures, which were accounting-oriented, were the standard deviation and the coefficient of variation of book equity returns (STDROE and CVROE) over the last 10 years. The final group of companies consised of those companies with market risk less than the average and whose accounting measures of risk were less than half the average. Table 3-3 shows the list of companies and the summary statistics for the companies that survived the screens. It is interesting to note that several utilities appear in the surviving sample, attesting to its comparability, reasonableness, and accuracy.

Another interesting variation on the above risk screens is to rank individual companies in descending order of risk for each of several risk measures individually. The sum of the individual ranks for each measure of risk provides a composite overall measure of risk for each company. Those companies located on the same portion of the risk spectrum as the utility in question, say the bottom decile (10% of the sample) are then designated as comparable companies. The procedure is illustrated in Table 3-4 for 10

TABLE 3-3
AVERAGE RETURN ON EQUITY 1982-1991 AND RISK MEASURES

Company	Status	10-year Mean ROE	STDROE	CVROE	Beta	Residual Risk
1 BCE Enterprises	R	12.33	2.34	0.1895	0.74	2.02
2 B.C. Telephone Co.	R	12.99	0.93	0.0712	0.70	3.19
3 Canada Malting Co. Ltd.	U	10.54	3.57	0.3393	0.68	9.37
4 Canadian Utilities Ltd.	R	14.98	2.40	0.1604	0.62	3.56
5 Chum Ltd.	U	13.68	1.56	0.1142	0.71	9.44
6 Corby Distilleries-CLA	U	13.81	1.80	0.1301	0.31	9.78
7 Corporate Foods Ltd.	U	23.39	1.59	0.0679	0.75	13.40
8 CT Financial Services	U	16.81	2.61	0.1551	0.52	8.09
9 Dover Industries Ltd.	U	17.91	2.66	0.1485	0.54	5.91
10 Fortis Inc.	R	14.34	1.66	0.1156	0.59	2.35
11 Hawker Siddeley Canada	U	8.45	1.72	0.2032	0.60	10.78
12 Imperial Oil Ltd.	U	9.12	3.31	0.3634	0.74	6.14
13 Island Telephone Co. Ltd	R	14.18	1.00	0.0702	0.47	4.76
14 Laurentian Bank Of CDA	U	11.34	3.45	0.3043	0.58	8.25
15 Loblaw Companies Ltd.	U	13.81	1.88	0.1363	0.61	8.12
16 Maple Leaf Foods Inc.	U	8.29	2.20	0.2656	0.72	15.41
17 Maritime Electric Co.	R	14.81	1.09	0.0735	0.54	4.57
18 Maritime Tel & Tel Co.	R	13.94	1.34	0.0961	0.58	3.04
19 MDS Health	U	14.75	3.77	0.2555	0.57	8.55
20 National Trustco Inc.	U	13.82	2.45	0.1772	0.63	9.83
21 Newtel Enterprises	R	13.07	2.26	0.1726	0.56	3.51
22 Pacific Northern	R	14.78	0.69	0.0469	0.51	4.88
23 Quebec-Telephone	R	14.36	1.20	0.0839	0.51	3.06
24 Scott Paper Ltd.	U	14.08	2.17	0.1539	0.72	11.13
25 Toromont Industries	U	10.10	3.66	0.3624	0.41	7.43
26 Trans Mountain Pipe Line	R	12.63	2.95	0.2335	0.60	7.03
27 UAP Inc.	U	10.80	2.41	0.2230	0.48	4.42
28 United Corporations Ltd	U	5.24	2.04	0.3894	0.72	10.47
29 Westcoast Energy Inc.	R	10.57	2.03	0.1916	0.66	3.61
30 Weston Ltd. (GEO)	U	12.94	2.35	0.1814	0.73	4.41
		13.06	2.17	0.1825	0.60	6.88

Source: Morin (1993)

TABLE 3-4

INDIVIDUAL COMPANY RANKS AND TOTAL COMPOSITE RISK SCORE

		Risk Measure (1)	Risk Measure (2)	Risk Measure (3)	Risk Measure (4)	Total Score
Company	F	10	7	5	8	30
Company	B	8	2	8	10	28
Company	C	4	8	10	3	25
Company	I	3	10	9	1	23
Company	A	7	1	6	7	21
Company	D	1	9	7	4	21
Company	J	9	3	3	5	20
Company	E	6	6	2	6	20
Company	H	2	5	1	9	17
Company	G	5	4	4	2	15

companies and 4 different risk measures. The first column shows the companies in the sample, the next 4 columns display the rank of each individual company according to each of 4 risk measures. The last column adds the 4 individual ranks to arrive at a composite score of the company, ranked in descending order of risk, from highest to lowest risk. The companies whose scores are closest to that of the utility are defined as comparable risk companies.

3.6 Risk Estimation and Call Option Pricing

Evidence of investor risk perceptions of utility common stocks over time can be extracted from market data on utility call options listed on the Chicago Board Option Exchange (CBOE). Options on the common stock of several utilities are traded daily in large volumes on the CBOE. Listed option quotations are available daily from the *Wall Street Journal*.

A call option is simply a right to buy a share of common stock at a predetermined price ("exercise price") over a stated period of time ("maturity"). The holder of an option can exercise the right to purchase the stock at the stated price anytime before or at maturity, or let the option expire unexercised.

A well-established body of financial theory has emerged in recent years on the valuation and pricing of call options. Essentially, three factors determine the price that an investor will pay for a call option. First, the maturity or time before expiration of the option; the longer the maturity, the more valuable the option, since the probability is greater that the actual common stock price will exceed the exercise price and make exercise attractive. Second, the exercise price; the lower the exercise price, the more valuable the option. Third, the volatility of the underlying stock; the more volatile the underlying stock, the more valuable the option, since the probability that the stock price will exceed the exercise price is greater, the more variable the stock price's behavior.

The valuation process of options by investors was formalized by Professors Black and Scholes (1973). The seminal Black-Scholes option valuation model is reproduced in Appendix 3-A, along with a numerical example. The Black-Scholes option pricing formula formally incorporates the three determinants of an option's value discussed above.

The market's consensus on the future volatility of a public utility's common stock is contained implicitly in the market price of the option. By taking the price of the option, and working backward through the Black-Scholes pricing formula, the volatility that is implicit within that option price can be obtained. Referring to the example of Appendix 3A, upon observing that the value of an option with S = $60, T = .241 and r = 6% was $10.60, one would discover that the implicit price volatility of that option is 0.40, since if that volatility were used in the pricing formula the price of the option observed in the market would be replicated.

Figure 3-7 shows the standard deviation of return implied by US Tel call option prices over various time periods. These hypothetical calculations of implied risk could have been performed by means of the Fischer Black Option Analysis Program, available commercially through Chase Econometrics/Interactive Data Corporation. The obvious trend implied by US Tel's call option data during that time period is the steady upward trend in the risk perceived by investors, which the traditional historical beta risk measure is unable to discern clearly. The advantage of the option-based technique is that risk perceptions can be tracked on a daily basis and that changes in risk can be readily detected. The drawback of the technique is that it can only be applied to utilities with traded options. The apparent complexity of the technique is likely to be a deterrent as well.

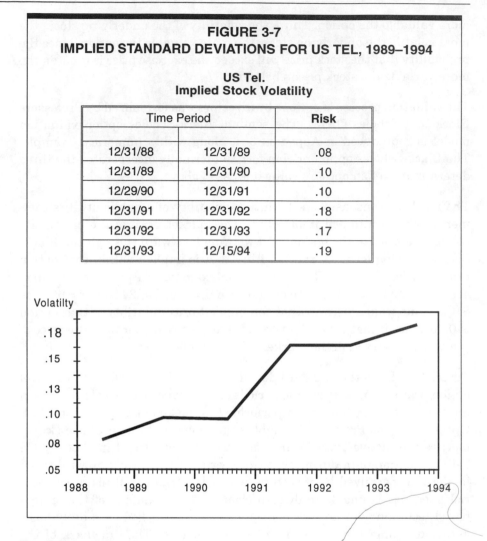

FIGURE 3-7
IMPLIED STANDARD DEVIATIONS FOR US TEL, 1989–1994

US Tel.
Implied Stock Volatility

Time Period		Risk
12/31/88	12/31/89	.08
12/31/89	12/31/90	.10
12/29/90	12/31/91	.10
12/31/91	12/31/92	.18
12/31/92	12/31/93	.17
12/31/93	12/15/94	.19

References

Andrews, V. L. North Carolina Natural Gas, Prepared Testimony, North Carolina Public Service Commission on Behalf of, G-21, Sub 293, 1990.

Archer, S.H. "The Regulatory Effects on Cost of Capital in Electric Utilities." *Public Utilities Fortnightly,* February 26, 1981.

Beaver, W.H., Kettler, P. and Scholes, M. "The Association Between Market Determined and Accounting Determined Risk Measures." *Accounting Review,* October 1970, 654-682.

Berndt, E.R. "Utility Bond Rates and Tax Normalization." *Journal of Finance,* December 1979, 1211-1220.

Black, F. and Scholes, M. "The Pricing of Options and Corporate Liabilities." *Journal of Political Economy,* May-June 1973, 637-659.

Blume, M.E. "On the Assessment of Risk." *Journal of Finance,* March 1971, 1-10.

Blume, M.E. "Betas and Their Regression Tendencies." *Journal of Finance,* June 1975, 785-796.

Brealey, R. and Myers, S. *Principles of Corporate Finance,* 4th ed. New York: McGraw-Hill, 1991.

Brigham. E.F. "The Changing Investment Risk of Public Utilities." Public Utility Research Center Working Paper 2-79, University of Florida, 1979.

Brigham, E.F. and Crum, R.L. "On the Use of the CAPM in Public Utility Rate Cases." *Financial Management,* Summer 1977,7-15.

Brigham, E.F. and Gapenski, L.C. *Financial Management: Theory and Practice,* 6th ed. Hinsdale IL: Dryden Press, 1991.

Brigham, E.F. and Shome, D.K. "Equity Risk Premium in the 1980's," Washington DC: Institute for Study of Regulation, 1982.

Buck, L.E. and Groth, J.C. "Regulatory Uncertainty and the Cost of Capital for Utilities." *Public Utilities Fortnightly,* February 20, 1986, 23-27.

Chan, L. and Lakonishok, J. "Are the Reports of Beta's Death Premature?" Illinois University, 1992.

Chandrasekaran, P.R. and Dukes, W.P. "Risk Variables Affecting Rate of Return of Public Utilities." *Public Utilities Fortnightly,* February 26, 1981, 32.

Chen, N.F. "Beta Nonstationarity, Portfolio Residual Risk, and Diversification." *Journal of Financial and Quantitative Analysis,* March 1981.

Davidson, W.N. and Chandy, P.R. "The Regulatory Environment for Public Utilities: Indications of the Importance of Political Process." *Financial Analysts' Journal,* November-December 1983, 50-53.

Dimson, E. "Risk Adjustment When Shares Are Subject to Infrequent Trading." *Journal of Financial Economics,* June 1979, 197-226.

Dubin, J.A. and Navarro, P. "The Effect of Rate Suppression on Utilities' Cost of Capital." *Public Utilities Fortnightly,* March 31, 1983, 18-22.

Dukes, W.P. and Chandy, P.R. "Rate of Return and Risk for Public Utilities," *Public Utilities Fortnightly,* September 1, 1983, 35-41.

Elton, E.J. and Gruber, M.J. *Modern Portfolio Theory and Investment Analysis.* New York: Wiley and Sons, 1991.

Fairchild, B. H. and MacKenzie, S. M. "The Impact of Regulatory Climate on Utility Capital Costs: An Alternative Test." *Public Utilities Fortnightly,* May 25, 1989, 6-8.

Fama, E.F. and French, K. R. "The Cross-Section of Expected Stock Returns." *Journal of Finance,* June 1992, 427-465.

Fanara Jr., P. and Gorman, R. "The Effects of Regulatory Risk on the Cost of Capital." *Public Utilities Fortnightly,* March 6, 1986, 32-36.

Fitzpatrick, D.B. and Stitzel, T.E. "Capitalizing an Allowance for Funds Used During Construction: The Impact on Earnings Quality." *Public Utilities Fortnightly,* January 19, 1978, 18-22.

Francis, J.C. "Skewness and Investors' Decisions." *Journal of Financial and Quantitative Analysis,* March 1975, 163-172.

Friend, I., Westerfield, R., and Granito, M. "New Evidence on the Capital Asset Pricing Model." *Journal of Finance,* June 1978, 903-916.

Fuller, R.J. and Kerr, W. "Estimating the Divisional Cost of Capital: An Analysis of the Pure-Play Technique." *Journal of Finance,* December 1981, 997-1009.

Gapenski, L.C. "An Hypothesis on the Impact of Regulatory Climate on Utility Capital Costs." *Public Utilities Fortnightly,* March 30, 1989, 28.

Gombola, M.J. and Kahl, D. R. "Time-Series Processes of Utility Betas: Implications for Forecasting Systematic Risk." *Financial Management,* Autumn 1990, 84-92.

Gordon, M.J. and Halpern, P. "The Cost of Capital to a Division of a Firm." *Journal of Finance,* September 1974, 1153-1163.

Hadaway, S.C., Heidebrecht, R., and Nash, J. "A Cost-Benefit Analysis of Alternative Bond Ratings Among Electric Utility." Economic Research Division, Public Utility Commission of Texas, 1982.

Hagin, R.L. *Modern Portfolio Theory.* Homewood IL: Dow Jones-Irwin, 1979.

Harrington, D.R. "Whose Beta is Best?" *Financial Analysts' Journal,* July-August 1983, 67-73.

Hickman, W.B. *Corporate Bond Quality and Investor Experience.* Princeton NJ: Princeton University Press, 1958.

Hyman, L.S. *America's Electric Utilities: Past, Present, and Future.* Arlington VA: Public Utilities Reports Inc., 1992.

Kothari, S.P., Shanken, J., and Sloan. R.G. "Another Look at the Cross-section of Expected Stock Returns." Bradley Policy Research Center of the University of Rochester, W. Simon Graduate School of Business Administration, No. 93-01,1993.

Kraus, A. and Litzenberger, R.H. "Skewness Preference and the Valuation of Risk Assets." *Journal of Finance,* September 1976, 1085-1099.

Kryzanowski. L. and Jalilvand, A. "Statistical Tests of the Accuracy of Alternative Forecasts: Some Results for U.S. Utility Betas." *The Financial Review,* Fall 1983, 319-335.

Lerner, E.M. and Breen, W.J. "The Changing Significance of AFUDC for Public Utilities." *Public Utilities Fortnightly,* January 1, 1981, 17-25.

Levy, H. "The CAPM and Beta in an Imperfect Market." *The Journal of Portfolio Management,* Winter 1980, 5-11.

Levy, R.A. "On the Short-term Stationarity of Beta Coefficients." *Financial Analysts' Journal,* November-December 1971, 55-62.

Litzenberger, R.H. "Determination of a Target Market to Book Value Ratio for a Public Utility in an Inflationary Environment." In *Proceedings: Iowa State University, Regulatory Conference on Public Utility Value and the Rate-Making Process,* 1980.

Litzenberger, R.H. Prepared testimony on behalf of Southern Bell (1979),

Malkiel, B.G. *A Random Walk Down Wall Street,* New York: W.W. Norton and Co., 1990.

McShane, K. C. Prepared testimony on Fair Return on Equity for Bell Canada, Foster Associates, Inc., February 1993.

Melicher, R.W. "Financial Factors which Influence Beta Variations within an Homogeneous Industry Environment." *Journal of Financial and Quantitative Analysis,* March 1974, 231-241.

Melicher, R.W. "Risk Measurement and Rate of Return under Regulation." In *Issues in Public Utility Regulation,* edited by H.M. Trebing, 325-341. East Lansing MI: Michigan State University, 1979.

Morin, R.A. "Market Line Theory and the Canadian Equity Market." *Journal of Business Administration,* Fall 1980, 57-76.

Morin, R.A. US West Communications (Mountain Bell), Rebuttal Testimony, Arizona Corporation Commission, March 1989.

Morin, R.A. California Water Association, Prepared Testimony, "Financial and Operational Risk Analysis of California Water Utilities." California Public Utilities Commission, Docket No. 90-11-033,1992.

Morin, R.A. Bell Canada, Prepared Testimony, Canadian Radio and Telecommunications Commission, 1993.

Morris III, R.B. "The Effect of Tax Flow Through on the Cost of Public Utility Debt." *Public Utilities Fortnightly,* November 6, 1980, 22-24.

Navarro, P. "How Wall Street Ranks the Public Utility Commissions." *Financial Analysts' Journal,* November-December 1983, 46-49.

Patterson, C.S. "CV Or Not CV? That is the Question." *Accounting and Finance,* May 1989.

Perry, P.R. "Instructor's Manual to Accompany Brealey and Myers' *Principles of Corporate Finance,*" 4th ed., New York: McGraw-Hill, 1991.

Pogue. G.A. Williams Pipeline Co., Prepared testimony, Federal Energy Regulatory Commission, Docket No. OR79-1, 1979.

Reilly, F.K. *Investment Analysis and Portfolio Management.* Hinsdale IL: Dryden Press, 1989.

Reilly, F.K. and Wright, D. J. "A Comparison of Published Betas." *Journal of Portfolio Management,* Spring 1988, 64-69.

Roll, R.W. and Ross, S.A. "On the Cross-Sectional Relation Between Expected Return and Betas." Working Paper, Yale University, 1993.

Rosenberg, J.I. "Risk, Return, and Regulation Among Energy Industries." *Public Utilities Fortnightly,* August 1986, 31-38.

Rosenberg, V. and Guy, J. "Prediction of Beta from Investment Fundamentals." *Financial Analysts' Journal,* 32, July-August 1976, 62-70.

Rosenberg, V. and McKibben, W. "The Prediction of Systematic Risk in Common Stocks." *Journal of Financial and Quantitative Analysis,* March 1973, 317-333.

Ross, S., Westerfield, R., and Jaffee, J. *Corporate Finance,* 3rd ed. Homewood IL: Irwin, 1993.

Scholes, M. and Williams, J. "Estimating Betas From Nonsynchronous Data." *Journal of Financial Economics,* 1977, 309-327.

Schwendiman, C.J. and Pinches, G.E. "An Analysis of Alternative Measures of Investment Risk." *Journal of Finance,* March 1975, 193-200.

Sharpe, W.F. and Alexander, G.J. *Investments,* 4th ed. New York: Prentice-Hall, 1990.

Sharpe, W. and Cooper, G.M. "Risk-Return Classes of New York Stock Exchange Common Stocks, 1931-1967." *Financial Analysts' Journal,* March-April 1972, 35-43.

Standard & Poor. *Credit Overview: Corporate and International Ratings.* New York: Standard & Poor's Corp., 1982.

Statman, M. "Betas Compared: Merrill Lynch vs. Value Line." *Journal of Portfolio Management,* Winter 1981, 41-44.

Trout, R.R. "The Regulatory Factor and Electric Utility Common Stock Investment Values." *Public Utilities Fortnightly,* November 22, 1979.

Wagner, W.H. and Lau, S.C. "The Effect of Diversification on Risk." *Financial Analysts' Journal,* November-December 1971, 48-57.

Wakeman, L.M. "Bond Rating Agencies and Capital Markets." Working Paper, UCLA Graduate School of Management, 1982.

Weinstein, M.I. "The Seasoning Process of New Corporate Bond Issues." *Journal of Finance,* December 1978, 1343-54.

Westmoreland, G. "Electric Utilities' Accounting for CWIP: The Effects of Alternative Methods on the Financial Statements, Utility Rates, and Market-to-book Ratio." PhD dissertation, University of Florida, 1979.

Additional References

Morin, R.A. "Risk Aversion Revisited." *Journal of Finance,* September 1983.

Morin, R.A. "Intervention Analysis and the Dynamics of Market Efficiency." In *Time-Series Applications,* New York: North Holland, 1983. (with K. El-Sheshai)

Myers, S. "The Relationship Between Real and Financial Measures of Risk and Return." In *Risk And Return In Finance*, edited by I. Friend and J. Bicksler. Cambridge: Ballinger Publishing Co., 1977.

Appendix 3-A
Call Option Valuation

Black-Scholes Formula:

$$C = S N(d_1) - E e^{-rt} N(d_2)$$

where
- C = price of a call option
- S = price of the stock
- T = time to expiration
- N = cumulative normal probability distribution function
- E = exercise price
- r = interest rate
- σ = volatility of the stock

$$d_1 = \frac{\ln(S/E) + (r + \tfrac{1}{2}\sigma^2 T)}{\sigma\sqrt{T}}$$

$$d_2 = d_1 - \sigma\sqrt{T}$$

EXAMPLE 3-A

Use of the formula requires the input of 5 variables: stock price, exercise price, time to maturity, interest rate, volatility of the stock. To calculate the value of a Utility X October 60 option with 88 days to expiration, and with particular observable values of the 5 variables as follows:

$$S = 68$$
$$E = 60$$
$$T = 88/365 = 0.241 \text{ years}$$
$$r = 6\%$$
$$\sigma = .40$$

Substituting the values of the variables in the formula, we have the option price as:

$$C = 68\, N(d_1) - 60 e^{-.06 \times .241}\, N(d_2)$$

where

$$d_1 = \frac{\ln \tfrac{68}{60} + (0.06 + \tfrac{1}{2} \times 0.40^2 \times 0.241)}{0.40 \times \sqrt{0.141}}$$

$$d_2 = .808 - .196 = .612$$

and using the normal distribution tables:

$$N(d_1) = N(.808) = .79$$

$$N(d_2) = N(.612) = .73$$

we obtain the call option price:

$$-0.01446$$

$$C = 68 \ X \ 0.79 - 60e^{-.01446} \times 0.73$$

$$= \$10.60$$

Chapter 4
Discounted Cash Flow Concepts

Consistent with the basic premises of rate of return regulation enunciated in Chapter 1, a public utility's allowed rate of return on equity must be sufficient to enable it to attract capital, and must be commensurate with the return on investments in other firms with similar risks. Otherwise, the ability to attract funds is impaired. The return required by equity owners for a given risk class is implicitly embedded in the share price of that firm. In order to estimate the required return on equity, or cost of equity, the determinants of stock price must be understood, which requires knowledge of the investor's valuation process.

Discounted Cash Flow (DCF) models occupy the next 5 chapters. This chapter outlines the basic theory of DCF. In Section 4.1 the classical theory of security valuation is reviewed. A generalized stock valuation model is derived in Section 4.2. Section 4.3 describes the standard DCF model prevalent in most regulatory hearings. The determinants of the dividend growth rate, which appear in most DCF models, are analyzed in Section 4.4. The Earnings/Price approach to cost of equity determination, which is a special case of the standard DCF model, is reviewed in Section 4.5. In Section 4.6, several refinements and more advanced versions of the standard DCF approach are described. The necessary assumptions behind all the models are discussed extensively throughout the chapter.

The actual implementation of the DCF models and the difficulties encountered in actual regulatory proceedings are discussed in the next 4 chapters of the DCF sequence. Chapter 5 discusses the practical implementation of DCF. Chapters 6 and 7 address two special issues of interest, namely, the treatment of flotation cost and alternate functional forms of the model. The last chapter in the DCF sequence discusses the construction of comparable groups of companies.

4.1 The Basics of Valuation

The Concept of Value

Classical valuation theory focuses on the true, or intrinsic, value of a security. This theory holds that the value of a financial asset is determined by its earning power, its ability to generate future cash flows. The fundamental value of the asset is the discounted sum of all future income flows that will be received by the owner of the asset. The fundamental notion that the value of an asset stems from the discounted present value of its future cash flow stream was first advanced by Fisher (1907) and later expanded by J. B. Williams in his classic 1938 book, *The Theory of Investment Value*. Molodovsky (1974) disseminated the use of the technique among financial analysts. In essence, the application of classical valuation theory by analysts involves estimating and adding up the present values of the future cash flows expected by the security holder.

Present Value. The concept of present value is designed to estimate how much an investment is worth today, given its expected future cash flows. Consider an investment that is expected to pay $100 one year from now. Its value today depends on the return one expects to make on other investments of comparable risk. If competing investments of similar risk are offering a return of 10%, an investment of $90.91 today, that is $100/1.1, is also expected to produce $100 one year from now. So, the original investment has a present value of $90.91. The process of computing present values of future sums is known as discounting or capitalizing. To determine the present value of a future sum, the future amount is multiplied by a discount factor available from standardized financial tables for various combinations of discount rate and number of time periods. The discount factor reflects the investor's opportunity, or foregone, rate of return on investments in a given risk class. The present value of any future stream of cash flows can be determined by this approach.

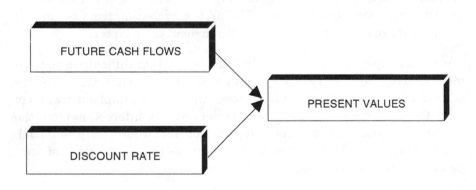

The formula for the present value of an amount, F, due in n years, given i as the time value of money, is given by:

$$PV = \frac{F}{(1+i)^n} = F(1 + i)^{-n} \tag{4-1}$$

For example, what is the worth of a bond that will pay $150 per year for three years, and an additional amount of $1,000 3 years from now, given that the opportunity cost of money for investments of comparable risk is

15%? Using the assumed discount rate of 15% and the corresponding discount factors available from a set of present value tables, or applying Equation 4-1 directly, the present value of $150 1 year from now is $130.43, the present value of $150 2 years from now is $113.42. The present value of the final $1,150 to be received 3 years from now is $756.14. Adding each separate present value, the present value of the bond investment is $1000.

$$PV = \$150/(1 + .15) + \$150/(1 + .15)^2 + (\$150 + \$1000)/(1 + .15)^3$$

$$= \$130.43 + \$113.42 + \$756.14$$

$$= \$1,000$$

This procedure is equally applicable to the case of common stocks. The aggregate present value of the discounted cash flows from holding the stock will equal the present value of the stock. Two characteristics distinguish the case of common stocks from bonds. First, the future cash flows from the stock are uncertain and probably uneven over time, unlike the cash flows from bonds, which are contractually set and known with relative certainty. Second, since the risk of holding stock exceeds that of holding bonds, the expected future cash flows from the stock must be discounted at a higher opportunity rate of interest, reflecting the additional risk.

Common Stock Valuation

The cash flows expected by investors holding common stock are dividends and changes in stock price. The following examples illustrate common stock valuation.

One-year Holding Period. Consider an investor with a 1-year holding period. For example, if a dividend of $5 and a resale price of $26 are expected at the end of the first year, and the stock is currently trading at $25, then the net cash flow expected by the investor is:

cash flow = expected dividend + change in stock price

$$= \$5 + (\$26 - \$25)$$

$$= \$6$$

By dividing the cash flow expected from the investment by the current stock price, the cash flow can be expressed as a rate of return per dollar of investment:

$$return = cashflow/investment$$

$$= \$6/\$25$$

$$= 24\%$$

The investor's return can be broken down into its two component parts, dividend yield and capital appreciation:

$$return = \frac{first\text{–}year\ dividend}{current\ stockprice} + \frac{change\ in\ stockprice}{current\ stock\ price}$$

$$= \$5/\$25 + (\$26 - \$25)/\$25$$

$$= 20\% + 4\% = 24\%$$

Generalizing the above example using algebraic notation, where D_1 is next year's expected dividend, P_1 is the price expected to prevail at the end of the year, and P_0, the current stock price, the 1-year return expected by the shareholder, denoted by the symbol K_e, can be expressed as:

$$K_e = D_1/P_0 + (P_1 - P_0)/P_0 \qquad (4\text{-}2)$$

Equation 4-2 demonstrates how the return required by the shareholder, or cost of equity, is set by the market through the market price. That return is the sum of the expected dividend yield, D_1/P_0 and the expected capital gains or losses, $P_1 - P_0/P_0$. The stock price at any time is set so that shareholders obtain a return of $K\%$ on their investment, reflecting their opportunity cost. If the current price of the stock is above P_0, the shareholder will not buy the stock since the dividends and end-of-period stock price are insufficient to cover opportunity cost. Conversely, if the current price is less than P_0, the investor will buy the stock since the return offered exceeds the opportunity cost.

By rearranging Equation 4-2 and solving for the stock price, an expression is obtained that is consistent with the basic tenet of classical valuation theory, namely, that the value of the stock is the present value of the cash flows expected from the investment discounted at the investor's required rate of return.

$$P_O = \frac{D_1}{1+K} + \frac{P_1}{1+k}$$

In the numerical example:

$$\$25 = \$5/1.24 + \$26/1.24$$

Two-year Holding Period.   If in the above numerical example, the investor possesses a 2-year holding period, the stock price can be expressed as the sum of cash flows for both future periods, discounted at the average required rate of return for the 2 periods. If, for example, a dividend of $5.25 and a resale price of $27.30 are expected at the end of the second year, we have:

$$25 = \frac{5.00}{1+K} + \frac{5.25}{(1+K)^2} + \frac{27.30}{(1+K)^2}$$

Solving for K, the investor's required return up to year 2 on the stock is 24%.

Thus, the DCF valuation framework is easily extensible over as many periods as desired, provided that reasonable estimates of future cash flows are available.

Realized Returns

The cost of common equity capital is sometimes estimated by calculating realized returns on equity over arbitrarily chosen historical time periods. The historical rate of return for a given period is the actual dividend yield plus the actual capital gain or loss. The basic measure of realized return is the same as Equation 4-2, except that actual realized data are used.

For example, to find the realized return to holders of a common stock over two periods, the first period return, K_1, is:

$$K_1 = \frac{D_1 + (P_1 - P_0)}{P_0}$$

and the second period return, K_2, is:

$$K_2 = \frac{D_2 + (P_2 - P_1)}{P_1}$$

The average return over the 2 periods can be computed by either the arithmetic average of the 2 period returns or by their geometric average. Chapter 11 will discuss the issue of whether the arithmetic or geometric mean is preferable and under what circumstances. The arithmetic average is simply $(K_1 + K_2)/2$. The geometric average of the 2 period returns is computed by:

$$K_e = \sqrt[2]{(1 + K_1)(1 + K_2)} - 1$$

Since the first period return is 24% and the second period is 21%, the average arithmetic average is $(24\% + 21\%) / 2 = 22.5\%$. The geometric average for the period is:

$$K_e = \sqrt[2]{(1 + .24)(1 + .21)} - 1)$$

$$= .2245 \text{ or } 22.45\%$$

The realized return approach is frequently encountered in measuring the cost of equity. Typically, the monthly realized returns are computed as above over a 10-year period and the arithmetic or geometric mean of the monthly returns is computed to arrive at the average realized return. The latter is then used as an estimate of cost of capital.

This procedure is suspect. Cost of capital is a forward-looking, long-run expectational concept, while realized return reflects only one of many outcomes initially envisaged by the investor in a probability distribution of several outcomes. It is important to keep in mind when using realized return as a proxy for expected return that the former measures what actually happened, and not necessarily what investors expected to happen.

Averaging realized returns provides only a broad indication of the relevant range over which expectations lie. These averages provide useful information only to the extent that they cover a long period of time and many securities, and that no major change has occurred in the economy. It would be hazardous to rely on 5 years of historical returns for a particular public utility as a guide to investors' expectations for the future. A simple example will illustrate this.

In the 1-year holding period example of the previous section, suppose that the actual resale price turns out to be $20 instead of the expected $25. Then, the after-the-fact realized return is:

$$K_1 = \frac{D_1 + (P_1 - P_0)}{P_0} = \frac{D_1}{P_0} + \frac{P_1 - P_0}{P_0}$$

$$= \$5/\$25 + (\$24 - \$25)/\$25$$

$$= 20\% - 4\% = 16\%$$

versus the expected 24%. Reliance on realized return provides a distorted measure of investors' expected return.

Or suppose investors become disenchanted with utility stocks because of unfavorable regulation, and now require a 30% return. With the increase in required return, the stock price will fall to $23.85 in order for investors who purchase the stock now to get a 30% return:

$$P_0 = \frac{D_1}{1+K} + \frac{P_1}{1+K}$$

$$= \$5/1.30 + \$26/1.30$$

$$= \$3.85 + \$20 = \$23.85$$

4.2 The General DCF Model

Extending the concepts of the previous section from a 1-year and 2-year holding period to a multi-year holding period, consider an investor with a horizon of n periods. The investor buys stock at the beginning of year 1, expects to receive dividends of D_1 at the end of year 1, D_2 at the end of year 2, D_3 at the end of year 3, etc., and expects to sell the stock at a price of P_n at the end of year n. If the investor's required return corresponding to the riskiness of those expected cash flows is K, the present value of the first year's expected dividend D_1, is:

$$\frac{D_1}{1+K}$$

The present value of the second year's dividend D_2 is:

$$\frac{D_2}{(1+K)^2}$$

and similarly for the other cash flows. The present value, and hence the price, of all the future expected cash flows from owning the stock is:

$$P_0 = \frac{D_1}{1+K} + \frac{D_2}{(1+K)^2} + \frac{D_3}{(1+K)^3} + \ldots + \frac{D_n}{(1+K)^n} + \frac{P_n}{(1+K)^n} \qquad (4\text{-}3)$$

In abbreviated form, the equation can be expressed as:

$$P_0 = \sum_{t=1}^{n} \frac{D_t}{(1+K)^t} + \frac{P_n}{(1+K)^n} \qquad (4\text{-}4)$$

Given the current price, the expected dividends up to period n and the price in period n, an estimate of the cost of equity, K, can be obtained. Alternately, the value of common stock can be expressed as the present value of a stream of dividends extending to infinity. This can be justified either by assuming that the investor has an infinite investment horizon, or by assuming that the expected resale price at the end of a limited horizon, P_n, is itself a present value of the expected dividends following year n to the new purchaser:

$$\text{Present Value} = \frac{D_1}{1 + K} + \frac{D_2}{(1 + K)^2} + \frac{D_3}{(1 + K)^3} \dots \text{ and so on indefinitely}$$

In abbreviated form, the equation can be expressed as:

$$P_0 = \sum_{t=1}^{n} \frac{D_t}{(1 + K)^t} \tag{4-5}$$

Equation 4-5 is the seminal DCF dividend valuation model of common stocks, the crucial equation for all the various DCF approaches discussed in this book.

General DCF Assumptions

The 4 crucial assumptions of the general DCF model are:

1. That investors, in fact, evaluate common stocks in the classical valuation framework, and trade securities rationally at prices reflecting their perceptions of value. Given the universality and pervasiveness of the classical valuation framework in investment education and in the professional investment community, this assumption is plausible.

2. That investors discount the expected cash flows at the same rate K in every future period. In other words, a flat yield curve is assumed. If K varies over time, there is no single required return rate, and practical estimates of the required return must be considered as weighted averages of K_1, K_2, $K_3 \dots K_n$. Since each of the 1-period return requirements can be thought of as an interest rate plus a risk premium, the required return to a multiple time horizon can be viewed as an average interest rate plus an average risk premium. More complex discounting models that incorporate these varying "yield curve effects" are available, but are of limited practical usefulness.

3. That the K obtained from the fundamental DCF equation corresponds to that specific stream of future cash flows alone, and no other. There may be alternate company policies that would generate the

same future cash flows, but these policies may alter the risk of the cash flow stream, and hence modify the investor's required return, *K*.

4. That dividends, rather than earnings, constitute the source of value. The rationale for computing the value of common stock from dividends is that the only cash values ever received by investors are dividends. Earnings are important only insofar as they provide dividends.

Focusing on the present value of expected earnings can be misleading. It is earnings net of any investment required to produce the earnings that are of interest, and not earnings alone. For example, a company expects earnings per share of $1.00 per year; but to sustain the stream of future earnings, the company needs to invest in real assets at the rate of $1.00 per year. Since an amount equal to each year's earnings must be channeled into new asset investment, no sustainable dividend payout, hence value, is possible. In general, even for a non-dividend paying company, earnings will eventually outrun the firm's need for additional asset investment, creating the capacity to pay dividends.

The finance literature has produced 3 general approaches to determine value, each involving discounting 3 different streams of money: (1) the present value of expected dividends, (2) the present value of expected earnings net of required investment, and (3) the present value of the cash flows produced by assets. All 3 approaches are equivalent, provided they are properly formulated.[1]

In summary, classical valuation theory states that the present value of a share of common stock can be derived from the discount rate and the expected dividend stream:

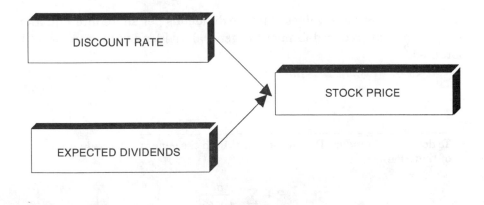

---

[1] The equivalence between the three approaches is demonstrated in several financial texts. See for example Francis (1988), Chapter 9.

The process can be reversed to arrive at the implicit discount rate from the present value (current price) and the dividend stream. This is the heart of the DCF procedure. Given estimates of the current price and future dividends, the stock's implicit discount rate can be calculated. The discount rate is that rate of return (cost of equity) that equates the current price with the forecasted dividend stream:

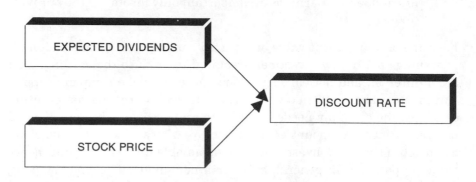

4.3 The Standard DCF Model

The general common stock valuation model embodied in Equation 4-5 is not very operational, since it requires an estimation of an infinite stream of dividends. But by assigning a particular configuration to the dividend stream, a more operational formula can be derived. Assuming that dividends grow at a constant rate forever, that is,

$$D_t = D_0 (1 + g)^t \qquad (4\text{-}6)$$

where g = expected dividend per share growth

and substituting these values of future dividends per share into Equation 4-5, the familiar reduced form of the general dividend valuation model is obtained:[2]

$$P_0 = \frac{D_1}{K - g} \qquad (4\text{-}7)$$

---

[2] To derive the standard DCF model, start with the general DCF valuation model of Equation 4-5:

$$P + \sum_{t=1}^{n} \frac{d_t}{(1 + K)^t}$$

If future dividens are growing at a constant rate of g, then:

In words, this fundamental equation states that the market price of a share of common stock is the value of next year's expected dividend discounted at the market's required return net of the effect of growth. Solving the equation for K, the cost of equity capital, the standard DCF formulation widely used in regulatory proceedings is obtained:

$$K = D_1/P_0 + g \qquad\qquad (4\text{-}8)$$

This formula states that under certain simplifying assumptions discussed below, which investors frequently make, the equity investor's expected return, K, can be envisaged as the sum of an expected dividend yield, D_1/P_0, plus the expected growth rate of future dividends, g. Investors set the equity price so as to obtain an appropriate return consistent with the risk of the investment and with the return foregone in investments of comparable risk. The basic idea of the standard DCF approach to estimating the cost of equity capital is to infer K from the observed share price and from an estimate of investors' expected future dividends. The principal appeal of the approach is its simplicity and its correspondence with the intuitive notion of dividends plus capital appreciation as a measure of investors' total expected return. The assumptions underlying the model are discussed in detail below. Essentially, a constant average growth trend for both dividends and earnings, a stable dividend payout and capital structure policy, and a discount rate in excess of the expected growth rate are assumed. A simple example will illustrate the standard DCF model.

---

2   (continued)

$$P = \frac{D_1}{(1 + K)} + \frac{D_1\,(1 + g)}{(1 + K)^2} + \frac{D_1\,(1 + g)^2}{(1 + K)^3} + \frac{D_1\,(1 + g)^{n-1}}{(1 + K)^n}$$

where n is the number of years. Hence, stock price P is the sum of an infinite geometric progression whose first term f is $\dfrac{D_1}{1+K}$ and whose constant ratio R is $\dfrac{1 + g}{1 + K}$. The standard formula for the sum of a geometric series is: $\dfrac{f}{1-R}$

Applying this formula:

$$P = \frac{D_1}{1 + K} \left/ \left(1 - \frac{1 + g}{1 + K}\right)\right. = \left(\frac{D_1}{1 + K}\right) \left/ \frac{K - g}{1 + K}\right. = \frac{D_1}{K - g}$$

Solving for the required rate of return (cost of equity):

$$K = \frac{D_1}{P} + g$$

EXAMPLE 4-1

We have the following market data for Utility X:

current dividend per share = $1.62

current stock price = $13.00

expected dividend growth = 4%

From Equation 4-8, the standard DCF model produces a cost of equity of:

$$K = D_1/P_0 + g$$

$$= D_0(1 + g)/P_0 + g$$

$$= \$1.62(1.04)/\$13 + .04$$

Note that next year's expected dividend is the current spot dividend increased by the expected growth rate in dividends. In general, implementation of the approach requires finding D_0 and P_0 from readily available sources of market data; the growth rate, g, can be estimated using several techniques. One way is to extrapolate the historical compound growth of dividends over some past period. Chapter 5 will discuss the applicational aspects of the DCF formulation in detail.

Standard DCF Model Assumptions

The assumptions underlying the standard DCF model have been the source of controversy, confusion, and misunderstanding in rate hearings. This section will attempt to clarify these assumptions.

Theories are simplifications of reality and the models articulated from theories are necessarily abstractions from the existing world so as to facilitate understanding and explanation of the real world. The DCF model is no exception to the rule. A model should not be judged by the severity and surrealism of its assumptions, but rather by its intended use and ability to predict, explain, and help the decision-maker attain his or her goal. The assumptions of the standard DCF model are as follows:

Assumption #1. The 4 assumptions discussed earlier in conjunction with the general classical theory of security valuation still remain in force.

Assumption #2. The discount rate, *K*, must exceed the growth rate, *g*. In other words, the standard DCF model does not apply to growth stocks. In Equation 4-7, it is clear that as *g* approaches *K*, the denominator gets progressively smaller, and the price of the stock infinitely large. If *g* exceeds *K*, the price becomes negative, an implausible situation. In the derivation of the standard DCF equation (4-7) from the general stock valuation equation (4-5), it was necessary to assume *g* less than *K* in order for the series of terms to converge toward a finite number. With this assumption, the present value of steadily growing dividends becomes smaller as the discounting effect of *K* in the denominator more than offsets the effect of such growth in the numerator.

This assumption is realistic for most public utilities. Investors require a return commensurate with the amount of risk assumed, and this return likely exceeds the expected growth rate in dividends for most public utilities. Although it is possible that a firm could sustain very high growth rates for a few years, no firm could double or triple its earnings and dividends indefinitely.

Assumption #3. The dividend growth rate is constant in every year to infinity. This assumption is not as problematic as it appears. It is not necessary that *g* be constant year after year to make the model valid. The growth rate may vary randomly around some average expected value. Random variations around trend are perfectly acceptable, as long as the mean expected growth is constant. The growth rate must be "expectationally constant," to use formal statistical jargon. This assumption greatly simplifies the model without detracting from its usefulness.

If investors expect growth patterns to prevail in the future other than constant infinite growth, more complex DCF models are available. For example, investors may expect dividends to grow at a relatively modest pace for the first 5 years and to resume a higher normal steady-state course thereafter, or conversely. The general valuation framework of Equation 4-5 can handle such situations. The "non-constant growth" model presented later in the chapter is an example of such a model.

It should be pointed out that the standard DCF model does not require infinite holding periods to remain valid. It simply assumes that the stock will be yielding the same rate of return at the time of sale as it is currently yielding.

EXAMPLE 4-2

To illustrate this point, consider a 3-year holding period in the previous numerical example. If both price and dividend grow at the 4% expected rate, dividends for each of the next 3 years are $1.68,

---

$1.75, and $1.82, respectively, and the price at the end of the third year is $13 $(1 + .04)^3$ = $14.62. If the investor sells the stock at the end of the third year, the return expected by the investor is still 17%, because the present value of the dividend stream and the stock price at resale is exactly equal to the current purchase price:

$$P_0 = \frac{1.68}{1.17} + \frac{1.75}{1.17^2} + \frac{1.82}{1.17^3} + \frac{14.62}{1.17^3}$$

$$= \$13$$

This will be true for any length of holding period. The main result of the DCF model does not depend on the value of n.

Another way of stating this assumption is that the DCF model assumes that market price grows at the same rate as dividends. Although g has been specified in the model to be the expected rate of growth in dividends, it is also implicitly the expected rate of increase in stock price (expected capital gain) as well as the expected growth rate in earnings per share. This can be seen from Equation 4-7, which in period 1 would give:

$$P_1 = D_2/(K - g)$$

but $\qquad D_2 = D_1 (1 + g)$, and $P_0 = D_1/(k - g)$

so that $\qquad P_1 = D_1 (1 + g)/(K - g) = P_0 (1 + g)$

Hence, g is the expected growth in stock price. Similarly, if a fixed fraction of earnings are distributed in dividends, then:

$$D_1 = aE_1$$

$$D_2 = aE_2$$

where a is the constant payout ratio and E the earnings per share. Since $D_2 = D_1 (1 + g)$, we also have $E_2 = E_1 (1 + g)$ and, hence, g is the expected growth in earnings per share.

Still another way to express the idea that the validity of the standard DCF model does not depend on the value of the investor's holding period is to say that investors expect the ratio of market price to dividends (or earnings) in year n, P_n/D_n, to be the same as the current price/dividend ratio, P_0/D_0. This must be true if the infinite growth assumption is made. Investors will only expect $(P/E)_n$ to differ from $(P/E)_0$ if they believe that the growth following year n will differ from the growth expected before year n, since the price in year n is the present value of all subsequent dividends from $n + 1$ to infinity.

The constancy of the price/earnings (P/E) assumption is not prohibitive to DCF usage. If there is reason to believe that stock price will grow at a different rate than dividends, for example, if the stock price is expected to converge to book value, a slightly more complex model is warranted. Such a model is presented in section 4.6.

Assumption #4. Investors require the same return K every year. The assumption of a flat yield curve was alluded to earlier, but requires elaboration. A firm's cost of capital, K, varies directly with the risk of the firm. By assuming the constancy of K, the model abstracts from the effects of a change in risk on the value of the firm. If K is to remain constant, the firm's capital structure policy and dividend payout policy must be assumed to remain stable so as to neutralize any effect of capital structure changes or dividend policy changes on K.

The assumption of a constant dividend payout policy not only simplifies the mathematics but also insulates the model from any effects of dividend policy on risk, if any, and hence on K. Besides, this assumption was indirectly stated earlier; a constant dividend policy implies that dividends and earnings grow at the same rate. The assumption of constant dividend payout is realistic. Most firms, including utilities, tend to maintain a fixed payout rate when it is averaged over several years.

The simplification of a constant capital structure may be acceptable if the utility exhibits a near constant debt-equity ratio over time and is expected to do so in the future.

Assumption #5. The standard DCF model assumes no external financing. All financing is assumed to be conducted by the retention of earnings. No new equity issues are used or, if they are, they are neutral in effect with respect to existing shareholders. The latter neutrality occurs if the market-to-book ratio is 1. Without this assumption, the per share dividends could be watered down by a new stock issue, violating the constant growth assumption. A more comprehensive model allowing for external stock financing is presented in a later section.

4.4 The Determinants of Dividend Growth

It is instructive to describe the factors that cause growth in dividends to occur and to disaggregate the g term in the standard DCF model into its contributory elements.

The "retention ratio" is defined as the percentage of earnings retained by the firm for reinvestment. The fraction of earnings not ploughed back into the firm's asset base is paid out as dividends, and is referred to as the "dividend payout ratio." Under the DCF assumption of no external financing, if a firm is expected to retain a fraction b of its earnings and expected to earn a book return of r on common equity investments, then its earnings, dividends, book value, and market price will all grow at the rate br. In short, a firm's sustainable dividend growth rate is its expected return on book equity times its retention ratio if all incremental equity investments are financed by the ploughback of earnings.

The relationship between a utility's book return on equity, retention ratio, payout ratio, book value, and dividend growth rate can best be understood by reference to the following numerical illustration.

Table 4-1 shows a firm earning a 10% book return on an initial equity capital base of $100. Its dividend policy consists of paying out 50% of its earnings in dividends, and retaining 50% of earnings for reinvestment. Earnings on an initial capital base of $100 are thus $10, from which $5 are paid in dividends, and $5 are retained and added back to the initial equity base of $100. An equity base of $105 is carried forward to the second year. Repeating the cycle in the second year, earnings are $10.50, or 10% on equity, $5.25 are paid out in dividends, and 50%, or $5.25, are reinvested, bringing the equity base to $110.25 in the third year. The process continues in an identical manner in each subsequent year. The stock price is shown in the last column at an arbitrarily assumed price/earnings multiple of 10 times earnings, in keeping with the DCF assumption of a constant price/earnings ratio. Note that if the book return on equity, r, and the retention ratio, b, remain constant, the dividends per share grow by r times b, or .10 x .50 = 5% per year. The book value of equity, earnings, and stock price also grow at the same rate of 5%.

TABLE 4-1
THE DETERMINANTS OF DIVIDEND GROWTH

Year	Equity Base	Earnings	Dividends	Retained Earnings	Stock Price
1	$100.00	$10.00	$5.00	$5.00	$100.00
2	105.00	10.50	5.25	5.25	105.00
3	110.25	11.02	5.51	5.51	110.25
4	115.76	11.58	5.79	5.79	115.76
	etc.	etc.	etc.	etc.	etc.
	g=5%	g=5%	g=5%	g=5%	g=5%

In summary:

$$K = D_1/P_0 + g \qquad (4\text{-}9)$$

but
$$g = br$$

so that
$$K = D_1/P_0 + br \qquad (4\text{-}10)$$

4.5 The Earnings/Price Ratio

Another method to estimate the cost of equity is the Earnings/Price Ratio. The rationale for the relationship of earnings to current stock price as a measure of equity cost is as follows. The legal claim of common shares relates to the residual income earned after all operating and all other financial charges against revenue have been met. By definition, the current return to shareholders is the after-tax earnings remaining after subtracting dividends owing to preferred stock. Irrespective of whether earnings are retained or paid out as dividends, they are the property of common equity holders. Dividends and earnings retained from current net income are simply the division of a stream of earnings into parts. The shareholders claim is against both parts. Implicitly, the common shares also enjoy the claim to the future dividends generated by incremental assets financed by earnings retained. In short, the stream of net earnings in total is the return to common stock. Thus, the market price of common stock is the valuation of the stream of anticipated earnings, and the relationship of earnings to price per share is the current rate of return on market value. If anticipated earnings per share are E_1 and current price per share is P_0, this measure of equity rate of return K is:

$$K = E_1/P_0 \qquad (4\text{-}11)$$

An alternate interpretation of this relationship as a measure of equity cost is to view this return of earnings to shareholders as a cost to the company of equity funds. Under this interpretation, the same rate of return must be earned on equity-financed assets to equal the cost rate. Otherwise, earnings produced will fall short of the requirement implied in the current earnings/price relationship.

The earnings/price ratio was discussed extensively in the corporate finance literature in the 1960s, and enjoyed some notoriety in regulatory hearings in that period. Today, the method has almost vanished from use because it can produce unreliable results if not properly applied. In fact, there are only 2 limiting cases in which the earnings/price yield constitutes an accurate measure of the cost of equity and reduces to the standard constant-growth DCF model. The specific circumstances under which the E/P ratio collapses to the standard DCF model are 2-fold: (1) the case where all earnings are paid out in dividends, and (2) the case of an "ordinary" firm.

1. All Earnings are Paid in Dividends

Consider the seminal DCF equation:

$$K = D_1/P_0 + g$$

If all earnings are paid out as dividends, then D_1 equals earnings per share, E_1, and growth is zero. The above equation is rewritten as:

$$K = E_1/P_0 + 0$$

and the cost of equity is simply the earnings/price ratio. This case lacks realism since most companies, including regulated utilities do in fact retain earnings.

2. The "Ordinary Firm"

An ordinary firm is defined as one without profitable opportunities; the firm earns a return on its new equity investments that is just equal to the cost of equity, that is, to investors' required return. In this case, $r = K$. If assets financed by the equity base at book value are allowed to earn the rate of return on equity's market value, the standard DCF model resolves into the Earnings/Price model. This is shown as follows. Starting with the standard DCF equation with the growth term $g = br$:

$$K = D_1/P_0 + br$$

If $r = K$, the latter can be substituted for r. Also, if the fraction of earnings retained is b, the fraction of earnings paid as dividends is $(1 - b)$. Hence, anticipated dividends are equal to the fraction of earnings distributed as $D_1 = (1 - b) E_1$. Substituting K for r and $(1-b)E_1$ in place of D_1, Equation 4-10 can be simplified as follows:

$$K = \frac{(1-b)\, E_1}{P_0} + bK \qquad (4\text{-}12)$$

$$K(1 - b) = \frac{(1 - b)\, E_1}{P_0}$$

Dividing both sides of the equation by $(1 - b)$ reduces the equality to:

$$K = E_1 / P_0 \qquad (4\text{-}13)$$

which is the earnings/price ratio model. Thus the earnings/price ratio is an estimate of the cost of equity when there are no investments that yield returns different in magnitude than the cost of equity; in a regulated utility, this will occur when the allowed return equals the overall cost of capital.

Solving the latter equation for the stock price P_0:

$$P_0 = E_1 / K \qquad (4\text{-}14)$$

Hence, stock price exceeds the earnings yield E_1 / K only when $r > K$, that is, when the firm earns on its incremental equity investments a return in excess of the discount rate employed by investors to value its shares. In the case of profitable investment, the earnings/price ratio underestimates the cost of equity capital. To demonstrate this, suppose that the rate of return to equity holders due to investment were to exceed the required return by $a\%$, that is, $r = K + a$. Substituting for $r = K + a$ in Equation 4-10, and following the same algebraic substitution as above, the equation would reduce to:

$$E_1 / P_0 = K - (b / 1 - b)\, a \qquad (4\text{-}15)$$

confirming that the earnings/price ratio understates the cost of equity when there are profitable investments. Intuitively, if a firm invests in projects whose returns are just equal to shareholders' opportunity costs, no impact on stock price will occur, although the firm's future earnings will expand. If very attractive investments are undertaken, the stock price will increase, although the earnings figure E does not reflect the very large increase in earnings expected. So, the earnings/price ratio underestimates the cost of equity K.

EXAMPLE 4-3

As a matter of policy, a corporation distributes all of its net income per share. Anticipated earnings for the coming year are $10 per share, and current market price, P_0 is $50 per share.

$$K = E_1 / P_0 = \$10 / \$50 = 20\%$$

EXAMPLE 4-4

The same corporation chooses to divide its net income fifty-fifty between dividends and retained earnings. Therefore,

$$b = .5 \text{ and } 1 - b = .5$$

Through its capital expenditure policy, the company succeeds in choosing assets so that earnings on the rate base in turn produce a return on the book value of equity equal to market value cost of equity of 20%. Earnings per share are $10 and market price is $50.

$$K = r = 20\%$$

$$K = D_1 / P_0 + br$$

$$K = (1 - b) E_1 / P_0 + br$$

$$= .5 \times \$10 / \$50 + (.5 \times .20)$$

It is interesting to speculate that if regulation worked perfectly at all times with no regulatory lag and with the allowed rate of return continuously set equal to the cost of equity at all times, the earnings/price ratio would constitute a simple yet ideal method to compute cost of equity. Because this is not generally the case, the earnings/price ratio is rarely used in rate cases. If it is, extreme care and caution must be exercised so that the assumptions underlying its use are not violated. One practical difficulty is to obtain an estimate of anticipated earnings, E_1, especially if earnings are subject to substantial seasonal fluctuation. Extrapolating historical earnings would pose additional problems if unrepresentative growth rates have distorted past earnings. Finally, the numerator of the earnings/price ratio is subject to the vagaries of accounting treatment and to the differences between companies with respect to the impact of inflation.

4.6 DCF Model Extensions

This section describes alternate formulations and refinements of the basic DCF approach. Essentially, the enhanced DCF models result from relaxing some of the more restrictive assumptions of the standard DCF model and from introducing some real world institutional elements in the standard DCF model. In the first discussion, the assumption of constant growth is dropped, and a more general DCF model is derived that is capable of handling various assumed growth profiles. The second discussion relaxes the assumption of no external stock financing, and restates the standard DCF model under more general conditions. Adjustment of the DCF model for flotation costs is analysed in Chapter 6.

The Non-Constant Growth DCF Model

In previous sections, a generalized security valuation model was presented. The central idea was that the price of a share of common stock is the present value of the stream of expected dividends discounted at the cost of equity capital. The general DCF model equation was given by:

$$P_0 = \sum_{t=1}^{n} \frac{D_t}{(1+K)^t} \qquad (4\text{-}16)$$

where P_0 = current price per share

D_t = dividend payment in period t

K = cost of equity capital

This general valuation model can be adapted to suit a variety of growth situations. The simplest assumption is that dollar dividends are constant; this reduces to the earnings/price model, as discussed in the previous section. The most popular assumption is that future dividends and earnings are expected to grow indefinitely at a constant rate due to future investments financed through the retention of earnings; this assumption gives rise to the standard DCF model, also discussed in the previous section.

Dividends need not be, and probably are not, constant from period to period. Moreover, there are circumstances where the standard DCF model cannot be used to assess investor return requirements. For example, if a utility's common stock is selling at a significant discount or premium from book value, and there is reason to believe that investors expect a convergence of stock price to book value, the standard DCF model is invalid. This is because the expected growth in stock price has to be different from that of dividends, earnings, and book value if the market price is to converge toward book value.

The DCF model will now be restated under more plausible and realistic estimates of future dividend growth rates. In essence, the following question will be answered: Given the actual stock price, and given a forecast of growth in dividends for the next n years and a subsequent constant normal growth rate thereafter, what is the implied rate of return required by investors? Expanding the above general stock price equation for a limited horizon of n years on the part of investors, we obtain:

$$P_0 = \frac{D_1}{1+K} + \frac{D_2}{(1+K)^2} + \dots + \frac{D_n}{(1+K)^n} + \frac{P_n}{(1+K)^n} \qquad (4\text{-}17)$$

where $D_1, D_2 \dots D_n$ = expected dividends in each year

P_n = expected stock price in year n

P_0 = current stock price

K = required return on equity

In words, Equation 4-17 states that current stock price P_0 is the present value of the dividends to be received in each of the next n years and of the stock price prevailing at the end of the nth year. Returns to common equity holders consist of dividends to a finite time horizon and the sale price, or liquidation value, of the equity at that time. The cost of common equity in market terms is the rate of discount required to equate the flow of future dividends plus market price at the horizon to current price.

If the growth rate beyond year n is to be constant, the expected value of P_n is then:

$$P_n = \frac{D_{n+1}}{K-g} = \frac{D_n(1+g)}{K-g} \, , \qquad (4\text{-}18)$$

that is, the standard constant growth DCF model prevails beyond year n. Substituting Equation 4-18 into Equation 4-19:

$$P_0 = \frac{D_1}{1+K} + \frac{D_2}{(1+K)^2} + \dots + \frac{D_n}{(1+K)^n} + \frac{D_n(1+g)}{K-g} \times \frac{1}{(1+K)^n} \qquad (4\text{-}19)$$

Knowing the current stock price, P_0, and given estimates of D_1 through D_n and of the constant growth beyond year n, g, one can solve Equation 4-19 for the implicit return on equity required by investors.

It should be stressed that the Non-Constant Growth model embodied in Equation 4-19 is quite consistent with current valuation practices of institutional investors and is a common estimation technique used by financial analysts[3]. The model is known under various names, including the Limited Horizon Model and Finite Horizon Model, and is used by many financial

---

[3] The majority of college-level investment and corporate finance textbooks describe the Finite Horizon DCF model. See, for example, Reilly (1994), Sharpe and Alexander (1990), Brigham and Gapenski (1991).

institutions to improve security valuation. Security analysts routinely estimate the model's required inputs, basing their forecasts on historical and on current and foreseeable future conditions for the economy and the company. Forecasts of earnings, dividends, earnings growth rates and payout ratios are used to derive anticipated future dividends, and the rate that equates the discounted stream of these anticipated future dividends to the current price is the required return on equity.

EXAMPLE 4-5

Assume a two-year time horizon. Current market price is $50 per share, dividends are predicted to be $5 in the first year and $5.40 per share in the second year. Dividend growth at the rate of 8% per year will prevail in third year and perpetually thereafter.

$$P_0 = \$50$$

$$D_1 = \$5$$

$$D_2 = \$5.40$$

$$g = 8\%$$

From Equation 4-19 the market price prevailing at the end of year 2 will equal:

$$P_2 = \frac{D_2(1+g)}{K-g} = \$5.40\frac{(1.08)}{K-0.08} \tag{4-20}$$

Therefore, from Equation 4-20:

$$P_0 = \frac{D_1}{1+K} + \frac{D_2}{(1+K)^2} + \frac{P_2}{(1+K)^2}$$

$$\$50 = \frac{\$5.00}{1+K} + \frac{5.40}{(1+K)^2} + \frac{5.40\,(1.08)}{K-0.08} \times \frac{1}{(1+K)^2}$$

Solving this equation for K by successive iteration, the cost of equity is obtained:

$$K = 21.8\%$$

Dividend estimates can be found by direct means or taken from an independent source such as Value Line Investment Service, one of many firms in the securities industry that provide estimates for the values of the variables in Equation 4-4. To illustrate the latter methodology,[4] the following example derives an explicit estimate of Utility X's cost of equity, based on data from Value Line.

EXAMPLE 4-6

The current issue of Value Line Investment Survey projects Utility X's earnings and dividends for 1995 and averages for 1997-1999. Interpolating for 1996, 1997, and 1998, and using the 1997-1999 forecast as the 1999 estimate, the following earnings and dividends per share estimates are obtained, along with the implied retention ratio, b.

	1994	1995	1996	1997	1998	1999
	Actual		Projected			
Earnings per Share	$2.38	2.45	2.63	2.82	3.00	3.18
Dividends per Share	1.66	1.74	1.83	1.92	2.00	2.08
Retention Ratio	30%	29%	30%	32%	33%	35%

The resulting compound growth rate in earnings for 1995 - 1999 is 6.74%, while the growth in dividends is 4.56% for the same period. Following this 5-year period, dividends will resume a constant normal growth rate, which can be obtained by multiplying the 1999 implied retention ratio of 35% by the 1998-2000 return on equity of 15% forecast by Value Line. The estimated constant growth rate is:

$$g = br = .35 \times .15 = 5.25\%$$

Substituting these estimates into Equation 4-20 with $n = 5$ years, and using the current stock price of $15 5/8, we obtain:

$$\$15.625 =$$

$$\frac{1.74}{1+K} + \frac{1.83}{(1+K)^2} + \frac{1.92}{(1+K)^3} + \frac{2.00}{(1+K)^4} + \frac{2.08}{(1+K)^5} + \frac{2.08\,(1.0525)}{K - 0.0525} \times \frac{1}{(1+K)^5}$$

Solving this equation for K, the implied expected rate of return on common equity is 16.2%.

---

[4] For an example of this approach in regulatory proceedings, see Morin (1991).

It is also possible for dividend growth to exceed earnings growth. However, it is unreasonable to postulate a growth in dividends that exceeds growth in earnings forever, because dividends would eventually exceed earnings. Investors could, however, expect a transitory change in payout ratios, say over the next 5 years. The converse is also true. If investors do expect a transitory change in payout, projection of a declining or rising retention ratio is inconsistent with the use of the Standard DCF model. A changing ROE and a changing retention ratio imply changing growth rates. A Non-Constant Growth DCF model is appropriate whenever the growth rate is expected to change, and the only way to produce a change in the forecast payout ratio is by introducing an intermediate growth rate that is different from the long-term growth rate, as in the previous example.

Another application of the Non-Constant Growth DCF model is when stock price and dividends cannot grow at the same rate by virtue of realistic circumstances in the capital markets.[5] A projected change in the price-to-earnings ratio or a shift in dividend growth for periods beyond the investment horizon will produce a capital gain or loss to the investor that is a legitimate part of investor return requirements. When estimating the cost of equity for utilities whose market price differs from book value, the standard DCF model must be corrected because the growth in stock price has to differ from the growth in dividends if the stock price is to converge to book value. The standard DCF model suppresses such capital gains or losses by assuming an infinite investment horizon.

When a utility's stock price is below book value or when regulatory lag is present, it is reasonable to assume that investors expect future increases in the utility's market-to-book ratio through upward adjustments in the allowed rate of return. This is because proper regulation requires a market-to-book ratio of at least 1. The expected increase in market-to-book ratio would result in the rate of price appreciation that exceeds the growth in earnings, contrary to the standard DCF model's assumptions that the firm's earnings per share grow at a constant rate forever and/or that the firm's price-to-earnings ratio is constant. Application of the standard DCF model would result in a downward-biased estimate of the cost of equity to a public utility whose current market-to-book ratio is less than 1 and that is expected to converge toward 1 by investors. It is not reasonable to postulate a growth in earnings that exceeds growth in book value forever, because earnings would eventually exceed book value on which such earnings are based. That is to say, it is unreasonable to expect a continued

---

5   This discussion draws on Carleton (1980).

increase in earned ROE forever. It is possible, however, that investors expect a transitory change in earned returns, say over the next 5 years. If investors do expect a transitory change in earned return, projection of a declining or rising earned ROE is inconsistent with the use of a single growth rate or Standard DCF model.

In the context of Equation 4-19, a forecast by investors that the stock price will ultimately reach book value after a regulatory lag period of n years means that $P_n = B_n$ where B_n is the book value per share in year n.

If the eventual recovery of stock price to book value is assumed to occur in n years, and that 2 growth rates can be estimated, 1 for dividends per share, g, and 1 for book value per share, g_B, to year n, Equation 4-19 becomes:

$$P_0 = \frac{D_0(1+g)}{1+K} + \frac{D_0(1+g)^2}{(1+K)^2} + \dots + \frac{D_0(1+g)^n}{(1+K)^n} + \frac{B_0(1+g_B)^n}{(1+K)^n}$$

where B_0 is the current book value per share. K is then the return expected over the following n years during which the periodic cash flows are the growing dividends, and for which the final cash flow is the market price at that date, assumed equal to book value at that date, $B_0(1+g_B)^n$.

EXAMPLE 4-7

If the current dividend is $6 per share, dividend growth is 2%, book value growth is 5%, current stock price is $80, and current book value per share is $100, for a recovery period of 2 years $(n=2)$, we obtain from Equation 4-19:

$$\$80 = \frac{6 \times 1.02}{1+K} + \frac{6 \times 1.02^2}{(1+K)^2} + \frac{100(1.05)^2}{(1+K)^2}$$

from which $K = 24.6\%$.

For a recovery period of 4 years $n = 4$ we obtain:

$$\$80 = \frac{6 \times 1.02}{1+K} + \frac{6 \times 1.02^2}{(1+K)^2} + \dots + \frac{6 \times 1.02^4}{(1+K)^4} + \frac{100(1.05)^4}{(1+K)^4}$$

from which $K = 17.8\%$.

The DCF Model with External Stock Financing

In developing the standard DCF model, only 1 source of equity financing was recognized, namely the retention of earnings. But growth in earnings and dividends can also be achieved by the sale of new common equity. The standard DCF model can be expanded to explicitly allow for the case of continuous new equity financing, as is discussed in Gordon (1974).

In Gordon's expanded DCF model, which is derived in Appendix 4-A, utilities are seen as engaging in 2 kinds of operations: (1) investment decisions on which they earn the rate of return r, and (2) stock financing operations on which they earn at the rate sv. If a utility is expected to finance stock at the rate s, the standard cost of equity model:

$$K = D_1/P + g$$

is altered as follows. Since growth in book value per share results from both types of operations, now $g = br + sv$ and not simply br, where

> s = funds raised from the sale of stock as a fraction of existing
> common equity

> v = fraction of the funds raised from sale of stock that accrues
> to shareholders at the start of the period

The only change required in the standard DCF model to recognize the expectation of continuous stock financing at the rate s is the change in the expected rate of growth from br to $br + sv$, as demonstrated by Gordon. The expanded DCF model of the cost of equity takes the form:

$$K = D_1/P + br + sv \qquad (4\text{-}21)$$

In this expanded DCF model, v is the fraction of earnings and dividends generated by the new funds accruing to existing shareholders. To understand the meaning of v, consider a new stock issue sold at a price equal to book value, $P = B$. The equity of the new shareholders is equal to the funds they invest, and the existing shareholders' equity is not changed. But if the stock is sold at a price greater than book value, $P > B$, a portion of the funds accrues to the existing shareholders. And if the stock is sold at a price less than book value, $P < B$, existing shareholders experience a dilution of their equity position. Specifically, Gordon[6] has shown that

$$v = 1 - B/P \qquad (4\text{-}22)$$

---

[6] Gordon (1974) provides a more rigorous development of the term v.

is the portion of the new funds raised that increases/decreases the book value of the existing shareholders' equity, depending on whether $P > B$ or $P < B$.

The expanded DCF model in Equation 4-21 reduces to the standard DCF version if either the company does not regularly sell new stock, $s = 0$, or if new stock is sold at a price equal to book value, $v = 0$. In the latter case, new stock financing has no impact on stock price. $B/P = 1$ in Equation 4-21, and v is thus 0. An alternate way of expressing this condition is that if the expected book return on equity is set equal to the cost of equity, then $P/B = 1$, and v is 0. A simple manipulation of Equation 4-21 is most revealing in that regard. Starting from the extended growth expression of Equation 4-21, it can be shown[7] that:

$$v = (r - K)/(1 - b)r \qquad (4\text{-}23)$$

Substituting Equation 4-23 into the extended growth expression $g = br + sv$, we obtain:

$$g = br + s(r - K)/(1 - b)r \qquad (4\text{-}24)$$

If the utility does not engage in external stock financing, then $s = 0$ and growth is simply the product of the retention ratio and book profitability. Positive common stock financing increases this growth only if return on investment exceeds the cost of equity, that is, only if the proceeds of the stock issue are invested to earn more than the cost of capital.

---

[7] This can be shown as follows. By definition, $v = 1 - B/P$. But from the standard DCF valuation equation $P = E(1 - b)/K - g$ and since $E = rB$, then $P = rB(1 - b)/K - g$ and $P/B = r(1 - b)/K - g$. Inverting the latter expression and substituting in the definition of v, Equation 4-23 follows:

$$v = (r - K)/(1 - b)r$$

EXAMPLE 4-8

To estimate the cost of equity of Utility X, where:

expected dividend yield	$D_1/P = .12$
expected return on book equity	$r = .13$
expected retention ratio	$b = .40$
expected growth in the number of shares (historical 10-year average)	$s = .05$
expected profitability of stock investment (market-to-book ratio of 0.90)	$v = -.11$

The expanded growth expression is given by:

$g = br + sv$

$= .40 \times .13 + .05 \times (-.11)$

$= .0520 - .0056$

$- .0464 \; or \; 4.64\%$

Combined with the expected dividend yield of 12%, the cost of equity is estimated as 12% + 4.64% = 16.64%.

An analogous extended DCF model was derived by Miller and Modigliani (1963), who used a slightly different valuation approach to arrive at an expression which is equivalent to Gordon's model in Equation 4-21. Miller and Modigliani obtained:

$$K = D_1/P + r(br + bs(1 - B/P)) \qquad (4\text{-}25)$$

where br = fraction of earnings retained

bs = new equity raised by stock sale as a fraction of earnings

Using the appropriate notational translations, several authors, including Davis and Sparrow (1972) and Arzac and Marcus (1981), have shown the equivalence of the Gordon and the Miller and Modigliani versions. One difficulty in applying the extended DCF model in regulatory proceedings is that the quantities s and v are not easily measurable nor intuitively understandable. By effecting the following simple notational translation:[8]

$$G = br + s \qquad (4\text{-}26)$$

The following equation for the allowed rate of return on equity is obtained (see derivation in Appendix 4-B):

$$r = G + (M/B)\ (K - G) \qquad (4\text{-}27)$$

where G is now the growth rate in total, not per share, book equity, and M/B is the market-to-book ratio. Equation 4-27 effectively tranforms the investor's required rate of return, K, into the utility's required return on book equity. This notational translation results in a more empirically tractable equation, since the quantity G is likely to be be more understandable and measurable than the quantities s and v. As discussed further in Chapter 10, the application of this equation depends upon the M/B value that is used. If a target M/B ratio of 1 is selected, then $r = K$ in Equation 4-12, as in the standard DCF model. New stock issues at a price equal to book value do not exert any dilutive or expansive impact on existing shareholders, so that $g=br$. Setting the allowed return on equity equal to the standard DCF cost of equity is appropriate under these circumstances.

References

Arzac, E.R. and Marcus, M. "Flotation Cost Allowance in Rate of Return Regulation: A Note." *Journal of Finance,* December 1981, 1199-1202.

Brigham, E.F. and Gapenski, L.C. *Financial Management: Theory and Practice,* 6th ed., Hinsdale IL: Dryden Press, 1991.

Carleton, W.T. "Alternative Formulations and Extensions of the Basic DCF Equation in the Context of a Regulated Public Utility." Reproduced in North Carolina Utilities Commission, Prepared Testimony, Docket No. P-55, Sub. 784, 1980.

Carleton, W.T. Prepared testimony on behalf of Southern Bell (1980).

---

[8] See Richter (1982) for a formal demonstration of this approach.

Davis, B.E. and Sparrow, F.T. "Valuation Models in Regulation." *Bell Journal of Economics and Management Science,* Autumn 1972, 544-567.

Fisher, I. *The Theory of Interest. London:* MacMillan & Co., 1930.

Francis, J.C. *Investment Analysis and Management,* 3rd. ed. New York: McGraw-Hill, 1988.

Gordon, M.J. *The Cost of Capital to a Public Utility.* East Lansing MI: Michigan State University, 1974.

Litzenberger, R.H. "Determination of a Target Market to Book Value Ratio for a Public Utility in an Inflationary Environment." In *Proceedings: Iowa State University, Regulatory Conference on Public Utility Value and the Rate-Making Process,* 1980.

Modigliani, F. and Miller, M.H. "The Cost of Capital, Corporation Finance, and the Theory of Investments." *American Economic Review,* June 1958, 261-297.

Modigliani, F. and Miller, M.H. "Taxes and the Cost of Capital: A Correction." *American Economic Review,* June 1963, 433-443.

Molodovsky, N. *Investment Values in a Dynamic World: Collected Papers of Nicholas Molodovsky.* Homewood IL: Richard D. Irwin, Inc., 1974.

Morin, R.A. Georgia Power Company, Prepared Testimony, Georgia Public Service Commission, 1991.

Reilly, F.K. *Investment Analysis and Portfolio Management.* Hinsdale IL: Dryden Press, 1989.

Richter, P.H. "The Ever-present Need for an Underpricing Allowance." *Public Utilities Fortnightly,* February 18, 1982, 58-61.

Sharpe, W.F. and Alexander, G.J. *Investments,* 4th ed. New York: Prentice-Hall, 1990.

Williams, J.B. *The Theory of Investment Value,* Cambridge, MA: Harvard University Press, 1938. Reprinted in *Modern Developments in Investment Management: A Book of Readings,* 2nd ed., edited by Lorie, J. and Brealey, R., 471-491. Hinsdale IL: Dryden Press, 1978.

Appendix 4-A
Derivation of Extended DCF Model

Gordon's DCF model with continuous new equity financing is derived as follows. Starting with the general stock valuation formula:

$$P = \sum_{t=1}^{n} \frac{D_t}{(1 + K)^t} \tag{4-A}$$

But dividends, D_t, equal earnings, E_t, times the payout ratio, $(1 - b)$, where b is the fraction of earnings retained:

$$D_t = E_t \, (1 - b) \tag{4-B}$$

Substituting (4-B) into (4-A):

$$P = \sum_{t=1}^{n} \frac{E_t \, (1 - b)}{(1 + K)^t} \tag{4-C}$$

An expression for future earnings, E_t, and future dividends, D_t, with continuous equity financing is now developed. If a firm's initial book equity is B_0, next year's book equity, B_1, will be B_0 plus additional equity generated by the retention of earnings, plus new equity raised from sale of new stock. If earnings per share of E_1 are generated in the first year on N_1 shares outstanding, the additional equity from retention is given by $bE_1 N_1$. The additional equity from new issues is s B_0, where $s =$ funds raised from sale of stock as a fraction of existing book equity. So, we have:

$$B_1 = B_0 + bE_1 N_1 + sB_0 \tag{4-D}$$

Since the return on equity, r, equals $N_1 E_1 / B_0$ by definition, $N_1 E1 = rB_0$. Substituting in (4-D):

$$B_1 = B_0 + brB_0 + sB_0 \tag{4-E}$$

$$B_1 = B_0 + (1 + br + s)$$

Generalizing, the book equity in any given year t is therefore:

$$B_t = B_0 \, (1 + br + s)^{t-1} \tag{4-F}$$

In other words, total equity in any period is increased by the retention of earnings, br, and the sale of additional shares, s.

Not all the equity accrues to existing shares. In any year t, the total equity includes the equity of the initial shareholders at $t=0$, and the equity arising from new stock during the period. Letting B_{t^*} be that portion of the total equity that belongs to the shares outstanding at $t=0$, and letting v be the fraction of the new funds provided during the period that accrues to the original shareholders at the start, then:

$$B_t^* = B_0 (1 + br + sv)^{t-1} \qquad \text{(4-G)}$$

A fuller explanation of the meaning of v is contained in the main body of the text and in Gordon (1974).

Multiplying both sides of (4-G) by r, and dividing both sides by the original number of shares outstanding, N, an expression for earnings per share in any given year t is obtained:

$$\frac{rB_t^*}{N} = \frac{rB_0}{N} (1 + br + sv)^{t-1}$$

$$E_t^* = E_0 (1 + br + sv)^{t-1} \qquad \text{(4-H)}$$

Multiplying both sides of (4-H) by $(1 + b)$, the payout ratio, an expression for per share dividends in any given year t is obtained:

$$(1 - b) \, E_t^* = (1 - b) \, E_0 (1 + br + sv)^{t-1}$$

$$D_t = D_0 (1 + br + sv)^{t-1} \qquad \text{(4-I)}$$

Substituting (4-I) in (4-A):

$$P = \sum_{t=1}^{n} \frac{D_0 (1 + br + sv)^{t-1}}{(1 + K)^t} \qquad \text{(4-J)}$$

(4-J) is a geometric progression whose sum converges to:

$$P = \frac{D_1}{K - br - sv} \qquad \text{(4-K)}$$

Solving for K:

$$K = \frac{D_1}{P} + br + sv \qquad \text{(4-L)}$$

Appendix 4-B
The Cost of Equity and the Allowed Return on Book Equity

This appendix derives an equation that transforms the investor's required return on equity into the firm's allowed return on book equity. From Equation K in Appendix 4-A:

$$P = \frac{D_1}{K - br - sv}$$

but $D_1 = E_1 (1 - b)$ and $E_1 = rB_0$ substituting and dividing both sides by B:

$$P/B = \frac{(1 - b)\, r}{K - br - sv}$$

$$P/B\,(K - br) - P/B\,sv = (1 - b)\, r$$

but $v = (1 - B/P)$ substituting and rearranging:

$$P/B\,(K - br) - P/B\,s + s = (1 - b)\, r$$

$$P/B\,(K - br - s) + s = (1 - b)\, r$$

but $G = br + s$ by definition, so:

$$P/B\,(K - G) + s = (1 - b)\, r = r - br$$

solving for r.

$$r = br + P/B\,(K - G) + s$$

$$r = G + P/B\,(K - G)$$

Chapter 5
DCF Application

The purpose of the DCF model is to estimate the opportunity cost of shareholders, or cost of equity capital. From the standard DCF model, the cost of equity is the sum of the expected dividend yield, D_1/P_0 and the expected growth, g. It would be a relatively simple matter to calculate a company's cost of equity capital if investor expectations were readily observable. Projections of dividends and growth for that company would be looked up, its stock price observed, and the cost of equity calculated, based on this one-firm sample. Reality is not so convenient, however, and the purpose of this chapter is to analyze the practical problems involved in applying the DCF model. The conceptual material of the previous chapter will be cast into practical perspective. The chapter reviews the practical implementation of the DCF model, the difficulties encountered, and potential tools and solutions to circumvent those difficulties.

Section 5.1 briefly describes readily available computerized sources of investment information useful in the implementation of the DCF approach. In Section 5.2, the issues of the appropriate dividend yield and stock price to employ are discussed. In Sections 5.3 through 5.5, methods of estimating expected growth are outlined, including historical growth, analysts' forecasts, and sustainable growth. Chapters 6 and 7 discuss two additional issues, both of which are reflected in the dividend yield component: the flotation cost allowance and the quarterly version of the annual DCF model. Chapter 8 stresses the need to broaden the sample to include other investment alternatives, and discusses the design of comparable risk groups of companies through the use of risk filters. Other complications that arise in determining the cost of equity, such as the absence of market data, the case of subsidiary utilities, and violation of DCF assumptions are also discussed in that chapter.

5.1 Data Sources

Several techniques described in this and subsequent chapters rely on the availability of historical and forecast information. The most widely used and comprehensive data bases in the determination of the cost of capital are briefly reviewed in this section[1] A wealth of investment information is

---

[1] An exhaustive catalogue of sources of investment information is contained in the following investments textbooks: Cohen, Zinbarg, and Zeikel (1987), Sharpe and Alexander (1990), and Francis (1988).

available in the publications of investment advisory services. The major services include:

- Moody's Investor Services Inc.

- Standard & Poor's Corporation

- The Value Line Investment Survey

A comprehensive and abundant flow of bulletins and reports emerges daily, weekly, and monthly from these services, compiled in reference volumes each year for various industry groups, including public utilities. Compendiums of information on individual companies are also available from Moody's and Standard & Poor's[2].

Of particular interest are the computerized data bases and computer-generated reports and tabulations offered by the major services to investors. Standard & Poor's Compustat's PCPLUS data base provides a wealth of historical information. This data base is available via magnetic tape or CDROMs directly from Standard & Poor's. Interactive Data Corp (IDC) and Lotus One Source provide a number of electronic data services and access to additional financial data banks. Both maintain or make available a number of large-scale financial data bases and a variety of software programs to access and process the data, such as[3]:

- The Security Master Data Base

- The Prices Data Base

- The Split and Dividend Data Base

- The Compustat Data Bases

- The Value Line Data Bases

- The IBES Summary Data Base

---

[2] Services offered by Standard & Poor's are described in a booklet entitled "Standard & Poor's Services and Publications Cover Every Financial Information Need," which may be obtained by writing to Standard & Poor's at 345 Hudson St., New York NY 10014. Moody's services are described in a publication entitled "How Moody's Can Help You," and may be obtained by writing to Moody's Investor Service Inc., 99 Church St. New York NY 10007.

[3] For a description of IDC/Chase Econometrics financial services, write to IDC/Chase Econometrics at 486 Totten Rd., Waltham MA 02154.

The Compustat tapes and CDROMs contain 20 years of annual financial and market information, updated regularly, for over 7,000 public industrial corporations, banks, utilities, and telecommunications companies. Quarterly data are available for the industrial companies for the past 10 years and for utilities over the past 12 years. Composite company group data can be extracted from the Compustat tapes based on various selected financial criteria and a multitude of financial ratios.

The Value Line Investment Survey covers over 1,600 stocks in 90 industries, and essentially provides a reference and current valuation service. Each stock in the list is reviewed in detail quarterly. Each week a new edition of the Value Line Survey covers approximately 125 individual companies in 4 to 8 different industries on a rotating basis. After all 1,600 stocks have been covered in 13 weeks, the cycle is repeated. A plethora of investment information and historical information is made available for each of these 1,600 companies, including growth rates risk measurements, quality rating, historical performance data, and financial ratios. Comprehensive financial statements, precalculated financial ratios, rate of return rates, per share data, measures of risk and earnings predictability, dividends and earnings forecasts, and countless other investment data are easily accessed. Value Line provides a shortened computerized version of its data base on diskette updated monthly under the "Value Screen III" brand name.

Personal computers and communications software provide ready access to financial data bases, including the Dow Jones News Retrieval, Compuserve, Lotus One Source, and The Source, which offer on-line access to comprehensive financial information on a paid subscription basis.

5.2 Dividend Yield Estimation

According to the standard DCF formulation, the cost of equity is estimated by the formula:

$$K = D_1/P_0 + g \qquad\qquad (5\text{-}1)$$

The measurement of K can be broken down into two components: measurement of the expected dividend yield, D_1/P_0, and the measurement of expected growth, g. The next two sections will consider each in turn. This section focuses on the dividend yield component.

Two major issues are involved in the determination of the dividend yield. First, the appropriate stock price to employ, and second, the relative merits of using a spot dividend yield versus an expected dividend yield.

Stock Price

Conceptually, the stock price to employ is the current price of the security at the time of estimating the cost of equity, rather than some historical high-low or weighted average stock price over an arbitrary historical time period. The reason is that the analyst is attempting to determine a utility's cost of equity in the future, and since current stock prices provide a better indication of expected future prices than any other price according to the basic tenets of the Efficient Market Hypothesis[4], the most relevant stock price is the most recent one. In other words, current stock prices reflect the most recent information. Use of any other price violates market efficiency.

Market Efficiency

The purpose of the equity market is to allow risk bearing in the economy in an efficient manner. An efficient market is one in which, at any time, security prices fully reflect all the relevant information available at that time. An efficient market implies that prices adjust instantaneously to the arrival of new information, and that therefore prices reflect the intrinsic fundamental economic value of a security. The market is efficient with respect to a given set of information if there is no way for investors to use that information set to select stocks and reap abnormal risk-adjusted returns. A considerable body of empirical evidence indicates that U.S. capital markets are efficient with respect to a broad set of information, including historical and publicly available information.[5]

The efficiency of the stock market has several implications. First, it indicates that observed prices at any time represent the true fundamental equilibrium value of a security, and that a cost of capital estimate should be based on current prices rather than on an average of past prices. Conceptually, there is no validity to smoothing stock price series over some past historical period. The measurement of K rests on the assumption that a utility's stock is accurately priced relative to other equivalent-risk investments. The Efficient Market Hypothesis validates that assumption. Second, the assumption of perfect markets that is embodied in DCF valuation models is validated by the existence of efficient markets. And

---

[4] The Efficient Market Hypothesis, pioneered by Fama (1970), is the cornerstone of modern investment theory, and is described in most college-level investment textbooks. For an excellent treatment, see Reilly (1994), Sharpe and Alexander (1990), and Brealey and Myers (1991).

[5] An excellent summary of the empirical evidence can be found in Reilly (1994). Of course, some well-documented market inefficiencies remain, such as the size effect, the January effect, and market-to-book anomalies.

third, under ideal circumstances, market efficiency suggests that the estimated K reflects returns in investments of similar risks, since observed stock prices reflect information about possible alternative investments with different risks and returns.

There is yet another justification for using current stock prices. In measuring K as the sum of dividend yield and growth, the period used in measuring the dividend yield component must be consistent with the estimate of growth that is paired with it. Since the current stock price P_0, is caused by the growth foreseen by investors at the present time and not at any other time, it is clear that the use of spot prices is preferable.

A frequent objection to the use of current stock prices is that they may reflect abnormal conditions, making it more useful to use average prices over a period of time for purposes of estimating the cost of capital. Average stock prices is appropriate during volatile market periods, when stock prices experience large random fluctuations. Visual inspection of a chart of daily closing prices over the last few weeks should reveal whether the current stock price is representative or is an outlier. If the current stock price is not an outlier, the use of the current stock price is corroborated. If the current stock price is indeed an outlier there is some justification for averaging over several trading days to smooth out market aberrations, as would be the case after a stock goes ex-dividend or after a large block sale of stock held by a financial institution, for example. But the longer the past period over which stock prices are averaged, the more severe the violation of market efficiency. A stock price dating back to the previous year, as some analysts advocate, reflects stale information and is not representative of current market conditions.

An analogy with interest rates will clarify this point. If, for example, interest rates have climbed from 10% to 12% over the past 6 months, it would be incorrect to state that the current interest rate is in the range of 10% to 12% just because this is the interest rate range for the past 6 months. Analogously, it is incorrect to state that the cost of equity, which has also risen along with interest rates, is in some given 6-month range. Just as the current interest rate is 12%, the cost of equity is currently that which is obtained from the standard DCF using current spot prices.

To guard against the possibility that the current stock price reflects abnormal conditions or constitutes a temporary aberration, while at the same time retaining the spirit of market efficiency, averaging stock prices over several recent trading days is a reasonable compromise. When estimating a current or near-term cost of equity, averaging stock prices over a short period is appropriate. The average closing stock price calculated over the most recent 10 trading days period at the time of estimating the cost of equity is a reasonable procedure. A similar average computed over a 1-month period rather than a 10-day period would not be unreasonable. Averaging the high and low stock prices for the most recent month is also a reasonable procedure. Closing stock prices can be obtained via modem from Dow Jones News Retrieval's Historical Quotes service or from Standard & Poor's Stock Guide.

It should be pointed out that averaging stock prices in periods when stock prices are rising will understate the stock price and overstate the current cost of common equity, and conversely.

In the special case of certain utility stocks traded over the counter, an estimate of current price may be obtained by averaging the most recent bid and ask prices. If the stock is thinly traded, there is some justification for averaging over several trading days, at the expense of market efficiency.

One compromise approach that eliminates the bias caused by averaging stock prices and yet is consistent with market efficiency principles is the random-walk model. Under this statistical approach, the correct price is the current observable price. The variability of stock price, as measured by the standard deviation of the residuals from the model, measures the stability of the stock price. The random-walk model takes the following form:

$$P_t = P_{t-1} + \varepsilon \tag{5-2}$$

where P_t = stock price in period t

P_{t-1} = stock price in period t–1

ε = forecast error

In words, the random-walk model asserts that the best forecast of today's stock price is yesterday's stock price, along with some forecasting error, and not some combination of previous stock prices. In practice, the analyst observes the current stock price, along with its volatility over the past year, as measured by the standard deviation. The standard deviation around the current stock price provides a 95% confidence interval. For example, if the current stock price is $50 and the standard deviation measured over the last year is $3.00, the random-walk model would employ a stock price ranging from $47 to $53. An example and exposition of this approach is found in Kihm and Rankin (1988).

Dividend Yield

The DCF model, and the discipline of finance in general, is forward-looking in nature and based on expected future cash flows. Therefore, the appropriate dividend to use in a DCF model is the prospective dividend rather than the current dividend because an investor expects it to grow over the next year. DCF theory states very clearly that the expected rate of return on a stock is equal to the expected dividend for the next period divided by the current stock price, plus the expected growth rate. In implementing the standard DCF model, it is the dividend that an investor who purchases the stock today expects a company to pay during the next 12 months that should be used, and not the dividend that was paid last year. The dividend for the next period is just equal to the current dividend times the growth rate, that is:

$$D_1 = D_0 (1 + g) \tag{5-3}$$

If dividends are paid once a year and increased each year in response to the growth in earnings, as is assumed in the standard DCF model, then the appropriate adjustment is to multiply the spot dividend yield, D_0/P_0 by $1 + g$. The spot dividend yield is obtained by dividing the dividends paid over the year ending on the purchase date by the stock price on that date.

If the spot dividend yield is used instead of the expected dividend yield, it creates a downward bias in the dividend yield component, and underestimates the cost of equity. For example, for a spot dividend yield of 6% and a growth rate of 8%, the cost of equity equals 14% unadjusted for the expected dividend yield. The correct dividend yield to employ is 6%(1 + .08) = 6.48%, yielding a cost of equity of 14.48% instead of 14%.

Comprehensive dividend information for stocks is available from Value Line, Dow Jones News Retrieval, and the Wall Street Journal on a regular basis.

One of the assumptions of the standard DCF model is that dividend payments are made annually, whereas, in fact, most utilities pay dividends on a quarterly basis.[6] Clearly, quarterly dividends are preferred by investors rather than a lump sum payment at the end of the year that is equal to the sum of the quarterly payments. This is due to the time value of money. The quarterly dividends, when reinvested until the end of the year, are worth more to the investor. As will be discussed at length in

---

[6] For a derivation, discussion, and implementation of the quarterly DCF model in regulatory hearings, see Friend (1983), Litzenberger (1988), and Chapter 7 of this book.

Chapter 7, the exact nature of the adjustment to the dividend yield becomes more complex and lies in excess of $1 + g$ if the quarterly timing of dividends and the interval between dividend payments are recognized.

Finally, if the conventional method of flotation cost adjustment is used by the regulator as discussed in the following chapter, the expected dividend yield must be adjusted for the underpricing allowance by dividing it by $1 - f$, where f is the underpricing allowance factor:

$$K = D_1 / P_0 (1 - f) + g \qquad (5\text{-}4)$$

5.3 Growth Estimates: Historical Growth

The principal difficulty in calculating the required return by the DCF approach is in ascertaining the growth rate that investors are currently expecting. While there is no infallible method for assessing what the growth rate is precisely, an explicit assumption about its magnitude cannot be avoided. Estimating the growth component is the most difficult and controversial step in implementing DCF since it is a quantity that lies buried in the minds of investors. Three general approaches to estimating expected growth can be used:

- historical growth rates

- analysts' forecasts

- sustainable growth rates

This section describes the historical growth approach while the next two sections address the other two approaches.

Historical growth rates in dividends, earnings, and book value are often used as proxies for investor expectations in DCF analysis. Investors are certainly influenced to some extent by historical growth rates in formulating their future growth expectations. In addition, these historical indicators are widely used by analysts, investors, and expert witnesses. A simple inventory of cost of capital testimonies over a reasonable time period in a given jurisdiction will reveal that DCF is widely used by academic and staff witnesses and that historical indicators are in wide usage in such testimonies. Professional certified financial analysts are also well versed in the use of historical growth indicators. To wit, the calculation of historical growth rates is normally one of the first steps in security analysis.

Historical indicators are also used extensively in scholarly research. There exists a vast literature in empirical finance designed to evaluate the use of historical information as surrogates for expected quantities.

When using historical growth rates in a regulatory environment, a convenient starting point is to focus on the utility in question, and to assume that its future growth is relatively stable and predictable. It is therefore reasonable to use past growth trends as one of many proxies for investor expectations. Historical rates of growth in earnings, dividends, market prices, and book values during some past period are among the most widely used proxies for expected growth. The fundamental assumption is made that investors arrive at their expected *g* by simply extrapolating past history. In other words, historical growth rates influence investor anticipations of long-run dividend growth rate.

In computing historical growth rates, three decisions must be made: (1) which historical data series is most relevant; (2) over what past period; and (3) which computational method is most appropriate.

Historical Series

DCF proponents have variously based their historical computations on earnings per share, dividends per share, and book value per share. Of the three possible growth rate measures, growth in dividends per share is likely to be preferable. After all, DCF theory states clearly that it is expected future cash flows in the form of dividends that constitute investment value.

Since the ability to pay dividends stems from a company's ability to generate earnings, growth in earnings per share can be expected to influence the market's dividend growth expectations. Dividend growth can only be sustained if there is growth in earnings. Using earnings growth as a surrogate for expected dividend growth can be difficult, however, since historical earnings per share are frequently more volatile than dividends per share.

Past growth rates of price and earnings per share tend to be very volatile and lead to unreasonable results, such as consistently negative growth rates. For example, in the 1970s and beginning of the 1980s especially, utility earnings growth rates were so unstable and volatile that they could not reasonably be expected to continue. Several empirical studies have shown that earnings growth rates are not persistent.[7] Dividend growth rates are considerably more stable as shown here in Table 5-1.

---

[7] The lack of persistence of earnings growth rates is documented in studies by Little (1962), Murphy (1966), and Lintner and Glauber (1967). The time series properties of earnings data are analysed in Brown and Rozeff (1978).

TABLE 5-1
GROWTH COMPUTATIONS FOR CONSOLIDATED NATURAL GAS

Year	Earnings Per Share	Dividends Per Share
1981	$1.86	$0.90
1982	$1.95	$0.96
1983	$1.96	$1.02
1984	$2.54	$1.10
1985	$2.58	$1.20
1986	$2.11	$1.37
1987	$2.24	$1.54
1988	$2.34	$1.67
1989	$2.20	$1.76
1990	$1.91	$1.85
1991	$1.94	$1.89
1992	$2.19	$1.90

Source: The Value Line Investment Survey

	Earnings Growth	Dividends Growth
- 3-year compound growth (1988-1991)	-1.32%	2.61%
- 10-year compound growth (1983-1992)	1.12%	6.42%
- 5-year compound growth (1988-1991) three year base periods	-2.06%	4.21%
- 10-year compound growth (1981-1991) three year base periods	0.46%	6.95%
- 5-year exponential growth (1988-1991)	-2.58%	3.29%
- 10-year exponential growth (1983-1991)	-1.35%	7.51%

Dividend growth rates are not nearly as affected by year-to-year inconsistencies in accounting procedures as are earnings growth rates, and they are not as likely to be distorted by an unusually poor or bad year. The relative stability of dividends versus earnings is discussed in the vast majority of college-level finance textbooks that discuss dividend policy. Because dividends track normalized earnings with a lag, and because of the information effect of dividend payments, they are necessarily more stable. Most companies, and utilities in particular, are reluctant to alter their dividend policy in response to transitory earnings variations.

Therefore, historical dividend growth is a more reliable proxy than historical earnings growth. Dividend growth is more stable than earnings growth, because dividends reflect normalized long-term earnings, rather than transitory earnings. Moreover, the DCF model clearly requires dividends as inputs to the model, for it is cash flows in the form of dividends that are the value generators.

One disadvantage of using dividends rather than earnings, however, is the discretionary aspect of dividends. Frequently, dividend increases are made in discrete, sometimes large steps, at management's discretion, and historical dividend growth may not be an adequate surrogate of the average expected growth over some future time period. Historical growth rates derived over specific periods can be biased by short-run changes in the dividend payout of a firm or through abnormal earnings that are unsustainable. A change in dividend policy would create growth in dividends that is more fictitious than real. Of course, if no change in long-run payout policy is anticipated, the expected average growth in dividends will equal the expected average growth in earnings.

Sustainable Versus Unsustainable Historical Growth

Past growth rates in earnings/dividends may be misleading if the past growth rates reflect an increase or a decrease in earned ROEs that are unsustainable or cannot be reasonably expected to continue in the distant future.

If historical ROEs have not been constant over the past 5 years, the mechanical extrapolation of historical earnings/dividends growth could imply that a similar pattern is expected to prevail over the next 5 years. In such a case, historical growth would not be an adequate proxy for expected growth to the extent that the trend in past ROEs is unsustainable or not expected to continue by investors. Under such circumstances, caution must be exercised in extrapolating past trends into the distant future. A more prudent procedure is to rely on analysts' growth forecasts that capture historical trends, the sustainability of such trends, and industry circumstances expected by investors.

It should be pointed out that if an increase in ROEs is expected by investors, the expected rate of growth in earnings will exceed the expected rate of growth in book value. Expected changes in ROE would result in the expected rate of growth in earnings per share being different from the expected rate of growth in book value per share. The converse is also true.

The standard infinite horizon DCF model projects the company's dividends into perpetuity. However, any single-growth variant of the standard DCF model is based on the assumption that dividends per share (DPS) and earnings per share (EPS) are expected to grow at some constant rate into perpetuity. The standard DCF model would be incorrectly specified when the investors' expected intermediate term EPS growth rate differs from the long-term sustainable EPS growth rate. When uneven growth is expected, it is inappropriate to use only the long-term sustainable EPS growth rate in the standard single-growth rate model. When growth rates are expected to vary, a two-growth rate DCF model is required to correctly identify the entire expected stream of future dividends reflected in the observed stock price. This was discussed earlier in Chapter 4.

Year to year changes in earnings and dividends can also be unduly influenced by changes in earned returns and/or changes in the dividend payout ratio. Past growth rates in earnings and dividends may be misleading if the past growth rates reflect an increase or a decrease in payout ratios that are unsustainable or cannot be reasonably expected to continue in the future forever.

If historical payout ratios have not been constant over the past 5 years, the extrapolation of historical earnings and dividends growth implies that a similar pattern is expected to prevail over the next 5 years. In such a case, historical growth may not be an adequate proxy for expected growth to the extent that the trend in past payout ratios is unsustainable or not expected to continue by investors. As stated previously, a more prudent procedure is to rely on analysts' growth forecasts.

If indeed the payout ratio is expected to change, the intermediate growth rate in dividends is not equal to the long-term growth rate, because dividend/earnings growth must adjust to the changing payout ratio. The implementation of a two-growth DCF model is required whenever assuming changing ROEs and/or payout ratios. For further discussion of the two-growth DCF model refer to Section 4.6 of Chapter 4.

Historical Growth of Book Value Per Share

Historical growth in book value per share may be a useful proxy for future dividend growth under certain limited circumstances. Book value per share tends to be less volatile than earnings per share or dividends per share. While book value is largely irrelevant for unregulated companies, it is a principal determinant of earnings for utilities in original cost jurisdictions because allowed earnings are determined by regulatory commissions on the basis of the level of book assets. Earnings per share is the product of book value per share and rate of return on book equity, so historical growth in book value per share may provide an indication of the growth in earnings that would have occurred if past rates of return had remained constant. Past growth in book value per share is an adequate proxy for future growth only if two crucial assumptions are met, however. First, that investors expect no change in earnings per share arising from changes in future book rate of return on equity. Second, that market-to-book ratios have remained stable. The latter assumption is vital, because book value may increase or decrease based on issuances of common stock at a premium or discount from existing book value. Growth from this source alone is largely unsustainable. An analysis of the historical relationship between per share earnings, book value, dividends, and the stability of earned returns on book equity and market-to-book ratios should provide valuable insights in assessing the merits of looking at history as a valid proxy for the future.[8]

Other historical series sometimes used by analysts as proxies for future dividend growth are revenues, assets, and net plant. Too many explicit assumptions are required to link the growth of these series with dividend growth. Reliance on such proxies is dangerous and unlikely to provide insights into future dividend growth. Some analysts average together the growth rate in customers, revenues, earnings, dividends, and book value. This procedure is highly questionable because only dividends and earnings are of interest. One might want to conduct a regression analysis to determine how growth in customers, sales, or book value influence growth in earnings and dividends, but otherwise the procedure is unjustified.

Time Period

Once an appropriate historical series has been selected, the period over which the growth is to be measured must be determined. The period must be long enough to avoid undue distortions by short-term influences and by abnormal years, and short enough to encompass current and foreseeable conditions relevant for investors' assessment of the future. Dividend growth over the past year is hardly representative of a trend. Similarly, it is meaningless to measure growth during a long period when dividend payout ratio was 60% and earned returns on book equity were 10% if investors, based on existing trends, expect the future payout to be 40% and future returns to be 13%.

Historical growth rates are customarily computed over the last 5 and 10 years. An average of the 5-year and 10-year growth rates is a reasonable compromise between the conflicting requirements of representativity and statistical adequacy.

A useful test of the reliability of historical growth as a surrogate for future growth is to measure its sensitivity to the period selected. If historical dividend growth is between 5% and 6%, regardless of the length of the period over which it is measured, one can conclude that the relationship between the historical growth rate and investors' expected growth rate is

---

[8] Changes in accounting practices can create problems of data comparability and consistency; the analysis should thus be confined to those years following the accounting changes. When using per share data series, care must be taken to include changes in capitalization, such as stock splits and stock dividends.

reliable. If the computed growth rate is highly sensitive to the length of the period, then it does not provide useful information.

The computation of historical growth rates requires a time period that is long enough to be statistically valid and short enough to be topical and current. Five- and 10-year periods have been adopted by several investment advisory services in reporting such historical growth rates as well as the forecasts of such growth rates. A 5- or 10-year measurement period is the accepted compromise in finance literature and the securities industry. Five-year horizons are routinely employed by financial analysts.

Value Line reports both 5- and 10-year historical growth in earnings, dividends, book value, cash flow, and revenues. Computerized data bases such as Compustat, and Value Line's "Value Screen III" software also report 5-year historical growth rates. In addition, many long term analysts' forecasts are reported for 5-year periods, such as those for Institutional Brokers Estimate System (IBES) and Zack's Earnings Estimator. Such information would not be reported unless it possessed value in excess of its production costs to investors, whether for informational, forecasting, or analytical purposes.

Growth Rate Computation

The method of calculating growth is most meaningful in the context of compound interest. If dividends grow from $2 to $3 over a 10-year period, for example, the total growth is 50%, or a simple average per annum rate of 5%. But 5% is not a meaningful expression of the growth rate because it ignores compounding, that is, the accrual of interest on interest as well as on the original value. Assuming annual compounding, $2 grows to $3 in 10 years at a rate of 4.1%. The latter can be obtained either from standard compound interest tables or from a specialized financial calculator.

Use of the compounding method of calculating growth is vulnerable to a potential distortion. If either the initial or terminal values are unrepresentative because they are unusually high or low, the resulting growth rate will not truly reflect the developments during the period. For example, if the terminal year happens to be one of severely depressed earnings due to inflation or acute regulatory lag, and the initial year one of boom, the indicated growth rate will be unrealistically low. The reverse may also be true. This potential distortion can be avoided in one of two ways. Either select initial and terminal end points that have similar economic characteristics, or do not use single year's data, but rather the averages of the first few and last few years' data as end points. The latter method is preferable because it involves less subjective judgement. The historical 5-year and 10-year compound growth rates available in the

Value Line Data Base for earnings, dividends, book value, revenues, and cash flows are computed in this manner. Base periods used by Value Line are 3-year averages in order to temper cyclicality and to mitigate any potential distortion due to sensitivity to end points in the calculation.

A more sophisticated method of calculating a growth rate is to fit a "least-squares line" to the logarithms of all the data in the series. This method is known under various names, such as log-linear trend line, log-linear regression, or least-squares exponential regression analysis. To implement the method, as demonstrated in Kihm and Rankin (1988), express the expected dividend for any year t as the current dividend compounded over t years:

$$D_t = D_0 \, (1 + g)^t \qquad (5\text{-}4)$$

Taking natural logarithms on both sides, hence the name log-linear trend line, we get:

$$\ln D_t = \ln D_0 \, (1 + g)^t$$

$$\ln D_t = \ln D_0 + t \ln (1 + g)^t$$

$$\ln D_t - \ln D_0 = t \ln (1 + g)^t \qquad (5\text{-}5)$$

The reason for employing the logarithm of dividends rather than raw dividends is because the slope of a line fitted through the raw data points represents a percentage increase, or growth rate per year, instead of merely a fixed dollar increase per period. A constant dollar increase per period implies a declining growth rate. The average growth rate computed using the log-linear approach is more useful because log-linear growth rates are not distorted by changes in the dollar level. In essence, the log-linear approach solves the so-called scale problem. The log-linear approach is therefore preferable to the raw linear approach.

Letting $\ln D_t - \ln D_0 = y$ and $\ln (1 + g)^t = b$, we have the simple expression:

$$y = tb \qquad (5\text{-}6)$$

The y is the historical dividends and t the time periods. Since both y and t are known, the term b can easily be estimated by simple regression, with the constant suppressed. The historical growth rate over the period can then be inferred from the estimate of b as follows:

$$b = \ln(1 + g)$$

$$e^b = e^{\ln(1 + g)} = 1 + g$$

$$g = e^b - 1 \tag{5-7}$$

The log-linear method is theoretically more precise than the compound growth rate method in that it weighs each observation equally rather than including just the end points. In normal circumstances, however, the added precision is not worth the substantial extra calculation effort. In certain extreme cases, the usefulness of the growth proxy may be improved if one or more abnormal years are omitted or adjusted.

The numerical example shown in Table 5-1 portrays a history of Consolidated Natural Gas Company's earnings and dividends per share. Compound growth rates, smoothed compound growth rates, and exponential growth rates for earnings and dividends are computed for the last 10 and 5 years. Compound growth is computed by solving the orthodox compound value formula for g:

$$F = P(1 + g)^n \tag{5-8}$$

where F = terminal value, P = initial value, and n = number of periods. For example, to get the 10-year dividend growth rate, the following formula is solved for g by either consulting standard compound interest tables or by using a financial calculator:

$$1.90 = 1.02(1 + g)^{10}$$

Base periods used in the computation of the smoothed compound growth rates are 3-year averages in order to temper cyclicality and reduce sensitivity to end points. For cxample, base periods for the 5-year and 10-year growth rate calculations through the end of 1992 are 1990-1992 versus 1986-1988 and 1981-1983, respectively. The exponential growth rates are obtained from Equation 5-7 through least-squares regression techniques.

Kihm and Rankin (1988) investigated the accuracy of various historical methods to estimate growth by checking actual dividend growth over 5- and 10-year periods with forecast dividend growth rates derived from various methods. The log-linear least-squares estimate based on 10 years of historical data outperformed other techniques. A simple 10-year or 5-year average of dividend growth rates also produced low forecast error. Dividend-based methods outperformed earnings-based methods. The sustainable growth method, discussed in Section 5.5, fared poorly.

Hazards of Historical Growth Rates

Past growth rates in earnings or dividends may be misleading, since past growth rates may reflect changes in the underlying relevant variables that cannot reasonably be expected to continue in the future, or may fail to capture known future changes.

The future need not be like the past. For example, assets may grow at a different rate, or utilities may be more or less profitable. Since investors take such factors into account in assessing future earnings and dividends, historical growth rates could provide a misleading proxy for future growth.

The standard DCF model assumes that a company will have a stable dividend payout policy and a stable earned return on book equity, and thus that earnings, dividends, and book value per share will in the future grow at the same rate. The DCF model also assumes that the financing mix, that is the proportions used of retained earnings, debt, and new stock issues, remains constant. If they change, the growth rates will change and the past growth rates will not reflect future growth rates. While it is appropriate to make such assumptions for forecasting purposes, these assumptions are frequently violated when examining historical data. Payout ratios or earned returns on equity may have been historically unstable, and hence earnings, dividends, and book value did not grow at the same growth rate.

It is customary and conceptually correct for forecasting purposes to assume that a utility will experience a constant payout ratio and thus that earnings and dividends will in the future grow at comparable rates over some given time period. As a matter of fact, these are the core assumptions incorporated in the DCF model. But if one is looking at historical data, or at short-term growth forecasts where payout ratios are not stable, then earnings and dividends may not grow at the same rate over some past historical period or over some short forecast period. But from a prospective viewpoint, the DCF fundamentally assumes that earnings and dividends will grow at the same rate.

This was certainly the case for most utilities in the 1970s and beginning of the 1980s when double-digit inflation increased plant, capital, and operating costs while regulatory lag held down price increases. The depressing effect of inflation on utility earnings, dividend, and book value growth was compounded by the necessity to sell stock at prices below book value, which diluted book value and retarded growth further. These low historical growth rates were not representative of future growth rates and could not be extrapolated into the future. The utility industry experienced a turnaround starting in the early 1980s. Inflation abated, utilities were authorized and were earning higher rates of return than in earlier years, and market-to-book ratios increased, so that stock sales no longer diluted book value to the same extent they did earlier. As a result, security analysts and investors were forecasting higher growth rates in the future compared to the past.

A good example of the danger of relying on historical growth rates is provided by the telecommunications industry in the early 1990s. The 5-year historical period before the early 1990s was characterized by non-recurring events that biased historical growth rates, such as cellular investments with heavy startup costs, acquisitions, diversification programs, or write-offs. The latter activities exerted a dilutive effect on historical earnings and dividends for several telephone companies during that period. Several of these companies' earnings growth were unrepresentative of future growth. Analysts' growth forecasts provided a more realistic and representative growth proxy for what was likely to happen in the future. If historical growth rates are to be representative of long-term future growth rates, they must not be biased by non-recurring events or by structural shifts in the fundamentals of the company.

Table 5-2 and Figure 5-1, taken from Brigham (1983), provide an interesting demonstration of how historical book value growth rate is a downward-biased estimator of future growth if the book return on equity has been rising. Brigham's demonstration works in reverse as well, that is, if earned returns were falling, historical growth would overestimate future growth.

To illustrate the dangers of historical growth, Gordon (1974, 1977) showed what happens to historical earnings growth when return on equity is increased. As displayed in Table 5-3, with a 4% earnings growth before period 4, and a 6% growth rate after period 4, the arithmetic mean rate of growth over the 5 years is 18%. This is due to an increase in book equity return from 10% to 15% and the 56% earnings growth in period 4. Extrapolation of the 18% growth rate over this 5-year period would appear to be quite unreasonable.

TABLE 5-2
ILLUSTRATION OF GROWTH RATE ESTIMATES

Year (1)	ROE (2)	Book Value Per Share, BVPS (Beginning of Year) (3)	Earnings Per Share, EPS (BVPS x ROE) (4)	Payout Rate (POR) (5)	Dividends Per Share, DPS (EPS x POR) (6)	Past Data (5-Year Averages) BVPS (7)	EPS (8)	Predicated Growth Rate, Based On DPS (9)	Expected Date g = b (ROE) = (1-POR) (ROE) (10)	Actual Growth Rates in EPS, DPS (11)
1	0.08	$10.0000	$0.8000	0.60	0.4800	-	-	-	3.20	3.20%
2	0.08	$10.3200	$0.8256	0.60	0.4954	-	-	-	3.20	3.20%
3	0.08	$10.6502	$0.8520	0.60	0.5112	-	-	-	3.20	3.20%
4	0.08	$10.9910	$0.8793	0.60	0.5276	-	-	-	3.20	3.20%
5	0.08	$11.3427	$0.9074	0.60	0.5445	3.15%	3.15%	3.15%	3.20	3.20%
6	0.08	$11.7056	$0.9365	0.60	0.5619	3.15%	3.15%	3.15%	3.20	3.20%
7	0.10	$12.0802	$1.2080	0.60	0.7248	3.15%	7.61%	7.61%	4.00	28.99%
8	0.10	$12.5636	$1.2564	0.60	0.7538	3.30%	10.00%	10.00%	4.00	4.00%
9	0.10	$13.0662	$1.3066	0.60	0.7840	3.54%	10.23%	10.23%	4.00	4.00%
10	0.10	$13.5888	$1.3589	0.60	0.8153	3.77%	8.23%	8.23%	4.00	4.00%
11	0.10	$14.1324	$1.4132	0.60	0.8479	3.92%	3.92%	3.92%	4.00	4.00%
12	0.10	$14.6977	$1.4698	0.60	0.8819	3.92%	3.92%	3.92%	4.00	4.00%
13	0.13	$15.2856	$1.9871	0.60	1.1923	3.92%	9.17%	9.17%	5.20	35.20%
14	0.13	$16.0804	$2.0905	0.60	1.2543	4.15%	12.02%	12.02%	5.20	5.20%
15	0.13	$16.9166	$2.1992	0.60	1.3195	4.50%	12.37%	12.37%	5.20	5.20%
16	0.13	$17.7963	$2.3135	0.60	1.3881	4.84%	10.09%	10.09%	5.20	5.20%
17	0.13	$18.7217	$2.4338	0.60	1.4603	5.07%	5.07%	5.07%	5.20	5.20%
18	0.13	$19.6952	$2.5604	0.60	1.5362	5.07%	5.07%	5.07%	5.20	5.20%

Source: Brigham (1983)

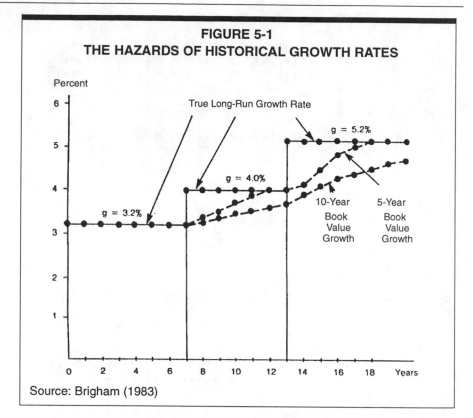

FIGURE 5-1
THE HAZARDS OF HISTORICAL GROWTH RATES

Source: Brigham (1983)

TABLE 5-3
THE IMPACT OF A CHANGE IN RATE OF RETURN ON EARNINGS GROWTH

Year	Book Value	Earnings Per Share	Dividends Per Share	Retained Earnings	Growth Rate of Earnings
	1	2	3	4	5
1	$10.00	$1.00	$0.60	$0.40	
2	$10.40	$1.04	$0.62	$0.42	4.00%
3	$10.82	$1.08	$0.65	$0.43	4.00%
4	$11.25	$1.69	$1.01	$0.67	56.00%
5	$11.92	$1.79	$1.07	$0.72	6.00%
6	$12.64	$1.90	$1.14	$0.76	6.00%

Column (1): Value for previous year plus retained earnings in previous year

Column (2): 10% of book value in first 3 years, and 15% of book value in last 3 years

Column (3): 60% of earnings

Column (4): 40% of earnings

Source: Gordon (1974, 1977)

Another potential problem with the use of historical growth rates is that there is no convenient method to adjust the results if the company's risk changes. For example, the stock price of an electric utility that diversifies into oil exploration or solar conservation reflects both the risk of electric generation and of peripheral energy activities. Historical growth rates may be quite different from those expected in the future.

The major point of all this is that it is perilous to apply historical growth when a utility is in a transition between growth paths. When payout ratios, equity return, and market-to-book ratios are changing, reliance on historical growth is hazardous. Such transitions can occur under variable inflation environments, and under fundamental environmental shifts, such as deregulation.

Given the choice of variables, length of historical period, and the choice of statistical methodologies, the number of permutations and combinations of historical growth rates is such that other methods and proxies for expected growth must be explored. Historical growth rates constitute a useful starting point and provide useful information as long as the necessary conditions and assumptions outlined in this section are not dramatically violated. Although historical information provides a primary foundation for expectations, investors use additional information to supplement past growth rates. Extrapolating past history alone without consideration of historical trends and anticipated economic events would assume either that past rates will persist over time or that investors' expectations are based entirely on history. Analysts' forecasts provide a supplementary source of information on growth expectations.

5.4 Growth Estimates: Analysts' Forecasts

Since investor growth expectations are the quantities desired in the DCF model, the use of forecast growth published by investment services merits serious consideration. The growth rates assumed by investors can be determined by a study of the analyses of future earnings and projected long-run growth rates made by the investment community. The anticipated long-run growth rates actually used by institutional investors to determine the desirability of investing in different securities influence investors' growth anticipations.

Typically, growth forecasts are in the form of earnings per share and dividends per share over periods ranging from 1 to 5 years, and are supported by extensive financial analysis. The average growth rate estimate for dividends and earnings measures the consensus expectation of the investment community.

In many cases, it is necessary to use earnings forecasts rather than dividend forecasts due to the extreme scarcity of dividend forecasts compared to the availability of earnings forecasts. Given the paucity and variability of dividend forecasts, using the latter would produce unreliable DCF results. In any event, the use of the DCF model prospectively assumes constant growth in both earnings and dividends. Moreover, there is an abundance of empirical research that shows the validity and superiority of earnings forecasts to estimate the cost of capital.

The uniformity of such growth projections are a test of whether they are typical of the market as a whole. If, for example, 10 out of 15 analysts forecast growth in the 7%–9% range, the probability is high that their analysis reflects a degree of consensus in the market as a whole.

Because of the dominance of institutional investors and their influence on individual investors, analysts' forecasts of long-run growth rates provide a sound basis for estimating required returns.[9] Financial analysts also exert a strong influence on the expectations of many investors who do not possess the resources to make their own forecasts, that is, they are a cause of g. The accuracy of these forecasts in the sense of whether they turn out to be correct is not at issue here, as long as they reflect widely held expectations. As long as the forecasts are typical and/or influential in that they are consistent with current stock price levels, they are relevant. The use of analysts' forecasts in the DCF model is sometimes denounced on the grounds that it is difficult to forecast earnings and dividends for only one year, let alone for longer time periods. This objection is unfounded, however, because it is present investor expectations that are being priced; it is the consensus forecast that is embedded in price and therefore in required return, not the future as it will turn out to be.

Published studies in the academic literature demonstrate that growth forecasts made by security analysts represent an appropriate source of DCF growth rates, are reasonable indicators of investor expectations and are more accurate than forecasts based on historical growth. These studies show that investors rely on analysts' forecasts to a greater extent than on historic data only. A study by Brown and Rozeff (1978) showed that analysts, as proxied by Value Line analysts, make better forecasts than could be obtained using only historical data, because analysts have available not only past data but also a knowledge of such crucial factors as rate case decisions, construction programs, new products, cost data, and so on. Brown and Rozeff tested the accuracy of analysts' forecasts versus fore-

---

[9] The rest of this section is adapted from Brigham (1983).

casts based on past data only, and concluded that their evidence of superior analyses means that analysts' forecasts should be used in studies of cost of capital. Their evidence supports the hypothesis that Value Line analysts consistently make better predictions than time series models.

Cragg and Malkiel (1982) presented detailed empirical evidence that the average analyst's expectation is more similar to expectations being reflected in the marketplace than are historical growth rates, and that they represent the best possible source of DCF growth rates. Cragg and Malkiel showed that historical growth rates do not contain any information that is not already impounded in analysts' growth forecasts. A study by Vander Weide and Carleton (1988) also confirmed the superiority of analysts' forecasts over historical growth extrapolations. A study by Timme and Eiseman (1989) produced similar results. Empirical studies have also been conducted showing that investors who rely primarily on data obtained from several large reputable investment research houses and security dealers obtain better results than those who do not.[10] Thus, both empirical research and common sense indicate that investors rely primarily on analysts' growth rate forecasts rather than on historical growth rates alone.

Ideally, one could decide which analysts make the most reliable forecasts and then confine the analysis to those forecasts. This would be impractical since reliable data on past forecasts are generally not available. Moreover, analysts with poor track records are replaced by more competent analysts, so that a poor forecasting record by a particular firm is not necessarily indicative of poor future forecasts. In any event, analysts working for large brokerage firms typically have a following, and investors who heed a particular analyst's recommendations do exert an influence on the market. So, an average of all the available forecasts from large reputable investment houses is likely to produce the best DCF growth rate.

Growth rate forecasts of several analysts are available from published sources. For example, the IBES (Institutional Brokers Estimate System) publication tabulates analysts' earnings forecasts on a regular basis by conducting a monthly survey of the earnings growth forecasts of a large number of investment advisors, brokerage houses, and other firms that engage in fundamental research on U.S. corporations. IBES forecasts are a product of Lynch, Jones, and Ryan, a major brokerage firm that collects and disseminates such forecasts. Data in IBES represent a compilation of earnings per share estimates of about 2,000 individual analysts from 100

---

[10] Examples of such studies include Stanley, Lewellen, and Schlarbaum (1981) and Touche Ross Co. (1982).

brokerage firms on over 2,000 corporations. The client base includes most large institutional investors, such as pension funds, banks, and insurance companies. Representative of industry practices, IBES contains estimates of earnings per share for the upcoming 2 fiscal years, and a projected 5-year growth rate in such earnings per share. Each item is available at monthly intervals. IBES collection procedures are designed to obtain timely forecasts made on a consistent basis. IBES requests normalized 5-year growth rates from analysts. Such normalization is designed to remove short-term distortions. Forecasts are updated when analysts formally change their stated predictions. IBES does, however, verify prior forecasts monthly to make sure that analysts still hold to them. Zacks Investment Service also provides analysts' growth forecasts, and these are conveniently available on-line through the Dow Jones News Retrieval Service.

Exclusive reliance on a single analyst's growth forecast runs the risk of being unrepresentative of investors' consensus forecast. One would expect that averages of analysts' growth forecasts, such as those contained in IBES or Zacks, are more reliable estimates of investors' consensus expectations likely to be impounded in stock prices. Moreover, the empirical finance literature has shown that consensus analysts' growth forecasts are reflected in stock prices, possess a high explanatory power of equity values, and are used by investors. Averages of analysts' growth forecasts are more reliable estimates of investors' consensus expectations.

One problem with the use of published analysts' forecasts is that some forecasts cover only the next 1 or 2 years. If these are abnormal years, they may not be indicative of longer-run average growth expectations. Another problem is that forecasts may not be available in sufficient quantities or may not be available at all for certain utilities, for example water utilities, in which case, alternate methods of growth estimation must be employed.

Some analysts are uncomfortable with the assumption that the DCF growth rates are perpetual growth rates, and argue that above average growth can be expected to prevail for a fixed number of years and then the growth rate will settle down to a steady-state, long-run level, consistent with that of the economy. The converse can also be true whereby below average growth can be expected to prevail for a fixed number of years and then the growth rate will resume a higher steady-state, long-run level. Extended DCF models are available to accomodate such assumptions, and were discussed in Chapter 4.

Historical Growth Rates Versus Analysts' Forecasts

Obviously, historical growth rates as well as analysts' forecasts provide relevant information to the investor with regard to growth expectations. In view of the empirical evidence and the conceptual discussion of the previous sections, and provided no structural shift in industry fundamentals have occurred, equal weight should be accorded to DCF results based on history and those based on analysts' forecasts. Each proxy for expected growth brings information to the judgment process from a different light. Neither proxy is without blemish, each has advantages and shortcomings. Historical growth rates are available and easily verifiable, but may no longer be applicable if structural shifts have occurred. Analysts' growth forecasts may be more relevant since they encompass both history and current changes, but are nevertheless imperfect proxies.

5.5 Growth Estimates: Sustainable Growth Method

Another method, alternately referred to as the "ploughback," "sustainable growth," and "retention ratio" method, can be used by investment analysts to predict future growth in earnings and dividends. In this method the fraction of earnings expected to be retained by the company, b, is multiplied by the expected return on book equity, r. That is,

$$g = b \times r$$

The conceptual premise of the method, enunciated in Chapter 4, Section 4.4, is that future growth in dividends for existing equity can only occur if a portion of the overall return to investors is reinvested into the firm instead of being distributed as dividends.

For example, if a company earns 12% on equity, and pays all the earnings out in dividends, the retention factor, b, is zero and earnings per share will not grow. Conversely, if the company retains all its earnings and pays no dividends, it would grow at an annual rate of 12%. Or again, if the company earns 12% on equity and pays out 60% of the earnings in dividends, the retention factor is 40%, and earnings growth will be 40% x 12% = 4.8% per year.

In implementing the method, the retention rate, b, should be the rate that the market expects to prevail in the future. If no explicit forecast is available, it is reasonable to assume that the utility's future retention ratio will, on average, remain unchanged from its present level. Or, it can be estimated by taking a weighted average of past retention ratios as a proxy for the future on the grounds that utilities' target retention ratios are usually, although not always, stable.[11]

Both historical and forecast values of r can be used to estimate g, although forecast values are superior. The use of historical realized book returns on equity rather than the expected return on equity is questionable since reliance on achieved results involves circular reasoning. Realized returns are the results of the regulatory process itself, and are also subject to tests of fairness and reasonableness. As a gauge of the expected return on book equity, either direct published analysts' forecasts of the long-run expected return on equity, or authorized rates of return in recent regulatory cases can be used as a guide. As a floor estimate, it seems reasonable for investors to expect allowed equity returns by state regulatory commissions to be in excess of the current cost of debt to the utility in question.

Another way of estimating the return on equity investors are expecting was proposed by Copeland (1979). Since earnings per share, E, can be stated as dividends per share, D, divided by the payout ratio $(1 - b)$, the earnings per share capitalized by investors can be inferred by dividing the current dividend by an expected payout ratio. Since most utilities follow a fairly stable dividend policy, the possibility of error is less when estimating the payout than when estimating the expected return on equity or the expected growth rate. Using this approach, and denoting book value per share by B, the expected return on equity is:

$$r = E/B = (D/(1 - b))/B \qquad (5\text{-}9)$$

Estimates of the expected payout ratio can be inferred from historical 10-year average payout ratio data for utilities. Since individual averages frequently tend to regress toward the grand mean, the historical payout ratio needs to be adjusted for this tendency, using statistical techniques for predicting future values based on this tendency of individual values to regress toward the grand mean over time.

An application of the sustainable growth method is shown in the following hypothetical example.

---

[11] Statistically superior predictions of future averages are made by weighting individual past averages with the grand mean, with the variance within the individual averages and the variance across individual averages serving as weights. See Efron and Morris (1975) for an excellent discussion of this method.

EXAMPLE 5-1

Southeastern Electric's sustainable growth rate is required for an upcoming rate case testimony. As a gauge of the expected return on equity, authorized rates of return in recent decisions for Eastern U.S. electric utilities as reported by Value Line for 1993 and 1994 averaged 12%, with a standard deviation of 1%. In other words, the majority of those utilities were authorized to earn 12%, with the allowed return on equity ranging from 11% to 13%. As a gauge of the expected retention ratio, the average 1993 payout ratio of 34 eastern electric utilities as compiled by Value Line was 60%, which indicates an average retention ratio of 40%, with a standard deviation of some 5%. This was consistent with the long-run target retention ratio indicated by the management of The Southeastern Electric. It is therefore reasonable to postulate that investors expect a retention ratio ranging from 35% to 45% for the company with a likely value of 40%. In Table 5-4 below, expected retention ratios of 35% to 45% and assumed returns on equity from 11% to 13% are combined to produce growth rates ranging from 3.8% to 5.4% with a likely value of 4.6%.

TABLE 5-4
ILLUSTRATION OF THE SUSTAINABLE GROWTH METHOD
EXPECTED GROWTH RATE: $g + br$

Expected Retention Ratio (b)	Expected Return on Book Equity (r)		
	11%	12%	13%
35%	3.85%	4.20%	4.55%
40%	4.40%	4.80%	5.20%
45%	4.95%	5.40%	5.85%

It should be pointed out that published forecasts of the expected return on equity by analysts such as Value Line are sometimes based on end-of-period book equity rather than on average book equity. The following formula[12] adjusts the reported end-of-year values so that they are based on average common equity, which is the common regulatory practice:

---

[12] The return on year-end common equity, r, is defined as $r = E/B_t$, where E is earnings per share, and B is the year-end book value per share. The return on average common equity, r_a, is defined as:

$$r_a = E/B_a$$

$$r_a = r_t \frac{2B_t}{B_t + B_{t-1}} \tag{5-10}$$

where r_a = return on average equity

r_t = return on year-end equity as reported

B_t = reported year-end book equity of the current year

B_{t-1} = reported year-end book equity of the previous year

The sustainable growth method can also be extended to include external financing. From Chapter 4, the expanded growth estimate is given by:

$$g = br + sv$$

where b and r are defined as previously, s is the expected percent growth in number of shares to finance investment, and v is the profitability of the equity investment. The variable s measures the long-run expected stock financing that the utility will undertake. If the utility's investments are growing at a stable rate and if the earnings retention rate is also stable, then s will grow at a stable rate. The variable s can be estimated by taking a weighted average of past percentage increases in the number of shares. This measurement is difficult, however, owing to the sporadic and episodic nature of stock financing, and smoothing techniques must be employed. The variable v is the profitability of the equity investment and can be measured as the difference of market price and book value per share divided by the latter, as discussed in Chapter 4.

---

[12] (continued)

where B_a = average book value per share. The latter is by definition:

$$B_a = \frac{B_t + B_{t-1}}{2}$$

where B_t, is the year-end book equity per share and B_{t-1} is the beginning-of-year book equity per share. Dividing r by r_a and substituting:

$$\frac{r}{r_a} = \frac{E/B_t}{E/B_a} = \frac{B_a}{B_t} + \frac{B_t + b_{t-1}}{2B_t}$$

Solving for r_a, a formula for translating the return on year-end equity into the return on average equity is obtained, using reported beginning-of-the year and end-of-year common equity figures:

$$r_a = r \frac{2B_t}{B_t + B_{t-1}}$$

Generally, there are three problems in the practical application of the sustainable growth method. The first is that it may be even more difficult to estimate what b, r, s, and v investors have in mind than it is to estimate what g they envisage. It would appear far more economical and expeditious to use available growth forecasts and obtain g directly instead of relying on four individual forecasts of the determinants of such growth. It seems only logical that the measurement and forecasting errors inherent in using four different variables to predict growth far exceed the forecasting error inherent in a direct forecast of growth itself.

Second, there is a potential element of circularity in estimating g by a forecast of b and ROE for the utility being regulated, since ROE is determined in large part by regulation. To estimate what ROE resides in the minds of investors is equivalent to estimating the market's assessment of the outcome of regulatory hearings. Expected ROE is exactly what regulatory commissions set in determining an allowed rate of return. If the ROE input required by the model differs from the recommended return on equity, a fundamental contradiction in logic follows. In other words, the method requires an estimate of return on equity before it can even be implemented. Common sense would dictate the inconsistency of a return on equity recommendation that is different than the expected ROE that the method assumes the utility will earn forever. For example, using an expected return on equity ROE of 13% to determine the growth rate and using the growth rate to recommend a return on equity of 11.5% is inconsistent. It is not reasonable to assume that this company is expected to earn 13% forever, but recommend an 11.5% return on equity. The only way this utility can earn 13% is that rates be set by the regulator so that the utility will in fact earn 13%.

One is assuming, in effect, that the company will earn at a return rate exceeding the recommended cost of equity forever, but then one is recommending that a different rate be granted by the regulator. In essence, using an ROE in the sustainable growth formula that differs from the final estimated cost of equity is asking the regulator to adopt two different returns.

The circularity problem is somewhat dampened by the self-correcting nature of the DCF model. If a high equity return is granted the stock price will increase in response to the unanticipated favorable return allowance, lowering the dividend yield component of market return in compensation for the high g induced by the high allowed return. At the next regulatory hearing, more conservative forecasts of r would prevail. The impact on the dual components of the DCF formula, yield and growth, are at least partially offsetting.

Thirdly, the empirical finance literature demonstrates that the sustainable growth method of determining growth is not as significantly correlated to measures of value, such as stock price and price/earnings ratios, as other historical growth measures or analysts' growth forecasts. Other proxies for growth, such as historical growth rates and analysts' growth forecasts, outperform retention growth estimates. See for example Kihm and Rankin (1988) and Timme and Eiseman (1989).

In summary, of the three proxies for the expected growth component of the DCF model, historical growth rates, analysts' forecasts, and the sustainable growth method, the latter is the least desirable. Criteria in choosing among the three proxies should include ease of use, ease of understanding, theoretical and mathematical correctness, and empirical validation. The latter two are crucial. The method should be logically valid and consistent, and should possess an adequate track record in predicting and explaining security value. The retention growth method is the weakest of the three proxies on both conceptual and empirical grounds. The empirical validity of the method is crucial in deciding which of the three proxies to employ. The research in this area has shown that the first two growth proxies do a better job of explaining variations in market valuation (M/B and P/E ratios) and are more highly correlated to measures of value than is the retention growth proxy.

References

Brealey, R. and Myers, S. *Principles of Corporate Finance,* 4th ed. New York: McGraw-Hill, 1991.

Brigham, E.F. Pennsylvania Electric Company, Rebuttal Testimony, Pennsylvania Public Utility Commission, Docket No. ER79-88, 1983.

Brown. L.D. and Rozeff, M.S. "The Superiority of Analyst Forecasts as Measures of Expectations: Evidence from Earnings." *Journal of Finance,* March 1978, 1-16.

Cohen, J.B., Zinbarg, E.D., and Zeikel A. *Investment Analysis and Portfolio Management,* 5th ed. Homewood IL: Richard D. Irwin, 1987.

Copeland, B.L. "The Cost of Equity Capital: A Model for Regulatory Review." In *Issues in Public Utility Regulation,* edited by H.M. Trebing, 342-366. East Lansing MI: Michigan State University, 1979.

Cragg, J.G. and Malkiel, B.G. "Expectations and the Structure of Share Prices." National Bureau of Economic Research. Chicago: University of Chicago Press, 1982.

Fama, E.F. "Efficient Capital Markets: A Review of Theory and Empirical Work." *Journal of Finance,* May 1970, 383-417.

Francis, J.C. *Investment Analysis and Management,* 3rd. ed. New York: McGraw-Hill, 1988.

Friend, I. The Bell Telephone Company of Pennsylvania, Prepared Testimony, Pennsylvania Public Utility Commission, Docket No. 2316, 1983.

Gordon, M.J. *The Cost of Capital to a Public Utility.* East Lansing, MI: Michigan State University, 1974.

Gordon, M.J. "Rate of Return Regulation in the Current Economic Environment." In *Adapting Regulation to Shortages, Curtailments, and Inflation,* edited by J.L. O'Donnell, 15-28. East Lansing MI: Michigan State University, 1977.

Kihm, S.G. and Rankin, W.F. "An Evaluation of Various Forms of the DCF Model." Office of the Chief Economist, Public Service Commission of Wisconsin, January 1988.

Lintner, J. and Glauber, R. "Higgledly Piggledy Growth in America?" Paper presented to the Seminar on the Analysis of Security Prices, University of Chicago, May 1967.

Little, I.M. "Higgledy Piggledy Growth." Institute of Statistics, Oxford, November 1962.

Murphy, J.E. "Relative Growth in Earnings per Share--Past and Future." *Financial Analysts' Journal,* November-December 1966.

Reilly, F.K. *Investment Analysis and Portfolio Management.* Hinsdale IL: Dryden Press, 1989.

Sharpe, W.F. and Alexander, G.J. *Investments,* 4th ed., New York: Prentice-Hall, 1990.

Stanley, L., Lewellen, W., and Schlarbaum, G. "Further Evidence on the Value of Professional Investment Research," *Journal of Financial Research,* Spring 1981, 1-9.

Timme, S.G. and Eiseman, P.C. "On the Use of Consensus Forecasts of Growth in the Constant Growth Model: The Case of Electric Utilities." *Financial Management,* Winter 1989, 23-35.

Touche Ross Co. "Proxy Disclosures and Stockholder Attitude Survey." Washington DC: National Association of Corporate Directors, May 1982.

Vander Weide, J.H. and Carleton, W. T. "Investor Growth Expectations: Analysts vs. History." *The Journal of Portfolio Management,* Spring 1988, 78-87.

Additional References

Brennan, J. F. *Estimating the Cost of Public Utility Common Equity: An Empirical Test of the DCF Assumptions,* Washington DC: Associated Utility Services Inc., 1988.

Brennan, J.F. and Moul, P.R. "Does the Constant Growth Discounted Cash Flow Model Portray Reality?" *Public Utilities Fortnightly,* January 21, 1988, 24-29.

Cragg, J.G. and Malkiel, B.G. "The Consensus and Accuracy of Some Predictions of the Growth of Corporate Earnings." *Journal of Finance,* March 1968, 67-84.

Efron, B. and Morris, C. "Data Analysis Using Stein's Estimator and its Generalizations." *Journal of the American Statistical Association,* June 1975, 311-19.

Elton, E.J., Gruber, M.J., and Gultekin, J. "Expectations and Share Prices." *Management Science,* September 1981, 975-981.

Siegel, J.J. "The Application of the DCF Methodology for Determining the Cost of Equity Capital." *Financial Management,* Spring 1985, 46-53.

Chapter 6
Flotation Cost Adjustment

This chapter demonstrates that an adjustment to the market-based cost of capital is necessary for flotation costs associated with the procurement of equity capital, and discusses the mechanics and controversies involved in applying this adjustment.

A typical utility is continuously issuing stock through its dividend reinvestment plan and employee stock option plan, or is selling new shares to the public on a regular basis in order to maintain its construction program and meet its mandated service requirements. The costs of issuing these securities are just as real as operating and maintenance expenses or costs incurred to build utility plants, and fair regulatory treatment must permit the recovery of these costs.

6.1 Flotation Cost Allowance

The simple fact of the matter is that common equity capital is not free. Flotation costs associated with stock issues are exactly like the flotation costs associated with bonds and preferred stocks. Flotation costs are incurred, and if they are not expensed at the time of issue, they must be recovered through a rate of return adjustment. This is routinely done for bond and preferred stock issues by most regulatory commissions. The flotation cost allowance to the cost of common equity capital is routinely discussed and applied in most corporate finance textbooks.

Flotation costs are very similar to the closing costs on a home mortgage. In the case of issues of new equity, flotation costs represent the discounts that must be provided to place the new securities. Flotation costs have three components: (1) the direct component, which is the compensation to the security underwriter for his marketing/consulting services, for the risks involved in distributing the issue, and for any operating-administrative expenses associated with the issue (printing, legal, prospectus, registration, etc.); (2) the indirect component, or market pressure, which represents the downward pressure on the stock price as a result of the increased supply of stock from the new issue, reflecting the basic economic fact that when the supply of securities is increased following a stock or bond issue, the price falls; and (3) the potential market price decline related to external market variables; this is often referred to as the allowance for "market break."

To prevent the dilution of existing shareholders' investment resulting from these three factors, an amount must be added to the rate of return on common equity to obtain the final cost of equity financing.[1] This incremental return is referred to as the "flotation cost allowance," and is the sum total of direct flotation expenses, market pressure, and market break.

To demonstrate the need for adjusting the market-determined return on equity for flotation costs, consider the following simple example. Shareholders invest $100 of capital on which they expect to earn a return of 10%, or $10, but the company nets $95 because of issuance costs. It is obvious that the company will have to earn more than 10% on its net book investment (rate base) of $95 to provide investors with a $10 return on the money actually invested. To provide the same earnings of $10 on a reduced capital base of $95 clearly requires a return higher than the shareholder expected return of 10%, namely $10/$95 = 10.53%. This is because only the net proceeds from an equity issue are used to add to the rate base on which the investor earns.

6.2 Magnitude of Flotation Costs

The flotation cost allowance requires an estimated adjustment to the return on equity of approximately 5% to 10%, depending on the size and risk of the issue. A more precise figure can be obtained by surveying empirical studies on utility security offerings.

According to empirical studies by Borum and Malley (1986) and Logue and Jarrow (1978), underwriting costs and expenses average 4% - 5.5% of gross proceeds for utility stock offerings in the U.S. Eckbo and Masulis (1987) found an average flotation cost of 4.175% for utility common stock offerings, and found that flotation costs increased progressively for smaller size issues.

As far as the market pressure effect is concerned, empirical studies clearly show that the market pressure effect is real, tangible, and measurable. Appendix 6-A describes one method of measuring the market pressure effect. Logue and Jarrow (1978) found that the absolute magnitude of the relative price decline due to market pressure was less than 1.5%. Bowyer and Yawitz (1980) examined 278 public utility stock issues and found an average market pressure of 0.72%. In a classic and monumental study published in the *Journal of Financial Economics,* which reviewed the aggregate empirical evidence on market pressure from several studies, Smith (1986) found a market pressure effect of 3.14% for industrial stock

---

[1] An alternate way of stating this requirement is that the utility's stock must be maintained at some minimum market-to-book ratio in such a way that the proceeds from new stock issues will not decline below book value per share.

issues and 0.75% for utility common stock issues. Other studies of market pressure are reported in Logue (1973), Pettway (1984), and Reilly and Hatfield (1969). In Pettway's study, the market pressure effect for a sample of 368 public utility equity sales was in the range of 2% to 3%. Eckbo and Masulis (1987) found that the relative price decline due to market pressure in the days surrounding the announcement amounted to slightly more than 1.5%.

The Eckbo and Masulis study also confirmed that the percentage flotation cost allowance is higher for small issues than for large issues in view of the high fixed cost component of total costs involved in the process of security underwriting. Although total costs of issuing securities vary according to size of the issue and the degree of risk, there are certain expenses that are fixed, regardless of issue size. These include legal fees and prospectus preparation. With respect to the balance, or underwriting costs, there is greater risk assumed with smaller issues.

In summary, based on empirical studies of U.S. utility security offerings, total flotation costs including market pressure conservatively amount to 5% of gross proceeds for U.S. security offerings. This is consistent with the fact that several utilities raise a substantial portion of their external equity every year through an automatic dividend reinvestment plan and offer a 5% discount, suggesting that the savings from abstaining from a public issue of common stock are at least 5%. The flotation cost allowance of 5% is likely to be conservative, since no explicit allowance for market break is incorporated. If negative events should occur during the time period from announcement of a public issue to actual pricing, the price could fall below book value unless a sufficient margin is maintained. Moreover, the 1% allowance for market pressure is probably conservative for large stock issues.

6.3 Application of the Flotation Cost Adjustment

This section formally demonstrates: (1) how and why it is necessary to apply a flotation cost allowance to the dividend yield component of the DCF model in order to obtain the fair return on equity capital; (2) why the flotation adjustment is permanently required to avoid confiscation even if no further stock issues are contemplated; and (3) why flotation costs are only recovered if the rate of return is applied to total equity, including retained earnings, in all future years.

An analogy with bond issues, as discussed in Brigham, Aberwald, and Gapenski (1985), is useful here in order to understand the treatment of issue costs in the case of common stock issues. In the case of bonds, flotation costs are recovered over the life of the bond in two steps: (1) flotation costs are amortized over the life of the bond and the annual amortization charge is incorporated into revenue requirements, in much the same way that funds invested in utility plant is recovered through depreciation charges; (2) the unamortized portion of flotation costs is included in rate base, and a return is earned on the unamortized costs, in the same way that a return is earned on the undepreciated portion of a utility's plant. The recovery continues year after year until the recovery process is terminated, regardless of whether the utility raises new debt capital. This is analogous to the process of depreciation, which allows the recovery of funds invested in utility plant. The recovery continues whether the utility constructs new facilities or not.

Unlike the case of bonds, common stock has no finite life so that flotation costs cannot be amortized and must therefore be recovered by way of an upward adjustment to the allowed return on equity.

In theory, underpricing costs could be expensed and recovered through rates as they are incurred. This procedure is not considered appropriate, however, because the equity capital raised in a given stock issue remains on the utility's common equity account and continues to provide benefits to ratepayers indefinitely. It would be unfair to burden the current generation of ratepayers with the full costs of raising capital when the benefits of that capital extend indefinitely. The common practice of capitalizing rather than expensing eliminates the intergenerational transfers that would prevail if today's ratepayers were asked to bear the full burden of flotation costs of bond/stock issues in order finance capital projects designed to serve future as well as current generations. Moreover, expensing flotation costs requires an estimate of the market pressure effect for each individual issue, which is likely to prove unreliable. A more reliable aproach is to estimate market pressure for a large sample of stock offerings rather than for one individual issue.

An alternative regulatory treatment is to incorporate flotation costs into the rate base as an intangible asset. While this solves the intergenerational problem and compensates investors fairly for their investment, the method clashes with the "used and useful" principle of rate base inclusions. An intangible asset related to flotation costs is unlikely to be viewed as a used and useful asset in the public service by regulators.

The conventional approach to flotation cost adjustment can be derived as follows. From the standard DCF model, the investor's required return on equity capital is expressed as:

$$K = D_1/P_0 + g \qquad \text{(6-1)}$$

If P_0 is regarded as the proceeds per share actually received by the company from which dividends and earnings will be generated, that is, P_0 equals B_0, the book value per share, then the company's required return is:

$$r = D_1/B_0 + g \qquad\qquad (6\text{-}2)$$

Denoting the percentage flotation costs f, proceeds per share B_0 are related to market price P_0 as follows:

$$P - fP = B_0$$

$$P(1-f) = B_0 \qquad\qquad (6\text{-}3)$$

Substituting Equation 6-3 into 6-2, we obtain:

$$r = D_1/P(1-f) + g \qquad\qquad (6\text{-}4)$$

which is the utility's required return adjusted for underpricing.[2]

Equation 6-4 is often referred to as the "conventional approach" to flotation cost adjustment. Its use in regulatory proceedings by cost of capital witnesses is widespread. The formula is discussed in several college-level corporate finance textbooks, such as Brigham and Gapenski (1991).

EXAMPLE 6-1

For flotation costs of 5%, dividing the expected dividend by 0.95 will produce the adjusted cost of equity capital. For a dividend yield of 6%, for example, the magnitude of the adjustment is 32 basis points: $.06/.95 = .0632$.

---

[2] Another way to look at it is that in order to prevent dilution of book value per share, the market-to-book ratio must be at least $1/(1-f)$. The Target Market-to-Book method discussed in Chapter 10 can be used to translate the DCF cost of equity figure into an appropriate allowed return on book equity. As shown in Chapter 10, the allowed return consistent with a target M/B ratio that allows for the recapture of flotation costs is:

$$r = M/B(K-g) + g$$

Brigham, Aberwald, and Gapenski (1985) performed an excellent analysis regarding the need for a flotation cost adjustment.

The following illustration adapted from Brigham, Aberwald, and Gapenski (1985) shows that: (1) even if no further stock issues are contemplated, the flotation adjustment is still permanently required to keep shareholders whole, and (2) flotation costs are only recovered if the rate of return is applied to total equity, including retained earnings, in all future years, even if no future financing is contemplated.

The flotation cost adjustment process is shown here in Tables 6-1 through 6-3 using illustrative market data.

The assumptions used in the computation are shown in Table 6-1. The stock is selling in the market for $25, and investors expect the firm to pay a dividend of $2.25, which will grow at a rate of 5% thereafter. The traditional DCF cost of equity is thus $k = D/P + g = 2.25/25 + .05 = 14\%$, or $3.50 in the first year. Nine percent of the 14%, or $2.25, will come from dividends, so that the remaining 5%, or $1.25, must then come from capital gains. To get a capital gain of $1.25 from $1.188 of retained earnings, the earnings retained must clearly earn more than 14%. Therefore, if the firm sells one share of stock, incurring a flotation cost of 5%, the traditional DCF cost of equity adjusted for flotation cost is thus $ROE = D/P(1-f) + g = .09/.95 + .05 = 14.47\%$.

TABLE 6-1
ASSUMPTIONS

Issue Price =	$25.00
Flotation Cost =	5.00%
Dividend Yield =	9.00%
Growth =	5.00%
Equity Return =	14.00
(D/P = g)	
Allowed Return on Equity =	14.47%
(D/P(1-f) + g)	

As shown in Table 6-2, the initial book value (rate base) is the net proceeds from the stock issue, which are $23.75, that is, the market price less the 5% flotation costs.

TABLE 6-2
$D/P(1-f) = g$ APPLIED ON ALL COMMON EQUITY
BEGINNING OF YEAR: 14.47 % ALLOWED RETURN

Year	Common Stock (1)	Retained Earnings (2)	Total Equity (3)	Stock Price (4)	Market/ Book Ratio (5)	EPS (6)	DPS (7)	Payout (8)
1	$23.75	$0.00	$23.75	$25.00	1.0526	$3.44	$2.25	65.45%
2	$23.75	$1.19	$24.94	$26.25	1.0526	$3.61	$2.36	65.45%
3	$23.75	$2.43	$26.18	$27.56	1.0526	$3.79	$2.48	65.45%
4	$23.75	$3.74	$27.49	$28.94	1.0526	$3.98	$2.61	65.45%
5	$23.75	$5.12	$28.87	$30.39	1.0526	$4.18	$2.74	65.45%
6	$23.75	$6.56	$30.31	$31.91	1.0526	$4.39	$2.87	65.45%
7	$23.75	$8.08	$31.83	$33.50	1.0526	$4.61	$3.02	65.45%
8	$23.75	$9.67	$33.42	$35.18	1.0526	$4.84	$3.17	65.45%
9	$23.75	$11.34	$35.09	$36.94	1.0526	$5.08	$3.32	65.45%
10	$23.75	$13.09	$36.84	$38.78	1.0526	$5.33	$3.49	65.45%
			5.00%	5.00%		5.00%	5.00%	

The table demonstrates that only if the company is allowed to earn 14.47% on rate base will investors earn their cost of equity of 14%. Column 1 shows the initial common stock account, while Column 2 shows the cumulative retained earnings balance, starting at zero, and steadily increasing from the retention of earnings. Total equity in Column 3 is the sum of common stock capital and retained earnings. The stock price in Column 4 is obtained from the seminal DCF formula: $D_1/(k-g)$. Earnings per share in Column 6 is simply the allowed return of 14.47% times the total common equity base. Dividends start at $2.25 and grow at 5% thereafter, which they must do if investors are to earn a 14% return. The dividend payout ratio remains constant, as per the assumption of the DCF model. All quantities, stock price, book value, earnings, and dividends grow at a 5% rate, as shown at the bottom of the relevant columns.

Only if the company is allowed to earn 14.47% on equity do investors earn 14%. For example, if the company is allowed only 14%, the stock price drops from $26.25 to $26.13 in the second year, inflicting a loss on shareholders. This is shown in Table 6-3. The growth rate drops from 5% to 4.53%. Thus, investors only earn 9% + 4.53% = 13.53% on their investment. It is noteworthy that the adjustment is always required each and every year, whether or not new stock issues are sold in the future, and that the allowed return on equity must be earned on total equity, including retained earnings, for investors to earn the cost of equity.

TABLE 6-3
$D/P(1-f) + g$ APPLIED ON ALL COMMON EQUITY
BEGINNING OF YEAR: 14% ALLOWED RETURN

Year	Common Stock (1)	Retained Earnings (2)	Total Equity (3)	Stock Price (4)	Mrkt/Book Ratio (5)	EPS (6)	DPS (7)	Payout (8)
1	$23.75	$0.00	$23.75	$25.00	1.0526	$3.33	$2.25	67.67%
2	$23.75	$1.08	$24.83	$26.13	1.0526	$3.48	$2.35	67.67%
3	$23.75	$2.20	$25.95	$27.31	1.0526	$3.63	$2.46	67.67%
4	$23.75	$3.37	$27.12	$28.55	1.0526	$3.80	$2.57	67.67%
5	$23.75	$4.60	$28.35	$29.84	1.0526	$3.97	$2.69	67.67%
6	$23.75	$5.88	$29.63	$31.19	1.0526	$4.15	$2.81	67.67%
7	$23.75	$7.23	$30.98	$32.61	1.0526	$4.34	$2.94	67.67%
8	$23.75	$8.63	$32.38	$34.08	1.0526	$4.53	$3.07	67.67%
9	$23.75	$10.09	$33.84	$35.62	1.0526	$4.74	$3.21	67.67%
10	$23.75	$11.63	$35.38	$37.24	1.0526	$4.95	$3.35	67.67%
			4.53%	4.53%		4.53%	4.53%	

Flotation Cost and the Extended DCF Model

The flotation cost adjustment can also be approached in the context of the more general extended DCF model discussed in Chapter 4. Recall the extended DCF expression for cost of equity capital under the assumption of continuous external stock financing:

$$K = D_1/P + br + sv \tag{6-5}$$

The expression for v was $v = 1 - B/P$. To incorporate underpricing, v needs to be redefined as:

$$v = 1 - B/P(1-f) \tag{6-6}$$

where $P(1-f)$ is the net proceeds from a stock issue. This recognizes that when a utility engages in external financing, it is the net proceeds per share that have an impact on existing shareholders rather than the full market price. To avoid any dilution in the existing shareholders' claim, v must be set equal to zero. Setting Equation 6-6 equal to zero, we obtain $B = P(1-f)$. By substituting Equation 6-6 into Equation 6-5, and by recognizing also that setting $v = 0$ implies $g = br$, Equation 6-5 is restated as follows to incorporate the effect of underpricing:

$$r = D_1/P(1-f) + g \tag{6-7}$$

The latter expression is identical to that obtained from the standard DCF model adjusted for underpricing in Equation 6-4.

The more practical version of the extended DCF model cast in terms of G, the growth rate in total book equity, also collapses to an identical expression:

$$r = G + (M/B)(K-G) \qquad (6\text{-}8)$$

To avoid dilution, $v = 0$, which in turn implies $G = g = br$. Equation 6-8 reduces to Equation 6-7 under the condition that $M/B = 1/(1-f)$:

$$r = g + (1/(1-f))(K-g)$$

$$= g + (1/(1-f)) D_1/P$$

$$= D_1/P(1-f) + g$$

6.4 Flotation Cost Controversies

Several important controversies have surfaced regarding the underpricing allowance. The first is the contention that an underpricing allowance is inappropriate if the utility is a subsidiary whose equity capital is obtained from its parent. This objection is unfounded since the parent-subsidiary relationship does not eliminate the costs of a new issue, but merely transfers them to the parent. It would be unfair and discriminatory to subject parent shareholders to dilution while individual shareholders are absolved from such dilution. Fair treatment must consider that if the utility subsidiary had gone to the capital marketplace directly, flotation costs would have been incurred.

A second controversy is whether a flotation cost allowance should be allowed because a company can always obtain equity from sources other than a public issue of common stock, such as a rights issue for example. There are several sources of equity capital available to a firm, including: public common stock issues, conversions of convertible preferred stock, dividend reinvestment plans, employees' savings plans, warrants, and stock dividend programs. Each carries its own set of administrative costs and flotation cost components, including discounts, commissions, corporate expenses, offering spread, and market pressure.

Equity capital raised through a public issue is typically more expensive than alternate sources of equity. Rights issues, when available, are less expensive, but direct costs would still be incurred. Of course, a rights issue assumes that a willing underwriter and a willing market could be found for such offerings in the first place, an unlikely event in public capital markets for small unproven companies. Internal sources of equity, including dividend reinvestment and/or employee stock option plans, are also typically less expensive, unless a discount on the purchase price is inherent in the plan, in which case they are often equivalent to a public issue. Direct costs are also incurred in an employee stock savings plan and/or a shareholder dividend reinvestment plan.

The flotation cost allowance is still warranted, however, because it is a composite factor that reflects the historical mix of all these sources of equity. The flotation cost allowance factor is a build-up of historical flotation cost adjustments associated and traceable to each component of equity source, and more specifically, is a weighted average cost factor designed to capture the average cost of various equity vintages and types of equity capital raised by the company. It is impractical and prohibitive to start from the inception of a company and source all present equity. A practical solution is to rely on the results of the empirical studies discussed earlier that quantify the average flotation cost factor of a large sample of utility stock offerings.

Richter (1982) demonstrated that the flotation cost allowance applicable to all the company's book equity is a weighted average of the current allowances required for each past financing, and suggested some practical means of circumventing the problem of vintaging each equity source. Richter essentially suggested sourcing book equity by broad categories of equity, such as dividend reinvestment plan equity, stock option equity, and public issue equity, and calculating a weighted average underpricing factor.

A third controversy centers around the argument that the omission of flotation cost is justified on the grounds that, in an efficient market, the stock price already reflects any accretion or dilution resulting from new issuances of securities and that a flotation cost adjustment results in a double counting effect. The simple fact of the matter is that whatever stock price is set by the market, the company issuing stock will always net an amount less than the stock price due to the presence of intermediation and flotation costs. As a result, the company must earn slightly more on its reduced rate base in order to produce a return equal to that required by shareholders.

It has also been argued that a flotation cost allowance is inequitable since it results in a windfall gain to shareholders. This argument is erroneous. As stated previously, the company's common equity account is credited by an amount less than the market value of the issue, so that the company must earn slightly more on its reduced rate base in order to produce a return equal to that required by shareholders.

The suggestion that the flotation cost allowance is unwarranted because investors factor this shortcoming in the stock price implies that it is appropriate to use a deficient model because such a deficiency is reflected in stock prices. In other words, it is appropriate to use a deficient model because investors are aware of this. Such circular reasoning could be used to justify any regulatory policy. For example, under this reasoning, it would be appropriate to authorize a return on equity of 1% because investors reflect this fact in the stock price. This is clearly illogical and erroneous. Any regulatory policy, as irrational as it may be, can be justified using this argument.

Another controversy is whether the underpricing allowance should still be applied when the utility is not contemplating an imminent common stock issue. Some argue that flotation costs are real and should be recognized in calculating the fair return on equity, but only at the time when the expenses are incurred. In other words, the flotation cost allowance should not continue indefinitely, but should be made in the year in which the sale of securities occurs, with no need for continuing compensation in future years. This argument implies that the company has already been compensated for these costs and/or the initial contributed capital was obtained freely, devoid of any flotation costs, which is an unlikely assumption, and certainly not applicable to most utilities. If the flotation costs of past stock issues have been fully recovered, the argument has merit. If that assumption is not met, the argument is without merit. The flotation cost adjustment cannot be strictly forward-looking unless all past flotation costs associated with past issues have been recovered.

A related controversy is whether or not the retained earnings component of equity requires a flotation cost adjustment. There is no flotation cost allowance made to retained earnings because it is implicitly embedded and recognized in the flotation cost adjustment formula. The conventional flotation cost adjustment formula deals with the fact that flotation costs are incurred only when new stock is sold, and not when earnings are retained. This is done by applying the flotation adjustment only to the dividend yield of the DCF formula and not to the growth component. The larger the fraction of earnings retained, the higher the growth rate, the lower the dividend yield component, and the smaller the flotation cost adjustment. In other words, larger retained earnings result in lower flotation costs adjustments as the costs are postponed into the future.

Some have argued that underwriters' discounts are not out-of-pocket expenses and thus should not be included in rates. On the basis of this argument, one might be foolish enough to believe that depreciation of utility plant should not be included in rates on the same grounds that depreciation is not an out-of-pocket expense. Obviously, the argument is without merit.

Lastly, some suggest that the flotation cost allowance should be based on a company's own actual flotation cost experience rather than on empirical studies that pertain to a large sample of stock offerings. To base a flotation cost allowance on a one-company sample, although company specific, would not provide a sufficiently reliable statistical and economic basis to infer a utility's appropriate flotation cost allowance. While it is conceptually correct to rely on the particular company circumstances in quantifying the flotation cost allowance, it is not a practical alternative. As discussed earlier, the flotation cost allowance is a weighted average cost factor designed to capture the average cost of various equity vintages and types of equity capital raised by the company.

As an additional practical matter, the market pressure effect is difficult to measure accurately for a specific issue. This is because one must disentangle the downward effect on stock price resulting from the increased supply of stock from the effect of general movement in the stock market. One must also measure the actual stock price following a common stock issue in relation to a hypothetical benchmark price without the issue over some arbitrary time period. This can be performed more reliably and more rigorously using a sample of utility stock offerings.

Alternative Flotation Cost Adjustment Formulas

Arzac and Marcus (1981) developed an alternative approach to accounting for flotation costs in regulatory hearings. To avoid dilution of the initial shareholders' equity, the allowed rate of return should equal:

$$R = \frac{K}{1 - \frac{fh}{1-f}} \qquad (6\text{-}9)$$

where $h = $ *external equity financing rate*, as a percentage of earnings, and the other symbols are as before.

Patterson (1983A and 1983B) formally compared the properties of the Arzac and Marcus adjustment with those of the conventional adjustment, and showed that the former is equivalent to expensing issue costs in each period when a stock issue occurs. In other words, if Equation 6-9 is consistently applied, the utility is reimbursed for its flotation costs in each year as they are incurred. Patterson also showed that the present value of flotation cost adjustments received by the utility is the same for both the conventional and the Arzac and Marcus adjustments.[3] The only difference between the two methods, if properly applied, is in the intergenerational allocation of flotation costs. The conventional approach amortizes them over an infinite period, while the Arzac and Marcus approach expenses them. The choice of method is a matter of public policy. It is important that whatever method is selected be applied consistently over the life of the utility.

It should be pointed out that the Arzac and Marcus method is based on the assumption that the flotation costs of past stock issues have been fully recovered, and hence, the recovery of future flotation costs is the primary basis for adjustment. The method is inappropriate if that assumption is not met.

On grounds of fairness alone, the conventional approach would seem preferable. Since the equity capital has long-term implications for both the company and ratepayers, imputing the flotation costs to ratepayers who happen to be extant at the time of each specific stock issue appears unreasonable. The conventional approach in effect normalizes the potential dilution issue over a period of years. To charge ratepayers for the full magnitude of stock issue costs at the time of each stock issue would impose an unfair burden on ratepayers at that time.

Hunter (1989) suggested an alternative formula to quantify the flotation cost allowance. In contrast to the conventional formula, however, the Hunter formula is cumbersome and laborious. It requires several inputs, some of which are highly arbitrary and difficult to quantify, and requires solving a complex quadratic equation involving a multitude of terms to obtain the stock price. As a practical matter, the Hunter formula produces the same order of magnitude of flotation cost adjustment as the conventional formula.

Howe and Beranek (1992) proposed a "weighted average" approach for adjusting ROE for flotation cost that provides solutions for a wide variety of operating conditions and circumstances. They also showed that the conventional formula is a special case of their approach, which weighs the pure equity rate by the retention ratio b and the adjusted equity rate by its converse $1-b$. The Howe and Beranek procedure consists of three steps: (1) obtain the cost of each individual source of equity financing; (2) determine the present value of each source; and (3) fix the weights by forming the ratio of each present value to their sum.

---

[3] Howe (1984) also compared the two flotation cost adjustment methods, and provided guidance for implementation. He showed that the conventional method actually slightly underestimates the adjustment, and that the Arzac and Marcus method slightly overestimates the magnitude of the adjustment.

While this procedure is theoretically correct, it has several operational difficulties. The main thrust of the Howe and Beranek approach is to source the equity. As discussed earlier, it is impractical and prohibitive to start from the inception of a company and source all present equity. The Howe and Beranek approach also implies that it is incorrect to apply a flotation cost adjustment to retained earnings. The conventional flotation cost adjustment formula deals with the fact that flotation costs are incurred only when new stock is sold, and not when earnings are retained. This is because the flotation adjustment is only applied to the dividend yield of the DCF formula, and not the growth component. This was discussed earlier.

References

Arzac, E.R. and Marcus, M. "Flotation Cost Allowance in Rate of Return Regulation: A Note." *Journal of Finance,* December 1981, 1199-1202.

Borum, V.M. and Malley, S.L. "Total Flotation Cost for Electric Company Equity Issues." *Public Utilities Fortnightly,* February 20, 1986, 33-39.

Bowyer Jr., J.W. and Yawitz, J.B. "The Effect of New Equity Issues on Utility Stock Prices." *Public Utilities Fortnightly,* May 22, 1980, 25-28.

Brigham, E.F., Aberwald, D.A., and Gapenski, L.C. "Common Equity Flotation Costs and Ratemaking," *Public Utilities Fortnightly,* May 2, 1985, 28-36.

Brigham, E.F. and Gapenski, L.C. *Financial Management: Theory and Practice,* 6th ed., Hinsdale IL: Dryden Press, 1991.

Eckbo, R. and Masulis, R. "Rights vs. Underwritten Stock Offerings: An Empirical Analysis." University of British Columbia, Working Paper No. 1208, September 1987.

Howe, K.M. "Flotation Cost Allowance for the Regulated Firm: A Comparison of Alternatives." *Journal of Finance,* March 1984, 289-91.

Howe, K.M. and Beranek, W. "Issue Costs and Regulated Returns: A General Approach." *Journal of Regulatory Economics,* December 1992.

Hunter, S.R. "The Complex Area of Flotation Cost Adjustment." *Public Utilities Fortnightly,* June 22, 1989, 23-26.

Logue, D. E. "On the Pricing of Unseasoned Equity Offerings." *Journal of Financial and Quantitative Analysis,* January 1973, 91-103.

Logue, D. E. and Jarrow, R. A. "Negotiations vs. Competitive Bidding in the Sale of Securities by Public Utilities." *Financial Management,* Autumn 1978, 31-39.

Patterson, C.S. "Flotation Cost Allowance in Rate of Return Regulation: Comment." *Journal of Finance,* September 1983A, 1335-1338.

Patterson, C.S. "Dilution Compensation versus Dilution Prevention: Some Clarifications." *Public Utilities Fortnightly,* November 10, 1983B, 49-51.

Pettway, R.H. "The Effects of New Equity Sales Upon Utility Share Prices." *Public Utilities Fortnightly,* May 10, 1984, 35-39.

Reilly, F.K. and Hatfield, K. "Investor Experience with New Stock Issues." *Financial Analysts' Journal,* September-October 1969, 73-80.

Richter, P.H. "The Ever-present Need for an Underpricing Allowance." *Public Utilities Fortnightly,* February 18, 1982, 58-61.

Smith, C.W. "Investment Banking and the Capital Acquisition Process." *Journal of Financial Economics,* 1986, 3-29.

Additional References

Berry, S.K. "Flotation Cost Allowance Methodologies: A Synthesis Using Present Value Analysis." *Financial Review,* August 1990, 487-500.

Patterson, C.S. *Methods for the Estimation of the Cost of Common Equity Capital,* Bell Canada, 1973.

Pettway, R.H. and Radcliffe, R.C. "Impacts of New Equity Sales upon Electric Utility Share Prices." *Financial Management,* Spring 1985, 16-25.

Appendix 6-A
Measuring Market Pressure Effects

The problem in measuring market pressure effects is to disentangle the downward effect on stock price resulting from the increased supply of stock from the effect of general movement in the stock market. Patterson (1973) has proposed one simple and effective method of isolating the market pressure effects from the market's aggregate effect. This method computes the following statistic for a series of past stock offerings, and uses the average as a measure of the market pressure effect:

$$\text{market pressure} = 1 - \frac{P_{LOW} + R}{\dfrac{P_{ANN} \, I_{LOW}}{I_{ANN}}} \qquad (6\text{-A})$$

where

P_{LOW} = low market price during the issue period

P_{ANN} = market price two days before announcement of the issue

I_{LOW} = level of the market index on the date of P_{LOW}

I_{ANN} = level of the market index two days before announcement date

R = value of one right on date if a rights issue

EXAMPLE 6A-1

Two days before the announcement of a common stock issue, Utility X's stock price is $60, while the Dow Jones Industrial Index is at 1200. During the issue period, Utility X's stock price reaches a low of $56 while the Dow Jones is at 1220 on the corresponding date. The market pressure effect can be computed as:

market pressure = 1 – $56/$60 (1220/1200)

= 1 – .949

= .051 or 5.1%

The allowance for market break is even more complex to gauge accurately. Some cushion should be provided against market declines from external causes. Regulated utilities are mandated to provide quality service and to expand when warranted by demand. Unlike unregulated companies, who have the luxury of postponing the issuance of new securities when market conditions are unfavorable, utilities do not have the same flexibility, and they must obtain capital when needed regardless of market conditions. A precise quantification of this effect is difficult. One way to assess the magnitude of market break is to compare current utility Price/Earnings ratios with their historical levels, and the higher the current P/E ratios, the greater is the possible decline.

Chapter 7
Alternative DCF Models

7.1 The Quarterly DCF Model

The standard annual form of the DCF model:

$$K = D_1/P_0 + g$$

assumes an annual dividend payment, a yearly increase in dividends starting exactly one year from the present, a constant rate of dividend growth, and a stock price P_0 that is determined on a dividend payment date. But because dividends are normally paid quarterly, the investor's required return should be assessed with a DCF model that recognizes quarterly payments.

It is a rudimentary tenet of security valuation theory discussed in Chapter 4 that when determining investor return requirements, the cost of equity is the discount rate that equates the present value of future cash receipts to the observed market price. Clearly, given that dividends are paid quarterly and given that the observed stock price reflects the quarterly nature of dividend payments, the market required return must recognize quarterly compounding, for the investor receives dividend checks and reinvests the proceeds on a quarterly schedule. Perforce, a stock that pays 4 quarterly dividends of one dollar commands a higher price than a stock that pays a 4-dollar dividend a year hence. Since investors are aware of the quarterly timing of dividend payments and since the stock price already fully reflects the quarterly payment of dividends, it is essential that the DCF model used to estimate equity costs also reflect the actual timing of quarterly dividends.

The traditional annual DCF model is based on the limiting assumptions that dividends are paid annually, and that dividends increase once a year starting exactly one year from the present. These assumptions are unnecessarily restrictive. Most companies, including utilities, in fact pay dividends on a quarterly basis. The quarterly DCF model discussed in subsequent sections of this chapter rests on the exact same assumptions as the annual DCF model except that the DCF model is refined to reflect the actual corporate practice of paying dividends quarterly rather than once a year. The quarterly version of the DCF model also assumes that the dividend rate is raised once a year instead of every quarter.

As both a practical and theoretical matter, stock yield calculations must be adjusted for the receipt of cash flows on a quarterly basis. The annual DCF model inherently produces incorrect results because it assumes that all cash flows received by investors are paid annually. By analogy, a bank rate on deposits that does not take into consideration the timing of the interest payments understates the true yield if the customer receives the interest payments more than once a year. The actual yield will exceed the stated nominal rate. Bond yield calculations are also routinely adjusted for the receipts of semi-annual interest payments. What is true for bank deposits and for bonds is equally germane for common stocks.

Most, if not all, finance textbooks discuss frequency of compounding in computing the yield on a financial security. The handbooks that accompany popular financial calculators used almost universally by the financial community contain abundant directions with respect to frequency of compounding.

Appendix 7-A formally derives the quarterly DCF model, which has the following form:

$$K = \frac{[D_1 (1 + K)^{3/4} + D_2 (1 + K)^{1/2} + D_3 (1 + K)^{1/4} + D_4]}{P_0} + g \qquad (7\text{-}1)$$

where D_1, D_2, D_3, D_4 = quarterly dividends expected over the coming year

g = expected growth in dividends

P_0 = current stock price

K = required return on equity

Equation 7-1 must be solved by iteration because K appears on both sides of the equation. Note that an even more general form of the quarterly DCF model can be derived for the case where the stock price is not determined on a dividend payment date. If we let f_1, f_2, f_3, and f_4 denote the fraction of the year before the quarterly dividends are received, Equation 7-1 becomes:

$$K = \frac{[D_1 (1 + K)^{1-f_1} + D_2 (1 + K)^{1-f_2} + D_3 (1 + K)^{1-f_3} + D_4{}^{1-f_4}]}{P_0} + g \qquad (7\text{-}2)$$

In the special case where the stock price happens to be determined on a dividend payment date, f_1, f_2, f_3, and f_4 are equal to 0.25, 0.50, 0.75 and 1.00 and Equation 7-2 reduces back to Equation 7-1.

The two-stage non-constant growth DCF model described in Chapter 4 has a quarterly counterpart:

$$P_0 = \frac{D_1\,(1+g)}{(1+K)^{0.25}} + \frac{D_2\,(1+g)}{(1+K)^{0.50}}$$

$$+ \frac{D_3\,(1+g)}{(1+K)^{0.75}} + \frac{D_3\,(1+g)}{(1+K)^{1.00}}$$

$$+ \frac{D_1(1+g)^2}{(1+K)^{1.25}} + \frac{D_2\,(1+g)^2}{(1+K)^{1.50}}$$

$$+ \frac{D_3\,(1+g)^2}{(1+K)^{1.75}} + \frac{D_3\,(1+g)^2}{(1+K)^{2.00}}$$

$$+ \frac{P_2}{(1+K)^{2.00}} \qquad (7\text{-}3)$$

The symbol g represents the first stage growth rate while P_2 represents the stock price in period 2 that is obtained by applying the quarterly DCF model using the second-stage growth rate.

Intuitively, the quarterly form of the DCF model described by Equation 7-1 resembles the standard annual form, but with a slightly modified dividend yield component. Letting $D_1' = D_1\,(1+K)^{3/4} + D_2\,(1+K)^{1/2} + D_3\,(1+K)^{1/4} + D_4$ in Equation 7-1, the quarterly DCF equation becomes:

$$K = D_1'/P_0 + g \qquad (7\text{-}4)$$

which is very similar to the annual version. One can think of the D_1' term as an augmented D_1 term that simply captures the added time value of money associated with investors receiving successive quarterly dividends and reinvesting them over the remainder of the year at $K\%$. That is to say, during the course of one year, the investor has the value of the first quarter's dividend for 3/4 of the year; the second quarter dividend for 1/2 of the year; the third quarter dividend for 1/4 of the year, and the fourth quarter dividend is received at the end of the year. The following illustration shows how to implement the quarterly DCF model and estimate the investor's required market return.

EXAMPLE 7-1

The common stock of Consolidated Natural Gas (CNG) is trading at $52.13. The dividend is expected to increase annually at a constant rate of 8.8%. The current quarterly dividend rate is $0.48 and has been in effect for two quarters. Thus, an investor buying CNG stock expects to receive, in the next year, two more dividends at the existing rate of $0.48 and two dividends at the new rate of $0.48(1 + g). The cost of equity capital is obtained by solving iteratively the quarterly version of the DCF model in Equation 7-1 by means of a computer spreadsheet. To solve that equation, the following input data for CNG:

$$D_1 = \$0.48$$

$$D_2 = \$0.48$$

$$D_3 = \$0.48 \, (1 + .0880) = \$0.52$$

$$D_4 = \$0.48 \, (1 + .0880) = \$0.52$$

$$P_0 = \$52.13$$

$$g = 8.80\%$$

are substituted into Equation 7-1 as follows:

$$K = \frac{[0.48 \, (1 + K)^{3/4} + 0.48 \, (1 + K)^{1/2} + 0.52 \, (1 + K)^{1/4} + 0.52]}{\$52.13} + .0880$$

The equation is solved iteratively by successive approximations for K_e, the cost of equity. Here, $K_e = 12.82\%$.

Note that the annual DCF model produces an estimate of 12.64%, which is less than the 12.82% estimate derived from the quarterly DCF model.

$$K = D_1/P_0 + g = \$2.00/\$52.13 + .088 = 12.64\%$$

The difference is attributable to the time value of money associated with receiving quarterly dividends. The annual version of the DCF model typically understates the cost of equity by approximately 30-40 basis points, depending on the magnitude of the dividend yield component.

The cost of equity capital estimate of 12.82% should be translated into a fair return on equity by allowing for a 5% flotation costs factor. This is accomplished by dividing the dividend yield component of the cost of equity figure by 0.95 to produce a fair DCF rate of return on equity of 13.03%.

7.2 Other Alternative DCF Models

Other alternative functional forms of the DCF model are available but are largely unrealistic and/or theoretically incorrect. The continuous compounding DCF model, for example, is developed assuming that dividends are paid continuously rather than at discrete time intervals.[1] Clearly, this model does not reflect reality, any more than does the annual DCF model, which assumes that dividends are paid once a year at the end of the year. The continuous DCF model has the following form:

$$K_c = D_0/P_0 + g \qquad (7\text{-}5)$$

where K_c = investor's expected return from the continuous DCF model

D_0 = annual per share dividend at time 0, i.e., current dividend

Another DCF model sometimes used by analysts, notably by the Federal Energy Regulatory Commission in its determination of the electric utility industry's generic rate of return on equity before 1993, lies halfway between the continuous and annual forms of the DCF model:

$$K_{ad\ hoc} = D_0\,(1 + 0.5G)/P_0 + g \qquad (7\text{-}6)$$

where $K_{ad\ hoc}$ = investor's expected return from the ad hoc DCF model

This "ad hoc" DCF model is based on the arbitrary assumption that the firm is halfway into its quarterly dividend cycle and assigns half a year's growth to the dividend. Of course, the model does not reflect reality and is arbitrary in nature. Only the quarterly compounding DCF model reflects reality, is theoretically correct, and is computationally tractable.

---

[1] The effective return under continuous compounding is computed with the following formula:

$$K_c = \frac{D_0\,[K_c/\ln\,(1 + k_e\,)\,] + g}{P_0}$$

7.3 Effective Rate Versus Nominal Rate of Return

This section shows that the investor required rate of return obtained from the quarterly DCF model must be adapted to the method of ratemaking. Kihm and Rankin (1988), Cichetti (1989), and Linke and Zumwalt (1984) contain excellent discussions of this point. The DCF quarterly rate is in fact an effective market-based rate of return that, although appropriate for unregulated companies, requires modification because of the manner in which revenue requirements are set. The adjustment is linked to the reinvestment assumptions of retained earnings.

By analogy, in a bank savings account that pays interest several times a year, the nominal rate and not the effective rate is used to compute the interest. Although the effective rate is used by investors to compare investment alternatives and to compute annual requirements, it is not used by the bank to compute interest on the principal balance on an unadjusted basis. An example drawn from Kihm and Rankin (1988) will clarify this point. Consider an investor requiring a 10% return from a bank savings account. The bank can satisfy the investor's return requirement by paying 9.57% compounded monthly. If the bank pays 10% compounded monthly, the investor will earn a 10.47% return, that is more than his 10% required return. In other words, paying the nominal annual return of 9.57% on a monthly compounded basis will yield the effective annual return of 10%, that is, the bank can meet the investor's objective by paying the nominal return. The situation is somewhat analogous for utilities, because the regulatory commission, like the bank, can meet the utility equity investor's objective by paying the nominal return.

The regulatory commission differs from a bank in one important respect, however. Unlike the bank that applies a nominal rate to the investor's opening balance, say $1,000, the regulator does not apply the return to the actual equity balance at the time of compounding but rather to an average common equity balance for the year, that is, to an amount in excess of $1,000 typically. Most often, the regulator applies the rate of return to an average common equity balance for a test year.

In the case of a forward test year, the use of the nominal return is preferable to the use of the effective return. This is because in the case of a forward test year for a growing utility, the equity balance at the end of the test period exceeds the equity balance at the beginning of the test period. Applying the effective return from the quarterly DCF model to the average equity balance will produce a higher actual effective return to the investor. Therefore, in jurisdictions with a forward test period and for a utility with a growing rate base, the use of a nominal return is preferable. Authorizing the nominal return from the quarterly DCF model yields a return comparable to the effective return from that model. The reverse is true in the case of a historical test year or a utility with a declining rate base. In jurisdictions where a historical test period is used, the use of the effective return is highly preferable and will in fact produce a downward-biased estimate of the investor's required return. The use of the effective return will produce a fair return to the investor in the case of a current test year jurisdiction.

To convert the effective return from the quarterly DCF model to its nominal equivalent, the n-period compounded equivalent of the quarterly DCF return is computed as follows:

$$K_{nom} = (\,[1 + K_{eff}]^{1/n} - 1)\; x\; n \qquad\qquad (7\text{-}7)$$

where $\quad K_{nom}\quad$ = the nominal rate of return

$\qquad\qquad K_{eff}\quad$ = the effective quarterly DCF rate of return

$\qquad\qquad n \qquad$ = the number of compounding periods

The number of compounding periods should match the number of compounding periods used in compounding the utility's reinvestment of retained earnings. Assuming a monthly compounding period, which is often used by regulators to compute the average rate base, the monthly compounded equivalent of the quarterly DCF return is obtained by substituting $n = 12$ in Equation 7-7:

$$K_{nom} = (\,[1 + K_{eff}]^{1/12} - 1)\; x\; 12$$

Returning to the Consolidated Natural Gas illustration above, the nominal rate of return corresponding to the 12.82% effective rate obtained from the quarterly DCF model is given by:

$$K_{nom} = (\,[1 + .1282]^{1/12} - 1)\; x\; 12 = 12.12\%$$

EXAMPLE 7-2

Consider the following simple example. A stock is trading at $50, with an annual dividend of $2.00, representing a current dividend yield of 4%. The dividend is expected to grow at a yearly 10% rate. The table below summarizes the nominal and effective returns from the four DCF models discussed so far: annual, quarterly, continous, and ad hoc.

TABLE 7-1
NOMINAL V. EFFECTIVE RETURN FOR 4 DCF MODELS

Compounding Assumption	Nominal Return	Effective Return
Annual	14.40%	14.40%
Quarterly	13.89%	14.63%
Continuous	14.00%	14.72%
Ad Hoc	14.20%	14.20%

Note that the nominal and effective return for both the annual and ad hoc DCF models are identical because they are both annual models to begin with. Note also that the effective returns for the continuous and the quarterly DCF models exceed the nominal returns because the more frequent the compounding the higher the return.

The applicability of the effective quarterly DCF return as a proper basis for setting rates is shown through the following illustration adapted from Cichetti (1989). Tables 7-2 to 7-4 demonstrate what happens to an investor when the quarterly DCF model is applied to a utility with a growing rate base in in a forward test year jurisdiction. Table 7-2 contains the assumptions of the illustration. Tables 7-3 and 7-4 show what happens to the investor if (1) the unadjusted, or effective, quarterly DCF return is allowed, and (2) the adjusted, or nominal return, is allowed.

TABLE 7-2
REQUIRED RETURN AND REQUIRED EARNINGS:
QUARTERLY DCF MODEL

ASSUMPTIONS:

Stock Price	=	$30.85
Quarterly Dividend	=	$ 0.70
Annual Dividend	=	$ 2.80
Growth Rate	=	4.50%

In this example, the effective return demanded by investors is 14.04%. The effective return from the quarterly DCF model of 14.04%, K_{eff}, is routinely converted to an equivalent monthly rate $K_{nom,12}$ by means of Equation 7-6 with $n = 12$:

$$K_{nom,\,12} = [1 + K_{eff}]^{1/12} - 1$$

The nominal equivalent is 13.86%, or 1.10% per month.

Table 7-3 shows what happens to investors if the utility is allowed to earn the nominal return of 13.86% on its equity rate base. By applying the nominal return to each future equity balance, the utility has enough earnings to satisfy investor return requirements. The required earnings are obtained by multiplying the equivalent monthly required equity return of 1.10% by the beginning of the month equity book value for the year. This produces earnings of $4.19. By allowing the nominal return to the beginning of period equity rate base each month, the investor receives the required dividends of $2.80 for the year and a capital appreciation from $30.85 to $32.24, that is, the expected 4.50% growth rate.

TABLE 7-3
APPLICATION OF THE NOMINAL RETURN

Step 1: Determine Investors' Required Return (market-based)

Dividend Yield	=	9.08%
Growth	=	4.50%
DCF Return	=	14.04%

Step 2: Convert Quarterly Return To Monthly Return (market-based)

Monthly Market Required Return = 1.1009%
Nominal Equivalent of 13.86%

Step 3: Determine "Effective Ratemaking Return"

Month	BOM Equity Book Value Per Share	Monthly Earnings Per Share	Quarterly Dividend Per Share	EOM Equity Book Value Per Share
Jan-94	$30.850	$0.340		$31.190
Feb-94	$31.190	$0.343		$31.533
Mar-94	$31.533	$0.347	$0.700	$31.180
Apr-94	$31.180	$0.343		$31.523
May-94	$31.523	$0.347		$31.870
Jun-94	$31.870	$0.351	$0.700	$31.521
Jul-94	$31.521	$0.347		$31.868
Aug-94	$31.868	$0.351		$32.219
Sep-94	$32.219	$0.355	$0.700	$31.874
Oct-94	$31.874	$0.351		$32.225
Nov-94	$32.225	$0.355		$32.580
Dec-94	$32.580	$0.359	$0.700	$32.238
Total		$4.188	$2.800	
Growth	4.50			

Table 7-4 shows that if the full unadjusted effective return from the quarterly DCF model is applied in setting rates instead of the nominal return, the investor will realize excess returns. The effective quarterly DCF of 14.04%, or 1.12% per month, produces a windfall. This is due to the compounding associated with the utility's reinvestment of accumulated equity. The total required earnings of $4.05 are more than sufficient to fulfill shareholders' return requirement, as evidenced by the appreciation in stock price from $30.85 to $32.10, which is a gain of 4.75% versus the 4.50% expected by investors. Only if the nominal rate is used in setting rates will the investor realize his required return.

TABLE 7-4
APPLICATION OF THE FULL UNADJUSTED EFFECTIVE RETURN

Step 1:   Determine Investors' Required Return (market-based)

Dividend Yield	=	9.08%
Growth	=	4.75%
DCF Return	=	14.30%

Step 2: Convert Quarterly Return To Monthly Return (market-based)

Monthly Market Required Return   =   1.1200%
Nominal Equivalent of 14.04%

Step 3: Determine "Effective Ratemaking Return"

Month	BOM Equity Book Value Per Share	Monthly Earnings Per Share	Quarterly Dividend Per Share	EOM Equity Book Value Per Share
Jan-94	$30.850	$0.346		$31.196
Feb-94	$31.196	$0.349		$31.545
Mar-94	$31.545	$0.353	$0.700	$31.198
Apr-94	$31.198	$0.349		$31.548
May-94	$31.548	$0.353		$31.901
Jun-94	$31.901	$0.357	$0.700	$31.558
Jul-94	$31.558	$0.353		$31.912
Aug-94	$31.912	$0.357		$32.269
Sep-94	$32.269	$0.361	$0.700	$31.930
Oct-94	$31.930	$0.358		$32.288
Nov-94	$32.288	$0.362		$32.650
Dec-94	$32.650	$0.366	$0.700	$32.315
Total		$4.265	$2.800	
Growth	4.75%			

It is important to note from Example 7-2 that the return estimate that gives proper recognition to the fact that utilities pay quarterly rather than annual dividends must also be properly related to the equity rate base implicit in the DCF analysis when determining the utility's required quantity of earnings. In other words, the rate base definition must match the rate of return construct. Recall that a utility's earnings are set as the product of the relative proportion of equity in the rate base and the cost of equity. A DCF equity cost of analysis implicitly defines the relevant rate base construct to be used. The procedure employed in calculating a utility's earnings must give proper recognition to the fact that the rate of return measure and the rate base measure are inextricably linked. That is, there must be consistency between rate of return and the rate base construct that it is paired with it. In Table 7-3, the monthly accumulation of retained earnings in the rate base reflects the application of the monthly nominal rate of return to the beginning of the month equity rate base.

It is difficult to determine the appropriate form of the DCF model to employ for ratemaking, however, given the methods of applying equity returns to the average utility common equity balance found in practice. Given the variety of rate base definitions (historical, current, forward, 13-month average, etc.), given the month-to-month seasonal behavior of the equity rate base, given the lack of consistency between the rate base definition and the capital actually invested by shareholders, there is no theoretically correct functional DCF form that matches actual regulatory practices with what the investor observes. To take all these considerations into account would require an intractable and complex theoretical DCF model. As a practical matter, the estimate provided by the standard annual DCF model is a reasonable compromise. For those utilities with a fully forward test year, a growing rate base, and a rate base that is in reasonable equality with invested capital, the application of the nominal return from a quarterly DCF model produces reasonable results. For those utilities with a current test year, a fairly stable rate base, and a rate base that is in reasonable equality with invested capital, the application of the effective return from a quarterly DCF model produces reasonable results. For those utilities with a historical test year, a declining rate base, and a rate base that is in reasonable equality with invested capital, the application of the effective return from a quarterly DCF model produces downward-biased results.

7.4 Controversies Surrounding the Quarterly DCF Model

One argument directed at the quarterly DCF model is that it assumes that dividends are increased every quarter by a constant growth factor. This argument is erroneous. The quarterly DCF model does not assume that dividends are increased every quarter. It does, however, assume that dividends are increased once a year, just as the basic annual DCF model does. The short-form approximation to the quarterly DCF model shown in Equation 7-B of Appendix 7-A does assume that dividends are increased at a constant rate every quarter. The discrepancy between the full-fledged quarterly DCF model and the short-form approximation is small.

The effect of using the shortcut approximation of Equation 7-B in Appendix 7-A instead of the full-fledged quarterly model of Equation 7-1 depends on the company's actual dividend cycle, and can be easily determined by using the sensitivity analysis of a computer spreadsheet. If a company's number of quarters left at the current rate n is less than 2, the approximation will understate the return on equity by about 15-20 basis points, depending on the relative magnitude of the growth rate and the dividend yield component. Conversely, if a company's number of quarters left at the current rate n is greater than 2, the approximation will overstate the return on equity by about 20-25 basis points. If n is equal to 2, that is, the firm is halfway into the dividend cycle, the discrepancy is negligible. Given that the various dividend cycles n of a large sample of companies are uniformly spread out, the overstatements and understatements will offset one another, and the net effect of the approximation is likely to be very small. The following table illustrates the discrepancy between the full-fledged quarterly DCF model of Equation 7-1 and its shortcut approximation for values of n ranging from 0 to 4.

n	g=3%	g=4%
0	0.1268%	0.1704%
1	0.0411%	0.0552%
2	-0.0419%	-0.0560%
3	-0.1222%	-0.1633%
4	-0.1999%	-0.2669%

A company's capital attraction ability is diminished unless its investors are allowed the effective DCF quarterly return. This is simply because investors are able to earn a larger return from competing comparable risk investments, and unless the company can earn at the same market-based rate of return as its investors can earn externally, the company's capital-raising ability is endangered. If an investor is confronted with a choice between an investment in stock of a public utility that is only allowed to earn the annual DCF return of 10%, and an investment in stock of another company of comparable risk that is expected to earn the quarterly DCF return of 10.38%, the investor would clearly choose the latter. At the end of the year, the investor's wealth would only be $1,100.00 with the first investment, compared to $1,103.80 for the second investment. Therefore, the investor will not invest funds in a public utility stock that is only allowed to earn the annual DCF return when comparable risk alternatives are earning more.

A second controversy regarding the quarterly DCF model centers around the argument that the use of quarterly timing implies questionable dividend reinvestment assumptions. The argument that a regulator awards investors a return on dividend reinvestment by using the quarterly DCF model is not peculiar to the quarterly DCF model for it could be directed at any DCF model, including the annual DCF model. All DCF models share the common assumption that cash dividends are reinvested at the cost of equity. The quarterly DCF model contains the same dividend reinvestment assumptions as does the annual DCF model.

Some analysts argue that the annual DCF model rather than the quarterly DCF model should be used because investors are aware of the difference in return and this shortcoming in the model is already reflected in the stock price. This position implies that it is appropriate to use a deficient model because such a deficiency is reflected in stock prices. In other words, it is appropriate to use a deficient model because investors are aware of this. We have encountered this type of convoluted logic before in the flotation cost discussion of Chapter 6. This kind of circular reasoning could be used to justify any regulatory policy. The quarterly adjustment is required because it is theoretically and practically correct.

References

Cichetti, M. "The Quarterly DCF Model, Effective and Nominal Rates of Return and the Determination of Revenue Requirements for Regulated Public Utilities." *National Regulatory Research Institute Quarterly Bulletin,* Fall 1989, 249-259.

Kihm, S.G. and Rankin, W.F. "An Evaluation of Various Forms of the DCF Model." Office of the Chief Economist, Public Service Commission of Wisconsin, Jan. 1988.

Linke, C.M. and Zumwalt, J.K. "Estimation Biases in Discounted Cash Flow Analyses of Equity Capital Cost in Rate Regulation." *Financial Management,* Autumn 1984, 15-21.

Additional References

Brigham, E.F. and Gapenski, L.C. *Financial Management: Theory and Practice,* 4th ed., Hinsdale IL: Dryden Press, 1985.

Bussa, R.G. "Rate of Return - Rate Base Issues in Utility Regulation." *The Engineering Economist,* Spring 1987, 231-245.

Linke, C.M. and Zumwalt, J.K. "The Irrelevance of Compounding Frequency in Determining a Utility's Cost of Equity." *Financial Management,* Autumn 1987, 65-69.

Appendix 7-A
DCF Model: Quarterly Timing Adjustment

Part I: Present Value of Expected Future Cash Flows

One starts with the fundamental notion that market price is the present value of expected future cash flows and assume for simplicity a 1-year holding period. If D_1, D_2, D_3, and D_4 represent the dividends that will be paid each quarter in the year following the purchase date, P_0 is the stock price, and P_1 the stock price one year from now, we can write:

$$P_0 = \frac{D_1}{(1+K)^{1/4}} + \frac{D_2}{(1+K)^{2/4}} \qquad (7\text{-A})$$

$$+ \frac{D_3}{(1+K)^{3/4}} + \frac{D_4}{(1+K)} + \frac{P_1}{1+K}$$

We multiply the numerator and denominator of each term by the following factors so as to facilitate algebraic manipulation.

$$P_0 = \frac{D_1(1+K)^{3/4}}{(1+K)^{1/4}(1+K)^{3/4}} + \frac{D_2(1+K)^{1/2}}{(1+K)^{1/2}(1+K)^{1/2}}$$

$$+ \frac{D_3(1+K)^{1/4}}{(1+K)^{3/4}(1+K)^{1/4}} + \frac{D_4}{(1+K)} + \frac{P_1}{1+K}$$

$$\frac{D_1(1+K)^{3/4}}{1+K} + \frac{D_2(1+K)^{1/2}}{1+K} + \frac{D_3(1+K)^{1/4}}{1+K}$$

$$+ \frac{D_4}{1+K} + \frac{P_1}{1+K}$$

Noting that $P_1 = P_0(1+g)$, we can solve for K by multiplying through by $1+K$ and dividing through by P_0 to get:

$$K = \frac{D_1(1+K)^{3/4} + D_2(1+K)^{1/2} + D_3(1+K)^{1/4} + D_4}{P_0} + g \qquad 7\text{-B}$$

197

where $g =$ *annual growth rate on earnings* and *dividends* The standard DCF model by analogy is

$$K = \frac{D_0(1+g)}{P_0} + g \qquad (7\text{-C})$$

Part II: A Useful Approximation

Although the above quarterly DCF model allows for the quarterly timing of dividend payments, growth in dividend payments, and recognizes that quarterly dividend payments can be constant within a given year, the model is computationally laborious. The quarterly DCF model below is a useful approximation and is far less laborious, although it does require the assumption that the company increases its dividend payments each quarter. If it is assumed that dividends grow at a constant rate of $g\%$ every quarter starting from a base of D_0, the current quarterly rate, the company's stock price is given by:

$$P_0 = \sum_{n=1} \frac{D_0(1+g)^{n/4}}{(1+k)^{n/4}} + g$$

which simplifies to:

$$P_0 = \frac{D_0(1+g)^{1/4}}{(1+k)^{1/4} - (1+g)^{1/4}} \qquad (7\text{-D})$$

Solving the above equation for K, the simplified DCF formula for estimating the cost of equity under quarterly dividend payments emerges as Equation 7-E.

$$K = \left[\frac{D_0(1+g)^{1/4}}{P_0} + (1+g)^{1/4} \right] - 1 \qquad (7\text{-E})$$

Part III: Quarterly Versus Annual

The difference in the cost of capital estimate between the quarterly and annual model can be substantial. Subtracting Equation 7-C from Equation 7-B, we obtain the difference between the annual and quarterly DCF estimates:

$$\frac{[D_1 (1 + K)^{3/4} + D_2 (1 + K)^{1/2} + D_3 (1 + K)^{1/4} + D_4) - D_0](1 + g)}{P_0} \qquad \text{(7-F)}$$

To obtain an idea of the magnitude of the difference, take representative values for the parameters of the above equation applicable to the illustrative company. Assume the quarterly dividends on the current year are 0.425, the range in growth rate g is 7% - 9%, the stock price P_0 = $32. The magnitude of the difference in cost of capital estimates from the above equation is approximately 30 basis points:

	Quarterly DCF	Annual DCF	Difference
$g = 7\%$	12.95%	12.68%	.27%
$g = 8\%$	14.03%	13.74%	.29%
$g = 9\%$	15.10%	14.79%	.31%

Chapter 8
DCF Applications and Comparable Groups

8.1 The Use of Comparable Groups

There are several reasons why the determination of cost of capital should not rest on a sample of one firm:

(1) **Consistency with the notions of fair and reasonable return promulgated in the *Hope* and *Bluefield* cases.** The basic premise in determining a fair return is that the allowed return on equity should be commensurate with returns on investments in other firms with comparable risk, hence the need to extend the sample to firms of comparable risk. Moreover, the equity costs of other firms represent economic opportunity costs that have a direct impact on the cost of equity for the utility being studied.

(2) **Added reliability.** Confidence in the reliability of the estimate of equity cost can be enhanced by estimating the cost of equity capital for a variety of risk-equivalent companies. Such group comparisons not only act as a useful check on the magnitude of the cost of equity estimate obtained from a single company, but also mitigate any distortion introduced by measurement errors in the two components of equity return, namely dividend yield and growth. Utilizing a portfolio of similar companies along with the company-specific DCF acts to reduce the chance of either overestimating or underestimating the cost of equity for an individual company. By relying solely on a single-company DCF estimate or for that matter on a single methodology, a regulatory commission limits its flexibility and increases the risk of authorizing unreasonable rates of return. For example, in a large group of companies, positive and negative deviations from the expected growth will tend to cancel out owing to the law of large numbers, provided that the errors are independent.[1] The average growth

---

[1] If $\bar{\sigma}_i^2$ represents the average variance of the errors in a group of N companies, and $\bar{\sigma}_{ij}$ the average covariance between the errors, then the variance of the error for the group of N companies, σ_N^2 is given by:

$$\sigma_N^2 = \frac{1}{N}\bar{\sigma}_i^2 + \frac{N-1}{N}\bar{\sigma}_{ij}$$

If the errors are independent, the covariance between them is zero, and the variance of the error for the group is reduced to:

$$\sigma_N^2 = \frac{1}{N}\sigma_i^2$$

As N gets progressively larger, the variance gets smaller and smaller.

rate of several comparable firms is less likely to diverge from expected growth than is the estimate of growth for a single firm. More generally, the assumptions of the DCF model are more likely to be fulfilled for a group of companies than for any single firm.

(3) **Abnormal conditions.** When there is reason to believe that the standard DCF model is inapplicable to a particular utility, or when a utility is experiencing extraordinary circumstances, the use of a bench-mark group of companies is the only viable alternative to measure equity costs through the DCF method. Appropriate risk adjustments must, of course, be rendered. Such extraordinary circumstances would include a corporate restructuring, a major plant cancellation, or situations such as those of General Public Utilities following the Three Mile Island accident or of Washington Power Public Service following the default on its bonds.

(4) **Circularity problem.** Stock price, hence cost of equity capital, depends on investors' growth expectations, which in turn depend partially on investors' perception of the regulatory process. The net result is that the cost of equity depends in part on anticipated regulatory action, since both components of equity return—yield and growth—are influenced by the regulatory process. Carried to its extreme, this implies that regulation would in effect deliver whatever equity return investors expect.

This calls to mind Myers' (1972) reference to the gaming aspects of regulation. Suppose that a stock price is initially below book value, and that regulators announce that they will subscribe to the standard DCF method of measurement. Stock price will then rise, since investors expect a higher allowed return to come out of the rate hearing. But if the stock price rises, the regulators will underestimate the cost of equity if they assume that investors expect a continuation of historical growth. If investors in turn recognize the regulator's error in assessing their expectations, a complex circular game between investors and regulators ensues. Myers' solution to this predicament is to extend the sample to include several comparable risk firms. It is thus imperative to examine market data not related to the firm's financial statistics as a check on the standard DCF model. The circularity problem, to the extent that it exists, can be mitigated by referencing data on non-regulated companies as well as on other utilities.

By means of comprehensive actual case studies and by drawing on the material of previous DCF chapters, this chapter illustrates the implementation of DCF in actual practice, discusses the design of comparable risk groups, and presents solutions to special problems encountered in applying

DCF. The case studies are carefully chosen from actual testimonial proceedings to illustrate a variety of practical issues.

8.2 DCF Case Studies

Case I: Georgia Power Company

Parent Company as Proxy

This case study is drawn from an actual 1991 regulatory proceeding (Morin 1991). Georgia Power's stock is not publicly traded since the Company is a wholly-owned subsidiary of The Southern Company. Therefore, any market value approach to determine the investor's expected return on equity must be applied indirectly. The stock of The Southern Company, however, is publicly traded. Therefore, as a starting point, DCF techniques are applied to The Southern Company as a proxy for Georgia Power. The procedure is conservative since Georgia Power was, at the time, more risky than The Southern Company as a whole in view of the former's high regulatory and business risks, and the latter's size and its regional and regulatory diversification. The DCF model is also applied to two groups of comparable companies to produce proxies for Georgia Power.

DCF Analysis of Parent Company

The DCF model is applied to The Southern Company data using three proxies for growth: (1) historical dividend growth rates, (2) security analysts' growth expectations, and (3) sustainable growth rate estimates. Because Georgia Power has nuclear risk exposure, because its bonds were rated Baa and because the company had above-average risks, the DCF formula is applied to two control groups of comparable risk companies with similar features, using historical growth rates and analysts' growth forecasts as proxies for growth: (1) a group of nuclear electric utilities, with a Baa/BBB bond rating, and (2) a group of high-beta electric utilities. These two groups present the same risk profile to investors as does Georgia Power.

The historical growth rate in dividends for The Southern Company over the past 5 years, as reported in the Value Line Investment Survey, is 4%. The Value Line historical growth rate is employed as indicative of the long-term dividend growth potential of The Southern Company in the DCF model.

TABLE 8-1
REQUIRED MARKET RETURN,
DCF ILLUSTRATIONS

(1)	Stock Price (2)	Qrtly Divid (3)	No. of Qtrs Left (4)	Expect Divid (5)	Divid Yield (6)	Growth (7)	Cost of Equity (8)	Fair Return (9)
Georgia Power	$26.50	$0.535	0	$2.23	8.40%	4.00%	12.79%	13.25%
Georgia Power	$26.50	$0.535	0	$2.20	8.32%	3.00%	11.67%	12.13%
Georgia Power	$26.50	$0.535	0	$2.21	8.35%	3.36%	12.08%	12.53%

Application of the DCF formulation using the historical dividend growth rate as a proxy is shown on the first row of Table 8-1. The historical growth rate of 4% (Column 7) is combined with the expected dividend yield in the first year (Column 6), to produce an estimate of the cost of common equity of 12.79% (Column 8). The stock price (Column 2) used, $26.50, is the average closing stock price for the 10 trading days in the period before the date of exercise. Closing stock prices are obtained from the Dow Jones Historical Quote Service. The expected dividend is obtained by multiplying the current indicated quarterly dividend rate (Column 3) of 4 x $0.535 = $2.14 by a growth factor, which depends on how long the current quarterly dividend rate has been in effect and on the timing of the anticipated dividend increase (Column 4). Since the current quarterly rate has been in effect for at least 4 quarters, an investor buying The Southern Company stock expects to receive in the next year four dividends at the new rate of $0.535 (1 + g). The expected dividend without the quarterly timing adjustment is therefore computed by multiplying the current indicated dividend by an appropriate growth factor, here (1 + g).

The cost of capital, K_e, is obtained by solving iteratively the quarterly version of the DCF model embodied in Equation 7-2 in Chapter 7. The following input data for The Southern Company are used:

$$D_1 = \$0.535 \ (1 + .0400 \ ) = \$0.5564$$

$$D_2 = \$0.535 \ (1 + .0400 \ ) = \$0.5564$$

$$D_3 = \$0.535 \ (1 + .0400 \ ) = \$0.5564$$

$$D_4 = \$0.535 \ (1 + .0400 \ ) = \$0.5564$$

$$P_0 = \$26.50$$

$$g = 4.00\%$$

Here, K_e = 12.79%. The cost of equity capital estimate of 12.79% must be translated into a fair return on equity by allowing for flotation costs, as discussed in Chapter 6. This is accomplished by dividing the dividend yield component of the cost of equity figure by 0.95. In Column 9 of Table 8-1, a conservative allowance of 5% is applied to the dividend yield component by dividing by 0.95 (100%–5%) to produce a fair DCF rate of return on equity for the The Southern Company of 13.25%. In addition, 25 basis points are added in order to account for the difference in risk between the The Southern Company and Georgia Power, bringing the estimate to 13.50%.

Application of the DCF formulation using analysts' growth expectations as a proxy is shown in the middle row of Table 8-1 and is developed in an identical manner to that of the previous method shown in the top row. The expected growth rate of 3% obtained from IBES's growth forecasts is combined with the expected dividend yield and the flotation cost adjustment. The estimate of The Southern Company's cost of equity using this particular method is 12.13%. An additional 25 basis points are added for the risk differential between The Southern Company and Georgia Power, bringing the estimate to 12.38%.

To apply the sustainable growth formula, two quantities are required, the expected retention ratio b and the expected return on equity r. As an estimate for r, Value Line's projected long-term return on common equity of 12% is used. It should be pointed out that Value Line's 12% estimate of r is based on the year-end common equity balance rather than on the customary average common equity balance commonly used for ratemaking, and is therefore substantially downward-biased. For the expected retention ratio, Value Line's expected ratio for The Southern Company is 28% over the next several years. The implied growth rate is obtained by multiplying the expected return on book equity of 12% by the retention ratio of 28% to produce a growth rate of 3.36%.

Application of the DCF formulation using the sustainable growth rate estimate as a proxy is shown on the third row of Table 8-1. The growth rate of 3.36% is combined with the expected dividend yield to produce a fair return on equity of 12.53%. An additional 25 basis points are added for the risk differential between The Southern Company and Georgia Power, bringing the estimate to 12.78%.

In summary, the three DCF estimates derived from The Southern Company data using three different growth proxies, including flotation costs, range from about 12.38% to 13.50%.

Adjustment for Differential Risk

The DCF results derived from The Southern Company market data must then be adjusted in order to apply them to Georgia Power. The Southern Company's cost of equity reflects the weighted average risk of its constituent subsidiaries. Since at the time, four of its five operating subsidiaries are rated A/A and have less business and regulatory risks, relative to its sister companies, while the fifth subsidiary, Georgia Power, is rated Baa/BBB and experiences greater business and regulatory risk, the expected equity return applicable to Georgia Power, to the extent that it was partially derived from market data based on The Southern Company, is slightly downward-biased.

The downward bias is 25 basis points. This estimate is based on two sources. First, the average spread between A-rated and Baa-rated utility bonds in recent years has been about 40 basis points. Given that Georgia Power represents a little more than half of The Southern Company, the bias from applying The Southern Company-based market data to Georgia Power is therefore about 20 basis points. Second, the Capital Asset Pricing Model (CAPM) provides a conceptual framework for determining a subsidiary's cost of capital. This is discussed extensively in Chapter 12, as are the computational details of the risk adjustment. Suffice it to say that the CAPM formula can be used to approximate the return (cost of equity) differences implied by the differences in the betas between The Southern Company and Georgia Power. The risk adjustment from the CAPM technique is 30 basis points.

In conclusion, the yield spread method indicates a downward bias of about 20 basis points, and the CAPM method indicates a downward bias of 30 basis points. The average of the two estimates is 25 basis points, Therefore, an amount of 25 basis points is added to each of the The Southern Company-based DCF result.

Comparable Groups

Two groups of companies are studied that are similar in risk to Georgia Power, one based on bond rating and nuclear content, and one based on the beta risk measure. The initial sample consisted of the 100 electric utilities monitored in Salomon Brothers' Electric Utility Monthly. The companies also had to be included in the Value Line Data Base and in the IBES summary of analysts' growth forecasts. Companies that have suspended dividends were eliminated from the sample. The sample of surviving companies then consisted of 87 electric utilities, for which data were available in all the aforementioned data sources.

Because of Georgia Power's nuclear content and its bond rating of Baa/BBB by Standard & Poor's and Moody's, respectively, the first group of companies consisted of all those nuclear electric utilities from the sample whose bonds are currently rated in the same rating category as Georgia Power, Baa/BBB. Companies with chronic deficient earnings that have not increased dividends for several years were omitted from the sample, as the DCF model assumption of constant growth is of questionable applicability for these companies.

Eleven companies survived the screening process, as shown in Table 8-2. Although there may be substantial differences in characteristics between these companies, which may result in varying risk assessments by investors, they are all subject to similar kinds of economic and regulatory risk influences, and the average risk of the group can be considered comparable to Georgia Power. This is confirmed by the homogeneity of the beta and common equity risk measures for the companies in the group, shown in Columns 3 and 4 of Table 8-2. All the company betas cluster around an average of 0.70, which is coincidentally the same as The Southern Company's beta.

Application of the DCF formulation to each of the companies in the reference group proceeds in an identical manner to that of the previous application to The Southern Company. Table 8-2 displays the DCF analysis using Value Line's 5-year historical dividend growth rate estimate as a proxy for expected growth. Table 8-3 shows the DCF analysis using the IBES median growth forecast by analysts as a proxy for expected growth. Proceeding for each company in the group exactly as before in the DCF analysis of The Southern Company, the average cost of common equity estimate for the group is 13.38% using analysts' growth forecasts, and 13.23% using historical growth. These results are adjusted for flotation costs and quarterly dividend payments.

Given that Georgia Power's business and regulatory risks are above the industry average, the second group of companies consisted of all those electric utilities from the master list whose beta is at the upper end of the risk spectrum for electric utilities. All the companies with a beta risk measure of 0.70 or higher were retained. Thirty-one companies survived the screen, as shown in Table 8-4. The 0.70 cutoff point was chosen because it is The Southern Company's beta. The average beta for the group is 0.72, versus The Southern Company's 0.70, while the common equity ratio of 46 percent for the group somewhat exceeds The Southern Company's 43 percent and Georgia Power's 43 percent.

Tables 8-4 and 8-5 show the DCF analysis for each company using Value Line's 5-year historical dividend growth rate estimate and the IBES

TABLE 8-2
REQUIRED MARKET RETURN AND MEASURES OF RISK
FOR NUCLEAR Baa-RATED ELECTRIC UTILITIES:
HISTORICAL GROWTH

Company (1)	Quality Rating (2)	Beta (3)	Common Equity Ratio (4)	Inter Cover (5)	Stock Price (6)	Qtrly Divid (7)	No. of Qtrs Left (8)	Expected Dividend (9)	Divid Yield (10)	Historical Growth (11)	Cost of Equity (12)	Fair Return (13)
1 Central Hudson	Baa/BBB	0.55	0.39	2.6	$24.00	$0.46	3	$1.86	7.74%	4.00%	12.08%	12.51%
2 Central Vermont	Baa/BBB	0.60	0.49	3.6	$27.00	$0.52	3	$2.10	7.77%	3.50%	11.60%	12.02%
3 Commonwealth Energy	Baa/BBB	0.70	0.42	2.9	$32.00	$0.73	1	$3.05	9.54%	6.00%	16.08%	16.62%
4 DQE Inc	Baa/BBB	0.65	0.39	2.5	$24.00	$0.36	3	$1.46	6.08%	5.00%	11.32%	11.66%
5 Eastern Utilities	Baa/BBB	0.70	0.36	0.8	$25.00	$0.65	1	$2.71	10.83%	5.50%	16.99%	17.59%
6 Entergy Corp	Baa/BBB	0.80	0.38	1.9	$23.00	$0.30	3	$1.22	5.30%	6.00%	11.52%	11.81%
7 Kansas G&E	Baa/BBB	0.65	0.46	2.1	$27.00	$0.43	0	$1.79	6.63%	4.00%	10.89%	11.25%
8 Long Island Lighting	Baa/BBB	0.85	0.29	1.4	$21.00	$0.38	3	$1.52	7.23%	5.00%	12.56%	12.96%
9 NY State E & G	Baa/BBB	0.75	0.42	3.0	$25.00	$0.52	2	$2.11	8.44%	3.00%	11.81%	12.27%
10 Rochester Gas & Electric	Baa/BBB	0.70	0.41	2.5	$20.00	$0.41	3	$1.63	8.16%	3.00%	11.50%	11.95%
11 Texas Utilities	Baa/BBB	0.70	0.47	1.8	$37.00	$0.74	0	$3.12	8.44%	5.50%	14.38%	14.85%
Average		0.70	0.40	2.3								13.23%

TABLE 8-3
REQUIRED MARKET RETURN AND MEASURES OF RISK
FOR NUCLEAR Baa-RATED ELECTRIC UTILITIES :
ANALYSTS' GROWTH FORECASTS

Company	Quality Rating	Beta	Common Equity Ratio	Total Interest Cover	Stock Price	Current Qtrly Dividend	No. of Qtrs Left	Expected Dividend	Dividend Yield	Analysts' Growth Forecasts	Cost of Equity	Fair Return
(1)	(2)	(3)	(4)	(5)	(6)	(7)	(8)	(9)	(10)	(11)	(12)	(13)
1 Central Hudson G & E	Baa/BBB	0.55	0.39	2.6	$24.00	$0.46	3	$1.86	7.74%	4.00%	12.08%	12.51%
2 Central Vermont	Baa/BBB	0.60	0.49	3.6	$27.00	$0.52	3	$2.09	7.74%	2.00%	10.03%	10.45%
3 Commonwealth Energy	Baa/BBB	0.70	0.42	2.9	$32.00	$0.73	1	$3.18	9.95%	12.00%	22.74%	23.30%
4 DQE Inc	Baa/BBB	0.65	0.39	2.5	$24.00	$0.36	3	$1.46	6.08%	5.00%	11.32%	11.66%
5 Eastern Utilities	Baa/BBB	0.70	0.36	0.8	$25.00	$0.65	1	$2.70	10.79%	5.00%	16.43%	17.03%
6 Entergy Corp	Baa/BBB	0.80	0.38	1.9	$23.00	$0.30	3	$1.22	5.30%	6.00%	11.52%	11.81%
7 Kansas G&E	Baa/BBB	0.65	0.46	2.1	$27.00	$0.43	0	$1.79	6.63%	4.00%	10.89%	11.25%
8 Long Island Lighting	Baa/BBB	0.85	0.29	1.4	$21.00	$0.38	3	$1.52	7.23%	5.00%	12.56%	12.96%
9 NY State E & G	Baa/BBB	0.75	0.42	3.0	$25.00	$0.52	2	$2.11	8.44%	3.00%	11.81%	12.27%
10 Rochester Gas & Electric	Baa/BBB	0.70	0.41	2.5	$20.00	$0.41	3	$1.63	8.16%	3.00%	11.50%	11.95%
11 Texas Utilities	Baa/BBB	0.70	0.47	1.8	$37.00	$0.74	0	$3.05	8.24%	3.00%	11.59%	12.04%
Average		0.70	0.40	2.3								13.38%

TABLE 8-4
REQUIRED MARKET RETURN AND MEASURES OF RISK
FOR HIGH BETA ELECTRIC UTILITIES: HISTORICAL GROWTH

	Company	Beta	Common Equity Ratio	Total Interest Cover	Stock Price	Current Qtrly Divid	No. of Qtrs Left	Expected Divid	Dividend Yield	Historical Growth	Cost of Equity	Fair Return
	(1)	(2)	(3)	(4)	(5)	(6)	(7)	(8)	(9)	(10)	(11)	(12)
1	American Electric Power	0.75	0.46		$28.00	$0.60	0	$2.41	8.61%	0.50%	9.41%	9.88%
2	Baltimore Gas & Electric	0.70	0.43	3.1	$27.00	$0.53	3	$2.13	7.88%	6.00%	14.18%	14.61%
3	Central Maine & Power	0.70	0.46	2.4	$17.00	$0.39	0	$1.61	9.45%	3.00%	12.90%	13.42%
4	Central & South West	0.70	0.48	2.8	$44.00	$0.73	3	$2.97	6.74%	6.50%	13.57%	13.95%
5	Cincinnati Gas & Electric	0.70	0.44	3.4	$30.00	$0.62	3	$2.49	8.29%	1.00%	9.58%	10.03%
6	Commonwealth Energy	0.70	0.42	2.9	$32.00	$0.73	3	$3.05	9.54%	6.00%	16.08%	16.62%
7	Con Ed NY	0.75	0.54	4.2	$23.00	$0.47	1	$1.91	8.31%	11.00%	19.89%	20.36%
8	Duke Power Co.	0.70	0.50	4.3	$28.00	$0.41	2	$1.68	5.99%	4.50%	10.72%	11.05%
9	Eastern Utilities	0.70	0.36	0.8	$25.00	$0.65	1	$2.71	10.83%	5.50%	16.99%	17.59%
10	Entergy Corp.	0.80	0.38	1.9	$23.00	$0.30	3	$1.22	5.30%	6.00%	11.52%	11.81%
11	Florida Progress Corp.	0.70	0.48	3.8	$38.00	$0.69	3	$2.77	7.30%	5.00%	12.63%	13.04%
12	FPL Group	0.70	0.44	2.9	$29.00	$0.59	1	$2.44	8.41%	4.50%	13.32%	13.78%
13	General Public Utilities	0.70	0.47	4.3	$44.00	$0.65	1	$2.70	6.13%	5.00%	11.38%	11.72%
14	IPALCO Enterprises	0.70	0.56	4.4	$26.00	$0.45	0	$1.88	7.23%	4.50%	12.05%	12.45%
15	Kansas P & L	0.70	0.50	3.1	$23.00	$0.47	3	$1.89	8.21%	6.00%	14.64%	15.09%
16	Long Island Lighting	0.85	0.29	1.4	$21.00	$0.38	3	$1.52	7.23%	5.00%	12.56%	12.96%
17	Minnesota P & L	0.70	0.49	3.0	$26.00	$0.48	3	$1.94	7.44%	7.50%	15.35%	15.77%
18	New York State E & G	0.75	0.42	3.0	$25.00	$0.52	2	$2.11	8.44%	3.00%	11.81%	12.27%
19	NIPSCO	0.80	0.42	2.6	$19.00	$0.29	3	$1.18	6.20%	6.00%	12.48%	12.82%
20	Northern States	0.75	0.49	4.5	$33.00	$0.58	1	$2.45	7.43%	7.50%	15.33%	15.74%
21	Northwestern PSC	0.70	0.55	3.7	$22.00	$0.38	3	$1.54	7.01%	6.00%	13.35%	13.74%
22	Pacificorp	0.70	0.45	2.8	$22.00	$0.36	1	$1.48	6.72%	3.50%	10.47%	10.84%
23	Pennsylvania P & L	0.70	0.40	3.3	$43.00	$0.75	2	$3.02	7.03%	3.00%	10.30%	10.68%
24	Public Svc Ent Grp	0.75	0.46	2.9	$26.00	$0.53	3	$2.14	8.22%	3.00%	11.56%	12.01%
25	Rochester Gas & Electric	0.70	0.41	2.5	$20.00	$0.41	3	$1.63	8.16%	3.00%	11.50%	11.95%
26	San Diego Gas & Electric	0.70	0.50	4.6	$45.00	$0.68	0	$2.86	6.36%	6.00%	12.65%	13.00%
27	SCE Corp.	0.75	0.47	4.2	$38.00	$0.66	1	$2.76	7.26%	6.00%	13.62%	14.02%
28	Southwestern PSC	0.70	0.51	4.4	$28.00	$0.55	0	$2.33	8.33%	6.00%	14.78%	15.24%
29	Texas Utilities	0.70	0.47	1.8	$37.00	$0.74	0	$3.12	8.44%	5.50%	14.38%	14.85%
30	Union Electric	0.75	0.48	3.7	$30.00	$0.54	3	$2.18	7.26%	3.50%	11.06%	11.45%
31	Utilicorp	0.70	0.39	1.9	$21.00	$0.38	3	$1.57	7.48%	13.50%	21.54%	21.97%
	Average	0.72	0.45	3.05								13.70%

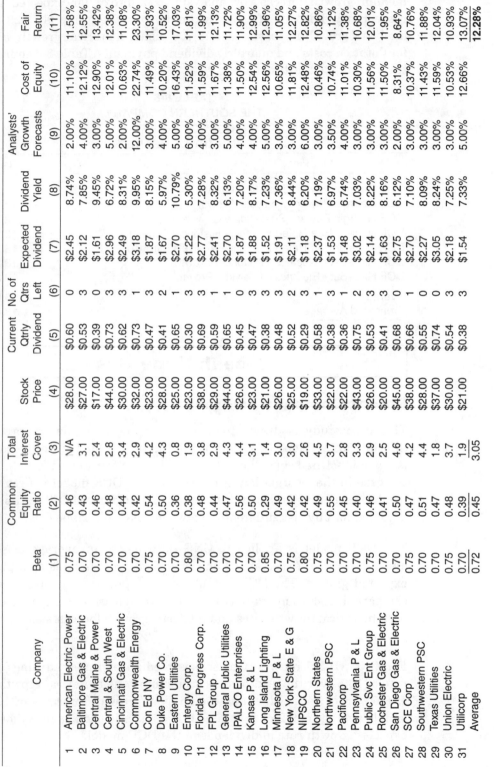

TABLE 8-5
REQUIRED MARKET RETURN AND MEASURES OF RISK
FOR HIGH-BETA ELECTRIC UTILITIES : ANALYSTS' GROWTH FORECASTS

	Company	Beta	Common Equity Ratio	Total Interest Cover	Stock Price	Current Qtrly Dividend	No. of Qtrs Left	Expected Dividend	Dividend Yield	Analysts' Growth Forecasts	Cost of Equity	Fair Return
		(1)	(2)	(3)	(4)	(5)	(6)	(7)	(8)	(9)	(10)	(11)
1	American Electric Power	0.75	0.46	N/A	$28.00	$0.60	0	$2.45	8.74%	2.00%	11.10%	11.58%
2	Baltimore Gas & Electric	0.70	0.43	3.1	$27.00	$0.53	3	$2.12	7.85%	4.00%	12.12%	12.55%
3	Central Maine & Power	0.70	0.46	2.4	$17.00	$0.39	0	$1.61	9.45%	3.00%	12.90%	13.42%
4	Central & South West	0.70	0.48	2.8	$44.00	$0.73	3	$2.96	6.72%	5.00%	12.01%	12.38%
5	Cincinnati Gas & Electric	0.70	0.44	3.4	$30.00	$0.62	3	$2.49	8.31%	2.00%	10.63%	11.08%
6	Commonwealth Energy	0.70	0.42	2.9	$32.00	$0.73	1	$3.18	9.95%	12.00%	22.74%	23.30%
7	Con Ed NY	0.75	0.54	4.2	$23.00	$0.47	3	$1.87	8.15%	3.00%	11.49%	11.93%
8	Duke Power Co.	0.70	0.50	4.3	$28.00	$0.41	2	$1.67	5.97%	4.00%	10.20%	10.52%
9	Eastern Utilities	0.70	0.36	0.8	$25.00	$0.65	1	$2.70	10.79%	5.00%	16.43%	17.03%
10	Entergy Corp.	0.80	0.38	1.9	$23.00	$0.30	3	$1.22	5.30%	6.00%	11.52%	11.81%
11	Florida Progress Corp.	0.70	0.48	3.8	$38.00	$0.69	3	$2.77	7.28%	4.00%	11.59%	11.99%
12	FPL Group	0.70	0.44	2.9	$29.00	$0.59	1	$2.41	8.32%	3.00%	11.67%	12.13%
13	General Public Utilities	0.70	0.47	4.3	$44.00	$0.65	1	$2.70	6.13%	5.00%	11.38%	11.72%
14	IPALCO Enterprises	0.70	0.56	4.4	$26.00	$0.45	0	$1.87	7.20%	4.00%	11.50%	11.90%
15	Kansas P & L	0.70	0.50	3.1	$23.00	$0.47	3	$1.88	8.17%	4.00%	12.54%	12.99%
16	Long Island Lighting	0.85	0.29	1.4	$21.00	$0.38	3	$1.52	7.23%	5.00%	12.56%	12.96%
17	Minnesota P & L	0.70	0.49	3.0	$26.00	$0.48	3	$1.91	7.36%	3.00%	10.65%	11.05%
18	New York State E & G	0.75	0.42	3.0	$25.00	$0.52	2	$2.11	8.44%	3.00%	11.81%	12.27%
19	NIPSCO	0.80	0.42	2.6	$19.00	$0.29	3	$1.18	6.20%	6.00%	12.48%	12.82%
20	Northern States	0.75	0.49	4.5	$33.00	$0.58	1	$2.37	7.19%	3.00%	10.46%	10.86%
21	Northwestern PSC	0.70	0.55	3.7	$22.00	$0.38	3	$1.53	6.97%	3.50%	10.74%	11.12%
22	Pacificorp	0.70	0.45	2.8	$22.00	$0.36	1	$1.48	6.74%	4.00%	11.01%	11.38%
23	Pennsylvania P & L	0.70	0.40	3.3	$43.00	$0.75	2	$3.02	7.03%	3.00%	10.30%	10.68%
24	Public Svc Ent Group	0.75	0.46	2.9	$26.00	$0.53	3	$2.14	8.22%	3.00%	11.56%	12.01%
25	Rochester Gas & Electric	0.70	0.41	2.5	$20.00	$0.41	3	$1.63	8.16%	3.00%	11.50%	11.95%
26	San Diego Gas & Electric	0.70	0.50	4.6	$45.00	$0.68	0	$2.75	6.12%	2.00%	8.31%	8.64%
27	SCE Corp	0.75	0.47	4.2	$38.00	$0.66	1	$2.70	7.10%	3.00%	10.37%	10.76%
28	Southwestern PSC	0.70	0.51	4.4	$28.00	$0.55	0	$2.27	8.09%	3.00%	11.43%	11.88%
29	Texas Utilities	0.70	0.47	1.8	$37.00	$0.74	0	$3.05	8.24%	3.00%	11.59%	12.04%
30	Union Electric	0.75	0.48	3.7	$30.00	$0.54	3	$2.18	7.25%	3.00%	10.53%	10.93%
31	Utilicorp	0.70	0.39	1.9	$21.00	$0.38	3	$1.54	7.33%	5.00%	12.66%	13.07%
	Average	0.72	0.45	3.05								12.28%

median growth forecast by analysts as a proxy for expected growth, respectively. The cost of equity estimate from the group is 12.28% using analysts' growth forecasts, and 13.70% using historical growth, adjusted for flotation costs and quarterly dividend payments. Table 8-6 summarizes the various DCF estimates.

TABLE 8-6
THE SOUTHERN COMPANY
COST OF EQUITY:
SUMMARY OF RESULTS

Method	Results
DCF Georgia Power - Historical Growth	13.50%
DCF Georgia Power - Analysts' Growth	12.38%
DCF Georgia Power - Sustainable Growth	12.78%
DCF Nuclear Baa Rated Electrics- Historical Growth	13.23%
DCF Nuclear Baa Rated Electrics - Analysts' Growth	13.38%
DCF High-Beta Electrics - Historical Growth	13.70%
DCF High-Beta Electrics - Analysts' Growth	12.28%
Average	**13.04%**
Truncated Average	**13.05%**

Case II: Hope Gas

Parent Company as Proxy

This case study is drawn from an actual 1992 regulatory proceeding (Morin 1992A). Hope Gas' stock is not publicly traded since the company is a wholly-owned subsidiary of Consolidated Natural Gas (CNG). As was the case in the Georgia Power case study, the DCF model is first applied to CNG as a proxy for Hope Gas and the parent-derived DCF estimate was adjusted for any risk differential between CNG and Hope Gas.

The DCF model is applied to CNG data using an average of security analysts' growth expectations and historical growth rates as a proxy for expected growth. The DCF formula is also applied to a control group of comparable risk companies as a means of comparison, using an average of both historical growth rates and analysts' growth forecasts as a proxy for growth.

For CNG, IBES reports a consensus median expected earnings growth rate of 10% over the next 5 years. Combining the historical growth figure of 8.5% from Value Line, and the analysts' growth forecasts of 10.0%, a simple average of 9.25% is obtained. The latter is used as proxy for CNG's expected growth rate in dividends in the DCF model.

Application of the DCF formulation is shown in Table 8-7.

TABLE 8-7
REQUIRED MARKET RETURN,
CNG:
DCF ANALYSIS

Company	Stock Price	Qtrly Divid	No. of Qtrs Left	Expected Dividend	Dividend Yield	Growth	Cost of Equity	Fair Return
(1)	(2)	(3)	(4)	(5)	(6)	(7)	(8)	(9)
C N G	$46.11	$0.475	1	$2.03	4.41%	9.25%	13.87%	14.12%

The growth rate of 9.25% (Column 7) is combined with the expected dividend yield in the first year (Column 6), to produce an estimate of the cost of common equity (Column 8). The stock price (Column 2) used, $46.11, is the average closing stock price for the 10 previous trading days. The expected dividend is obtained by multiplying the current indicated quarterly dividend rate (Column 3) of 4 x $0.475 = $1.90 by a growth factor, which depends on how long the current quarterly dividend rate has been in effect and on the timing of the anticipated dividend increase (Column 4). Since the current quarterly rate has been in effect for three quarters, an investor buying CNG stock expects to receive in the next year one more dividend at the existing rate of $0.475 and three dividends at the new rate of $0.475 $(1 + g)$. The expected dividend without the quarterly timing adjustment is therefore computed by multiplying the current indicated dividend by an appropriate growth factor, here $(1+0.75g)$.

The expected growth rate (Column 7) of 9.25% is combined with the expected dividend yield (Column 6) of 4.41% to produce the cost of capital estimate of 13.87% (Column 8). As in the previous Georgia Power case study, the latter is obtained by solving iteratively the quarterly version of the DCF model using the following input data for CNG:

$D_1 = \$0.475$

$D_2 = \$0.475 \ (1 + .0925)$

$D_3 = \$0.475 \ (1 + .0925)$

$D_4 = \$0.475 \ (1 + .0925)$

$P_0 = \$46.11$

$g \ = 9.25\%$

213

Here, the cost of equity, $Ke = 13.87\%$. The dividend yield component of the cost of equity figure is divided by 0.95 to allow for flotation cost. As shown in Table 8-7, a fair DCF rate of return on equity of 14.12% is obtained.

Risk Adjustment

At the time of the 1992 regulatory proceeding, the DCF estimate of CNG's cost of equity was not applicable to Hope Gas. CNG's cost of equity reflects the weighted average risk of its constituent subsidiaries. Since the operating subsidiaries other than Hope Gas and its sister gas distribution companies are riskier than Hope Gas, the expected equity return applicable to Hope Gas, to the extent that it is derived from CNG market data, is therefore upward-biased. The bias is estimated to be on the order of 87 basis points (0.87%). This adjustment brings the DCF estimate of Hope Gas's cost of equity from 14.12% to 13.25%.

The DCF results derived from CNG market data were adjusted as follows in order to apply them to Hope Gas. Although the adjustment is based on CAPM theory, which is the subject of Chapter 12, a brief explanation follows here. CNG has a beta risk factor of 0.75, versus 0.62 for the average gas distribution utility, as shown in Table 8-8. The CAPM formula can be used to measure the return (cost of equity) differences implied by the differences in the betas between CNG and the average LDC. The basic form of the CAPM states that the return differential is given by the differential in beta, times the excess return on the market, $R_M - R_F$. R_M is defined as the return on the overall equity market, and R_F denotes the risk-free rate. If beta is reduced from 0.75 to 0.62, that is by 0.13, the return differential implied by the difference in beta between Hope Gas (0.62) and CNG (0.75) is given by 0.13 times $R_M - R_F$. Using an estimate of 7.4% for $R_M - R_F$, the return adjustment is 96 basis points; using an estimate of 6.0% for $R_M - R_F$, the return adjustment is 78 basis points, for an average of 87 basis points. The difference in return is thus about 0.87%, which reduces the DCF estimate of CNG's equity costs from 14.12% to 13.25%.

Comparable Groups

The basic notion underlying the cost of common equity capital is that at any time, securities are priced so that all securities of equivalent risk offer the same expected rate of return. For Hope Gas, the basic problem is thus to determine the expected rate of return for its particular risk class.

The group of comparable risk companies consists of the 7 natural gas distribution utilities included in Moody's Gas Distribution Industry composite. These utilities are primarily in the same industry and face similar

TABLE 8-8
REQUIRED MARKET RETURN AND MEASURES OF
RISK FOR MOODY'S GAS DISTRIBUTION UTILITIES:
5-YEAR HISTORICAL GROWTH

Company	Beta	1991 Common Equity	Total Interest Cover	Stock Price	Current Qtrly Dividend	No. of Qtrs Left	Expected Dividend	Dividend Yield	Historical Growth	Cost of Equity	Fair Return
(1)	(2)	(3)	(4)	(5)	(6)	(7)	(8)	(9)	(10)	(11)	(12)
1 Atlanta Gas Light	0.65	0.49	3.6	$35.00	$0.52	2	$2.179	6.23%	9.50%	16.08%	16.42%
2 Brooklyn Union	0.50	0.45	3.4	$33.00	$0.49	1	$1.991	6.03%	3.50%	9.75%	10.08%
3 Indiana Energy	0.70	0.53	3.5	$29.00	$0.37	3	$1.500	5.17%	5.50%	10.88%	11.16%
4 Laclede Gas	0.55	0.53	3.7	$40.00	$0.60	0	$2.556	6.39%	6.50%	13.20%	13.55%
5 NW Natural Gas	0.60	0.43	1.7	$29.00	$0.43	0	$1.763	6.08%	2.50%	8.78%	9.11%
6 Peoples Energy	0.80	0.52	3.2	$31.00	$0.44	1	$1.852	5.98%	7.00%	13.26%	13.59%
7 Washington Gas	0.55	0.59	3.7	$37.00	$0.54	2	$2.199	5.94%	5.50%	11.69%	12.02%
Average	0.62	0.51	3.3					5.97%	5.71%	11.95%	12.28%

investment risks as Hope Gas. Although there may be substantial differences in characteristics between these companies, which may result in varying risk assessments by investors, as a group they are all subject to similar kinds of economic and regulatory risk influences, and the average risk of the group can be considered comparable to Hope Gas.

Application of the DCF formulation to each of the companies in the reference group proceeds in an identical manner to that of the previous application to CNG. Tables 8-8 and 8-9 display the DCF analysis for each company using Value Line's 5-year historical dividend growth rate and the IBES consensus growth forecast by analysts as proxies for expected growth.

Proceeding for each company in the group exactly as before in the DCF analysis of CNG, the average cost of common equity estimate for the group is 12.28% using historical growth, and 11.89% using growth forecasts. These results are adjusted for flotation costs and quarterly dividend payments.

Case III: Central Telephone Co. of Nevada

Parent Company as Proxy

This case study is drawn from an actual 1992 regulatory proceeding (Morin 1992B). Central Telephone-Nevada's stock is not publicly traded since the company is a division of Central Telephone Company, which is a wholly-owned subsidiary of Centel Corporation (Centel). Therefore, the DCF model is applied to two control groups of companies as proxies for Central Telephone-Nevada, using analysts' growth forecasts and historical growth rates, when applicable: a group of independent telephone companies and a group made up of the seven Bell Regional Holding Companies (RHCs). The DCF model could not be applied to parent company Centel as a proxy for Central Telephone-Nevada because Centel market data is likely to be distorted by the ongoing merger-acquisition negotiations with Sprint and because of Centel's high component of unregulated activities.

The first group of comparable companies, listed in Table 8-10, is comprised of 7 independent telephone companies that for the most part provide local telecommunication services in a number of different state jurisdictions in different economic regions. Although there are many differences in characteristics between these independent telephone companies, which result in varying risk assessments by investors, they are all subject to similar kinds of economic and regulatory risk influences.

Application of the DCF formulation to each of the companies is shown in Table 8-10, and proceeds in an identical manner to that of the previous

TABLE 8-9
REQUIRED MARKET RETURN AND MEASURES OF
RISK FOR MOODY'S GAS DISTRIBUTION UTILITIES:
ANALYSTS' GROWTH FORECASTS

Company	Beta	1991 Common Equity	Total Interest Cover	Stock Price	Current Qtrly Dividend	Qtrs Left	Expected Dividend	Dividend Yield	Analysts' Growth Forecasts	Cost of Equity	Fair Return
(1)	(2)	(3)	(4)	(5)	(6)	(7)	(8)	(9)	(10)	(11)	(12)
1 Atlanta Gas Light	0.65	0.49	3.6	$35.00	$0.52	2	$2.142	6.12%	6.00%	12.39%	12.73%
2 Brooklyn Union	0.50	0.45	3.4	$33.00	$0.49	1	$1.998	6.06%	4.00%	10.28%	10.61%
3 Indiana Energy	0.70	0.53	3.5	$29.00	$0.37	3	$1.510	5.21%	8.00%	13.46%	13.74%
4 Laclede Gas	0.55	0.53	3.7	$40.00	$0.60	0	$2.556	6.39%	6.50%	13.20%	13.55%
5 NW Natural Gas	0.60	0.43	1.7	$29.00	$0.43	0	$1.789	6.17%	4.00%	10.40%	10.74%
6 Peoples Energy	0.80	0.52	3.2	$31.00	$0.44	1	$1.813	5.85%	4.00%	10.06%	10.38%
7 Washington Gas	0.55	0.59	3.7	$37.00	$0.54	2	$2.194	5.93%	5.00%	11.17%	11.49%
Average	0.62	0.51	3.3					5.96%	5.36%	11.57%	11.89%

TABLE 8-10
REQUIRED MARKET RETURN AND MEASURES OF
RISK FOR INDEPENDENT TELEPHONE COMPANIES:
ANALYSTS' GROWTH FORECASTS

Company	Beta	1991 Common Equity	Total Interest Cover	Stock Price	Current Qrtly Dividend	No. of Qtrs Left	Expected Dividend	Dividend Yield	Analysts' Growth Forecasts	Cost of Equity	Fair Return
(1)	(2)	(3)	(4)	(5)	(6)	(7)	(8)	(9)	(10)	(11)	(12)
1 Alltel Corp	0.95	0.51	4.2	$38.89	$0.370	2	$1.547	3.98%	9.00%	13.16%	13.38%
2 Century Tel	1.15	0.56	3.6	$32.93	$0.110	3	$0.459	1.39%	17.00%	18.48%	18.56%
3 Cincinnati Bell	0.90	0.54	2.3	$18.13	$0.200	0	$0.864	4.77%	8.00%	12.99%	13.25%
4 GTE Corp	0.95	0.38	2.8	$31.83	$0.425	0	$1.853	5.82%	9.00%	15.14%	15.47%
5 Rochester Tel	0.80	0.48	3.1	$32.01	$0.385	3	$1.567	4.90%	7.00%	12.11%	12.38%
6 So. New Eng Tel	0.85	0.52	2.2	$32.75	$0.440	0	$1.883	5.75%	7.00%	13.02%	13.34%
7 Sprint Corp	0.95	0.37	2.3	$24.18	$0.250	0	$1.150	4.76%	15.00%	20.10%	20.37%
Average	0.94	0.48	2.93					4.48%	10.29%	15.00%	15.25%
Average w/o Sprint											14.40%

DCF illustrations. The growth component for the DCF model is based on the analysts' 5-year growth forecasts. As shown in Column 12, the average return on equity estimate for the group without Sprint Corporation is 14.40%.

The DCF results using historical growth rates yield unreliable estimates for these companies, clearly outside the limits of reasonable probability, and are not representative of investors' expected growth rates, as attested by the wide gap between historical growth and analysts' growth forecasts. Several of the companies' historical growth rates in earnings and dividends are distorted by non-recurring transitional factors, such as acquisitions, reorganizations, and divestitures.

To illustrate, Rochester Telephone's aggressive acquisition program in the past few years, while enhancing long-term growth prospects, has diluted historical earnings growth. Similarly, Centel's cellular growth and the associated startup costs in the past few years has drained earnings growth. Likewise, Cincinnati Bell's diversification effort into the telecommunications software business has had a negative impact on earnings.

If historical growth rates are to be representative of long-term future growth rates, they must not be biased by non-recurring events or by structural shifts in the fundamentals of the company. If the period used in measuring historical growth is characterized by non-recurring events that bias historical growth rates, such as cellular investments with heavy startup costs, acquisitions, diversification programs or write-offs, that period is not representative of the future. Instead, analysts' growth forecasts should be used in measuring expected growth. This was certainly the case for several independent telephone companies in the late 1980s and early 1990s, where diversification, acquisition, or write-off activities diluted historical earnings and dividends. Earnings growth for some of the independent telephone companies has been erratic in recent years and unrepresentative of future growth. In some cases, dividends and earnings growth were downward-biased by the building of cellular networks. Such undertakings require large capital investments and intense marketing programs that retard earnings growth. Under these circumstances, analysts' growth forecasts provide a more realistic and representative growth proxy for what is likely to happen in the future.

Adjustment for Unregulated Operations

The cost of equity estimate from the telephone independents reflects the weighted average risk of regulated telephone operations and unregulated telecommunications activities. To the extent that the unregulated operations are riskier, the expected equity return of applicable regulated telephone operations is upward-biased. The bias is of the order of 50 basis points. This adjustment lowers the DCF estimate from 14.40% to 13.90%. The details of the adjustment for differential risk are shown in Chapter 11.

The second group of companies, listed in Table 8-11, includes the 7 Bell RHCs. Application of the DCF formulation to each of the Bell RHCs proceeds in an identical manner to that of previous DCF analyses. Both the mean 5-year growth forecast by analysts contained in IBES and the 5-year historical growth rate in dividends for each company were used as proxies for expected growth. As shown in Column 10, the average return on equity estimate for the group is 12.59% using analysts' forecasts. The corresponding figure using historical growth is 13.34%, as shown in Table 8-12. The historical growth rate was used here because of its stability at the time and because, unlike the independent telephone companies, it was less affected by acquisitions, write-offs, and asset reevaluations at the time.

No adjustment for unregulated activities was applied, because the telephone operations of the RHCs at the time comprised some 90% of their activities. Moreover, any upward bias from the presence of riskier unregulated operations is likely to be offset by Central Telephone-Nevada's greater risk relative to the telephone operating companies of the RHCs.

8.3 Special Situations

A frequent deterrent to applying the DCF approach is the absence of investor-based market data. This situation usually prevails in the case of a utility company that is a subsidiary of a publicly listed parent company or in the case of a private unlisted company. Another deterrent is that the strategic assumptions of the DCF model are sometimes violated and the DCF model cannot be applied. Examples of such violations include dividend interruption, severe financial distress, limited access to capital markets, or a structural shift in the fundamentals of the utility's operations. Remedies are available to salvage the DCF approach in such situations.

Case IV: Public Service of Indiana

This case study is drawn from an actual 1993 regulatory proceeding (Morin 1993). The situation of Public Service of Indiana (PSI) in 1993 provides a vivid illustration of DCF assumptions being violated. The principal difficulty in calculating the required return by the DCF approach is in estimating the growth rates that investors are currently expecting. Three

TABLE 8-11
REQUIRED MARKET RETURN AND MEASURES OF
RISK FOR BELL RHCS:
ANALYSTS' GROWTH FORECASTS

Company	Beta	Stock Price	Current Qtrly Dividend	No. of Qtrs Left	Expected Dividend	Dividend Yield	Analysts' Growth Forecasts	Cost of Equity	Fair Return
(1)	(2)	(3)	(4)	(5)	(6)	(7)	(8)	(9)	(10)
1 Ameritech	0.80	$63.01	$0.880	3	$3.57	5.67%	6.00%	11.91%	12.23%
2 Bell Atlantic	0.85	$43.69	$0.650	3	$2.64	6.04%	6.00%	12.31%	12.64%
3 Bellsouth	0.85	$48.73	$0.690	0	$2.93	6.00%	6.00%	12.27%	12.60%
4 NYNEX	0.80	$76.89	$1.160	3	$4.71	6.13%	6.00%	12.40%	12.74%
5 Pacific Tel	0.85	$42.24	$0.545	3	$2.22	5.25%	7.00%	12.49%	12.78%
6 Southwestern Bell	0.90	$61.78	$0.730	3	$2.97	4.81%	7.00%	12.02%	12.28%
7 U.S. West	0.90	$35.41	$0.520	0	$2.20	6.23%	6.00%	12.51%	12.85%
Average	0.85					5.73%	6.29%	12.27%	12.59%

221

TABLE 8-12
REQUIRED MARKET RETURN AND MEASURES OF
RISK FOR BELL RHCS :
HISTORICAL GROWTH

Company	Beta	Stock Price	Current Qtrly Dividend	No. of Qtrs Left	Expected Dividend	Dividend Yield	Historical Growth	Cost of Equity	Fair Return
(1)	(2)	(3)	(4)	(5)	(6)	(7)	(8)	(9)	(10)
1 Ameritech	0.80	$63.01	$0.880	3	$3.59	5.70%	8.00%	13.98%	14.30%
2 Bell Atlantic	0.85	$43.69	$0.650	3	$2.65	6.06%	7.00%	13.35%	13.68%
3 Bellsouth	0.85	$48.73	$0.690	0	$2.95	6.06%	7.00%	13.36%	13.69%
4 NYNEX	0.80	$76.89	$1.160	3	$4.72	6.14%	7.00%	13.44%	13.78%
5 Pacific Tel	0.85	$42.24	$0.545	3	$2.22	5.25%	7.00%	12.49%	12.78%
6 Southwestern Bell	0.90	$61.78	$0.730	3	$2.96	4.80%	6.00%	10.99%	11.25%
7 U.S. West	0.90	$35.41	$0.520	0	$2.23	6.29%	7.00%	13.60%	13.94%
Average	0.85					5.76%	7.00%	13.03%	13.34%

procedures can be employed to estimate the growth in dividends expected by investors:

(1) historical growth of dividends or earnings per share

(2) security analysts' growth expectations

(3) sustainable growth method, with growth as the product of the expected retention ratio and the expected return on equity

In the case of PSI data in 1993, however, the application of these techniques was impaired. For example, a meaningful longer-term historical growth rate in dividends could not be computed because of the interruption of dividends following the Marble Hill nuclear plant cancellation and the resumption of dividends only in 1989. As another example, PSI's earnings per share over the previous 5 years were as follows:

1988	$2.41
1989	$2.32
1990	$2.20
1991	$1.97
1992	$1.60

The negative historical growth rates implied in those earnings figures are clearly not representative of future growth, as they are severely distorted by the Marble Hill incident and subsequent related events. PSI's 5-year historical growth rate was downward-biased by the impact of cessation and eventual resumption of dividends following the Marble Hill incident. Similar distortions apply to dividend payout and earned return on equity data. By the same token, prospective data may be distorted by the unrepresentative starting values for such data.

It was thus difficult and speculative to apply any of the growth estimating techniques directly to historical PSI data. More fundamentally, the basic assumptions of constant growth, constant ROE, and constant measures of financial performance that underlie the DCF model are likely to be violated in the case of PSI data.

Whenever the payout ratio of a company is expected to change, the intermediate growth rate in dividends is not equal to the long-term growth rate, because dividend/earnings growth must adjust to the changing payout ratio. The implementation of the standard DCF model to PSI was of questionable relevance in this circumstance.

Given that PSI is one of Moody's group of 24 electric common stocks, DCF analysis can be applied to a comparable group of companies consisting of the remaining 23 companies included in Moody's electric utility composite. The analysis proceeds in an identical manner to the DCF analyses presented in the various case studies presented at the beginning of the chapter. Because a cost of equity estimate from the Moody's group reflects the risk of the average electric utility and because PSI is riskier than average, a risk adjustment must be applied. This can be done with the beta-based risk differential technique described in the earlier case studies.

Use of Parent Company Data

In order to estimate a subsidiary's cost of equity using the DCF technique, one approach is to estimate the parent company's cost of equity based on market information. This is necessary for the DCF approach because the subsidiary's common stock has no separate market value and all new common equity for the subsidiary is frequently obtained by the parent company. As was seen earlier in the case studies, the parent company's cost of equity is then assigned to the subsidiary's equity component. If the subsidiary conducts its own debt and preferred stock financing, the parent cost of equity is combined with the subsidiary's individual debt and pre-ferred stock costs to arrive at a weighted average cost of capital. While this procedure accounts for the unique costs of the subsidiary's debt and preferred stock, it presumes the risk of the subsidiary to be similar to that of the consolidated parent company. If the subsidiary does not engage in any financing at all, the parent's consolidated weighted average cost of capital can be assigned to the subsidiary, again provided that the relative risks of the parent and subsidiary are similar. If the parent's risk differs from that of the subsidiary, risk adjustment techniques must be applied, as was seen in the case studies presented earlier.

In the case of an electric utility company that is a subsidiary of an electric utility parent holding company, it is usually reasonable to assume that the subsidiary's risk and therefore its cost of equity is not substantially different from that of the consolidated parent company. The subsidiary's cost of common equity is not likely to change materially, although it may be higher, if it is not part of the parent company system. As a large multi-unit company, the parent company enjoys greater diversification than its individual operating subsidiaries. In effect, risks are pooled, so the risk of the whole is less than the sum of the risks of the parts because of diversification. Moreover, holding companies may be able to operate on a more cost-effective basis by shifting energy resources in line with the relative supply-demand situation of the geographic areas of operation.

If the riskiness of all the subsidiaries in the system are the same, the assumption that a given subsidiary's risk, and therefore its cost of equity, is similar to that of the consolidated parent is viable. This condition can be verified by an empirical comparison of the relative bond ratings, coverage ratios, debt-to-equity ratios, and volatilities of book return on equity for each subsidiary in the group over the past decade. Such comparisons will reveal whether the subsidiary's risk is greater, the same, or less than the average of the consolidated parent company.

To verify whether this assumption is met, a more formal study of the risk-return relationship between utility holding companies and utility operating companies in general can be performed as follows. The risks and returns of a sample of operating electric power companies, not part of a holding complex, and those of a sample of holding companies can be compared using beta and standard deviation as risk measures and the standard DCF model as a measure of return. The results of such a comparison should reveal whether the holding company arrangement improves earnings and reduces risk, and whether the cost of capital for firms in the group are reduced by diversification.

Analyzing one particular holding company arrangement can clarify the risk comparability of a subsidiary and its parent company. To illustrate, Public Service Enterprises (PSE) can be seen as a portfolio of companies, including both regulated companies and unregulated companies. From a conceptual viewpoint, on a stand-alone basis, the regulated companies are probably slightly less risky than the unregulated portions of the portfolio. But as a practical matter, since the regulated operation, Public Service Electric & Gas (PSEG), still constitutes at this time the vast majority of PSE's activities and value, there is little distinction to be made between PSE and PSEG. The risk-return properties of the PSE portfolio are vastly dominated by the risk-return properties of the regulated operations component. Therefore, it is appropriate to assume that PSE derives its revenues predominantly from its regulated business, and is perceived by investors as an energy utility company.

As an additional practical matter, to the extent that equity investors in PSE stock are less than perfectly diversified, PSE's diversification activities actually reduce investor risk. Financial theory clearly states that portfolio diversification reduces risk for a given return if the components of the portfolio are less than perfectly correlated. As an added practical matter, the diversification activities of PSE may further reduce PSEG's risk through a co-insurance effect stemming from its subsidiary activities.

In short, if there is no quantifiable significant risk differential between PSE and PSEG at this time, then their respective costs of debt and equity capital are virtually indistinguishable from one another. To the extent that the aforementioned co-insurance effect exists, and to the extent that corporate diversification benefits investors rather than homemade individual diversification, ratepayers have benefited from PSEG's diversification efforts.

225

Bond Rating Approach

Another approach to salvage the DCF approach in the absence of investor-based market data is to apply the DCF model to a sample of utilities whose bond rating is similar to that of the utility in question, assuming that the subsidiary or company in question does in fact conduct its own debt financing and is rated by credit agencies. An example of this approach was actually provided in the case study discussed in the previous section where the second reference group of companies consisted of utilities whose bond rating matched that of Georgia Power. The assumption underlying this approach is that there is a one-to-one correspondence between a utility's equity risk and its debt risk. This is usually a plausible assumption as long as the proportion of preferred stock outstanding is comparable for each company in the reference group and that the regulatory risks confronted by each company in the group are similar, as revealed by regulatory climate rankings.

Bond Yield Spread Approach

In the absence of market data or in the case of clear violations of DCF assumptions, the following approach can be employed. First, the cost of equity is estimated for a group of typical utilities with the orthodox DCF method. Second, an appropriate risk increment is added to or subtracted from the equity return allowance, based on the bond and preferred yield relationships between the utility in question and the benchmark group of typical utilities. A case study will illustrate.

Case V: General Public Utilities

At the risk of oversimplification, the problem was to estimate the cost of equity in 1983 to The Metropolitan Edison Company and The Pennsylvania Electric Company, two subsidiaries of General Public Utilities, in the aftermath of the Three Mile Island nuclear accident in 1979. None of the growth estimating techniques in the DCF model was directly applicable as a result of the accident. Since no dividends had been paid from 1979 until 1983 and since past and current earnings were severely depressed, the extrapolation of historical dividend growth rates into the future was unreasonable, and the retention ratio method of estimating growth was inoperative as well. The paucity of analysts' earnings and dividends forecasts and the wide divergence of opinion among analysts in the few forecasts that were available underscored the uncertainty and unreliability of such forecasts. The assumptions of constant perpetual growth and constant payout ratio were clearly not met. The dividend forecasts required for implementation of the non-constant growth model were also unreliable.

Since any estimate based on General Public Utilities corporate data was unreliable, an indirect two-step procedure was used. First, the cost of common equity was derived for three barometer groups of companies: a group of 34 eastern electric utilities, a group of 7 electric utilities operating under comparable regulation, and a barometer group of industrial companies. This phase of the analysis proceeded in much the same way as in the earlier case example of The Southern Company. The average cost of equity figure for the three benchmark groups from all the DCF techniques was 16.75% at the time.

Secondly, an appropriate risk increment was added to the DCF equity return for the reference utility groups. The magnitude of the risk increment was based on the amount by which the yields on the senior securities of the General Public Utilities' operating companies exceeded those of the groups of electric utilities. To illustrate, Figure 8-1 shows the yield spreads between Standard & Poor's BBB Bond Average and Metropolitan Edison and Pennsylvania Electric bonds in graphical form for eleven months in 1982.

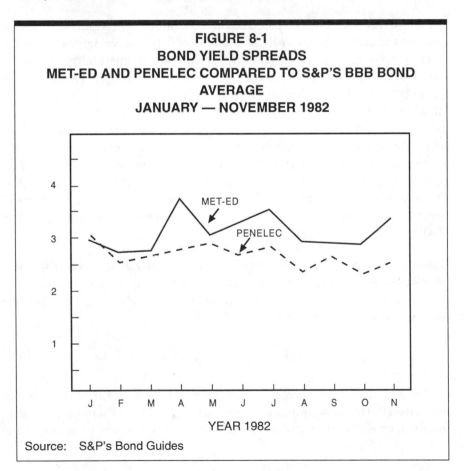

FIGURE 8-1
BOND YIELD SPREADS
MET-ED AND PENELEC COMPARED TO S&P'S BBB BOND AVERAGE
JANUARY — NOVEMBER 1982

YEAR 1982

Source: S&P's Bond Guides

227

Care must be taken to compare bonds with similar characteristics in regard to maturity, coupon, and callability. The bond yield spread fluctuated narrowly around 3% and 2.5% for the two companies respectively, with a current value of 2.5% and 2%. Similar patterns were uncovered for preferred stock yields. The 16.75% cost of capital estimate obtained by applying DCF to the reference groups was therefore conservatively adjusted upward by 2% and 1.5% to obtain Metropolitan Edison's and Pennsylvania Electric's cost of equity capital.

Cluster Analysis

Vander Weide (1993) developed an interesting approach to estimate the cost of equity of a company whose stock is not publicly traded. He applied the DCF method to a group of publicly traded companies comparable in risk to the company in question, and used the average DCF cost of equity for these companies as an estimate of equity costs.

Vander Weide selected the comparable companies on the basis of "closeness" to the company in question in terms of four risk variables: after-tax interest coverage, equity ratio, total capital, and predictability of operating income. After determining the location of each publicly traded firm on a graph whose coordinates are the four basic risk measures, he measures "closeness" by the length of a straight line between the point associated with the company in question and the points associated with each other firm. This measurement process is illustrated graphically on Figure 8-2 for two risk measures. Firm A has an interest coverage ratio of 3 and an equity ratio of 50%, and corresponds to point A on the graph. Firm A is closer to Firm B than to Firm C, despite its greater distance in terms of coverage alone. Vander Weide's measure of closeness considers the effect of all risk variables simultaneously.

Distance, or closeness, is measured mathematically as follows: If X and Y are two axes on a graph corresponding to two risk measures, and if there are two points on a graph with coordinates $(X1, Y1)$ and $(X2, Y2)$, then the distance between the two points is given by:

$$\sqrt{(X_2 - X_1)^2 + (Y_2 - Y_1)^2} \qquad (8\text{-}1)$$

If the X and Y axes corresponding to the two risk variables are not measured in the same units, it is necessary to convert them to a common measure using the standard deviation of the sample as scale factors. If the

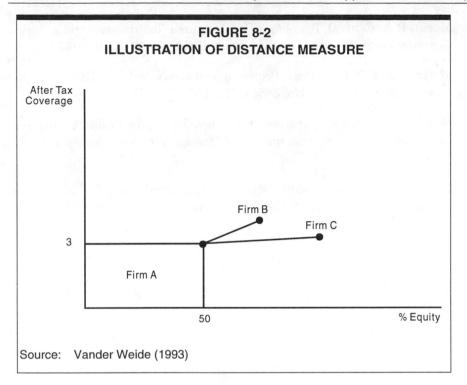

FIGURE 8-2
ILLUSTRATION OF DISTANCE MEASURE

Source: Vander Weide (1993)

X axis scale factor is S_1 and the Y axis scale factor is S_2, the distance formula becomes:

$$\sqrt{\frac{(X_1 - X_1)^2}{S_1^2} + \frac{(Y_2 - Y_1)^2}{S_2^2}} \qquad (8\text{-}2)$$

This process can be easily extended to include as many risk variables as desired. Vander Weide developed a comparable sample of firms by identifying publicly-traded firms that cluster closest to the company in question in terms of the four aforementioned risk variables on the basis of the distance measurement process described in Equation 8-2.

References

Morin, R.A. Georgia Power Company, Prepared Testimony, Georgia Public Service Commission, 1991.

Morin, R.A. Hope Gas Inc., Prepared Testimony, Public Service Commission of West Virginia, Case No. 91-025-G-42T, 1992A.

Morin, R.A. Central Telephone Co., Prepared Testimony, Public Service Commission of Nevada, Docket Nos. 92-7069 and 92-7070, 1992B.

Morin, R.A. PSI Resources, Prepared Testimony, Indiana Utility Regulatory Commission, Case No. 38584-S1, 1993.

Myers, S. C. "The Application of Finance Theory to Public Utility Rate Case." *Bell Journal of Economics and Management Science,* Spring 1972, 58-97.

Vander Weide, J.H. Pacific Bell, Prepared Testimony, Public Utilities Commission of the State of California, Docket No. 92-05-004, 1993.

Chapter 9
Reflections on Cost of Capital Methodology

9.1 Sole Reliance on the DCF Methodology

While the DCF model is presently fashionable in regulatory proceedings, although not nearly as much in financial theory circles, uncritical acceptance of the standard DCF equation vests the model with a degree of accuracy that simply is not there. One of the leading experts on regulation, Dr. C. F. Phillips discussed the dangers of relying on the DCF model:

> [U]se of the DCF model for regulatory purposes involves both theoretical and practical difficulties. The theoretical issues include the assumption of a constant retention ratio (i.e., a fixed payout ratio) and the assumption that dividends will continue to grow at a rate g in perpetuity. Neither of these assumptions has any validity, particularly in recent years. Further, the investors' capitalization rate and the cost of equity capital to a utility for application to book value (i.e., an original cost rate base) are identical only when market price is equal to book value. Indeed, DCF advocates assume that if the market price of a utility's common stock exceeds its book value, the allowable rate of return on common equity is too high and should be lowered; and vice versa. Many question the assumption that market price should equal book value, believing that the earnings of utilities should be sufficiently high to achieve market-to-book ratios which are consistent with those prevailing for stocks of unregulated companies.
>
> . . . [T]here remains the circularity problem: Since regulation establishes a level of authorized earnings which, in turn, implicitly influences dividends per share, estimation of the growth rate from such data is an inherently circular process. For all of these reasons, the DCF model suggests a degree of precision which is in fact not present' and leaves 'wide room for controversy about the level of k [cost of equity].[1]

Sole reliance on the DCF model ignores the capital market evidence and financial theory formalized in the CAPM and other risk premium methods. The DCF model is one of many tools to be employed in conjunction

---

[1] See Phillips (1993), pp. 395-96.

with other methods to estimate the cost of equity. It is not a superior methodology that supplants other financial theory and market evidence. The broad usage of the DCF methodology in regulatory proceedings does not make it superior to other methods.

9.2 Reservations on DCF

Notwithstanding the fundamental thesis that several methods and/or variants of such methods should be used in measuring equity costs, the DCF methodology can be particularly fragile in a given capital market environment. Two reservations concerning the application of the DCF method are in order. The first reservation concerns the applicability of the DCF model to utility stocks in general at this time in the current capital market environment. The second reservation concerns the estimation of the expected growth component required by the DCF model.

Applicability of the DCF Model

Caution has to be used in applying the DCF model to utility stocks for three reasons. The first reason is that the stock price used as input in the dividend yield component may be unduly influenced by structural changes and changing investor expectations in the utility industry. Stock prices can also be influenced by mergers and acquisitions possibilities, by speculation concerning asset restructurings and deregulation of certain assets, and by corporate takeover rumors.

The second reason is that the traditional DCF model is based on a number of assumptions, some of which are unrealistic in a given capital market environment. For example, the standard infinite growth DCF model assumes a constant market valuation multiple, that is, a constant price/earnings (P/E) ratio. In other words, the model assumes that investors expect the ratio of market price to dividends (or earnings) in any given year to be the same as the current price/dividend (or earnings) ratio. This must be true if the infinite growth assumption is made. This is somewhat unrealistic under current conditions. The DCF model is not equipped to deal with sudden surges in market-to-book (M/B) and price/earnings (P/E) ratios, as was experienced by several utility stocks in recent years. Figures 9-1A and 9-1B show the volatile behavior of price/earnings and market-to-book ratios for gas distribution utility stocks in the last 10 years.

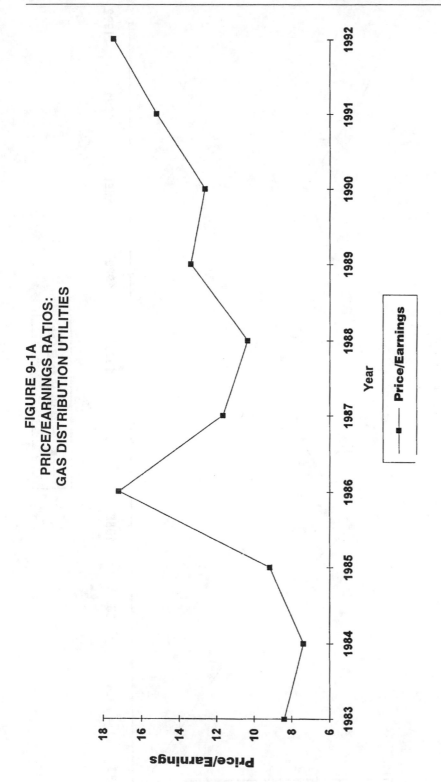

FIGURE 9-1A
PRICE/EARNINGS RATIOS:
GAS DISTRIBUTION UTILITIES

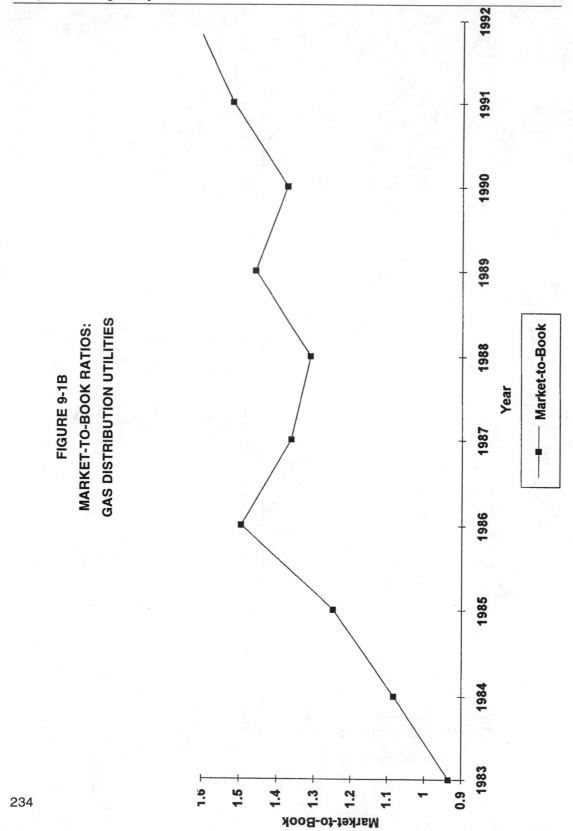

FIGURE 9-1B
MARKET-TO-BOOK RATIOS:
GAS DISTRIBUTION UTILITIES

The equity market's behavior in the 1980s and early 1990s, particularly after 1986, does not comport well with the assumptions of the basic standard DCF model. Several fundamental and structural changes have transformed the utility industry from the times when the standard DCF model and its assumptions were developed by Professor Gordon. Increased competition triggered by national policy, such as the divestiture of AT&T, FERC Order 636, the new Energy Act, accounting rule changes, representation of capital recovery rates, changes in customer attitudes regarding utility services, the evolution of alternative energy and information sources, deregulation, and mergers-acquisitions have all influenced stock prices in ways vastly different from the early assumptions of the DCF model. These changes suggest that some of the raw assumptions underlying the standard DCF model are questionable, and that the DCF model should be at least complemented by alternate methodologies to estimate the cost of common equity.

Contrary to the standard DCF assumption of a constant price/earnings ratio, stock price may not necessarily be expected to grow at the same rate as earnings and dividends by investors. This is especially true in the short run. Investors may very well assume that the price/earnings ratio will in fact continue to increase in the short run, fueling the expected rate of return. The converse is also true. Price/earnings ratios have proved volatile and unstable in recent years. The essential point is that the constancy of the price/earnings ratio required in the standard DCF model may not always be a valid assumption. To the extent that increases (decreases) in relative market valuation are anticipated by investors, especially myopic investors with short-term investment horizons, the standard DCF model will understate (overstate) the cost of equity.

Another way of stating the same point is that the DCF model does not account for the ebb and flow of investor sentiments over the course of the business cycle. The problem was particularly acute in the early 1990s where investors, faced with very low returns on short-term fixed-income securities and an uncertain market outlook, sought the higher yields offered by utility stocks in a so-called flight to quality, boosting their stock price and lowering their dividend yield.

The effect of erratic market valuation multiples on the DCF model can be illustrated with the following example. Assume that a utility's stock is trading at $100. Assume further that its earnings per share are expected to be $8.00 for the current year, and are expected to grow at 10% per year in the future. Finally, assume that the company pays out one-half of its earnings as dividends. If the stock is initially trading at 12.5 times earnings, the dividend yield is 4%. If investors do not expect the price/earnings ratio of 12.5 to change in the next year, the estimated expected return from holding the stock for one year using the standard DCF model is as follows: a dividend yield of 4%, plus growth in value (stock price) from $100 to $110, or 10%, for a total return of 14%. The ending stock price is $110, that is, 12.5 times next year's earnings of $8.80.

But what if investors expect an increase in the price/earnings ratio from 12.5 to 13.0? Then, the growth in value is from $100 to $114.40, or 13.0 times next year's earnings of $8.80, for a total return of 18.40% (dividend yield of 4%, plus growth in value of 14.40%). The orthodox DCF model would indicate returns of 14%, whereas the investors' true expected return is 18.4%. Investor expected returns are substantially understated whenever investors anticipate increases in relative market valuation, and conversely.

The third reason for caution and skepticism is that application of the DCF model produces estimates of common equity cost that are consistent with investors' expected return only when stock price and book value are reasonably similar, that is, when the M/B is close to unity. As shown below, application of the standard DCF model to utility stocks understates the investor's expected return when the market-to-book ratio of a given stock exceeds unity. This is particularly relevant in the capital market environment of the 1990s where utility stocks are trading at M/B ratios well above unity. The converse is also true, that is, the DCF model overstates the investor's return when the stock's M/B ratio is less than unity. The reason for the distortion is that the DCF market return is applied to a book value rate base by the regulator, that is, a utility's earnings are limited to earnings on a book value rate base.

The simple numerical illustration shown in Table 9-1 below demonstrates the impact of market-to-book ratios on the DCF market return. The example shows the result of applying a market value cost rate to book value rate base under three different M/B scenarios. The three columns correspond to three M/B situations: the stock trades below, equal to, and above book value, respectively. The latter situation is noteworthy and representative of the current capital market environment. The DCF cost rate of 10%, made up of a 5% dividend yield and a 5% growth rate, is applied to the book value rate base of $50 to produce $5.00 of earnings. Of the $5.00 of earnings, the full $5.00 are required for dividends to produce a dividend yield of 5% on a stock price of $100.00, and no dollars are available for growth. The investor's return is therefore only 5% versus his required return of 10%. A DCF cost rate of 10%, which implies $10.00 of earnings, translates to only $5.00 of earnings on book value, or a 5% return. The situation is reversed in the first column when the stock trades below book value. The $5.00 of earnings are more than enough to satisfy the investor's dividend requirements of $1.25, leaving $3.75 for growth, for a total return of 20%. This is because the DCF cost rate is applied to a book value rate base well above the market price. Therefore, the DCF cost rate understates the investor's required return when stock prices are well above book, as is the case presently.

TABLE 9-1
EFFECT OF MARKET-TO-BOOK RATIO ON MARKET RETURN

	Situation 1	Situation 2	Situation 3
1 Initial purchase price	$25.00	$50.00	$100.00
2 Initial book value	$50.00	$50.00	$50.00
3 Initial M/B	0.50	1.00	2.00
4 DCF Return 10% = 5% + 5%	10.00%	10.00%	10.00%
5 Dollar Return	$ 5.00	$ 5.00	$ 5.00
6 Dollar Dividends 5% Yield	$ 1.25	$ 2.50	$ 5.00
7 Dollar Growth 5% Growth	$ 3.75	$ 2.50	$ 0.00
8 Market Return	20.00%	10.00%	5.00%

The DCF Growth Component

A second concern deals with the realism of the constant growth rate assumption and with the difficulty of finding an adequate proxy for that growth rate. The standard DCF model assumes that a single growth rate of dividends is applicable in perpetuity. Not only is the constant growth rate assumption somewhat unrealistic, but it is difficult to proxy. Analysts' growth forecasts are usually made for not more than 2 to 5 years, or if they are made for more than a few years, they are dominated by the near-term earnings and dividends picture. In short, the perpetual growth term of the DCF model does not square well with the shorter-term focus of institutional investors.

A note of caution is also necessary when dealing with historical growth rates and their use in the DCF model. Historical growth rates can be downward-biased by the impact of diversification and restructuring activities and by the impact of abnormal weather patterns in the case of energy utilities. Acquisitions, start-up expenses, and front-end capital investments associated with diversification and restructuring efforts, and unfavorable weather patterns can retard and dilute historical earnings growth, and such growth is not representative of a company's long-term growth potential. Therefore, caution must be exercised when applying any of the growth estimating techniques directly to recent historical utility company data.

Given a dramatic change in a utility's operating environment, the need to be forward-looking is apparent. Historically-based measures of risk and growth can be downward-biased in assessing present circumstances. This type of bias certainly applied to telephone stocks following the divestiture of AT&T in 1984, and certainly apply to gas distribution utilities following the FERC's Order 636 in 1993. The fundamental risks and growth prospects of electric utilities are also changing rapidly following the passage of the Energy Bill in 1993. These shifts in growth prospects take some time before they are fully reflected in the historical growth rates. Hence, backward-looking growth and statistical analysis may fail to fully reflect the fact that the risks and growth prospects of utilities have escalated, and may only provide limited evidence that the risk and the cost of capital to these utilities have increased. Of course, the converse may also be true under certain circumstances.

Also, there is an element of logical circularity inherent in the growth component of the DCF model. The cost of equity capital depends in part on anticipated regulatory action, since both components of the cost of equity, dividend yield and growth, are influenced by the regulatory process. One solution to this potential predicament is to employ other market-based techniques, such as the CAPM, that examine market data not directly related to the firm's financial statistics. Another solution is to examine the DCF returns for comparable risk industrial stocks.

In summary, caution and judgment are required in interpreting the results of the DCF model because of (1) the questionable applicability of the DCF model to utility stocks in certain capital market environments, (2) the effect of declining earnings and dividends on financial inputs to the DCF model and biases caused by the effect of changes in risk and growth, and (3) the conceptual and practical difficulties associated with the growth component of the DCF model. Hence, there is a clear need to go beyond, to the results produced by alternate methodologies.

9.3 Use of Multiple Methods

When measuring equity costs, which essentially deal with the measurement of investor expectations, no one single methodology provides a foolproof panacea. If the cost of equity estimation process is limited to one methodology, such as DCF, it may severely bias the results. One major problem that results from using only one methodology is the lack of corroborating evidence. There is simply no objective cross check on the result. All the market data and financial theory available at the time should be used in making an estimate.

There are four broad generic methodologies available to measure the cost of equity: DCF, Risk Premium, and Capital Asset Pricing Model (CAPM), which are market-oriented, and Comparable Earnings, which is accounting-oriented. Each generic market-based methodology in turn contains several variants: For example, the Empirical CAPM and Arbitrage Pricing Model are sub-species of the CAPM methodology.

Each methodology requires the exercise of considerable judgment on the reasonableness of the assumptions underlying the methodology and on the reasonableness of the proxies used to validate the theory. The failure of the traditional infinite growth DCF model to account for changes in relative market valuation, discussed above, is a vivid example of the potential shortcomings of the DCF model when applied to a given company. It follows that more than one methodology should be employed in arriving at a judgment on the cost of equity and that these methodologies should be applied across a series of comparable risk companies.

There is no single model that conclusively determines or estimates the expected return for an individual firm. Each methodology possesses its own way of examining investor behavior, its own premises, and its own set of simplifications of reality. Each method proceeds from different fundamental premises that cannot be validated empirically. Investors do not necessarily subscribe to any one method, nor does the stock price reflect the application of any one single method by the price-setting investor. There is no monopoly as to which method is used by investors. In the absence of any hard evidence as to which method outdoes the other, all relevant evidence should be used and weighted equally, in order to minimize judgmental error, measurement error, and conceptual infirmities. A regulator should rely on the results of a variety of methods applied to a variety of comparable groups, and not on one particular method. There is no guarantee that a single DCF result is necessarily the ideal predictor of the stock price and of the cost of equity reflected in that price, just as there is no guarantee that a single CAPM or Risk Premium result constitutes the perfect explanation of that stock price.

If a regulatory commission relies solely on a single cost of equity estimate, the commission greatly limits its flexibility and increases the risk of authorizing unreasonable rates of return. The results from a one-company sample are likely to contain a high degree of measurement error and may be distorted by short-term aberrations. The commission's hands should not be bound to one single company-specific estimate of equity costs, nor should the commission ignore relevant evidence and back itself into a corner.

Financial literature supports the use of multiple methods. Professor Eugene Brigham, a widely respected scholar and finance academician, asserted:

> In practical work, it is often best to use all three methods—CAPM, bond yield plus risk premium, and DCF—and then apply judgement when the methods produce different results. People experienced in estimating capital costs recognize that both careful analysis and some very fine judgements are required. It would be nice to pretend that these judgements are

unnecessary and to specify an easy, precise way of determining the exact cost of equity capital. Unfortunately, this is not possible.[2]

Another prominent finance scholar, Professor Stewart Myers, in his best-selling corporate finance textbook, stated:

> The constant growth formula and the capital asset pricing model are two different ways of getting a handle on the same problem.[3]

In an earlier article, Professor Myers explained the point more fully:

> Use more than one model when you can. Because estimating the opportunity cost of capital is difficult, only a fool throws away useful information. That means you should not use any one model or measure mechanically and exclusively. Beta is helpful as one tool in a kit, to be used in parallel with DCF models or other techniques for interpreting capital market data.[4]

9.4 Financial Integrity and DCF

According to the seminal standards underlying the notion of fair return, as laid down in the landmark *Hope* and *Bluefield* cases, the return allowed by the regulator must be such as (1) to permit the utility to attract capital and maintain integrity, and (2) to be comparable with returns on similar risk investments.

It is transparent that return on equity and interest coverage, which is a pivotal standard used by capital markets with respect to the attraction of debt capital, are related. A return on equity that produces inadequate interest coverages, endangers debt capital attraction. If the coverage implied by a recommended return on equity is below current bond rating benchmarks, then an anemic coverage would almost guarantee a further downgrading of a company's bonds, particularly if coverages were already marginal. This can be further damaging if the company is pursuing a substantial construction expenditure program and requires external financing in a volatile and quality-conscious capital market. If the coverage ratio implied by any cost of equity estimate is well outside that of its peers, then this should attest to the inadequacy of the estimate. As a result, existing bondholders would be inflicted a capital loss, and the cost

---

[2] See Brigham and Gapenski (1991), p. 256.
[3] See Brealey and Myers (1991), p. 182.
[4] See Myers (1978), p. 67.

of capital, hence ratepayer burden, would increase. This is in direct violation of the fundamental doctrine of capital attraction and financial integrity promulgated by the landmark *Hope* and *Bluefield* cases.

The essence and the ultimate test of the validity of a rate of return estimate is whether it will permit the company to attract capital on reasonable terms and maintain the company's financial integrity.

There are many dimensions and factors that determine a utility's financial integrity. The notion of integrity is fluid and encompasses several considerations, and no one single measure can capture the adequacy of integrity. The return on equity should certainly be designed at a minimum to keep the stock price at competitive levels. The return should also be high enough to produce coverages consistent with an optimal bond rating.

Both capital attraction and financial integrity standards must be fulfilled in determining a fair rate of return. Despite a deterioration in credit standing, a utility may be able to attract capital temporarily, but at prohibitive costs and under unfavorable terms. Eventually, the utility will face capital funds rationing and/or the costs of financing will become prohibitive, and the utility will no longer be able to attract capital at a reasonable price.

To assess the reasonableness of the allowed return on equity, the coverage ratio that results from a given allowed equity return can be computed and compared to norms of reasonableness. The coverage ratio measures the ability of a firm's earnings to meet its fixed obligations, and is an important determinant of creditworthiness scrutinized by bond rating agencies and by the investment community. The simplest calculation of coverage is the interest coverage based on pre-tax operating income, calculated as follows:

$$\frac{\text{Pre–tax operating income}}{\text{Interest charges}}$$

The calculation excludes AFUDC, which is a non-cash item, and other income. An equivalent formulation is the traditional and widely used times interest earned ratio (TIE), calculated as:

$$TIE = \frac{\text{Profit before Taxes} + \text{Interest Charges}}{\text{Interest Charges}}$$

Another variant is to include AFUDC income and miscellaneous income in the numerator of the ratio. The formula for the so-called Securities Exchange Commission (SEC) coverage, which is used in bond prospectuses approved by the SEC, is obtained by including not only AFUDC and miscellaneous income but also the interest component of leasing payments in the numerator, and by including the latter charges in the denominator as part of the financial burden to be covered. Sometimes, depreciation charges are added in the numerator to produce a cash income coverage.

To verify the reasonableness of the estimated equity return, the coverage implied by the latter is calculated, and compared to a benchmark target ratio, such as the median ratio for utilities in a similar bond rating category. Table 9-2 illustrates the calculation of the TIE ratio that would obtain using the utility's projected embedded costs of debt and preferred stock, projected capital structure, and a tax rate of 50%, and a series of allowed return on equity values. The calculations are based on idealized circumstances, and assume that all reported income can be used to meet the coverage requirements, that interest is the only fixed charge to be covered, and that rate base equals total invested capital. The equation used to calculate TIE is:

$$TIE = \frac{W_d K_d + W_p K_p / (1 - T) + W_e K_e / (1 - T)}{W_d K_d} \qquad (9\text{-}1)$$

where W_d, W_p, and W_e represent the percentage of debt, preferred, and common stock in the capital structure; K_d, K_p, and K_e are the embedded cost of debt and preferred and the cost of common equity; and T is the tax rate.

Not only does the coverage ratio serve as a useful check on the reasonableness of an estimate of equity cost, but it also forms the basis for estimating the cost of equity for publicly-owned utilities subject to rate regulation. For several water utilities and municipally-owned electric utilities, there are two approaches used to calculate the allowed return on common equity capital. One approach is the "stand alone" approach, whereby the cost of equity of comparable privately-owned utilities is applied, based on cost of equity estimates for private companies of equivalent bond and stock ratings. The rationale for this method is that from the point of view of efficient economic pricing, the rate of return on equity for publicly-owned utilities should essentially be the same, on a risk adjusted basis, as the rate of return on equity for privately-owned utilities.

TABLE 9-2
COVERAGE RATIOS AT VARIOUS RETURNS ON COMMON EQUITY

GIVEN CAPITAL STRUCTURE

Source	% of Capital		% Cost		Weighted Cost
Debt	50%	x	10%	=	5.0%
Preferred	10%	x	12%	=	1.2%
Equity	40%	x	K_e		

K_e	TIE
18.0%	4.36
17.5%	4.28
17.0%	4.20
16.5%	4.12
16.0%	4.04
15.5%	3.96
14.5%	3.88
14.0%	3.72

Illustration of calculation where $K_e = 16\%$:

$$TIE = \frac{.50\,(10.0) + .10\,(12.0)/1 - .50 + .40\,(16.0)/1 - .50}{.50\,(10.0)}$$

$$= 4.04$$

Otherwise, the ratepayers-owners of publicly-owned utilities would be better off if all earnings were paid out to them in the form of lower taxes so that they could reinvest the savings in other enterprises of similar risk. Moreover, the standards of *Hope* and *Bluefield* were articulated without reference to the ownership of the utility, so that the use of capital attraction and financial integrity standards as a starting point for analyzing the fair return to publicly-owned utilities is consistent with *Hope* and *Bluefield*. Another approach is to set the allowed return on equity so as to produce a coverage ratio that will allow the utility to maintain its integrity and to attract capital on reasonable terms. The coverage ratios of other publicly-owned utilities or of non-regulated entities of the same quality can be used as benchmarks. Copan (1983) provides a good description of coverage ratios as measures of publicly-owned firms' revenue requirements.

9.5 Judgment and the DCF Method

It is clear from the material of the four chapters that have dealt with the DCF method that the permutations and combinations of estimates based on alternate time periods, measures, companies, models, and statistical methodology are unbounded. The only solid generalization about DCF is that the final cost of equity recommendation is a judgment based on a wide variety of data and techniques. The important point is that judgmental estimates of equity cost rest on sound factual economic logic. Plausible and defensible DCF estimates within a narrow range can be developed, provided the tools of this and previous chapters are used intelligently and objectively.

The DCF method cannot be applied in a robotic, mechanistic manner. Mechanical approaches designed to simply insert numbers into an algebraic equation without regard to the reasonableness of such inputs in a regulatory setting must be avoided. For example, the determination of expected growth is judgmental, since expected growth lies buried in the minds of investors, unobservable. Any inconsistency between historically-based growth estimates, analysts' growth forecasts, and sustainable growth estimates should be explainable by objective common-sense economic reasoning. The tools described in the previous DCF chapters provide diagnostic guides and calculating aids only. The vast arsenal of techniques described apply differently to different companies, or differently to the same company at different times. Each rate case possesses different circumstances. More than one cost of equity capital estimating technique must be consulted.

Capital markets are highly volatile and uncertain. The determination of cost of capital should thus take a more accommodating and flexible stance and should resist the temptation of simply inserting today's numbers into an algebraic equation without regard to the purpose of the exercise. Given that rates set by regulators are likely to remain in effect for several years, the allowed rate of return should reflect this circumstance and should not reflect day-to-day fluctuations in interest rates and current spot circumstances. In the early 1980s when long-term interest rates were extraordinarily high, when DCF—Risk Premium—CAPM results were accordingly high, allowed rates of return were not set correspondingly, but rather were set at a lower level so as to keep a longer-term perspective. The same rationale should prevail when interest rates are low.

The need to broaden the sample and extend the analysis to include comparable risk firms is evident in order to verify the reasonableness of the single company estimate and to abide with the spirit of the *Hope-Bluefield* doctrines. Referencing data on other utilities and other unregulated companies will mitigate the circularity problem as well. Other cost of capital estimation techniques must be employed as an additional check on the reliability and reasonableness of the DCF estimate. These methods are the subject of subsequent chapters.

Several complications in estimating the cost of equity are discussed in later chapters, such as the impact of capital structure and dividend policy. It is important to keep in mind that the DCF model does not explicitly supply any evidence as to what the cost of equity would be under different circumstances, such as a different capital structure. The DCF model produces a cost of equity estimate predicated on current conditions. Alternate conditions may produce higher or lower growth rates, hence different equity cost estimates, depending on investor reaction to the change in conditions as manifested by the market price.

References

Brealey, R. and Myers, S. *Principles of Corporate Finance,* 4th. ed. New York: McGraw-Hill, 1991.

Brigham, E.F. and Gapenski, L.C. *Financial Management: Theory and Practice,* 6th ed. Hinsdale IL: Dryden Press, 1991.

Copan, J.A. "Debt Coverage as a Measure of a Firm's Revenue Requirements." *Public Utilities Fortnightly,* August 18, 1983, 27-33.

Myers, S. C. "On the Use of Modern Portfolio Theory in Public Utility Rate Cases: Comment." *Financial Management,* Autumn 1978, 66-68.

Phillips, C.F. *The Regulation of Public Utilities: Theory and Practice,* Arlington VA: Public Utilities Reports Inc., 1993.

Additional References

Whittaker. W. and Sefton, R. "The DCF Methodology: A Fair Return in Today's Market?" *Public Utilities Fortnightly,* July 9, 1987, 16-20.

Chapter 10
Market-to-Book and Q-Ratios

This chapter discusses the Market-to-Book (M/B) Ratio and its relationship with the cost of capital. Section 10.1 establishes the formal relationship between the allowed return on equity, the cost of equity, and the M/B ratio. Section 10.2 demonstrates how the DCF cost of equity figure can be theoretically transformed into an appropriate allowed return on equity, based on a target M/B ratio. The importance of maintaining an M/B slightly in excess of 1.0 is underscored. Section 10.3 discusses the estimation of cost of equity capital based on the multivariate statistical analysis of the determinants of M/B ratios. Section 10.4 describes the Q-Ratio approach to determining the cost of equity capital. Section 10.5 critically evaluates the role of M/B ratios in regulation and concludes that regulators should largely remain unconcerned with such ratios because they are determined by exogenous market forces and are outside the direct control of regulators. M/B ratios are largely the end result of the regulatory process itself rather than its starting point.

In Chapter 1, it was suggested that if regulators set the allowed rate of return equal to the cost of capital, the utility's earnings will be just sufficient to cover the claims of the bondholders and shareholders. No wealth transfer between ratepayers and shareholders will occur.

The direct financial consequence of setting the allowed return on equity, r, equal to the cost of equity capital, K, is that share price is driven toward book value per share. Intuitively, if $r > K$, and is expected to remain so, then market price will exceed book value per share since shareholders are obtaining a return in excess of their opportunity cost. But if $r < K$, and is expected to remain so, market price will be below book value per share since the utility is failing to achieve its opportunity cost. A simple idealized example will illustrate this important point.

EXAMPLE 10-1

Consider a utility with a book value of equity per share of $10, and let us say that the market's required return on equity is 12% for firms in that risk class. If the $10 book value of equity is allowed to earn $1.20 per share, or 12%, the market price will set at $10, since the market's required return at that price will be also $1.20/$10, or 12%. If, on the other hand, the $10 book equity per share is allowed to earn say only 6%, the market price has to fall to $5.00 in order for the market's required return to be 12%, that is, $0.60/$5, or 12%.

10.1 The M/B Ratio and the Cost of Capital in Theory

The theoretical relationship between r, K, and M/B can be demonstrated by a simple manipulation of the standard DCF equation. Starting from the seminal DCF model:

$$P_0 = \frac{D_1}{K - g} \qquad (10\text{-}1)$$

and expressing next year's dividend, D_1, as next year's earnings per share, E_1, times the earnings payout ratio, $1 - b$, we have:

$$D_1 = (1 - b) E_1 \qquad (10\text{-}2)$$

Substituting the latter equation into Equation 10-1:

$$P_0 = \frac{E_1 (1 - b)}{K - g} \qquad (10\text{-}3)$$

But next year's earnings per share, E_1, are equal to the expected rate of return on equity, r, times the book value of equity per share, B, at the end of the current year:

$$E_1 = rB \qquad (10\text{-}4)$$

Substituting Equation 10-4 in Equation 10-3:

$$P_0 = \frac{r B (1 - b)}{K - g} \qquad (10\text{-}5)$$

Dividing both sides of the equation by B, and noting that $g = br$:

$$P_0/B = \frac{r(1 - b)}{K - br} = \frac{r - br}{K - br} \qquad (10\text{-}6)$$

From Equation 10-6, it is clear that the market-to-book, or P_0/B, will be unity if $r = K$, greater than unity if $r > K$, and less than unity if $r < K$:

$$M/B \;\; \overset{>}{\underset{<}{=}} \;\; 1.0 \text{ as } r \;\; \overset{>}{\underset{>}{=}} \;\; K$$

Solving Equation 10-6 for K, a basic measure of cost of equity adjusted for the prevailing M/B ratio can be obtained:

$$K = \frac{r(1-b)}{M/B} + br \qquad \qquad (10\text{-}7)$$

In words, Equation 10-7 demonstrates that finding a cost of equity that is reconcilable to the book return on common equity requires that the latter be increased or decreased by the M/B ratio in proportion to the fraction of income distributed as dividends. Equation 10-7 provides a method of finding the cost of equity capital that is consistent with the observed M/B ratio.

EXAMPLE 10-2

The market value of a utility's common stock has fallen to 75% of its book value. Realized return on book equity expected by investors is 15%. Earnings are divided evenly between dividends and retentions.

$$b = .50 = (1 - b)$$

$$r = .15$$

The cost of common equity reconcilable with the observed M/B ratio is:

$$K - \frac{r(1-b)}{M/B} + br$$

$$= \frac{.15 \times .50}{.75} + (.50 \times .15)$$

$$= .10 + .075$$

$$= .175 \; or \; 17.5\%$$

Several cautions are in order. First, the expected return on book equity rather than the currently allowed return on equity must be used, because the M/B ratio is determined by what investors expect regulators to do, and not by what the regulators did in the past. A serious circularity problem arises if the current allowed return on equity is used because the numerator of the M/B ratio is stock price, which reflects the expected allowed return and not the currently allowed return.

Second, while straightforward application of the DCF approach will theoretically drive share price toward book value per share, it must also be true that the utility can actually be expected to earn the rate set for regulatory purposes. Several factors can cause the utility to earn more or less than is nominally allowed. Delay in instituting new regulatory proceedings, or regulatory lag, can cause the utility to earn more or less than is prescribed. If cost trends deviate from expectations in the case of a forward test year jurisdiction, or if unexpected future changes in cost and output levels occur, regulatory lag will cause the utility to earn more or less than is allowed.

Third, other external factors impinge on the M/B. Diversification into non-regulated fields may cause the ratio to deviate from 1.0, even though the profitability of the regulated portion is restricted. Even if all the firm's activities are regulated, if assets are excluded from rate base, or if Construction Work in Progress (CWIP) does not appear in rate base and no Allowance for Funds Used During Construction (AFUDC) is allowed on CWIP, rate base will not equal net book value, and the M/B will not equal 1.0.

Fourth, in an inflationary period, the replacement cost of a firm's assets may increase more rapidly than its book equity. To avoid the resulting economic confiscation of shareholders' investment in real terms, the allowed rate of return should produce a M/B ratio that exceeds 1.0, as the subsequent section on Q-ratios will demonstrate.

10.2 Target Market-to-Book Ratios and the Cost of Equity

The previous section developed a method of estimating the cost of equity based on observed M/B ratios. The process can be reversed. This section demonstrates how the cost of equity figure obtained from standard DCF can be translated into an appropriate allowed rate of return on book equity to take into account any sanctioned difference between market price and book value. The magnitude of the adjustment will depend on the choice of target M/B ratio. The technique is labeled the Target Market-to-Book Method.

At least two arguments can be made to the effect that allowed rates of return on book equity should be sufficient to sustain a given market price. First, continued access to the equity capital market requires a market price at, or somewhat above, book value to insure salability of new equity issues. The costs of floating common stock, including the underwriter spread, market pressure, and allowance for market break, have been ignored thus far. The nature and magnitude of issue costs were treated in Chapter 6. To enable a company to attract capital on terms that do not dilute the value of existing shares, the market price must be sufficiently above book value so that the net proceeds after costs of issue from the sale of new stock are greater than book value. The return allowed by the regulator should be such that neither confiscation of old equity nor dilution of new equity occurs.

Second, if the goal of regulation is viewed as duplicating the result that would be obtained in an unregulated competitive environment, this requires a market-to-book premium similar to that which prevails for unregulated firms. This will be discussed further in the Q-ratio section of the chapter.

Capital Attraction and Market-to-Book Ratios

A strong case can be made for a market price at least equal to book value. One of the fundamental indicators of a utility's financial integrity is the ability to raise equity capital under favorable conditions. This is especially crucial in the case of public utilities whose needs for external equity are frequent, inflexible, and large. It is a well known fact noted by several finance scholars that if a company sells stock for less than book value, the book value of the previously outstanding shares will be diluted, and so will the earnings per share, dividends per share, and earnings growth. Moreover, it becomes increasingly difficult to distribute the same dollar dividends on an increased number of shares outstanding, and investors will become increasingly reticent in accepting any further stock issues.

The following numerical example illustrates the adverse consequences for both ratepayers and stockholders of selling stock below book value.

EXAMPLE 10-3

Consider a utility with $500 of plant investments, all equity financed, with 20 common shares outstanding. The book value per share is therefore $500/20, or $25. The allowed rate of return is 10%, and the market's required return is 20%.

Earnings will total 10% x $500 = $50, and earnings per share will be $50/20 = $2.50. The stock price is therefore $2.50/.20 = $12.50, or half of the book value per share since the allowed return is one half of the required return. The M/B ratio is $12.50/$25.00 = .50.

What happens if the utility requires an additional $500 of assets to be financed by a $500 stock issue with each share selling for $12.50? The company is allowed to earn an additional $50 on this incremental investment (.10 x $500), for a total earnings figure of $100. To finance an amount of $500 at $12.50 per share requires the issuance of 40 additional shares, bringing the total number of shares from 20 to 60. Earnings per share decline to $100/60 = $1.67, and the price of each share drops to $1.67/.20 = $8.35 in order for shareholders to continue earning 20%. The book value per share drops from $25 to $1000/60 = $16.67. Summarizing the results in tabular form:

	Before	After
Equity capital	$500	$1000
Number of shares	20	60
Book value per share	$25	$16.67
Earnings (10% of equity)	$50	$100
Earnings per share	$2.50	$1.67
Market price (20% return)	$12.50	$8.35
Market-to-book ratio	.50	.50

Therefore, sale of stock when the M/B ratio is less than 1.0 dilutes the share in ownership of the original holders of the 20 shares. The book value for each share they own declines from $25 to $16.67, since the new equity capital base is now divided among 60 shares. The market price drops by 33% as a consequence of the equity dilution.

The above example does not imply that utilities cannot, in fact, raise capital when share prices are below book value, but that they can only do so at the expense of existing shareholders. When expected earnings are less than investors' requirements and a sale of stock occurs, new shareholders can only expect to gain their return requirement at the expense of the old shareholders. The market recognizes the potential dilution impact and reprices the shares downward as protection of the required return. A regulatory policy of setting the allowed return so as to obtain a M/B ratio of at least 1.0 avoids such deliberate economic confiscation and abides by the financial integrity criterion of the *Hope* case and the financial soundness criterion of the *Bluefield* case. Such a policy is also in the interests of ratepayers. Systematic dilution of equity imposed on shareholders, because of deficient earnings, endangers the success of the next stock issue. Investor uncertainties are raised as to whether reasonable earnings will be allowed are raised, thereby increasing the cost of debt and equity.

Adjustment for Target Market-to-Book Ratio

The allowed return on book equity must be revised to account for any sanctioned difference between market price and book value. This adjustment to the cost of equity capital can be obtained using the annual DCF model. Solving Equation 10-6 for r:

$$r = M/B\,(K - g) + g \tag{10-8}$$

Equation 10-8 defines the return on book value required to be earned such that the investor will receive his required rate of return and the target M/B ratio will be maintained.

EXAMPLE 10-4

The cost of equity for a utility is 15%, as determined by the standard DCF process. The growth component of that return is 5%. The commission that regulates the utility is on record as stating that its regulatory intention is to allow a rate of return such that the utility's stock will sell at 1.1 times book value to avoid dilution. The allowed return on book equity follows from Equation 10-8:

$$r = 1.1(.15 - .05) + .05 = .16 \; or \; 16\% \tag{10-9}$$

To illustrate yet another use of the DCF formula, the next example combines the Target Market-to-Book Ratio approach with the Non-Constant Growth model enunciated in Chapter 4.

EXAMPLE 10-5

A regulatory commission advocates an M/B of 1.1. This fact is known to investors, but, at present, the stock is trading at book value exactly. It is assumed that current dividends are $5, book value per share is $76.43, the long-term expected growth is 7%, and that investors expect the recovery of stock price to take place in one period. In other words, regulatory lag lasts one period. From the general Non-Constant Growth Model, also known as the Finite Horizon or Limited Horizon Model, of Equation 4-17 in Chapter 4:

$$P_0 = \frac{D_0(1+G)}{1+K} + \frac{1.1 B_0 (1+g)}{1+K}$$

$$\$76.43 = \frac{\$5 (1 + .07)}{1+K} + \frac{1.10 \times \$76.43(1 + .07)}{1+K} \tag{10-10}$$

from which $K = 24.70\%$. Alternate assumptions on the length of the recovery period can easily be handled by the general model of Equation 4-17.

10.3 Econometric Models of the Market-to-Book Ratio

Another approach to measuring the cost of equity capital consists of statistically estimating the M/B ratios for a sample of companies as a function of several explanatory variables, one of which is the expected book return on equity. Using the statistically-estimated relationship, the expected book return on equity that causes the M/B ratio to be 1.0 is the estimate of cost of equity capital.

Equation 10-6 is the conceptual departure point for the statistical model. From Equation 10-6, the M/B ratio is approximately a linear function of the expected book return on equity, r. At first glance, it seems reasonable to relate statistically the M/B ratios and book equity returns for a sample of companies by the following linear relationship:

$$M/B = a_0 + a_1 r \qquad (10\text{-}11)$$

where a_1 and a_0 are constants.

Equation 10-11 is the basis for the so-called Comparable Earnings Pricing Technique (CEPT) employed by some analysts. The CEPT method assumes the M/B ratio achieved by a company is a function of the return on equity actually earned by that company. To implement the technique, Equation 10-11 is estimated statistically by regression techniques over a large sample of unregulated companies. From the estimated relationship, the return on equity that produces a M/B ratio of slightly above 1.0 is the cost of equity capital.

The technique has several flaws, both conceptually and empirically. The simplistic linear relation assumed between the M/B ratio and r does not fully explain the M/B ratios of the companies in a given sample. A simple regression of M/B ratios on expected return on equity is inappropriate because it presumes that every company in a given sample has the same risk and growth rate. Additional variables are needed to fully explain actual M/B ratios. Studies that use the empirical relationship between return on equity and M/B ratios to infer the return necessary to produce a M/B ratio of 1.0 are misleading because they assume a constant invariant relationship between M/B ratios and equity returns for all firms, irrespective of their risk, growth, and dividend yield. Empirically, the regression relationship can be falsified by outlying points that distort the regression line away from the trends set by most of the points. The technique can also be criticized for failing to include other risk measures in addition to the

M/B ratio in its selection of comparable companies. A wide range of returns may correspond with a specified range of M/B ratio.

A more realistic and general explanatory equation would take the form:

$$M/B = a_0 + a_1F_1 + a_2F_2 + a_3F_3 + \ldots\ldots a_nF_n \qquad (10\text{-}12)$$

This equation asserts that a company's M/B ratio is a linear function of several explanatory factors, F_1, F_2, $F_3 \ldots F_n$, including the expected book return on equity. The magnitude and direction of the variables' effects on M/B ratios are measured by the factor coefficients, a_1, a_2, $\ldots a_n$. Typical explanatory variables include expected return on book equity, expected dividend growth, dividend yield, standard deviation, proxies for earnings quality, regulatory climate, accounting convention, and various risk variables designed to capture financial, business, and regulatory risk. The risk variables include the equity ratio, beta, CWIP treatment, regulatory climate ranking, and the relative importance of construction expenditures. Multiple regression techniques are applied to Equation 10-12 over a sample of companies to produce estimates of the magnitude of these effects. Two actual case examples will illustrate the methodology.

EXAMPLE 10-6

Brigham, Shome, and Bankston (1979) specified the following M/B model for the electric utility industry:

$$M/B = a_0 + a_1 \text{ (Book yield)} + a_2(\text{Growth}) + a_3(\text{Equity Ratio})$$

$$+ a_4(\text{AFUDC}) + a_5(\text{Commission Ranking Dummy})$$

$$+ a_6(\text{Flow--through Dummy}) \qquad (10\text{-}13)$$

Book yield is measured by multiplying the expected book return on equity, r, by the expected dividend payout rate, $1 - b$. Growth is measured by the retention ratio method as br. The equity ratio measures financial risk, and the percentage of net income made up of AFUDC measures earnings quality. A dummy variable to distinguish among utilities' regulatory climate, and a dummy variable to differentiate flow-through from normalized accounting companies were added. The model was estimated for 100 electric utilities from annual reports data. The coefficients of the above equation were estimated by multiple regression techniques. The resulting equation was:

$$(M/B) = -0.10 + 10.310 \,(\text{Book Yield}) + 1.32 \,(\text{Growth})$$

$$+ 0.36 \,(\text{Equity Ratio}) - .04 \,(\text{AFUDC})$$

$$+ 0.08 \,(\text{Commission Ranking Dummy})$$

$$- 0.08 \,(\text{Flow--through Dummy})$$

$$R^2 = 74\%$$

The explanatory power of the regression, as measured by R^2, was 74%, which indicates a high degree of accuracy on the part of model's ability to explain M/B ratios. The coefficients all had the anticipated signs; companies with high book yields and high growth rates had higher M/B ratios; the first dummy variable, Commision Ranking, a proxy for regulatory climate, exerts a positive effect on market valuation. The second dummy variable had a negative coefficient, indicating that flow-through accounting companies sell for lower M/B ratios than normalized accounting companies.

Inserting a specified company's actual values for the explanatory variables in the fitted equation, the cost of equity is obtained by solving the fitted equation for the level of book equity return that makes the M/B ratio 1.0. Inserting the values for Wisconsin Public Service, a 13.51% cost of equity was obtained by solving the above equation for the value of r, which produced a M/B ratio of 1.0. If the estimated equation is valid, and if the target M/B ratio is 1.0, then

EXAMPLE 10-7

Morin (1986A, 1986B) investigated the impact of varying amounts of CWIP in the rate base on the cost of equity of investor-owned electric utilities using multiple regression analysis of M/B ratios. Using the statistically-estimated relationship, the expected book return on equity, which causes the M/B ratio to be 1.0, is the estimate of cost of equity capital.

As shown above, a realistic and general explanatory equation of the M/B ratio takes the form:

$$M/B = a_0 + a_1 F_1 + a_2 F_2 + a_3 F_3 + \ldots \ldots a_n F_n$$

The advantage of estimating the above equation by regression technique is that all the variables that affect cost of capital are held constant, allowing a consistent comparison of the effect of the each factor separately.

Typical explanatory variables are the same as those listed earlier. To test the effect of CWIP inclusion on the M/B ratio, Morin estimated the following 5-factor model each year:

$$M/B = a_o + a_1 ROE + a_2 G + a_3 E/C + a_4 CONST + a_5 CWIP\} \quad (10\text{-}14)$$

where   ROE   = expected book return on equity

              G = expected growth rate

              E/C = common equity ratio as a % of total capital

            CONST = size of construction program as a % of total capital

            CWIP = % of CWIP in rate base

The construction variable a_4 is intended to capture the financial burdens of a utility's plant construction activities perceived by the investment company. The sign and magnitude of the CWIP coefficient a_5 in the above equation provide the basis for assessing the impact of CWIP on equity costs. The effect of CWIP on the M/B ratio can be translated into the effect on the cost of equity capital as follows:

(1) Substitute the mean values for each of the five independent variables in the estimated regression equation, except ROE, and solve for ROE, which will produce a M/B = 1.0.

(2) Remove the effect of CWIP on the M/B ratio by assuming a value of 0 for the CWIP variable in the regression equation, and solve for the required return on equity ROE as above.

(3) The effect of CWIP on the cost of equity capital is simply the difference between the two calculated ROE's.

Two different approaches to capturing CWIP were employed in the 1986A and 1986B4 Morin studies. First, a zero-one dummy variable was used, set equal to 1 if the utility had any CWIP included in rate base; zero otherwise. Second, the percentage of CWIP included in rate base was obtained from Argus for each company individually as of year-end. The regression models were estimated with both definitions.

The explanatory power of the model estimated was quite high for a cross-sectional regression study such as this one, as evidenced by the consistent R^2s of .40 to .46. The expected growth and expected ROE exerted a consistent, strong positive influence on the M/B ratio. The construction variable consistently exerted a strong negative influence, indicating that the greater the importance of a utility's construction program, the lower the M/B ratio, and thus the higher the cost of equity capital. Both CWIP variables exerted a positive influence on the M/B ratio, indicating that the inclusion of CWIP in rate base increases the M/B ratio and thus lowers the cost of equity capital.

As expected, the equity ratio coefficient was consistently positive, indicating that the lower the financial risk, the higher the M/B ratio and the lower the cost of equity capital. The beta and regulatory climate variables yielded mixed results.

When historical growth variables and realized return on equity were also used as explanatory variables instead of forward-looking versions of those variables, inferior regression results were obtained. These results provided convincing evidence that growth forecasts and ROE forecasts provide a superior explanation of M/B ratios and cost of equity capital than historically-oriented measures.

The results of the study also provided convincing evidence that the inclusion of CWIP in rate base produces significantly lower equity costs for a public utility, by a factor varying from a low of 0.42% for a modest level of CWIP inclusion to a high of 1.66% for 100% inclusion. The savings in equity costs imply correspondingly lower ratepayer burdens.

Pitfalls of M/B Models

Like all other cost of capital estimation methods, M/B-based econometric models of equity costs have advantages and shortcomings. On the positive side, such models are firmly anchored on the foundations of DCF theory. The data required to implement the models are easily accessible in computer-readable form. The method makes the required judgment explicit, in contrast to other methods; econometric techniques facilitate the specification of confidence limits, which can be used to establish a range of reasonableness for ratemaking purposes. The major contribution of the models is that they allow the user to make cost of capital comparisons between firms, while holding constant all the factors that differentiate firms from one another.

On the negative side, the method is vulnerable to "curve fitting" excesses. The temptation is strong to include a multitude of explanatory variables that may or may not have any economic validity. The inclusion of explanatory variables should rest on strong defensible economic arguments, rather than on empirical elegance and spectacular explanatory power. Another drawback of the approach is that the user requires a solid understanding of econometric estimation techniques. It is important that the assumptions of linear regression techniques be well understood and verified for possible violation. Checks for multicolinearity between the explanatory variables, measurement error biases, omitted variables biases, and scale effects should be conducted. The stability of the coefficients over time is also necessary if the econometric model is to be useful for forecasting equity-costs. The major drawback of the approach is that it is only as valid as the DCF model on which its rests. As discussed in the previous chapter, the DCF model is very fragile in particular capital market conditions.

One common error in specifying M/B models is to use the currently allowed book return on equity, rather than the expected return, as one of the explanatory variables. The stock price that appears in the numerator of the M/B ratio reflects the return expected by investors to be granted, and not the return currently allowed or currently earned. If the model is estimated using actual return, the estimated coefficient for that variable will be biased, since the actual M/B ratio will be different from what is justified by the current return on equity. The coefficient of return on equity will thus be invalid, and use of the method to infer the cost of equity capital will lead to distorted values of equity costs.

All the earlier caveats that share price will only be driven toward book value under knife-edge circumstances deserve reiteration.

10.4 The Q-Ratio

The Q-ratio can be used to establish an appropriate target M/B ratio for a company. The Q-ratio is defined as the ratio of the market value of a firm's securities to the replacement cost of its assets. A control group of comparable unregulated companies is used to establish an appropriate Q-ratio. This ratio is multiplied by the replacement cost value of equity-financed assets in a subject utility to obtain a target market price that measures the replacement cost market value of the equity. The target M/B ratio employs the target market price, and the return on book equity required to support the target M/B ratio is computed from the transformation relationship of Equation 10-8:

$$r = P_Q / B (K - g) + g \qquad (10\text{-}15)$$

where P_Q = target market price computed from the target Q-ratio.

Rationale

The market value of a firm's securities clearly exerts an important influence on the firm's incentive to invest in capital projects. If the market value of a firm's stocks and bonds exceeds the cost of establishing productive capacity, there is an incentive to raise capital and establish new productive capacity, since such investments increase stock price. Conversely, if the market value of a firm's securities is less than the current cost of establishing productive capacity, there is a disincentive to invest in new plant, since such investments would decrease stock price, and investors could exercise the option to liquidate the firm's assets at a value in excess of the equity value.

In the long-run, for a competitive industry, the possibility of free entry and exit of firms in a competitive industry would ensure that the market value of a firm's securities equals the replacement cost of its assets. Otherwise, the possibility of entry and exit into the industry would trigger the addition or deletion of further production, thereby altering product prices, profits, and finally market values until such an equality prevailed.

The relationship between the market value of a firm's securities and the replacement cost of its assets is embodied in the Q-ratio, first developed by Tobin and Brainard (1971). The Q-ratio is defined as follows:

$$Q = \frac{\text{Market Value of a Firm's Securities}}{\text{Replacement Cost of Firm's Assets}}$$

If $Q > 1.0$, a firm has an incentive to invest because the value of the firm's securities exceeds the replacement cost of assets, that is, the firm's return on its investments exceeds its cost of capital. Conversely, if $Q < 1.0$, a firm has a disincentive to invest in new plant. In final long-run equilibrium, the Q-ratio is driven to 1.0.

The Q-Ratio and Regulation

The language of the *Hope* decision strongly suggests that the objective of regulation is to target a utility's profits at a level commensurate with the profits earned by competitive firms of comparable risk. Since in the unregulated sector, competitive forces will assure that over long periods of time the Q-ratio will be 1.0, regulators should provide public utilities with a return sufficient to realize an expected average Q-ratio of 1.0.

In the short-run, temporary disequilibriums occur so that unregulated firms will not necessarily achieve Q-ratios of 1.0. Consistent with the comparable earnings doctrine and the capital attraction standard of *Hope*, a utility's profits should be targeted at a level commensurate with the actual profits earned by firms of similar risk. By this standard, the end result of the rate setting process is a stock price that implies a Q-ratio equal to the aggregate Q-ratio for a sample of comparable risk unregulated firms. In other words, under the Q-ratio standard, the allowed return should be set so that the ratio of market value to replacement cost is the same for regulated and unregulated firms of comparable risk.

Earlier in this chapter, it was argued that the cost of equity should be translated into an allowed rate of return such that the M/B ratio will be slightly in excess of 1.0 in order to prevent dilution of book value when new stock is sold. But these considerations only relate to dilution of nominal book value. The Q-ratio extends this argument to include protection from dilution in real terms. In an inflationary period, the replacement cost of a firm's assets may increase more rapidly than its book equity. To avoid the resulting economic confiscation of shareholders' investment in real terms the allowed rate of return should produce a M/B ratio that provides a Q-ratio of 1.0 or a Q-ratio equal to that of comparable firms.

To implement the standard, the cost of equity derived from DCF, CAPM, and Risk Premium methodologies is translated into the fair equity return consistent with a Q-ratio equivalent to that of comparable unregulated firms. In other words, the cost of book equity is the return required to be earned on the utility's book equity such that the investor will receive the required return K and the stock price maintains a Q-ratio equal to that of comparable firms. The issue of setting the allowed rate of return at a level sufficient to equate the Q-ratio of a regulated utility with the Q-ratio of comparable risk unregulated firms is discussed in Litzenberger (1980) and Harlow (1984a, 1984b).

Data Sources

The U.S. Council of Economic Advisers in a previous annual Economic Report of the President (1979) developed aggregate estimates of the Q-ratio for the corporate sector as a measure of the incentive for corporate investment in plant and equipment. These aggregate Q-ratio estimates employed data items from both the national income and product accounts and from the flow of funds accounts in order to arrive at the ratio of the market values of corporate debt and equity to the replacement cost of assets. As a proxy for asset replacement cost, an estimate of net depreciable assets and inventories repriced for the effects of inflation was used. These data items are not easily reconcilable with items in the balance sheet of an individual firm, however.

A simple balance sheet method to calculate Q-ratios for individual firms uses the following formula:

$$Q = \frac{MVE + FVD}{RC} \qquad (10\text{-}16)$$

where MVE = market value of equity, including convertible preferred, if any

           MVE = RC - FVD

           RC = replacement cost of "net assets"

           FVD = face value of debt, straight preferred, and investment tax credits

"Net assets" are total assets at replacement cost less current liabilities other than debt, and less deferred credits other than the investment tax credit. For the replacement cost of assets, either trended original cost or the actual replacement cost data required by the SEC in 10K reports can be used.

It is important to note that the face value of debt and preferred, rather than their market value, is used in calculating the numerator of the Q-ratio. This is due to the particular nature of the regulatory process. To determine a utility's overall allowed rate of return, the embedded cost of debt and preferred stock is used. As a result, ratepayers bear the gains and losses associated with the use of senior capital raised in the past. Utility's shareholders neither benefit nor lose by the change in the market prices of the senior capital brought about by changes in interest rates. Accordingly, the use of the market values of senior capital is not appropriate when computing utility Q-ratios.

Based on the latter qualification, a just and reasonable price for a public utility's stock should be determined by subtracting the book value rather than the market value of senior capital from the replacement cost of assets. Litzenberger (1980) describes the final regulatory standard implied by the Q-ratio as follows. A fair and reasonable stock price should result in a ratio Q_r of the market value of the utility's equity to the value of its equity at adjusted replacement cost that is equal to the Q-ratio for a comparable group of unregulated firms. The value of the utility's equity at adjusted replacement cost is in turn defined as the historical book value of its equity plus the difference between its net plant and equipment at replacement cost and at historical cost.

Implementation

The general procedure for applying the Q-ratio approach to the determination of equity cost consists of 4 steps:

Step 1:   Obtain a sample of comparable risk unregulated companies, using the risk filter techniques described in earlier chapters.

Step 2:   Calculate the Q-ratio for each company in the sample, as per Equation 10-16, using the replacement costs of their net plant and equipment and inventories contained in their 10K reports and the market value of their publicly traded debt and equity securities.

Step 3:   Calculate the target M/B ratio that would result in a Q_r ratio equal to the equity ratio for the comparable group of unregulated firms. The numerator of the target M/B ratio is the value of the specified utility's equity at replacement cost calculated using replacement cost data.

Step 4:   Use transformation Equation 10-8 to convert the utility's cost of equity capital into a fair return on equity.

EXAMPLE 10-8

The following example is adapted from Litzenberger (1988). The cost of equity capital for Eastern Power Company derived from the DCF, Risk Premium, and CAPM methodologies is 15%, consisting of a 5% growth and a 10% expected dividend yield. For reasons of consistency, the same group of unregulated comparable risk firms used in the execution of the DCF method is retained for computing the reference Q-ratio. The average Q-ratio for this group of risk-equivalent companies is 0.85, computed from the application of Equation 10-16 to each company. To estimate the target M/B ratio, the value of common equity at adjusted replacement cost is first estimated from the information contained in the current annual report:

VALUE OF EASTERN POWER COMPANY'S EQUITY
AT ADJUSTED REPLACEMENT COST
($000,000)

Common Equity	$150
Minority Interest Common Equity	$ 5
Convertible Preferred	$ 2
Value of Equity at Historical Cost	$157
Difference between Net Plant at Replacement and Historical Cost	$ 80
Value of Common Equity at Adjusted Replacement Cost	$237

The target M/B ratio for the Eastern Power Company is calculated as follows:

Value of Equity at Replacement Cost	$237
	x
Comparable risk firms Q-ratio	0.80
Target Market Value of Equity	$190
	÷
Value of Common Equity at Historical Cost	$157
Target M/B Ratio	1.21

Lastly, the cost of equity capital of 15% is translated into the allowed equity return, which will produce the target M/B ratio of 1.21, using Equation 10-8:

$$r = M/B(K-g) + g$$

$$= 1.21\,(15\% - 5\%) + 5\%$$

Drawbacks of the Approach

At the practical level, the results of the Q-ratio approach can only be as accurate as the replacement cost data on which it is based, typically derived from 10K reports. The lack of verifiability and the subjective nature of these data are likely deterrents from use of the method. For non-publicly traded companies, the problem of generating suitable replacement cost data is even more formidable; trended original cost proxies could serve instead. At the conceptual level, despite the convincing logic of the method and despite the economic foundation on which it rests, the basic premise that the M/B ratios of utilities should be more consistent with those prevailing for comparable industrials is controversial. A substantial burden would be imposed on utility ratepayers by implementing the method, while it is questionable whether investors' returns would be ameliorated. A quotation from Kahn makes the point:

> . . . any attempt of a regulatory commission to permit investors the higher return would only be self-defeating. Investors would respond to the higher earnings per share by bidding up the prices of the securities to the point at which new purchases would earn only the old cost of capital on their investments. The only beneficiaries would be those who happened to own the stock at the time the policy change was announced or anticipated.[1]

10.5 Reservations Regarding the Use of M/B Ratios in the Regulatory Process

It is sometimes argued that because current market-to-book (M/B) ratios are in excess of 1.0, this indicates that companies are expected by investors to be able to earn more than their cost of capital, and that the regulating authority should lower the authorized return on equity, so that the stock price will decline to book value. It is therefore plausible, under this argument, that stock prices drop from the current M/B value to the desired M/B ratio range of 1.0 times book.

There are several reasons why this view of the role of M/B ratios in regulation should be avoided.

(1) The inference that M/B ratios are relevant and that regulators should set an ROE so as to produce a M/B of 1.0 is erroneous. The stock price is set by the market, not by regulators. The M/B ratio is the end result of regulation, and not its starting point. The view that regulation should set an allowed rate of return so as to produce a M/B of 1.0, presumes that investors are masochistic. They commit capital to a utility with a M/B in excess of 1.0, knowing full well that they will be inflicted a capital loss by regulators. This is not a realistic or accurate view of regulation.

(2) The condition that the M/B will gravitate toward 1.0 if regulators set the allowed return equal to capital costs will be met only if the actual return expected to be earned by investors is at least equal to the cost of capital on a consistent long-term basis. The cost of capital of a company refers to the expected long-run earnings level of other firms with similar risk. If investors expect a utility to earn an ROE equal to its cost of equity in each period, then its M/B ratio would be approximately 1.0 or higher with the proper allowance for flotation cost.

(3) A company's achieved earnings in any given year are likely to exceed or be less than their long-run average. Depressed or inflated M/B ratios are to a considerable degree a function of forces outside the control of regulators, such as the general state of the economy, or general economic or financial circumstances that may affect the yields on securities of unregulated as well as regulated enterprises. The achievement of a 1.0 M/B ratio is appropriate, but only in a long-run sense. For utilities to exhibit a long-run M/B ratio of 1.0, it is clear that during economic upturns and more favorable capital market conditions, the M/B ratio must exceed its long-run average of 1.0 to compensate for the periods during which the

---

[1] See Kahn (1970), p. 52.

M/B ratio is less than its long-run average under less favorable economic and capital market conditions.

Historically, the M/B ratio for utilities has fluctuated above and below 1.0. It has been consistently above 1.0 during the 1980s and early 1990s. This indicates that earnings below capital costs and M/B ratios below 1.0 during less favorable economic and capital market conditions must necessarily be accompanied with earnings in excess of capital costs and M/B ratios above 1.00 during more favorable economic and capital market conditions.

It should also be pointed out that M/B ratios are determined by the marketplace, and utilities cannot be expected to attract capital in an environment where industrials are commanding M/B ratios well in excess of 1.0. Moreover, if regulators were to currently set rates so as to produce a M/B ratio of 1.0, not only would the long-run target M/B ratio of 1.0 be violated, but more importantly, the inevitable consequence would be to inflict severe capital losses on shareholders. Investors have not committed capital to utilities with the expectation of incurring capital losses from a misguided regulatory process.

(4) The fundamental goal of regulation should be to set the expected economic profit for a public utility equal to the level of profits expected to be earned by firms of comparable risk, in short, to emulate the competitive result. For unregulated firms, the natural forces of competition will ensure that in the long-run the ratio of the market value of these firms' securities equals the replacement cost of their assets. This suggests that a fair and reasonable price for a public utility's common stock is one that produces equality between the market price of its common equity and the replacement cost of its physical assets. The latter circumstance will not necessarily occur when the M/B ratio is 1.0. As the previous section demonstrated, only when the book value of the firm's common equity equals the value of the firm's equity at replacement assets will equality hold.

References

Brigham, E.F., Shome, D.K., and Bankston, T.A. "An Econometric Model for Estimating the Cost of Capital for a Public Utility." Public Utility Research Center Working Paper 5-79, University of Florida, 1979.

Callen, J.L. "Estimating the Cost of Equity Using Tobin's Q." *The Engineering Economist*, Summer 1988, 349-358.

Harlow, F. "Efficient Market Perspectives on Utility Rate of Return Adequacy." *Public Utilities Fortnightly*, March 29, 1984A, 38-40.

Harlow, F. "Q-Ratios and the Target Return on Equity for Utilities." *Public Utilities Fortnightly,* April 12, 1984B, 29-31.

Kahn, A.E. *The Economics of Regulation: Principles and Institutions.* New York: Wiley and Sons, 1970.

Litzenberger, R.H. "Determination of a Target Market to Book Value Ratio for a Public Utility in an Inflationary Environment." In *Proceedings: Iowa State University, Regulatory Conference on Public Utility Value and the Rate-Making Process,* 1980.

Litzenberger, R.H. Wisconsin Bell, Prepared testimony, Wisconsin Public Service Commission, 1988.

Morin, R.A. "An Empirical Study on the Effect of CWIP on Cost of Capital and Revenue Requirements, Part I." *Public Utilities Fortnightly,* July 10, 1986A, 21-27.

Morin, R.A. "An Empirical Study on the Effect of CWIP on Revenue Requirements and Cost of Capital." *Public Utilities Fortnightly,* July 24, 1986B, 24-28.

Tobin, J. and Brainard, W.C. "Pitfalls in Financial Model Building." *American Economic Review*, February 1968, 104.

Chapter 11
Risk Premium

The risk premium method of determining the cost of equity, sometimes referred to as the "stock-bond-yield spread method" or the "risk positioning method," or again the "bond-yield plus risk-premium" method, recognizes that common equity capital is more risky than debt from an investor's standpoint, and that investors require higher returns on stocks than on bonds to compensate for the additional risk. The general approach is relatively straightforward: First, determine the historical spread between the return on debt and the return on equity. Second, add this spread to the current debt yield to derive an estimate of current equity return requirements.

The risk premium approach to estimating the cost of equity derives its usefulness from the simple fact that while equity return requirements cannot be readily quantified at any given time, the returns on bonds can be assessed precisely at every instant in time. If the magnitude of the risk premium between stocks and bonds is known, then this information can be used to produce the cost of common equity. This can be accomplished retrospectively using historical risk premiums or prospectively using expected risk premiums.

11.1 Rationale and Issues

The basic idea behind the risk premium approach is portrayed graphically in Figure 11-1. The horizontal axis measures security risk; the further to the right a security lies, the greater its investment risk. U.S. government securities are shown at the origin since they are devoid of default risk. The vertical axis portrays the required returns. The straight line, labeled the capital market line (CML), shows at a point in time the risk return tradeoff in capital markets, that is, the relationship between a security's risk and its required return. The term R_F, which stands for "risk free," designates the rate of interest on default-free securities as measured by the rate of interest on U.S. Treasury bills.

Corporate bonds are riskier than U.S. Treasury securities, so their yields are higher. The risk premiums rise for lower quality corporate bonds. Therefore, the risks on corporate bonds are plotted higher than the risks of U. S. Treasury securities on the Capital Market Line, and their required returns are correspondingly higher. Common stocks are riskier than corporate bonds, and returns on stocks are correspondingly higher.

FIGURE 11-1
THE RELATIONSHIP BETWEEN RISK AND RETURN IN CAPITAL
MARKETS

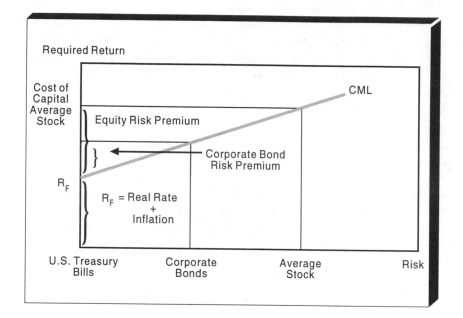

The Capital Market Line demonstrates the linkages between various segments of the capital market. Investor capital flows between the various markets depending on the risk-return relationship for each market segment, and the return for each type of capital increases with the risk of the security. Relative risk premiums, RPs, corresponding to the slope and shape of the Capital Market Line at a point in time, exist for each type of security as follows:

AAA Corporate Bond Yield = U. S. Treasury Bond Yield + RP_1

BAA Corporate Bond Yield = AAA Corporate Bond Yield + RP_2

Preferred Stock Yield = BAA Corporate Bond Yield + RP_3

Common Stock Return = BAA Corporate Bond Yield + RP_4

The magnitude of the relative risk premiums is determined by shifts in demand and supply in each capital market segment, which are in turn driven by investors' attitudes toward risk, and by the relative risk differentials perceived by investors between each type of security.

Notwithstanding the simplicity of the concept, there are three problems that must be resolved before the risk premium method can be implemented: measurement, stability, and risk adjustment. First, we must address the measurement issue. How should the general levels of these risk premiums be measured, or equivalently, how should the slope of the capital market line at a point in time be estimated? Several related questions must be answered. Over what historical period should the risk premium be established? Should the spreads be estimated using realized or expected returns? What specific debt and equity securities should be used?

Second, we must address the stability issue. Is the level of the risk premium constant? The customary assumption that underlies the use of the risk premium technique is that shifts in interest rates have no significant impact on the required risk premium; that is, the slope of the capital market line remains unchanged even though the height of the line rises and falls in response to changes in interest rates. Are the risk premiums in fact constant? Do they fluctuate in a predictable fashion over time as the factors that determine the risk premium change? Expressed in another way, is investor risk aversion constant?

Third, we address the risk adjustment issue. What is the relative size of the risk premium on utility and industrial stocks, and how is the return requirement derived from the risk premium method to be adjusted for the risk of a given utility? Answers to those three fundamental questions are offered in the remainder of this chapter.

11.2 Historical Risk Premium

One approach to estimating the risk premium is to examine the historical returns actually earned from investments in stocks and bonds. The risk premium is simply the difference between the historical realized returns on stocks and bonds. This approach can be expressed as follows:

$$K_e = K_d + \text{historical bond-equity spread}$$

where

$$K_e = \text{cost of common equity}$$

$$K_d = \text{incremental cost of debt}$$

For example, if the current cost of debt is 6% and the historical spread between stocks and bonds is 7%, then the cost of common equity equals 13%:

$$K_e = K_d + \text{historical bond-equity spread}$$

$$= 6\% + 7\% = 13\%$$

Of course, the essential requirement of the method is to obtain an estimate of the historical spread between bond and stock returns. Historical return data for common equities and bonds are compiled over some past period, and the mean return differential between stocks and bonds serves as the measure of the risk premium. The best example of this approach is the Ibbotson Associates compilation of historical returns and historical risk premiums from 1926 to the present, which compares realized holding period annual returns on equities, government long-term and short-term securities, corporate bonds, and inflation. Annual updates of the return results are published by Ibbotson Associates.[1]

Application of the method proceeds directly from the historical results. For example, since the average return realized from investing in U.S. Treasury long-term bonds over the 1926-1992 period has been 5.1% while the mean historical return from investing in stocks during the same period has been 12.4%, then the average bond-stock spread over the total period was 7.3%. If, for example, long-term Treasury bonds are currently yielding 6%, then a reasonable estimate of the current equity return for the average stock is 6.0% + 7.3% = 13.3%.

One variation of the historical risk premium method is to estimate the relationship between earned book returns on equity and bond yields over some reference period, and apply the resulting relationship to a specified utility's current borrowing costs. A similar approach can be employed with authorized (allowed) returns on equity instead of earned returns on equity.

Three implementation issues are involved when dealing with historical risk premiums: the choice of time period, the realized return trap, and the method of computing historical returns. The first two are related.

Time Period

Realized risk premium results are highly dependent on the choice of time period over which the security return data are compiled. Both the length of the period and the choice of end points can make a substantial difference in the final results obtained. For example, Table 11-1 reports the realized returns on stocks and bonds obtained by Ibbotson Associates for the last 10, 20, 30, and 50 years ending in 1992. The resulting risk premium varies from 2.2% to 7.7%. Keeping the length of the period unchanged, and altering the end point by 2 years, the corresponding results for various periods ending in 1990 instead of 1992 show a risk premium varying from 0.2% to 7.5%.

---

[1] See Ibbotson Associates, Inc. (1993).

TABLE 11-1
THE INSTABILITY OF RISK PREMIUMS COMPUTED FROM REALIZED
REALIZED RETURNS

Period	Stock Returns	Bond Returns	Risk Premium
1983-1992	16.2	12.6	3.6
1973-1992	11.3	9.1	2.2
1963-1992	10.9	6.8	4.1
1943-1992	12.6	4.9	7.7
1981-1990	13.9	13.7	0.2
1971-1990	11.2	8.7	2.5
1961-1990	10.2	6.2	4.0
1941-1990	12.0	4.5	7.5

Source: Ibbotson Associates (1993)

The historical risk premium approach assumes that the average realized return is an appropriate surrogate for expected return, or, in other words, that investor expectations are realized. However, realized returns can be substantially different from prospective returns anticipated by investors, especially when measured over short time periods. Therefore, a risk premium study should consider the longest possible period for which data are available. Short-run periods during which investors earn a lower risk premium than they expect are offset by short-run periods during which investors earn a higher risk premium than they expect. Only over long time periods will investor return expectations and realizations converge.

Risk premiums based on short time periods can be particularly volatile, changing with capital market conditions, inflationary expectations, and fiscal-monetary forces. One should therefore ignore the realized risk premiums measured over short time periods, since they are heavily dependent on these short term market movements, and instead rely on the long-term results, since periods of such length are long enough to smooth out short-term aberrations, and to encompass several business and interest rate cycles. In their comprehensive study of historical returns on stocks and bonds, Ibbotson Associates recommend the use of the entire study period in estimating the appropriate market risk premium, so as to minimize subjective judgment and to encompass as many diverse regimes of inflation, interest rate cycles, and economic cycles.

To the extent that the estimated historical equity risk premium follows what is known in statistics as a random walk, one should expect the equity risk premium to remain at its historical mean. Therefore, the best estimate of the future risk premium is the historical mean. Since the Ibbotson

Associates study finds no evidence that the market price of risk or the amount of risk in common stocks has changed over time, it is normally reasonable to assume that these quantities will remain stable in the future.[2] The practice of arbitrarily weighting certain time periods more or less than other time periods in order to obtain a weighted risk premium presupposes knowledge of how the risk premium varies over time and is highly subjective.

Expected Versus Realized Returns

The second problem involves the distinction between expected and realized return. The historical risk premium approach fundamentally assumes that average realized return is an appropriate surrogate for expected return, or in other words, that investor expectations are realized. Realized returns can be substantially different from prospective returns anticipated by investors, and therefore constitute a hazardous benchmark on which to base the risk premium between stocks and bonds, particularly when measured over short time periods.

Realized returns can be envisaged as the sum of an expected return plus a component of unanticipated return, which will be positive or negative depending on whether investors underestimated or overestimated expected future returns. Unless the mean unanticipated component of return on stocks equals that on bonds, historical spreads between stocks and bonds will not accurately reflect expected risk premiums. Only if investors do not systematically overestimate or underestimate future returns will spreads based on historical returns converge with those based on expected returns. For example, it is plausible that investors in the early 1980s consistently underestimated the phenomenal ascent in interest rates. The Federal Reserve's reversal in monetary policy in October 1979, whereby monetary aggregates were targeted instead of interest rates, was unanticipated by investors. The resulting gyrations in interest rates and increase in bond volatility in 1981-1982 led investors to expect higher returns from bonds, reducing the bond-stock spread. Reliance on historical risk premiums during this period would have produced an underestimate of the risk premium. The converse is also true as in the early 1990s, for example, when interest rates decreased consistently and substantially, unexpected by investors.

---

[2] Some analysts suggest adjusting the risk premium for any significant trend in risk premium behavior. Such trends, if any, can be detected by visual inspection of the results, or more formally, by computing serial correlation coefficients. To the extent that very little serial correlation between successive annual risk premiums exists, such adjustments are unwarranted.

The *Hope* and *Bluefield* cases established the fundamental premise that investors should receive a return commensurate with returns currently available on comparable risk investments, not that investors be guaranteed a return coinciding with their initial return expectations. Consequently, the determination of a fair and reasonable return on equity should rest preferably on investor expectations, and historical risk premiums should be based on expected returns rather than on realized returns, data permitting.

While forward-looking risk premiums based on expected returns are preferable, historical return studies over long periods still provide a useful guide for the future. This is because over long periods investor expectations and realizations converge. Otherwise, investors would never commit investment capital. Investors expectations are eventually revised to match historical realizations, as market prices adjust to bring anticipated and actual investment results into conformity. In the long-run, the difference between expected and realized risk premiums will decline because short-run periods during which investors earn a lower risk premium than they expect are offset by short-run periods during which investors earn a higher risk premium than they expect.

Computational Issues

The third problem in relying on historical return results is the method of averaging historical returns.

Geometric v. Arithmetic Averages.   One major issue relating to the use of realized returns is whether to use the ordinary average (arithmetic mean) or the geometric mean return. Only arithmetic means are correct for forecasting purposes and for estimating the cost of capital. When using historical risk premiums as a surrogate for the expected market risk premium, the relevant measure of the historical risk premium is the arithmetic average of annual risk premiums over a long period of time. This is formally shown in *Principles of Corporate Finance,* a widely used and respected textbook on corporate finance by Brealey and Myers (1991). Appendix 11-A illustrates that only arithmetic averages can be used as estimates of cost of capital, and that the geometric mean is not an appropriate measure of cost of capital. A widely-used Ibbotson Associates publication title contains a rigorous discussion of the impropriety of using geometric averages in estimating the cost of capital (Ibbotson Associates 1993).

The use of the arithmetic mean appears counter-intuitive at first glance, because we commonly use the geometric mean return to measure the average annual achieved return over some time period. In estimating the cost of capital, the goal is to obtain the rate of return that investors expect, that is, a target rate of return. On average, investors expect to achieve their target return. This target expected return is in effect an arithmetic average. The achieved or retrospective return is the geometric average. In statistical parlance, the arithmetic average is the unbiased measure of the expected value of repeated observations of a random variable, not the geometric mean.

The geometric mean answers the question of what constant return an investor would have to achieve in each year to have his or her investment growth match the return achieved by the stock market. The arithmetic mean answers the question of what growth rate is the best estimate of the future amount of money that will be produced by continually reinvesting in the stock market. It is the rate of return that, compounded over multiple periods, gives the mean of the probability distribution of ending wealth.

While the geometric mean is the best estimate of performance over a long period of time, this does not contradict the statement that the arithmetic mean compounded over a number of years that an investment is held provides the best estimate of the ending wealth value of the investment. The reason is that an investment with uncertain returns will have a higher ending wealth value than an investment that simply earns (with certainty) its compound or geometric rate of return every year. In other words, more money, or terminal wealth, is gained by the occurrence of higher than expected returns than is lost by lower than expected returns.

In capital markets, where returns are a probability distribution, the answer that takes account of uncertainty, the arithmetic mean, is the correct one for estimating discount rates and the cost of capital.

EXAMPLE 11-1

A historical risk premium for Peoples Gas, a subsidiary of Consolidated Natural Gas, was estimated with an annual time series analysis from 1954 to 1992 applied to the gas distribution industry as a whole, using Moody's Gas Distribution Utility Index as an industry proxy. The analysis is depicted in Figure 11-2.

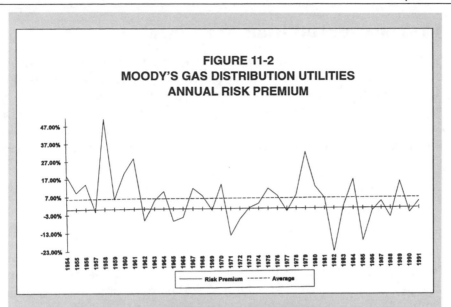

FIGURE 11-2
MOODY'S GAS DISTRIBUTION UTILITIES
ANNUAL RISK PREMIUM

The risk premium was estimated by computing the actual return on equity capital for *Moody's Gas Distribution Index* for each year from 1954 to 1992 using the actual stock prices and dividend yields of the index, and then subtracting the Moody's A-rated Utility Bond Index Return for that year. Moody's utility bond yields, dividend yields, and stock prices were obtained from *Moody's Public Utility Manual 1992*. To compute the annual stock return, the annual dividend yields reported on Moody's gas distribution utility index were converted to annual dividends by multiplying the yield by the stock price for that year. The dividends were then added to the stock price appreciation for the year and the total was divided by the stock price. The bond price information is obtained by calculating the present value of a bond due in 30 years with a $4.00 coupon and a yield to maturity of a particular year's indicated Moody's A-rated utility bond yield. See example calculations below:

$$\text{1990 Stock Return} = \frac{[\text{1991 Stock Price} - \text{1990 Stock Price} + \text{1990 dividend}]}{[\text{1990 Stock Price}]}$$

$$\text{1990 Bond Return} = \frac{[\text{1991 Bond Price} - \text{1990 Bond Price} + \text{1990 Interest}]}{[\text{1990 Bond Price}]}$$

where   Interest = $4.00

The average risk premium over the period was 5.69%. Given that Consolidated's current cost of debt at the time was 7.00%, and that the average risk premium is 5.69%, the implied cost of equity for Peoples is therefore 7.00% + 5.69% = 12.69%.

11.3 Expected Risk Premium

Another approach to estimating the risk premium is to examine the returns *expected* from investments in common equities and bonds. The risk premium is simply the difference between the expected returns on stocks and bonds. This approach is prospective in nature in contrast to the realized risk premium approach described in the previous section, which is retrospective in nature. The methodology can be expressed as follows:

where $\quad K_e = K_d +$ expected risk premium

$K_e =$ cost of common equity

$K_d =$ cost of debt

For example, if the current cost of debt is 6% and the expected risk premium between stocks and bonds is 7%, then the cost of common equity equals 13%:

$$K_e = K_d + \text{expected risk premium}$$

$$= 6\% + 7\% = 13\%$$

To estimate the expected risk premium, the expected rate of return on equity for a broad sample of companies is computed with the DCF model for each of several time periods (months, or quarters, or years) and the yields on debt for the corresponding period are subtracted from these estimates.

Implementing the Expected Risk Premium Method

To implement the method, several issues must be resolved. An appropriate debt security must be chosen, a representative selection of equity securities defined, a method of computing returns selected, and the risk premium adjusted for comparable risk. Each of those issues is discussed in turn.

Choice of Debt Security. As a practical matter, the choice of debt instrument in the risk premium analysis is largely immaterial, as long as it is consistently applied. To illustrate, if the risk premium of utility stocks is 4% measured over AA-rated utility bonds, and that the current AA bond yield is 8%, the implied cost of equity is 12%. If instead the risk premium of utility stocks is 5% measured over long-term Treasury bonds, and that the current yield on long-term Treasury bonds is 7%, the implied cost of equity is still 12%.

As a conceptual matter, however, several analysts prefer to use the yield on risk-free securities rather than the yield on corporate bonds in order to isolate the spread component of the return and avoid having to adjust the debt yield for default risk differentials. An added incentive for selecting risk-free government securities is the presence of well developed and active markets for interest rate futures contracts on government bonds. These markets contain market forecasts of rates on various Treasury securities.

Theoretically, the best surrogate for the risk-free rate is the yield on short-term Treasury bills. But the Treasury bills yield is highly volatile and dominated by short-term monetary and fiscal developments. More-over, the T-Bill rate incorporates a premium for short-term inflationary expectations rather than a premium for the long-run inflationary expectations embedded in bond yields and stock returns. Yields on default-free long-term Treasury bonds are thus more appropriate.

While long-term Treasury bonds possess a higher degree of interest rate risk than Treasury bills, this is only true if the bonds are sold before maturity. A substantial fraction of bond market participants, usually institutional investors with long-term liabilities (pension funds, insurance companies), in fact hold bonds until they mature, and therefore are not subject to interest rate risk. Institutional bondholders neutralize the impact of interest rate changes by engaging in hedging transactions in the financial futures markets or by matching the maturity of a bond portfolio with the investment planning period.

Some analysts believe that long-term bond yields embody investor expectations beyond the period for which utility rates will be in effect. As a compromise, they suggest the use of the yield on U.S. Treasury notes with approximately 3 to 5 years in maturity. However, the yields on intermediate-term Treasury notes reflect the impact of factors different from those influencing long-term securities such as common stock. The premium for expected inflation embedded into 5-year Treasury notes is likely to be far different than the inflationary premium embedded into long-term securities yields. The yields on long-term Treasury bonds match more closely with common stock returns. Therefore, the yield on intermediate-term Treasury notes is an inappropriate proxy for the risk-free rate.

Since common stock is a very long-term investment because the cash flows to investors in the form of dividends last indefinitely, the yield on very long-term government bonds is the best measure of the risk-free rate for use in the risk premium method. The expected common stock return is based on very long-term cash flows, regardless of an individual's holding time period. Moreover, utility asset investments generally have very long-term useful lives and should correspondingly be matched with very long-term maturity financing instruments.

Choice of Equity Securities. In order that the estimated risk premium be as stable as possible and be uncontaminated by the vagaries of a particular group of securities, the benchmark group of equity securities should be broadly representative and well diversified. There are several stock market indices on which comprehensive and easily accessible data are available. Value Line's Composite Market Index, Standard & Poor's 500 Index, and the Dow Jones Industrials Average are suitable proxies for the equity market portfolio. There are also several utility industry indices on which comprehensive and easily accessible data are available. Both Moody's and Standard & Poor's publish composite utility industry indices for the gas distribution, gas transmission, electric, and telecommunications industries.

Method of Computing Returns. In the case of bonds, the yield to maturity serves as a proxy for expected return, and is a suitable measure of the return expected by bondholders who anticipate holding the bond until maturity.[3] Yield to maturity data on government securities are widely available from published sources, including commercially available data bases on computers.

In the case of common stock, application of the DCF model to the market index as a whole can provide a reasonably precise estimate of the expected return for the market. The following two examples illustrate the methodology.

EXAMPLE 11-2

The aggregate expected market return is computed each year for a 10-year period, using data on Value Line's Composite Market Index by summing the dividend yields and the expected growth each year, as follows:

$$\text{Expected Equity Return}_t = \text{Expected Dividend Yield}_t + \text{Growth}_t$$

$$= \text{Spot Dividend Yield}_t\,(1+g) + \text{Growth}_t$$

$$= \frac{D_0(1+g)}{P_0} + g$$

---

[3] The yield to maturity of a bond is the return promised to the bondholder so long as the issuer meets all interest and principal obligations and the investor reinvests coupon income at a rate equal to the yield to maturity. See Homer and Leibowitz (1972) for a full discussion of bond return computations and of the pitfalls of yield to maturity as a valid return measure.

Expected growth on the market aggregate is proxied by the historical 5-year growth in earnings per share on the composite index.[4] The Value Line Data Base provides the necessary data on the index. The year-by-year analysis of expected equity market returns and bond yields over a 10-year period is shown in Table 11-2 using illustrative data.

TABLE 11-2
RISK PREMIUM ANALYSIS: AGGREGATE RETURN DATA

Year	Average Spot Dividend Yield	5-Year Growth Earnings Per Share	Expected Dividend Yield	Expected Equity Market Return	Moody's Newly Issued Corporate Bonds Composite	Risk Premium
(1)	(2)	(3)	(4)	(5)	(6)	(7)
1	2.28%	5.00%	2.39%	7.39%	7.50%	-0.11%
2	2.55%	6.50%	2.72%	9.22%	7.90%	1.32%
3	3.66%	9.00%	3.99%	12.99%	9.50%	3.49%
4	3.60%	10.00%	3.96%	13.96%	9.80%	4.16%
5	3.41%	11.50%	3.80%	15.30%	8.80%	6.50%
6	4.13%	12.00%	4.63%	16.63%	8.40%	8.23%
7	4.59%	11.50%	5.12%	16.62%	9.20%	7.42%
8	4.71%	11.50%	5.25%	16.75%	10.40%	6.35%
9	4.35%	12.50%	4.89%	17.39%	13.20%	4.19%
10	4.92%	12.00%	5.51%	17.51%	15.90%	1.61%

Average Risk Premium:

Years 5-10: 5.56%

Years 1-10: 4.32%

An estimate of the risk premium on the average stock is obtained each year by subtracting the yields on the average corporate bond, proxied by Moody's Newly Issued Corporate Bonds Composite, from the corresponding equity return. The results, depicted in Figure 11-3, indicate that the risk premium for the overall equity market averaged 4.32% above long-term corporate bonds over the 10-year period, and 5.56% over the last 5-year period. A similar and preferable analysis could be replicated using

---

[4] The growth in earnings is used instead of the growth in dividends because several stocks that make up the Value Line Composite Index do not pay dividends. In any event, for an index made up of a large number of companies, dividend growth and earnings growth are likely to coincide over the long-run, since in the aggregate dividend policies are stable.

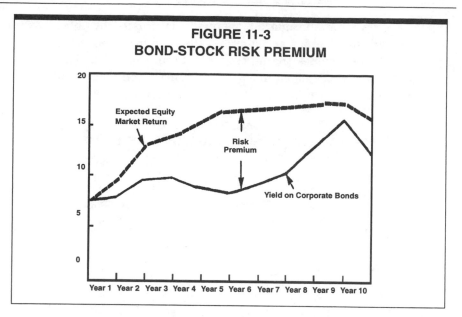

FIGURE 11-3
BOND-STOCK RISK PREMIUM

EXAMPLE 11-3

A technique that circumvents the difficulty of relying on historical growth was employed by Brigham, Shome, and Vinson (1985) in a comprehensive study of the risk premium approach to measuring a utility's cost of equity. For each company in the Dow Jones Industrials and Utility averages, they computed the equity return implicit in the Non-constant Growth DCF model by solving the following equation for K (see Chapter 4, Equation 4-19):

$$P_0 = \frac{D_1}{1+K} + \frac{D_2}{(1+K)^2} + \frac{D_3}{(1+K)^3} + \ldots + \frac{D_n}{(1+K)^n} + \frac{D_n(1+g)}{K-g} \times \frac{1}{(1+K)^n} \qquad (4\text{-}19)$$

As a proxy for the expected growth on the overall market, Brigham, Shome, and Vinson relied on Value Line's published forecast data for each year's dividend forecasts and for the terminal year dividend for each company in the index rather than on historical growth rates. The long-run, steady-state growth rate was computed by the sustainable growth method, whereby $g=br$, using Value Line's estimate of long-run expected return on book equity and long-run expected retention ratios for each firm in the index. Using the year-end stock price, they solved the model for K for each company in the sample for each year, and calculated an average DCF return for the industrials group and the utility group, weighted by the market value of each company as a proportion of the total market value. Subtracting the year-end long-term Treasury bond rate, a risk premium estimate was derived for each year.

long-term Treasury bonds instead of corporate bonds. There are a myriad of well-known academic and professional research studies published on the subject, using expected rates of return. Studies by Friend and Blume (1975), Malkiel (1979), Brigham and Shome (1982), and Brennan (1982) are examples.

One potential problem in the above approach is that historical growth may not be reflective of expected growth. Instead, the average 5-year earnings growth forecast of analysts reported by IBES for a large number of publicly-traded stocks can be used as a more suitable proxy for the expected growth on the overall market.

One drawback to this approach is that the Dow Jones Industrials Average may not be representative of the overall equity market, and that a more diversified cross-section of American industry may be preferable. On the other hand, the data requirements for application of the Brigham, Shome, and Vinson approach to each company in a large diversified index are computationally prohibitive.

Risk Adjustments.   The risk premium estimate derived from a composite market index must be adjusted for any risk differences between the equity market index employed in deriving the risk premium and a specified utility common stock. Several methods can be used to effect the proper risk adjustment.

First, the beta risk measure for the subject utility or the beta of a group of equivalent risk companies can serve as an adjustment device. The market risk premium, RP_M, is multiplied by the beta of the utility, β_i, to find the utility's own risk premium, RP_i:

$$RP_i = \beta_i\ RP_M$$

and the beta-adjusted risk premium is added to the bond yield to arrive at the utility's own cost of equity capital. For example, if the risk premium on the average stock is 5% over the bond yield, based on a broad-based index such as Value Line's Composite Market Index, and if the subject utility has a beta of 0.60, the adjusted risk premium is 5% x 0.60 = 3%. This method is very similar to the Empirical Capital Asset Pricing Model approach discussed in Chapter 13.

A second risk adjustment approach is to scale the risk premium up or down based on a comparison of the utility's risk relative to that of the overall market. Any of the objective quantitative measures of risk described in Chapter 3 are adequate for this purpose. For example, the ratio of the utility's standard deviation of returns to the average standard

283

deviation of the individual component stocks of the index can be computed and serve as a basis for relative risk adjustment. Alternately, in the case of non-publicly-traded utility stocks, the utility's average deviation around trend of earnings per share or of book return on equity relative to that of the market index could serve as the basis for the risk adjustment. The scaling can also be performed judgmentally on the basis of qualitative risk measures, such as relative bond ratings, Standard & Poor's stock ratings, and Value Line's safety ratings.

A third approach is to estimate a utility risk premium directly using an aggregate utility stock market index. Several examples of this approach appear in the next section.

Utility Industry Risk Premiums

Another way of tailoring the risk premium approach to a specific group of companies, such as regulated utilities, is to estimate a specialized risk premium for securities in a given industry, and then to base the risk premium for a specific company on the industry-wide risk premium. Example 11-4 illustrates this approach.

Company-Specific Risk Premium

Instead of relying on an aggregate stock market index or an industry specific index, the risk premium can be estimated by focusing on company specific data directly. Under this approach, a forward-looking risk premium can be estimated by computing the required market rate of return for the company's stock based on the DCF method for each month, or quarter, over a specified period, and then subtracting from these returns the spot yield on the utility's bond at the end of the same month or quarter.

Computation of the expected equity return is based on the standard DCF model, whereby the expected dividend yield is added to the long-run expected growth rate for each month. The latter can be proxied by a simple average of stock analysts' estimates of the long-term growth rate of the company's earnings and/or dividends during the past six months if such forecasts are available, or else on historical growth. The company's own risk premium is obtained for each month by subtracting from the equity return estimate the yield to maturity of its bonds for that month. The monthly risk premiums are averaged to produce the mean historical risk premium for the company.

One drawback of this approach is that the risk premium estimate is only as good as the DCF estimate of equity return used in deriving it and is thus susceptible to the singular vagaries of that particular company. An

EXAMPLE 11-4

A forward-looking or prospective risk premium for Peoples Gas, a subsidiary of Consolidated Natural Gas, was estimated with a month-to-month time series analysis over the past 9 years applied on the gas distribution industry as a whole, using Moody's Gas Distribution Utility Index as an industry proxy. The reason for performing the risk premium study on an industry composite rather than on individual company data is to mitigate the possible vagaries of individual company results. The analysis is depicted in Figure 11-4.

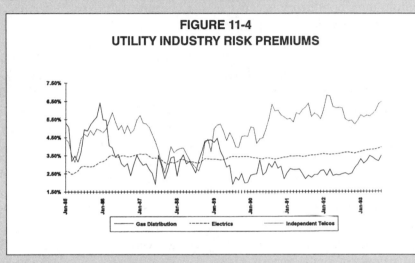

FIGURE 11-4
UTILITY INDUSTRY RISK PREMIUMS

The risk premium was estimated by computing the cost of equity capital for each month from 1985 to 1993 using the quarterly DCF model, and then subtracting the yield on Moody's A-rated Utility Bond index for that month. The monthly cost of equity was computed using the DCF model. The monthly spot dividend yields reported on the Moody's index were converted to expected dividend yields by multiplying the spot yield by $(1 + g)$, where g is the expected growth rate. The expected growth rates were obtained for each company in the index for each month from the analysts' consensus forecast reported in IBES. The growth rates were then averaged for each month for the index of companies. The cost of equity was computed using the quarterly DCF model approximation (see Chapter 7, Appendix 7-A). The average risk premium over the period was 3.36%, adjusted for flotation cost and quarterly timing.

Given that the cost of debt at the time was 7.00%, and that the average risk premium is 3.36%, the implied cost of equity for Peoples' Gas is therefore 7.00% + 3.36% = 10.36%.

Figure 11-4 also shows the evolution of risk premiums for the electric and telephone utility industries that were computed using a similar procedure.

abnormally low or high risk premium can result from a biased DCF estimate. For example, a negative risk premium can arise from a low or even negative historical growth rate, caused in turn by an inadequate earnings level, or by a low dividend yield component. The reverse conditions may cause an upward-biased risk premium. The estimated risk premium may be illusory because of the inability to measure accurately the equity return on the company's stock.

If the risk premium is based on the company's own bond yields rather than on Treasury bond yields, distortions can occur due to characteristics of the company's bonds. For example, the spread between Treasury bond yields and corporate bond yields widens during volatile capital market periods because of call provision effects. If the company's bonds are callable after 5 years from the issue date, and if investors expect falling interest rates, the relative probability of recall on the corporate bonds is thus increased, and a greater yield premium is required from such bonds.

Another potential drawback of the approach is that rate of return analysts sometimes use the approach as a check on their DCF estimate. This is circular to the extent that the risk premium computation relies on the DCF estimate of equity return.

11.4 Negative Risk Premium

In the 1980-1981 era of turbulent capital markets and volatile interest rates, several cost of capital experts testifying in regulatory proceedings advanced the notion that utility debt securities had become riskier than equity securities, and that the bond-stock risk premium had become negative. This section will review the arguments underlying this view.

The notion of a negative risk premium refers to the situation where the expected market return of common equity is less than that of the bonds of the same issuer. Expressed in another way, the debt securities having prior claims are more costly to the issuer than the securities having residual claims.

Such a view is not consistent with the basic precepts of finance, economics, and business law. By simple legal fact, common shareholders are residual claimants to a company's earnings and assets, while bondholders are priority claimants on corporate assets and earnings. The interest payments to bondholders take precedence and must be serviced first, before any distribution of dividends to common shareholders can be contemplated. It follows that the basic business risks of a company will fall much more heavily upon the earnings available to shareholders than upon the earnings available to service the priority claims of bondholders, and that therefore stocks are riskier than bonds.

Financial theory has always asserted that the greater a security's risk, the greater the return required from that security, with risk defined as the uncertainty of the return. Setting aside the question of bankruptcy and default, which by itself makes stocks riskier investment vehicles than bonds, the return on a bond, represented by fixed interest payments and repayment of principal, is contractual in nature. But there is no such guarantee in the case of common stocks. Dividend payments are not guaranteed, and the shareholders' claim on assets and earnings is junior to that of the bondholders. Bondholders expect that they will earn the prevailing coupon rate or yield-to-maturity when they purchase a bond, and shareholders expect a return made up of dividends and capital gains. To subscribe to the idea of a negative risk premium is synonymous with believing that investors price securities so that they assign a higher probability of earning the stock's non-contractual return than of earning the bond's guaranteed return, which seems highly unlikely.

If the expected return on bonds were to momentarily exceed the expected return on common equity, rational profit-maximizing and risk-averse investors could both enhance the yield of their portfolios and reduce the risk of their holdings by simply switching out of common stocks and into bonds. Such portfolio-switching behavior would lower stock prices and increase bond prices, thereby raising the yield on stocks and lowering the yield on bonds. This portfolio substitution of bonds for stocks would continue until a normal positive risk premium was restored. The existence of a negative risk premium could not persist for any length of time in efficient capital markets.

The allegation of a negative risk premium sometimes rests on empirical studies of historical "realized" risk spreads of stocks over bonds as opposed to the study of "expected" risk premiums. Clearly, during depressed stock market periods, common stocks do worse than bonds, and realized stock returns are lower than realized bond returns. The realized return of bonds has in fact exceeded the return on stocks in several instances in the past, but this only shows that investor expectations simply were not realized for those periods. In a forward-looking sense, expected stock returns will exceed expected bond returns. Risk premium studies should always be conducted on the basis of expectations, and not on the basis of realizations.

The view that common equity capital is more risky than bonds is certainly consistent with the empirical data. The seminal Ibbotson Associates study (1993) estimated the risk premium between the average stock and risk-free government bonds to have been 7.3% during the 1926-1992 period, and the risk premium between the average stock and the average corporate bond to have been about 6.6% during the same period. Granted that utility stocks are less risky than the average stock, as evidenced by their lower betas, the risk difference does not even begin to explain the remaining return differential. There is no logical or empirical support for the notion that bonds are riskier than common equity.

Outstanding bonds are in fact exposed to interest rate risk, that is, the risk that interest rates will rise and bond prices will fall, inflicting a capital loss on bondholders. This risk can rise substantially in periods of volatile interest rates, such as the 1980-1981 period. It should be kept in mind, however, that some stocks, utility stocks in particular, are highly interest-sensitive. These stocks provide a return to their holders predominantly in the form of dividend yield, which is interest-rate sensitive. There is a well known bond theorem that states that the longer the maturity of a security, the greater its price volatility. It is also a fact that common stocks do not mature, and therefore bonds have a shorter maturity. If interest rates fall, the price of a public utility's stock would increase more than the price of its bonds. But the converse is also true. If interest rates were to rise, the common stock price would fall more. And this is precisely why interest-sensitive common stocks would be riskier than bonds.

Leaving aside the interest-sensitivity argument, negative risk premiums can only prevail if the interest rate risk of bonds exceeds the combined business risk and financial risk of stocks. Advocates of negative risk premiums argue that such a situation indeed exists during inflationary periods. During such periods, utility stocks are safer investments than bonds since equity returns can be increased by regulators while bond returns are fixed. In other words, utility common shareholders are not subject to interest rate risk because regulators will increase allowed common equity returns as inflationary pressures intensify. The dollar returns received by bondholders are fixed and cannot be adjusted for inflation, whereas the returns received by shareholders are indexed to inflation by the regulatory process itself. This argument is often characterized as the "hedging" argument, in which it is said that bonds are poor inflation hedges and utility stocks are a good hedge against inflation.

The argument regarding the hedging advantage of stocks over bonds is misstated right from the start. While bonds are not hedged against unanticipated inflation, they are hedged against anticipated inflation since bond yields increase in step with anticipated inflation. So, if bonds are indeed superior hedges, it is against the unanticipated component of inflation only. Theoretically, equity investments represent claims against physical assets whose real returns should remain unaffected by inflation. In reality, equities have not provided a hedge against inflation. Up until 1982, the stock market indices had not progressed substantially since the upward inflationary spiral started in the late 1960s, and declined severely in real inflation-adjusted terms. The view that equities are a hedge against inflation is unsupported by the facts. The tax system erroneously taxes inflation profits, and historical cost-based depreciation charges do not cover replacement costs adequately in inflationary times. Inflation increases financing requirements at the very time that such financing is expensive, depressing earnings.

As far as utilities are concerned, several studies by both practitioners and academicians have documented the fact that the average returns on common equity for the utility industry have not kept pace with inflation.[5] Even casual empiricism will reveal that despite increases in equity return allowances, the equity returns actually earned by utilities have not increased commensurately. The record of the last decade indicates that the returns earned by utilities cannot be readily adjusted in response to adverse interest rate changes.

In fact, even if stocks in general were inflation hedges, utility stocks are likely to be poor hedges. During the period of regulatory lag, which is likely to lengthen during inflationary periods, the utility shareholder is not protected against changes in expected inflation. Compared to unregulated companies, the utilities have few of the characteristics that would make them good inflation hedges; they are more capital intensive, enjoy relatively little pricing flexibility, and have more rigid financing requirements.

To mitigate further the argument that interest rate risk affects bonds more than stocks, a substantial fraction of bond market participants, usually institutional, are able to attenuate interest rate risk by hedging this risk either through appropriate positions in financial futures contracts, or by pursuing so-called immunization strategies. Institutional bondholders neutralize the impact of interest rate changes by matching the maturity of a bond portfolio with the investment planning period, or by engaging in hedging transactions in the financial futures markets. The merits and mechanics of such strategies are well documented by both academicians

---

[5] Several studies have documented the poor performance of common stocks as inflation hedges. See Reilly (1994) for a discussion and review of these studies.

and practitioners[6]. Stocks are not so easily immunized, being of infinite maturity. Moreover, the mechanisms and market techniques for minimizing the effects of interest rate risk on stock portfolios are still embryonic in nature, compared to similar techniques for bond portfolios.

To further assess the likelihood of negative risk premiums, if negative risk premiums do exist, they should be associated with sharply upward sloping yield curves. If investors are deeply concerned with inflation, the maturity premium of long-term bonds over short-term bonds should expand, compressing the stock-bond risk premium. In fact, the reverse situation usually prevails in times of interest rate volatility. The yield curve is negative, with short-term rates higher than long-term rates. This is inconsistent with negative yield spreads.

Some analysts contend that after-tax return factors can justify the existence of a negative risk premium. By applying tax adjustments to the raw returns on stocks and bonds, a negative risk premium emerges. The adjustments reflect the favorable tax treatment accorded to the capital gains component of stock returns and the tax incentives available for dividend income received from electric utilities. Such adjustments are unnecessary as they are already impounded in stock prices. To the extent that such advantages exist, investors are willing to pay higher market prices, and accept lower expected returns. Any forward-looking cost of capital calculation already embodies tax effects since investors price securities on the basis of after-tax returns.

The existence of a negative risk premium is highly unlikely, as it is at serious odds with the basic tenets of finance and law. Using proper definitions for expected rates of return of equity and debt, the preponderance of the evidence indicates that the negative risk premium does not exist. Several risk premium studies cited in Section 11.3 of this chapter have found positive risk premiums well in excess of 3% over the last decade. Risk premiums do narrow during unusually turbulent and volatile interest rate environments, but then return to normal levels. They are most unlikely to ever become negative.

11.5 Risk Premium Determinants

Fundamentally, the primary determinant of expected returns is risk. To wit, the various paradigms of financial theory, including the Capital Asset

---

[6] See McNally (1980) and Kolb and Gay (1982) for a discussion of immunization strategies for bond portfolios.

Pricing Model and the Arbitrage Pricing Model, posit fundamental relationships between return and risk. There are also secondary influences on the relative magnitude of the risk premium, however, including the level of interest rates, default risk, and taxes.

Interest Rates

Published studies by Brigham, Shome, and Vinson (1985), Harris (1986), Harris and Marston (1992), Carleton, Chambers, and Lakonishok (1983), McShane (1993), and others demonstrate that, beginning in 1980, risk premiums varied inversely with the level of interest rates—rising when rates fell and declining when interest rates rose. The reason for this relationship is that when interest rates rise, bondholders suffer a capital loss. This is referred to as interest rate risk. Stockholders, on the other hand, are more concerned with the firm's earning power. So, if bondholders' fear of interest rate risk exceeds shareholders' fear of loss of earning power, the risk differential will narrow and hence the risk premium will shrink. This is particularly true in high inflation environments. Interest rates rise as a result of accelerating inflation, and the interest rate risk of bonds intensifies more than the earnings risk of common stocks, which are partially hedged from the ravages of inflation. This phenomenon has been termed as a "lock-in" premium. Conversely in low interest rate environments, when bondholders' interest rate fears subside and shareholders' loss of earning power dominate, the risk differential will widen and hence the risk premium will increase.

Harris (1986) showed that for every 100 basis point change in government bond yields, the equity risk premium for utilities changes 51 basis points in the opposite direction, for a net change in the cost of equity of 49 basis points. For example, a 100 basis point decline in government bond yields would lead to a 51 basis point increase in the equity risk premium and therefore an overall decrease in the cost of equity of 49 basis points. Similar results were uncovered by McShane (1993) who examined the statistical relationship between DCF-derived risk premiums, interest rates, and inflation, using a sample of high-grade utilities. Example 11-5 is extracted from the McShane risk premium analysis to illustrate the methodology.

EXAMPLE 11-5
DCF-Based Risk Premium Study

Dependent Variable:

Equity Risk Premium, defined as the DCF cost of equity less the yield on long-term government bonds.

Independent Variables:

1. Yield on long-term government bonds.

2. Time (year)

The statistical relationship obtained by ordinary least-squares regression is as follows:

Equity Risk Premium = 11.25 - 0.51 (Long Government Bonds) - 0.26 Time

$$(t=-5.56) \quad (t=-7.48)$$

By substituting the level of the long-term government bond yield and the year, an estimate of the risk premium is obtained.

Carleton (1984) found that for a 100 basis point change in government bond yields, the equity risk premium changes 63 basis points in the opposite direction for a net change of 37 basis points. These studies imply that the cost of equity changes only half as much as interest rates change. The knowledge that risk premiums vary inversely to the level of interest rates can be used to adjust historical risk premiums to better reflect current market conditions. Thus, when interest rates are unusually high (low), the appropriate current risk premium is somewhat below (above) that long-run average. The empirical research cited above provides guidance as to the magnitude of the adjustment.

Risk premiums also tend to fluctuate with changes in investor risk aversion. Such changes can be tracked by observing the yield spreads between different bond rating categories over time. Brigham, Shome, and Vinson (1985) examined the relationship between risk premium and bond rating and found, unsurprisingly, that the risk premiums are higher for lower rated firms than for higher rated firms. Figure 11-5 shows the results graphically.

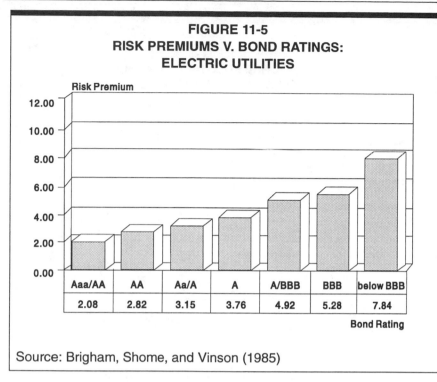

FIGURE 11-5
RISK PREMIUMS V. BOND RATINGS:
ELECTRIC UTILITIES

Aaa/AA	AA	Aa/A	A	A/BBB	BBB	below BBB
2.08	2.82	3.15	3.76	4.92	5.28	7.84

Bond Rating

Source: Brigham, Shome, and Vinson (1985)

EXAMPLE 11-6

Figure 11-6 shows the month-to-month evolution of the risk premium of Bell Regional Holding Companies over the 1985-1993 period along with the corresponding level of interest rates. On a month-to-month basis over the period, the risk premium fluctuated in a manner inversely related to interest rates. As interest rates increased, the yield spread of stocks over bonds narrowed, owing to the increasing interest rate risk faced by bond investors, and conversely. The inverse relationship between the risk premium and interest rates is depicted graphically in Figure 11-7. The functional relationship between the two can be determined by statistical regression techniques. The exact statistical relationship between interest rates and the risk premium from 1985 to 1993 is as follows:

RISK PREMIUM = 0.070014 − 0.36946 (INTEREST RATE)

Given that Moody's AA Utility Bond Yield Average stood at approximately 7.25% at that time, the risk premium implied by the above relationship is 4.32%, that is, 0.070014 - 0.36946 x .0725 = .0432. The implied cost of equity was therefore 7.25% + 4.32% = 11.57%.

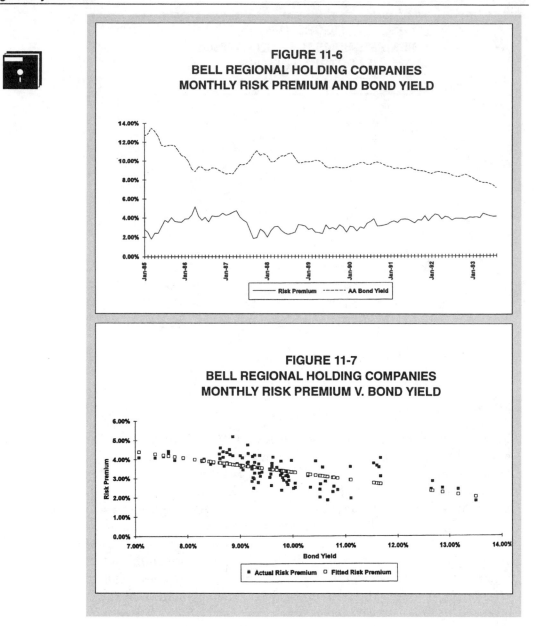

FIGURE 11-6
BELL REGIONAL HOLDING COMPANIES
MONTHLY RISK PREMIUM AND BOND YIELD

FIGURE 11-7
BELL REGIONAL HOLDING COMPANIES
MONTHLY RISK PREMIUM V. BOND YIELD

Taxes

Significant changes in the relative taxation of returns received from stocks and bonds can also influence risk premiums. Measured risk premiums will in fact incorporate investor adjustments to relative taxation rates, since it is pre-tax risk premiums that are measured from capital market data rather than post-tax quantities.

Some analysts have therefore argued that there should be an adjustment for taxation differentials between securities and investors. This presents a gargantuan practical problem, however. If a regulatory commission were to seek to enable the utility to compensate investors for their after-tax returns, there could be as many returns as there are tax bracket variations, and they would defy analysis. It is impractical to determine the constellation of tax brackets for all the company's shareholders, and to determine the identity and tax bracket of the marginal price-setting investor. This argument ignores the fact that several institutional investors are not taxable, such as pension funds, and they engage in very large amounts of trading on security markets. Taxable retail investors are relatively inactive traders when compared to large non-taxable investors who have a substantial influence on capital markets.

Fundamentally, the core determinant of expected returns is not taxability, it is risk. Taxable investors will examine the risk-return tradeoff offered by various securities first, and as a secondary matter, the taxability issue.

Not only is it unrealistic to attempt to target tax clienteles in issuing securities but this presents investors with a serious practical dilemma. If a utility could target non-taxable investors only for bonds, it would follow that a coupon considerably less than the current return on common equity would be acceptable, since the bonds have much lower risk. But when the buyer of such bonds decided to sell securities, he or she would confront a serious dilemma because the taxable would-be buyers would require vastly higher returns (would be willing to pay a much lower price). The seller would face a large capital loss on resale, or would be forced to sell the bonds to other non-taxable investors. But the latter would have no incentive to trade with the seller, because they would have the opportunity of purchasing many other alternative securities providing a higher yield.

11.6 Conclusions

The risk premium method is conceptually sound and firmly rooted in the conceptual framework of Capital Market Theory, which is the subject of the next chapter. Data requirements to implement the method are not prohibitive. The methodology is responsive to changes in capital market conditions and provides a timely signaling device for current interest rate trends in contrast to the DCF method, which may be sluggish in detecting changes in return requirements, especially when based on historical data. For example, a DCF estimate anchored on historical growth trends may actually decline during a steep rise in interest rates. The high costs of borrowing erode utility earnings, producing low earnings growth rates, and a downward biased DCF estimate. The reverse scenario occurs in a period of declining interest costs, producing upward-biased DCF estimates.

One advantage of risk premium over DCF is that the former is a period-by-period study of the cost of equity over the cost of debt, in contrast to the latter which is a point-in-time cross-sectional estimate. In other words, the risk premium approach takes a broader time-series perspective rather than a snapshot point-in-time viewpoint, and is therefore less vulnerable to the vagaries of any one particular capital market environment. The risk premium test relies on a succession of DCF observations over long periods, and is not as vulnerable to a given capital market environment as a spot DCF test.

Equal emphasis should be accorded to risk premium results based on history and those based on prospective data. Each proxy for expected risk premium brings information to the judgment process from a different light. Neither proxy is without blemish, each has advantages and short-comings. Historical risk premiums over long periods are available and verifiable, but may no longer be applicable if structural shifts have occurred. Prospective risk premiums, which are DCF-based, may be more relevant since they encompass both history and current changes, but are nevertheless imperfect proxies and are subject to measurement error and to the vagaries of the DCF input proxies.

References

Brealey, R. and Myers, S. *Principles of Corporate Finance,* 4th ed. New York: McGraw-Hill, 1991.

Brennan, J.F. "Does Utility Long-term Debt Really Cost More than Common Equity?" *Public Utilities Fortnightly,* February 18, 1982.

Brigham, E.F. and Shome, D.K. "Equity Risk Premium in the 1980's." Washington DC: Institute for Study of Regulation, 1982.

Brigham, E.F., Shome, D.K., and Vinson, S. R. "The Risk Premium Approach to Measuring a Utility's Cost of Equity." *Financial Management,* Spring 1985, 33-45.

Carleton, W.T. "Rate of Return, Rate Base, and Regulatory Lag Under Conditions of Changing Capital Costs." *Land Economics,* May 1974, 145-151.

Carleton, W.T., Chambers, W., and Lakonishok, J. "Inflation Risk and Regulatory Lag." *Journal of Finance,* May 1983.

Friend, I. and Blume, M. E. "The Demand for Risky Assets." *American Economic Review,* December 1975, 900-922.

Harris, R.S. "Using Analysts' Growth Forecasts to Estimate Shareholder Required Rates of Return." *Financial Management,* Spring 1986, 58-67.

Harris, R.S. and Marston, F.C. "Estimating Shareholder Risk Premia Using Analysts' Growth Forecasts." *Financial Management,* Summer 1992, 63-70.

Homer, S. and Leibowitz, M.L. *Inside the Yield Book: New Tools for Bond Market Strategy.* Englewood Cliffs NJ: Prentice-Hall, 1972.

Ibbotson Associates. *Stocks, Bonds, Bills, and Inflation, 1992 Yearbook.* Chicago: Ibbotson Associates, 1993.

Ibbotson, R.G. and Sinquefield, R.A. *Stocks, Bonds, Bills, and Inflation: The Past and the Future.* Financial Analysts Research Foundation, 1982 ed., Monograph No. 15.

Kolb, R.W. and Gay, G.D. "Immunizing Bond Portfolios with Interest Rate Futures." *Financial Management,* Summer 1982, 81-89.

Litzenberger, R.H. Prepared Testimony on Behalf of NYNEX, FCC Docket No. 84-800, 1984.

Malkiel, B.G. "The Capital Formation Problem in the United States." *Journal of Finance,* May 1979, 291-306.

McNally, R.W. "How to Neutralize Reinvestment Rate Risk." *Journal of Portfolio Management,* Spring 1980.

McShane, K.C. Prepared Testimony on Fair Return on Equity for Bell Canada, Foster Associates, Inc., February 1993.

Reilly, F.K. *Investment Analysis and Portfolio Management,* Hinsdale IL: Dryden Press, 1994.

Additional References

Carleton, W.T. and Lakonishok, J. "Risk and Return on Equity; The Use and Misuse of Historical Estimates." *Financial Analysts' Journal,* January-February 1985, 38-47.

Appendix 11-A
Comparison of the Use of Arithmetic and Geometric Means in Estimating the Cost of Capital

This appendix shows why arithmetic rather than geometric means should be used for forecasting, discounting, and estimating the cost of capital. Similar treatments and demonstrations are available from Brealey and Myers (1991), Ibbotson Associates (1993), and Litzenberger (1984). This appendix draws from the three aforementioned sources, particularly the latter.

By definition, the cost of equity capital is the annual discount rate that equates the discounted value of expected future cash flows (from dividends and the sale of the stock at the end of the investor's investment horizon) to the current market price of a share in the firm. The discount rate that equates the discounted value of future expected dividends and the end of period expected stock price to the current stock price is a prospective arithmetic, rather than a prospective geometric mean rate of return. Since future dividends and stock prices cannot be predicted with certainty, the "expected" annual rate of return that investors require is an average "target" percentage rate around which the actual, year-by-year returns will vary. This target rate is, in effect, an arithmetic average.

A numerical illustration adapted from Litzenberger (1984) will clarify this important point. Consider a non-dividend paying stock trading for $100 which has, in every year, an equal chance of appreciating by 20% or declining by 10%. Thus, after one year, there is an equal chance that the stock's price will be $120 and an equal chance the price will be $90. Figure 11A-1 presents all possible eventualities after two periods have elapsed (the rates of return are presented at the end of the lines in the diagram).

The possible stock prices are shown in the following table.

TABLE 11A-1
STOCK PRICES AFTER TWO PERIODS

Price	Chance
$144	1 chance in 4
$108	2 chances in 4
$ 81	1 chance in 4

The expected future stock price after two periods is then:

$$1/4 \ (\$144) + 2/4 \ (\$108) + 1/4(\$81) = \$110.25$$

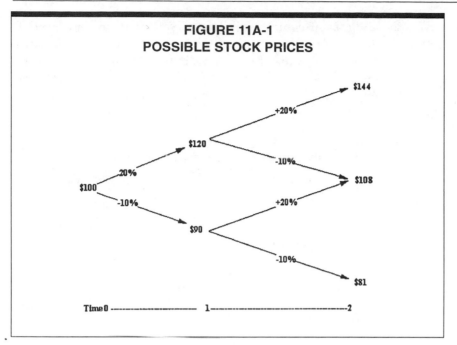

FIGURE 11A-1
POSSIBLE STOCK PRICES

The cost of equity capital is calculated as the discount rate that equates the present value of the future expected cash flows to the current stock price. In the present simple example, the only cash flow is the gain from selling the stock after two periods have elapsed. Thus, using the expected stock price of $110.25 calculated above, the expected rate of return is that r, which solves the following equation:

$$\text{Current Stock Price} = \frac{\text{Expected Stock Price}}{(1+r)^2}$$

The factor $(1+r)^2$ discounts the expected stock price to the present. Substituting the numerical values, we have:

$$\$100 = \frac{\$100.25}{(1+r)^2}$$

$$r = 5\%$$

Thus, the cost of equity capital is 5%. This 5% cost of equity capital is equal to the prospective arithmetic mean rate of return, which is the probability-weighted average single period rate of return on equity. Since in every period there is an equal chance that the stock's return will be 20% or -10%, the probability-weighted average is:

$$1/2\,(\,20\%\,) + 1/2\,(-10\%\,) = 5\%$$

However, the 5% cost of equity capital is not equal to the prospective geometric mean rate of return, which is a probability-weighted average of the possible compounded rates of return over the two periods. Now consider the prospective geometric mean rate of return. Table 11A-2 shows the possible compounded rates of return over two periods, and the probability of each.

TABLE 11A-2
STOCK PRICES AND RETURNS AFTER TWO PERIODS

Price	Chance	Compounded Return
$144	1 chance in 4	20.00%
$108	2 chances in 4	3.92%
$ 81	1 chance in 4	-10.00%

Thus, the prospective geometric mean rate of return is:

$$1/4\ (\ 20\%\ ) = 2/4\ (\ 3.92\%\ ) + 1/4\ (\ -10\%\ ) = 4.46\%$$

This return is not equal to the 5% cost of equity capital.

Litzenberger (1984) extended the example to include the case of a dividend-paying company and reached the same conclusion: the implied discount rate calculated in the DCF model is an expected arithmetic rather than an expected geometric mean rate of return.

The foregoing analysis shows that it is erroneous to use a prospective multi-year geometric mean rate of return as a "target" rate of return for each year of the period. If, for example, investors currently require an expected future rate of return on an investment of 13% each year, then 13% is the appropriate annual rate of return on equity for ratemaking purposes. Consequently, in using a risk premium approach for the purposes of rate of return regulation, the single-year annual required rate of return should be estimated using arithmetic mean risk premiums.

Chapter 12
Capital Asset Pricing Model

This chapter describes the Capital Asset Pricing Model (CAPM) approach to cost of capital estimation, and explores the model's applicability to public utilities. Conceptual, empirical, and computational issues are raised. Section 12.1 provides a succinct conceptual background of the model. Formal theoretical development of the model is only briefly considered; comprehensive and detailed presentations of the theory are generously available in most finance or investment textbooks.[1] Section 12.2 examines the interrelationships between the CAPM, DCF, and Risk Premium models. Section 12.3 examines the CAPM's consistency with public utility regulation. Section 12.4 discusses problems in application, potential remedies, and the model's required inputs. Section 12.5 discusses the concerns and practical usefulness of the model. This chapter lays the groundwork for the next 3 chapters, which consider this model and the Arbitrage Pricing Model in some detail. Chapter 13 summarizes the empirical evidence on the CAPM's validity, and explores extensions of the model in light of its conceptual and empirical limitations, setting the stage for the Arbitrage Pricing Model. Chapter 14 will present a variety of applications of CAPM theory germane to utility ratemaking, such as divisional cost of capital, risk adjustment as between parent and utility subsidiary, and the impact of diversification activities. Chapter 15 presents the Arbitrage Pricing Model.

12.1 Conceptual Background

The concept and measurement of risk were treated extensively in Chapters 2 and 3. Risk was defined as the variability of outcomes around an expected result. For an undiversified investor who views a security in isolation, the standard deviation of realized returns provides a valid estimate of the security's risk.

An underpinning of the CAPM is that an investor diversifies by combining risky securities into a portfolio. The result is such that the risk of the total portfolio is less than that of any of its parts. Diversification reduces portfolio risk because security returns do not move perfectly together. Complete

---

[1] For a complete development of the CAPM, see Brealey and Myers (1991), Sharpe and Alexander (1990), Copeland and Weston (1993); Hagin (1979) presents a straightforward non-mathematical treatment of the model.

elimination of risk is impossible, however, since securities all move together to a certain extent because of the influence of pervasive market-wide forces.

A security's total risk can be partitioned into "specific risk," the portion unique to the company, and "market risk," the nondiversifiable portion related to the general movement of security markets. The core idea of the CAPM is that investors can eliminate company-unique risks by appropriate diversification, and should therefore not be rewarded for bearing this superfluous risk. Diversified risk-averse investors are only exposed to market risk, and are therefore rewarded with higher expected returns for bearing only market-related risk. Beta is a measure of market risk, and captures the extent to which a security's returns move in tandem with the returns of the overall market.

A fundamental notion underlying the CAPM is that risk-averse investors demand higher returns for assuming additional risk, and higher-risk securities are priced to yield higher expected returns than are lower-risk securities. The CAPM quantifies the additional return required for bearing incremental risk, and provides a formal risk-return relationship anchored on the basic idea that only market risk matters, as measured by beta. Formally, all securities are priced such that:

Expected Return = Risk-free Rate + Risk Premium

= Risk-free Rate + Relevant Risk x Market Price of Risk

= Risk-free Rate + Beta x Market Price of Risk

The formal CAPM expression takes the form:

$$K = R_F + \beta (R_M - R_F) \qquad (12\text{-}1)$$

where K = required return

R_F = risk-free rate

R_M = required return on the overall market

β = security's beta risk measure

Equation 12-1 is the standard CAPM expression and provides a simple and useful tool to estimate the cost of capital for securities having risks different from that of the overall market. A formal derivation of the model can be found in Appendix 12-A. The CAPM asserts that an investor expects to earn a return, K, that could be gained on a riskless investment,

R_F, plus a risk premium for assuming risk, proportional to the security's market risk, β, and the market price of risk $R_M - R_F$.

The CAPM risk-return relationship, often referred to as the Security Market Line (SML), is portrayed graphically in Figure 12-1.

FIGURE 12-1
THE SECURITY MARKET LINE

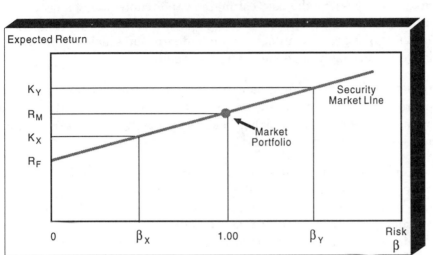

The intercept of the line is the expected risk-free rate, R_F, which has a beta of zero, and the slope is the expected market return, R_M, less the risk-free rate, R_F, that is, the slope equals the market price of risk. The expected return on the market has a beta of 1.00 by definition. Utility X on the graph has a beta less than 1.00 and thus an expected return (cost of capital), K_X, less than the overall market return, R_M, while Utility Y has a beta greater than 1.00 and an expected return K_Y greater than R_M.

The CAPM can be viewed as a equilibrium pricing schedule for capital of varying risk, depicting the going rate of return prevailing in capital markets on investments of varying risk. The model states that in well-functioning capital markets, the expected risk premium on each investment is proportional to its beta. This implies that each security should lie on the Security Market Line. Competition in capital markets among investments of differing risk produces the CAPM risk-return relationship. Any security selling at a price low enough to yield more than its appropriate return on the SML attracts profit-maximizing investors who bid up its price until it expected return falls to its appropriate position on the SML. Conversely, investors will dispose of any security selling at a price high enough to put its expected return below the SML, exerting downward pressure on price until the security's return rises to the level justified by its beta.

A multitude of assumptions are required to obtain the CAPM. Two general assumptions overshadow the others. The first general assumption is that capital markets are competitive and efficient, and information is freely available to all investors. This information is absorbed so quickly into security prices that the security prices can be trusted to represent the best estimate of the true value of a security at any time. An important body of empirical evidence amassed by researchers generally points to a high degree of efficiency in capital markets,[2] although some inefficiencies remain.

The second general assumption is that investors are rational profit-maximizers who pursue their monetary self-interests, and in the process demand higher returns for higher risks and drive expected returns toward their levels predicted by the SML.

The remaining assumptions are more stringent and specialized. For example, investors hold diversified portfolios and operate in capital markets unencumbered by transaction costs, taxes, and restrictions on borrowing and short-selling. Investors possess homogeneous expectations, thereby agreeing on the likely prospects of securities over a common time horizon. Finally, investor preferences and the statistical nature of security returns follow rigid definite patterns.

In spite of the lack of realism of some of these assumptions, the true test of the CAPM is whether the model possesses explanatory power and forecasting ability. It is worthwhile asking whether the assumptions underlying the CAPM are any less confining than those underlying the standard growth DCF model. This is unlikely. According to the "end result" doctrine of the *Hope* case, and according to the dictates of economic positivism, a model should be judged by its ability to predict and explain rather than by the robustness of its assumptions. In any event, the CAPM is remarkably robust in its basic formulation. Several extensions of the basic CAPM have been developed, relaxing the assumptions, without tarnishing the fundamental nature of the model.

The CAPM is not a static once-and-for-all relationship. The height and slope of the SML fluctuate in response to macroeconomic forces and changes in investor behavior. For example, Figure 12-2 shows the new SML following an increase in expected inflation from 0% to 6%. At every level of risk, the

---

[2] Reilly (1989) presents a synthesis of the empirical evidence on market efficiency.

real inflation-free cost of capital rises by 6% to adjust to its new nominal level. Figure 12-2, adapted from Brigham & Gapenski (1991), also demonstrates the higher risk premium that results from a steepening of the slope of the SML in response to a higher degree of investor risk aversion.

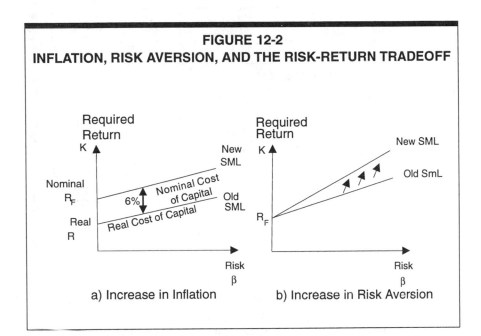

FIGURE 12-2
INFLATION, RISK AVERSION, AND THE RISK-RETURN TRADEOFF

12.2 CAPM, DCF, and Risk Premium Interrelationship

For added perspective, it is useful at this point to spell out the link among the three broad approaches to cost of capital estimation studied so far. The interrelationships among DCF, risk premium, and the CAPM are configured in Figure 12-3.

Starting at the top of the diagram, DCF valuation theory defines the value of any equity security as the discounted present value of its future stream of dividend payments. Given the market price of the security and its forecast dividend stream, the implicit expected return from the security can be derived. The risk premium approach, as shown in the middle of the diagram, holds that the expected return for a security can be derived by adding to the risk-free return an appropriate premium return to reflect the security's risk. The premium for bearing risk is empirically derived. The CAPM, shown at the bottom of the diagram, also asserts that the expected return depends on the risk-free rate and a risk premium, but formally quantifies the exact nature of the risk premium as a linear function of market risk, or beta.

FIGURE 12-3
THE RELATIONSHIP AMONG DCF, RISK PREMIUM, AND CAPM

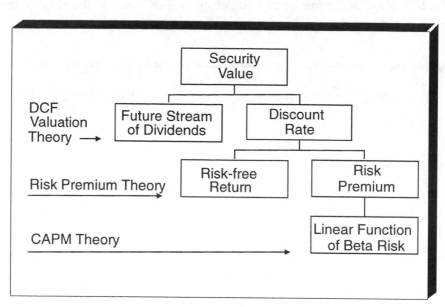

FIGURE 12-4
ESTIMATES OF UTILITY COST OF CAPITAL USING THE
CAPM: A NUMERICAL ILLUSTRATION

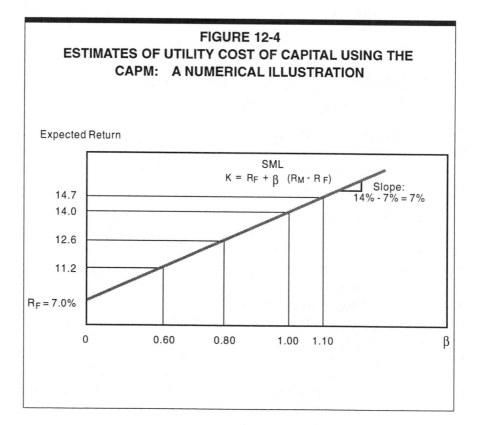

12.3 The CAPM and Public Utility Regulation

The cornerstone of public utility rate of return regulation is the principle enunciated in the *Hope* case that "the return to the equity owner should be commensurate with returns on investments in other enterprises having corresponding risk." The CAPM presents a conceptual framework that meets the legal criteria for the establishment of a fair return and that operationalizes the *Hope* doctrine. The "return commensurate with the return foregone from comparable risk opportunities" is the return that investors expect when they purchase other equity shares of comparable risk. The *Hope* decision requires consideration of relative risk, which can be measured by beta. Provided that estimates for the relevant risk and attendant return quoted in the *Hope* doctrine can be obtained, the CAPM relationship can be used to determine a fair and reasonable return.

In the *Bluefield* decision, the U.S. Supreme Court required that the allowed return be sufficient to assure a utility's financial soundness, which implies that market returns be considered. The CAPM-based cost of capital is the rate of return prevailing in capital markets on investments of similar risk, and is therefore the return necessary to attract capital to investments of a given risk, taking into account the soundness criterion of *Bluefield*.

12.4 CAPM Application

At first glance, the CAPM appears simple in application. The values of the CAPM's three input parameters, R_F, β, and R_M, are estimated and inserted into the CAPM formula to produce the cost of equity estimate, or used in reading the cost of equity directly from the SML. A numerical example is shown in Figure 12-4.

Assuming a 7% risk-free rate, and a 17% market return, that is, a market risk premium of 7%, the cost of equity estimates for Utilities X, Y, and Z are 11.2%, 12.6%, and 14.7%, respectively, corresponding to their respective betas of 0.60, 0.80, and 1.10.

Despite the CAPM's conceptual appeal and mechanistic simplicity, operationalizing the CAPM to estimate a fair return on equity presents several practical difficulties. From the start, the model itself is an expectational, forward-looking model. To stress this point, the following equation restates the CAPM formula with expectational operators attached to each input variable:

$$E(K) = E(R_F) + E(\beta) \times [E(R_M) - E(R_F)] \qquad (12\text{-}2)$$

where $\quad E(K) \quad$ = expected return, or cost of capital

$\quad\quad\quad\quad E(R_F) \quad$ = expected risk-free rate

$\quad\quad\quad\quad E(\beta) \quad$ = expected beta

$\quad\quad\quad\quad E(R_M) \quad$ = expected market return

The difficulty is that the CAPM model is a prospective model while most of the available capital market data required to match the three theoretical input variables (expected risk-free return, expected beta, and expected market return) are historical. None of the input variables exists as a separate identifiable entity. It is thus necessary in practice to employ different proxies, with different results obtained with each set of proxy variables. Each of the three required inputs to the CAPM is examined below.

Risk-free Rate

Theoretically, the yield on 90-day Treasury bills is virtually devoid of default risk and subject to a negligible amount of interest rate risk. But, as seen in the previous chapter, the T-bill rate fluctuates widely, leading to volatile and unreliable equity return estimates, and it does not match the equity investor's planning horizon. Equity investors generally have an investment horizon far in excess of 90 days. More importantly, short-term Treasury bill yields reflect the impact of factors different from those influencing long-term securities, such as common stock. For example, the premium for expected inflation absorbed into 90-day Treasury bills is likely to be far different than the inflationary premium absorbed into long-term securities yields. The yields on long-term Treasury bonds match more closely with common stock returns. For investors with a long time horizon, a long-term government bond is almost risk-free.

In their well-known corporate finance textbook, Brigham and Gapenski (1991) stated the following:[3]

> Treasury bill rates are subject to more random disturbances than are Treasury bond rates. For example, bills are used by the Federal Reserve System to control the money supply, and bills are also used by foreign governments, firms, and individuals as a temporary safe-house for money. Thus, if the Fed decides to stimulate the economy, it drives down the bill rate, and the same thing happens if trouble erupts somewhere in the world and money flows into the United States seeking a temporary haven.

---

[3] See Brigham and Gapenski (1991).

Harrington (1987) took an even more practical approach in estimating the risk-free rate. Unlike most theoretical textbooks, Harrington suggests looking at this from the point of view of a practitioner who has a real problem:

> Because of the empirical evidence, the intercept is consistently higher than a Treasury security and the fact that a Treasury bill rate is heavily influenced by Federal Reserve activity and is thus not a free-market rate, many practitioners suggest the use of a long-term government rate or an AA industrial bond rate as a proxy for the risk-free rate . . . . Because U.S. Treasury bills are usually considered the closest available approximation to a risk-free investment, the discount rate on Treasury bills is often used as a risk-free rate. This creates some very serious problems, however, because the rate of Treasury bills like that on most short-term marketable instruments is quite volatile. One way to approach the problem of dealing with the risk premium factor is to use the long-term interest rate instead of the risk-free rate....The most widely used proxies, 30 or 90-day Treasury bill rates, are empirically inadequate and theoretically suspect.[4]

While the spot yield on long-term Treasury bonds provides a reasonable proxy for the risk-free rate, the CAPM specifically requires the expected spot yield. Market forecasts of rates on Treasury bonds are available in the form of interest rate futures contract yields, and can be employed as proxies for the expected yields on Treasury securities.

Over the last 50 years, the Treasury bill rate has approximately equaled the annual inflation rate, as demonstrated in Fama (1975) and Ibbotson Associates (1993). Refined techniques to forecast inflation based on the current shape of the yield curve could thus be employed to obtain the expected risk-free rate.[5] Alternately, the consensus inflation forecast by economists over the requisite horizon could be employed to derive the risk-free rate estimate. However, none of these techniques is likely to provide superior estimates to that supplied by current yield data. The complexity and computational costs are likely to outweigh their marginal usefulness.

In practice, sensitivity analyses employing various input values for the risk-free rate can produce a reasonably good range of estimates of equity costs. For example, for a risk-free rate range of 7% to 8% and a market

---

[4] See Harrington (1987).

[5] See Ibbotson and Sinquefield (1982) for a description of the methodology of forecasting future security yields based on yield curve analysis.

return of 14%, the CAPM cost of equity for a public utility with a beta of 0.80 ranges from 12.6% to 12.8%. This is shown graphically in Figure 12-5.

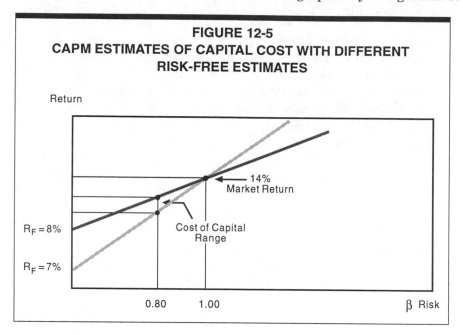

FIGURE 12-5
CAPM ESTIMATES OF CAPITAL COST WITH DIFFERENT RISK-FREE ESTIMATES

Beta Estimate

In Chapter 3, it was argued that beta is a useful, simple, objective measure of risk when used to gauge the relative risks of securities. The relative risk ranking of securities is somewhat immune to the beta estimation method. The situation is different when the objective of estimating beta is to obtain an absolute estimate of the cost of equity for an individual security. In this case, the reliability of the beta-estimation technique has a direct effect on the confidence in the estimate of equity cost.

A useful starting point is the utility's historical beta. Historical price and dividend data are easily obtainable from computerized data bases. Using a software package that performs statistical regression, betas can be estimated by examining the past variability of the utility's stock in relation to the market. Commercially available betas can also be employed. Several investment firms supply beta estimates, the most noteworthy being Value Line and Merrill Lynch. Published betas have the advantage of being already adjusted for their natural tendencies to revert to 1.00. Recall from Chapter 3 that only adjusted betas are appropriate, not raw betas. If the utility's past market risk seems likely to continue, based on an examination of company fundamentals, historical beta calculations can be used to estimate the cost of equity. In the case of a non-publicly-traded, regulated entity, Chapter 14 will offer several applications of the CAPM to estimate the beta of separate divisions and regulated operating subsidiaries.

Historically estimated betas for individual securities are frequently unstable and sensitive to the estimation technique. The CAPM was initially developed in the context of portfolio theory and was aimed at portfolio management practices, and not at utility cost of equity estimation. When portfolios of securities are considered, the statistical estimation errors for each individual security's beta cancel out, so that historically estimated betas for portfolios are reliable and constitute reliable predictors of the portfolio's future beta. But when using the CAPM to estimate a utility's cost of capital, only one security is considered, accentuating the statistical estimation problem. One remedy is to rely on an industry beta instead of a one-security sample, or on the average beta for a portfolio of comparable risk securities.

The perils and biases of relying on historical beta as a proxy for the true fundamental future beta were discussed in Chapter 3, and several remedies were offered. Since betas change over time as both company fundamentals and capital structures change, examination of possible future changes in company fundamentals can reveal the future likely trend and value of beta. Clues to such changes can be obtained by studying the behavior of key accounting variables, such as payout ratios, capital structure ratios, and earnings stability trends. Comparison of historical betas with "fundamental betas" and "accounting betas" can reveal changes in the utility's risk fundamentals.

If listed call options are traded on the utility's stock, a time series of the standard deviation implied in daily call option premiums can reveal on a timely basis whether investor risk perceptions are changing and whether beta is changing in some predictable manner.

The final CAPM estimate of equity cost should be sensitized over a range of beta estimates to produce a range of estimates of the cost of equity. A 95% confidence interval, based on the standard error of estimate, around the best estimate of the beta coefficient, could be utilized. For example, for a risk-free rate of 8% and a market return of 16%, the CAPM estimate of equity cost for a utility with a beta of 0.80 is 14.4%; if the standard error of estimate of beta is 0.15, beta estimates range from 0.65 to 0.95, with a corresponding range of equity cost of 13.2% to 15.6%. This is shown in Figure 12-6.

Market Return

The last required input to the CAPM is the expected market risk premium return, $R_M - R_F$, which is the difference between the market return and the risk-free rate. Some analysts estimate the two components of the

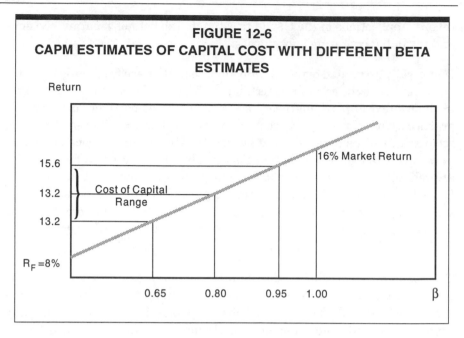

FIGURE 12-6
CAPM ESTIMATES OF CAPITAL COST WITH DIFFERENT BETA ESTIMATES

market risk premium separately, while others focus on the market risk premium directly. There are essentially two methods of estimating the market risk premium: prospective and historical.

The prospective method is implemented by applying the DCF methodology to a representative market index, such as the Standard & Poor's 500 Index, Value Line Composite, or the New York Stock Exchange Index. For reasons of consistency, the market index employed should be the same as the market index used in deriving estimates of beta. If risk premiums are volatile, this method of directly measuring R_M is preferred. Subtracting the current risk-free rate from that estimate produces a valid estimate of the market risk premium. The previous chapter outlined the specifics of the methodology to measure the aggregate market return based on the DCF method.

Another method of estimating the expected market return is based on a procedure described in detail by Ibbotson Associatesand Sinquefield (1982), which relies on the analysis of the current yield curve. Ibbotson and Sinquefield present forecasts of stocks, bonds, bills, and inflation rates based on the current yield curve. Essentially, the forward rates implied in the current curve are computed each year into the future. Forecasts of the nominal riskless rate are derived by subtracting the expected maturity premiums from the 1982 forward rates. Adding the historical equity risk premium to the riskless rate forecasts gives the common stock nominal return. The advantage of the method is that equity return forecasts are directly obtained, and that is what the CAPM requires. The disadvantage is the relative complexity and burdensome computational requirements of the method.

The second broad approach to estimate the expected market risk premium is to measure $R_M - R_F$ directly from historically-derived risk premiums. A common procedure is to assume that investors anticipate about the same risk premium in the future as in the past. The long-term market risk premium is estimated as the arithmetic mean excess of total equity returns over the long-term government bond yield.[6] For example, from 1926 to 1992, the risk premium on the Standard & Poor's 500 Index averaged 7.3%, based on the Ibbotson Associates historical return series (1993). If the expected Treasury bond yield is 7%, a benchmark estimate of 7.3% for the risk premium implies an estimated R_M of 14.3%. The benchmark risk premium estimate of 7.3% was derived from a long series of historical returns, nearly 70 years.

The importance of using a long historical period for estimation purposes was described in the last chapter. Clearly, the accuracy of the realized risk premium as an estimator of the prospective risk premium is enhanced by increasing the number of years used to estimate it. By analogy, one cannot predict with any reasonable degree of accuracy the result of a single, or even a few, flips of a balanced coin. But one can predict with a good deal of confidence that approximately 50 heads will appear in 100 tosses of the coin. Under these circumstances, it is most appropriate to estimate future experience from long-run evidence of investment performance. Therefore, the historical or realized market risk premium used to estimate the prospective or expected market risk premium should be based on the longest period available, such as Ibbotson Associates' historical estimates from 1926 to the present.

The danger in using too short a period involves the distinction between expected and realized return. The historical risk premium approach fundamentally assumes that average realized return is an appropriate surrogate for expected return, or in other words, that investor expectations are

---

[6] Note that the long-term government bond *income* (yield) returns are subtracted. The reason for subtracting the bond *income* returns instead of the total return is that the yield of the bond reflects the market's expectations at the time of purchase. This is not the case with total returns, which can be biased by unanticipated capital losses due to adverse interest rate movements. Bond income returns are a valid measure of expectation, whereas historical bond total returns are biased estimates of the expected return. Stocks do not have an easily observable measure of expected return comparable to a bond's yield to maturity, and total stock returns must therefore be employed. This is discussed in Ibbotson Associates (1993).

realized. Realized returns can be substantially different from prospective returns anticipated by investors especially over short time periods. But over very long periods, such as the 1926-1992 period, investor expectations coincide with realizations; otherwise, investors would never invest any money. Note also that the entire period for which data are available should be used and all years weighted equally. There is no reason to weigh recent returns more heavily than distant returns because of the random behavior of the market risk premium.

In Chapter 11, it was shown that the arithmetic average of year-to-year risk premiums over an extended time period is the appropriate one for measuring the cost of capital, and not the geometric mean return. This is because the arithmetic mean return, compounded over the number of years that an investment is held, provides the best estimate of the ending wealth value of that investment.

Cost of capital is synonymous with investor expected return. The expected return is not guaranteed, of course. Deviations around the expected return are likely to occur. In good years, the actual return will exceed the expected return, and conversely in bad years. But on average, over long time periods, investors expectations are achieved, or else no one would invest funds. Looking forward, the expected return is an arithmetic mean. Looking backward, the historical achieved return is a geometric average. When looking at the future, the arithmetic mean is relevant. When examining the past, the geometric mean is relevant. In statistical parlance, the arithmetic average is the unbiased measure of the expected value of repeated observations of a random variable, not the geometric mean.

As in the case of the beta estimate and risk-free rate estimate, a sensitivity analysis of possible CAPM cost of capital estimates should be conducted for a specified utility using a reasonable range of estimates for the market return. See Figure 12-7 for an illustration.

The range of cost of capital estimates obtained using a separate range for each of the three input variables to the CAPM—beta, risk-free rate, and market return—can be combined to produce an overall sensitivity analysis for the cost of equity value. This is illustrated in Figure 12-8, where the range of estimates obtained is 12.55% to 16.65%, with a midpoint value of 14.6%. See Rhyne (1982) for a similar illustration.

The broad range of estimates obtained is typical of CAPM application. The results obtained will vary somewhat depending upon the choice of proxies.

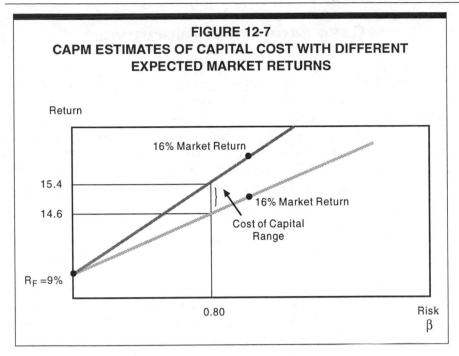

FIGURE 12-7
CAPM ESTIMATES OF CAPITAL COST WITH DIFFERENT
EXPECTED MARKET RETURNS

FIGURE 12-8
RANGE OF CAPM COST OF EQUITY CAPITAL ESTIMATES

β Range	R_F Range	R_M		
		15%	*16%*	*17%*
	8%	12.55	13.20	13.85
0.65	9%	12.90	13.55	14.20
	10%	13.25	13.90	14.55
	8%	13.60	14.40	15.20
0.80	9%	13.80	14.60	15.40
	10%	14.00	14.80	15.60
	8%	14.65	15.60	16.55
0.95	9%	14.70	15.65	16.60
	10%	14.75	15.70	16.65
Range:	*Low*	*12.55%*	*Mid 14.60%*	*High 16.65%*

Case Study: GTE Northwest

The following example from Morin (1993), extracted from an actual 1993 rate case, illustrates the prospective approach to estimating the market return. To apply the CAPM to GTE Northwest, a telephone operating subsidiary of GTE Corporation, three quantities are required: the risk-free rate, beta, and the market risk premium. As a proxy for the risk-free rate, the current yield at the time on long-term Treasury bonds of 7.7% was used. As a proxy for GTE Northwest's beta, the average beta of the Bell RHCs and the independent telcos of 0.89 was used, which was remarkably close to GTE Corporation's own beta of 0.90.

For the market risk premium, a range of 6.0% to 7.4% was used. This range was based on the results of both forward-looking and historical studies of long-term market risk premiums. Two studies guided the assumed range. For the upper estimate, the Ibbotson Associates compilation of historical returns shows that a broad market sample of common stocks outperformed the income return to long-term U.S. government bonds by 7.4% from 1926 to 1991. Since long-term government bonds were yielding 7.7% at the time, the implied market return was 7.4% + 7.7% = 15.1%.

For the lower estimate of the 6.0% - 7.4% market risk premium range, a DCF analysis was applied to the market as a whole. The DCF methodology requires the estimation of certain components of the market index, such as the dividend yield and growth rate. These estimates can be made with the use of Value Line's "Value Screen III" software, which is made available to investors on a paid subscription basis for a modest fee on computer diskettes updated on a monthly basis. This Value Line data base is a replica of the most current Value Line company reports. These reports are widely circulated in the investment community and are used extensively by analysts.

The Value Line universe comprises some 1,600 stocks, representing over 90% of the market value of all publicly-traded common stocks. This index is clearly representative of the aggregate equity market. All dividend-paying stocks in the Value Line universe were screened; those companies with negative growth rates and with growth rates in excess of 20% were excluded. Companies with growth rates in excess of 20% were excluded because the DCF model does not apply to companies with growth rates in excess of the cost of equity.

The average spot dividend yield for the remaining universe of about 800 dividend-paying stocks was added to the average dividends and earnings growth forecasts for the universe of stocks. The latter was derived by averaging the Value Line growth forecast in earnings and dividends per share for each stock in the universe.

The individual growth rate estimates for each company were labeled "Projected EPS Growth Rate (%)" and "Projected DPS Growth Rate (%)" by Value Line, and were defined by Value Line as the compound annual rate of growth of earnings/dividends projected for the next 3 to 5 years from the time of publication. They were calculated by dividing the average actual result for the latest 3 years into the average projected result for the period 3 to 5 years hence.

At the time, excluding high-growth stocks, the expected dividend yield on the aggregate market was 3.3% (Value Line Screen III average dividend yield on dividend-paying stocks), and the projected growth for the Value Line common stocks was in the range of 8.5% to 11.2%. Adding the two components together produced an expected return on the aggregate equity market in the range of 11.8% to 14.5%, with a midpoint of about 13.2%. Recognition of quarterly dividend payments, and an expected dividend yield rather than a spot dividend yield, brought this estimate to about 13.6%, or a risk premium of approximately 6.0% over long-term U.S. Treasury bonds, which were yielding 7.7% at the time.

Using those input values, the CAPM estimates of equity costs ranged from 13.04% to 14.29%, with a midpoint of 13.66%. For example, with a beta of 0.89 and a market risk premium of 6.0%, the CAPM equation became:

$$K = 7.7\% + 0.89\,(13.7\% - 7.7\%) = 13.04\%$$

12.5 Conclusions

It is important to remember that the CAPM provides a powerful conceptual framework to understand the process of determining security returns, and is a central paradigm of financial theory. By producing an easily interpretable and parsimonious single measure of risk, the model provides a useful simplification and focus for the pricing of financial securities. It also provides a useful expository device to formalize the relationship between risk and return. But like all models in the social sciences, it is nevertheless an abstraction from reality, analogous to the model of perfect competition in economics. Applying any model to social problems is an uncomfortable and difficult task. As in the case of the DCF model, the CAPM is more than just an equation in which arbitrary numbers are inserted, and requires detailed and logical analysis for each of its components, supplemented by enlightened judgment.

While the CAPM provides a valid and rigorous conceptual framework to determine capital costs, the implementation problems are challenging. None of the inputs to the CAPM is known with certainty so that only estimates of equity costs are obtained. The true equity return is unobtainable. It is possible, however, to develop a range of estimates based on the application of several methodologies supplemented by the exercise of informed judgment throughout the estimation process.

References

Brealey, R. and Myers, S. *Principles of Corporate Finance,* 4th ed. New York: McGraw-Hill, 1991.

Brigham, E.F. and Gapenski, L.C. *Financial Management: Theory and Practice,* 6th ed. Hinsdale IL: Dryden Press, 1991.

Copeland, T. E. and Weston, F. *Financial Theory and Corporate Policy,* 3rd ed. Reading MA: Addison Wesley, 1993.

Fama, E.F. "Short-term Interest Rates as Predictors of Inflation." *American Economic Review,* June 1975, 269-282.

Hagin, R.L. *Modern Portfolio Theory.* Homewood IL: Dow Jones-Irwin, 1979.

Harrington, D.R. *Modern Portfolio Theory, The Capital Asset Pricing Model, and Arbitrage Pricing Theory: A User's Guide.* New York: Prentice-Hall, 1987.

Ibbotson Associates. *Stocks, Bonds, Bills, and Inflation, 1992 Yearbook.* Chicago: Ibbotson Associates, 1993.

Ibbotson, R.G. and Sinquefield, R. A. *Stocks, Bonds, Bills, and Inflation: The Past and the Future.* Financial Analysts Research Foundation, Monograph No. 15, 1982.

Morin, R.A. GTE Northwest Inc., Prepared Testimony, Public Utility Commission of Oregon, Advice No. 412 and 413, 1993.

Reilly, F.K. *Investment Analysis and Portfolio Management,* Hinsdale IL: Dryden Press, 1994.

Sharpe, W.F. and Alexander, G.J. *Investments,* 4th ed. New York: Prentice-Hall, 1990.

Rhyne, R.G. "Can the Capital Asset Pricing Model Give Reliable Estimates of The Cost of Equity?" *Public Utilities Fortnightly,* Feb. 18, 1982, 58-60.

Appendix 12-A
Capital Asset Pricing Model

The necessary assumptions underlying the CAPM are:

1. Capital markets are perfect with no transaction costs, taxes, or impediments to trading. All assets are perfectly marketable, and no one trader is significant enough to influence price.

2. There are no restrictions to short-selling securities.

3. Investors can lend or borrow funds at the risk-free rate

4. Investors possess similar beliefs on the expected returns and risks of securities, that is, investors have homogeneous expectations.

5. Investors construct portfolios on the basis of expected return and variance of return only, implying that security returns are normally distributed.

6. Investors maximize the expected utility of the terminal value of their investment at the end of one period.

If a fractional investment of X_1 is invested in the market portfolio, and $(1 - x_1)$ in a risk-free securitiy, the expected return on the combined portfolio is given by:

$$E(R_P) = x_1 E(R_M) + (1 - x_1)R_F \qquad \text{(12-A)}$$

The portfolio's beta is, by definitions

$$\beta_p = \frac{cov(R_P, R_M)}{\sigma^2(R_M)} = \frac{\sigma_{pM}}{\sigma_M^2} \qquad \text{(12-B)}$$

Substituting for R_P in (12-b):

$$\beta_p = \frac{cov(x_1 R_M + (1 - x_1)R_F, R_M)}{\sigma_M^2}$$

$$= \frac{x_1\sigma_M^2 + (1 - x_1)\sigma_{FM}}{\sigma_M^2}$$

Since the return on the risk-free security is certain, $\sigma_{FM} = 0$.

Thus,

$$\beta_p = \frac{x_1 \sigma_M^2}{\sigma_M^2} = x_1 \tag{12-C}$$

Substituting (12-C) into (12-A)

$$E(R_p) = R_f + \beta_p(E(R_M) - (1 - \beta_p)R_F \tag{12-D}$$

Rearranging:

$$E(R_p) = R_F + \beta_p(E(R_M) - R_F) \tag{12-E}$$

Equation (12-E) is the CAPM. A similar expression can be shown to hold not only for portfolios, but for each risky security in the market portfolio (see Sharpe (1981):

$$\boxed{E(R_i) = R_F + \beta_i(E(R_M) - R_F)} \tag{12-E}$$

Chapter 13
CAPM Extensions

13.1 Empirical Validation

The last chapter showed that the practical difficulties of implementing the CAPM approach are surmountable. Conceptual and empirical problems remain, however.

At the conceptual level, the CAPM has been submitted to criticisms by academicians and practitioners.[1] Contrary to the core assumption of the CAPM, investors may choose not to diversify, and bear company-specific risk if abnormal returns are expected. A substantial percentage of individual investors are indeed inadequately diversified. Short selling is somewhat restricted, in violation of CAPM assumptions. Factors other than market risk (beta) may also influence investor behavior, such as taxation, firm size, and restrictions on borrowing.

At the empirical level, there have been countless tests of the CAPM to determine to what extent security returns and betas are related in the manner predicted by the CAPM.[2] The results of the tests support the idea that beta is related to security returns, that the risk-return tradeoff is positive, and that the relationship is linear. The contradictory finding is that the empirical Security Market Line (SML) is not as steeply sloped as the predicted SML. With few exceptions, the empirical studies agree that the implied intercept term exceeds the risk-free rate and the slope term is less than predicted by the CAPM. That is, low-beta securities earn returns somewhat higher than the CAPM would predict, and high-beta securities earn less than predicted. This is shown in Figure 13-1.

---

[1] The use of the CAPM in regulatory proceedings has not escaped criticism. See for example Malko and Enholm (1985), Chartoff, Mayo, and Smith (1982), and the Autumn 1978 issue of *Financial Management,* in which several prominent finance scholars address the use of the CAPM in regulatory proceedings.

[2] For a summary of the empirical evidence on the CAPM, see Jensen (1972) and Ross (1978). The major empirical tests of the CAPM were published by Friend and Blume (1975), Black, Jensen, and Scholes (1972), Miller and Scholes (1972), Blume and Friend (1973), Blume and Husic (1973), Fama and Macbeth (1973), Basu (1977), Reinganum (1981B), Litzenberger and Ramaswamy (1979), Banz (1981), Gibbons (1982), Stambaugh (1982), and Shanken (1985). CAPM evidence in the Canadian context is available in Morin (1981).

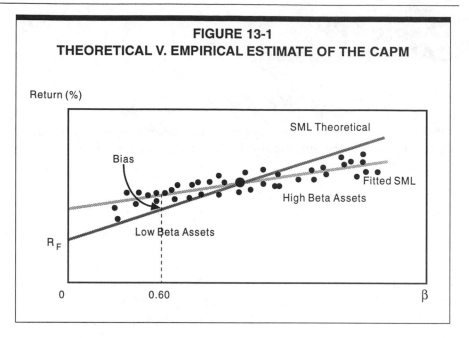

FIGURE 13-1
THEORETICAL V. EMPIRICAL ESTIMATE OF THE CAPM

The slope is less than predicted by the CAPM, and the intercept term is greater than the risk-free rate. This result is particularly pertinent for public utilities whose betas are typically less than 1.00. Based on the evidence, as shown in Figure 13-1, a CAPM-based estimate of the cost of capital underestimates the return required from such securities.

The empirical evidence also demonstrates that the SML is highly unstable over short periods and differs significantly from the long-run relationship. This evidence underscores the potential for error in cost of capital estimates that apply the CAPM using historical data over short time periods. The evidence[3] also shows that the addition of specific company risk, as measured by standard deviation, adds explanatory power to the risk-return relationship.

Roll (1977) argued that the CAPM has never been tested and that such a test is infeasible. Roll argued, moreover, that the market index proxy used in empirical tests of the CAPM is inadequate; since a true comprehensive market index is unavailable, such tests will be biased in the direction shown by the actual empirical results. Deviations of empirical results from the predictions of the CAPM does not necessarily mean that the CAPM is misspecified, but rather that the market index used in testing is inefficient. Roll's conclusion is that the CAPM is not testable unless the exact composition of the true market portfolio is known and used in the tests. Moreover,

---

[3] See Friend, Westerfield, and Granito (1978) and Morin (1980).

the CAPM is a forward-looking expectational model and to test the model it is necessary to predict investor expectations correctly. Any empirical test of the CAPM is thus a test of the joint hypothesis of the model's validity and of the function used to generate expected returns from historical returns.

In short, the currently available empirical evidence indicates that the simple version of the CAPM does not provide a perfectly accurate description of the process determining security returns. Explanations for this shortcoming include some or all of the following:

1. The CAPM excludes other important variables that are important in determining security returns, such as size, skewness, taxes, and uncertain inflation.

2. The market index used in the tests excludes important classes of securities, such as bonds, mortgages, and business investments.

3. Constraints on investor borrowing exist contrary to the assumption of the CAPM.

4. Investors may value the hedging value of assets in protecting them against shifts in later investment opportunities. See Merton (1973) and Morin (1981).

Revised CAPM models have been proposed relaxing the above constraints, each model varying in complexity, each model attempting to inject more realism into the assumptions. Ross (1978) and, more recently, Tallman (1989) presented excellent surveys of the various asset pricing theories and related empirical evidence. These enhanced CAPMs produce broadly similar expressions for the relationship between risk and return and a SML that is flatter than the CAPM prediction. Section 13.2 focuses on the more tractable extensions of the CAPM that possess some applicability to public utility regulation.

13.2 CAPM Extensions

Several attempts to enrich the model's conceptual validity and to salvage the CAPM's applicability have been advanced. In this section, extensions of the CAPM and pragmatic solutions to safeguard the model's applicability are discussed. The first explanation of the CAPM's inability to explain security returns satisfactorily is that beta is insufficient and that other systematic risk factors affect security returns. The implication is that the effects of these other independent variables should be quantified and used in estimating the cost of equity capital. The impact of the supplementary variables can be expressed as an additive element to the standard CAPM equation as follows:

Letting a stand for these other effects, the CAPM equation becomes:

$$K = R_F + a + \beta (R_M - R_F)$$ (13-1)

To capture the variables' impact on the slope of the relationship, a coefficient b is substituted for the market risk premium. The revised CAPM equation becomes:

$$K = R_F + a + b \times \beta$$ {13-2}

The constants a and b capture all the market-wide effects that influence security returns, and must be estimated by econometric techniques. Factors purported to affect security returns include dividend yield, skewness, and size effects.

Dividend Yield Effect

Empirical studies by Litzenberger and Ramaswamy (1979), Litzenberger, Ramaswamy, and Sosin (1980), and Rosenberg and Marathe (1975) find that security returns are positively related to dividend yield as well as to beta. These results are consistent with after-tax extensions of the CAPM developed by Brennan (1970) and Litzenberger and Ramaswamy (1979) and suggest that the relationship between return, beta, and dividend yield should be estimated and employed to calculate the cost of equity capital.

The dividend yield effects stem from the differential taxation on corporate dividends and capital gains. The standard CAPM does not consider the regularity of dividends received by investors. Utilities generally maintain high dividend payout ratios relative to the market, and by ignoring dividend yield, the CAPM provides biased cost of capital estimates. To the extent that dividend income is taxed at a higher rate than capital gains, investors will require higher pre-tax returns in order to equalize the after-tax returns provided by high-yielding stocks with those of low-yielding stocks. In other words, high-yielding stocks must offer investors higher pre-tax returns.[4] Even if dividends and capital gains are undifferentiated for tax purposes, there is still a tax bias in favor of earnings retention (lower dividend payout), as capital gains taxes are paid only when gains are realized.

---

[4] The strength of the tax effect on yield is diluted by non-taxable institutional ownership and by the personal tax exemption on dividend income from electric utility stocks.

The traditional return-beta relationship described by the SML fails to recognize the dividend yield dimension. But the two-dimensional SML can be expanded into a three-dimensional security market plane (SMP) by adding a dividend yield line as in Figure 13-2, which portrays the relationship among return, beta, and dividend yield. The positive effect of yield on return can be seen on the graph. In a given risk class, the required return increases with the dividend yield. Some institutional portfolio managers have in fact implemented the SMP approach for actual investment management decision making, in effect recommending for purchase undervalued securities situated above the SMP.

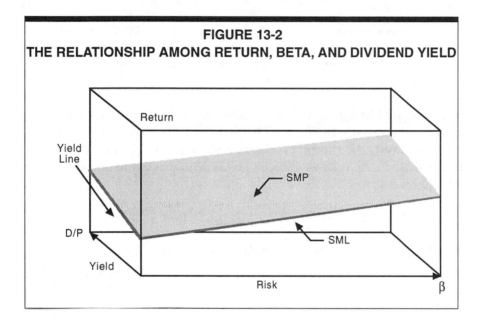

FIGURE 13-2
THE RELATIONSHIP AMONG RETURN, BETA, AND DIVIDEND YIELD

Skewness Effects

Investors are more concerned with losing money than with total variability of return. If risk is defined as the probability of loss, it appears more logical to measure risk as the probability of achieving a return that is below the expected return. Figure 13-3 shows three frequency distribution of returns, one symmetrical, one skewed left, and one skewed right. If the probability distribution is symmetrical, specialized measures of downside risk are unnecessary, since a normal symmetrical distribution has no skewness; the areas on either side of the mean expected return are mirror images of one another.

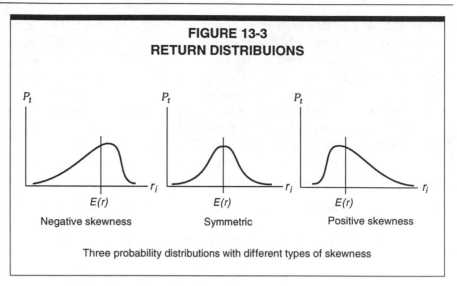

FIGURE 13-3
RETURN DISTRIBUIONS

Negative skewness Symmetric Positive skewness

Three probability distributions with different types of skewness

In the context of the CAPM, the traditional CAPM provides downward-biased estimates of cost of capital to the extent that these skewness effects are significant. As shown by Kraus and Litzenberger (1976), expected return depends on both on a stock's systematic risk (beta) and the systematic skewness:

RETURN = RISK-FREE RATE + MARKET RISK + SKEWNESS RISK

Denoting the risk-free rate by R_F, the return on the market as a whole by R_M, the stock's systematic market risk by β, the stock's systematic skewness by γ, and the market price of skewness reduction by S_M, the amended CAPM is stated as follows:

$$K_e = R_F + \beta\,(\,R_M - R_F\,) + \gamma\,(\,S_M - R_F\,) \qquad (13\text{-}3)$$

Systematic skewness, γ, is measured as the ratio of the co-skewness of the stock with the market to the skewness of the market.

Empirical studies by Kraus and Litzenberger (1976), Friend, Westerfield, and Granito (1978), and Morin (1980) found that, in addition to beta, skewness of returns has a significant negative relationship with security returns. This result is consistent with the skewness version of the CAPM developed by Rubinstein (1973) and Kraus and Litzenberger (1976).

This may be particularly relevant for public utilities whose future profitability is constrained by the regulatory process on the upside and relatively unconstrained on the downside in the face of socio-political realities of public utility regulation. The distribution of security returns for regulated utilities is more likely to resemble the negatively skewed distribution displayed in the left-hand portion of Figure 13-3. The process of regulation, by restricting the upward potential for returns and responding sluggishly on the downward side, may impart some asymmetry to the distribution of returns, and is more likely to result in utilities earning less, rather than more, than their cost of capital. The traditional CAPM provides downward-biased estimates of the cost of capital to the extent that these skewness effects are significant. A security market plane (SMP) similar to that envisaged in the case of dividend yield effects can be imagined, substituting a skewness line for the dividend yield line.

Skewness effects can be illustrated by the nature of the probability distribution of security returns for California water utilities in the 1990s. Because of the asymmetry in the future water supply, there is a greater probability of downside returns to investors under adverse supply conditions, but essentially no probability of correspondingly large positive returns. That is, these water utilities' future profitability is constrained by both the regulatory process and by a negatively skewed water supply. Hence, measures of variability and covariability, such as standard deviation and beta, are likely to provide downward-biased estimates of the true risk relative to that of unregulated firms and other utilities.

The implication is that an additional risk premium must be added to the business-as-usual return on equity to compensate for the added risks. The lack of symmetry in investor returns must be considered. A risk premium sufficient to compensate investors for the limited upside returns/unlimited downside returns versus comparable risk companies and other utilities is required.

To illustrate, Figure 13-4 shows the hypothetical probability distributions of revenues, earnings before interest and taxes (EBIT), and net income under normal conditions for a California water utility. Note that fluctuations in revenues are magnified when transmitted to EBIT because of operating leverage, and further magnified when transmitted to net income because of financial leverage. The coefficient of variation of revenue, EBIT, and net income are 0.14, 0.47, and 1.11, respectively.

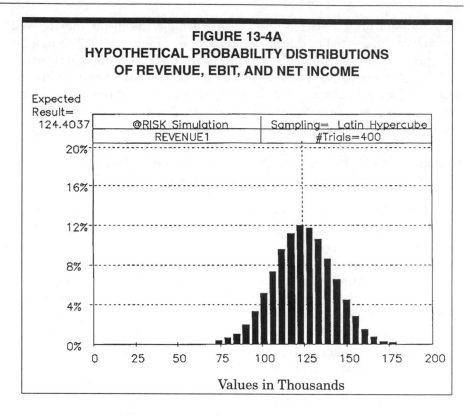

FIGURE 13-4A
HYPOTHETICAL PROBABILITY DISTRIBUTIONS
OF REVENUE, EBIT, AND NET INCOME

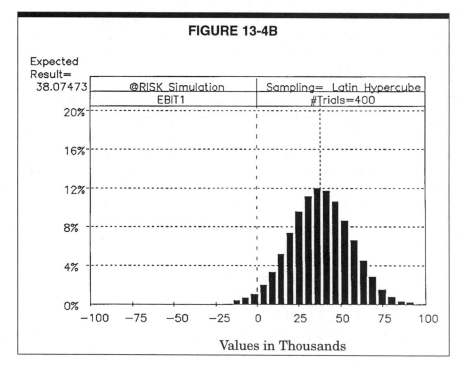

FIGURE 13-4B

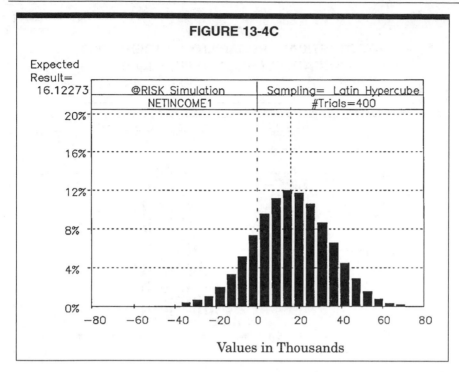

FIGURE 13-4C

Expected
Result=
16.12273

@RISK Simulation
NETINCOME1

Sampling= Latin Hypercube
#Trials=400

Values in Thousands

Figure 13-5 shows the same probability distributions if revenues are negatively skewed. Note the increased downside net income potential and, hence, the increased risk. The coefficient of variation of revenue, EBIT, and net income become 0.12, 0.43, and 1.41, respectively. The risk to the shareholder increases from 1.11 to 1.41 as a result of leverage and skewness effects.

This result reinforces that notion that an added premium is required to offset the lack of upside potential. The added premium must be sufficient to produce the same average return that would prevail under conditions of perfect symmetry.

Size Effects

Investment risk increases as company size diminishes, all else remaining constant. The size phenomenon is well documented in the finance literature. Empirical studies by Banz (1981) and Reinganum (1981A) have found that investors in small-capitalization stocks require higher returns than predicted by the standard CAPM. Reinganum (1981A) examined the relationship between the size of the firm and its P/E ratio, and found that small firms experienced average returns greater than those of large firms that were of equivalent systematic risk (beta). He found that small firms produce greater returns than could be explained by their risks. These results were confirmed in a separate test by Banz (1981) who examined stock returns

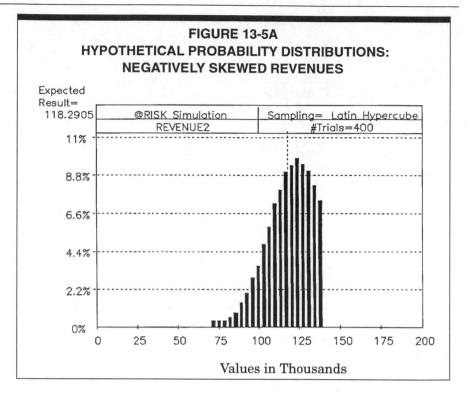

FIGURE 13-5A
HYPOTHETICAL PROBABILITY DISTRIBUTIONS:
NEGATIVELY SKEWED REVENUES

Values in Thousands

over the much longer 1936-1975 period, finding that stocks of small firms earned higher risk-adjusted abnormal returns than those of large firms.

Small companies have very different returns than large ones, and on average they have been higher. The greater risk of small stocks does not fully account for their higher returns over many historical periods. Ibbotson Associates' widely-used annual historical return series publication covering the period 1926 to the present reinforces this evidence (Ibbotson Associates, 1993). They found that for the period 1926-1992 the average small stock premium was 6% over the average stock, more than could be expected by risk differences alone, suggesting that the cost of equity for small stocks is considerably larger than for large capitalization stocks. One plausible explanation for the size effect is the higher information search costs incurred by investors for small companies relative to large companies. This effect is likely to be negligible for all but the very small public utilities whose equity market value is less than $60 million.

In addition to earning the highest average rates of return, the small stocks also had the highest volatility, as measured by the standard deviation of returns. Ibbotson defines small stocks as those in the lowest size decile among NYSE stocks, with size defined as the dollar value of shares outstanding. The size trigger point occurs at a market value of $60 million.

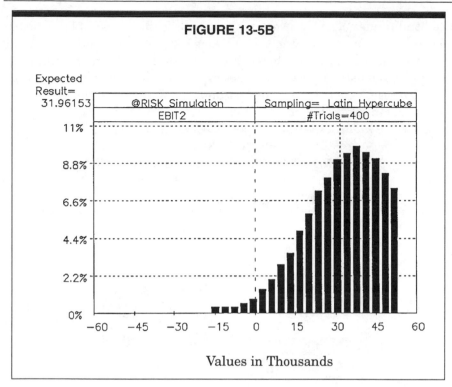

FIGURE 13-5B

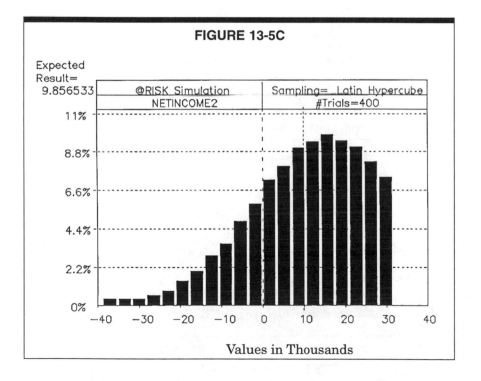

FIGURE 13-5C

331

The bond ratings of small firms are typically less than those of large firms. Figure 13-6 contrasts the Standard & Poor's bond and stock ratings of small versus large capitalization stocks. For bond ratings, the first quintile of companies ranked in descending order of market value of equity is ranked A- on average, versus CC for the last quintile. For stock ratings, the first quintile of companies is ranked A- to B+, versus C for the last quintile.

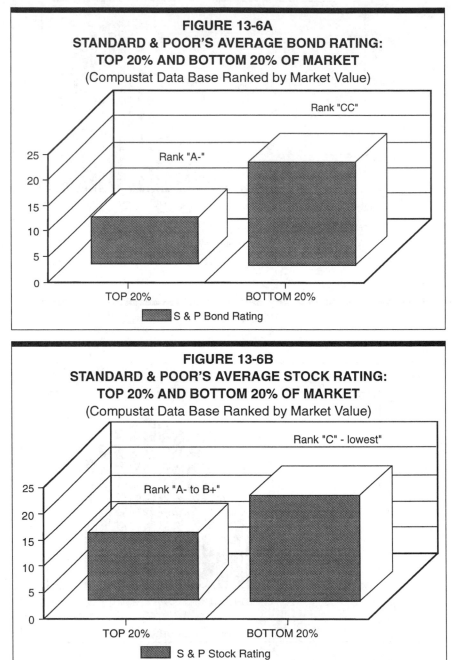

FIGURE 13-6A
STANDARD & POOR'S AVERAGE BOND RATING:
TOP 20% AND BOTTOM 20% OF MARKET
(Compustat Data Base Ranked by Market Value)

Rank "CC"

Rank "A-"

25
20
15
10
5
0

TOP 20%   BOTTOM 20%

S & P Bond Rating

FIGURE 13-6B
STANDARD & POOR'S AVERAGE STOCK RATING:
TOP 20% AND BOTTOM 20% OF MARKET
(Compustat Data Base Ranked by Market Value)

Rank "C" - lowest"

Rank "A- to B+"

25
20
15
10
5
0

TOP 20%   BOTTOM 20%

S & P Stock Rating

Much research effort has gone into investigating the size effect. In addition to statistical measurement problems, the economic rationale for the size effect is difficult to unravel. In fact, Roll (1981) even questioned the evidence on the small firm effect. Presumably, small stocks provided less utility to the investor, and require a higher return. The size effect may be a statistical mirage, whereby size is proxying for the effect of different economic variables. Small firms may have low price-earnings ratios or low market prices, for example. The size effect is most likely the result of a liquidity premium, whereby investors in small stocks demand greater returns as compensation for lack of marketability and liquidity. Investors prefer high to low liquidity, and demand higher returns from less liquid investments, holding other factors constant.

Market Index and Missing Assets

A second explanation for the CAPM's inability to fully explain the process determining security returns involves the use of an inadequate or incomplete market index. Empirical studies to validate the CAPM invariably rely on some stock market index as a proxy for the true market portfolio. The exclusion of several asset categories from the definition of market index misspecifies the CAPM and biases the results found using only stock market data. Kolbe and Read (1983) provide an illustration of the biases in beta estimates that result from applying the CAPM to public utilities. Unfortunately, no comprehensive and easily accessible data exist for several classes of assets, such as mortgages and business investments, so that the exact relationship between return and stock betas predicted by the CAPM does not exist. This suggests that the empirical relationship between returns and stock betas is best estimated empirically rather than by relying on theoretical and elegant CAPM models expanded to include missing assets effects. In any event, stock betas may be highly correlated with the true beta measured with the true market index.

Constraints on Investor Borrowing

The third explanation for the CAPM's deficiency involves the possibility of constraints on investor borrowing that run counter to the assumptions of the CAPM. In response to this inadequacy, several versions of the CAPM have been developed by researchers. One of these versions is the so-called zero-beta, or two-factor, CAPM which provides for a risk-free return in a market where borrowing and lending rates are divergent. If borrowing rates and lending rates differ, or there is no risk-free borrowing or lending, or there is risk-free lending but no risk-free borrowing, then the CAPM has the following form:

$$K = R_Z + \beta (R_M - R_F) \qquad (13\text{-}4)$$

The model is analogous to the standard CAPM, but with the return on a minimum risk portfolio that is unrelated to market returns, R_Z, replacing the risk-free rate, R_F. The model has been empirically tested by Black, Jensen, and Scholes (1972), who found a flatter than predicted SML, consistent with the model and other researchers' findings.

The zero-beta CAPM cannot be literally employed in cost of capital projections, since the zero-beta portfolio is a statistical construct difficult to replicate. Attempts to estimate the model are formally equivalent to estimating the constants, *a* and *b*, in Equation 13-2.

13.3 Empirical CAPM

Whatever the explanation for the flatter than predicted SML, whether it be dividend yield, skewness, size, missing assets, or constrained borrowing effects, the general suggestion is that the empirical relationship between returns and betas should be estimated empirically rather than asserted on an a priori basis. Equation 13-2 has gradually evolved to become known as the Empirical Capital Asset Pricing Model (ECAPM), and represents a pragmatic solution to the limitations of the standard CAPM, whether it be data limitations, unrealistic assumptions, or omitted variables. All the potential vagaries of the model are telescoped into the 2 constants, *a* and *b*, which must be estimated econometrically from market data. The technique is formally applied by Litzenberger, Ramaswamy, and Sosin (1980) to public utilities in order to rectify the CAPM's basic shortcomings. Not only do they summarize the criticisms of the CAPM insofar as they affect public utilities, but they also describe the econometric intricacies involved and the methods of circumventing the statistical problems. Essentially, the average monthly returns over a lengthy time period on a large cross-section of securities grouped into portfolios, are related to their corresponding betas by statistical regression techniques; that is, Equation 13-2 is estimated from market data. The utility's beta value is substituted into the equation to produce the cost of equity figure. Their own results demonstrate how the standard CAPM underestimates the cost of equity capital of public utilities because of the utilities' high dividend yield and return skewness.

As discussed in Section 13.1, empirical tests of the CAPM have shown that the risk-return tradeoff is not as steeply sloped as that predicted by the CAPM. That is, low-beta securities earn returns somewhat higher than the CAPM would predict, and high-beta securities earn less than predicted.

Several finance scholars have developed refined and expanded versions of the standard CAPM by relaxing the constraints imposed on the CAPM, such as dividend yield, size, and skewness effects. In doing so, they obtained broadly similar expressions for the relationship between risk and expected return. These enhanced CAPMs typically produce a risk-return relationship that is flatter than the CAPM prediction. In other words, they obtained a result that is closer to the actual risk-return relationship.[5]

The empirical CAPM formula described below produces a risk-return trade-off that is flatter than the predicted tradeoff, and approximates the observed relationship between risk and return on capital markets. The empirical approximation to the CAPM is consistent with both theory and empirical evidence, and has the added advantage of computational simplicity. Whereas the traditional version of the CAPM is given by the following:

$$K = R_F + \beta \left(R_M - R_F \right)$$

the empirical evidence found by Morin (1989) indicates that the expected return on a security over the period 1926-1984 was actually given by:

$$\text{RETURN} = .0829 + .0520\beta$$

Given that the risk-free rate over the estimation period was approximately 6%, this relationship implies that the intercept of the risk-return relationship is higher than the 6% risk-free rate, contrary to the CAPM's prediction. Given the Ibbotson Associates' result that the average return on an average risk stock exceeded the risk-free rate by about 8% during the period from 1926 through 1984, that is $(R_M - R_F) = 8\%$, the intercept of the observed relationship between return and beta exceeds the risk-free rate by about 2%, or 1/4 of 8%, and that the slope of the relationship, .0520, is close to 3/4 of 8%. Therefore, the empirical evidence suggests that the expected return on a security is related to its risk by the following approximation:

$$K = R_F + x \left(R_M - R_F \right) + \left(1 - x \right) \beta \left(R_M - R_F \right) \qquad (13\text{-}5)$$

where x is a fraction to be determined empirically. The value of x is actually derived by systematically varying the constant x in that equation from zero

---

[5]   An excellent overview of variants of the CAPM is provided in the corporate finance textbook by Brealey and Myers (1991A), Chapter 8, and particularly in the accompanying instructor's manual (1991B).

to 1.00 in steps of 0.05 and choosing that value of x that minimized the mean square error between the observed relationship,

$$RETURN = .0829 + .0520\,\beta$$

and the empirical shortcut CAPM formula.[6] The value of x that best explains the observed relationship is between 0.25 and 0.30. If $x = 0.25$, the equation becomes:

$$K = R_F + 0.25\,(R_M - R_F) + 0.75\,\beta\,(R_M - R_F) \qquad (13\text{-}6)$$

Using a simple numerical example, assuming a risk-free rate of 7%, a market risk premium of 7%, and a beta of 0.80, the empirical CAPM equation above yields a cost of equity estimate of 12.95% as follows:

$$K = 7\% + 0.25\,(14\% - 7\%) + 0.75 \times 0.80\,(14\% - 7\%)$$

$$= 7\% + 1.75\% + 4.2\%$$

$$= 12.95\%$$

The actual historical relationship between risk premiums and the risk of a large population of common stocks can be observed over a long time period and used to estimate the appropriate risk premium for a given utility. The utility's cost of equity can then be estimated as the yield on long-term Treasury bonds plus the estimated risk premium. To illustrate, the actual relationship between risk premiums and betas on common stocks over a long time period can be estimated, and this historical relationship be used to estimate the risk premium on the utility's common equity, on the grounds that over long time periods, investors' expectations are realized.

To execute this method, monthly rates of return for all common stocks listed on the New York Stock Exchange from 1926 to the present are obtained from the University of Chicago's Center for Research in Security Prices (CRISP) data tapes. Five-year betas are then computed for each month for each company. For each month, the securities are assigned to one of 10 portfolios on the basis of ranked betas, from the lowest to the highest beta. Monthly returns for each of the portfolios are compounded to produce annual rates of return on each of the 10 portfolios from 1931 to the

---

[6] The corresponding evidence for Canadian capital markets is scant. For studies of the relationship between return and risk in Canada, see Morin (1980) and Jobson and Korkie (1985)

present. Historical risk premiums for each of the 10 portfolios are calculated for the period 1931 to the present by averaging the difference between the portfolio's annual rate of return and the government bond yield. For example, if the following hypothetical relationship between the risk premium and the portfolios' betas is obtained for the period 1931 - 1992[7]:

$$Risk\ Premium \ = \ 4.21\% + (3.94\% \ x \ Beta\ )$$

Using the utility's beta of 0.60, for example, the risk premium for the hypothetical utility is:

$$4.21\% + (3.94\% \ x \ 0.60) = 6.6\%$$

A long-term cost of equity capital estimate for the company is obtained by adding the risk premium of 6.6% to the current yield on long-term Treasury bonds or to the projected long-term yield implied by the closing prices on the Treasury bond futures contract traded on the Chicago Board of Trade. The latter measures the consensus long-term interest rate expectation of investors.[8] If the yield on long-term Treasury bonds is 6%, then the cost of equity implied by the empirical relationship is 6.00% + 6.60% = 12.60%. A similar procedure could be developed based on the standard deviation of return rather than on beta as risk measure.

13.4 Conclusions

Although financial theory has shown that beta is a sufficient risk measure for diversified investors and although most of the empirical literature has confirmed its importance in determining expected return, there are notable exceptions. Over the course of its history, the death of beta has been peridically announced, inevitably followed by its rebirth. The Fama and French (1992) article is a case in point. These authors found little explanatory power in beta. But here again the autopsy of beta was premature, and "reports of beta's death are greatly exaggerated." For one thing, the CAPM specifies a relationship between expected returns and beta, whereas Fama and French employed realized returns. Moreover, in a subsequent re-

---

[7] See Litzenberger (1988) for an excellent example of this empirical CAPM technique.

[8] The average market forecasts of rates in the form of interest rate Treasury securities futures contracts data can be used as a proxy for the expected risk-free rate.

compensation for beta risk and little relation to M/B ratios, unlike Fama and French. They also found that market risk premiums are much larger when betas are estimated using annual rather than monthly data.

On the positive side, as a tool in the regulatory arena, the CAPM is a rigorous conceptual framework, and is logical insofar as it is not subject to circularity problems, since its inputs are objective, market-based quantities, largely immune to regulatory decisions. The data requirements of the model are not prohibitive, although the amount of data analysis required can be substantial, especially if CAPM extensions are implemented.

On the negative side, the input quantities required for implementing the CAPM are difficult to estimate precisely. These problems are not insurmountable, however, provided that judgment is exercised and that the logic underlying the methodology is well supported. The techniques outlined in this chapter should prove helpful in this regard. Sensitivity analysis over a reasonable range of risk-free rate, market return, and beta is strongly recommended to enhance the credibility of the estimates.

The standard form of the CAPM must be used with some caution. There is strong evidence that the CAPM does not describe security returns perfectly, especially for public utilities. Beta is helpful in explaining security returns only when complemented with other risk indicators, such as dividend yield, size, and skewness variables. Rather than theorize on the effects of such extraneous variables, a more expedient approach to estimating the cost of equity capital is to estimate directly the empirical relationship between return and beta, and let the capital markets speak for themselves as to the relative impact of such variables. The empirical form of the CAPM provides an adequate model of security returns. If a utility's beta can be estimated for a given period, then by knowing the empirical relationship between risk and return, the security's expected return, or cost of capital, can be estimated. Here again, the cost of capital estimates produced by an ECAPM procedure should be sensitized to produce a range of estimates.

The CAPM is one of several tools in the arsenal of techniques to determine the cost of equity capital. Caution, appropriate training in finance and econometrics, and judgment are required for its successful execution, as is the case with the DCF or risk premium methodologies.

It is only natural that the next generation of CAPM models formally account for the presence of several factors influencing security returns. A new finance theory, which extends the standard CAPM to include sensitivity to several market factors other than market risk, has been proposed to replace the CAPM. Proponents of the Arbitrage Pricing Model (APM) contend that APM provides better results than does the CAPM and is not plagued by the shortcomings of the CAPM, while retaining its basic intuition. Chapter 15 discusses this latest paradigm in financial theory, and explores its pertinence in cost of capital determination. But first, Chapter 14 presents numerous applications of the CAPM that are relevant to utilities.

References

Banz, R.W. "The Relationship Between Return and Market Value of Common Stock." *Journal of Financial Economics,* March 1981, 3-18.

Basu, S. "Investment Performance of Common Stocks in Relation to Their Price-Earnings Ratios: A Test of the Efficient Markets Hypothesis." *Journal of Finance,* June 1977, 663-682.

Black, F., Jensen, M.C., and Scholes, M. "The Capital Asset Pricing Model: Some Empirical Tests." Reprinted in *Studies in the Theory of Capital Markets,* edited by M.C. Jensen, 79-124. New York: Praeger, 1972.

Blume, M.E. and Friend, I. "A New Look at the Capital Asset Pricing Model." *Journal of Finance,* March 1973, 19-34.

Blume, M.E. and Husic, F. "Price, Beta, and Exchange Listing." *Journal of Finance,* May 1973, 283-299.

Brealey, R. and Myers, S. *Principles of Corporate Finance,* 4th ed. New York: McGraw-Hill, 1991A.

Brealey, R. and Myers, S. *Principles of Corporate Finance,* Instructors' Manual, Appendix C. New York: McGraw-Hill, 1991B.

Brennan, M. J. "Taxes, Market Valuation, and Corporate Financial Policy." *National Tax Journal,* December 1970, 417-427.

Chartoff, J., Mayo, G.W., and Smith, W.A. "The Case Against the Use of the CAPM in Public Utility Ratemaking." *Energy Law Journal,* 1982, 62-93.

Fama, E.F. and French, K. R. "The Cross-Section of Expected Stock Returns." *Journal of Finance,* June 1992, 427-465.

Fama, E.F. and Macbeth, J. "Risk, Return, and Equilibrium: Empirical Tests." *Journal of Political Economy,* June 1973, 607-636.

Friend, I. and Blume, M.E. "The Demand for Risky Assets." *American Economic Review,* December 1975, 900-922.

Friend, I., Westerfield, R., and Granito, M. "New Evidence on the Capital Asset Pricing Model." *Journal of Finance,* June 1978, 903-916.

Gibbons, M.R. "Multivariate Tests of Financial Models: A New Approach." *Journal of Financial Economics,* March 1982, 3-28.

Ibbotson Associates. *Stocks, Bonds, Bills, and Inflation, 1992 Yearbook.* Chicago: Ibbotson Associates, 1993.

Jensen, M.C. "Capital Markets: Theory and Evidence." *Bell Journal of Economics and Management Science,* Autumn 1972, 357-398.

Jobson, J.D. and Korkie, R.M. "Some Tests of Linear Asset Pricing with Multivariate Normality." *Canadian Journal of Administrative Sciences,* June 1985, 114-138.

Kolbe, A.L. and Read, J.A. *Missing Assets and the Systematic Risk of Public Utility Shares.* Boston MA: Charles River Associates, May 1983.

Kothari, S.P., Shanken, J., and Sloan. R.G. "Another Look at the Cross-section of Expected Stock Returns." Bradley Policy Research Center of the University of Rochester, W. Simon Graduate School of Business Admin., No. 93-01,1993.

Kraus, A. and Litzenberger, R.H. "Skewness Preference and the Valuation of Risk Assets." *Journal of Finance,* September 1976, 1085-1099.

Litzenberger, R. H. and Ramaswamy, K. "The Effect of Personal Taxes and Dividends on Capital Asset Prices: Theory and Empirical Evidence." *Journal of Financial Economics,* June 1979, 163-196.

Litzenberger, R.H., Ramaswamy, K., and Sosin, H. "On the CAPM Approach to the Estimation of a Public Utility's Cost of Equity Capital." *Journal of Finance,* May 1980, 369-383.

Malko, J.B. and Enholm, G.B. "Applying CAPM in a Utility Rate Case: Current Issues and Future Directions." *Electric Ratemaking,* September-October 1985, 29-34.

Merton, R.C. "An Intertemporal Capital Asset Pricing Model." *Econometrica,* Sept. 1973, 867-887.

Miller, M. and Scholes, M. "Rates of Return in Relation to Risk: A Re-examination of Some Recent Findings." In *Studies in the Theory of Capital Markets,* edited by M. C. Jensen, 47-78. New York: Praeger, 1972.

Morin, R.A. "Market Line Theory and the Canadian Equity Market." *Journal of Business Administration,* Fall 1980, 57-76.

Morin, R.A. "Intertemporal Market-Line Theory: An Empirical Test." *Financial Review,* Proceedings of the Eastern Finance Association, 1981.

Morin, R.A. US West Communications (Mountain Bell), Rebuttal Testimony, Arizona Corporation Commission, March 1989.

Reinganum, M.R. "Misspecification of Capital Asset Pricing: Empirical Anomalies Based on Earnings, Yields and Market Values." *Journal of Financial Economics,* March 1981A, 19-46.

Reinganum, M.R. "The Arbitrage Pricing Theory: Some Empirical Results." *Journal of Finance,* May 1981B, 313-321.

Roll, R.W. "A Critique of the Asset Pricing Theory's Tests." *Journal of Financial Economics,* March 1977, 129-176.

Roll, R.W. "A Possible Explanation of the Small Firm Effect." *Journal of Finance,* Sept. 1981, 879-888.

Rosenberg, V. and Marathe, V. "The Prediction of Investment Risk: Systematic and Residual Risk." Proceedings of the Seminar on the Analysis of Security Prices. Chicago: University of Chicago, 20, November 1975.

Ross, S.A. "The Current Status of the Capital Asset Pricing Model." *Journal of Finance,* September 1978, 885-902.

Rubinstein, M.E. "A Mean-Variance Synthesis of Corporate Financial Theory." *Journal of Financial Economics,* March 1973, 167-182.

Shanken, J. "Multivariate Tests of the Zero-Beta CAPM." *Journal of Financial Economics,* September 1985, 327-348.

Stambaugh, R.F. "On the Exclusion of Assets from Tests of the Two-Parameter Model: A Sensitivity Analysis." *Journal of Financial Economics,* Nov. 1982, 237-268.

Tallman, E.W. "Financial Asset Pricing theory: A Review of Recent Developments." *Economic Review,* Federal Reserve Bank of Atlanta, November-December 1989, 26-41.

Additional References

Litzenberger, R.H. Wisconsin Bell, Prepared Testimony, Wisconsin Public Service Commission, 1988.

Roll, R.W. and Ross, S.A. "An Empirical Investigation of the Arbitrage Pricing Theory." *Journal of Finance,* December 1980, 1073-1103.

Chapter 14
Divisional Cost of Capital and CAPM Applications

The objective of this chapter is to explore the theoretical and practical aspects of estimating cost of capital rates for non-traded entities within public utilities. These include operating subsidiaries, divisions, lines of business, individual projects, customer classes, and service categories. The term *division* is employed broadly to signify any such entity. The chapter provides several techniques to develop groups of comparable risk companies in applying DCF and CAPM methodologies to estimating divisional cost of capital rates.

The divisional cost of capital issue encompasses a dual problem: (1) the concept of risk adjustment, and (2) the application mechanics inherent in developing divisional cost of capital estimates.

With respect to risk adjustment, both common sense and financial theory assert that risk-averse investors require higher returns from higher risk investments. This implies that the expected return, or cost of capital, for a higher risk investment exceeds that of a lower risk investment.

Utility companies are not homogeneous in risk. One can think of a utility company as a portfolio, or bundle, of assets, with each entity within the company carrying a different degree of risk. For example, monopolistic services differ in risk from competitive services; capacity expansion projects are riskier than routine maintenance projects; residential utility services differ in risk from commercial-industrial services. Viewing these divisional investments on a stand-alone basis just like any other corporate investment, the higher the risk of that investment, the higher the cost of capital.

The company-wide cost of capital is not necessarily appropriate for individual divisions because it superimposes one cost of capital and its implicit risk level on all aspects of the company. A corporate-wide cost of capital estimate assumes that all divisions have the same degree of risk. This effect is demonstrated graphically by the horizontal line CC in Figure 14-1, which plots an array of divisional investments on a risk-return graph.

The horizontal line is the corporate-wide cost of capital (CC) applied across the board to all projects and divisions of the company. The upward-sloping risk-return line RR represents a risk-adjusted divisional cost of capital system whereby investors require higher returns for investing in projects with higher risks. In region I of the graph, investors are overcompensated for bearing risk. The company-wide cost of capital is too high and

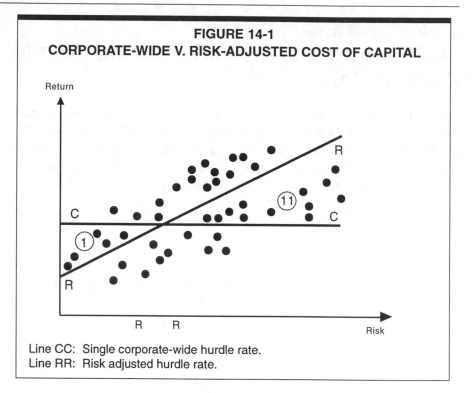

FIGURE 14-1
CORPORATE-WIDE V. RISK-ADJUSTED COST OF CAPITAL

Line CC: Single corporate-wide hurdle rate.
Line RR: Risk adjusted hurdle rate.

unduly rewards investors, given the low risk incurred. In region II, investors are undercompensated for bearing risk. The company-wide cost of capital is too low and unduly penalizes investors, given the high risk incurred.

The risk-return tradeoff given by the CAPM, which is line RR in Figure 14-1, requires that all divisions earn at least the rate of return required by the market on investments of equivalent risk. The implication is that each investment has its own cost of capital because each investment has different risk. The company-wide cost of capital is only an average cost of capital appropriate for the entire portfolio of corporate investments. It is only applicable to divisions that are clones of the company as a whole; in other words, to divisions with the same risk profile as the company.

Incidentally, Figure 14-1 bears a crucial message: the cost of capital for a division, investment project, or specific asset investment depends on the riskiness of that investment, and not on the identity of the company undertaking the project. The cost of capital depends on the use of funds and not on the source of funds. This is because the cost of capital is fundamentally the opportunity cost of the investor, that is, the foregone return on comparable risk investments.

Another reason to be concerned with the divisional cost of capital issue is that for a non-traded regulated entity, such as a company division, subsidiary, service category, or individual project, the traditional cost of capital techniques (DCF, CAPM, etc.) cannot be applied directly, but rather must be estimated indirectly, as is frequently done for companies that are regulated operating subsidiaries of holding companies. The usual procedure consists of applying the traditional cost of capital techniques to parent company data as a proxy for the division. This procedure is adequate provided that the regulated entity possesses the same degree of risk as the parent company, or provided that the regulated entity represents the vast majority of the parent's value, as measured by assets, net operating income, or net income.

However, many utility services are provided by companies with a mixture of different regulated and non-regulated activities, such as telephone utilities, combined gas and electric utilities, and diversified gas utilities with exploration, distribution, and transmission subsidiaries. Telephone companies are frequently disaggregated into a regulated utility segment and a competitive services segment, and it is necessary to estimate equity costs for the individual segments. Even for a publicly-traded company, the application of traditional methods can be misleading if the risk of the utility differs from that of the more diversified parent company. In other words, parent company data may not be an adequate proxy for the utility component of that company, and divisional cost of capital estimates are in order.

With respect to the application mechanics, there are several methodologies available to determine the cost of equity for a division, as shown in Table 14-1: (1) Management Comparisons, (2) Pure-Play Companies, (3) Residual Beta, (4) Multiple Regression, (5) Accounting Beta, and (6) Determinants of Beta. The Pure-Play approach can in turn be applied through Cluster Analysis and Spanning Portfolio techniques. The Accounting Beta approach also possesses several derivatives: Pure-Play Beta, Earnings Beta, Regression Beta, and Fundamental Beta. Comparatively speaking, the Pure-Play, Accounting Beta, and Cluster Analysis methodologies have enjoyed more exposure and application in regulatory settings. Each of these methodologies is explored in greater detail in the following sections of this chapter.

The CAPM, discussed in Chapters 12 and 13, provides the conceptual underpinnings for much of the material in this chapter. Recall that risk-averse investors demand higher returns for assuming additional risk, and higher-risk securities are priced to yield higher expected returns than lower-risk securities. The CAPM quantifies the additional return required for bearing incremental risk, and provides a formal risk-return relationship anchored on the basic idea that only market risk matters, as measured by beta. There is no formal financial theory that links return with any other single measure of risk, such as standard deviation of return or variability of earnings. According to the CAPM, as illustrated in Chapter 12, Equation 12-1, securities are priced such that:

EXPECTED RETURN = RISK-FREE RATE + RISK PREMIUM

$$K = R_F + \beta (R_M - R_F)$$

If a divisional beta can be estimated, the CAPM equation can be employed to estimate the cost of capital consistent with that beta. This chapter provides a variety of tools designed to infer a divisional beta.

TABLE 14-1
DIVISIONAL COST OF CAPITAL ESTIMATION TECHNIQUES

A. Management Comparisons

B. Pure-play Companies
   (1) Cluster Analysis
   (2) Spanning Portfolios

C. Residual Beta

D. Multiple Regression

E. Accounting Beta
   (1) Pure-play Betas
   (2) Earnings Beta
   (3) Regression
   (4) Fundamental Beta

F. Determinants of Beta

14.1 Management Comparisons

The first technique to estimate the risk of a non-traded asset, or division, is the Management Comparisons approach. Under this approach, company management subjectively assesses the risk position of the division relative to a list of industries, as shown in the list of Value Line Industry Betas in Table 14-2, and identifies the industry with risk closest to the division. After reaching a consensus agreement on identifying the closest industry clone, the beta of that industry is used as a proxy for the common stock beta of the division. For example, from Table 14-2, if the division most closely resembles the "Electronics" industry in terms of risk, a Beta of 1.09 is appropriate for that division. The CAPM or ECAPM equations can then be employed to estimate the cost of equity for that division using the proxy beta.

TABLE 14-2
VALUE LINE INDUSTRY BETAS

Industry Name	Beta
Security Brokerage	1.58
Semiconductor	1.49
Computer/Peripherals	1.37
Homebuilding	1.35
Medical Services	1.34
Computer Software/Services	1.29
Banks	1.27
Financial Services	1.25
Medical Supplies	1.21
Drug	1.20
Retail Building Supplies	1.19
Aluminum	1.18
Toys/School Supplies	1.18
Broadcasting/Cable	1.17
Banks: Midwest	1.16
Railroads	1.15
Truck/Trans Lsg	1.15
Apparel	1.12
Household Products	1.10
Insurance: Life	1.09
Electronics	1.09
Maritime	1.08
Advertising	1.07
Restaurant	1.06
Grocery	1.04
Telecommunication Services	1.04
Newspapers	0.99
Publishing	0.99
Auto Parts: Repl	0.99
Office Equipment/Supplies	0.98
Electrical Equipment	0.98
Insurance: P/C	0.97
Aerosp/Def	0.97
Metals/Mining: Industry	0.96
Cement & Aggreg	0.95
Foreign Telecom	0.95
Telecommunications Equipment	0.94
Precision Instruments	0.93
Chemical: Diver	0.92
Bank: Canadian	0.92
Beverages: Alcohol	0.91
Home Furnishings	0.87
Coal/Alternate Energy	0.85
European Divers	0.83
Food: Wholesale	0.79
Auto/Truck: For	0.76
Petro: Producing	0.72
Electric Utilities: East	0.65
Natural Gas: Distribution	0.61
Canadian Energy	0.57
Water Utilities	0.56
Gold/Silver Mining	0.29

Source: Value Screen III, 1993

On the practical side, the approach is arbitrary and judgmental. A consensus on relative divisional risks may be difficult to reach. For example, the analysis may not distinguish those risk factors in each division that are diversifiable and those that are not. Even if arbitrary and qualitative risk differentials can be identified, there exists no financial model to translate those risk differences into rate of return differentials.

14.2 Pure-Play Companies

A second approach is to identify publicly-traded companies that are most similar to the division and then apply the traditional techniques of DCF and CAPM to the proxy firms. The average cost of equity for these companies can be used as an estimate of equity cost for the division. For example, the average beta of a group of gas distribution utilities can be used as a proxy for a similar non-traded gas distribution utility's unobservable beta and used in the CAPM to infer that utility's cost of capital.

One difficulty with the pure-play approach is that although the reference companies may have the same business risk, they may have different capital structures. Observed betas reflect both business risk and financial risk. The fundamental idea is contained in the following relationship:

OBSERVED BETA = BUSINESS RISK BETA + FINANCIAL RISK PREMIUM

Hence, when a group of companies are considered comparable in every way except for financial structure, their betas are not directly comparable. Fortunately, there is a technique for adjusting betas for capital structure differences, based on CAPM theory. The following equation expresses the decomposition of observed beta between a business risk-related component, or unlevered beta, and a financial risk component related to the use of debt financing:

$$\beta_L = \beta_U \left[1 + (1-T) D/E\right] \qquad (14\text{-}1)$$

where β_L is the observed levered beta of a company, β_U is the unlevered beta of the same company with no debt in its capital structure, D/E is the ratio of debt to equity, and T the corporate income tax rate. Intuitively, one can think of the above equation as expressing the total risk of a company, β_L, as the sum of business risk, β_U, and a financial risk premium that depends on the magnitude of the company's debt ratio, D/E.

The relationship between beta and financial risk is depicted in Figure 14-2.

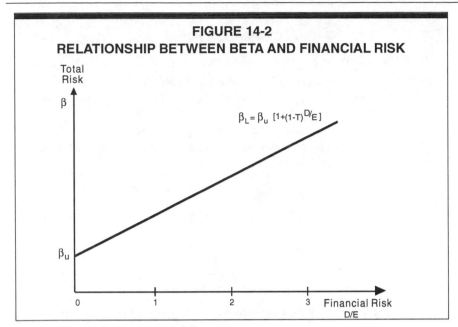

FIGURE 14-2
RELATIONSHIP BETWEEN BETA AND FINANCIAL RISK

$$\beta_L = \beta_u \; [1+(1-T)^{D/E}]$$

The vertical axis represents the beta, or total risk, of the company. The horizontal axis denotes the degree of financial risk measured by the debt-equity ratio. For an all-equity financed company with no financial risk, the levered beta coincides with the unlevered beta. In other words, the company's total risk equals its business risk, as the financial risk is nil. As the financial risk increases, the total risk of the company increases steadily.

The important issue here is that beta is a measure of the systematic risk of the levered equity of the proxy firms, and these proxy companies will often employ leverage different from that used by the division for which the cost of equity is being measured. If we assume that the proxy companies are considered comparable in every way except for capital structure, their betas are not directly comparable. To circumvent this difficulty, the observed "levered" betas of the proxy firms must be "unlevered" in order to isolate their pure business risk component, then "relevered" using the division's own target capital structure. The unlevering of the company betas removes the effect of financial risk to focus on the pure business risk component of the pure-play companies. The relevering of the pure business risk betas accounts for the division's own financial leverage.

The following example demonstrates a two-step procedure for estimating the impact of a change in capital structure on beta. First, the "unlevered" beta of each company in the reference group is estimated and averaged so that the resulting group beta is purged of financial risk and is reflective of business risk only. Second, the business risk beta is relevered, or "recapitalized" to reflect the utility's own capital structure.

349

EXAMPLE 14-1

The levered beta of a pure-play company is 0.80 and its debt-equity ratio is 35%/65%. The division's target debt-equity ratio is 45%/55%. A corporate tax rate of 40% is applicable to both the pure-play company and the division, and book values are assumed equal to market values. The first step of the methodology is to purge the pure-play company's beta from the effects of financial leverage and obtain the unlevered beta using Equation 14-1:

$$\beta_L = \beta_U [1 + (1-T)\ D/E]$$

$$0.80 = \beta_U [1 + (1-.40)35/65]$$

Solving the above equation, $\beta_U = 0.60$. The second step is to estimate the levered beta of the division using the same equation in reverse, only this time using the division's own financial leverage:

$$\beta_L = \beta_U[1 + (1-T)D/E] = 0.60\ [1 + (1 - 0.40)\ 45/55] = 0.90$$

The estimated beta for the division of 0.90 is then used in the CAPM or in an extended form of the model such as the ECAPM to estimate the cost of equity capital consistent with the division's own debt ratio.

EXAMPLE 14-2

The General Gas Company, a regulated distributor of natural gas, is a subsidiary of a holding company engaged in several business ventures, both regulated and unregulated. The utility's capital structure consists of 45% debt and 55% equity. The companies presented in Table 14-3 below are considered comparable in terms of business risk. The second and third columns of the table show the published beta and capital structure for each company, obtained from Value Line. The fourth column computes the unlevered beta for each company, by solving Equation 14-1 for β_U using each company's D/E. A 50% tax rate is assumed, and book values are assumed to be equal to market values. The average unlevered beta for the industry is 0.60, and reflects the business risk of the gas distribution industry and hence of General Gas Company. To estimate the levered beta associated with General Gas Company's own capital structure, Equation 14-1 is solved for β_L using the unlevered beta for the industry and the new D/E as follows:

$$\beta L = \beta U [1 + (1-T)\, D/E]$$

$$= 0.60 + (1-.50)\ .45/.55$$

$$= 1.01$$

The estimated beta for the new debt ratio is then used in the CAPM or in an extended form of the model such as the ECAPM to estimate the cost of equity capital consistent with General Gas Company's own debt ratio.

TABLE 14-3
THE COMPUTATION OF UNLEVERED BETAS
GENERAL GAS COMPANY: MARKET DATA

Company	Beta	Estimated Debt Ratio	Unlevered Beta
Diversified Energy Inc.	0.45	36.5%	0.35
Piedmont Natural Gas Co.	0.50	44.3%	0.36
Laclede Gas	0.65	40.1%	0.49
Consolidated Natural Gas	0.85	37.7%	0.65
Nicor Inc.	0.90	44.5%	0.64
KN Energy Inc.	0.95	46.1%	0.67
Columbia Gas	0.95	49.6%	0.64
Mountain Fuel	1.05	45.5%	0.74
Entex Inc.	1.20	50.1%	0.80
Northwest Energy Co.	1.30	64.1%	0.69
Average	0.88	45.9%	0.60

Source: Value Line

The pure-play methodology assumes that the pure-play companies have the same business risk as the division, and that, indeed, such pure-play companies can be identified to begin with. One difficulty with the approach is to identify undiversified "single line of business" proxy companies. The pool of pure-play companies is shrinking as utilities become more diversified over time. In fact, most companies, including utilities, are not perfectly homogeneous in risk and have multiple lines of business. Moreover, to the extent that the universe of pure-play companies is dwindling, the influence of abnormal observations, or outliers, on the proxy cost of capital estimate increases. Finally, the choice of screening parameters and cutoff points in defining a sample of pure-plays is arbitrary and judgmental. The analyst possesses a fair amount of latitude in defining screening criteria, such as degree of diversification, company size, and non-utility business.

EXAMPLE 14-3

An interesting example of the levered-unlevered beta methodology is provided in Table 14-4. The table compares and quantifies the relative business risk of the telecommunications, gas, and electric utilities industries. Relative beta differentials are inadequate to make such comparisons because beta is a measure of total risk, which includes both business risk and financial risk. Unlevered (business risk) betas can be computed, however, using Equation 14-1. Table 14-4 displays the calculations as of late 1993. The first column shows the Value Line average beta for each industry, and the second column the reported debt ratio. The latter can easily be converted into a debt-equity ratio. Assuming a corporate tax rate of 40%, the last column computes the unlevered beta as per Equation 14-1. Clearly, the telecommunications industry possessed a far greater degree of business risk than the energy utilities at the time.

TABLE 14-4
CALCULATION OF BUSINESS RISK USING
UNLEVERED BETA

Segment	Reported Beta (1)	Debt Ratio (2)	Tax Rate (3)	Unlevered Beta (4)
7 Bell Regionals	0.86	41%	40%	0.61
Independent Telephones	1.00	50%	40%	0.63
Gas Distribution Utilities	0.58	50%	40%	0.36
Electric Utilities	0.67	56%	40%	0.38
Source: Value Line				

Another difficulty is that although the task of applying the pure-play approach to the broader utility segment of a diversified company is practically feasible, the task of applying the method at the more micro level, to each service category or customer class for example, becomes operationally prohibitive. A sample of market-traded firms comparable in risk to each of the individual service categories can be difficult to locate.

Another limitation of the technique is that it is does not consider corporate synergies, that is to say, it assumes that the risk of a total company is simply the sum of the risk of its parts.

Cluster Analysis

With the Cluster Analysis approach, comparable companies are selected on the basis of "closeness" to the targeted entity in terms of such predetermined risk variables as bond rating, after-tax interest coverage, equity ratio, total capital, and variability of operating income. Cluster analysis, briefly introduced in Chapter 8, generates a small group of publicly-traded firms that are comparable in risk to a target division or firm from a much larger universe of diverse companies.

After determining the location of each publicly-traded firm on a graph whose coordinates are the selected risk measures, closeness can be measured by the length of a straight line between the point associated with the division in question and the points associated with each other firm. This measurement process is illustrated graphically in Figure 14-3 for two risk measures: bond rating and income variability. Firm A has a lower income variability and a higher bond rating than firm B, as shown by points A and B on the graph.

The risk comparability of firms A and B is measured mathematically by the distance on the graph, or closeness, between the two points A and B as follows: If X and Y are two axes on a graph corresponding to two risk measures, and there are two points on a graph with coordinates (X_1, Y_1) and (X_2, Y_2), then the distance, D, between the two points is given by:

$$D = (X_2 - X_1)^2 + (Y_2 - Y_1)^2 \qquad (14\text{-}2)$$

If the X and Y axes corresponding to the two risk variables are not measured in the same units, it is necessary to convert them to a common measure using the standard deviation of the sample as scale factors.

This process can be easily extended to include as many risk variables as desired. Figure 14-4 displays the cluster analysis in simplified form using two risk variables. Two clusters of companies are shown on the graph in the form of two small circles, one cluster similar in risk to firm A and the other cluster similar in risk to firm B. Firms A and B could just as well be divisions rather than publicly-traded firms. Operationally, the clustering criteria must be loose enough so as to include a sufficient number of companies, but also stringent enough so as to provide a comparable group of companies close to the candidate firm. This tradeoff can be seen by comparing the distance, D, between the two clusters and the diameter, d, of the two circles in Figure 14-4.

The distance between clusters has to be significantly larger than the distance within clusters if risk comparability is to be achieved, but d has

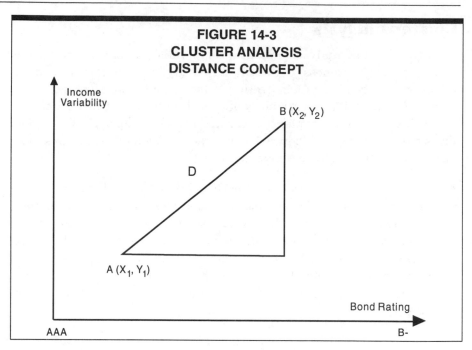

**FIGURE 14-3
CLUSTER ANALYSIS
DISTANCE CONCEPT**

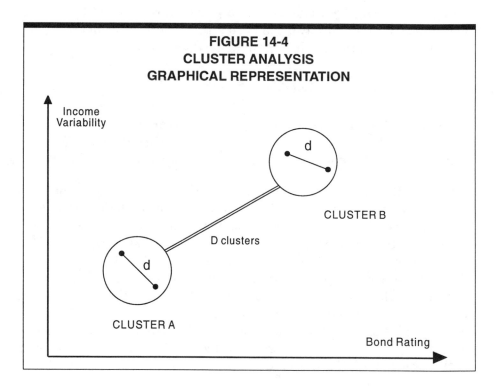

**FIGURE 14-4
CLUSTER ANALYSIS
GRAPHICAL REPRESENTATION**

to be large enough to allow the entry of a sufficient number of companies. A cluster size of 15 to 30 firms is reasonable. Once a cluster of comparable companies is identified for each firm or division, the average DCF and CAPM/ECAPM cost of equity estimates for the publicly-traded companies are used as estimate of equity costs for the divisions.

An excellent example of cluster analysis is provided by Vander Weide (1993) who implemented the approach in 5 distinct steps. First, an adequate universe of companies is defined with sufficient market data to enable a DCF calculation and sufficient accounting data to compute the risk variables. Second, relevant risk variables that define the overall investment risk of the companies are selected. Vander Weide used the following 5 dimensions of investment risk and their associated measurement:

Risk Dimension	Risk Measurement
Variability	Operating income variability
Growth	Sales growth
Operating risk	Cash flow/assets ratio
Financial risk	Bond rating
Size	Total assets

Third, the risk variables are standardized for each firm because the risk variables are not measured in the same units. It is thus necessary to convert them to a common measure using the standard deviation of the sample as scale factors. Fourth, redundancies are eliminated by checking for the degree of correlation between each pair of risk variables. Highly correlated risk variables are eliminated. This is necessary to avoid the double counting of any particular risk dimension. Lastly, those firms among the remaining population that most resemble the target firm are identified by means of a cluster analysis computer program. CAPM and DCF cost of equity calculations are then performed on the comparable firms.

Spanning Portfolios

Another method of identifying comparable risk firms is Spanning Portfolios. With this method, portfolios of companies that display the same responsiveness to predetermined common macroeconomic factors as the division are found. Because the method is spawned from the Arbitrage Pricing Model (APM), it is discussed in Chapter 15, along with numerical illustrations. Once these "mimicking" portfolios of companies are found, the average DCF and CAPM/ECAPM cost of equity estimates for these publicly traded companies comparable in risk to the division are used to estimate equity costs.

The spanning portfolio approach is inexorably linked with the APM and is still undergoing empirical fine-tuning. The company data requirements for implementing the approach are prohibitive and the method requires historical cash flow information for each division extending well back in time. The relative merits of the approach versus other divisional cost of capital methodologies are assessed in Ingram and Morin (1993).

14.3 Residual Beta

The CAPM framework provides yet another methodology for determining a division's cost of capital. A parent company can be viewed as a portfolio of beta assets or divisions. In the absence of significant synergy, the risk of the parent's common stock, as measured by beta, is a weighted average of the risks (betas) associated with each of its divisions. A parent company's risk is the sum of the risks of its components, that is, a parent's beta β_p is equal to the weighted average of the betas of its divisions, say division 1, 2, and 3, as follows:

$$\beta_p = W_1\beta_1 + W_2\beta_2 + W_3\beta_3 \qquad (14\text{-}3)$$

where, W_1, W_2, and W_3 represent the weight of the three divisions, and β_1, β_2, and β_3 the betas of those divisions. For the weights applicable to the divisions, the average percentage contribution of each division to consolidated operating income over a reasonable historical period can be used. Given that the weighted betas of all of the parent's divisions must add up to its aggregate beta and given the weighted betas of two of the three divisions, the residual beta applicable to the remaining division can be calculated. The CAPM formula can be used to measure the cost of equity of the "residual" division.

The practical difficulty with this approach is that it is only applicable in the limited case of one unknown division. The method also presumes that if a company has n divisions, the risks and relative weights of all divisions but one must be known, that is, market data must be available on $n-1$ divisions. Otherwise, the method is unusable.

This method is very useful in cases where an adjustment to the parent company's DCF estimate is warranted based upon the risk differential among segments or divisions of the parent company. Since the beta of the parent represents the weighted average of the betas associated with each division or segment of the parent, these betas can be used to adjust the DCF results derived from parent company market data by applying them to a division of the parent with a different degree of risk than the parent.

The two examples below are drawn from actual rate case testimonies and illustrate the method.

Case Study 14-1: Central Telephone

Parent company data are used in many rate cases as a proxy for a non-publicly-traded utility subsidiary when determining a cost of equity estimate using the DCF or CAPM methodologies. This indirect approach of using the parent company as a proxy for the utility component is necessary since there are no observable market valuation signals for the non-traded subsidiary. The following case study is drawn from an actual 1992 rate case testimony by Morin (1992A) involving Central Telephone's Nevada operations (Central), a wholly-owned subsidiary of Centel Corporation, before Centel's merger with Sprint.

The DCF cost of equity estimate for Centel, the parent company, was initially used as a proxy for Central. However, to the extent that the unregulated operations are riskier, for example cellular operations, the expected equity return applicable to Centel's regulated telephone operations is upward-biased. An adjustment for the risk differential between the parent company and the regulated entity is necessary.

In order to approximate the beta applicable to Centel's regulated telephone operations, the following procedure was used. The parent company's beta (β_{Centel}) is equal to the weighted average of the betas of its regulated telephone operations and unregulated telecommunications activities:

$$\beta_{Centel} = W_r \beta_r + W_u \beta_u \tag{14-4}$$

where, W_r and W_u represent the weight of the regulated and unregulated segments of Centel, and β_r and β_u the betas of the regulated and unregulated segments. The parent company's beta, β_{Centel}, on the left-hand side of the equation was easily obtained from Value Line. On the right-hand side, if the weights W_r and W_u of the two segments of Centel's operations are known, and if the risk (beta) of the unregulated segment, β_u, is known, the equation can be solved for the beta applicable to the regulated segment, β_r.

This analysis is shown in Table 14-5.

TABLE 14-5
CENTEL: BETA BY SEGMENTS

Segment (1)	Beta (2)	Weight (3)	Weighted Beta (4)
Unregulated	1.25	20%	0.25
Regulated	0.86	80%	0.69
CENTEL			0.94

	CAPM	ECAPM
Return differential = (Ibbotson 7.1% risk premium)	0.54%	0.41%
Return differential = (6% market risk premium)	0.47%	0.35%

For the weights applicable to the two segments, the percentage contribution to value of the regulated and unregulated segments were assumed to be 80% and 20%, respectively. As an approximation, a beta of 1.25 for the unregulated segment (cellular properties, information services, telecommunications software, network system products, and others) was assumed. In other words, the unregulated portion was assumed to be 25% riskier than the average common stock investment, which has a beta of 1.00.

Given that the weighted betas of Centel's segments must add up to its aggregate beta of 0.94 in the absence of synergies, and given the weighted beta of the unregulated component, the residual beta must therefore be applicable to the remaining regulated telephone component. Solving for the beta of the regulated segment, which represents Central, we obtained 0.86.

The CAPM formula was used to approximate the return (cost of equity) differences implied by the differences in the betas between the parent company and the regulated telephone operations. The basic form of the CAPM states that the return differential is given by the differential in beta times the excess return on the market, $R_M - R_F$. If beta is reduced from 0.94 to 0.86, that is by 0.08, the return differential implied by the difference in beta between the regulated segment (0.86) and the parent (0.94) is given by 0.08 times $R_M - R_F$. Using an estimate of 6% for $R_M - R_F$, the return adjustment is 47 basis points. Using an estimate of 7% for $R_M - R_F$, the return adjustment is about 54 basis points, for an average of 51 basis points. Using the empirical version of the CAPM, as discussed in Chapter 13, the corresponding adjustments are smaller.

Case Study 14-2: The Peoples Natural Gas Company

As in the previous case study, parent company data were initially used as a proxy in determining a cost of equity estimate for the subsidiary in a Morin (1993) rate case testimony involving The Peoples Natural Gas Company (Peoples), a gas distribution subsididary of Consolidated Natural Gas Company (Consolidated). The parent company cost of equity reflected the weighted average risk of its constituent subsidiaries, which included three principal divisions: exploration-production, transmission, and distribution. Since the operating subsidiaries other than Peoples and its sister gas distribution companies might have been riskier than Peoples at the time, the expected equity return applicable to Peoples, to the extent that it is derived from Consolidated market data, may be upward-biased.

Consolidated's beta, β_{CNG}, is 0.80, and is in turn equal to the weighted average of the betas of its three principal divisions: exploration-production, transmission, and distribution.

$$\beta_{CNG} = W_e \beta_e + W_t \beta_t + W_d \beta_d$$

where, W_e, W_t, and W_d represent the weight of the exploration-production, transmission, and distribution divisions of Consolidated, and β_e, β_t, and β_d the betas of those divisions. The Value Line beta for Consolidated, β_{CNG}, as seen on the left-hand side of the equation, is 0.80. On the right-hand side, if the weights of the three major divisions of Consolidated's operations and the risks (betas) of the two non-distribution divisions are known, the equation can be solved for the beta applicable to the distribution division, which represents Peoples. This analysis is shown in Table 14-6.

TABLE 14-6
CONSOLIDATED NATURAL GAS:
BETA BY SEGMENTS

Segment (1)	Beta (2)	Weight (3)	Weighted Beta (4)
Exploration-production	0.90	26%	0.23
Transmission	1.06	27%	0.29
Distribution	0.60	47%	0.28
CNG			0.80
		CAPM	ECAPM
Return differential = (Ibbotson 7.1% risk premium)		1.44%	1.08%
Return differential = (6% market risk premium)		1.22%	0.91%

For the weights applicable to the divisions, the average percentage contribution of each division to consolidated operating income over the last three years was used. Ideally, one should employ market value weights. Market value data for corporate divisions were not available, however. As a proxy for market value, contribution to operating income was used, as it is more highly correlated to value than any size variable, such as assets or revenues. As an approximation for the beta of the transmission division, the average of the Value Line betas of the 7 companies that make up the Transmission component of Moody's Natural Gas Industry Index was used. This was 1.06. As an approximation for the beta of the exploration-production component, the average beta of the 16 companies in Value Line's Petroleum Index was used. This was 0.90. Given that the weighted betas of all of Consolidated's divisions must add up to Consolidated's aggregate beta of 0.80, and given the weighted betas of two of the three divisions, the residual beta of 0.60 was applicable to the remaining gas distribution component, which represented Peoples.

Using the CAPM and following the same procedure that we used for Centel in the first case study, the return differential is given by the differential in beta times the excess return on the market, $R_M - R_F$. If beta is reduced from 0.80 to 0.60, that is by 0.20, the return differential implied by the difference in beta between Peoples (0.60) and Consolidated (0.80) is given by 0.20 times $R_M - R_F$. Using an estimate of 6% for $R_M - R_F$, the return adjustment is about 122 basis points; using an estimate of 7.1% for $R_M - R_F$, the return adjustment is about 144 basis points, for an average of 133 basis points. Using the empirical version of the CAPM, as discussed in Chapter 13, the corresponding adjustments are 91 and 108 basis points, for an average of about 100 basis points. Averaging the two results, the difference in return is about 1.15%.

14.4 Multiple Regression

One difficulty with the pure-play approach previously discussed is the identification of undiversified "single-line of business" proxy companies. In fact, most companies are not homogeneous in risk and have multiple lines of business. This difficulty can be circumvented by recognizing that the risk of a multidivisional company is a weighted average of the risks of each of its divisions. More specifically, a multidivisional company's unlevered beta β_U equals the weighted average of the unlevered betas of its divisions. For example, for a two-division firm:

$$\beta_U = W_1 \beta_{U1} + W_2 \beta_{U2} \qquad (14\text{-}5)$$

If we consider two multidivisional companies, A and B, each with two lines of business, then for each company:

$$\beta_{UA} = W_1\beta_{U1} + W_2\beta_{U2}$$

$$\beta_{UB} = W_1\beta_{U1} + W_2\beta_{U2}$$

The above two equations with two unknowns can be solved for the unlevered line-of-business betas, β_{U1} and β_{U2}. In other words, if data exist on two companies, each with two lines of business, and the company unlevered betas as well as the weights of the two lines of business are known, the above two equations can easily be solved for β_{U1} and β_{U2}.

More generally, if there are more companies than lines of business, the unlevered divisional betas can be estimated by running a multiple regression of the unlevered multidivisional company betas against the line of business weights. The estimated regression coefficients become the divisional unlevered betas. The levered division betas can be computed from Equation 14-1. The CAPM can be used to measure the divisional cost of equity.

14.5 Accounting Beta

Of course, the betas of individual divisions are not observable. In the Accounting Beta approach, the beta of the division is inferred from accounting data and is then inserted into the CAPM to calculate the cost of equity. Proxies for the true unobservable divisional beta include the Pure-Play Beta, Earnings Beta, Regression Beta, and Fundamental Beta.

Pure-Play Beta

In the Pure-Play Beta approach, a sample of firms with publicly-traded securities whose operations are as similar as possible to the entity in question is found. The average beta of the sample is then used as a surrogate for the non-traded entity's beta. Methods of identifying valid proxy firms were discussed earlier, including industry betas, cluster analysis, and spanning portfolios. One underlying assumption of this approach is that the beta and capital structure of the pure-play companies are similar to those of the division. If not, the levering and unlevering procedures discussed previously must be utilized.

Earnings Beta

One attempt to circumvent the absence of stock market data for a division is to compute an "earnings beta." Since beta is a measure of the co-movement between the returns of an individual company and those of the overall market, and since such co-movement is to a large extent determined by the co-movement of a company's earnings and the overall economy-wide corporate earnings, an "earnings beta" can be computed. A time series of the division's quarterly earnings can be regressed on the corresponding index of aggregate quarterly corporate earnings over the last ten years, and the slope coefficient from such a relationship is the "earnings beta." Since stock prices respond to earnings, the earnings beta and the usual stock beta should be highly correlated. The earnings beta is basically a measure of earnings cyclicality, that is, the extent to which fluctuations in a company's earnings mirror the fluctuations in aggregate earnings of all firms. Growth in earnings per share and growth in after-tax cash flow per share are likely to be related to market return as well, and could be used instead of divisional earnings.

EXAMPLE 14-4

Two steps are required to implement the Earnings Beta approach. First, a general relationship between beta and earnings beta must be established for a large sample of publicly-traded stocks. Second, the estimated relationship is used to infer the division's beta. For example, the following statistical relationship between the published betas of a large sample of publicly-traded stocks and their earnings beta is found by regression techniques:

STOCK MARKET BETA = .564 + 0.251 EARNINGS BETA   (14-6)

If a division's beta, obtained by regressing a time series of the division's quarterly earnings on an index of aggregate quarterly corporate earnings over the last 10 years, is 0.90, then the stock market beta of that division, obtained by inserting the division's earnings beta into the above equation, is 0.73:

STOCK MARKET BETA = $0.564 + 0.251 \times 0.90 = 0.73$

Regression Beta

Given that accounting data capture the same events and information that influence market prices, and given that accounting data constitute an important source of information to investors in setting security prices, it stands to reason that accounting variables and market risk are related.

In the Regression Beta approach, the effects of company fundamentals on beta are estimated by relating beta to several fundamental accounting variables through multiple regression techniques. As discussed in Chapter 3, an equation of the following form is estimated using a large sample of publicly-traded companies:

$$\beta = a_0 + a_1 X_1 + a_2 X_2 + a_3 X_3 + \ldots + a_n X_n + e$$

in which each X variable is one of the variables assumed to influence beta, and e is the residual error term. The estimated historical relationship between accounting variables and beta for a large sample of publicly-traded companies can then be used to forecast the beta of an individual company or division. This is done by inserting the division's own accounting data in the estimated regression equation. Using the derived beta, the cost of equity capital can be measured with the CAPM. An example of the regression beta approach was supplied in Chapter 3.

The advantage of the Regression Beta approach is that, unlike the historical beta, the estimated beta responds more quickly to a change in a company's fundamentals. This is because more current values of the division's accounting variables can be substituted in the regression equation. However, the weakness of the methodology is that the accounting betas are computed under the assumption that all companies respond in a similar manner to a change in fundamentals, that is, the regression coefficients in the above equation are equally applicable to all companies. It is also important that the coefficients be stable over time, that is, that the estimated relationship remain consistent historically. Otherwise, the technique is inappropriate.

Fundamental Beta

The Fundamental Beta approach combines the techniques of historical betas and Regression Betas into one system. It stands to reason that fundamental beta is more accurate in predicting future beta than either historically derived estimates or accounting-based estimates alone.

Fundamental betas are developed through "relative response coefficients," defined as the ratio of the expected response of a security to the expected response of the market if both the security and the market are affected by the same event, say inflation or changes in energy costs. Those securities that react to an economic event in the same manner as the market will have high response coefficients, and vice-versa. The security's fundamental beta is determined by both the relative response of security returns to economic events and by the relative contributions of various types of economic events to market variance. The fundamental beta of a security is the weighted average of its relative response coefficients, each weighted by the proportion of total variance in market returns due to that specific event. To compute fundamental beta, it is necessary to consider the sources of economic events, to project the reaction of the security to such moves, and to assign probabilities to the likelihood of each possible type of economic event.

To forecast fundamental betas, a multiple regression equation similar to the one above is used, but with considerably more variables. A vast array of variables on market variability, earnings variability, financial risk, size, growth, and a multitude of company and industry characteristics is used to capture differences between the betas of various companies and industries.

On the practical side, the Earnings Beta approach requires a sufficient amount of historical accounting data and suffers from the rather arbitrary and numerous allocation and separation decisions of the accounting information. If the historical availability of divisional earnings data is limited, the technique is statistically unreliable. Similarly, the Regression Beta and Fundamental Beta approaches require growth, earnings volatility, capital structure, and other extensive divisional data that may not be available in sufficient quantity to render the analysis meaningful or reliable. Beta estimates from the Regression Beta approach are typically subject to large estimation errors even when performed at the company level. The Residual Beta approach is subject to a similar fate, since it is impossible to remove the implied betas from parent company data when there exists more than one non-traded division.

14.6 Determinants of Beta

Another technique, labeled Determinants of Beta, or sometimes Beta Decomposition, decomposes the beta coefficient into fundamental components that can be observed directly for the division. Rather than relying on historical measures, this approach links beta to its fundamental economic determinants. The beta "drivers" can be estimated from historical data and used to quantify beta and therefore the cost of capital.

Several authors in the finance literature have formalized the joint impacts of risk factors on beta and shown that beta has three main components: demand risk, operating leverage, and financial leverage:

BETA = DEMAND RISK x OPERATING LEVERAGE x FINANCIAL LEVERAGE

Utilities are exposed to a number of significant risks that have an impact on their beta and, hence, on their cost of equity capital. These risks can be conveniently catalogued under the headings of demand risk, operating leverage, and financial leverage. Demand risk refers to the unanticipated variability in demand and prices caused by macroeconomic conditions, regulation, competition, and supply imbalances and to the unanticipated variability in operating and financing costs caused by macroeconomic conditions, regulation, competition, and technological change. Leverage refers to the extent to which these demand and cost uncertainties are magnified by the operating cost and financial cost structures of the company.

Two findings in the literature are noteworthy. Chung (1989) developed a theoretical model of the determinants of beta, whereby beta is a function of three factors: (1) the sensitivity of revenues to general macroeconomic conditions, (2) the degree to which this sensitivity is levered up (magnified) by the operating cost structure of the firm, and (3) the degree to which it is further levered up by the financial structure of the firm. Specifically, Chung showed that for a given firm:

$$BETA = m\,(E/P)\,(BETA_{rev})(DOL)(DFL) \qquad (14\text{-}7)$$

where $BETA_{rev}$ = sensitivity of changes in firm's revenues to changes in the aggregate revenues of a broad market proxy (demand risk)

   DOL = a measure of the degree of the firm's operating leverage, defined as the change in Earnings Before Interest and Taxes (EBIT) associated with a given change in revenues

   DFL = a measure of the degree of the firm's financial leverage, defined as the change in net income associated with a given change in EBIT

   m = a coefficient that reflects the DOL and DFL levels of the market proxy

   E/P = the company's earnings to stock price ratio

Therefore, a security's systematic risk is a function of: (1) the degrees of financial and operating leverage, which are determined principally by the firm's asset and capital structure, (2) the firm's demand beta, which measures the demand volatility of the firm's output to general economic conditions, and (3) the earnings to price ratio.

The demand beta captures the fundamental business risk of the firm in the output market. If a company has neither operating nor financial leverage, that is, all costs are variable and there is no debt (DFL = DOL = 1 in Equation 14-7), then the risk of common stocks is driven entirely by its demand risk. But if the firm is levered operationally and/or financially (DFL and/or DOL >1), the risk of common stocks is determined by its demand risk, augmented by the effects of leverage.

Under the simplifying assumption that a firm's price/earnings multiple is constant, or conversely that its earnings/price ratio is constant, then the market equity beta in the above equation reduces to:

$$BETA = m\,(BETA_{rev})(DOL)(DFL) \qquad (14\text{-}8)$$

In a similar vein, Gahlon and Gentry (1982) demonstrated that beta is a function of the degrees of operating and financial leverage, the coefficient of variation (cyclicality) of the revenues, and the correlation coefficient between the cash flows to the owners and the aggregate dollar return to all capital assets. They derived the following relationship for a firm's beta:

$$BETA = R_F\varphi/[STDDEV(R_M) - L\varphi] \qquad (14\text{-}9)$$

where φ $= (DOL)(DFL)CV(REV)\,\rho$

DOL = degree of operating leverage

DFL = degree of financial leverage

$CV(REV)$ = coefficient of variation of revenues

ρ = correlation between the firm's cash flows and the cash flows of the market proxy

R_F = risk-free rate

R_M = market return

$STDDEV(R_M)$ = standard deviation of the market return proxy

L = market risk premium

Equation 14-9, which is very similar to the Chung model, asserts that a stock's systematic risk is a function of three macroeconomic variables and four types of real-asset risk. The macroeconomic variables, R_F, $STDDEV(R_M)$, and L, are common to all firms. Therefore, risk differentials among firms stem from the remaining variables, that is, asset structure, capital structure, and general management decisions about the types of real-asset risk. These risk elements are reflected in the equation:

$$\varphi = DOL \times DFL \times CV(REV) \times \rho \qquad (14\text{-}10)$$

where *DOL* and *DFL* are as defined before, *CV(REV)*, or the coefficient of variation of revenues, is the variability of revenues scaled by size in terms of expected revenues, which is a measure of demand risk, and ρ is the sensitivity of the firm's cash flows to changes in the macro economy.

If a company has no fixed operating costs or uses no debt financing (*DOL* = *DFL* = 1 in Equation 14-10), its systematic risk simply reflects its demand risk. However, as fixed costs or operating leverage increases, margins increase. Margins reflect the difference between sales revenue and variable costs, and measure the fraction of revenues available to cover fixed costs and generate profits. The larger the margin, the greater the impact on profits for a given level of sales fluctuation. Higher margins, due to increased fixed cost or operating leverage, magnify the effect of demand risk on beta. A similar magnification effect is associated with the fixed costs of financing. If fixed-income securities are issued to raise the capital required to meet service obligations, the degree of financial leverage, hence investment risk, increases.

The magnification effect of leverage and the role of margin can be seen in the following equations. Denoting expected revenues by *E(REV)*, contribution margin by *C*, and fixed operating costs by *F*, *DOL* is defined as the change in pre-tax operating cash flow attributable to a given change in expected revenue, and equals:

$$DOL = [C \times E(REV)] / [C \times E(REV) - F] \qquad (14\text{-}11)$$

Denoting fixed financing costs by *I*, financial leverage is similarly defined as the change in expected cash flow to shareholders attributable to a given change in pre-tax operating cash flow, and equals:

$$DFL = \frac{C \times E(REV) - F}{C \times E(REV) - F - I} \qquad (14\text{-}12)$$

Theoretically, the Determinants of Beta model can be applied to each division. Provided that sufficient historical information exists for each division and that reliable accounting data are available to estimate the components of the above equations for *DOL* and *DFL*, the approach can be used to estimate beta for each division. Current values for the necessary macroeconomic variables, including the risk-free rate, market return, market volatility, and the tax rate are easily obtainable. *DOL* and *DFL* are measured by Equations 14-11 and 14-12, and *BETA* is measured by Equation 14-8. The coefficient of variation of revenues is obtained by dividing the expected revenue by its standard deviation. The CAPM is then used to measure the resulting cost of equity capital. Waddell and Takis (1988) provided a comprehensive application of this approach and discussed the estimation of each parameter within the decomposition equation using historical data.

This model is particularly useful in quantifying relative changes in risk and required return. The following case study, taken from an actual rate case testimony by Morin (1992B), illustrates the usefulness and application of the approach. The case explores the effects of increasing operating and financial leverage on the risk and cost of capital of the water utility industry following the passage of the Safe Drinking Water Act (SDWA) in the early 1990s.

Case Study 14-3: California Water Association

This rate case for the California Water Association was concerned with the extensive non-revenue-producing capital and operating requirements that occurred as a result of increased water quality regulations contained in the Safe Drinking Water Act. These regulations increased the water utility industry's operating leverage (DOL) by mandating incremental treatment investment to wholesalers and retailers. They also increased rate base and fixed costs since any additional plant was depreciated over a constant retail ratepayer base, and they resulted in an increased amount of fixed costs being passed on by wholesalers to retailers.

Financial leverage (DFL) increased as well because large mandated capital investments, which exceeded the availability of internally generated funds, had to be funded externally, most likely in the form of additional debt. Stock issuances were not a viable alternative for many water companies due to the lack of visibility and marketability of thinly traded securities and the accompanying dilution potential and high flotation costs associated with such offerings.

The risk and the investors' required return in the water utility industry was altered with the implementation of the SDWA. Quantifying that change in risk and return was the key issue in this 1993 California case. The use of historical betas in this situation was, of course, unreliable since the prospective changes in the financial and operating leverage would not be reflected in the historical numbers. The Determinants of Beta model was used to capture the relative changes in risk and return.

Table 14-7 applies the model to representative data from the California Water Service Company (CWS).

TABLE 14-7
SYSTEMATIC RISK AND LEVERAGE:
CALIFORNIA WATER SERVICE COMPANY

	Base Case	New Regime
Macroeconomic Variables		
Expected Market Return, R_M	14%	14%
Standard Deviation of Market Return	21%	21%
Risk-free Rate, R_F	8%	8%
Tax Rate, T	40%	40%
λ	0.29	0.29
Cash Flows		
Expected Revenues, E(REV)	$124	$124
Standard Deviation of Revenue, STD(REV)	$18	$18
Contribution Margin	67%	67%
Fixed Operating Expenses	$46	$51
Interest Expense	$10	$11
Risk Measures		
Degree of Operating Leverage, DOL	2.24	2.59
Degree of Financial Leverage, DFL	1.37	1.52
Coefficient of Variation of Revenue, CV(REV)	0.1452	0.1452
Correlation Coefficient	0.90	0.90
Risk and Return		
φ	0.4016	0.5149
β	0.57	0.84
Cost of Equity, CAPM	11.45%	13.03%

The first group of variables includes current values for the necessary macroeconomic variables, including the risk-free rate; market return; market volatility, or standard deviation of market return; and the tax rate. The second group shows the cash flow characteristics for CWS, under status quo conditions and under new water regulation requirements, that is, with the estimated incremental capital investments and operating costs required to comply with the SDWA. In the illustration, expected revenues are $124 million, with a standard deviation of $18 million, estimated from 10-year historical sales data. The contribution margin is set at 67%. Fixed operating expenses are assumed to increase from $46 million to $51 million in response to estimated SDWA compliance requirements. Interest expense increases by $1 million in response to the incremental debt burden required to finance incremental compliance capital investments.

The third and fourth groups report the resulting values for the risk parameters, including beta, DOL, and DFL under both scenarios. DOL and DFL are measured according to Equations 14-11 and 14-12; beta is measured according to Equation 14-8. The coefficient of variation of revenues is obtained by dividing the expected revenue by its standard deviation. The CAPM is used to measure the resulting cost of equity capital. Comparing the results from the two columns, both measures of leverage increase as a result of the increase in fixed costs provoked by SDWA compliance requirements. Hence, beta increases from 0.57 to 0.84 in the example, and the CAPM cost of equity rises from 11.45% to 13.03%, or about 150 basis points as a result.

A comprehensive illustration of the Determinants of Beta approach was provided by Waddell and Takis (1988), who calculated the cost of capital of various customer classes for Connecticut Light and Power using the definitions of variables that are contained in Equation 14-9. Table 14-8 presents the calculations, results, and input assumptions. The class cost of capital computations are performed with the CAPM.

Waddell and Takis (1988) also offered some interesting insights into the relative risks of customer classes. Some analysts argue that industrial customer sales are more risky than residential sales, because revenue variability is greater, and that therefore a higher cost of equity capital rate should be assigned to the industrial class. This point of view misses the crucial connection between revenue variability and earnings variability and its critical role in determining investor risk.

If, indeed, industrial sales volatility translates into net income volatility, then the industrial class is indeed riskier than the other classes, and should be assigned a higher return component. But in order to support

TABLE 14-8
CLASS COST OF CAPITAL CALCULATIONS:
CONNECTICUT LIGHT AND POWER

	Residential	Small Industrial	Large Industrial
Class-Specific Risk Parameters			
Degree of Operating Leverage, DOL	2.181	1.924	1.661
Degree of Financial Leverage, DFL	2.441	1.497	1.757
Coefficient of Variation, CV(REV)	0.082	0.132	0.090
Correlation Coefficient of Sales	0.963	0.999	0.966
Market Related Parameters			
Market Risk Premium (lambda)	0.052	0.052	0.052
Standard Deviation of Market Returns	0.083	0.083	0.083
Current Risk-free Rate	0.088	0.088	0.088
Historical Risk-free Rate	0.108	0.108	0.108
Class Cost of Capital Calculations			
β	0.740	0.650	0.391
$K(e)$	12.61%	12.41%	10.79%

that position, it must first be demonstrated that differences in sales variability do translate into differences in earnings variability. The critical link between revenue variability and earnings variability and the crucial role of the latter in determining risk cannot be ignored. It is earnings volatility rather than sales volatility that is the determinant of risk and investor required return. Two classes of customers can have the same sales variability, yet vastly different earnings variability, because of the variability in cost structure, more specifically, the ratio of fixed to variable costs. It is therefore inappropriate to connect capital costs to sales variability directly without examining the relative underlying cost structures.

The Determinants of Beta approach is fairly complex and possesses burdensome accounting requirements, requiring reliable historical accounting information to compute historical variability, DOL, DFL, etc. It also assumes that fixed operating costs and interest charges are allocated properly across each division.

14.7 Conclusions

This chapter has explored the theoretical and practical aspects of estimating distinctive cost of capital rates for non-traded entities, such as operating subsidiaries, divisions, lines of business, individual projects, and service categories. The major conclusion is that it is conceptually desirable to employ divisional cost of capital in decision-making and ratemaking. The chapter has provided a myriad of techniques for specifying the divisional cost of capital.

While these techniques function adequately at a fairly aggregate level, the practical difficulties involved in measuring the divisional cost of capital become progressively more difficult and unreliable as one increases the degree of disaggregation. At a macro level, it is possible to obtain reliable estimates of equity costs. For example, if a utility is segregated into a regulated division and a competitive division, it is quite feasible to estimate equity costs for the two broad divisions. But at a more micro level, the task becomes more difficult as one goes down to individual customer class or service category levels, particularly if there is a lack of reliable historical data and/or there is a paucity of pure-play comparable risk companies for the division. Of course, the task of estimating divisional cost of capital rates for non-traded entities is academic if there are no significant risk differences between the entities. In the latter case, the company cost of capital provides a useful and reliable estimate of individual division cost rates.

The divisional cost of capital techniques are fairly complex and require reliable historical data. Even if reliable historical data on individual divisions are available, any change in the utility's operating environment underscores the need to be forward-looking. Historically-based measures of risk are necessarily biased in assessing current circumstances. For example, in the telecommunications industry in the late 1980s and early 1990s, the fundamental risks of telephone companies and of their component parts were changing rapidly. At that time, the estimation of individual cost of equity rates for individual telephone service segments was questionable and largely academic because growing competition was quickly blurring any risk-return differential between utility and competitive services. Any risk distinctions between divisions in the telephone utility industry were diminishing with each new leap in technology and with the gradual penetration of competition across the entire spectrum of telecommunications services, including the local loop.

The important point is that statistical analysis runs the risk of not fully reflecting the fact that the risks of a given industry have changed, and will only provide limited evidence that the risk and the cost of capital have changed. Therefore, to the extent that divisional cost of capital estimates are based on history, they are likely to be biased for an industry that is experiencing change in its risk profile.

Determining the cost of equity for various pieces of a company is not a simple, mechanical, number-crunching exercise. It requires sufficient time as well as expert judgment to interpret the results of these various approaches.

References

Chung, K.H. "The Impact of the Demand Volatility and Leverages on the Systematic Risk of Common Stocks." *Journal of Business Finance and Accounting,* Summer 1989.

Gahlon, J.M. and Gentry, J.A. "On the Relationship Between Systematic Risk and the Degrees of Operating and Financial Leverage." *Financial Management,* Summer 1982, 15-23.

Ingram, M. and Morin, R.A. "Using Cluster Analysis to Identify Proxies for Divisional Cost of Capital." Working Paper 93-12, Center for the Study of Regulated Industry, Georgia State University School of Business, 1993.

Morin, R.A. Central Telephone Co., Prepared Testimony, Public Service Commission of Nevada, Docket Nos. 92-7069 and 92-7070, 1992A.

Morin, R.A. California Water Association, Prepared Testimony, "Financial and Operational Risk Analysis of California Water Utilities," California Public Utilities Commission, Docket No. 90-11-033, 1992B.

Morin, R.A. Peoples Natural Gas Company, Prepared Testimony, Pennsylvania Public Utility Commission, Docket No. R-932886, 1993.

Vander Weide, J.H. Pacific Bell, Prepared Testimony, Public Utilities Commission of the State of California, 1993, Docket No. 92-05-004.

Waddell. J.A. and Takis, W.M. "Cost of Capital Differentials by Customer Class: An Analysis." *Public Utilities Fortnightly,* October 27, 1988.

Additional References

Ingram, M. "Theoretical and Empirical Foundations of the Spanning Portfolio Approach to Estimating Divisional Cost of Capital." Working Paper No. 91-3 Center for the Study of Regulated Industry, Georgia State University School of Business, 1991.

Chapter 15
Arbitrage Pricing Model

The Arbitrage Pricing Model (APM), developed by Ross (1976), is a model of the expected return on a security, that is, the cost of capital. It imposes fewer restrictive assumptions in its derivation of security returns and preserves the intuitive appeal of the CAPM, yet is more flexible, and eliminates some of the conceptual problems and troublesome aspects of the CAPM. The fundamental underpinnings of the CAPM, that (1) higher risk is associated with higher return, (2) security risk can be partitioned into a diversifiable and a non-diversifiable risk component, (3) market-wide systematic forces exert an influence on security returns, and (4) security returns are made up of a risk-free rate and a risk premium, are preserved by the APM. The inability to test the CAPM adequately and the naive nature of the model are somewhat circumvented by the APM.

The APM is essentially a generalized, multiple-factor version of the CAPM. It can be viewed as an augmented CAPM with multiple betas and multiple risk premiums. The CAPM suggests that investors should only be recompensed for market risk, namely beta. But what if there are systematic elements of risk other than beta that permeate across all securities? Other plausible risk elements affect all securities include changes in economic activity, changes in inflationary expectations, and changes in interest rates. For example, securities with low systematic risk with respect to the market (beta), such as public utilities, may very well possess high systematic risk with respect to inflation, given their capital intensive nature. So, even if a security has a beta of 1.00, it may not track overall stock market returns when inflationary expectations intensify. Note that the CAPM does not deny the existence of more than one factor in stock returns. Rather, it asserts that only one such factor, namely the market, is priced.

The APM rests on two central building blocks. First, security returns are influenced by several economy-wide systematic factors and by a specific company-related component. Second, assets that are close substitutes will sell for the same price. Section 15.1 of the chapter describes the two conceptual building blocks of the APM in more detail. Section 15.2 contrasts the APM with the CAPM. Empirical evidence to support the APM is presented in Section 15.3. Section 15.4 discusses the applicability of the APM to utility cost of capital, and Section 15.5 offers some concluding remarks.

15.1 Conceptual Background

The first of the APM's two conceptual building blocks is that security returns are assumed to be a linear function of an unknown number of unspecified factors. Investors anticipate individual security returns based on predictions of a variety of changes in the economy that systematically affect all securities. If the predictions are correct and if the process that converts the factor predictions into security return predictions is also correct, then investor predictions are fulfilled. But if there are unanticipated changes in the economy, then returns realized by investors will deviate from what is expected. It is therefore possible to envisage realized returns as the sum of the return initially expected by investors and a deviation component, or surprise effect, caused by inaccurate factor predictions. The extent of the discrepancy will depend on the security's own response to the economic factors.

Suppose, for example, that inflation and industrial production are the only two economic factors impinging on security returns. Then, actual returns will consist of the predicted returns plus the surprise effects caused by the unanticipated deviations of interest rates and inflation from expectation. The magnitude of the surprise effect will depend on the security's own sensitivity to inflation and interest rates:

Actual Return = Expected Return +

Inflation Surprise x Sensitivity to Inflation +

Interest Rate Surprise x Sensitivity to Interest Rates

In equation form:

$$R = E(R) + \beta_1 F_1 + \beta_2 F_2 \qquad (15\text{-}1)$$

where
R	= actual return
$E(R)$	= expected return
β_1	= sensitivity to factor 1
β_2	= sensitivity to factor 2
F_1	= economic factor 1
F_2	= economic factor 2

To illustrate, consider a utility that has a sensitivity of 2 to inflation. Investors were predicting an inflation rate of 8%, but the actual inflation rate turned out to be 10%, then actual returns will deviate by 2 times the deviation of 2%, or 4%, from prediction. The 2% surprise in inflation is magnified into a 4% discrepancy between actual and expected return. The sensitivity factor can be thought of as an inflation beta of 2. A similar "factor beta" exists for interest rate effects, and for any other systematic economic factors acting pervasively upon all security returns. The higher the security's factor sensitivity, the greater its exposure risk to that factor.

Actual security returns are also influenced by factors unique to the company, factors unrelated to macroeconomic developments. These forces were referred to as "specific risk" in earlier discussions of the CAPM. An additional term must be added to the actual return equation above in order to recognize the impact of unexpected company-specific events.

$$R = E(R) + \beta_1 F_1 + \beta_2 F_2 + \varepsilon \qquad (15\text{-}2)$$

where ε = return on specific residual factors

As was the case with the CAPM, company-specific risks can be eliminated by diversification, whereby the impacts of specific events on a portfolio will cancel out by virtue of the law of large numbers. The returns on portfolios will be dominated by systematic factors and will be largely immune to company-specific effects. It follows that the only risk of concern to investors will be the exposure to factor risks.

Equation 15-2 represents the first fundamental assumption of the APM, and describes the process that is assumed to generate security returns. Expression 15-2 can be generalized to accommodate any number of factors:

$$R = E(R) + \beta_1 F_1 + \beta_2 F_2 + \beta_3 F_3 + \dots + \beta_k F_k + \varepsilon \qquad (15\text{-}3)$$

In summary, the APM asserts that security returns are generated by the linear multifactor model of Equation 15-3. In words, the equation says that for each security, investors have an expected return in mind, but that certain economic forces, or factors, may lead to actual results that differ from initial investor expectations. This feature of the APM is reasonable and quite consistent with the prevailing practice by investment managers of fitting securities into different behavioral groups, for example defensive stocks, cyclical stocks, growth stocks, etc.

The second conceptual building block underlying the APM is that there must be a particular relationship between expected return (cost of capital) and the systematic risk measures for a given security if no riskless profit opportunities are to be found in capital markets. This relationship is developed as follows.

If there is a risk-free asset with no systematic exposure to economic factors, then investors will require at least this much return from a security plus a premium for compensation to factor risks:

EXPECTED RETURN = RISK-FREE RETURN + FACTOR RISK PREMIUMS

Only the risks of exposure to unanticipated changes in the economic factors are systematic and thus deserve compensation. All other risks can be eliminated by diversification. The amount of extra return for a given risk factor will depend on the security's exposure to that factor, as measured by its sensitivity to that factor, and on the price of risk associated with the factor. Going back to the initial example of two systematic factors, namely inflation exposure and interest rate exposure, the expected return on a security can be represented as in Figure 15-1:

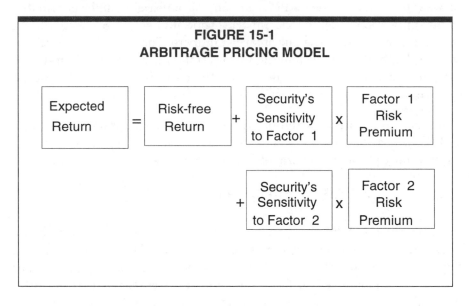

FIGURE 15-1
ARBITRAGE PRICING MODEL

In equation form:

$$E(R) = R_F + \beta_1(F_1 - R_F) + \beta_2(F_2 - R_F) \qquad (15\text{-}4)$$

Equation 15-4 asserts that a security's expected return will be a linear function of the security's sensitivity to the two common factor movements. Generalizing to the case of n factors, the fundamental APM relationship emerges:

$$E(R) = R_F + \beta_1(F_1 - R_F) + \beta_2(F_2 - R_F) + ... + \beta_n(F_n - R_F) \qquad (15\text{-}5)$$

EXAMPLE 15-1

Consider the three-factor APM model:

$$E(R) = R_F + \beta_1(F_1 - R_F) + \beta_2(F_2 - R_F) + \beta_3(F_3 - R_F)$$

The risk-free return is 8%, and a public utility has the following risk coefficients with respect to the three factors: $\beta_1 = 0.40$, $\beta_2 = 0.10$, $\beta_3 = 0.80$. The risk premiums are 7%, 2%, and 5% for each of the three factors, respectively. The cost of capital is then computed by substituting the requisite values in the above equation:

$$K = 8\% + 0.40 \times 7\% + 0.10 \times 2\% + 0.80 \times 5\%$$

$$= 15\%$$

The crux of the APM is that an arbitrage process ensures that Equation 15-5 will prevail. The term arbitrage refers to the buying and selling pressures exerted on security prices by investors. If returns deviate from what the APM equation predicts, profit-seeking investors step in and buy undervalued securities and sell overvalued securities thereby causing the cquation to be true. To see how this "no free lunch" arbitrage principle operates, consider for expository convenience the simple case of only one factor, say the market factor, as shown in Figure 15-2. Since there is only one factor, Equation 15-5 reduces to:

$$E(R) = R_F + \beta_1(F_1 - R_F)$$

which is the equation of the straight line depicted in Figure 15-2.

Consider three well-diversified portfolios A, B, C, with factor betas of 0.80, 0.90, 1.00 and expected returns of 14%, 17%, and 18%, respectively, as shown in Figure 15-2. Portfolio C is mispriced and lies above the predicted APM risk-return relationship, presenting investors with an opportunity for arbitrage profits. By combining portfolio A and B into a new portfolio D, investors can create a new portfolio with the same risks as C. The risks of D will be a weighted average of the risks of A and B, and the expected return on D will also be a weighted average of the expected returns on A and B. If portfolio D consists of equal dollar amounts of A and B, the expected return on D will be 16%, the average of the returns on A and B. The risk of D will be 0.90, the average of A and B's risks.

Investors will note that security C has the same risk as D, namely 0.90, but offers a higher return, 17%. Investors can capture a riskless arbitrage

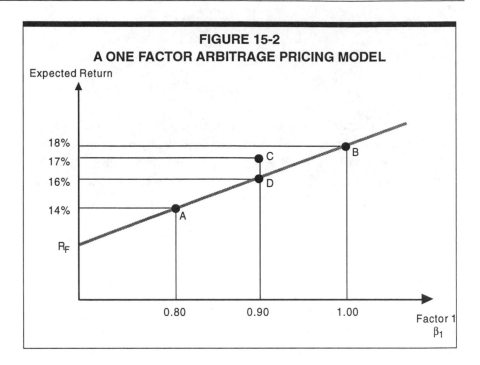

FIGURE 15-2
A ONE FACTOR ARBITRAGE PRICING MODEL

profit by selling short D, which is a combination of A and B, and by using the proceeds of the short sale to buy C. In doing so, investors will drive up C's price, and drive down A and B's prices, lowering the expected return on C and increasing the expected returns on A and B. The buying and selling will continue until all securities are located on the straight line. At this point, final equilibrium is reached and each security's return will be a linear function of its systematic risk.

The important point in the above example is that the arbitrage profit is achieved with no net dollar outlay by investors and with no risk, since the long and short positions are perfectly offsetting. The APM equilibrium pricing relationship must prevail because riskless and costless arbitrage profit opportunities cannot exist in an efficient market.

The same idea can be extended to the case of more than one factor. In the case of two factors, each security's return will be a linear combination of its systematic risks with respect to the two factors and will plot on a plane in final equilibrium, as illustrated schematically in Figure 15-3. Securities that are located above the plane are underpriced and offer a riskless profit opportunity. All security returns will adjust until riskless arbitrage profits are eliminated, and all returns reside on plane ABCD. In the case of more than two factors, each security plots on a "hyperplane" with the appropriate number of dimensions.

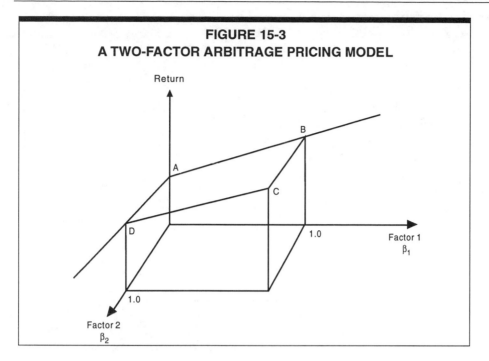

FIGURE 15-3
A TWO-FACTOR ARBITRAGE PRICING MODEL

15.2 CAPM Versus APM

The APM relationship embodied in Equation 15-5 asserts that the return on any risky security is equal to the risk-free rate plus a linear combination of risk premiums, as was shown in Figure 15-1. Each risk premium is the expected return in excess of the risk-free rate associated with an asset that has a systematic risk with respect to that factor only. The CAPM is a special case of the APM if only one factor influences security prices and if that factor happens to be the market portfolio. Under this circumstance, the APM collapses into the CAPM as shown in Figure 15-4, and Equation 15-5 reduces to the CAPM with the coefficient β_1 transformed into the traditional security beta.

The assumptions underlying the APM are far less stringent than the assumptions required for the standard CAPM to obtain. The APM derives from two major assumptions: that security returns are linear functions of several economic factors as per Equation 15-2, and that no profitable arbitrage opportunities exist since investors are able to eliminate such opportunities through riskless arbitrage transactions. The other assumptions required by the APM are that investors are greedy, risk averse, that they can diversify company-specific risks by holding large portfolios, and that enough investors possess similar expectations to trigger the arbitrage process.

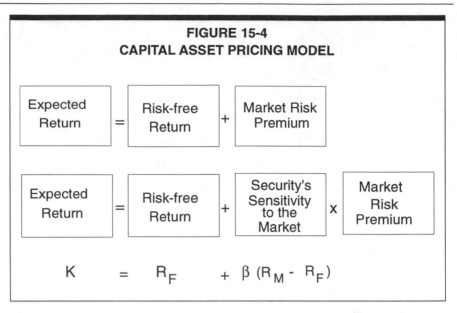

FIGURE 15-4
CAPITAL ASSET PRICING MODEL

The market portfolio plays no special role in the APM. It may or may not be one of the relevant factors affecting security prices. As such, the APM is immune to Roll's critique that the CAPM is inherently untestable. Unlike the CAPM, the APM has a more general theoretical structure. It does not require the assumptions of a single holding period and can easily be extended to a multi-period framework. Neither does it require unrestricted borrowing and lending at the risk-free rate, nor that investors select portfolios solely on the basis of their expected returns and standard deviation of returns. The APM makes no explicit assumptions about the empirical distribution of asset returns. The APM is a statement about the relative pricing of any subset of securities, and therefore one need not measure the entire universe of securities in order to test the model.

The chief attraction of the APM is that it allows security returns to depend on more than one factor, not just the market factor. The APM can easily accommodate the effect of changes in several economic factors on security returns. For example, it is quite plausible that a public utility has a different pattern of sensitivities to underlying economic forces than the average industrial stock. But since the traditional CAPM beta of a utility only measures how sensitive the utility is to the particular mix of economic factors in an aggregate stock index such as the Value Line Composite Index, the CAPM provides a distorted estimate of a utility's cost of capital. It could very well be that utilities are more inflation-sensitive and less GNP- sensitive than the average stock. An APM-based cost of capital estimate would recognize this differential sensitivity, while a CAPM-based estimate would ignore it.

In summary, the APM is based on less stringent assumptions than the CAPM, does not require the identification of the true market portfolio, and is not restricted to a single holding-period. The disadvantage of the APM is that the number or identity of the factors is unspecified.

15.3 Empirical Evidence

Studies by Gehr (1975), Roll and Ross (1980), Reinganum (1981), Chen (1983) and Dhrymes, Friend, and Gultekin (1984) have tested the APM using historical daily return data on publicly listed common stocks. These studies are generally supportive of the APM and typically employ a statistical technique known as "factor analysis" to establish if multiple factors explain security returns better than a single factor. Factor analysis determines the number of variables driving a given series of observations, here security returns, based on the observed covariance relationships between series of observations. The number of factors and their sensitivity coefficients are statistically derived from the data itself, rather than postulated as predetermined economic phenomena, based on the ability of the factors to reproduce the covariance structure observed within a set of historical returns.

For cost of capital estimation purposes, the important issue is to identify the actual factors at work. Empirical research based on Equation 15-5 suggests that there are no more than three to five common factors affecting stock returns. The results obtained by Chen, Roll, and Ross (1986) indicate that there are three and possibly four factors that systematically influence security prices. The four factors mentioned most frequently are related to unanticipated changes in inflation, industrial production, bond risk premiums, and the slope of the term structure of interest rates. Bond risk premiums are measured as the return differential between low-grade corporate bonds and Treasury bonds, and capture the degree of risk aversion of investors. The term structure factor refers to the difference between the yield on a long-term and a short-term Treasury security. Based on numerous empirical studies, it is also reasonable to include the market portfolio (beta) as one of the factors. These variables all make intuitive sense as valid risk factors because unexpected changes in these variables influence the market value of all securities.

In most of these empirical studies, addition of specific company variables such as size or standard deviation risk does not contribute significantly to the explanation of security returns, consistent with the APM. Chen (1983) found that the CAPM anomaly known as the size effect is mostly eliminated by the APM, and that the APM can explain CAPM residuals but not vice-versa. This finding suggests that the APM is an improvement over the CAPM. In the same vein, Lehmann and Modest (1988) could not reject the APM when security portfolios were formed on the basis of dividend yield or standard deviation risk. This finding also suggests that the APM is an improvement over the CAPM because CAPM research has found an anomaly with regard to dividend yield and standard deviation risk. Both Lehmann and Modest (1988) and Korajczyk (1988), however, found a significant relationship between company size and expected return that is not captured by the APM.

Paradoxically, it is important to point out that it is not necessary to identify the factors in order to use the APM as a cost of capital determination device, as long as the number of factors is known. The relationship between security returns and the associated factors can be expressed in terms of observable portfolios of securities. Since portfolio returns are dominated by systematic factors, different portfolios can be carefully selected in such a way that they each have different sensitivities to the systematic factors, and these portfolios can be used as indices for the factors. An example from Roll and Ross (1983) will illustrate. Suppose that there are two unknown factors that systematically influence returns. To estimate the cost of capital for a particular company, we need only find two large imperfectly correlated portfolios. If the two portfolios are not perfectly correlated, it follows that one is more heavily weighted toward one of the two unknown economic factors than the other. So, to determine a company's cost of capital, it is only necessary to calculate the security's sensitivity to each of these proxy or "mimicking" portfolios and use these sensitivities to calculate the cost of capital.

Chen (1983) performed a direct empirical comparison of the APM and the CAPM by fitting both models to historical return data. The unexplained residual portion of the returns explained by the CAPM was statistically related to the APM's factor coefficients; similarly, the unexplained residual portion of the returns explained by the APM was statistically related to the CAPM coefficients. The results showed that the APM could explain a significant portion of the CAPM's unexplained return portion but that the CAPM could not explain the APM return residual. Chen concluded that the APM was a more potent model for explaining security returns. Fogler (1982) addressed the more general question of whether the APM is really any different from the more general multiple-factor extensions of the CAPM enunciated in the previous chapter, and concluded that the severity of the required assumptions and the testability requirements favor the APM. Whether one subscribes to the APM or to the multiple-factor CAPM, Fogler argues correctly that although the theoretical framework of the models differ, the empirical issue boils down to identifying the factors and developing the indices necessary to capture the systematic sources of security returns.

15.4 APM and Utility Cost of Capital

At the time of this writing, few APM empirical studies specifically directed at public utilities' cost of capital are available. Four studies are noteworthy. Using a three-factor model, Roll and Ross (1983) calculated the difference between the average historical monthly return and the return obtained by the standard CAPM for each of a sample of 131 regulated utility companies over the period 1925-1980. Consistently positive differences were obtained, indicating that the CAPM consistently underestimated the cost of capital for the sample utilities relative to their historical costs in that time period. They also calculated the difference between historical returns and the returns using the APM. The differences between actual capital costs and those predicted by the APM model were much smaller and essentially random, neither predominantly positive nor negative. The estimated costs of capital were on average significantly greater for the APM than for the CAPM. Roll and Ross concluded that by including additional forces that influence security risks, the APM does a better job of explaining security returns than does the CAPM. The CAPM is unable to capture the greater sensitivity of utility stocks to unanticipated inflation compared to unregulated companies, while the APM recognizes the sensitivity to inflation as a risk for which investors require compensation.

Bower, Bower, and Logue (1984A, 1984B) also presented evidence that the APM may lead to different and better estimates of the cost of capital than the CAPM, particularly in the case of electric utility stock returns. The authors found that the APM's multiple factors provide a better indication of asset risk and a better estimate of expected return. They concluded that regulators should not discard CAPM results but should place greater weight on APM estimates when the two models disagree.

Pettway and Jordan (1987) performed statistical tests to compare the relative performance of the CAPM and APM to estimate the cost of equity capital for electric and natural gas utilities. While both models generated reasonably good results, the APM estimates were superior.

Berry and Burmeister (1988) estimated the sensitivities of individual securities and portfolios to five risk factors and explored variations in sensitivities to different types of risk across industries. The risk factors include unanticipated changes in five macroeconomic variables: default risk, the term structure of interest rates, inflation, the long-run expected growth rate of profits in the economy, and residual market risk. The authors found that the utility sector is relatively insensitive to unexpected inflation and unexpected changes in growth rate of profits risk. This is not surprising given the utilities' ability to pass through cost increases more readily than other industries and given that the effects of unexpected inflation are cushioned by regulation. Also, because profitability is constrained by regulation, there is less exposure to growth rate of profits risk. The authors found several other interesting patterns of risk exposure across industries and economic sectors that correspond closely to intuition.

Spanning Portfolios

One APM-based utility cost of capital application deserves mention. Chapter 14 alluded to the Spanning Portfolios method of estimating the divisional cost of capital and identifying comparable risk firms. This method was developed by Krueger and Linke (1988) and used in an actual rate case. With this method, portfolios of companies that display the same responsiveness to predetermined common macroeconomic factors as the division are found. The traditional cost of capital estimating techniques are then applied to the proxy companies.

Four steps are required to implement the method. First, a sufficient time-series of historical cash flows is collected for a sample of publicly-traded companies. Figure 15-5 shows a hypothetical data matrix of historical quarterly cash flow information for a sample of 100 companies over a 12-year time period.

**FIGURE 15-5
SPANNING PORTFOLIOS
STEP 1
DATA MATRIX**

	Q1'79	Q2'79	Q3'79	....	....	....	Q4'90
XYZ	1.003	1.31	0.986	1.065	"	"	1.653
IBM	1.121	"					
ATT	1.664	"					
USX	1.036	"					
GM	1.274	"					
GTE	1.413	"					
ITT	0.996	"		LOG Δ CASH FLOWS			
"	"	"					
"	"	"		LOG (CFT/CFT-1)			
"	"	"					
"	"	"					
"	"	"					
"	"	"					
100							

Second, a statistical technique known as Factor Analysis is applied to the sample in order to identify the number of common factors required to explain the behavior of the firms' cash flows and to determine the sensitivity ("beta") of each company's cash flows to the common macroeconomic factors. Figure 15-6 displays the hypothetical factor loadings for each company for a three-factor case. The target division's cash flow sensitivity to the same factors is also calculated.

FIGURE 15-6
SPANNING PORTFOLIOS
STEP 2
FACTOR ANALYSIS

Macroeconomic Factors
Factor Analysis
          Sensitivity of Log (C.F.) to Factors
3 Factors

	F1	F2	F3
XYZ	0.251	−0.633	0.888
IBM	0.109	0.611	0.345
ATT	0.905	0.698	−0.105
USX	0.342	−0.186	0.626
GM	0.611	0.456	0.536
GTE	0.853	−0.061	0.469
ITT	0.492	0.085	0.316
.	.	.	.
.	.	.	.
.	.	.	.
.	.	.	.
.	.	.	.
.	.	.	.
100			

Figure 15-7 shows the same information in abbreviated form for the target division XYZ and three of the 100 companies, IBM, AT&T, and US Steel.

Third, spanning, or "mimicking" portfolios of companies are formed with the same factor loadings as division XYZ. Figure 15-8 shows the method of finding the weights of each stock in the portfolio, which consists essentially of solving a set of three equations, one for each company, and for the three unknown weights of the stocks in the portfolios.

FIGURE 15-7
SPANNING PORTFOLIOS
STEP 2 (CONTINUED)
FACTOR ANALYSIS

	F1	F2	F3
XYZ	0.251	-0.633	0.888
IBM	0.109	0.611	0.345
ATT	0.905	0.698	-0.105
USX	0.342	-0.186	0.626

XYZ	= 0.251F1 - 0633F2 + 0.888F3
IBM	= 0.109F1 + 0.611F2 - 0.345F3
ATT	= 0.905F1 + 0.698F2 - 0.105F3
USX	= 0.342F1 - 0.186F2 + 0.626F3

FIGURE 15-8
SPANNING PORTFOLIOS
STEP 3
MIMICKING PORTFOLIOS

To find weights, solve:

0.251 = 0.109W1 + 0.905W2 + 0.342W3
0.633 = 0.611W1 + 0.698W2 - 0.186W3
0.888 = -0.345W1 - 0.105W2 + 0.626W3

W1 = 0.484
W2 = 0.865
W3 = - 0.518

Portfolio of: 0.484 units of IBM
0.865 units of ATT
- 0.518 units of USX

Same factor sensitivities as XYZ

F1 = 0.251   F2 = -0.633   F3 = 0.888

The portfolios are formed so as to exhibit the same risk factor coefficients as the target division. The figure shows how a portfolio made up of 0.48

units of IBM, 0.87 units of AT&T, and -.52 of USX will display the same factor sensitivities as the target division XYZ, and must therefore have the same expected return as the division. Several spanning portfolios can be constructed. Lastly, the average DCF and CAPM/ECAPM cost of equity estimates for these publicly-traded companies comparable in risk to the division are then used as estimates of equity costs. The cost of capital of the target division, K_{XYZ} is obtained as the weighted average of the cost of capital of the securities in the portfolio:

$$EK_{XYZ} = 0.48\ K_{IBM} + 0.87\ K_{ATT} - 0.52\ K_{USX}$$

The spanning portfolios approach is inexorably linked with the APM, which is still undergoing empirical fine-tuning. The company data requirements for implementing the approach are prohibitive and the method requires historical cash flow information for each division extending well back in time. The relative merits of the approach versus other divisional cost of capital methodologies are assessed in Ingram and Morin (1993).

15.5 Conclusions

The chief advantage of the APM is that it can accomodate several common risk factors while the CAPM is limited to one common risk factor. While the APM provides a superior method from both a conceptual and practical perspective for computing the cost of equity capital, the final verdict on the APM is still pending. There is a great deal of ongoing research on the APM. It is still premature to proclaim the APM as the natural successor to the CAPM. Empirical problems and testing controversies remain, and much empirical work remains to be done.

One troublesome aspect of the APM at this time is the inability to specify precisely the identity of the explanatory factors and to identify clearly the economic forces underlying these factors and their linkages with security returns. For example, it is conceivable that each factor may be a statistical construct that captures the joint effects of several economic variables. Inflation and bond risk premiums are two examples. Voluminous research on identifying factors and providing economic content to the APM is continuing.

The process of delineating factors must extend beyond statistical estimation. The danger of developing statistically estimated factors based on the factor analysis approach is that they may represent statistical artifacts devoid of economic meaning. Even if economically meaningful factors could be located, the question of their stability over time must be resolved. Perhaps from a practical perspective, easily observable factors on capital markets, such as the risk-free rate, stock market returns, and stock portfolios are more tractable than macroeconomic variables.

One important criterion in the search for relevant factors and indices is that they remain stable in order of importance from period to period if they are to be used for predictive purposes. For example, if inflation sensitivity is found to be a crucial factor based on an analysis of the 1980s, and inflation abates in the 1990s because of more stringent monetary and fiscal policies, the question arises as to whether an inflation index remains relevant for explaining security returns. The question also arises as to whether the covariance relationships between factors remain stable under a changed economic environment.

Another difficulty is that the APM and the CAPM sometimes provide conflicting signals concerning the riskiness of a security. To illustrate, the CAPM portrays utilities as low-risk defensive stocks while the APM depicts them to be sensitive to inflation risk, and thus risky in a high-inflation environment. This is shown in Roll and Ross (1983) and in Bower, Bower, and Logue (1984A and 1984B).

The APM literature is burgeoning, following the same path the CAPM did over the last two decades. The identity of the factors, the method of calculating the factors, and the stability of such factors are being explored. Controversies as to the testability and logical consistency of the APM are being raised, for example by Shanken (1982). Replies, rejoinders, and retaliations by academicians follow suit. Refinements and extensions to the APM are being formulated to enrich the content of the theory.

The advent of various software tools and the results of empirical research make the APM progressively more usable and flexible as a tool for estimating the cost of capital. It is only a matter of time before the model gains more prominence and before cost of capital analysts introduce the APM in testimony before regulatory boards. Pending the results of current research, the ECAPM provides a viable temporary alternative, with the impact of the systematic factors buried in the estimated coefficients.

References

Berry, M.A. and Burmeister, E. "Sorting Out Risks Using Known APT Factors." *Financial Analysts' Journal,* March - April 1988, 65-78.

Bower, D., Bower, R.S., and Logue, D.E. "A Primer on Arbitrage Pricing Theory." *Midland Corporate Finance Journal,* Fall 1984A.

Bower, D., Bower, R.S., and Logue, D.E. "Arbitrage Pricing Theory and Utility Stock Returns." *Journal of Finance,* September 1984B 1041-1054.

Chen, N.F. "Some Empirical Tests of the Theory of Arbitrage Pricing." *Journal of Finance,* December 1983, 1393-1414.

Chen, N.F., Roll, R., and Ross, S.A. "Economic Forces and the Stock Market." *Journal of Business,* July 1986, 383-426.

Dhrymes, P., Friend, I., and Gultekin, B. "A Critical Reexamination of the Empirical Evidence on the Arbitrage Pricing Theory." *Journal of Finance,* June 1984, 323-346.

Fogler, H.R. "Common Sense on CAPM, APT, and Correlated Residuals." *Journal of Portfolio Management,* Summer 1982, 20-28.

Gehr, A. "Some Tests of the Arbitrage Pricing Theory." *Journal of the Midwest Finance Association,* 1975, 91-105.

Ingram, M. and Morin, R.A. "Using Cluster Analysis to Identify Proxies for Divisional Cost of Capital." Working Paper 93-12, Center for the Study of Regulated Industry, Georgia State University School of Business, 1993.

Krueger, M.K. and Linke, C.M. "Estimating the Cost of Equity Capital for a Division of a Firm: A Spanning Approach." OPUR Faculty Working Paper, College of Commerce and Bus. Admin., Univ. of Illinois at Urbana-Champaign, November 1988.

Lehmann, B. and Modest D. "The Empirical Foundations of the Arbitrage Pricing Theory." *Journal of Financial Economics,* January 1988, 213-254.

Pettway, R.H. and Jordan, B.D. "APT vs. CAPM Estimates of the Return-Generating Function Parameters for Regulated Public Utilities." *Journal of Financial Research,* Fall 1987, 224-238.

Reinganum, M.R. "The Arbitrage Pricing Theory: Some Empirical Results." *Journal of Finance,* May 1981, 313-321.

Roll, R.W. and Ross, S.A. "An Empirical Investigation of the Arbitrage Pricing Theory." *Journal of Finance,* December 1980, 1073-1103.

Roll, R.W. and Ross, S.A. "Regulation, the Capital Asset Pricing Model, and the Arbitrage Pricing Theory." *Public Utilities Fortnightly,* May 26, 1983, 22-28.

Ross, S.A. "The Arbitrage Theory of Capital Asset Pricing." *Journal of Economic Theory,* December 1976, 341-360.

Shanken, J. "The Arbitrage Pricing Theory: Is It Testable?" *Journal of Finance,* December 1982, 1129-1140.

Additional References

Chen, N.F. "Arbitrage Asset Pricing: Theory and Evidence." Unpublished PhD Thesis, UCLA, Graduate School of Management, 1981.

Ingram, M. "Theoretical and Empirical Foundations of the Spanning Portfolio Approach to Estimating Divisional Cost of Capital." Working Paper No. 91-3, Center for the Study of Regulated Industry, Georgia State University School of Business, 1991.

Chapter 16
Comparable Earnings

The Comparable Earnings standard has a long and rich history in regulatory proceedings, and finds its origins in the fair return doctrine enunciated by the U.S. Supreme Court in the landmark *Hope* case. The governing principle for setting a fair return decreed in *Hope* is that the allowable return on equity should be commensurate with returns on investments in other firms having comparable risks, and that the allowed return should be sufficient to assure confidence in the financial integrity of the firm, in order to maintain creditworthiness and ability to attract capital on reasonable terms. Two distinct standards emerge from this basic premise: a Standard of Capital Attraction and a standard of Comparable Earnings. The Capital Attraction Standard focuses on investors' return requirements, and is applied through market value methods described in prior chapters, such as DCF, CAPM, or Risk Premium. The Comparable Earnings standard, which is the subject of this chapter, uses the return earned on book equity investment by enterprises of comparable risks as the measure of fair return.

16.1 Rationale

The Comparable Earnings approach stems from a particular interpretation of the *Hope* language that states that returns are to be defined as book rates of return on equity (ROE) of other comparable firms. Book return on common equity is computed by dividing the earnings available to common shareholders by the average book common equity. ROE should be measured using "normalized" earnings, that is, earnings before extraordinary items and unusual charges. To implement the approach, a group of companies comparable in risk to a specified utility is defined, the book return on equity is computed for each company, and the allowed return is set equal to the aggregate return on book value for the sample. The reference group of companies is usually made up of unregulated industrial companies of similar risk.

The rationale of the method is that regulation is a duplicate for competition. The profitability of unregulated firms is set by the free forces of competition. In the long run, the free entry of competitors would limit the profits earned by these unregulated companies, and, conversely, unprofitable ventures and product lines would be abandoned by the unregulated companies. In other words, the free entry and exit of competitors should ensure that the profits earned by non-regulated firms are normal in the economic sense of the term. Aggregating book rates of return over a large number of unregulated companies would even out any abnormal short-run profit aberrations, while averaging over time would dampen any cyclical aberrations. Thus, by averaging the book profitability of a large number of unregulated companies over time, an appropriate measure of the fair return on equity for a public utility is obtained.[1]

16.2 Implementation

To implement the Comparable Earnings standard, three steps are required. First, a sample of unregulated companies of reasonably comparable risk is developed. Second, an appropriate time period over which book rates of return on equity are measured is chosen. Third, the result is adjusted for any risk differential between the sample of unregulated companies and the utility, to the extent that such a differential exists. The three steps are discussed in more detail below. The apparent simplicity of the method is overshadowed by various practical difficulties encountered in executing the method, some of which are more illusory than real.

Risk Comparability

The arsenal of quantitative and qualitative measures of risk described in Chapters 2 and 3 provides a solid basis for identifying firms in a comparable risk class. Chapter 8 presented several methodologies and case examples for identifying a group of comparable risk companies in the context of the DCF model. For example, a list of companies comparable in risk to a specified utility might be screened from a computer data base according to the following criteria: (1) they should have a standard deviation of market return and/or beta as close as possible to the subject utility; (2) they should be publicly-traded companies to ensure data availability; (3) they should have a given Value Line rating indicating a degree of safety similar to the subject utility; (4) they should have a given Standard & Poor's quality rating, comparable to the subject utility; and (5) the companies should be non-regulated industrials so as to avoid circularity problems, as discussed below.

A myriad of risk screening criteria can be used, such as bond ratings, betas, coverage ratios, earnings or ROE volatility, and stability of dividends. Some analysts impose additional qualitative criteria for constraining the sample of comparable firms to resemble utilities. For example, the universe of companies could be limited to consumer-oriented

---

[1] For illustrative implementation of the Comparable Earnings approach, see Morin (1993A and 1993B) and Mc Shane (1993).

industries on the grounds that they, like utilities, exhibit more stability than other industries, such as cyclical, durable goods, construction, and natural resource industries. Others exclude financial institutions (banks, real estate companies, investment companies, etc.) because of their very high degree of financial leverage and capital turnover relative to utilities. Other analysts impose minimum size constraints, minimum volume of trading on public exchanges, and a ceiling on the amount of dividend cuts over a past period.

In defining a population of comparable-risk companies, care must be taken not to include other utilities in the sample, since the rate of return on other utilities depends on the allowed rate of return. The book return on equity for regulated firms is not determined by competitive forces but instead reflects the past actions of regulatory commissions. It would be hopelessly circular to set a fair return based on the past actions of other regulators, much like observing a series of duplicate images in multiple mirrors. The rates of return earned by other regulated utilities may very well have been reasonable under historical conditions, but they are still subject to tests of reasonableness under current and prospective conditions.

Time Period

The cost of capital of a company refers to the expected long-run earnings level of other firms with similar risk. But a company's achieved earnings in any given year are likely to exceed or be less than their long-run average. Such deviations from expectations occur at the macroeconomic level as well. At the peak of the business cycle, firms generally earn more than their cost of capital, while at the trough the reverse is typical. Aggregating returns over a large number of comparable-risk unregulated firms averages the abnormally high and low rates of profitability in any given year. Furthermore, to dampen cyclical aberrations and remove the effects of cyclical peaks and troughs in profitability, an average over several time periods should be employed. The time period should include at least one full business cycle that is representative of prospective economic conditions for the next cycle. Such cyclical variations can be gauged by the official turning points in the U.S. business cycle, reported in *Business Conditions Digest*.

Averaging achieved returns over a historical 10-year period can serve as a reasonable compromise between the dual objectives of being representative of current economic conditions and of smoothing out cyclical fluctuations in earnings on unregulated firms. Moreover, the previous decade usually has witnessed sufficiently diverse inflationary, interest rate, and business cycle environments to be representative of long-term trends and investor expectations.

Some analysts confine their return study to the most recent time period. The most serious flaw of this approach is that historical returns on equity vary from year to year, responding to the cyclical forces of recession and expansion and to economic, industry-specific and company-specific trends. The most recent period is not likely to mirror expectations and be representative of prospective business conditions. Moreover, in the short run, reported book profitability frequently moves in the opposite direction to interest rates and to investors' required returns. For example, a period of disinflation and falling interest rates will increase company earnings and earned equity returns, while investors' return requirements are falling, and conversely.

The fundamental issue is whether realized book returns are an adequate surrogate for expected returns. To visualize the problem, Figure 16-1 represents a probability distribution of returns envisaged by investors.

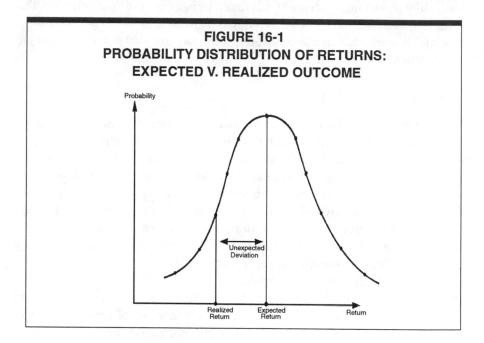

FIGURE 16-1
PROBABILITY DISTRIBUTION OF RETURNS:
EXPECTED V. REALIZED OUTCOME

The Comparable Earnings standard attempts to measure the expected book return, that is, the mean of the probability distribution. But the actual realized return in any given time period represents but a single outcome on the distribution, which may be far removed from original investor expectations. The problem is not unique to the Comparable Earnings method. Any method that relies on historical data is vulnerable to this deficiency. To maximize the possibility that historical results will match expectations, the sample of companies studied should be large enough so that deviations from the mean return will cancel out. But such deviations will only cancel out if there are no systematic economy-wide effects acting upon all companies at the same time, such as recession or expansion cycles. The remedy is to average actual book returns over long periods of time over several economic cycles.

One practical difficulty with Comparable Earnings is the lag in the availability of accounting data. Frequently, the most recent accounting data available is already one year old, notwithstanding the fact that rates will not become effective until an even later date. A remedy does exist, however. An estimate of the current year's ROE and of next year's expected ROE can be derived from analysts' earnings forecasts. The consensus earnings forecasts from IBES or Zacks for a given company is divided by an estimate of the per share book value of common equity. The latter is equal to the previous year's book value per share plus the projected addition to retained earnings. The latter is simply the projected earnings per share for the coming year less the projected dividends per share. Therefore, it is possible to devise projected Comparable Earnings results and circumvent the tardiness of accounting data.

"Real Comparable Earnings."   Under the "real comparable earnings" approach, the adequacy of unregulated companies' current book returns is examined in relation to varying inflationary environments. For example, suppose that a given utility has the same degree of risk as the average stock market investment. The Standard & Poor's 400 Industrials Index provides a ready-made comparable risk group of companies. If from 1974-1993, the book equity returns of the S&P 400 averaged 15%, and the rate of inflation over the corresponding period was 6%, then annual real return must have averaged 9%. If the current or forecast inflation rate is 4%, an average prospective return on book equity for the S&P 400 index of 13% would be required to maintain a real return comparable to past experience.

Inflation accounting remains a controversial topic. The relationship between comparable earnings and inflation is tenuous. To assess real returns, that is, inflation-adjusted ROEs, one must work with formal inflation-adjusted financial statements where reported earnings and equity book values are adjusted for inventory profits, replacement cost depreciation, and the monetary gains of debt financing. Holland and Myers (1979) studied the real returns of U.S. corporations using the national income accounts. They found that the complexity and data requirements involved in deriving and applying inflation-adjusted returns are probably not worth the practical benefits. Inflation accounting or current cost accounting concepts are not yet officially recognized or used. More importantly, accounting rates of return possess conceptual blemishes that far outweigh any the benefits of applying formal inflation adjustments.

In times of variable inflation, it is obvious that accounting rates of return are not accurate measures of true economic rates of return. What is less obvious is that accounting returns are generally not valid measures of economic returns even under non-inflationary conditions. Accounting or book return is, in many cases, a poor measure of true economic return. The relationship between the two rates is a complex function of the age structure of a firm's assets, the company's growth, depreciation policy, and inflation. To illustrate, the book return of a utility with aged assets will exceed that of a company with relatively new assets, all else remaining constant.

Several academic studies, notably by Solomon (1970), Solomon and Laya (1967), and Fisher and McGowan (1983), have confirmed that the strong disparity between accounting and true economic return and the biases inherent in book returns are systematic and do not cancel out in the averaging process. It was suggested earlier that the reference group of companies be made up of unregulated companies in order to avoid the circularity problem. But, given that rates are set on the basis of a book value rate base in most jurisdictions, the economic value of a utility is likely to be in closer concordance with its book value. Thus, the biases in book returns of unregulated firms are inherently more serious than the biases for regulated firms.

Risk Adjustment

The risk comparability of the two groups can be verified by comparing the summary risk statistics of the utility group and the industrials group. Typically, if the risk filter is constructed correctly, no adjustment to the comparable earnings result is necessary for any risk differential between utilities and the industrial group. If the risk filter is valid, the industrial group will be, by definition, virtually identical to the utility group.

If risk differences between the utility and the unregulated group do exist perhaps because of the scarcity of low-risk industrial companies and/or because of liberal screening criteria, a risk adjustment may be in order. There are several ways to quantify the risk adjustment. One way is to compare the average beta of the two groups and use the CAPM to quantify the return differences implied by the differences in the betas between the two groups. For example, if the difference in beta between the utility group and the industrials group is 0.05, the return differential is given by 0.05 times the excess return on the market, $(R_M - R_F)$. Using an estimate of 6% for $(R_M - R_F)$, the return adjustment is 30 basis points. Assuming the industrial group has the higher average beta, the Comparable Earnings result is therefore adjusted downward by 30 basis points.

Another method is to estimate the DCF cost of equity implied by the relative price/earnings (P/E) ratios of the two groups. Because P/E ratio differences between the two groups are due to differences in growth and risk, and because growth differentials can be factored out, the difference in DCF cost of equity reflects the difference in risk. The following DCF formula using the dividend payout, D/E, reconciles the cost of common equity with the observed P/E ratio[2] and takes growth differentials into account:

$$K = \frac{D/E}{P/E} + g \qquad (16\text{-}1)$$

The DCF return for each group can be calculated using the above formula. The return differential between the two groups will determine the magnitude of the adjustment to the industrial returns.

A third method is based on market-to-book (M/B) ratios. If the average M/B ratio for the group of comparable risk companies is reasonably close to 1.0, if there is no inflation, and if the standard DCF model is applicable to the companies in the group, then the sample companies are earning their cost of capital. This is because in an inflation-free, competitive environment, firm market values are driven to book values. If the average M/B ratio exceeds 1.0, the industrial group may be suspected of earning monopolistic returns in excess of the cost of capital, and the group's average book return is not an adequate measure of cost of capital. One way

---

2 The following equation transforms the observed P/E ratio into the investor's required return on equity. From the formal DCF statement of the value of a share of common stock, from Chapter 4, Equation 4-7:

$$P = \frac{D_1}{K - g}$$

but $D_1 = E_1(1 - b)$. Substituting and dividing both sides by E:

$$P/E = \frac{(1 - b)}{K - g}$$

$$P/E\,(K - g) = (1 - b)$$

Dividing both sides of the equation by P/E and solving for K:

$$K = (1 - b)/P/E + g$$

to circumvent this problem is to eliminate from the sample those industries that are characterized by high concentrations of market share.

This argument is valid only if actual realized book returns are, in fact, reflective of expected book returns and if inflation is absent. In the absence of inflation, if realized book returns averaged over a long time period for a large aggregate of comparable risk companies are taken as valid surrogates for expected book returns, then it is appropriate to compute M/B ratios in order to gauge whether these companies are expected to earn an amount more, less, or equal to their cost of capital. To maximize the possibility that the average book returns of the reference companies are in fact reflective of their cost of capital, a specified M/B ratio constraint can be applied on the sample companies as an additional screening criterion.

The picture changes when inflation is introduced. For unregulated firms, the natural forces of competition will ensure over the long-run that the ratio of the market value of these firms' securities equals the replacement cost of their assets, and not their book value. As discussed in Chapter 10, this suggests that a fair and reasonable price for a public utility's common stock is one that produces equality between the market price of its common equity and the replacement cost of its physical assets. The latter circumstance will not necessarily occur when the M/B ratio is 1.0. Therefore, a M/B in excess of 1.0 is not necessarily indicative of monopoly returns.

The appropriate manner of testing for the existence of monopoly profits is therefore to determine the Q-ratio of the industrial firms. If the Q-ratio exceeds 1.0, excess returns are indicated, and vice-versa. If the Q-ratio is reasonably close to 1.0, the firms in the comparable group are indeed competitive and earning fair returns equal to the cost of capital. McShane (1993) suggested an expedient technique for computing the Q-ratio. Because reliable replacement cost data are unavailable for industrial firms, they repriced the common equity by adding annual increments to book value to reflect cumulative inflation, using the Consumer Price Index of GNP Deflator. They then compare the market value of the equity to its restated book value to determine if the Q-ratio differs significantly from 1.0. In the absence of any evidence of monopolistic returns, no adjustment to the industrial returns is warranted due to high M/B ratios. If the Q-ratio departs significantly from 1.0, a return adjustment is required.

Some Comparable Earnings enthusiasts argue that the achieved ROEs can be used to determine the cost of capital, and to that end, they adjust the industrial ROEs to a value that would produce a M/B ratio of 1.0. In other words, these analysts take the position that because current M/B ratios are in excess of 1.0, this indicates that companies are expected by investors to be able to earn more than their cost of capital, and that the regulating authority should lower the authorized return on equity, so that the stock price will decline to book value.

Chapter 10 offered several reasons why this view of the role of M/B ratios in regulation should be avoided. The fundamental goal of regulation should be to set the expected economic profit for a public utility equal to the level of profits expected to be earned by firms of comparable risk, in short, to emulate the competitive result.

Case Study 16-1

In this actual rate case study drawn from Morin (1993A), a sample of comparable-risk industrials and public utilities was composed using four risk measures as screening guides. Only those companies whose risk and variability characteristics were at the low end of the risk spectrum survived the stringent screening process. The first risk measure was the beta coefficient, a market-oriented measure. The betas were taken from The Value Line Investment Survey, the largest and most widely circulated independent investment advisory service. The second, third, and fourth risk measures, which are accounting-oriented, were the standard deviation of achieved book returns on equity (STDROE), the coefficient of variation of book equity returns (CVROE), and total interest coverage. The book equity returns in the last 10 years were averaged for each company. Both the STDROE and the CVROE were then computed for each company. The CVROE was obtained by dividing the STDROE by the mean.

The interest coverage ratio measures the ability of a firm's earnings to meet its fixed obligations, and is an important determinant of creditworthiness scrutinized by bond rating agencies and by the investment community. Total interest coverage figures were obtained from Standard & Poor's Compustat PCPlus (Compustat). Compustat's definition of total interest coverage is "income before extraordinary items" (the income of a company after all expenses, but before provisions for common and/or preferred dividends), plus "interest expense" (the periodic expense to the company of securing short- and long-term debt).

The initial screening process to derive the sample of comparable-risk, publicly-traded industrial and utility companies was as follows: (1) Companies listed in The Value Line Investment Survey and for which information was available on Standard & Poor's Compustat PCPlus yielded an initial sample of 1,475 companies. (2) Companies that did not have current year interest coverage data and companies with negative interest coverage were omitted from the sample, reducing the sample size to 1,352. (3) Companies that did not have ROE data for each of the last 10 years and companies with negative mean ROEs were omitted from the sample, reducing the sample size to 967. (4) Companies with STDROE greater than 100 and CVROE greater than 10 were deleted from the sample, leaving a total of 953 companies ready to be screened. (5) Finally, to simulate the coverage environment of the utility industry, companies with total interest coverage of less than 1.00 and greater than 4.00 were eliminated from the sample, leaving a total sample of 551 companies.

The companies were then screened as follows. The average beta and total interest coverage of the sample of 551 companies were 0.97 and 2.20, respectively. The third and fourth risk measures yielded an average STDROE and CVROE for the sample of 6.45 and 0.7744, respectively. All companies with market risk and total interest coverage less than or equal to the average and whose STDROE and CVROE measures of risk were less than or equal to half the average were retained, that is, companies with a beta less than or equal to 0.97, total interest coverage less than or equal to 2.20, STDROE less than or equal to 3.22 and CVROE less than or equal to 0.3872.

Table 16-1 shows the list of companies and the summary statistics for the 46 companies that survived the screens. It is interesting to note that several utilities appear in the surviving sample, attesting to its comparability, reasonableness, and accuracy. Of the 46 surviving companies, 18 are industrials and 28 are utilities, 8 of which are gas distribution companies.

Table 16-2 shows the summary statistics for the 18 industrials that survived the stringent screening process. The group of 18 comparable-risk companies experienced a mean return on book equity of 13.13% over the last 10 years. As indicated at the bottom of the various columns, the average adjusted beta for this sample of low risk industrials is 0.84. The average total interest coverage is 1.41, the average CVROE is 0.1588, and the average STDROE is 1.80. To place the results for the industrial group in perspective, the statistics for the entire screened database of 551 companies were the following: average beta 0.97, average total interest coverage 2.20, average CVROE 0.7744, and average STDROE 6.45.

Another way of constructing the screen is to rank the companies on each of the risk criteria, and then array the companies by their composite ordinal risk score, as illustrated in Chapter 3, Table 3-4.

TABLE 16-1
AVERAGE RETURN ON EQUITY 1983-1992 AND RISK MEASURES, I

Company	Status	10-Year Mean ROE	STDROE	CVROE	Beta	Total Int Cov
1 Amer. Elec Pwr	R	12.71	1.21	0.0954	0.75	2.16
2 Amer. Water Wks	R	12.77	1.55	0.1211	0.65	1.70
3 Ameron, Inc.	U	8.12	2.14	0.2635	0.50	1.50
4 AMSouth Bancorp	U	14.03	1.49	0.1063	0.90	1.34
5 Atlanta Gas Lt	R	12.52	1.69	0.1352	0.65	2.12
6 BCE Inc.	R	12.55	1.56	0.1245	0.60	1.67
7 Boatmen's Bncsh	U	13.68	2.78	0.2033	0.95	1.30
8 Calif Water	R	13.55	1.68	0.1236	0.50	2.05
9 Canon Inc (ADR)	U	8.52	3.18	0.3728	0.75	1.68
10 Commerce Bancsh	U	12.68	1.15	0.0911	0.75	1.35
11 Conn. Energy	R	11.60	1.34	0.1156	0.55	1.89
12 Conn. Nat Gas	R	13.14	1.38	0.1052	0.60	2.11
13 Consumers Water	R	13.82	2.91	0.2107	0.50	1.70
14 Fifth Third Banc	U	17.38	0.82	0.0470	0.95	1.55
15 First Alabama	U	14.43	0.82	0.0569	0.95	1.42
16 First Of Amer.	U	15.45	1.16	0.0753	0.95	1.23
17 First Tenn Natl	U	13.79	2.79	0.2020	0.85	1.32
18 Hawaiian Elec.	R	12.24	1.77	0.1445	0.70	1.42
19 Hitachi, Ltd.	U	8.25	3.09	0.3740	0.75	1.68
20 Houston Inds.	R	12.96	2.27	0.1750	0.60	1.91
21 Huntington Banc	U	13.89	2.55	0.1838	0.90	1.34
22 Idaho Power	R	11.30	2.86	0.2533	0.60	2.08
23 IES Industries	R	12.36	2.89	0.2339	0.55	2.11
24 Interstate Pwr	R	10.87	2.32	0.2136	0.55	2.14
25 Liberty Nat'l	U	14.07	0.86	0.0612	0.85	1.30
26 Marshall & Ilsley	U	15.57	1.33	0.0856	0.95	1.52
27 Nat'l Fuel Gas	R	11.82	2.24	0.1896	0.60	2.00
28 Northeast Util	R	14.41	2.91	0.2020	0.65	2.06
29 NW Natural Gas	R	10.98	2.84	0.2589	0.60	1.59
30 Ohio Edison	R	12.50	2.70	0.2222	0.80	1.98
31 Old Kent Fin'l	U	15.98	1.25	0.0785	0.90	1.37
32 Oneok Inc.	R	8.78	2.70	0.3077	0.80	1.90
33 Phila. Suburban	R	10.88	0.75	0.0686	0.60	1.71
34 Public Svc (co)	R	13.33	1.72	0.1291	0.65	2.09
35 Public Svc Ent.	R	12.77	1.36	0.1061	0.70	2.02
36 Sierra Pacific	R	11.13	1.68	0.1513	0.55	1.80
37 Sony Corp.(ADR)	U	8.49	3.12	0.3675	0.75	1.40
38 South Jersey In.	R	11.63	1.49	0.1278	0.50	1.95
39 Star Banc Corp.	U	13.41	0.62	0.0463	0.85	1.33
40 Synovus Fin'l	U	17.37	1.33	0.0767	0.65	1.32
41 Textron, Inc.	U	11.18	1.86	0.1663	0.95	1.44
42 United Water	R	11.97	1.88	0.1570	0.70	1.63
43 Utilicorp Untd.	R	13.35	3.05	0.2283	0.60	1.53
44 Washington Energy	R	9.56	3.07	0.3208	0.55	1.45
45 Westc'st Energy	R	9.95	1.52	0.1529	0.50	1.46
46 Wicor, Inc.	R	11.61	3.18	0.2736	0.60	2.14
		12.46	1.98	0.1697	0.70	1.69

Source: Compustat PCPlus and Value/Screen III

TABLE 16-2
AVERAGE RETURN ON EQUITY 1983-1992
AND RISK MEASURES, II

	Company	Status	10-Year Mean ROE	STDROE	CVROE	BETA	Total Int Cov
1	Ameron, Inc.	U	8.12	2.14	0.2635	0.50	1.50
2	Amsouth Bancorp	U	14.03	1.49	0.1063	0.90	1.34
3	Boatmen's Bncsh	U	13.68	2.78	0.2033	0.95	1.30
4	Canon Inc (ADR)	U	8.52	3.18	0.3728	0.75	1.68
5	Commerce Bancsh	U	12.68	1.15	0.0911	0.75	1.35
6	Fifth Third Banc	U	17.38	0.82	0.0470	0.95	1.55
7	First Alabama	U	14.43	0.82	0.0569	0.95	1.42
8	First of Amer.	U	15.45	1.16	0.0753	0.95	1.23
9	First Tenn National	U	13.79	2.79	0.2020	0.85	1.32
10	Hitachi, Ltd.	U	8.25	3.09	0.3740	0.75	1.68
11	Huntington Banc	U	13.89	2.55	0.1838	0.90	1.34
12	Liberty National	U	14.07	0.86	0.0612	0.85	1.30
13	Marshall & Ilsley	U	15.57	1.33	0.0856	0.95	1.52
14	Old Kent Fin'l	U	15.98	1.25	0.0785	0.90	1.37
15	Sony Corp.(ADR)	U	8.49	3.12	0.3675	0.75	1.40
16	Star Banc Corp.	U	13.41	0.62	0.0463	0.85	1.33
17	Synovus Fin'l	U	17.37	1.33	0.0767	0.65	1.32
18	Textron, Inc.	U	11.18	1.86	0.1663	0.95	1.44
			13.13	1.80	0.1588	0.84	1.41

Source: Compustat PCPlus and Value/Screen III

16.3 Assessment

On the plus side of the ledger, the Comparable Earnings standard is easy to calculate, and the amount of subjective judgment required is minimal. The method avoids several of the subjective factors involved in other cost of capital methodologies. For example, the DCF approach requires the determination of the growth rate contemplated by investors, which is a subjective factor. The CAPM requires the specification of several expectational variables, such as market return and beta. In contrast, the Comparable Earnings approach makes use of simple, readily available accounting data. Return on book equity data are widely available on computerized data bases for most public companies and for a wide variety of market indices.

The method is easily understood, and is firmly anchored in regulatory tradition. The method is not influenced by the regulatory process to the same extent as market-based methods, such as DCF and CAPM. The base to which the Comparable Earnings standard is applicable is the utility's book common equity, which is much less vulnerable to regulatory influences than stock price, which is the base to which the market-based standards are applied. Stock price can be influenced by the actions of regulators and investor expectations of those actions.

Although the analyst possesses a fair amount of latitude in selecting risk criteria to define the sample of comparable risk companies, it is easier to generate a set of comparable risk companies than it is to measure accurately the input quantities required in alternate cost of capital estimating techniques, such as DCF and CAPM. As a practical matter, although different risk measures may produce different groups of comparable companies, many of the same companies are selected over a wide range of risk measures.

On the minus side of the ledger, the Comparable Earnings approach rests on a particular notion of opportunity cost, namely that a utility should be allowed to earn what it would have earned had its capital been invested in other firms of comparable risk. A goal of fairness is said to be achieved by this. This legal interpretation of returns stands in contrast to financial theory, which interprets returns as forward-looking, market-determined returns, derived from the capital gains and dividends expectations of investors relative to stock prices.

Accounting rates of return are not based on opportunity cost in the economic sense, but reflect the average returns earned on past investments, and hence reflect past regulatory actions. The denominator of accounting return, book equity, is a historical cost-based concept, which is insensitive to changes in investor return requirements. Only stock market price is sensitive to a change in investor requirements. Investors can only purchase new shares of common stock at current market prices and not at book value.

Another way of expressing the above argument is that the Comparable Earnings standard ignores capital markets. If interest rates go up 2% for example, investor requirements and the cost of equity should increase commensurably, but if regulation is based on accounting returns, no change in equity cost results. Investors capitalize expected future cash flows and not current earnings, and what was earned on book value is not directly related to current market rates.

Another conceptual anomaly is that when the utility's current book rate of return is compared to that of firms of comparable risk, it is assumed that there is a fundamental theoretical relationship between accounting returns and risk. But no such relationship exists in financial theory. The risk return tradeoff found in financial theory is expressed in terms of market values rather than in terms of accounting values. Only if long time periods are examined and broad aggregates are used can an empirical relationship between risk and accounting return be found.

One objection to the Comparable Earnings method is that comparisons of book rates of return among companies are computationally misleading because of differences among companies in their accounting procedures. Despite the umbrella of generally acceptable accounting principles, areas of difference include the treatment of inventory valuation, depreciation, investment tax credits, deferred taxes, and extraordinary items. The lack of accounting homogeneity is exacerbated by the necessity of studying nonregulated companies, which are likely to exhibit greater accounting differences. As a practical matter, such differences are relatively minor in comparison to the problems of risk estimation and time period discussed earlier, and may be attenuated by employing reasonably diverse aggregates in the reference group and by excluding groups with vastly different asset and financing compositions from utilities, such as financial institutions and natural resource sectors. If the companies in a particular reference group have clear identifiable differences in accounting treatment, the latter should be used as an additional screening criterion to eliminate such companies, or the accounting rates of return should be restated on a consistent comparable basis.

More fundamentally, the basic premise of the Comparable Earnings approach is that regulation should emulate the competitive result. It is not clear from this premise which is the proper level of competition being referenced. Is the norm the perfect competition model of economics where no monopolistic elements exist, or is it the degree of competition actually prevailing in the economy? A strong case for the latter can be made on grounds of fairness alone.

Although the Comparable Earnings test does not square well with economic theory, the approach is nevertheless meritorious. If the basic purpose of comparable earnings is to set a fair return rather than determine the true economic return, then the argument is academic. If regulators consider a fair return as one that equals the book rates of return earned by comparable risk firms rather than one that is equal to the cost of capital of such firms, the Comparable Earnings test is relevant. This notion of fairness, rooted in the traditional legalistic interpretation of the *Hope* language, validates the Comparable Earnings test.

Moreover, if regulation is a substitute for competition, and if the cost of capital is to play the same role in the utility industry as in unregulated industries, then the allowed rate of return should be set in excess of the cost of capital. The reason, as articulated by Friend (1983), has to do with the economic criterion employed by corporations in their investment decisions.

This criterion is that the expected marginal return on new projects be greater than the cost of capital. Corporations rank investment projects in descending order of profitability, and successively adopt all investment projects to the point where the least attractive project has a return equal to the cost of capital. The average return on all new investment projects will then exceed the cost of capital. If the average, rather than the marginal, return is set equal to the cost of capital as is the case with Comparable Earnings, the implication is that a company also accepts investment projects that are less profitable than the cost of capital, so that the average return on all projects accepted is equal to the cost of capital. Corporate investment would largely cease under such a scheme. Moreover, if unregulated companies were to pursue such an investment policy, a serious misallocation of economic resources would ensue.

The Comparable Earnings approach is far more meaningful in the regulatory arena than in the sphere of competitive firms. Unlike industrial companies, the earnings requirement of utilities is determined by applying a percentage rate of return to the book value of a utility's investment, and not on the market value of that investment. Therefore, it stands to reason that a different percentage rate of return than the market cost of capital be applied when the investment base is stated in book value terms rather than market value terms. In a competitive market, investment decisions are taken on the basis of market prices, market values, and market cost of capital. If regulation's role was to duplicate the competitive result perfectly, then the market cost of capital would be applied to the current market value of rate base assets employed by utilities to provide service. But because the investment base for ratemaking purposes is expressed in book value terms, a rate of return on book value, as is the case with Comparable Earnings, is highly meaningful.

References

Friend, I. The Bell Telephone Company of Pennsylvania, Prepared Testimony, Pennsylvania Public Utility Commission, Docket No. 2316, 1983.

Fisher, F.M. and McGowan, J.J. "On the Misuse of Accounting Rates of Return to Infer Monopoly Profits." *American Economic Review,* March 1983, 82-97.

Holland, D.M and Myers, S.C. "Trends in Corporate Profitability and Capital Costs." In *The Nation's Capital Needs: Three Studies,* Edited by R. Lindsay, Committee for Economic Development, 1979.

McShane, K. C. Prepared testimony on Fair Return on Equity for Bell Canada, Foster Associates, Inc., February 1993.

Morin, R.A. Peoples Natural Gas Company, Prepared Testimony, Pennsylvania Public Utility Commission, Docket No. R-932886, 1993A.

Morin, R.A. Bell Canada, Prepared Testimony, Canadian Radio and Telecommunications Commission, 1993B.

Solomon, E. "Alternative Rate of Return Concepts and Their Implications for Utility Regulation." *Bell Journal of Economics and Management Science,* Spring 1970, 65-81.

Solomon, E. and Laya, J.E. "Measurement of Company Profitability: Some Systematic Errors in the Accounting Rate of Return." In *Financial Research and Management Decisions,* Edited by A.A. Robichek. New York: Wiley and Sons, 1967.

Chapter 17
Weighted Average Cost of Capital

Traditionally, the allowed rate of return in regulatory hearings is calculated as the weighted average of the cost of each individual component of the capital structure weighted by its book value. This is illustrated in Table 17-1, where the capital structure, expressed as percent of book value, consists of 40% debt, 10% preferred stock, and 50% common stock, with individual cost rates of 8%, 6%, and 12%, respectively.

TABLE 17-1
ILLUSTRATION OF COST OF CAPITAL CALCULATION

Source	% of Capital	% of Cost	Weighted Cost	Tax Factor*	Capital Cost Including Tax
Debt	40.00% X	8.00% =	3.20%	X 1 =	3.20%
Preferred	10.00% X	6.00% =	0.60%	X 2 =	1.20%
Equity	50.00% X	12.00% =	6.00%	X 2 =	12.00%
	100.00%		9.80%		16.40%

*The tax factor is 1/(1 - tax rate): assuming a 50% corporate tax rate

1/(1 - 0.50) = 1/0.50 = 2.00

The estimated allowed rate of return of 9.8%, also known as the weighted average cost of capital (WACC), is then applied to the book value of the rate base to determine the total revenue requirements (costs of service) needed to service the capital employed by the utility. Knowledge of the 9.8% allowed rate of return on total capital is not enough to determine the total cost of capital to the ratepayers, however, for it ignores the tax burden. Assuming a 50% tax rate, in order to provide a $1 return to the bondholders, the utility requires only $1 of revenue. But it takes $2 of revenue to provide a $1 return to the preferred and common equity holders because the utility must pay corporate income taxes. In the above example, if the rate base is $100 and the tax rate 50%, to provide a return of $3.20 on the bondholders' $40 investment, the utility requires $3.20 of pre-tax revenues. But to provide a return of $0.60 + $6.00 = $6.60 to the equity holders' $60 investment, the regulatory commission must allow a profit before taxes of 2 x $6.60 = $13.20. From the ratepayers' viewpoint, the total cost of capital inclusive of taxes is $3.20 + $13.20 = $16.40, or 16.4%.

An alternate and equivalent computational procedure, shown in Table 17-2, is to express the cost of debt directly on an after-tax basis, and then compute the weighted average cost of each component of capital.

TABLE 17-2
ILLUSTRATION OF COST OF CAPITAL CALCULATION: ALTERNATE VERSION

Source	% of Capital		% of Cost		Weighted Cost
Debt	40.00%	X	8.00%(1-.50)	=	1.60%
Preferred	10.00%	X	6.00%	=	0.60%
Equity	50.00%	X	12.00%	=	6.00%
	100.00%				8.20%

The resulting WACC is then multiplied by the tax factor to obtain directly the cost of capital inclusive of taxes. Going back to the above example, the after-tax cost of debt is 8% $(1 - T) = 8\%(1 - .50) = 4\%$, where T is the tax rate. The weighted cost of debt is then 1.6%, for a total WACC of 8.2%, instead of the 9.8% shown above. The pre-tax cost of capital is then simply the post-tax figure of 8.2% multiplied by the tax factor of 2, or 16.4%, the same figure obtained with the first procedure.

More generally, if K_d and K_e are the costs of debt and equity, and W_d and W_e are, respectively, the weights of debt and equity to the total value of capital, the weighted average cost of capital, K, can be expressed as:

$$K = K_d W_d + K_e W_e \qquad (17\text{-}1)$$

Several issues regarding the WACC arise in regulatory proceedings, particularly with regard to the optimal set of weights W_d and W_e. Section 17.1 of this chapter rationalizes the use of book value weights rather than market value weights in the computation of the WACC. Section 17.2 explores the effect of capital structure on cost of capital in an informal and intuitive manner, while Section 17.3 addresses the same topic in a more formal manner. Section 17.4 briefly discusses the empirical evidence on the existence of an optimal financing mix of debt and equity that would minimize the utility's cost of capital and thus minimize ratepayer burden. Capital structure issues are further discussed in the next several chapters. Chapter 18 presents illustrative examples and practical implications of capital structure theory in regulatory settings, including the consequences of including or excluding certain components of capital in the WACC calculation, the treatment of zero-cost items of capital, and the consistency of the rate base and invested capital. Chapter 19 presents a model designed to determine the optimal capital structure for a regulated utility. Chapter 20 addresses the issue of double leverage.

17.1 Book Versus Market Value

In the context of rate making for regulated utilities,[1] it is almost universal practice to employ a hybrid computation consisting of embedded costs of debt and a market-based cost of equity, with costs of debt and equity both weighted at their respective book values in the determination of the WACC. Letting K_{em} stand for the market-based cost of equity, K_d for the embedded costs of debt at the coupon rate, and D/C and E/C for the ratios of debt and equity at book value to the total book value of capital, the traditional computation of weighted capital cost of capital, K, is expressed as:

$$K = K_d \; D/C + K_{em} \; E/C \qquad (17\text{-}2)$$

The orthodox WACC computation employs book-value weights attached to measures of cost of each component of the capital structure at the time of the rate proceeding. The return on common equity is a current cost rate, calculated using any one of several techniques described thus far in the book, such as DCF, Risk Premium, CAPM, and Comparable Earnings. The other rates are "embedded" costs, that is, total interest and preferred dividend costs divided by the book value of debt and preferred stock, respectively. They are not market-based costs. The dollar cost of debt capital is viewed narrowly as the explicitly-stated contractual obligation to pay interest during the life of the bond and to pay the principal amount at maturity. This accounting approach to debt cost stands in contrast to the economic approach, which views the cost of debt as the yield to maturity required by bondholders, related to the net proceeds of the issue. Moreover, the implicit "risk cost" of debt by way of the increased financial risk borne by shareholders as a result of introducing senior capital is not reflected in the debt cost component but rather in the equity component of the weighted cost of capital. Similar arguments apply to the cost of preferred stock, traditionally defined as the weighted average of the indicated dividend rate for each issue divided by its net proceeds.

Despite its wide acceptance in practice, the curious mixture of book and market values and costs in Equation 17-2 requires justification. The rationale for using embedded cost of debt is that the award of a rate of return on rate base to cover market yield on debt would only result in

---

[1] This section draws on Andrews in Morin and Andrews (1993).

windfall gains or losses to shareholders. That is, if market yields exceed embedded costs, rate coverage of the difference would not accrue to the bondholders, but rather to the shareholders, because of the contractual fixity of bondholders' claims. Any excess of market over book costs of debt falls upon the shareholders, and conversely. By allowing the utility to earn its actual embedded cost and equity earnings equal to the cost of equity times the equity book value, regulators prevent shareholders from windfall gains and losses when interest rates change. Hence, book value weights inflict no harm on bondholders beyond that produced by variability of market price when current yield deviates from the coupon rate.

The usage of book value weights is defended on several grounds. First, the relationship of debt and equity at book value is an expression of the utility's long-term capital structure policy. If incremental funds are raised in proportions such that a target debt/equity ratio in book value terms is maintained, the earnings requirements to cover capital costs must be computed using the actual weights in which funds are raised, that is, book value weights. Second, book value proportions are stable. Hence, their presentation to regulatory authority avoids the vagaries introduced by variability of market values. Lastly, if regulation performs adequately, the book value and market value of equity will be driven toward equality. The use of market value weights is defended on the countering observation that the reflection of capital structure in historical cost values of debt and equity is blemished over long periods by price level changes. Hence, relative proportions at book value are not free of distortion. One seemingly potent argument in favor of market value weights is that if cost of capital is not formulated in terms of current market costs, there is no assurance that the commitment of funds to investment projects by utilities will earn a rate sufficient to cover these costs. Presumably, the latter is a socially desirable goal of regulation, if the competitive result is to be emulated.

It can be shown, however, that if the regulatory authority adds the cost of the additional capital required by new investment projects into the allowed rate of return, and if there is no regulatory lag, the utility will realize an appropriate compensatory return on incremental investment. For example, let K' be the incremental market cost of capital for a new project requiring an investment of I dollars. Regulatory authority typically would not calculate K' as a separate return. But if the cost of capital is calculated as a weighted average of the embedded cost of debt and an estimated cost of equity, the incremental cost of capital for the additional asset will add $K' \times I$ dollars to the overall revenue requirements. In effect, then, if the regulatory commission incorporates the cost of additional capital into the allowed rate of return, the utility will realize K' on incremental investment, other things being equal. If there is regulatory lag, however, a utility's rate of return on new projects will deviate from the current capital costs. The only way to avoid this is through an arbitrary return adjustment, similar to an attrition allowance.

In summary, the use of book quantities instead of the more economically correct market quantities is not unreasonable for the purposes of setting utility rates.

17.2 The Effect of Capital Structure on Cost of Capital

This section describes the effects of capital structure changes on the cost of capital in an informal manner. The existence of an optimal capital structure emerges from simple and reasonable behavior postulates on the part of bondholders and equity holders. The next section presents a more formal theoretical treatment.

The relationship between capital structure and the cost of capital is shown graphically in Figure 17-1.

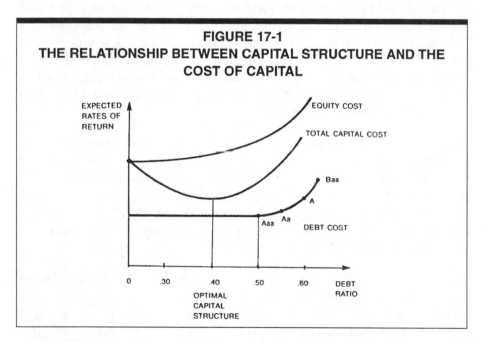

FIGURE 17-1
THE RELATIONSHIP BETWEEN CAPITAL STRUCTURE AND THE COST OF CAPITAL

The horizontal axis is the debt D to total capital C ratio, D/C, assuming that no other form of senior capital exists. The graph depicts the return requirements of bondholders and shareholders in response to a change in capital structure as the firm progressively substitutes debt for equity capital. Taxes are ignored for the moment.

413

The required return on debt is relatively flat from a debt ratio of zero up to a critical debt ratio value, say 50%. Beyond that point, an increase in debt ratio has an upward influence on bond returns as debt holders perceive a significant increase in financial risk. The actual value of the critical threshold can be determined by examining the debt ratio of utilities with the highest quality bonds (Aaa). Any reduction in debt ratio below the critical point would not yield significant reductions in interest costs. The security of the bondholders' investment is not substantially improved by additional reductions in the debt ratio. Beyond the critical point, bond returns increase in a manner consistent with the quality gradient observed for utility bond yields and debt ratios. The points on the bond graph in Figure 17-1 can be estimated by observing the actual bond yields and debt ratios for electric utilities rated Aaa, Aa, A, and Baa, respectively, at a moment in time. Access to debt financing is likely to be severely curbed beyond the Baa rating level.

The curve depicting the behavior of shareholders as the debt ratio is increased is developed as follows. At a zero debt ratio, the return on equity coincides with the return on total capital since the firm is all-equity financed at that point. Shareholders only have to contend with business risk and do not have to deal with financial risk at that juncture. Beyond that point, with each successive increase in the debt ratio, equity returns rise moderately at first in response to increasing financial risk to the point where the bond ratings begin to deteriorate. As the debt ratio reaches dangerous levels where the solvency of the firm is endangered, shareholders' required returns rise sharply.

This fundamental concept in finance was encountered in Chapter 2 when discussing financial risk. As a company increases the relative amount of debt capital in its capital structure, total fixed charges increase, and the probability of failing to meet the growing fixed charge burden increases also. The residual earnings available to common stockholders become increasingly volatile and riskier as the firm increases its financial leverage, causing shareholders to require a higher return on equity.

The relationship between the average cost of capital and capital structure emerges directly from the assumed behavior of bond returns and equity returns. This is also shown in Figure 17-1. At zero debt ratio, the cost of capital is coincident with the cost of equity. With each successive substitution of low-cost debt for high-cost equity, the average cost of capital declines as the weight of low-cost debt in the average increases. A low point is reached where the cost advantage of debt is exactly offset by the increased cost of equity. This is the optimal capital structure point. Beyond that point, the cost disadvantage of equity outweighs the cost advantage of debt, and the weighted cost of capital rises accordingly.

The most salient characteristic of the graph is the U-shaped nature of the cost of capital curve, pointing to the existence of an optimal capital structure whereby the cost of capital is minimized. Despite the rise of both debt and equity costs with increases in the debt ratio, the WACC reaches a minimum. Beyond this point, the low-cost and tax advantages of debt are outweighed by the increased equity costs. This occurs just before the point where bond ratings start deteriorating, and the cost of capital increases rapidly at higher debt ratios.

Utilities should strive for a capital structure that minimizes the composite capital cost, including taxes. Hypothetical capital structures are sometimes used by regulatory commissions to determine a fair allowed return if a utility is deemed to have deviated significantly from the optimum. Of course, the imputation of a capital structure different from the actual necessarily presupposes the existence of an optimal capital structure that must be demonstrated. A hypothetical capital structure may lower the cost of capital, which in turn may translate into lower rates for consumers as long as the use of more debt results in the cost and tax benefits of debt outweighing the increased equity costs. Finding the optimal structure is easier said than done, however. The imposition of an hypothetical structure by the regulator must rest on a determination of the optimal capital structure. The graphical relationships of Figure 17-1 are difficult to measure accurately. The bond return graph can be charted with some confidence by observing bond yields and attendant debt ratios for comparable companies in a given industry. The equity return graph is more difficult to construct accurately. Nevertheless, reasonable procedures for deriving the cost of capital curve can be devised as the examples of Chapters 18 and 19 will demonstrate. The next section outlines capital structure theory in more formal terms.

17.3 An Overview of Capital Structure Theory[2]

No-Tax Version

Assuming perfectly functioning capital markets and the absence of corporate taxes, Modigliani and Miller (1966) argued that the value of a corporation, hence its cost of capital, is independent of capital structure. Financing

i.e. value of a firm is indep. of how it is financed.

---

[2] Brigham (1985) provided an excellent review of capital structure theories and their application in an actual rate case setting. Brigham, Gapenski, and Aberwald (1987) investigated the relationship between capital structure, cost of capital, and revenue requirements, and review the major theoretical and empirical works on the subject. This section draws on both these works.

decisions are irrelevant under these conditions. The value of a firm is determined by the left-hand side of its balance sheet, that is, by the earning power of its assets. How the stream of operating income generated by the assets is apportioned among the bondholders and shareholders is irrelevant. By analogy, the value of a pie (operating income) should not depend on the manner in which it is sliced. Modigliani and Miller provided an arbitrage proof of this proposition, whereby two identical firms with differing capital structures must have the same value if riskless profit opportunities are to be avoided. Figure 17-2 shows how the riskless profit opportunities are to be avoided, and shows how the overall cost of capital, hence revenue requirements, are unaffected by the debt ratio under this theory.

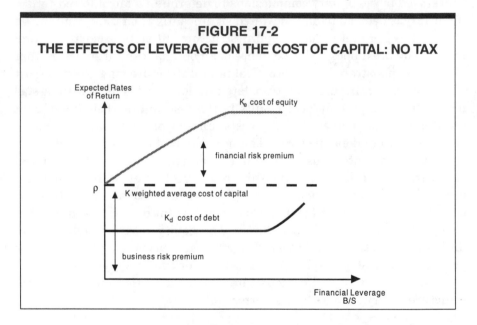

FIGURE 17-2
THE EFFECTS OF LEVERAGE ON THE COST OF CAPITAL: NO TAX

If the overall cost of capital remains unchanged with leverage, it follows that the increased required return on equity resulting from the added risk of leverage completely offsets the low-cost advantage of debt. Otherwise, the WACC could not remain constant. In other words, the total cost of capital remains unchanged regardless of the capital structure because the increase in required earnings resulting from greater leverage is exactly offset by the substitution of lower cost debt for higher cost of equity. The behavior of equity costs is shown in Figure 17-3.

The exact relationship between leverage and the cost of equity is linear and is expressed as:

$$K_e = \rho + (\rho - i)\, B/S \qquad (17\text{-}3)$$

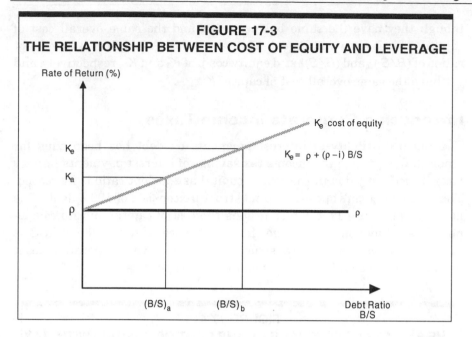

FIGURE 17-3
THE RELATIONSHIP BETWEEN COST OF EQUITY AND LEVERAGE

where ρ is the cost of equity for an all-equity firm, B/S is the market value leverage or debt ratio, and i is the current rate of interest. This equation states that the cost of equity is equal to the cost of capital of an unlevered (no debt) firm plus the after-tax difference between the cost of capital of an unlevered firm and the cost of debt, weighted by the leverage ratio. The cost of equity rises with the debt-equity ratio in a linear fashion, with the slope of the line equal to $(\rho - i)B/S$.

As derived in Appendix 17-A, the accounting analog to Equation 17-3, using actual returns instead of expected returns is:

$$r = R + (R - i) \, D/E \, (1 - t) \qquad (17\text{-}4)$$

where r = after-tax net income/book value of equity

           R = operating rate of return on assets

           i = interest rate on aggregate debt

           D = book value of all interest-bearing debt

           E = book value of equity

           t = marginal income tax rate

The major implication of either Equation 17-3 or Equation 17-4 is that two firms with different debt ratios will have different equity costs, even though they have the same business risk and the same overall cost of capital. This is shown in Figure 17-3 where firm A and firm B have debt ratios of $(B/S)_a$ and $(B/S)_b$ and equity costs of K_a and K_b, respectively, and yet have the same overall cost of capital K.

Introducing Corporate Income Taxes

The tax deductibility of interest payments on debt has been thus far ignored. Recognizing the income tax savings of interest payments implies a continued reduction in the cost of capital as the debt ratio is increased. Therefore, the firm's optimal capital structure consists of 100% debt. This is shown in Figure 17-4, which graphs the cost of capital and its components as a function of leverage. In the absence of taxes, the WACC is invariant to changes in capital structure. However, with corporate taxes it declines with each relative increment of debt capital.

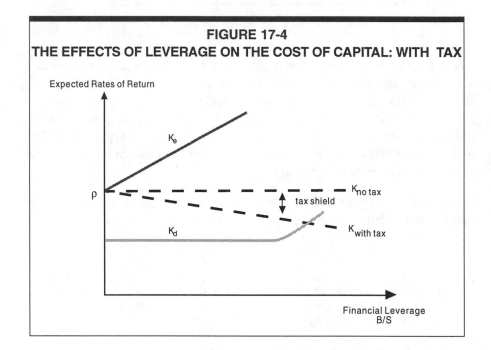

FIGURE 17-4
THE EFFECTS OF LEVERAGE ON THE COST OF CAPITAL: WITH TAX

The reason why substituting debt for equity reduces the cost of capital and revenue requirements is that the tax shelter increases the cash flows available to all claimants on the firm's assets, that is, the bondholders and shareholders. As the firm substitutes debt for equity capital, the fraction of operating income diverted to the tax authority becomes smaller, and the fraction accruing to shareholders becomes correspondingly larger. Adding debt thus enhances the value of the firm and reduces the overall cost of capital and ratepayer burden. The gain from debt financing, G, is the corporate tax rate, T, times the quantity of debt, D:

$$G = TD \qquad (17\text{-}5)$$

For example, if the corporate tax rate is 40%, for every dollar of debt financing, the tax shield gain is 0.40 times $1.00 = $0.40.

The linear relationship between the overall cost of capital and the debt ratio derived from the tax-adjusted theory shown in Figure 17-4 can be expressed as:

$$K = \rho \left(1 - T\frac{B}{C}\right) \qquad (17\text{-}6)$$

where K is the overall cost of capital for a levered firm, ρ is the cost of capital for an all-equity firm as before, T is the corporate income tax rate, and B/C is the debt to total capital ratio expressed in market value terms. In words, the equation asserts that a company's WACC equals the unlevered cost of equity reduced by the tax effect of leverage. If the firm has no debt, B/C equals zero in the above expression and the cost of capital reduces to ρ, which is the cost of capital of a unlevered firm. Note also that there is no inconsistency between the traditional definition of the WACC embodied in Equation 17-1 and the above definition in Equation 17-6, also known as the Modigliani-Miller definition. They are identical. Equation 17-6 can be easily obtained by susbtituting Equation 17-7 into Equation 17-1.

The implied relationship between the cost of equity and leverage remains linear as in the no-tax situation of Equations 17-3 and 17-4, but the rate of increase (slope) is lessened by the tax advantage of debt. Equation 17-3 becomes:

$$K_e = \rho + (\rho - i)(1 - T)\, B/S \qquad (17\text{-}7)$$

This crucial formula states that the levered cost of equity equals the unlevered cost plus a term reflecting the increase in financial risk precipitated by leverage. [3]

---

[3] These relationships can be easily extended to allow for the presence of preferred stock. Letting d represent the dividend rate on preferred stock, and P/S the market value ration of preferred stock to common equity, Equation 17-7 becomes:

$$K_e = P + (p - i)(1 - T)\, B/S + (p - d)\, P/S$$

The increase is linear and depends solely on the constancy of debt costs and tax effects. The accounting analog, shown in Equation 17-8, is derived in Appendix 17-A.

$$r = [R + (R - i) D/E] (1 - T) \qquad (17\text{-}8)$$

Corporate taxes are the only major factor that implies that debt lowers capital costs. All other factors discussed below imply the contrary.

Introducing Personal Income Taxes

Clearly, the conclusion of an all-debt capital structure suggested by the Modigliani-Miller cum-tax thesis is unrealistic, a situation easily verified not to exist. Therefore, the low-cost advantage and tax benefits of leverage must be offset by some disadvantage varying directly with leverage. One of those disadvantages is personal taxes. The importance of personal taxes in affecting investor return requirements is undeniable. One merely has to examine the yield differential between tax-exempt municipal bonds and corporate bonds of similar quality to see the effect of personal taxes, at least for taxable investors.

Miller (1977) presents an alternative capital structure theory that maintains that the value of debt tax shields disappears when both personal and corporate income taxes are considered. Even though interest income is not taxed at the firm level, it is taxed at the personal level. When debt replaces equity, the company pays less taxes, but investors pay more. The introduction of personal taxes into the picture diminishes the advantage of debt financing and offsets the effect of corporate taxes. This is attributable to the advantageous tax treatment of stocks versus bonds, because equity income is taxed at the firm level but may largely avoid personal taxes if it comes in the form of capital gains. The more favorable tax treatment of capital gains from stocks is such that equity income is favored over interest income. Even if the personal tax rate on interest income were equal to the capital gains tax rate on stocks, taxes on the latter are not paid until the gain is realized.

Miller explored the effect of personal taxes, in addition to corporate taxes, on the overall cost of capital, and concluded that when personal tax effects are considered, the tax advantages of debt financing dissipate. When both personal and corporate taxes are taken into account, the gain per dollar of debt financing, G, is given by the following expression:

$$G = 1 - \frac{(1 - T_c)(1 - T_{ps})}{(1 - T_{pb})} \tag{17-9}$$

where T_c = corporate tax rate

T_{ps} = personal tax rate on income from stocks

T_{pb} = personal tax rate on income from bonds

Over a wide range of values for the above three tax rates, the gain from debt financing disappears. Miller derives this result by analyzing the tax treatment of $1 of interest income and $1 of equity income as follows:

TAX ADVANTAGE OF DEBT FINANCING: MILLER'S THESIS
TAX TREATMENT: STOCKS AND BONDS

	Before Tax	After Corporate Taxes	After Personal Taxes
Interest Income from Bonds	$1	$1	$1(1 - T_{pb})$
Income from Common Stocks	$1	$1(1 - T_c)$	$1(1 - T_c)(1 - T_{ps})$

One dollar ($1) of interest income is taxed only at the personal level at the bondholder's tax rate while $1 of equity income is taxed at both the corporate level at the corporate tax rate and at the personal level at the shareholder's tax rate.

At the limit, if the corporate tax rate T_c equals the personal tax rate on interest income T_{pb} and if the personal tax rate on income from stocks T_{ps} is zero in the above equation, the tax gain from debt usage G equals zero. Or if $(1 - T_c)(1 - T_{ps})$ equals $1 - T_{pb}$ in the above equation, the tax gain from debt usage vanishes, that is, the corporate tax advantage of debt is exactly neutralized by the personal tax advantage of equity. Thus, Miller concludes that the relative advantage of debt depends on the relative magnitudes of the above tax rates.

Several studies have quantified the magnitude of these tax rates, and findings indicate that the tax advantage of debt financing is smaller than previously thought. The personal tax rate from stock income is very small, owing to the non-taxation of unrealized capital gains, the low tax bracket of recipients of dividend-paying stocks, and the non-taxable status of several institutional investors. The personal tax rate from bond income is almost equal to the corporate tax rate. Referring to Equation 17-9, and allowing for these findings, the gain from debt financing is therefore small. What Miller has made clear is that the tax advantage of debt is weaker than implied in the original Modigliani-Miller thesis with corporate taxes alone.

The implication of the Miller model is that there exists an optimal debt ratio for the aggregate of corporations, but that for any single tax-paying firm debt policy does not matter if the total supply of debt is to suit investors' needs. The reason there is no tax advantage to issuing more debt is that such tax advantage has already been priced.

By introducing both corporate and personal taxes into the analysis, Miller found the following relationship between the cost of equity and financial leverage, which bears a close family resemblance to the Modigliani-Miller version in Equation 17-7, which only considers corporate taxes:

$$K_e = \rho + [\rho - i(1- T)]B/S \qquad (17\text{-}10)$$

In the extreme, the Miller model takes us back full-circle to the original Modigliani-Miller position, whereby no tax advantage whatsoever to debt financing exists and no optimal capital structure exists. Empirical evidence and extensions to the Miller model suggest that Miller's conclusion is controversial. To the extent that the personal tax rate on equity income is less than the personal tax rate on interest income due to the deferral of capital gains taxes, there remains some advantage to debt financing.

Financial Distress

Another disadvantage of leverage that offsets the tax advantage is the cost of financial distress. Financial distress costs may include direct (legal fees, court costs, etc.) and indirect bankruptcy costs. The latter are more significant. Short of bankruptcy, they may include the costs of writing, monitoring, and enforcing debt contracts to avoid the natural conflicts of interest between bondholders and stockholders of firms with high debt ratios. Distress forces management decisions that constrain operations, decrease cash flows, and decrease investment opportunities. For example, the inability to perform proper maintenance on new installations on utility plant increases with distress.

As the firm increases its debt ratio, it increases the value of the tax shield but it also increases the costs of financial distress. Beyond some point, the additional tax shield is outweighed by the additional threat of financial distress. Corporate taxes together with debt-related bankruptcy costs and agency costs lead to a U-shaped relationship between cost of capital and leverage, and an optimal capital structure, as shown in Figure 17-5.

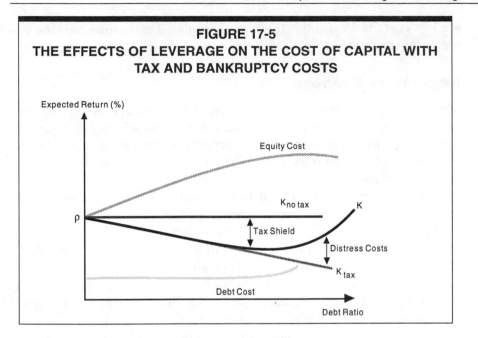

FIGURE 17-5
THE EFFECTS OF LEVERAGE ON THE COST OF CAPITAL WITH TAX AND BANKRUPTCY COSTS

Agency Costs

The existence of an optimal capital structure can be explained by causes other than debt tax shields and distress costs. One such explanation is the presence of agency costs. Agency costs refer to the costs of monitoring imposed by debt. To prevent the possibility that shareholders could take advantage of bondholders by engaging in risky ventures for example, bondholders are protected by restrictive covenants and monitoring devices that limit their risk. The costs of monitoring the firm to ensure that the covenants are respected constitute agency costs. The presence of agency costs increases the cost of debt and therefore reduces the attraction of debt financing, offsetting fully or partially any tax advantage of debt.

External common equity incurs agency costs as well. New shareholders may have an opposition of interests and costs with existing shareholders. For example, a new issue of common stock will redistribute the costs of structuring management perquisites and incentives between new and existing shareholders. The costs of preventive audits are also a form of an agency cost. Higher equity ratios lead to higher equity agency costs.

Jensen and Meckling (1976) suggest that an optimal capital structure exists, given increasing agency costs with higher equity ratios on the one hand and higher debt ratios on the other. The firm will select an optimum combination of debt and equity so as to minimize total agency costs. Unfortunately, these costs are difficult to quantify and can only be subjectively estimated. Moreover, it is reasonable to conclude that these costs

423

are less onerous for utilities than for unregulated companies because the regulatory process itself acts as a monitoring device.

Regulatory Process

Several authors have argued that although both regulated and unregulated firms benefit from debt through a lower cost of capital, regulated firms benefit less because a utility's operating income is decreased by the amount of tax savings from debt, unlike unregulated firms. For an excellent review of the applicability of capital structure theory to public utilities, the interested reader is directed to Patterson (1983). In the regulatory process, taxes are treated as an operating expense in the calculation of revenue requirements. If a utility issues more debt, the attendant tax savings will be passed on to ratepayers in the form of lower rates. Utility shareholders do not obtain the tax benefits of debt financing. If the tax advantage of debt is invalidated by the mechanics of the regulatory process, it would appear that the original Modigliani-Miller capital structure theory without taxes is applicable to utilities. Equation 17-3 rather than Equation 17-7 would be the correct formulation of equity costs.

This is not the complete story, however. Because the regulated price changes with leverage, the demand for utility services is likely to be altered. Hence, the precise relationship between cost of capital and capital structure for a regulated firm cannot be derived without specifying exactly its demand and supply curve, as demonstrated by Jaffee and Mandelker (1976). Under plausible assumptions of demand behavior, Jaffee and Mandelker showed that the value of a levered firm under regulation is understated in the Modigliani-Miller no-tax framework, that is, the cost of capital is overstated. In the context of Figures 17-2 and 17-4, the cost of capital line for a regulated firm probably lies between the no-tax scenario and the with-tax scenario for an unregulated firm. In other words, there is still some tax advantage to debt financing, but its magnitude is less than that predicted by the Modigliani-Miller thesis. The slope of the cost of equity equation lies between that predicted in the no-tax case (Equation 17-2) and that predicted in the with-tax case (Equation 17-4). The precise impact also depends on the exact manner in which regulators pass through the tax savings from debt financing to ratepayers. The demand effects would differ depending on whether the regulator lowers service rates or eliminates certain fixed charges.

Signalling Effects

Information costs also play a role in any decision to increase debt for a publicly-traded company. According to the "signalling" theory of capital structure, also referred to as the Asymmetric Information Theory, the substitution of debt for equity provides information to investors that future prospects are favorable, interest coverage is assured, and the tax shelters associated with debt, if any, are usable. The converse is also true. Managers have more information concerning the company than do investors. Because rational investors expect managers to issue securities that best serve the interests of existing shareholders as opposed to those of new investors, investors generally view the sale of common stock as a negative signal that the company's prospects are poor. If attractive investment opportunities did exist, management would want to retain these benefits for existing shareholders rather than share them with new shareholders. Thus, investors lower the company's stock price and raise the cost of common equity when a new common stock offering is announced. This implies that utilities should maintain a borrowing reserve, using less debt in normal times so as to build reserve debt capacity when needed. The greater the uncertainty of future prospects (business risk), the greater the reserve borrowing capacity should be. This argument does not apply when regulators are attempting to ascribe a particular capital structure to a utility, since no management signal is involved.

Intangibles

The last factor that palliates the tax advantage of leverage includes all the intangible disadvantages of added debt financing, including bond rating impact, loss of flexibility associated with a high debt ratio, less advantageous terms of security offerings, and higher transaction costs. With regard to the impact on bond rating, an increase in debt ratio is likely to produce a lower bond rating for debt, increasing the company's incremental cost of debt financing. Excessive additions of debt that would result in a downgrading of the firm's bonds will reduce the desirability of the firm's bonds to institutional demanders of corporate bonds.

Brigham (1985) provided a useful graphical synthesis of the various theoretical views on capital structure. Figure 17-6 reproduces Brigham's graphic view of capital structure viewpoints. The Modigliani-Miller (MM) model with corporate taxes, which suggests that the cost of capital declines steadily with added debt, is shown as line (1) on the graph. Miller's position that personal tax effects neutralize corporate tax effects appears as line (4). Line (2) modifies the Miller position to recognize that the various tax rates offset some, but not all, the corporate tax advantages of debt. Line (3) adds another refinement to recognize that the corporate tax rate declines with added debt financing as the firm's added interest burden lowers its taxable income and hence its tax rate. Line (5) on the graph, which represents the dominant view of academics, nets the personal and corporate tax effects against the costs of distress. At low levels of debt, the tax effects dominate and lower the cost of capital. As the debt ratio increases, distress costs intensify at an increasing rate and eventually overtake the tax advantages, and the cost of capital increases beyond that point. Point X on the graph shows that the optimal capital structure of the hypothetical company occurs at a debt ratio of 42%.

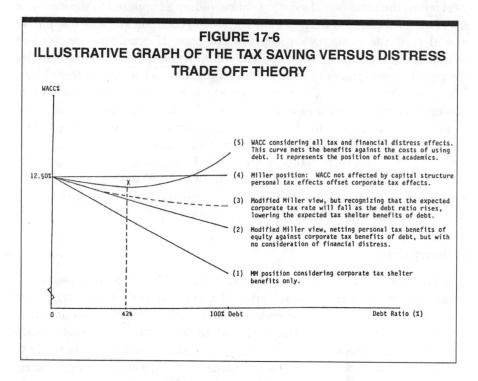

FIGURE 17-6
ILLUSTRATIVE GRAPH OF THE TAX SAVING VERSUS DISTRESS TRADE OFF THEORY

17.4 Empirical Evidence on Capital Structure

Several researchers have studied the empirical relationship between the cost of capital, capital-structure changes, and the value of the firm's securities. Comprehensive and rigorous empirical studies of the relationship between cost of capital and leverage for public utilities, summarized in Patterson (1983), include Modigliani and Miller (1958, 1963), Miller (1977), Brigham and Gordon (1968), Gordon (1974), Robichek, Higgins, and Kinsman (1973), Mehta, Moses, Deschamps, and Walker (1980), Brigham, Shome, and Vinson (1985), and Gapenski (1986). Copeland and Weston (1993) provided a comprehensive summary of the empirical evidence. Although it is not easy in such empirical tests to hold all other relevant factors constant, the evidence partially supports the existence of a tax benefit from leverage and that leverage increases firm value. The evidence also strongly favors a positive relationship between leverage and the cost of equity, which is consistent with the Modigliani-Miller propositions. However, there is still some controversy over the acceptance of the linear formulation in Equations 17-3 and 17-6. Some investigators believe the relationship is curvilinear, others believe its is linear but has a slope less than $R - i$.

In a study of public utility capital structures, Patterson (1983) concluded that firm value rises with leverage and revenue requirements decline at low levels of leverage, and he confirmed the existence of a cost-minimizing capital structure. Whether this optimal capital structure also minimizes revenue requirements depends on the effectiveness of regulation in passing interest tax savings through to ratepayers. Patterson also found that utilities tend to operate at a debt ratio slightly less than the optimal level, in the interest of flexibility and maintaining borrowing reserves.

The empirical effects of leverage on common equity return are summarized in Brigham, Gapenski, and Aberwald (1987). Tables 17-3 and 17-4 show the results of empirical studies and theoretical studies obtained when the debt ratio increases from 40% to 50%. The studies report that equity costs increase anywhere from a low of 34 to a high of 237 basis points when the debt ratio increases from 40% to 50%. The average increase is 138 basis points from the theoretical studies and 76 basis points from the empirical studies, or a range of 7.6 to 13.8 basis points per one percentage increase in the debt ratio. The more recent studies indicate that the upper end of that range is more indicative of the repercussions on equity costs.

TABLE 17-3
EFFECTS OF LEVERAGE ON COMMON EQUITY: EMPIRICAL STUDIES

Study	Result
MM (1958)	115 basis points
MM (1963)	62
Miller (1977)	237
Average	138

TABLE 17-4

Empirical

EFFECTS OF LEVERAGE ON COMMON EQUITY: THEORETICAL STUDIES

Study	Result
Brigham and Gordon (1968)	34 basis points
Gordon (1974)	45
Robichek, Higgins, and Kinsman (1973)	75
Mehta, Moses, Deschamps, and Walker (1980)	109
Gapenski (1986)	72
Brigham, Gapenski, and Aberwald (1987)	117
Average	76

Chapter 19 will show the results of a simulation model designed to investigate empirically the appropriate capital structure of a utility company using current market data and industry trends.

17.5 Conclusions

The benefits and costs of using debt, including taxes, agency costs, and distress costs, were identified and quantified by the various models of capital structure. Both the cost of debt and equity were seen to increase steadily with each increment in financial leverage. Despite the rise of both debt and equity costs with increases in the debt ratio, the WACC reaches a minimum as the weight of low-cost debt in the average increases. Beyond this optimal point, the low-cost and tax advantages of debt are outweighed by the rising distress costs, agency costs, personal tax disadvantages, and the overall cost of capital increases rapidly at higher debt ratios.

Despite the intuitive and conceptual appeal of this "trade-off" view of the optimal capital structure, it is difficult to quantify precisely the costs/benefits of various debt levels and to establish the optimal level of debt. Morever, the optimal capital structure shifts over time with changes in capital market conditions and changes in business risk. Chapter 19 will provide a simulation model that circumvents some of these difficulties and determines the optimal bond rating for a utility and the level of debt consistent with that bond rating. Finally, we also know from the signalling framework that utilities should maintain a borrowing reserve, using less debt in normal times so as to build reserve debt capacity when needed.

In the final analysis, finance theory provides limited guidance on what a company's capital structure should be precisely. Capital structure decisions must be determined by managerial judgment and market data in contrast to the exact mathematical formulas resulting from the theories presented in this chapter. Financial theory provides benchmarks and useful data to assist management in capital structure decisions. Capital structure decisions depend critically on each company's own situation and level of business risk as well. The higher the business risk, the lower the debt ratio.

As a practical matter, the effect of capital structure on total weighted average cost of capital is likely to be minor over the range of capital structures usually found in the utility industry. If one subscribes to the majority view that the cost of capital curve is U-shaped, the error committed by assuming a constant debt/equity ratio is not large given the flatness of the curve over the range of capital structures normally employed by utilities. Even if one subscribes to the pure Modigliani-Miller view that cost of capital is a declining function of leverage over a wide range of debt ratios, the magnitude of the error is still likely to be small, especially when compared to the range of reasonableness of cost of capital estimates in regulatory hearings. It is hard not to concur with Myers (1972) that it is fairly safe to estimate a utility's cost of capital on the assumption of a constant debt ratio, unless a major rapid shift in capital structure is contemplated. Similar arguments can be made for a change in dividend policy.

As far as the regulation of capital structure is concerned, the acceptability of a given capital structure is difficult to determine precisely. The debt and equity cost relationships necessary to derive the optimal capital structure are difficult to establish with any degree of precision. Yet, it is the responsibility of regulators to ensure that a utility's capital structure should reflect a proper balance between investors' interest and ratepayers' interests, and should be cost-minimizing. Given the analytical constraints, the acceptability of a utility's capital structure should be governed by a general guideline drawn from the capital structure principles enunciated in this chapter. Such a guideline would ensure that a utility should increase the relative amount of debt it employs to the point where the increased returns required by bond and equity investors exceed the total cost savings derived from substituting low-cost, tax-free debt for high-cost, taxable capital. It is also important that a reasonable safety margin against possible shifts in capital market conditions and investor risk attitudes be allowed.

The optimal capital structure simulation model presented in Chapter 19 suggests that long-term achievement of at least an A rating and preferably a AA rating is in a utility company's and its ratepayers' best interests. Debt leverage targets should be set in the lower part of the range required to attain this optimal rating. If the company maintains its debt ratio close to the bottom end of the optimal range required for a AA bond rating, its overall cost of capital should be minimized. If the company reduces its debt ratio below that point, it would be giving up the tax benefits associated with debt but would not reap the benefits from a lower cost of debt and equity. If the company operates at a debt ratio beyond that point, the cost of debt and equity will rise. The latter rise will occur at an increasing rate if the operating environment deteriorates. Moreover, the company will reduce its financing flexibility.

References

Brigham, E.F. and Gordon, M.J. "Leverage, Dividend Policy, and the Cost of Capital." *Journal of Finance,* March 1968. 85-103.

Brigham, E.F. New England Telephone and Telegraph Co., Prepared Testimony, State of New Hampshire, Docket No. DR 85-181. 1985.

Brigham, E.F., Gapenski, L.C., and Aberwald, D.A. "Capital Structure, Cost of Capital, and Revenue Requirements." *Public Utilities Fortnightly,* January 8, 1987, 15-24.

Brigham, E.F., Shome, D.K., and Vinson, S.R. "The Risk Premium Approach to Measuring a Utility's Cost of Equity." *Financial Management,* Spring 1985, 33-45.

Copeland, T. E. and Weston, F. *Financial Theory and Corporate Policy,* 3rd ed. Reading MA: Addison Wesley, 1993.

Gapenski, L.C. "An Empirical Study of the Relationship Between Equity Costs and Financial Leverage for Electric Utilities." Public Utility Research Center, Working Paper, University of Florida, 1986.

Gordon, M.J. *The Cost of Capital to a Public Utility.* East Lansing, MI: Michigan State University, Michigan, 1974.

Jaffee, J.F. and Mandelker, G. "The Value of the Firm Under Regulation." *Journal of Finance,* May 1976, 701-713.

Jensen, M.C. and Meckling, W. "Theory of the Firm: Managerial Behavior, Agency Costs, and Ownership Structure." *Journal of Financial Economics,* October 1976, 305-360.

Mehta, D., Moses, E.A., Deschamps, B., and Walker, M. "Influence of Dividends, Growth, and Leverage on Share Prices in the Electric Utility Industry: An Econometric Study." *Journal of Financial and Quantitative Analysis,* December 1980, 1163-1196.

Miller, M.H. "Debt and Taxes." *Journal of Finance,* May 1977, 261-276.

Modigliani, F. and Miller, M.H. "The Cost of Capital, Corporation Finance, and the Theory of Investments." *American Economic Review,* June 1958, 261-297.

Modigliani, F. and Miller, M.H. "Taxes and the Cost of Capital: A Correction." *American Economic Review,* June 1963, 433-443.

Modigliani, F. and Miller, M.H. "Some Estimates on the Cost of Capital to the Electric Utility Industry 1954-57." *American Economic Review,* June 1966, 333-348.

Morin, R.A. and Andrews, V.L. *Determining Cost of Capital for Regulated Industries,* Public Utilities Reports Inc. and The Management Exchange Inc., Washington DC, 1993.

Myers, S. C. "The Application of Finance Theory to Public Utility Rate Case." *Bell Journal of Economics and Management Science,* Spring 1972, 58-97.

Patterson, C.S. "The Effects of Leverage on the Revenue Requirements of Public Utilities." *Financial Management,* Autumn 1983, 29-39.

Robichek, A.A., Higgins, R.C., and Kinsman, M. "The Effect of Leverage on the Cost of Equity Capital of Electric Utility Firms." *Journal of Finance,* May 1973, 353-367.

Appendix 17-A
Derivation of Return on the Book Value of Equity[4]

This appendix derives an expression that decomposes the return on equity into its various components. Let r denote the after-tax Net Income/Book Value of equity.

The stream of income available to securities in the aggregate is earnings before interest and tax *EBIT*, or pre-tax net operating income (before financial charges). *EBIT* is the source of all income to financial claims. Denote R as the rate of return of this income stream relative to assets net of zero-rate debt, A. Then, $R = EBIT/A$ is the return on total asset investments. Also, adopt other symbols as follows:

t = marginal income tax rate

i = interest rate on aggregate debt

D = book value of all interest-bearing debt

E = book value of equity

These variables are substituted into the expressions appearing above and the resulting expressions are simplified.

$$r = \frac{\text{post–tax net income}}{\text{book value of equity}} = \frac{(RA - iD)(1 - t)}{E}$$

Since assets $A = E + D$ we can substitute and simplify:

$$r = \frac{(R(E + D) - iD)(1 - t)}{E}$$

$$r = [R + (RD/E) - (iD/E)](1 - t)$$

$$r = [r + (R - i)D/E](1 - t)$$

The final expression says that r, the return on book value of equity, is directly proportional to the overall pre-tax financial return on assets plus a differential (premium) of this rate over the interest rate (rate spread)

---

[4] This is taken from Morin and Andrews (1993).

levered by the debt/equity ratio, D/E. The term $1 - t$ multiplied by the pre-tax values reduces them to post-tax equivalents.

For simplicity, especially in graphing, the above expression may be translated to a form more readily recognizable as a linear equation:

$$r = R(1 - t) + (R - i)(D/E)(1 - t)$$

The debt/equity ratio and post-tax equivalent expression are constants and their product is the slope of the function.

Chapter 18
Capital Structure Issues

Section 18.1 of this chapter presents selected practical applications of capital structure theory for regulated utilities. Section 18.2 examines the interrelationship between the rate base and invested capital, and the consequences of including or excluding certain components of capital in the weighted average cost calculation.

18.1 Applications

Several practical implications and applications for regulatory finance emerge from the capital structure concepts expounded in the previous chapter.

Anticipated Capital Structure Changes

One immediate application of the material in the last chapter is that consideration should be given to changes in the leverage rate when estimating the cost of equity. Suppose that an unexpected change in the debt ratio from d_1 to d_2 is to be effected as per Figure 18-1. If the cost of equity is estimated from past data based on the debt ratio d_1, an estimate of K_1 is obtained. But this understates the true cost of equity of K_2, based on the new debt ratio d_2.

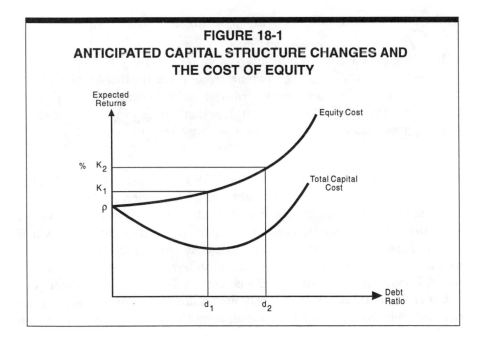

FIGURE 18-1
ANTICIPATED CAPITAL STRUCTURE CHANGES AND THE COST OF EQUITY

435

EXAMPLE 18-1

Eastern Power Company's cost of equity is estimated at 12% based on the company's existing capital structure, which consists of 35% debt and 65% equity in market value terms. The current borrowing rate is 8%, and the corporate income tax rate is 40%. The management of Eastern Power Company, perhaps at the urging of the regulatory commission, has decided to alter its capital structure to 40% debt and 60% equity. The revised cost of equity can be obtained by solving the Modigliani-Miller Equation 17-7 from Chapter 17, duplicated below, using the revised debt ratio:

$$K_e = \rho + (\rho - i)(1 - T)\, B/S \qquad (17\text{-}7)$$

But in order to solve for K_e, the cost of capital for an all-equity financed firm, ρ, is required. This can be done by solving the above equation for ρ under the old capital structure, and inserting the resulting ρ in the same equation under the new capital structure:

$$12\% = \rho + (\rho - .08)(1 - .40)\, .35/65$$

from which $\rho = 11.02\%$. Inserting the latter value of ρ in the equation and using the new capital structure, the revised cost of equity is obtained:

$$K_e = .1102 + (.1102 - .08)(1 - .40)\, .40/.60 = .1223 = 12.23\%$$

In using Equation 17-7, the market value of equity is easily obtained by multiplying the current stock price by the number of shares outstanding. The market value of debt is obtained by applying orthodox bond valuation formulas. Book values can be used as an approximation if market values are unobservable.

One of the assumptions underlying the DCF model discussed in Chapter 4 is the expected constancy of the debt ratio. The reason for this assumption should be evident from Example 18-1. The future dividends per share, which drive the DCF model, depend on expected earnings per share, which in turn depend on the expected debt ratio. As long as the debt ratio has been constant historically and is expected to be maintained in the future, the DCF model is salvaged. But if a change in debt ratio is expected, the cost of equity obtained from the DCF model must be altered based on the expected debt ratio, using the procedure outlined in the example. Two caveats are in order here. First, to the extent that the regulatory process inactivates the tax advantage of debt by passing on the savings to ratepayers, the no-tax equivalent of Equation 17-7 found in Equation 17-3 should be used instead. Replicating the calculations of the previous numerical example using the latter equation instead, a revised cost of equity of 12.33% is obtained, which is not significantly different from the 12.23% number obtained using the tax-adjusted form of the model. More generally, given the extreme nature of the no-tax effect assumption, the revised cost of equity probably lies between the two polar values obtained from the two formulations.

Second, while both Equations 17-7 and 17-3 require the use of market value capital structure, the use of book values is preferable because the equity return obtained is in fact applied to the book value of the equity by the regulator. If the stock is trading at or near book value, no problem arises. But if the stock is trading away from book value, the use of market values will lead to distorted cost of equity estimates.

There are other capital structure frameworks and other guides from financial theory available besides the Modigliani-Miller framework that can quantify the effects of a change in capital structure on the cost of equity. Recall that Modigliani-Miller brought only corporate taxes into the analysis, but no personal taxes. Miller introduced both corporate and personal taxes into the analysis and found the following relationship between the cost of equity and financial leverage, which bears a close family resemblance to the Modigliani-Miller version:

$$K_e = \rho + [\rho - i(1 - T)]\, B/S \qquad\qquad (17\text{-}10)$$

Returning to our numerical example, the revised cost of equity can be obtained by solving the above Miller Equation 17-10 instead of Equation 17-7. But in order to solve for K_e, the cost of capital for an all-equity financed firm, ρ, is required. This can be done by solving the above equation for ρ under the old capital structure, and inserting the resulting ρ in the same equation under the new capital structure:[1]

---

[1] An alternate methodology to find the cost of an all-equity financed firm, ρ, is to use Equation 17-6:

$$K = \rho\,(1 - T\, B/C))$$

Knowing the tax rate, T, and the weighted cost of capital, K, at the firm's eisting capital structure, B/C, the equation can be solved for ρ.

$$K_e = \rho + [\rho - i(1 - T)] \, B/S$$

$$12\% = \rho + [\rho - .08 \, (1 - .40)].35/.65$$

from which $\rho = 9.48\%$. Inserting the latter value of ρ in the equation and using the new capital structure, the revised cost of equity is obtained:

$$K_e = .0948 + [.0948 - .08 \, (1 - .40)] \, .40/.60 = .1260 = 12.60\%$$

Still another way to tackle the problem is to compute an unlevered beta, as in Example 1 of Chapter 14 using Equation 14-1, then relever the beta with the new capital structure. The CAPM formula is then employed to measure the cost of equity under the new capital structure.

The major thrust of this example is that an estimate of cost of capital on the basis of an observed capital structure is erroneous if the capital structure is expected to change. The revised cost of equity can be estimated with three methodologies: the Modigliani-Miller, Miller, and the levered beta-CAPM equations.

Comparable Groups

A measurement problem similar to that of the previous numerical example can arise when using the cost of equity capital of other companies as a check against estimates based on the market data for the utility itself. If the group of comparable companies has been carefully designed using adequate risk filters for both business risk and capital structure differences, this will not be a problem. But if substantial capital structure differences exist between the utility and the reference companies, all else being constant, the same remedial correction as in the above example is necessary, using Equation 17-7 and the average capital structure of the reference group to compute the cost of capital for an all-equity firm, and the subject utility's own capital structure to compute its cost of capital using the same equation in reverse. Here also the unlevered-relevered beta approach discussed in Chapter 14 and illustrated in the General Gas case example can be used to adjust the results of the comparable groups for differences in leverage.

Hypothetical Capital Structures

Another implication of leverage theory is that cost of capital estimates based on a utility's current market data and the capital structure expected by investors cannot be applied to any other capital structure without the adjustment described in previous examples. Regulators frequently assign hypothetical, or deemed, capital structures to utility companies for purposes of revenue requirements computation. This procedure is appropriate only if the cost of equity estimated from current investor expectations is revised to take into account the new capital structure prescribed by the regulator. The cost of equity estimate based on the actual capital structure is no longer consistent with the new capital structure. Of course, the imposition of an hypothetical capital structure presupposes that the existing actual capital structure is not optimal in the first place.

If it is assumed for a moment that it is proper to impute a capital structure consisting of substantially more debt, the higher common equity cost rate related to a changed common equity ratio must be reflected in the approach. In ascribing a capital structure different from the company's actual capital structure, which, for example, imputes a higher debt amount, the repercussions on equity costs must be recognized. As discussed in previous chapters, it is a rudimentary tenet of basic finance that the greater the amount of financial risk borne by common shareholders, the greater the return required by shareholders in order to be compensated for the added financial risk imparted by the greater use of senior debt financing. In other words, the greater the debt ratio, the greater is the return required by equity investors. Both the cost of incremental debt and the cost of equity must be adjusted to reflect the additional risk associated with the hypothetical capital structure. The arguments work in reverse if a hypothetical capital structure consisting of less debt than the actual were to be imputed.[2]

In summary, it is logically inconsistent to combine a fictitious capital structure with a return on equity estimate that excludes the effects of the proposed capital structure. By omitting the repercussions on equity costs and debt costs, a serious conceptual error would be committed in determining the cost of equity capital.

A similar problem arises in the double leverage approach to computing equity costs. If a cost of equity estimate based on a given capital structure is not modified to account for the double levered capital structure used by the regulator to determine the allowed return, a distorted measure of capital cost results. The double leverage issue is discussed at length in Chapter 20.

---

[2] The use of hypothetical capital structures necessarily entails the use of hypothetical equity costs, hypothetical debt costs, hypothetical interest payments, and hypothetical taxation.

The Decomposition of Return on Book Equity

The following equation, reproduced below from Equation 17-8 in the last chapter, expresses the book return on equity as a function of several underlying explanatory variables, and contains useful analytical properties.

$$r = [R + (R - i) D/E] (1 - T) \tag{17-8}$$

The expression formally links book equity returns with leverage. Specifically, the equity return is proportional to the utility's rate of return on assets plus a premium equal to the excess of the asset rate over the debt rate levered by the book value debt/equity ratio net of tax effects. It is highly instructive to apply the expression to a given utility on a historical basis in order to quantify the driving forces behind equity returns and explain the behavior and trends of such returns.

EXAMPLE 18-2

The levered return on book value of equity is given by:

$$r = [R + (R - i) D/E] (1 - T)$$

If the return on total assets, R, is 15%, the cost of debt, i, is 10%, the tax rate, T, is 50%, and the utility employs $50 million of equity capital and $50 million of debt capital, the return on book equity is given by:

$$r = [.15 + (.15 - .10) \$50/\$50] (1 - .50)$$

$$= [.15 + (.05) 1/1] (.50)$$

$$= [.15 + .05] (.50) = .10 \text{ or } 10\%$$

After-tax values of r with $R = 15\%$ and $T = 50\%$ for various degrees of leverage and debt costs are shown in the table below:

i	0	1	2
.05	.075	.125	.175
.075	.075	.1125	.150
.100	.075	.100	.125

D/E

EXAMPLE 18-3

Table 18-1, drawn from Andrews in Morin and Andrews (1993), shows the decomposition of book return on equity into its constituent parts for an hypothetical telephone utility over a four-year period, and provides an analysis of the direction and magnitude of the factors that drive equity returns. For example, the significant rise in realized equity returns in the last year is largely the result of a widening spread between the asset rate of return and debt cost. Table 18-2 shows a sample calculation for five selected years

TABLE 18-1
DISAGGREGATION OF BOOK RETURN ON EQUITY
(Dollars in Millions)

Earnings after tax	$ 624
Federal and state income tax	440
Interest expense	278
EBIT = Earnings before interest and income tax	$1,342

Assets net of zero-rate debt = A	= $7621
EBIT/Net assets = R	= $1342/$7621 = .176
Interest-bearing debt = D	= $2994
Interest expense	= $278
Average interest rate = i	= $278/$2994 = .093
Common equity = E	= $4628
Debt/Equity = D/E	= .647

Effective tax rate = Tax/Earnings before Tax = t
$$= \$440/\$1{,}064 = .414 \text{ or } 41.4\%$$

Return on equity = r = $[R + (R - i)D/E]$ (1-t)
$$= [.176 + (.176 - .093).647] (1 - .414)$$
$$= [.176 + (.083 \times .647)] (.586)$$
$$= [.176 + .054] (.586)$$
$$= .135 \text{ or } 13.5\%$$

or

$$r = R(1-t) + (R-i)(D/E)(1-t)$$
$$= .103 + .379 (R - i)$$

Source: Andrews (1993)

TABLE 18-2
COMPUTATION OF RETURN ON EQUITY

	Year 1	Year 2	Year 3	Year 4	Year 5
R(EBIT/A)	.176	.167	.154	.140	.143
i	.093	.095	.088	.081	.076
(R - i)	.083	.072	.066	.059	.067
X D/E	.647	.651	.673	.657	.660
+ R	.176	.167	.154	.140	.143
X (1 - t)	.586	.581	.590	.598	.557

Finding the Optimal Capital Structure

The management of National Electric Company is of the opinion that the cost of debt is a function of the debt ratio, and that this function is reflected in the schedule shown in the first and second columns of Table 18-3.

TABLE 18-3
THE RELATIONSHIP BETWEEN LEVERAGE AND COST OF CAPITAL

Debt Ratio	After-Tax Cost of Debt	Equity Cost	Composite Capital Cost
0%	5.00%	14.00%	14.00%
10%	5.00%	14.15%	13.24%
20%	5.00%	14.60%	12.68%
30%	5.00%	15.35%	12.25%
40%	6.00%	16.40%	12.24%
50%	7.00%	17.75%	12.38%
60%	9.00%	19.40%	13.16%
70%	12.00%	21.35%	14.81%

The second column shows the after-tax cost of debt, assuming a tax rate of 50%. In an actual situation, such a schedule could be derived from the actual bond yields and debt ratios for utility bonds in different quality rating groups averaged over a number of years.[3]

The utility's management also believes that the company's cost of equity can be expressed as the sum of the risk-free rate, R_F, a premium for business risk, b, and a premium for financial risk, f, as follows:

$$K_e = R_F + b + f \qquad (18\text{-}1)$$

The risk-free rate, as measured by the yield on long-term Treasury bonds, is currently 10%. The premium for business risk demanded by utility investors is estimated at 4%. The premium for financial risk is an increasing function of the debt ratio; the premium rises slowly at first, and then accelerates rapidly as the debt ratio reaches prohibitive levels. The behavior of the premium for financial risk is assumed to be proportional to the square of the debt ratio, and the proportionality constant is 0.15.[4] Substituting in Equation 18-1, the cost of equity function can be expressed as:

---

[3] Knowing any three points on the curved portion of the bond graph, a quadratic function can be fitted to approximate the shape of the graph.

[4] Empirical evidence on the shape of the equity graph can be found in Robichek, Higgins, and Kinsman (1973).

$$K_e = 10\% + 4\% + 0.20\,(D/C)^2 \qquad (18\text{-}2)$$

$$K_e = 14\% + 0.20\,(D/C)^2$$

This function is shown as a schedule of equity cost for various debt ratios in the third column of Table 18-3.

The weighted average cost of capital for each level of debt ratio is calculated by adding the cost of debt and the cost of equity corresponding to each debt ratio, weighted by their relative proportions. This calculation appears in the fourth column of Table 18-3. The cost of capital plotted in Figure 18-2 reaches a minimum at a debt ratio of 40%. National Electric Company's optimal capital structure thus consists of 40% debt and 60% equity. Once again, this result is derived from hypothetical cost curves resting on reasonable assumptions.

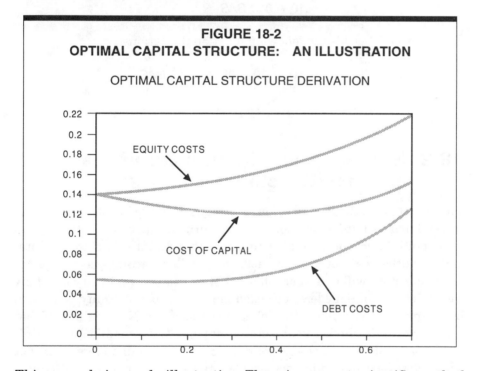

FIGURE 18-2
OPTIMAL CAPITAL STRUCTURE: AN ILLUSTRATION

OPTIMAL CAPITAL STRUCTURE DERIVATION

This example is purely illustrative. There is no exact scientific method or formula to derive a utility's optimal capital structure. The example is to be regarded as an exhibit of the approach only, and not as a precise prescription for finding the optimal capital structure. The simulation approach described in Chapter 19 represents a more realistic and pragmatic approach.

Another way to specify the functional relationship between the cost of equity and leverage is to employ the Modigliani-Miller and/or Miller expressions discussed earlier in the chapter and repeated below:

$$K_e = \rho + (\rho - i)(1 - T) \, B/S \qquad (17\text{-}7)$$

$$K_e = \rho + [\rho - i(1 - T)] \, B/S \qquad (17\text{-}10)$$

For example, with an unlevered cost of equity of 10%, a cost of debt of 8%, and a tax rate of 40%, Equation 17-7 yields the following functional relationship between the cost of equity and financial leverage:

$$K_e = .10 + (.10 - .08)(1 - .4) \, B/S$$

$$= .10 + .012 \, B/S$$

Equation 17-10 yields the following functional relationship:

$$K_e = .10 + [.10 - .08(1 - .4)] \, B/S$$

$$= .10 + .052 \, B/S$$

18.2 Rate Base and Capital Structure Interrelationship

The meaning and functioning of a utility's weighted cost of capital is interrelated with its companion rate of return on rate base.[5] If the regulator applies the cost of capital to a rate base that deviates from total capital and if authorized returns are achieved, dollar earnings available for common equity will exceed or fall short of the dollars necessary to satisfy the claims of shareholders. For example, if the cost of equity is 12% on book equity of $10 million, the dollars necessary are $1.20 million. If that rate of return is applied to an equity component of $9 million, the result would be equity earnings of $1.08 million, or $0.12 million less than that expected to be achieved by comparable risk investments.

In general, if there is a discrepancy between the total capital investment and the rate base, the fair return on common equity will not be achieved.

---

[5] Most of the content of this section is adapted from Andrews in Morin and Andrews (1993).

The dollars available to service equity capital will deviate from the number of dollars required to provide the earnings that investors require as compensation for the risk capital invested in the utility. Shareholders act as the residual bearers of the gain or loss consequences of rate base-invested capital discrepancies.

More formally, if the utility's weighted average cost of capital is K, and if investors have supplied C dollars of capital, the total dollar returns required to service capital are K times C, or KC. If the regulator applies the cost of capital to the rate base, W, and if the rate base equals invested capital C, then the net utility income produced to service capital will be K times W, or KW. Since the earnings permitted on assets are equal to the earnings necessary to service the capital put up by investors, then KW equals KC.

But what if the allowed return on the rate base does not equal K? If the regulator allows a return of y, which differs from K, the earnings available to investors are yW. The earnings will equal the requirement of returns to capital so that $yW = KC$ only if the regulator permits it. The allowed return on rate base will then be $y = K\ C/W$. Clearly, if the rate base W equals the capital C actually supplied by investors, then $y = K$.

If the rate base does not equal invested capital, then y cannot equal K. If y is set equal to K but the rate base is less than capital, then $yW < KC$, meaning that return on capital realized by the utility will be lower than its cost. The integrity of the invested equity capital will not be maintained. The converse is also true.

EXAMPLE 18-4

Cost of debt $K_d = 10\%$　　　　　　　Cost of equity $K_e = 15\%$

Debt $D = \$50$　　　　　　　　　　　Equity $E = \$50$

The revenue requirement is given by:

$$K_d \times D\ .10 \times \$50 = \$\ 5.00$$

$$K_e \times E\ .15 \times \$50 = \$\ 7.50$$

$$\text{Revenue Requirement} = \$12.50$$

The weighted average cost of capital is calculated as the dollars required to service investors as a fraction of the capital invested:

$$K = \$12.50/\$100 = 12.5\%$$

or by computing the weighted average cost of each component:

$$K = 0.50 \; x \; 10\% + 0.50 \; x \; 15\% = 12.5\%$$

If the rate base equals invested capital, then $K = \$100 \; x \; 12.50\% = \$12.50$. The return to the equity investor is calculated as follows:

Revenue	$12.50
Interest Expense	- $ 5.00
Return to Equity	$ 7.50

The return on equity is then $7.50/$50.00 = 15%. The equity investor's return equals the cost of equity of 15%. All is well because the rate base equals invested capital.

If the rate base exceeds invested capital, the equity investor will enjoy a windfall gain. To see this, assume that the rate base is $125 versus the $100 of capital invested. The revenue requirement equals 125 x $125 = $15.625. The return to the equity investor is then:

Revenue	$15.625
Interest Expense	- $ 5.000
Return to Equity	$10.625

The return on equity is then $10.625/$50.00 = 21.25%. The equity investor's return exceeds the cost of equity of 15%.

Conversely, if the rate base is less than invested capital, the equity investor will suffer a loss. To see this, assume that the rate base is $75 versus the $100 of capital invested. The revenue requirement equals .125 x $75 = $9.375. The return to the equity investor is then:

Revenue	$ 9.375
Interest Expense	- $ 5.000
Return to Equity	$ 4.375

The return on equity is then $4.375/$50.00 = 8.75%, well short of the cost of equity of 15%.

In practice, it is rarely true that the rate base and total capital are equal. For example, CWIP assets excluded from rate base without the AFUDC offset, or asset investments excluded from the rate base because such investments are not deemed "used and useful" and/or "prudent" by the regulator clearly violate the equality of rate base and invested capital. A more subtle example is the case of the working capital allowance. The working capital allowance incorporated into rate base in most jurisdictions bears little resemblance to the traditional accounting meaning of net working capital. If capital is equal to a total composed in part of net working capital, and if the working capital component of the rate base equals net working capital only by chance, then rate base and capital can only be equal by coincidence.

Rate Base Disallowance

Rate base disallowances present a dramatic example of the inequality between the rate base and invested capital. Investors supply dollars of capital, not physical plant. Each dollar of capital has an earnings requirement (interest, dividends, earnings) irrespective of the manner in which the utility employs that dollar. The exclusion of plant investment from rate base for any variety of reasons and the failure to provide earnings in the form of AFUDC on the excluded investment result in a part of total capital that has no earnings power, but which nevertheless has ongoing capital costs. These costs must be absorbed by earnings from existing investments, raising the possibility of severe losses.

The totality of a company's capital has to be serviced, whether through the medium of operating revenues or in part through the accrual of AFUDC. Therefore, the allowed rate of return on common equity is applicable to the total common equity component of the total investments of the utility company. Anything less than that has the direct and immediate effect of reducing common equity return below the level needed to meet the capital attraction and the comparable earnings standards articulated in the *Hope* and *Bluefield* decisions. To apply an allowed rate of return to a rate base that does not provide for total common equity investment does not maintain the integrity of that capital and does not enable the company to attract capital. If the allowed rate of return is applied to a rate base that reflects less than the total common equity investment, the rate of return on equity has to be proportionately increased so as to yield the same aggregate dollar amount of return that the allowed rate of return applied to the total common equity investment would provide for the servicing of the total common equity.

Disallowance can be justified on grounds of management imprudence, which in turn results only from a failure of management to control events that should be controlled by any basically sound management. It is important that if such a determination is to be made, it be done *ex-ante,* or in a forward-looking sense, rather than after the fact, or retroactively. Should imprudence be demonstrated, the risks associated with additions to the asset base will rise precipitously, and the institutional arrangements under which future assets are acquired will change accordingly. A utility company would require assurances that it can recover and earn a return on prudently invested capital before it engages in new construction, or the responsibility for providing future capacity will have to be transferred from the utility to a third party. The risk for ratepayers is that such arrangements will not be negotiated until inadequate capacity and poor service are unavoidable.

The exclusion of a portion of a plant from rate base undermines a utility's integrity. Instead of earning a return on the disallowed plant investment, a utility must write off this investment, thus reducing its equity by the amount of the disallowance. Its interest coverage, equity ratio, and return on equity all suffer, and access to capital markets may be jeopardized if the deterioration is sufficient. Moreover, it is important that regulation provide correct resource allocation signals to the utility, which will produce adequate capacity and service in the future.

It is vital that the entire plant should be included in rate base. Bond and equity investors expect and take comfort in the long-standing regulatory practice that once a plant goes into service, it be accorded the legal status of plant in service, thereby legitimizing the investment previously denied as CWIP. The removal of plant from rate base could result in severe and adverse financial impacts on the company and its ratepayers by increased capital costs flowing from lower coverages and increased risks. If cost responsibility is assigned to the shareholders, the risk of holding utility securities would increase substantially, reducing stock prices and bond ratings, and resulting in much higher capital costs.

Utility regulation constrains profitability on the upside but not on the downside. Utilities, unlike unregulated companies, frequently face a situation in which they are penalized for specific operating problems or failures, but not rewarded for good performance. An environment in which ratepayers obtain the benefits of successful operation or new technologies but investors bear the full costs of failure creates a game of "heads I win, tails you lose" and it increases the riskiness of any utility while bringing with it the attendant increase in capital costs. If there is a finite probability of total ruin under bad conditions, but essentially no probability of correspondingly large positive returns under current regulatory practices, then the expected return for normal expected conditions would have to be substantially higher than for unregulated companies, and utilities would have to earn high returns in normal times to offset large losses when major problems occur. Unregulated companies do not operate in this constrained environment; they can go bankrupt, but they have as an offset the possibility of earning very high returns.

Short-term Debt

Interest-rate bearing short-term debt is an issue in some jurisdictions. The omission of short-term debt from the debt component of the weighted cost of capital calculation is sometimes rationalized by the traditional practice of using short-term debt, bank borrowing and commercial paper, as interim financing during construction periods. Since this can be an expensive omission in periods of high short-term interest rates, the inclusion of short-term debt in rate filings has become more frequent.

EXAMPLE 18-5

This example shows that the omission of short-term debt from the capital structure, or more generally the omission of any component of capital, results in imputation of the resulting weighted average cost to the omitted element. Consider Table 18-4 below. A utility has a capital structure consisting of equal proportions of debt and equity of $50, with attaching costs of 10% and 20%, respectively, to give a weighted cost of 15%. By contrast, the Table also shows the calculated weighted cost of capital with another $50 of short-term debt included at an imputed weighted cost of 15%.

TABLE 18-4
SHORT-TERM DEBT AND THE WEIGHTED COST OF CAPITAL

	Weight			Weighted Cost	
	Case A	Case B	Cost	Case A	Case B
Debt	0.50	0.333	0.10	0.05	0.033
Short-term debt	—	0.333	0.15	—	0.050
Equity	0.50	0.333	0.20	0.10	0.067
Total Weighted Cost				15	0.15

In Case A, dollar earnings total .15 x $100 = $15, enough to service the $5 claim of bondholders and the $10 claim of shareholders. In Case B, dollar earnings total .15 x $150 = $22.50, from which $5 and $10 will cover the claims of bondholders and shareholders respectively, and the remaining $7.50 is available to service the $50 of short-term capital at a return rate of $7.50/$50 = 15%, which is the weighted average cost of capital.

Exclusion of the short-term debt capital from the weighted average calculation is equivalent to assigning the average otherwise computed, as long as the rate base is defined as equal to total capital. This result is obtained because of the behavior of the weights attached to the sources of funds when short-term debt is included or excluded. Inclusion of the short-term debt in the calculation will dilute the proportionate weights of other funds sources. However, attachment of the overall weighted cost to the short-term component adds exactly the costs of the diluted sources for a net difference of zero. This result is proven formally by Andrews in Morin and Andrews (1993), and depends on the independence of the rate base definition.

If the rate base is reduced by the amount of the short-term debt, equivalency of result no longer holds. This last point is demonstrated more formally by Andrews in Morin and Andrews (1993) as follows. Assuming that a weighted average cost of K applies to three rate-bearing components of capital, C_1, C_2, and C_3. The coverage of capital costs is provided by a rate base, W, equal to $C_1 + C_2 + C_3$. The rate base earns at the rate y, thus,

$$yW = K(C_1 + C_2 + C_3)$$

If $C2$ is excluded from capital, the missing coverage is KC_2. However, if the rate base is not altered, earnings will exceed $K(C_1 + C_3)$ by the amount $yC_2 = KC_2$. If the rate base is reduced by something less than C_2, partial coverage of C_2 will result. The main point is that these results only hold if the rate base W equals invested capital, $C_1 + C_2 + C_3$. Example 18-6 illustrates this proposition numerically.

EXAMPLE 18-6

Cost of long-term debt $K_d = 10\%$. Cost of short-term debt $K_{sd} = 8\%$

Cost of equity $K_e = 15\%$

Long-term Debt $D = \$33.33$ Short-term Debt $SD = \$33.33$

Equity $E = \$33.33$

The revenue requirement is given by:

$$Kd \times D \quad .10 \times \$33.33 \qquad = \$\ 3.33$$

$$Ksd \times SD \quad .08 \times \$33.33 \qquad = \$\ 2.66$$

$$Ke \times E \quad .15 \times \$33.33 \qquad \underline{= \$\ 5.00}$$

$$\text{Revenue Requirement} \qquad = \$11.00$$

The weighted average cost of capital is calculated either as the dollars required to service investors as a fraction of the capital invested:

$$K = \$11.00/\$100 = 11.0\%$$

or the weighted average cost of each component:

$$K = 0.33 \times 10\% + 0.33 \times .08 + 0.50 \times 15\% = 11.0\%$$

If short-term debt is excluded from the calculation, the weights revert back to 50/50. The revenue requirement is given by:

$$K_d \times D \quad .10 \times \$33.33 \qquad = \$3.33$$

$$K_e \times E \quad .15 \times \$33.33 \qquad \underline{= \$5.00}$$

$$\text{Revenue Requirement} \qquad \$8.33$$

Again, the weighted average cost of capital is calculated either as the dollars required to service investors as a fraction of the capital invested:

$$K = \$8.33/\$66.67 = 12.5\%$$

or as the weighted average cost of each component:

$$K = 0.50 \times 10\% + 0.50 \times 15\% = 12.5\%$$

The return to the equity investor is calculated as follows:

Revenue	$ 12.50
Interest Expense	
long-term	- $ 3.33
short-term	- $ 2.67
Return to Equity	$ 6.50

The return on equity is then $6.50/$33.33 = 19.5%. The equity investor experiences a windfall gain because the interest on the short-term debt of 8% is less than the overall return of 12.5%, and the excess accrues to the equity investor.

Now consider the situation where the rate base is $75. The revenue requirement equals .125 x $75 = $9.375. The return to the equity investor is:

Revenue	$9.375
Interest Expense	
long-term	- $3.333
short-term	- $2.666
Return to Equity	- $3.376

The return on equity is then $3.376/$33.33 = 10.13%, which is less than the required return on equity of 15%. The reasons for the return deficiency is that although the interest on short-term debt of 8% is less than the overall return of 11%, this is more than offset by the deficiency between the rate base and capital invested, $75 versus $100.

Zero-cost Capital Components[5]

Zero-cost components of capital arise from customer deposits, deferred income taxes accumulated from reporting of acceleration for tax purposes as opposed to straight-line book depreciation reported externally in utility financial statements, and deferred credits to income tax associated with investment tax credits. Most jurisdictions permit normalized or deferred recognition of at least one of these means of tax reduction, as opposed to immediate recognition (flow-through) of the tax savings for rate-making purposes. Current tax laws (1994) greatly reinforce this practice.

---

[5] This section is adapted from Andrews in Morin and Andrews (1993).

Most regulatory commissions consider deferred tax credits to be a part of the capital structure, but allow a zero rate of return on that capital component, on the grounds that deferred taxes are equivalent to an interest-free loan from the government and hence have no cost to the utility. An equivalent treatment is to subtract the zero-cost source of financing from the rate base.

To see this, consider the following example. As shown in Table 18-5, a utility has a capital structure consisting of equal proportions of debt and equity of $50 each with attaching costs of 10% and 20%, respectively, to give a weighted cost of 15%. By contrast, the table also shows the calculated weighted cost of capital with another $50 of deferred tax financing included at a zero-cost rate.

TABLE 18-5
ZERO-COST COMPONENTS AND THE WEIGHTED COST OF CAPITAL

	Weight			Weighted Cost	
	Case A	Case B	Cost	Case A	Case B
Debt	0.50	0.333	0.10	0.05	0.033
Deferred taxes	—	0.333	0.00	—	0.000
Equity	0.50	0.333	0.20	0.10	0.067
	Total Weighted Cost			0.15	0.10

One alternative treatment (Case B) is to include deferred taxes as a component of capital and find the allowed return as the weighted average of capital, including zero-cost capital sources. The weighted average cost of capital is 10% using this method. Applied to a rate base of $150, which includes deferred taxes, dollar earnings of .10 x $150 = $15 are produced, enough to service the claims of both bondholders, .10 x $50 = $5, and shareholders, .20 x $50 = $10.

Coverage of exactly the same dollar total of capital cost results from subtraction of the zero-rate capital from the rate base and the capital structure (Case A). The weighted average cost of capital is 15%, if deferred tax capital is excluded from the computation. Applied to a rate base of $150 - $50 = $100, dollar earnings of .15 x $100 = $15 are produced, the same dollar total of capital cost achievable under the first method. Note, however, that the two allowed rates cannot be equal (15% versus 10%). The divergence will be even greater if the rate base does not equal invested capital. Example 18-7 provides a numerical illustration.

EXAMPLE 18-7

Cost of long-term debt $K_d = 10\%$ Cost of equity $K_e = 15\%$

Long-term Debt $D = \$33.33$ Cost-free sources $F = \$33.33$

Equity $E = \$33.33$

The revenue requirement is given by:

$$K_d \times D \; .10 \times \$33.33 \quad = \quad \$3.33$$

$$K_d \times SD \; .00 \times \$33.33 = \quad \$0.00$$

$$K_e \times E \; .15 \times \$33.33 \quad = \quad \underline{\$5.00}$$

Revenue Requirement $\$8.33$

Assume the rate base equals $100. The weighted average cost of capital is calculated either as the dollars required to service investors as a fraction of the capital invested:

$$K = \$8.33 / \$66.66 = 12.5\%$$

or as the weighted average cost of each component:

$$K = 0.50 \times 10\% + 0.50 \times 15\% = 12.5\%$$

If the rate base equals the capital invested, the return to the cost-free sources equals the weighted average cost of capital. To show this, revenues are computed as the product of the rate base and the weighted cost of capital:

$$\text{Revenues} = .125 \times \$100 = \$12.50$$

The return to zero-cost sources is calculated as follows:

Revenue	$12.50
Interest Expense	- $ 3.33
Return to Equity @ 15%	- $ 5.00
Return to Zeros	$ 4.17

The return to zero-cost sources is then $4.17/$33.33 = 12.5%, which is equal to the weighted cost of capital. The crucial assumption tion underlying this result is the equality between rate base and invested capital.

Note that the actual return to the equity investor is given by:

Revenue	$12.50
Interest Expense	- $ 3.33
Return to Equity	$ 9.17

which represents a return of $9.17/$33.33 or 27.5%, which is far in excess of the required 15%.

To rectify this anomaly, let us say that the rate base is defined net of all zero-cost sources of financing, that is, $100 - $33.33 = $66.66. Revenues are computed as the product of the net rate base and the weighted cost of capital:

$$\text{Revenues} = .125 \times \$66.66 = \$8.33$$

The return to the equity investor is given by:

Revenue	$ 8.33
Interest Expense	- $ 3.33
Return to Equity	$ 5.00

which represents a return of $5.00/$33.33 or 15%, which equals the cost of equity.

The validity of this result depends on the magnitude of the rate base. If the rate base was $75 instead of $100 before subtraction of the zero-cost sources of financing in the example, the equity investor experiences a return deficiency. Revenues are computed as the product of the new net rate base, $75 - $33.33 = $41.67, and the weighted cost of capital:

$$\text{Revenues} = .125 \times \$41.67 = \$5.21$$

The return to the equity investor is given by:

Revenue	$ 5.21
Interest Expense	- $ 3.33
Return to Equity	$ 1.88

which represents a return of $1.88/$33.33 or only 5.6%, which is far less than the equity investor's required 15%.

As a result of current tax laws, some deferred tax credits must be allowed a rate of return. The impact on capital costs can be seen by referring back to the short-term debt example in Table 18-4, and substituting deferred tax of $50 for short-term debt. Exclusion of deferred tax from the weighted average is equivalent to assigning the average otherwise computed, as long as the rate base is defined to include total capital. It is noteworthy that if the return on the deferred credits is captured by the shareholders, the return on equity is in effect increased.

References

Morin, R. A. and Andrews, V.L. *Determining Cost of Capital for Regulated Industries,* Public Utilities Reports Inc. and The Management Exchange Inc., Washington DC, 1993.

Robichek, A.A., Higgins, R.C., and Kinsman, M. "The Effect of Leverage on the Cost of Equity Capital of Electric Utility Firms." *Journal of Finance,* May 1973, 353-367.

Additional References

Myers, S.C. "The Capital Structure Puzzle." *Journal of Finance,* July 1984, 575-592.

Chapter 19
Optimal Capital Structure

19.1 Introduction

The existence of an optimal capital structure for a public utility has been a controversial issue in corporate finance and utility regulation. The issue resurfaces periodically, particularly when the equity ratios become inflated in relation to historical standards. For example, when electric utilities enter a cash generation mode following the termination of base load construction programs and/or decrease in load growth, their equity ratios thicken. Or when a utility's equity ratio must be solidified in response to heightened business risk, regulators' concerns on the appropriate capital structure intensify as a result.

The correct proportion of debt and equity capital for a utility to employ is particularly relevant for utility ratepayers, since equity costs exceed debt costs owing to the tax deductibility of interest payments on debt. The debt ratio that minimizes capital costs, or conversely, the credit rating that is most cost effective, is the major concern of this chapter. Specifically, does maintaining a high or upper medium-grade credit rating, for example AA as opposed to A, or A as opposed to BBB, cause a company's overall capital costs, inclusive of taxes, to be minimized? This chapter is the empirical counterpart of Chapter 17 and provides an empirical resolution to the optimal capital structure issue by means of a simulation model. At what level of leverage is the low-cost advantage of debt financing offset by the rising risks? Conversely, given the intimate connection between bond rating and debt ratio, what is the optimal bond rating?

For expository convenience, a hypothetical utility company labeled as the Southeastern Electric Company or "Southeastern" is referenced throughout the chapter. The case example developed in this chapter is to be regarded as illustrative only, and not as a precise formula for finding the optimal capital structure.

In the way of background to the case, a management audit report alleges that Southeastern's capital structure plan for the next five years is not supported by a detailed analysis of the alternatives, and that the company should evaluate the feasibility of reducing equity ratio targets. More specifically, the report shows that increasing the debt ratio targets reduces capital costs. The report suggests that the costs of maintaining a given bond rating and the underlying costs to the ratepayer are not minimized by the current debt ratio. In contrast, the simulation model described in this chapter shows that electric utilities whose bonds are rated a strong A to AA enjoy lower capital costs and provide lower rates than BBB utilities, especially in adverse capital market conditions. The results of the model indicate that it is in Southeastern's interest and that of its ratepayers to maintain a strong A to AA bond rating over the next several years and to maintain a maximum debt ratio consistent with that target.

The chapter is divided into three sections. Section 19.1 outlines the basics of the methodology. Section 19.2 presents a simulation model designed to identify Southeastern's optimal bond rating from the ratepayers' viewpoint. Section 19.3 summarizes the chapter and offers conclusions and policy implications.

It should be pointed out that the general approach employed in this chapter is pragmatic rather than theoretical. The optimal capital structure issue is addressed from the point of view of investors or from the point of view of someone who is in close contact with investor concerns.

19.2 Model Fundamentals

As was evident from Chapter 17, capital structure theory provides limited quantitative guidance on where or whether there is, in fact, an optimal debt ratio or an optimal bond rating. The classic Modigliani-Miller argument asserts that a company's cost of capital is constant regardless of the debt ratio, but since interest payments are tax deductible, debt financing has a large cost advantage. Miller's introduction of personal taxes in the picture palliates the corporate tax advantage of debt. Since then, numerous theoreticians have debated the theory of capital structure, trading off the tax advantage of debt and the costs of distress and information signaling. Empirical investigations have generated controversy as well, although it is clear that there is a tax benefit from leverage and that leverage decreases overall cost of capital, at least over low levels of leverage. It is equally clear from these studies that the cost of equity increases with leverage.

Given the unsettled nature of financial theory, it is imperative that an empirical approach be implemented. The simulation model in the next section will investigate empirically the existence of an optimal bond rating, using current data and current industry realities.

In order to isolate the issues clearly and to facilitate comprehension of the full capital structure simulation model presented in Section 19.2, a simplified illustration is presented. The basic idea of the method along with the crucial variables and assumptions driving the model will emerge. [1]

---

[1] The simulation model presented in this chapter builds upon and extends the foundation laid by Hadaway (1986).

Consider an A-rated utility with the following capital structure before a change is contemplated: the rate base of $100 is financed 50% by debt and 50% by common equity, with cost rates of 10% and 14%, respectively. Note that the cost rates imply a risk premium of 4% of common equity returns over bond yields. The corporate tax rate is 34%, so that the tax conversion factor is 1/(1−.34) = 1.52. Referring to Table 19-1 below, the tax-inclusive cost of capital is 15.61%. That is, on a rate base of $1,000, $156.10 of revenue requirements are needed to service the capital contributed by investors.

TABLE 19-1
TAX-INCLUSIVE COMPOSITE COST OF CAPITAL BEFORE CHANGE

Type Of Capital	Amount	Weight	Cost	Weighted Cost	Tax Factor	Weighted Return
Debt	$50	50.00%	10.00%	5.00%	1.00	5.00%
Equity	$50	50.00%	14.00%	7.00%	1.52	10.61%
	$100			12.00%		15.61%
Coverage =	3.12					

The coverage ratio measures the ability of the utility's earnings to meet its fixed obligations, and is an important determinant of creditworthiness scrutinized by bond rating agencies and by the investment community. In this example, the pre-tax operating revenues of $15.61 can be divided by the interest charges of $5 to find the coverage ratio of 3.12 that results from the allowed return. Conversely, had the target coverage of 3.12 been given, the implied debt ratio of 50% required to produce the coverage of 3.12 could be computed. This is an important pillar of the simulation model in the next section. Given the target coverage ratio, the required debt and equity ratios to produce that coverage can be computed.[2]

---

[2] The formula for accomplishing the transition from the required coverage to the debt ratio is derived as follows: Interest coverage COV is defined as the pre-tax, pre-interest earnings available to service the interest charges, or $WACC$/interest. $WACC$ is equal to $K = K_d W_d + K_e W_e$, where K_d and K_e are the cost of debt and equity, W_d and W_e are the percent weights of debt and equity. The interest burden is $K_d W_d$. It can easily be shown that coverage equals:

$$COV = \frac{K_e(1 - W_d)}{K_d W_d(1 - T)} + 1$$

Of course, given the interest coverage ratio, $K_e, K_d,$ and T, and given that the weights W_d and W_e must add up to 1, the above equation can be solved for the debt ratio W_d consistent with that coverage:

$$W_d = \frac{K_e}{K_d(COV - 1)(1 - T) + K_e}$$

The utility now alters its capital structure from 50% debt to 60% debt, as shown in Table 19-2 below. The company's bonds are downgraded from A to BBB in response to the higher financial risk borne by investors.

TABLE 19-2
TAX-INCLUSIVE COMPOSITE COST OF CAPITAL AFTER CHANGE

Type Of Capital	Amount	Weight	Cost	Weighted Cost	Tax Factor	Weighted Return
Debt	$60	60.00%	11.00%	6.60%	1.00	6.60%
Equity	$40	40.00%	15.00%	6.00%	1.52	9.09%
	$100			12.60%		15.69%

Coverage = 2.38

What happens to total capital costs depends on the impact of higher financial leverage on debt costs and equity costs. In the example, it is arbitrarily assumed that debt costs rise from 10% to 11% in response to the higher risk represented by the higher debt ratio. Given the stock-bond risk premium of 4%, equity costs rise to 15%. Overall capital costs rise to 15.69% as a result of the change in capital structure, and the coverage ratio deteriorates from 3.12 to 2.38. The crucial variables that determine the precise impact on overall capital costs are the revised debt and equity costs in response to the higher financial risks of the company. In the example, the utility is downgraded from A to BBB because of its higher debt ratio, and it is arbitrarily assumed in the example that the yield spread between A-rated and BBB-rated securities is 1%.

The example shows that the crucial determinants of eventual capital costs include the debt ratio (or coverage) benchmarks assigned by credit rating agencies for various bond rating classes, the yield spreads between bond rating categories, and the reaction of equity costs to increased leverage. The simulation model presented in the next section is predicated on these fundamental determinants, and proceeds directly from the example discussed here with a few more embellishments and refinements included. For example, Southeastern utilizes preferred stock financing and has approximately 90% of its assets as earning assets. Preferred stock financing and non-earning CWIP assets are therefore introduced in the model.

19.3 Capital Structure Simulation Model

Table 19-3 below presents the capital costs calculations and assumptions for an AAA-rated electric utility, the highest bond rating accorded by the bond rating agency Standard & Poor's (S&P). The input data should be representative of current capital market conditions.

TABLE 19-3
"AAA" UTILITY

Assumptions: AAA Bond Rating

Coverage		= 5.00			
Cost of debt		= 9.50%			
Cost of preferred		= 8.75%			
Cost of equity		= 13.50%			
Tax rate		= 38.00%			
Equity tax factor		= 1.61			

Component		Weighted Cost	Cost	Tax Factor	Overall Return
Debt	32.29%	9.50%	3.07%	1.00	3.07%
Preferred	10.00%	8.75%	0.88%	1.61	1.41%
Equity	57.71%	13.50%	7.79%	1.61	12.56%
Total	100.00%		11.73%		17.04%

Coverage = 5.00

The key initial input is the coverage requirement for a AAA electric utility. Given that the S&P coverage AAA guideline for electric utilities as of early 1993 is "greater than 4.5" and that the AA guideline is "3.5 - 5.0," a coverage requirement of 5.00 is assumed.

The second step is to translate the coverage requirement into a debt/equity ratio that will produce that coverage. For a coverage requirement of 5.00, a debt ratio of 32.29% is implied. The third step is to verify that the implied debt ratio is consistent with the S&P guidelines. It is imperative that both the coverage and debt ratio benchmarks be internally consistent. The implied ratio of 32.29% is consistent with the S&P guidelines. A preferred stock ratio of 10% is assumed throughout the analysis. The results of the study are not sensitive to this assumption. Given the debt ratio of 32.29% and the preferred ratio of 10%, the common equity ratio must be 57.71%, that is 100% - 42.29%.

The cost of debt for a AAA electric is assumed to be 9.5%. The cost of preferred stock is assumed to be 75 basis points less than the cost of debt throughout the analysis. This is based on an examination of the yield spread history between preferred stock and long-term bonds of electric utilities for the last twelve years. A risk premium of 4% is assumed to prevail between utility AAA bonds and common stocks. The behavior of equity costs in response to increasing leverage is discussed more fully later. A combined federal and state tax rate of 38% is assumed throughout, which in turn produces a tax conversion factor of $1/(1-.38) = 1.61$. With those plausible assumptions, the composite capital cost for a AAA electric is 17.04%, including taxes. As a check on the calculations, the coverage ratio is determined under these capital structure conditions and is indeed equal to 5.00, confirming the accuracy of the computation.

Table 19-4 presents the corresponding calculations for a AA utility instead of a AAA utility. The midpoint of the S&P coverage benchmark for a AA utility is 4.25, which translates into a debt ratio of 37% using the coverage-debt ratio relationship discussed earlier. The implied debt ratio lies outside the benchmark range, however. Lowering the coverage assumption to 3.75 produces a debt ratio of about 40%, which is now inside the target debt ratio range. The cost of debt has risen from 9.50% to 9.79% as a result of the higher risk. The increase in 29 basis points is based on a historical analysis of spreads between AAA- and AA-rated utility bond indices over the prior twelve years. Preferred costs are assumed to rise in corresponding fashion from 8.75% to 9.04% and common equity costs also rise from 13.5% to 13.79%. The composite capital cost for the AA utility decreases from 17.04% to 16.46%.

TABLE 19-4
"AA" UTILITY

Assumptions: AA Bond Rating

Coverage	= 3.75
Cost of debt	= 9.79%
Cost of preferred	= 9.04%
Cost of equity	= 13.79%
Tax rate	= 38.00%
Equity tax factor	= 1.61

Component		Weighted Cost	Cost	Tax Factor	Overall Return
Debt	40.33%	9.79%	3.95%	1.00	3.95%
Preferred	10.00%	9.04%	0.90%	1.61	1.46%
Equity	49.67%	13.79%	6.85%	1.61	11.05%
Total	100.00%		11.70%		16.46%

Coverage = 3.75

The same procedure is replicated for an A and BBB utility, using the appropriate coverage benchmarks and the historical yield spread average between A and BBB bonds over the past twelve years. For A-rated electric utilities, the midpoint of the coverage ratio range, 3.25, is used. This produces a debt ratio internally consistent with the benchmark range. For BBB-rated electrics, a coverage ratio of 2.8 is used, so as to produce a debt ratio consistent with the low end of the target range.

Tables 19-5 and 19-6 below show the results for A- and BBB-rated utilities, respectively. The composite capital cost decreases slightly to 16.40% for the A-rated utility and begins to increase below that rating, rising to 16.43% for a BBB utility.

TABLE 19-5
"A" UTILITY

Assumptions: AA Bond Rating

Coverage	= 3.25
Cost of debt	= 10.07%
Cost of preferred	= 9.32%
Cost of equity	= 14.32%
Tax rate	= 38.00%
Equity tax factor	= 1.61

Component		Weighted Cost	Cost	Tax Factor	Overall Return
Debt	45.13%	10.07%	4.54%	1.00	4.54%
Preferred	10.00%	9.32%	0.93%	1.61	1.50%
Equity	44.87%	14.32%	6.43%	1.61	10.36%
Total	100.00%		11.90%		16.40%

Coverage = 3.25

TABLE 19-6
"BBB" UTILITY

Assumptions: BBB Bond Rating

Coverage	= 2.80
Cost of debt	= 10.49%
Cost of preferred	= 9.74%
Cost of equity	= 14.99%
Tax rate	= 38.00%
Equity tax factor	= 1.61

Component		Weighted Cost	Cost	Tax Factor	Overall Return
Debt	50.37%	10.49%	5.28%	1.00	5.28%
Preferred	10.00%	9.74%	0.97%	1.61	1.57%
Equity	39.63%	14.99%	5.94%	1.61	9.58%
Total	100.00%		12.19%		16.43%

Coverage = 2.80

Assumptions and Results

The full set of assumptions along with a summary of the results are recapitulated in the tables below, taken directly from the electronic spreadsheet used to simulate capital structure conditions. Tables 19-7 and 19-8 present the detailed simulation results under normal and adverse economic conditions, respectively. As discussed later, the pattern of results is relatively insensitive to the majority of the quantitative assumptions over a wide range of reasonableness for those values.

TABLE 19-7
OPTIMAL CAPITAL STRUCTURE ANALYSIS,
ASSUMPTIONS AND SUMMARY OF RESULTS:
NORMAL ECONOMIC ENVIRONMENT

Assumptions:		Note
AAA Debt Cost	9.50%	assumed
AAA Equity Cost	13.50%	debt cost + risk premium
Debt-stock Risk Premium AAA	4.00%	assumed
Debt-stock Risk Premium AA	4.00%	"
Debt-stock Risk Premium A	4.25%	"
Debt-stock Risk Premium BBB	4.50%	"
Debt-preferred Risk Premium	0.75%	"
AAA Preferred Cost	8.75%	debt cost + risk premium
% Preferred Stock	10.00%	assumed
Tax Rate	38.00%	federal & state tax
Coverages		
AAA Coverage	5.00	S & P benchmarks
AA Coverage	3.75	"
A Coverage	3.25	"
BBB Coverage	2.80	"
Yield Spreads		
AAA-AA Spread	0.29%	1979-1990 yield spreads
AA-A Spread	0.28%	"
A-BBB Spread	0.42%	"
% Earning Assets In Rate Base	90.00%	assumed

SUMMARY OF RESULTS:
NORMAL ECONOMIC ENVIRONMENT

Bond Rating	%Debt	%WACC	Rev Reqt's	Incremental Rev Reqt's
AAA	32.29%	17.04%	$170.44	$0.00
AA	40.33%	16.46%	$164.53	($5.91)
A	45.13%	16.40%	$164.11	($0.42)
BBB	50.37%	16.43%	$164.37	$0.26

TABLE 19-8
OPTIMAL CAPITAL STRUCTURE ANALYSIS,
ASSUMPTIONS AND SUMMARY OF RESULTS:
ADVERSE ECONOMIC ENVIRONMENT

Assumptions:		Note
AAA Debt Cost	9.50%	assumed
AAA Equity Cost	13.50%	debt cost + risk premium
Debt-Stock Risk Premium AAA	4.00%	assumed
Debt-Stock Risk Premium AA	4.00%	"
Debt-Stock Risk Premium A	4.25%	"
Debt-Stock Risk Premium BBB	4.50%	"
Debt-Preferred Risk Premium	0.75%	"
AAA Preferred Cost	8.75%	debt cost + premium
% Preferred Stock	10.00%	assumed
Tax Rate	38.00%	federal & state tax

Coverages		
AAA Coverage	5.00	S & P benchmarks
AA Coverage	3.75	"
A Coverage	3.25	"
BBB Coverage	2.80	"

Yield Spreads		
AAA-AA Spread	0.62%	1979-1990 yield spreads
AA-A Spread	0.86%	"
A-BBB Spread	0.65%	"
% Earning Assets In Rate Base	90.00%	assumed

SUMMARY OF RESULTS:
ADVERSE ECONOMIC ENVIRONMENT

Bond Rating	%Debt	%WACC	Rev Reqt's	Incremental Rev Reqt's
AAA	32.29%	17.04%	$170.44	$0.00
AA	40.15%	16.93%	$169.28	($1.16)
A	44.63%	17.70%	$176.95	$7.67
BBB	49.77%	18.01%	$180.09	$3.14

The summary of the key results of the model contained in Table 19-7 shows the debt ratios, capital costs, and revenue requirements associated with the various bond ratings under normal capital market conditions. The revenue requirements are computed simply by multiplying the capital costs by an hypothetical rate base of $1,000. The last column shows the incremental revenue requirements impact. Those results indicate a marginal cost advantage for the A bond rating. The striking feature of the results is that capital structure changes have a modest effect on capital costs, at least under normal economic conditions. Capital structure changes do affect debt and equity costs, but changes in those variables are offset by changes in the proportions of each capital structure component. A similar result was obtained by Brigham, Gapenski, and Aberwald (1987) and Baptiste, Borges, and Carr (1988) in their studies of optimal utility capital structures.

Table 19-8 is the analog of Table 19-7 but under adverse economic conditions. The yield spreads prevailing in the turbulent 1981-1982 capital market environment were assumed to represent the spreads under adverse capital market conditions. The cost-minimizing optimal bond rating is now a clear AA, given the coverage assumptions. Capital costs at the AA rating level are 16.93% versus above 17% for any other bond rating. The fundamental difference between the two sets of results lies in the spread differences between a normal and an adverse capital market environment. Spreads typically widen under adverse capital market conditions, as investor quality consciousness and flight to quality increases. Table 19-9 shows that the yield advantage of a higher bond rating increases dramatically in poor years of difficult financial markets. The cumulative yield advantage of a AA rating over a BBB rating is 70 basis points under normal conditions versus 151 basis points under adverse capital market conditions.

TABLE 19-9
YIELD SPREADS: NORMAL v. POOR YEARS

SPREAD (basis points)

	Normal Years	Poor Years
AAA v. AA	29	62
AA v. A	28	86
A v. BBB	42	65

In assessing the wisdom of striving for a different bond rating, the adversity scenario results are far more meaningful and relevant. After all, the fundamental ideas of adequate debt capacity and prudent capital structure policy only make sense in the context of adverse economic circumstances. By analogy, when assessing the creditworthiness of a potential client applying for a loan, a prudent banker or creditor tries to determine the likelihood of interest and principal repayment should the client's operations encounter difficulty. If the lender concludes that the applicant's earnings are insufficient to cover its financial obligations under adversity conditions, the lender will not extend credit. Similarly, a firm elects not to increase its debt ratio for fear that its cash flows may be insufficient when it encounters major adversities in its operating environment.

Robustness of Results

Several sensitivity analyses of the model results were conducted with respect to some key assumptions. The fundamental nature of the results and the ultimate conclusion that the optimal bond rating is at least a strong A remain unaltered. One assumption made throughout the analysis is that earning assets constitute 90% of the rate base capital. The chief results of this study are not sensitive to the magnitude of this assumption. The preferred stock ratio was varied from 5% to 10%, and the preferred-bond yield spread was varied from 0 to 125 basis points with no significant differences in the results. The tax rate was varied from 20% to 40%, again with no substantial alteration in the pattern of the results; of course, the magnitude of the revenue requirements changes with the tax rate, but the fundamental U-shaped pattern (cost minimum at AA rating) of the results was preserved, especially when running the more relevant adversity scenario.

As shown in the upper portion of Tables 19-7 and 19-8, the stock-bond risk premium was initially assumed to be 4% for a AAA- and AA-rated utility, and to increase to 4.25% and 4.50% for A- and BBB-rated utilities, respectively. This was based on a rigorous analysis of how equity costs vary with leverage. Several formal theoretical models of how the cost of equity varies with leverage are available from the finance literature. The behavior of equity costs as leverage increases was alternatively modeled using Modigliani-Miller's approach, which recognizes corporate income taxes, as discussed in Chapter 17 using Equation 17-7, Miller's extension of that equation to allow for personal taxes, as illustrated in Equation 17-10, variations of the so-called Capital Asset Pricing Model, and empirical functional forms of the cost of equity-leverage relationship. The average estimate from the various cost of equity capital frameworks at varying amounts of leverage implied debt-stock risk premiums progressively increasing from 4% to 4.5% as bond quality deteriorates. The ultimate conclusion of the optimal A to AA bond rating remained robust when the model was amended to reflect more rigorous treatments of equity costs.

One particularly sensitive assumption was the coverage ratio assumption for BBB-rated utilities. The benchmark S&P range is 1.5 to 3.0. Below 2.3, the implied debt ratio lies outside the benchmark range of acceptability. In the narrow range of 2.3 to 2.5, the optimal bond rating under adverse conditions was in fact BBB, but this latter result did not take into explicit account all the intangible costs associated with a low bond rating that are not incorporated into the model. Any reasonable quantification of such costs reverses this result.

19.4 Conclusions

The model results show that on an incremental cost basis, a strong A bond rating generally results in the lowest pre-tax cost of capital for electric utilities under normal economic conditions. Under adverse economic conditions, which are far more relevant to the question of capital structure, the optimal bond rating is AA. This result prevails over a wide range of cost of common equity models and estimates utilized, and remains very robust to changes in key assumptions. The message from the model is clear: over the long run, a strong A to AA bond rating will minimize the pre-tax cost of capital to ratepayers, even on the basis of the embedded cost of debt. This is crucial for ratemaking purposes, where the embedded cost of debt is employed. Over the years, as the company replaces its funded debt issues through either retirement or call tenders, the pre-tax cost of incremental debt and overall capital is minimized at the A to AA level, depending on capital market conditions.

The implication is clear. Long-term achievement of at least an A rating and preferably a AA rating is in the electric utility company's and ratepayers' best interests. Debt leverage targets should be set in the lower part of the range required to attain this optimal rating. Progressive attainment of this goal will minimize rates, all else remaining constant.[3] If the company maintains its debt ratio close to the bottom end of the optimal range, its overall cost of capital should be minimized. If the company reduces its debt ratio below that point, it would be giving up the tax benefits associated with debt but would not reap the benefits from a lower cost of debt and equity. If the company operates at a debt ratio beyond that point, the cost of debt and equity will rise. The latter rise will occur at an increasing rate if the operating environment deteriorates. Moreover, the company will reduce its financing flexibility.

The case example developed in this chapter is to be regarded as illustrative only, and not as a precise formula for finding the optimal capital structure. While capital structure theory provides insights into the determinants of an optimal capital structure, it cannot state exactly the composition of a company's capital structure. Even though theory provides valuable insights

---

[3] In the utility regulation context, the New York Public Service Commission agreed that in the case of electric and gas utilities, based on data from 1981 and earlier, an "A" rating was optimal from the standpoint of both overall capital cost and availability. There have been significant changes since that 1982 decision, notably the tightening of electric utility bond rating criteria by Standard & Poor's in response to the increased business risks of electric utilities, tax reform, and a transformed capital market environment.

for management to make more informed decisions, capital structure decisions must be made on the basis of informed judgment rather than by the mechanical application of mathematical models.

There are several industry-specific and company-specific circumstances that the simulation model cannot readily quantify, including intangible costs, impact on bondholders, capital market losses, flotation costs, and impact on company flexibility. The simulation model was specifically applied to an electric utility company under circumstances prevailing at the time, and does not automatically extend to other industries, other companies, or other capital market conditions.

It is also important to point out that the case for a strong A to AA bond rating is understated by the model results to the extent that several intangible costs and distress costs associated with a higher debt ratio cannot be readily accommodated into the model, without the model becoming computationally prohibitive. The simulation model does not capture several intangible cost items associated with a low bond rating. Several examples of such costs follow.

The need to maintain borrowing capacity was developed in Chapter 17. During normal times a utility company should conserve enough unused borrowing capacity so that during periods of adversity it can use this capacity to avoid foregoing investment opportunities, selling stock at confiscatory prices, or jeopardizing its mandated obligation to serve.

Earlier, it was shown that the yield advantage of a higher bond rating increases dramatically in adverse capital market conditions. But bond flotation costs, which must be borne by ratepayers, increase also as bond ratings decline, particularly in years of difficult financial markets. Not only is lower bond quality associated with higher yields, but lower-rated utility bonds also carry shorter maturities, especially in poor years. The result is a maturity mismatch between the firm's long-term capital assets and its liabilities. Moreover, lower bond quality is associated with more years of call protection, particularly during difficult financial markets; since bonds are frequently called after a decrease in interest rates, bonds that carry call protection for a greater number of years are more costly to utility companies. Finally, as bond ratings decline, the probability that a company will reduce the dollar amount or shorten the maturity of their bond issues increases dramatically. This in turn reduces the marketability of a bond issue, and hence increases its yield. Any reasonable quantification of these implicit costs reinforces the case for a strong A to AA bond rating.

References

Baptiste, L., Borges, G., and Carr, G. "Utility Bond Ratings and the Cost of Capital." *Public Utilities Fortnightly,* October 27, 1988, 21-26.

Brigham, E.F., Gapenski, L.C., and Aberwald, D.A. "Capital Structure, Cost of Capital, and Revenue Requirements." *Public Utilities Fortnightly,* January 8, 1987, 15-24.

Hadaway, S.C. "A Cost Benefit Analysis of Alternative Regulatory Capital Structures," Center for the Study of Regulated Industry, Georgia State University, October 1986.

Additional References

Morin, R.A. Optimal Capital Structure for Central Illinois Co., Prepared Testimony, CILCORP, 1990.

New York PSC, Case 27679, Opinion and Order, Oct. 18, 1982, 49 PUR 4th 329, 333-334.

Chapter 20
Double Leverage

The purpose of this chapter is to critically address the Double Leverage (DL) approach to determining the cost of capital of a regulated utility. The double leverage approach has serious conceptual and practical limitations and is not consistent with basic financial theory and the notion of fairness. The assumptions and logic underlying the method are questionable. The double leverage argument violates the core notion that an investment's required return depends on its particular risks. The chapter concludes that the Double Leverage approach has no place in regulatory practice and should be discarded.

The chapter is divided into two sections. Section 20.1 introduces the basic notion of double leverage and describes the alternative approaches of determining the cost of capital for a subsidiary of a parent corporation. Section 20.2 critiques the double leverage approach at both the conceptual and practical levels.

20.1 Intercorporate Ownership and Double Leverage

Determining the cost of capital for a utility operating company owned by a holding company is a controversial capital structure issue. Intercorporate ownership opens the possibility of leveraging the common equity of one corporate entity at two or even more corporate levels. If a parent corporation issues its own debt and if a wholly-owned subsidiary also builds debt over the base of equity invested by the parent, leveraging takes place twice on the single layer of the parent's publicly-held equity. A parent company and a single subsidiary can thus create double leverage; even more extensive leveraging can occur through the existence of parent-subsidiary horizontal and vertical networks of subsidiaries. The situation is common among utilities with clusters of subsidiaries and their parents. The term "double leverage" stems from a situation in which there is initial leverage on the earnings for the operating company's common stock and then additional leverage for the holding company's common stock to the extent that the holding company obtains part of the funds invested in the subsidiary's common stock from debt sources.

The issue does not arise for electric and gas companies that are subsidiaries of holding companies because the Public Utility Holding Company Act limits the amount of borrowing these companies may undertake. Telecommunications and water utilities are not governed by this Act, however.

Even though the DL approach has largely disappeared from regulatory practice, the method is occasionally encountered in regulatory proceedings involving independent telecommunications and water utility companies.

There are two methods of computing the cost of capital under double leverage conditions: the Independent Company, or Stand-Alone, approach, and the Double Leverage approach. Consider the following numerical example. An operating company's capital structure consists of equal proportions of debt and equity, with attaching costs of 10% and 20%, respectively. The company is a wholly owned subsidiary of a parent company whose own source of capital is 25% debt and 75% equity. It is assumed that the cost of debt to the parent is also 10%, and that a reasonable return to parent stockholders is 15%. The latter assumption will be revisited in the Example at the end of the chapter. The situation is summarized in Table 20-1 below.

TABLE 20-1
OPERATING AND PARENT COMPANY COST OF CAPITAL

	Amount	Weight	Cost	Weighted Cost
Operating Company				
Debt	$ 50	.50	.10	.05
Equity	$ 50	.50	.20	.10
	$100	1.00		
			Total Cost	.15
Parent Company				
		Weight	Cost	Weighted Cost
Debt		.25	.10	.0250
Equity		.75	.15	.1125
			Total Cost	.1375

Independent Company Approach

One way to proceed is simply to ignore the parent-subsidiary relationship, and treat the operating company's cost of capital in the usual way as the weighted average cost of capital using the operating company's own capital structure and cost rates. Under this approach, often labeled the Stand-Alone Approach or Subsidiary Approach, the subsidiary is viewed as an independent operating company, and its cost of equity is inferred as the cost of equity of comparable risk firms. The methodology rests on the basic premise that the required return on an investment depends on its risk, rather than on the parent's financing costs.

In the example, the weighted cost is 15%. The allowed return of 20% on equity is derived from the techniques described in previous chapters, including DCF, Risk Premium, or CAPM. The equity return reflects the risk to which the equity capital is exposed and the opportunity return foregone by the company's shareholders in investments of similar risk. The identity of the shareholders is immaterial in determining the equity return.

Double Leverage Approach

Another approach is the Double Leverage methodology. This method has several variants. One treatment, shown in Table 20-2, traces the operating company's equity capital of $50 to its source, namely the parent's debt and equity capital. The cost of equity to the operating company is simply the overall weighted average of capital to the parent, since the equity capital is said to have been raised by the parent through a mixture of debt and equity. The parent's composite capital cost is imputed to the subsidiary's equity.

TABLE 20-2
OPERATING COMPANY COST OF CAPITAL: DOUBLE LEVERAGE CONCEPT

	Amount	Weight	Cost	Weighted Cost
Debt-Subsidiary	$50.00	.500	.10	.0500
Equity-provided by parent:				
Debt-parent (25%)	$12.50	.125	.10	.0125
Equity-parent (75%)	$37.50	.375	.15	.0563
			Weighted Cost	.1188

Advocates of the double leverage approach argue that the utility subsidiary only requires a 11.88% return on total capital rather than the 15.00% indicated in the previous calculation. Although the parent invested $50 in the company, it used leverage itself in raising its capital, so that the true cost of capital to the subsidiary is the cost of its own debt capital, plus the proportionate cost of its parent's debt and equity capital. Moreover, if the parent was allowed a 20% return on its $50 equity investment in the subsidiary, unreasonably high returns would be extracted by the parent's shareholders from ratepayers. In the example, gross dollar earnings of .20 x $50 = $10 would accrue to the parent company's shareholders; but since 25% of that $50, or $12.50, was borrowed at an interest rate of 10%, $1.25 must be subtracted from the gross earnings of $10 to produce net equity earnings of $8.75 on an equity investment of $37.50. That is a 23.33% return on equity. The theoretical and conceptual fallacies of this reasoning will be discussed shortly.

Modified Double Leverage Approach

One refinement to the double leverage method is to recognize that the parent's weighted cost of capital should only be imputed to the portion of equity actually contributed by the parent. The subsidiary's retained earnings should be removed from the double leverage imputation since none of the subsidiary's retained earnings are traceable to the capital raised by the parent. This will associate proportionately the components of parent capital and their respective costs with that part of subsidiary equity ostensibly financed in this way. The revised calculation with retained earnings removed is shown in Table 20-3. It is assumed that $40 of the $50 of subsidiary equity capital was contributed by the parent, and the remaining $10 is the subsidiary's own retained earnings, and the latter continues to be allowed a 20% return.

TABLE 20-3
OPERATING COMPANY COST OF CAPITAL: MODIFIED DOUBLE LEVERAGE CONCEPT

	Amount	Weight	Cost	Weighted Cost
Debt-Subsidiary	$50	.50	.10	.050
Retained Earnings—Subsidiary	$10	.10	.20	.020
Equity-provided by parent:				
Debt-parent (25%)	$10	.10	.10	.010
Equity-parent (75%)	$30	.30	.15	.045
			Weighted Cost	.125

One procedural flaw in the above double leverage computation is the failure to recognize that the debt ratio of the operating company has increased from 50% to 60%. Hence both debt and equity cost rates should be higher as a result of the increased financial risk. The 20% return on equity should be adjusted upward in recognition of the increased financial risk.

Consolidated Approach

Another method of computing the subsidiary's cost of capital uses consolidated data of the parent and subsidiary companies on the grounds that the holding company and its units are financed as an integrated whole, based on system-wide financing objectives. The cost rates for debt and preferred capital are system-wide averages, and the cost of equity is determined by traditional methods. Before to the divestiture of AT&T, the Bell System supported the use of a consolidated capital structure rather than a double-levered capital structure.

A few points regarding consolidated capital structures are in order. First, the debt of the consolidated company is the sum of the holding company's debt and the subsidiary's debt. Hence, the consolidated cost of debt is a weighted cost of parent and subsidiary debt. Second, the cost of equity of the holding company is identical to that of the consolidated entity. This is because the value of the parent holding company's stock expressly recognizes subsidiary income to parent investment if accounted on an equity basis. Accounting on the equity basis treats subsidiary net income as income to the parent's equity investment whether such income is received as dividends or not. The parent's retained earnings necessarily reflect this. Accordingly, the cost of equity associated with market valuation of holding company equity is also the cost of equity for the consolidated network. Third, a consolidated capital structure is equivalent to a double-levered capital structure when all the parent's subsidiaries have the same amounts of leverage. Lastly, some analysts contend that assignment of the consolidated weighted cost to the equity cost of the subsidiary is equivalent to imputation of the holding company's equity cost. This can only be true in the highly unlikely event that the costs of consolidated debt and equity are exactly equal, or, if they are unequal, that the differences in weights between the consolidated and the subsidiary capital structure exactly offset the differences in costs. This is proven formally in Morin and Andrews (1993).

20.2 Critique of Double Leverage

Adherents to the double leverage calculation argue that the true cost of capital to a utility subsidiary is the weighted cost of its own debt and the weighted cost of the parent's debt and equity funding. Moreover, unless the subsidiary's equity is assigned the parent's weighted cost of capital, parent shareholders will reap abnormally high returns. Although persuasive on the surface, these arguments conceal serious conceptual and practical problems. Moreover, the validity of double leverage rests on questionable assumptions.

The flaws associated with the double leverage approach have been discussed thoroughly in the following academic literature. Pettway and Jordan (1983) and Beranek and Miles (1988) pointed out the flaws in the double leverage argument, particularly the excess return argument, and also demonstrated that the stand-alone method is a superior procedure. Rozeff (1983) discussed the ratepayer cross-subsidies of one subsidiary by another when employing double leverage. Lerner (1973) concluded that the returns granted an equity investor must be based on the risks to which the investor's capital is exposed and not on the investor's source of funds.

Theoretical Issues

The double leverage approach contradicts the core of the cost of capital concept. Financial theory clearly establishes that the cost of equity is the risk-adjusted opportunity cost to the investors and not the cost of the specific capital sources employed by investors. The true cost of capital depends on the use to which the capital is put and not on its source. The *Hope* and *Bluefield* doctrines have made clear that the relevant considerations in calculating a company's cost of capital are the alternatives available to investors and the returns and risks associated with those alternatives. The specific source of funding and the cost of those funds to the investor are irrelevant considerations.

Carrying the double leverage standard to its logical conclusion leads to even more unreasonable prescriptions. If the common shares of the subsidiary were held by both the parent and by individual investors, the equity contributed by the parent would have one cost under the double leverage computation while the equity contributed by the public would have another. This is clearly illogical. Or, does double leverage require tracing the source of funds used by each individual investor so that its cost can be computed by applying double leverage to each individual investor? Of course not! Equity is equity, irrespective of its source, and the cost of that equity is governed by its use, by the risk to which it is exposed.

For example, if an individual investor borrows money at the bank at an after-tax cost of 8% and invests the funds in a speculative oil exploration venture, the required return on the investment is not the 8% cost but rather the return foregone in speculative projects of similar risk, say 20%. Yet, under the double leverage approach, the individual's fair return on this risky venture would be 8%, which is the cost of the capital source, and not 20%, which is the required return on investments of similar risk. Double leverage implies that for all investors who inherited stock or received stock as a gift, the allowed return on equity would be zero, since the cost of the stock to the investors is zero. It also implies that if, tomorrow morning, a subsidiary were sold to a company with a higher cost of capital than the parent, the subsidiary's cost of equity would suddenly become higher as a result of the change in ownership. If we assumed that the double leverage concept were appropriate, we would also have to assume that the day following AT&T's divestiture in 1984, the cost of equity of the newly created Bell Regional Holding Companies suddenly rose by a substantial amount. This is logically absurd, as it is the use of capital that governs its cost, and not its source. For example, if a subsidiary with a double leverage cost of equity of 12% were sold to another company with a higher cost of capital of, for example, 15%, would regulation alter the return accordingly just because of the change in ownership?

If so, the same utility with the same assets and providing the same service under the new management would have a higher cost of service to rate-payers because of the transfer of ownership. Clearly, if a utility subsidiary were allowed an equity return equal to the parent's weighted cost of capital while the same utility were allowed a fair, presumably higher, return were it not part of a holding company complex, an irresistible incentive to dissolve the holding company structure would exist in favor of the one-copany operating utility format. The attendant benefits of scale economies and diversification would then be lost to the ratepayers.

The cost of capital is governed by the risk to which to the capital is exposed and not by the cost of those funds or whether it is they were obtained from bondholders or common shareholders. The identity of the subsidiary's shareholders should have no bearing on its cost of equity because it is the risk to which the subsidiary's equity is exposed that governs its cost of money, not whether it is borrowed from bondholders or sold to common shareholders for issued shares. Had the parent company not been in the picture, and had the subsidiary's stock been widely held by the public, the subsidiary would be entitled to a return that would fully cover the cost of both its debt and equity.

Just as individual investors require different returns from different assets in managing their personal affairs, why should regulation cause parent companies making investment decisions on behalf of their shareholders to act any differently? A parent company normally invests money in many operating companies of varying sizes and varying risks. These operating subsidiaries pay different rates for the use of investor capital, such as long-term debt capital, because investors recognize the differences in capital structure, risk, and prospects between the subsidiaries. Yet, the double leverage calculation would assign the same return to each activity, based on the parent's cost of capital. Investors do recognize that different subsidiaries are exposed to different risks, as evidenced by the different bond ratings and cost rates of operating subsidiaries. The same argument carries over to common equity. If the cost rate for debt is different because the risk is different, the cost rate for common equity is also different, and the double leverage adjustment should not obscure this fact.

The double leverage concept is at odds with the opportunity cost concept of economics. According to this principle of economics, the cost of any resource is the cost of an alternative foregone. The cost of investing funds in an operating utility subsidiary is the return foregone on investments of similar risk. If the fair risk-adjusted return assigned by the market on utility investments is 15%, and the regulator assigns a return less than 15% because of a double leverage calculation, there is no incentive or defensible reason for a parent holding company to invest in that utility.

Fairness and Capital Attraction

The double leverage approach is highly discriminatory, and violates the doctrine of fairness. If a utility is not part of a holding company structure, the cost of equity is computed using one method, say the DCF method, while otherwise the cost of equity is computed using the double leverage adjustment. Estimating equity costs by one procedure for publicly held utilities and by another for utilities owned by a holding company is inconsistent with financial theory and discriminates against the holding company form of ownership. Two utilities identical in all respects but their ownership format should have the same set of rates. Yet, this would not be the case under the double leverage adjustment.

The capital attraction standard may also be impaired under the double leverage calculation. This is because a utility subsidiary must compete on its own in the market for debt capital, and therefore must earn an appropriate return on equity to support its credit rating. Imputing the parent's weighted cost to the utility's equity capital may result in inadequate equity returns and less favorable coverage, hence impairing the utility subsidiary's ability to attract debt capital under favorable terms.

Questionable Assumptions

Several assumptions underlying the double leverage standard are questionable. One assumption to which the previous numerical illustrations have already alluded, is the traceability of the subsidiary's equity capital to its parent. None of the subsidiary's retained earnings can be traced to the capital raised by the parent. Some analysts salvage the double leverage approach by assigning one cost rate to retained earnings and another to the common equity capital raised by the parent, with the curious result that equity has two cost rates. The traceability issue goes further. If a parent company issues bonds or preferred stock to acquire an operating subsidiary, the traceability assumption is broken. Corporate reorganizations and mergers further invalidate the traceability assumption.

By virtue of using the parent's weighted cost as the equity cost rate for the subsidiary, another questionable assumption is that the parent capital is invested in subsidiaries that all have the same risks. Lastly, the double leverage procedure makes the unlikely assumption that the parent holding company invest its funds in each subsidiary proportionately to each subsidiary's debt-equity ratio, which is unreasonable.

Double Leverage: A Tautology

The double leverage approach is a tautology. It is not the parent's weighted average cost of capital (WACC) that determines the subsidiary's cost of equity because the parent's WACC is itself a weighted average of equity costs of all subsidiaries. Double leverage adherents confuse the direction of cause and effect. The equity cost of subsidiaries must be found on a stand-alone basis.

The last nail in the double leverage coffin can be shown as follows. If capital market equilibrium is to hold, the cash flows to the parent company's bondholders and stockholders must equal the cash flows from the parent's equity in each subsidiary. Letting K denote the cost of capital, the subscripts p and s denote the parent and subsidiary, D and E the dollar amounts of debt and equity, and the subscripts d and e denote debt and equity, we can therefore say:

$$K_{dp} D_p + K_{ep} E_p = \sum_s^n K_{es} W_s \qquad (20\text{-}1)$$

The various unknowns, including the parent return on equity, can be found in terms of all the other given variables. What the above equation makes clear is that the parent cost of equity is determined by subsidiary cost of equity, and that parent capital costs cannot determine subsidiary capital costs. This can be seen even more clearly by dividing the above equation by total parent value V to obtain:

$$K_{dp} D_p/V + K_{ep} E_p/V = \sum_s^n K_{es} E_s/V \qquad (20\text{-}2)$$

The left side of the equation is the usual expression for the parent's WACC, and the right side is the weighted average of equity costs of all subsidiaries. However,

$$\sum_s^n E_s = V \qquad (20\text{-}3)$$

so that the parent's WACC is itself a weighted average of equity costs of all subsidiaries. The fundamental logical fault of double leverage is to arbitrarily equate the equity cost of each subsidiary to the left side of the above equation. The inescapable conclusion is that the subsidiary cost of equity must be found on a stand-alone basis, because the parent's WACC is itself a weighted average of subsidiary equity costs.

EXAMPLE 20-1

In the numerical example provided at the beginning of the chapter in Table 20-1, the parent's cost of equity capital was arbitrarily and wrongly assumed to be 15%. This example shows that the parent cost of equity consistent with the terms of the example is 23.33%, and not 15%. The fundamental point of the illustration was to show the logical inconsistency of the double leverage argument. When an illustration is constructed with an assumed subsidiary cost of equity, the assumed parent cost of equity must be consistent with it. This is shown below.

If the subsidiary was regulated in the standard correct way, the allowed return is computed as .50 x 10% + .50 x 20% = 15%. According to advocates of double leverage, this implies excess returns to the parent, that is:

Earnings from the subsidiary to the parent: $100 x 15% = $15.00
       less total interest: $50 x 10% + $12.50 x 10% = $ 6.25
Earnings to parent equity: $ 8.75

which represents a return of $8.75/$37.50 = 23.33%, far in excess of the *assumed* parent equity cost of 15%.

Double leverage advocates adjust for this alleged excess by assigning the parent's overall return of 13.75% to the subsidiary's equity. The subsidiary's overall return becomes 11.875%, as shown below:

	Amount	Weight	Cost	Weighted Cost
Debt-Subsidiary	$50.00	.500	.10	.05000
Equity-provided by parent:				
Debt-parent (25%)	$12.50	.125	.10	.01250
Equity-parent (75%)	$37.50	.375	.15	.05625
		Weighted Cost		.11875

The 11.875% becomes the double leverage allowed return on the subsidiary's total assets. Only with this allowed rate of return, according to the tenets of double leverage, does the parent's equity receive the *assumed* rate of return of 15%. That is, the parent receives $100 x 11.875% = $11.875, less the interest cost of $6.250, or $5.625, on an equity investment of $37.50, which is a is a 15% return. And, so it seems, the parent receives the required rate of return.

The fundamental flaw of this approach is that the assumptions of the example are internally inconsistent and illogical. When an illustration is constructed with assumed subsidiary cost of equity, the assumed parent cost of equity must be consistent with it. It is not the parent's weighted average cost of capital that determines the subsidiary's cost of equity because the parent's cost of capital is itself a weighted average of equity costs of all subsidiaries.

Equation 20-2 makes it clear that the parent cost of equity is determined by the subsidiary cost of equity, and that parent capital costs cannot determine subsidiary capital costs. Given the cost of debt K_{dp}, the subsidiary's cost of equity K_{es}, and the amounts of capital, the above equation implies that the parent equity cost consistent with 20% subsidiary cost of equity is 23.33%:

$$[\$50 \times 20\% - \$12.50 \times 10\%]/\,\$37.50 = 23.33\%$$

In summary, the double leverage adjustment has serious conceptual and practical limitations and violates basic notions of finance, economics, and fairness. The assumptions which underlie its use are questionable, if not unrealistic. The approach should not be used in regulatory proceedings.

References

Beranek, W. and Miles, J.A. "The Excess Return Argument and Double Leverage." *The Financial Review,* May 1988, 145-151.

Lerner, E.M. "What Are the Real Double Leverage Problems?" *Public Utilities Fortnightly,* June 7, 1973, 18-23.

Morin, R. A. and Andrews, V.L. *Determining Cost of Capital for Regulated Industries,* Public Utilities Reports Inc. and The Management Exchange Inc., Washington DC, 1993.

Pettway, R.H. and Jordan, B.D. "Diversification, Double Leverage, and the Cost of Capital." *Journal of Financial Research,* Winter 1983. 289-300.

Rozeff, M.S. "Modified Double Leverage: A New Approach." *Public Utilities Fortnightly,* March 1983, 31-36.

Stich, R.S. "The Four Fables of Double Leverage." *Public Utilities Fortnightly,* Aug. 8, 1985, 36-40.

Chapter 21
Alternative Regulatory Frameworks

21.1 Introduction

A review of the procedures and methods employed in orthodox rate of return regulation ("RORR") and an examination of alternatives is particularly timely in view of the profound technological, social, and political changes that are taking place in the utility industry.[1] On the one hand, policies designed to foster competition and efficiency have been promulgated, while at the same time a possibly outmoded regulatory regime based on cost and monopoly assumptions is prevalent. The cohabitation of competition and regulation, to the extent that it exists, is unhealthy. The potential result is that society will have the worst of both worlds, whereby the benefits and efficiency gains of competition and the advantages of traditional regulation are both denied.

The business environment of the utility industry is changing rapidly. Because of technology as well as governmental and regulatory actions, the traditional role of utility companies is undergoing a profound change. Competition now prevails in several of the utility companies' services and important markets (bypass, power wheeling, unbundling of services, etc.). Customers have alternative means of filling their communication, information, and energy needs. Given the intensification of competition and the attendant pressure on rate schedules to reflect cost, the need for reexamining the regulatory framework is apparent.

Not only is the new competitive environment of the utility industry challenging the relevance of RORR, but very broad economic factors are reinforcing the need to reexamine RORR. The role of the service economy is increasing. A competitive global economy is emerging, and current regulatory structures must be supportive of the ability to compete. In this environment, economic wealth, social welfare, and the ability to compete will clearly depend on the availability of innovative, reasonably-priced utility services. Utilities need to access new markets and need to respond in a timely manner to customer and competitive pressures.

Alternatives to RORR have already been adopted by several regulatory commissions. These include allowed ROE ranges, performance-linked allowed ROEs, return-sharing mechanisms between ratepayers and

---

[1] An excellent review of alternative regulatory frameworks and reference source for portions of this chapter is provided by Sikes (1987).

483

shareholders, price caps, social contract regulation, and incentive regulation, among others. The benefits of such plans provide the regulated company with the ability to respond to competitive pressures, provide socially beneficial differentiated prices, and avoid various administrative and compliance costs. Moreover, under these regimes, the companies possess the necessary incentives to be cost-efficient, which they do not entirely possess under traditional RORR.

The objectives of this chapter are to: (1) evaluate the present system of regulating utilities, and (2) describe and critically evaluate alternative forms of regulation according to several criteria. Of course, it is not intended to serve as an exhaustive treatment of alternative regulatory frameworks, but rather to provide an overview of the issues. Rigorous and exhaustive treatment of the subject abound elsewhere.

The chapter is organized as follows. Section 21.1 describes the role of regulation as a surrogate for competition and its appropriateness in a competitive environment and presents criteria by which a regulatory regime should be evaluated. Section 21.2 critically reviews various alternative regulatory frameworks ("ARFs") based on those criteria. Both Incentive Regulation and Price Regulation ARFs are considered. Concluding remarks appear in Section 21.3.

21.2 The Role of Regulation

As discussed in Chapter 1, public utility regulation replaces the free market system by establishing allowable prices for the rendering of public services. The purpose of regulation is to replicate the results that the competitive market system would achieve in the way of reasonable prices and profits. Public utilities can operate at substantially lower costs under monopolistic conditions than under competition by eliminating the duplication of costly plant facilities and distribution networks, or by facilitating the realization of optimal plant sizes and economies of demand diversity.

Figure 21-1 displays the traditional economics of a public utility's product and the reason for regulation.[2] The shaded area shows the excess profits earned by a monopolist, which can only be earned by restricting output. Figure 21-2 shows the difference between the regulated price and quantity $P_R Q_R$ and the monopoly result $P_M Q_M$. The regulated price will be such that the price equals the average cost, which includes a normal profit rate. RORR mitigates the effects of monopoly pricing by constraining total revenues (TR) toward the levels achieved under competition, as shown in Figure 21-2.

---

[2] This discussion can be found in most college-level microeconomics textbooks.

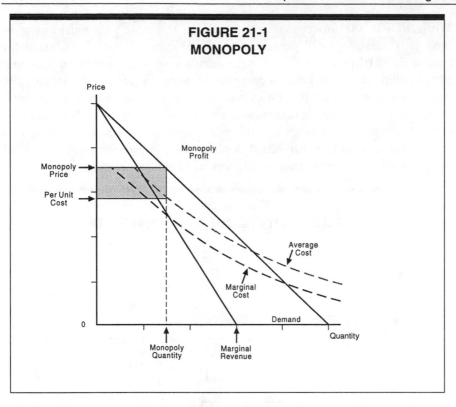

FIGURE 21-1
MONOPOLY

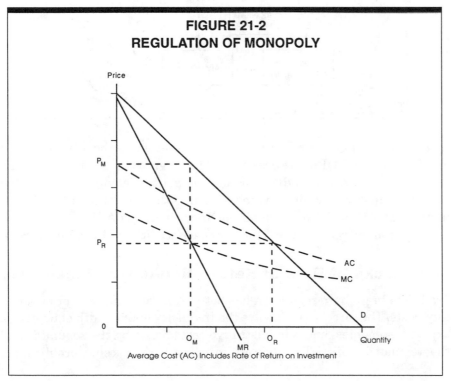

FIGURE 21-2
REGULATION OF MONOPOLY

Average Cost (AC) Includes Rate of Return on Investment

While RORR has functioned adequately in the past in a world of pure monopoly and may still provide a reasonable regulatory foundation for traditional utility services, its relevance in an industry with growing competition across a broad spectrum of services is questionable. The fundamental rationale for the existence of regulation is that it acts as a proxy for competition, and therefore regulation is largely redundant in a competitive market. Deregulation is always the preferred alternative in a competitive market. Figure 21-3 depicts the fundamental premise that competition should supplant regulation whenever market forces exist.

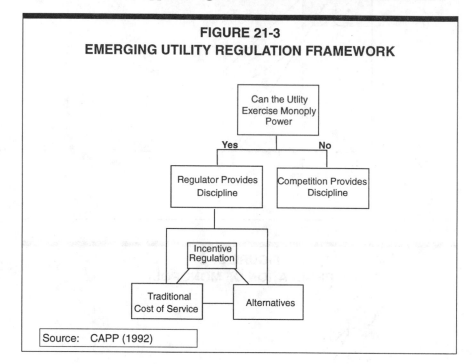

FIGURE 21-3
EMERGING UTILITY REGULATION FRAMEWORK

Source: CAPP (1992)

In the increasingly competitive global marketplace, the rigidities and inefficiencies of RORR are less tolerable. A growing awareness of the drawbacks of RORR in a dynamic and competitive environment has led several regulatory jurisdictions to reexamine the relevance of RORR and implement ARFs. Before examining these various ARFs, some soul-searching on the relevance and limitations of traditional RORR is in order.

Drawbacks of Rate of Return Regulation Incentives

Traditional rate base regulation has both direct and indirect, or opportunity, costs. The direct costs involve the frequency and breadth of hearings, expert testimonies, and administrative costs borne by the regulator and the regulated utility. The indirect costs, which are considerably more important than the direct costs in magnitude, involve the lack of incentives to minimize production cost and to innovate.

Generally, there are two aspects to these indirect opportunity costs: (1) the potential for over-capitalization and (2) the potential for inflated operating expenses, wages, and overhead. With regard to the over-capitalization argument, while there is no conclusive academic evidence of over- or under-capitalization, there is nevertheless some effect on managerial behavior. Additions to rate base are not necessarily guided by the discipline of the free marketplace under orthodox RORR. With respect to the distortion of operating costs, management is clearly disinclined to minimize operating costs under traditional "pass-through" regulation. There is the added temptation to shift costs from unregulated to regulated services in order to reduce prices of unregulated services. Of course, there are constraints on the inflation of operating costs in the existing regulatory regime, for example, the disallowances of certain imprudent and excessive costs. Consumer demand and price elasticity considerations will impose some constraints on distorted operating costs. Also, the presence of regulatory lag provides some incentive to reduce costs during the period of regulatory lag.

The inherent presence of regulatory lag in RORR dampens incentives to innovate and to introduce new services to the extent that the utility is unable to capture the cost savings of its innovations. Frequently, the payoff of its innovations and efficiency gains are asymmetric; cost savings from successful innovations are passed on to ratepayers, while unsuccessful ventures are disallowed and absorbed by investors. The net result is that utilities may use capital/labor ratios that are not cost-minimizing. Although regulatory lag can be dampened by the use of forward test years and interim rate provisions, any regulatory lag can be detrimental to the utility's ability to respond promptly to competitive challenges. The presence of regulatory lag also makes it difficult to earn a reasonable rate of return, especially in an inflationary environment.

Lack of Pricing Flexibility. With intensified competition in a given market, pricing flexibility is required in order to remove or constrain existing cross-subsidies. Cross-subsidies provide opportunities for competitors to bypass the utility's facilities and skim the profits from selected services. With traditional RORR, pricing flexibility can be stringent and burdensome if hearings are required for rate restructuring and if a tariff approval process is required to alter rates. Orthodox RORR can place utilities at a serious competitive disadvantage in a fast-moving and changing competitive marketplace. Regulatory lag further limits the pricing flexibility, and the company may be unable to respond to competitive pressures.

Regulatory Burden. Traditional RORR is costly. The process requires judgment on complex technical issues such as rate base, optimal capital structure, cost of capital, and the allocation of joint common costs. All this takes place in a quasi-judicial adversarial proceeding. Expert studies have demonstrated that traditional RORR creates undesirable incentives to overinvest and distort rate structures uneconomically, and fails to provide incentives to minimize operating costs. The process creates the danger of a "cost plus" mentality.

Other costs are created as a consequence of traditional RORR. Cost-shifting among regulated and competitive services and potential predatory pricing require costly controls such as accounting separations or structural separations. The typical basis for allocating joint and common costs is accounting mechanisms, which are arbitrary and imperfect. The resulting uneconomic allocation of costs produces inefficient prices and a further misallocation of resources.

The traditional regulatory process is ritualistic and susceptible to a lack of objectivity. One alleged ritual is that of excessive requests, in the hope of achieving a lower but acceptable level of rates. There are several wasteful and costly gaming aspects involved in regulatory activities. The process is somewhat intrusive, and frequently infringes on management prerogatives. A fairer, more effective, less manipulable, and less legalistic system is required. The adversarial, rigid, and procedural nature of the existing process must give way to a more flexible, lighter, and more expedient regime, which is also less administratively burdensome. This agility is crucial in the dynamic, fast-moving global marketplace.

It is sometimes argued that non-price dimensions of utility products may be ignored by strict adherence to the limitation of profits. Quality of service, reliability, and safety of service may be compromised according to this argument. But the fact that utilities are greatly exposed to public criticism for inadequate service tempers this argument. If anything, there is an inclination to expand the rate base and improve service in rate-of-return regulation. Besides, additional costs of improving service can always be included in the cost of service. A thorough reading of the literature leaves one with the feeling that in spite of its failings, rate of return regulation remains the best overall regulatory framework.

In summary, traditional RORR creates undesirable incentives to overinvest, to distort rate structures uneconomically, and to operate at inflated cost. There are compelling reasons to investigate alternatives to RORR regulation: (1) to provide superior incentives for cost-cutting and operational efficiency, (2) to pursue greater product and service innovation, (3) to be more responsive to competitive market pressures, and (4) to set more economically efficient prices. The question remains as to whether the alternatives to RORR are superior in achieving the objectives of regulation and satisfying the criteria enumerated below.

There are numerous precedents in several industries that regulatory reform improves efficiency and reduces costs. The role of government regulation has been reassessed in several industries, including airlines, telecommunications, and financial institutions. Entry restrictions have been liberalized, and the level and intensity of regulatory controls have been reduced. Comprehensive regulatory reform might generate similar benefits in the utility industry. Whatever mode of regulation is selected, it should be more cost-effective, encourage firms to offer innovative services and keep pace with technological change, provide incentives to minimize production costs, and provide ample flexibility and agility in pricing competitive services.

Modest advances and reforms have already been implemented within the confines of traditional RORR. Steps taken by regulators to improve regulation include return incentive bands, rigorous cost separation standards, miscellaneous stabilization and normalization accounts (weather, short-term interest rate variations), and expedited tariff approvals. Although such improvements have proved beneficial, a more fundamental reexamination and reform of traditional RORR is in order.

Traditional RORR has served us well in the past and may continue to do so in the future. Its positive attributes merit mention. First, under the approach of authorizing a range in ROE rather than a single point estimate as in some jurisdictions, with rates set at the midpoint, the ability of utilities to retain earnings in the upper portion of the range provides a modest incentive for efficiency. Second, traditional RORR does provide some assurance that investors will earn a fair and reasonable rate of return despite regulatory lag. Third, some pricing flexibility within the confines of traditional RORR has been achieved through removing tariffs on competitive services.

Framework for Analyzing Alternatives

Before proceeding to a critical review of ARFs, criteria are required in order to evaluate regulatory alternatives (Sikes, 1987). These criteria should reflect the fundamental socioeconomic goals of an effective regulatory regime. The criteria taken as a whole reflect a delicate balancing act. On the one hand, economic efficiency must be promoted by regulation. On the other hand, the regulatory regime must be reasonable, predictable, administrable, and equitable to investors and ratepayers. The specific criteria used to critically evaluate regulatory alternatives include:

1. *Efficiency Incentives*

   Incentives for cost minimization must be provided. Decreases in the direct and indirect costs of regulation, that is, operational efficiency, must be promoted.

2. *Innovation Incentives*

   Incentives to innovate and to invest in research and development and new technology must be present.

3. *Pricing Flexibility*

   Flexibility in pricing non-monopolistic services must be present. The flexibility to price individual services promotes the efficient allocation of resources and improves the utility's ability to respond to competitive forces and meet the customers' needs.

4. *Administrative Efficiency*

   Any regulatory regime must be simple to administer, predictable, flexible, and minimize the direct costs of regulation. Data and information requirements must be minimized as well.

5. *Adequate Returns to Investors*

   Any regulatory regime must provide investors with a fair and reasonable return commensurate with the risk of the investment and with a reasonable opportunity to earn that return.

6. *Fairness*

   Any regulatory plan must provide benefits to all parties involved: regulators, investors, ratepayers, and utility management. A regulatory regime must also provide a forum for ratepayers to air complaints. Public benefits must be provided.

7. *Quality of Service*

   Any regulatory plan must promote the quality of service rendered.

8. *Rate Predictability and Consistency*

   Any ARF must result in predictable and consistent service rates. Any viable alternative to RORR must also address the issues of: (1) predatory pricing, (2) cross-subsidization, and (3) market power.

Lastly, any ARF must proceed from the fundamental premise that service rates reflect true cost. If rates for one service are far below cost, while rates for another service are well above cost, the latter provides a significant social subsidy to the former and constitutes a major component of the total cost of providing that service. If there is competition in providing that service, the current cross-subsidy is unsustainable. Competitive entry will force subsidies out of the regulatory system. Given the increasingly competitive environment in the utility industry, any ARF must accomodate the transition to cost-based pricing methodologies. When the transition to a rational rate structure is complete, departure(s) from traditional RORR can then be contemplated.

In the telecommunications industry in the early 1990s, for example, as competition has shifted pricing schedules to a cost basis, telephone companies' ("telco") rate structure have been under pressure to reflect cost. Given the existing technological alternatives and a fragile rate structure (a structure that reflects public policy for many services rather than pricing based on economic costs), there are incentives for large-volume users to leave a telco's network and seek alternative providers to meet their telecommunications requirements. Because large-volume users typically represent a substantial proportion of total revenues, the loss of these customers would have serious financial consequences for both the telcos and their customers. This risk can be compounded by the lack of pricing flexibility in dealing with large users under status quo regulation. The ability of telcos to subsidize local rates using toll rates that are above cost continues to diminish. By providing local service at rates below cost, long-term business risks are increased since the rates for other services have to be priced in excess of the rates available from a competitor. A similar set of circumstances exists in the electric utility generation business.

To be successful, an ARF should be preceded by a rationalization of service rates and associated costs. To offset the revenue shortfalls caused by the reduction in rates from competitive services, rates on monopolistic services should first be realigned to achieve cost parity.

21.3 Alternatives to ROR Regulation

Although traditional RORR has served its purpose well until now, the introduction of competition questions its continued applicability, and alternatives must be examined.[3] The character of RORR has remained remarkably static in sharp contrast to the dynamic changes in the utility industry's environment. A wide spectrum of ARFs, which are more suited to a competitive environment and which purport to address the limitations of

---

[3] This section draws from Morin and Andrews (1993).

RORR, are available, ranging from minor variations of RORR, to radical departures from rate of return-style intervention, to outright deregulation.

The various ARFs can be classified into two broad species: Incentive Regulation (or Modified ROR) and Price Regulation. The first species works within the confines of traditional RORR but involves modifications, extensions, and refinements of RORR. The principal variants of Incentive Regulation include Incentive Return and Zone of Reasonableness—Sharing Mechanisms. The second species, frequently referred to as Social Contract regulation, involves a departure from rate of return regulation toward price of service regulation, and includes Banded Rates and Price Cap regulation. Other regulatory mechanisms involve Automatic Rate Adjustments, Focused Incentives, and Market-Basket/Yardstick.

Of course, the various frameworks are not mutually exclusive, as features of each can be combined. For example, the Federal Communications Commission's model of regulating interexchange telecommunications carriers represents a broad mixture of price caps, banded rates, earnings sharing, and zone of reasonabless regulation.

Incentive Regulation

Incentive Return: Overview. Formal company-wide comprehensive incentive plans centering on the allowed rate of return have been developed in several jurisdictions. In essence, an incentive premium in excess of the authorized rate of return is granted as an incentive device and/or to reward the attainment of a certain performance objective. Benefits accrue to both investors and ratepayers, the former in the form of enhanced profitability, and the latter in the form of reduced costs. The ROE increment is frequently tied to a specific performance target, for example a given ratio of actual/filed capital spending program. More importantly, the ROE increment is applied in order to reward overall management performance as opposed to the attainment of a narrow, specific objective. Two contrasting plans are representative and noteworthy.

Under the Alabama Public Service Commission's incentive plan, known as Rate Stabilization and Equalization (RSE), a range in allowable rate of return is allowed, instead of a single-point return figure. Rates are adjusted automatically on a quarterly basis whenever the earned ROE falls outside the allowed ROE band, without protracted hearings. There are no rate adjustments as long as the earned return falls within the allowed range. The idea of the plan is to provide some additional incentive for efficiency by allowing the company to keep some excess return.

The Mississippi Public Service Commission implemented a comprehensive incentive regulation plan, known as Performance Evaluation Plan (PEP), which provides a viable alternative to traditional RORR. The basic thrust of PEP is to replace "cost-plus" traditional RORR with a performance-based framework. Under PEP, management has the opportunity to earn a fair rate of return and, more importantly, has far more incentive to perform efficiently in relation to the old system, because the company, in this case Mississippi Power Company, has more to gain in the form of higher returns under PEP.

The plan takes the idea of the Alabama RSE plan one step further by indexing the allowed range of return to performance. The main purpose of the plan is to lessen the impact, frequency, and size of rate increase requests by permitting limited rate adjustments in order to maintain an approved return. At the same time, the purpose is to provide the company with an incentive to be efficient, reduce costs, and improve productivity by allowing an approved range of returns and allowing that range to increase with performance. The latter is measured by an index, obtained from scoring four aspects of performance, including rate comparisons with other utilities, customer satisfaction, service reliability, and equipment availability. The company's cost of capital is adjusted each quarter for this performance to obtain the Performance-Based Return on Investment. The company uses the earned return on overall capital rather than the earned return on common equity capital. This earned return on investment (EROI) is also the company's return on retail rate base, which is a commonly accepted measure in electric utility regulation.

Under PEP, retail rates may be increased, decreased, or remain the same, depending on the company's performance against predetermined financial and operational indicators. The company files information semi-annually, which allows the Commission to perform this evaluation. The incentive for the company arises from the fact that changes in monthly bills may not exceed two percentage points per semi-annual filling or four percent in any one calendar year.

After nearly eight years of experience with the PEP, rates have become more stable and lower, relative to traditional rate of return regulation, because of the performance incentive and the reduction in regulatory lag.

Since its inauguration in 1986, the plan has generally accomplished the objectives that any regulatory framework must accomplish. PEP has reduced the direct costs of regulation, by limiting the scope and frequency of rate cases. By permitting the allowed range of return to increase with improved performance, PEP has provided incentives that are considerably higher than orthodox RORR, resulting in lower indirect costs of regulation as well. Incentives for cost minimization and innovation have been provided. The plan has improved administrative efficiency, by virtue of its simplicity, predictability, and flexibility. The plan has also been equitable, in that benefits have been provided to all parties involved: regulators, investors, ratepayers, and utility employees. Lastly, PEP has reduced investor risk perceptions of the company as compared to other electric utilities. As shown in Morin (1993), the company's allowed and earned returns under the PEP procedure are fair and reasonable, and even conservative, as they are often less than those allowed for comparable electric utilities.

Incentive Return: Evaluation. Integrated incentive plans have advantages and disadvantages. The Alabama-style allowed ROE range does provide some additional incentive for efficiency by allowing the company to keep some excess return. The plan has reduced direct costs of regulation by limiting the scope and frequency of rate cases. But the plan has little pricing flexibility and limited options. The incentives are limited because any excess over range triggers rate reductions.

Under the more broadly-based performance-indexed plans, such as Mississippi's PEP plan, the company enjoys automatic rate relief so long as it remains within the adjustment limits. The relief increases or decreases with achieved performance. Under these conditions, returns will be more constant and predictable, and rates lower because of the performance incentive.

The plan certainly reduces the direct costs of regulation, by limiting the scope and frequency of rate cases. At the same time, the plan has little pricing flexibility and limited options. In contrast to the Alabama RSE plan, however, the incentives are considerably higher because the allowed range of return is permitted to increase with improved performance.

Although such comprehensive incentive plans represent minimal departure from orthodox RORR, the major drawback is that the performance standards are highly arbitrary, and so are the weights given to the performance components. This style of incentive plan is difficult to implement if performance benchmarks are scarce and/or the comparable companies are heterogeneous in terms of market and service territory circumstances. Moreover, there is no additional flexibility given to adjust prices in responses to competitive forces or to changes in cost/supply/demand.

Incentive plans generally offer little advantage if rates are misaligned with costs. If competition has entered those markets that generate rate subsidies, there is a chronic tendency to earn the low end of the allowed return range.

Zone of Reasonableness—Sharing: Overview. Under this regime, a range in rate of return is authorized instead of a point estimate following a traditional rate hearing. An allowed range of rate of return is established after a lengthy hearing, and rates are reduced if the upper limit is exceeded, and conversely. This style of regulation is certainly less stringent than orthodox RORR where profits are regulated by a single-value rate of return. More importantly, the range serves as an incentive device by motivating the company to minimize costs and operate efficiently so as to attain the top end of the authorized range.

Zone of reasonableness ARFs are frequently accompanied by a sharing mechanism that allows the company to retain a portion of earned profits above the upper bound of a "reasonableness zone," with the balance of overearnings refunded to ratepayers, and conversely. A limit is frequently imposed on the sharing arrangements.

Such profit-sharing plans are common with telcos and provide potent incentives to reduce costs and increase revenues. Attempts to avoid sharing by inflating costs or operating expenditures and attempts to absorb excess earnings by excessive capital expenditures are unlikely. The role of management is to maximize its shareholders' wealth, and this is accomplished by maximizing shareholders' earnings over time. Management would violate this mandate by raising expenses simply to avoid sharing. Any such attempt would simply hurt the company's investors.

These plans are frequently accompanied with a set of conditions and privileges. Often, the company agrees to a rate reduction or prohibition on future rate increases for a specified time period in exchange for price flexibility for its competitive services.

Zone of Reasonableness—Sharing: Evaluation. There are three advantages of authorizing a reasonable ROE range rather than a single point estimate. The first is that providing a zone of reasonableness for the authorized ROE permits the regulator the flexibility of weighing other factors, such as rate base, capital structure, and incentive provisions in its decision, with the assurance that the ROE estimate is within a reasonable range.

The second is that capital markets are volatile, and reasoned judgment is important. The results of mechanical approaches to estimating ROE are subject to measurement error, small sample bias, and turbulence in capital markets. Thus, estimating ROE for ratemaking purposes must take a longer-term and a more flexible view.

The third, and most important, is that a range serves as an incentive device by encouraging the company to minimize costs and operate efficiently so as to attain the top end of the authorized range. Allowing a range of permissible returns instead of a specific number, within which the utility's return could fluctuate, reaping some reward for success, and penalty for failure, provides utility management some incentive for efficiency. It does not entirely possess these incentives under traditional rate of return regulation. Moreover, authorizing a range in ROE provides the regulated company with some ability to respond to competitive pressures and avoid some administrative and compliance costs.

Five issues germane to zone of reasonableness ARFs include: the appropriate width of the band, the issue of symmetry, the incidence of capital additions, differential risk effects across companies, and the formula for sharing earned profits.

Width of the Band

Whether the zone is wide enough to provided adequate incentive is certainly an issue. Brigham and Aberwald (1988) provided an excellent analysis of the issue. Figure 21-4, drawn from their work, displays variations of the earned rate of of return over time with four alternative mechanisms for resetting the earned return back to the allowed return.

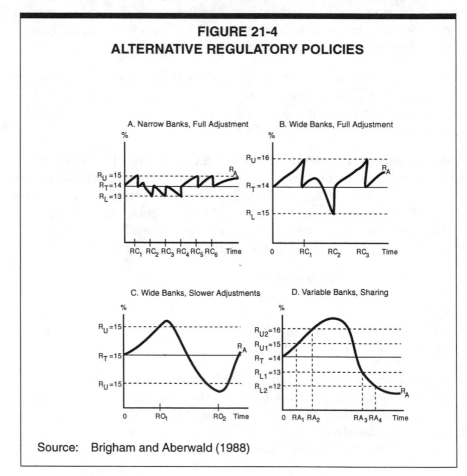

FIGURE 21-4
ALTERNATIVE REGULATORY POLICIES

Source: Brigham and Aberwald (1988)

The first of the four mechanisms in Figure 21-4 uses a narrow zone of reasonableness with instantaneous rapid adjustments. As a result, rate hearings are numerous and the earned return closely tracks the allowed return. Such a regime is remarkably close to the current cost-plus aspect of RORR, and offers limited incentives for operational efficiency and innovation. The second mechanism employs wider bands with instantaneous rapid adjustments. As a result, rate hearings are less frequent, and incentives to reduce costs and market new service offerings are promoted because of the opportunity to earn a reasonable return over a longer period. However, the incentives evaporate as the earned return approaches the upper limit of the zone and may even provide disincentives for further efficiency gains. Similarly at the lower end of the band, there are disincentives to perform so as to trigger a rate case. The third mechanism employs wider bands with slower rate adjustments. The fourth mechanism involves a dual wide band regime with slower adjustments along with provisions for ratepayer sharing. Two upper and lower bands are set. When the earned return touches one of the bands, rates are not immediately adjusted so as to drive the earned return toward the allowed return. Instead, the adjustment is designed to cause ratepayers to share in further efficiency gains in the upper portion of the zone and force investors to share in further innefficiencies in the lower portion. The latter regime is superior from the standpoint of providing continuous incentives for efficiency and continuous disincentives for cost increases.

Symmetry

It is important that the sharing mechanism be symmetrical in its apportionment of gains and losses between shareholders and ratepayers. While the preferred alternative is symmetry, if ratepayers are allowed to share gains in excess of the authorized range but not losses below the range, the effect on the plan's lack of symmetry on investor returns must be considered. A reasonable remedy is to add a risk premium that compensates investors for the limited upside returns/unlimited downside returns asymmetry versus comparable risk companies. Assuming some plausible probability distribution of investor equity returns both with and without the sharing plan, the added premium is required to offset the plan's lack of upside potential and produce the same average return that would prevail under orthodox regulation.

Capital Additions

It is also important that zone of reasonableness ARFs be consistent with the rate of capital additions and the concomitant increase in output for a given utility. For example, a utility with a growing rate base has an inherent tendency to earn the bottom of the range, and yet is unable to seek rate relief. Such a utility has an unfair opportunity to earn a fair return relative to other utilities, and possesses a disincentive to engage in capital investments.

Differential Risk Effects

Another source of individual company risk is that the effects of a zone of reasonableness band will vary greatly from company to company. Those companies with low Capital/Net Operating Income (C/X) ratios are more affected than companies with high C/X ratios for a given zone of reasonableness. For example,[4] a zone of reasonableness of +-2% around a given midpoint implies a swing of +- 16 % Net Operating Income (NOI) before a company with a C/X ratio of 4.8 is out of the zone. The lower the C/X, the greater is the effect of a change in operating profitability. Zone of reasonableness adjustment is much more likely for low C/X telcos than for high

---

[4] This is formally discussed in Morin and Andrews (1993) and in Andrews, V.L. (1992). The derivation is shown below:

Let $x = NOI$ and let C/X denote the capital/NOI ratio. Using a representative value of C/X = 4.8 times, that is, the company requires \$4.80 capital per dollar of NOI. Therefore, assuming a gain of 1% in NOI, a corporate tax rate (T) of 40%, the after tax gain is given by:

$$(1-T)(1\%) = (0.6)(1\%) = 0.6\%$$

Because the capital/NOI ratio is 4.8, then

$$ROR = [(0.6X)]/(C/X) = [(0.6)(1\%)]/4.8 = 0.6\%/4.8 = .125$$

In other words, a unit change in NOI results in a corresponding change of 12.5% in ROR. Put another way, given the stated parameters, a percentage point gain or loss in NOI corresponds to a gain or loss of 8 percentage points in ROE:

$$ROR = 0.125 \ NOI$$

$$8 \ ROR = NOI$$

$$8\% \ ROE = 1\% \ NOI$$

If the zone of reasonableness is +- 2 percentage points around the mid-point, companies can undergo swings of +-16 percentage points in NOI without hitting the upper and lower limits.

$$(8) \ (+2\% \ ROR) = +16\% \ NOI$$

or

$$(8) \ (-2\% \ ROR) = -16\% \ NOI$$

C/X telcos. Nor is a given zone of reasonableness band neutral with respect to the debt/equity mix of individual companies. The presence of leverage compounds functioning of the zone of reasonableness. Higher debt/equity ratios will widen swings of return on equity for a given change in returns to capital *ROI*. The major point of this is that an ARF is not neutral on its effect on risk and return.

Sharing Formula

Three broad options are possible: (1) funnel approach, (2) graduated approach, and (3) predetermined simple formula approach. In the first sharing option, any initial excess or deficiency above or below the benchmark for the first x% accrues entirely to the shareholders. Any further excess or deficiency is shared between customers and investors according to some linear progressive formula. In the case of excess earnings, the sharing is linearly progressive without a cap; in the case of an earnings deficiency, it accrues entirely to investors without any floor. However, investors could recoup a portion of any deficiency if the company has generated excess earnings during the contract period.

The second option is a graduated sharing mechanism. This option is theoretically superior because a properly structured graduated sharing mechanism could increase the incentives for efficiency improvements beyond that of simple formula sharing plans. Graduated sharing reflects the economic principle that each incremental unit of productivity improvement is more difficult to obtain than the prior unit. Therefore, as earnings increase above the benchmark level, management must be encouraged to increase productivity further by allowing shareholders to retain an increasing percentage of the shareable earnings.

The third option is that earnings above the benchmark rate of return are shared on a predetermined formula basis with ratepayers, for example 50/50, 75/25, or 25/75, with no floor or ceilings on the ROE. The sharing is accomplished through a surcredit applied to the monthly recurring charges for all services, or for those services under the auspices of the plan. The surcredit is applied to return a total of whatever agreed upon percentage sharing the earnings exceeded the benchmark ROE over a predetermined period, say one year.

One danger under this simple sharing formula option is that since there is no earnings ceiling or floor, and since the plan is to remain in force for several years, the exposure and risks to the shareholders could be higher than under traditional RORR. Under such circumstances, the payoff to investors is asymmetric, since there is sharing of gains beyond the benchmark but no sharing of losses below the benchmark. To compensate for the added risks inherent in this option, a risk premium could be added to the "business as usual" benchmark.

These simple formula plans have the advantage of simplicity and expediency, and are easy to administer. One possible disadvantage of the option is the added risks from the asymmetric nature of the payoff, and what constitutes an adequate compensation for those added risks. In contrast to the other sharing options, the simple formula sharing plan is less cumbersome to administer, but it produces less symmetry between ratepayers and investors.

Price Regulation

Banded Rates: Overview. In a banded pricing method, regulators set a midpoint price and then allow prices to vary in either direction by some prespecified amount. Another variant of this approach is to set minimum and maximum prices for each service as boundaries, and allow discretion between these boundaries. The widths are adjusted over time. The bands can apply to all services, or more typically to utility services only, while competitive services are deregulated.

Economic theory suggests that markets where monopoly power exists should be regulated, but not based on some predetermined ROR. Instead, regulation should be confined to the regulation of prices themselves. Prices should be regulated to be above the incremental cost and below the stand-alone cost [5] of a given product or service, because these benchmark prices comprise the range of prices observed in a competitive market. Therefore, in a banded pricing regime, the lower and upper bounds should be set at incremental cost and stand-alone cost, respectively. The regulated firm should set prices within this range, and the resulting price caps would insure that no profits above competitive levels could be earned. No additional constraints on profits or ROR are required, at least in theory.

Larson and Monson (1987) offered an original graphical analysis of economic pricing and of alternative regulatory pricing policies. Assuming a two-service regulated firm, Figure 21-5 illustrates possible combinations of prices for the two services, x and y. The curve AB represents combinations of prices that produce revenues and costs that exactly cover the firm's revenue requirement.

---

[5] The stand-alone price of a service is the total cost that an efficient company would incur to produce that service alone; if a company produces two products X and Y, the stand-alone cost of X would be the cost of producing X without the scale economies available from the joint production of X and Y.

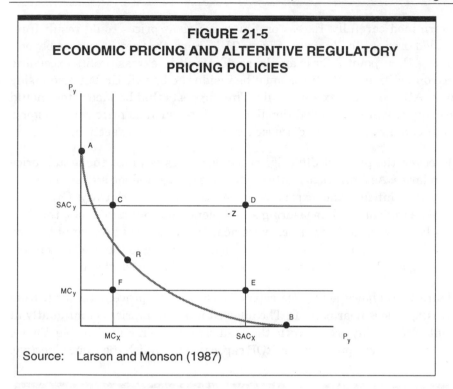

FIGURE 21-5
ECONOMIC PRICING AND ALTERNTIVE REGULATORY PRICING POLICIES

Source: Larson and Monson (1987)

The marginal cost and stand-alone benchmark prices are also shown in Figure 21-5, forming the feasible region CDEF. Point F represents the marginal cost pricing level for both services. In this latter case, the prices are insufficient to cover the company's costs of service. Point D represents the stand-alone cost pricing level for both services. Point R represents the Ramsay prices[6] for both services.

Banded Rates: Evaluation.   On the positive side, the banded pricing regime is simple and reduces the direct costs of regulation since fewer rate filings are required. The method grants some pricing flexibility to the regulated company, and creates incentives to minimize costs since any cost savings are not automatically passed through to ratepayers. The method also reduces cost misallocations because regulatory services are capped; any attempt to inflate costs signifies less profits. There is no threat of anti-competitive cross-subsidies.

On the negative side, the method does not ensure that investors will earn a reasonable rate of return, unless the lower and upper bounds are

---

[6] Ramsay prices allocate unattributable costs across customer classes in inverse proportion to price elasticity, and maximize producer-consumer surplus under perfect competition.

determined carefully. Excess profits or deficient prices could result from banded pricing. To illustrate, Figure 21-5 shows that setting prices beyond curve AB, at point Z for example, could result in excess profits exceeding the competitive level. Prices must be inside the box CDEF but also inside curve AB to prevent excess profits. This suggests that banded rates should be complemented with additional constraints, such as price caps and/or a profit cap. Price caps are discussed in detail in the next section.

Moreover, the greatest difficulty of banded rates is to set the actual price boundaries. As a practical matter, estimates of stand-alone and incremental costs are difficult and expensive to locate and are arbitrary. Given the extreme difficulties of measuring stand-alone and marginal costs, the firm may be allowed to choose price pairs near the upper right corner of the box CDEF, such as point Z in Figure 21-5, again pointing to the need of complementing banded rates with price cap and/or profit cap constraints.

Figure 21-6 shows how price caps can be used to prevent the firm from choosing prices near point D. The allowed maximum prices occur jointly at point D'. Now only price pairs in the shaded area C'D'E'F are feasible. Figure 21-7 shows how a profit cap, or ROE cap, can accomplish the same objective.

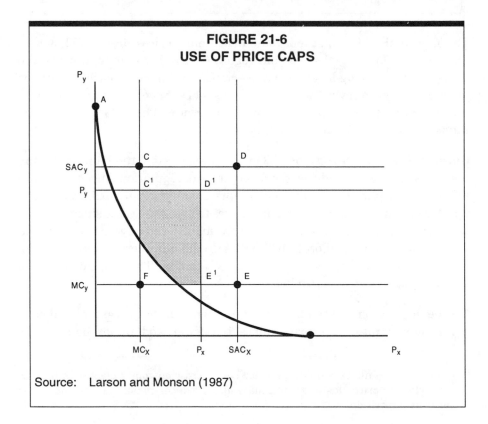

FIGURE 21-6
USE OF PRICE CAPS

Source: Larson and Monson (1987)

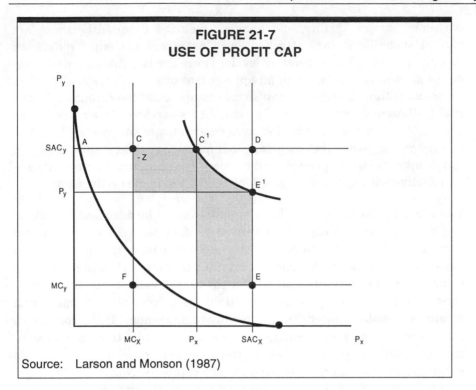

FIGURE 21-7
USE OF PROFIT CAP

Source: Larson and Monson (1987)

If only a profit cap is used, as shown in Figure 21-7, then any price in the truncated box C'CE'EF can be charged. Prices in the area C'DE' are excluded. If price caps were to be used to achieve the same price points, setting price caps P_x and P_y would also exclude the same points. But they also exclude the shaded area of Figure 21-7, which may be too restrictive a pricing policy when used alone.

Social Contract—Price Cap: Overview. Under Social Contract, or Price Cap, regulation prevalent in the regulation of U.S. telcos, local exchange rates are often fixed initially, typically at existing levels, and future adjustments are allowed only in accordance with a predetermined formula ("price cap"), often linked to an aggregate measure of inflation with a productivity offset. Provisions for exogenous uncontrollable factors are included. This system of regulation substitutes price caps in place of RORR for a pre-arranged period of time, typically three to five years. Price caps are imposed on monopoly services in order to protect monopoly subscribers and in competitive markets where the company occupies a dominant market position. Prices not subject to the social contract, typically competitive services, are deregulated.

The typical social contract form of regulation consists not only of a price cap imposed on local rates, but may also include provisions for monitoring

503

customer service, quality, and network security. Frequently, there are capital spending strings attached, such as a commitment for network modernization or R&D spending levels. There are two fundamental principles governing the design of an appropriate price cap regime. The first principle is that the revenue cap should compensate the company for the real (inflation-adjusted) costs of producing its services. Any revenue cap that fails to cover real production costs would ensure the insolvency of the company. The compensation principle implies that the rate of change in the company's output price should increase based on input price inflation and decline with the rate of growth of overall economic productivity.

The second principle is that the revenue cap must be designed to provide the company with economic incentives to promote cost reduction and innovation. The definition of the price cap factor is important. The compensation principle would suggest that it is the company's own input price inflation and productivity that should govern the rate at which its prices change. But such a cap would essentially be a "cost plus" formula and would provide little incentive to company management. If the company's own factor inputs are entered into the pricing formula, there is no incentive to take the risks and incur the expenses required to raise its productivity since there is no payoff to the company. Nor would management be penalized for poor productivity performance, since slow productivity growth would simply translate into a smaller productivity adjustment and a faster rate of growth in its prices.

Therefore, in order to promote efficiency and provide proper incentives, the revenue cap must not only reflect the compensation principle, it must also incorporate incentive features explicitly. What is required is that the final revenue cap incorporate some kind of target indices for both input price inflation and productivity growth. In order for the mechanism to be preserved, the key feature of any target rate is that it must be unaffected by the company's own operating and investment decisions. If the company is able to generate productivity growth in excess of this target rate, or keep input price increases below the level set forth in the target, the output price growth allowed by the cap will exceed the pure compensation level. Given the features contained in most plans that provide for sharing between the company and ratepayers of earnings above a predetermined benchmark rate of return, these target growth rates provide an important incentive for efficient performance.

The price cap mechanism also imposes an important penalty for inefficient operation. If the company's costs increase by more than the target rate for whatever reason, the output price growth allowed by the cap will not cover the actual costs incurred by the company. This shortfall is a penalty for inefficient operation that the company has a strong incentive to avoid.

It is important to emphasize that the provision of incentives for efficiency requires both the use of targets for productivity and input price indices and some kind of profit-sharing mechanism. Neither alone is sufficient. Figure 21-8 illustrates the inadequacy of price caps when used in isolation for a telephone utility.

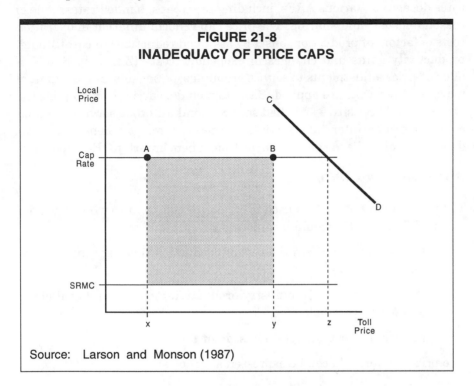

FIGURE 21-8
INADEQUACY OF PRICE CAPS

Source: Larson and Monson (1987)

Local rates are capped at a certain level, while business customer toll rates are bounded between X and Y; any price within the bounds is allowed. Line CD shows the combinations of prices required to produce a fair and reasonable rate of return. Business customer rates must be at least Z to fulfill investor requirements. Therefore, price caps must be developed with caution.

A variety of price cap models are in existence. Caps can be applicable to baskets of services or individual services, or even include a weighted average rate. Price cap ARFs can include profitability constraints, sharing mechanisms, and constraints on individual service rates so as to promote rate stability and/or preclude predatory pricing. Two milestone examples of comprehensive price cap regulation are the FCC's ratemaking procedures on interexchange carriers in the U.S. (Docket No. 89-624), and California's regulatory framework (Decision 89-10-031) for telcos. A price cap plan has been in operation for several years to regulate British Telecom, the so-called "RPI less 4.5%" formula as of 1994.

FCC Price Cap Plan

The FCC's comprehensive price cap framework serves as a useful case study to identify the issues and controversies in an ARF. The plan is illustrative because of its multi-dimensional nature. The plan incorporates dosages of various ARFs, including price caps, banded rates, zone of reasonableness, and sharing. The price cap reflects inflation in operation costs of factors of production, offset by assumed reductions in cost through productivity gains and changes in exogenous costs (Z-factor). Bands of allowed price adjustments to service groupings, or baskets, of +-5% annual movement per year are applied. Baskets include: carrier common line (no bands), traffic-sensitive switched services, and all other services (special access, corridor interstate services). A zone of reasonableness to limit departures of realized rate of returns from a benchmark ROE is specified.

Price Cap Index (PCI).

The price cap index formula used to measure the extent to which a carrier can modify its tariffs should incorporate several levers:

1. Effects of changes in the cost of production factors, that is, inflation.

2. Differences between industry productivity growth and that of the economy as a whole.

3. Exogenous cost changes adjustment factor.

The price cap formula can be expressed as follows:

$$GNPPI - X + [\pm\ Z] \qquad\qquad (21\text{-}1)$$

where $GNPPI$ = Gross National Product Price Index

X = Productivity offset

Z = Exogenous factor adjustment

The equation says that the output price of the company should change at the aggregate rate of output price inflation plus or minus an adjustment factor that represents the aggregate rate of productivity growth in the economy. To the extent that the productivity offset or X factor is positive, the plan ensures that the inflation-adjusted output prices for the company will decline over time at the rate given by the X factor.

As a proxy for the economy-wide input price inflation, the Gross National Product Deflator (GNPD) index is used. An alternative proxy is to use the

Consumer Price Index (CPI), although it is less representative of aggregate input factor inflation.

For the X productivity factor, a specific reasonable factor based on some historical aggregate index of productivity of the telecommunications industry over a full business cycle could be used. The X-Factor reflects changes in the unit cost of production due to total factor productivity growth in the industry, and is designed as a device to spur telcos to beat the index. The Z-factor captures exogenous changes in costs beyond management control such as tax rates, accounting rule changes, separation cost changes, and other decided ad hoc cost changes mandated by the regulator. In other words, the company is forgiven what it cannot control.

For example, with a productivity hurdle of 4% per year, GNPPI - X = GNPPI - 4%. In other words, the net of economy-wide price rise minus 4% target operating efficiencies is the allowed overall price increase. Telcos that are able to lower their costs by more than 4% per year earn more than the target rate, whereas telcos unable to lower costs by as much as 4% per year earn less than the target rate.

The FCC plan, as of 1994, offers two elective productivity targets: either a baseline productivity offset of 2.8% or 3.8%, each augmented with a consumer productivity dividend of 0.5%. Therefore, the productivity offset now is either 2.8% + 0.5% = 3.3% or 3.8% + 0.5% = 4.3% at the discretion of the carrier. A company is invited to gamble on the productivity offset. If you select the more stringent productivity target, a more liberal zone of allowed return is granted, as shown later.

To place proper perspective on the productivity factor of the order of 4%, recall from the mathematics of compound interest that 4% doubles in 17 years. One can speculate as to whether telephone carriers can cut costs in half in 17 years? What will be the source of the next generation of cost reductions after fiber technology and digital switching?

The key to the cap formula is that it provides an incentive mechanism to the company to economize on the use inputs and to promote productivity growth. If the company outperforms the national productivity growth average, the revenue cap is more than cost compensatory. Because of the profit sharing arrangement in place, the company and its employees can keep some of the additional revenues. The mechanism therefore provides the company with a positive incentive to generate productivity growth in excess of the target.

Zone of Reasonableness

The FCC adopted a zone of reasonableness with a baseline overall return (ROR) of 11.25% in 1993. The zones of allowed ROE varied, depending on the choice of productivity offset. The higher the productivity target selected, the higher the rate of return potential. The table below summarizes the bands of allowed return, coupled with the three levels of sharing allowed by the plan.

Productivity Offset Choice

	Election 1	Election 2
	3.3%	4.3%
No-Sharing Zone	11.25% - 12.25%	11.25%-13.25%
50-50 Sharing	12.25%-16.25%	13.25%-17.25%
100% Return	> 16.25%	> 17.25%

One noteworthy feature of the plan is that the safety net "Lower Adjustment Mark" is set at 10.25%, which is below the baseline ROR of 11.25%.

California's Price Cap Regime

In 1989, the California Commission sought alternatives to RORR that would motivate telephone utilities to: (1) cut costs and operate efficiently, (2) pursue greater product and service innovation, and (3) be more responsive to competitive market pressures, setting more economically efficient prices. As a result, the Commission adopted a regime of Price Cap regulation known as New Regulatory Framework (NRF).

The Commission's Decision 89-10-031 establishes a NRF for Pacific Bell and GTE of California (GTEC) that substitutes a Price Cap regulatory mechanism for traditional RORR, constrained by an earnings sharing mechanism. The latter is controlled by a market-based rate of return on overall capital in combination with a benchmark return level and additional return constraints.

Under the Commission's NRF, rates are set in accordance with a predetermined price cap formula linked to an exogenous aggregate measure of inflation (GNPPI) with an exogenous productivity offset (X) set at 4.5%. Provisions for exogenous uncontrollable factors (Z) are included. The price cap formula is similar to Equation 21-1.

A principal feature of the Commission's price cap formula is that it promotes efficiency and provides proper incentives because it is unaffected by the company's own operating and investment decisions. If the company is able to generate productivity growth in excess of the target rate, or keep input price (cost) increases below the level set forth in the target, the output price (service rate) growth allowed by the cap will exceed the company's own costs. Given the ability to earn a return set within a wide range, these target growth rates provide an important incentive for efficient performance.

As of 1994, the NRF also provided for a sharing mechanism, predicated on a market rate of return (MROR) of 11.5% and a benchmark rate of return (BROR) set at 150 basis points above MROR, that is, 13.0%. The company retains 100% of earnings between the MROR and the BROR and shares 50/50 of earnings above the BROR. Earnings in excess of a cap set at 500 basis points above MROR, that is, 16.5%, are returned to customers. The companies are unable to seek rate relief as long as the earned return exceeds a floor level set at 325 basis points below MROR, that is, 8.25%. Finally, the NRF plan contains a trigger mechanism for refiling market returns, linked to the yield on Treasury bonds. If the yield deviates 250 basis points from the level of 8.0% prevailing in 1989 (actually 7.99%), that is, if yields on long-term Treasury bonds fall outside a range of 5.5% to 10.5%, alterations to the return components may be sought.

Combining the various return components of the plan, the company can earn a return on total capital within a range of 8.25% to 14.75%. The latter figure is obtained by noting that returns above the BROR of 13.0% and the maximum level of 16.5% must be shared 50/50 with ratepayers, reducing the maximum achievable return from 16.5% to one-half of the difference between the cap and 13.0%.

It is important that the sharing mechanism be symmetrical in its apportionment of gains and losses between shareholders and ratepayers. If ratepayers are allowed to share gains in excess of the authorized range but not losses below the range, the effect on the plan's lack of symmetry on investor returns must be considered. One purpose of the 150 basis points return increment above the MROR in the NRF is to compensate investors for the limited upside returns/unlimited downside returns assymmetry relative to the symmetry in the returns of comparable risk industrials.

The role played by the rate of return in the Commission's NRF is minor. Whereas under traditional RORR, the rate of return plays a central role since rates are set so as to produce a fair and reasonable rate of return on the invested capital, the rate of return components under the NRF play a secondary role. There is no direct linkage between rates and return under NRF. The rate of return serves as a safety mechanism to protect ratepayers and investors from inadequate indices. This implies that double-precision accuracy in determining the various rate of return components of the NRF is unwarranted, and that far greater latitude and discretion are available in setting the return parameters of the plan.

Following the 1992 NRF review and a settlement agreement with GTE of California, sharing between the BROR and the ceiling ROR was eliminated as of January 1, 1994. The obvious implication of the elimination of sharing is that the determination of MROR and BROR becomes redundant, and therefore the settlement agreement does not provide for such returns. Should 50/50 sharing between the MROR and BROR be reimposed at a later date, or should a market-based and/or benchmark return be reinstituted, the agreement stipulates an assumed MROR of 10.5%.

Social Contract—Price Cap: Evaluation. On the positive side, price cap regulation avoids several direct costs of traditional RORR, since rate proceedings are only required to set initial rates for services. The plan allows for freedom to price and operate within the price caps, hence providing flexibility to reduce prices in response to competition. The plan provides large incentives to reduce costs and exceed the price cap parameters, because if the company outperforms the index through its efforts, innovation, or productivity gains, it retains the benefits. Incentives for over-capitalization essentially disappear because price caps break the direct linkage between the rate base and profitability. The incentive for cross-subsidization disappears as well, since the link between individual rates and profitability is severed.

More generally, price caps break any linkage between rates and company costs of service. For the ratepayer, price caps afford protection against market price changes and a possible reduction in real rates to the extent that the productivity parameter exceeds the price index parameter. Price caps also prevent rate shock and provides stability and predictability in rates. The plan also automatically polices cost allocations and eliminates the incentive to cross-subsidize competitive services by the utility services. If the company shifts costs from competitive services to monopoly services, any profits earned are reduced. Overall, price caps are better suited to an environment of emerging competition than is RORR.

Because a price cap plan is based on a productivity target that is invariant to the utility's own investment decisions, it removes the undesirable bias toward rate base padding that may be present in traditional RORR. Under the index approach, rate base considerations disappear, and only the company's shareholders would suffer from unwise business investment decisions and imprudent expenditures. If a sharing mechanism is present, the latter passes along to the ratepayers the benefit of extra profits realized from good decision-making and prudent expenditures. The use of a target productivity growth obviates the need for direct regulatory involvement in the micromanagement of the company's investment decisions.

On the negative side, price cap regulation always presents the risk of higher prices for regulated services if: (1) the rate adjustment index is inappropriate, and/or (2) a sharp decline in costs occurs through technological change. There is no assurance that shareholders will receive a fair return. The relationship between price caps and profit caps was discussed earlier. To guard agains the possibility of inadequate investor returns, a zone of reasonableness in authorized ROE can be established.

As shown below, benefits of price cap plans are tied to individual company circumstances. The risks of errant cost and productivity indices will vary from company to company. One fundamental difficulty inherent in any price cap regime is how to distinguish between productivity gains attributable to managerial effort versus exogenous uncontrollable factors. This is not an insurmountable obstacle, however.

In contrast to traditional RORR, any incentives from conscious use of regulatory lag are lost. Price caps may produce an incentive to reduce service quality in attempting to beat the inflation and productivity indices, although in a competitive environment, the incentive is to promote service quality rather than endanger it. Without the appropriate profitability constraints, the gains and losses may exceed an acceptable level. Price caps that govern aggregate prices may also result in inefficient pricing on individual services. The impact on risk and cost of capital may be significant, hinging on the degree of correlation between company-specific inflation and productivity data versus that of the macroeconomy.

It should also be pointed out that price cap regulation alone without a mechanism to rationalize rates will not necessarily produce adequate cost-based rates on monopolistic services as revenues are progressively squeezed by competition on competitive services. Any price cap regime would require inordinately high price caps in order to realign subsidized rates to offset competitive losses.

Price Cap Formula Risks

Price Cap ARFs carry their own set of risks, relative to traditional RORR. Major risk issues are associated with each component of the pricing formula. Moreover, the incidence of the plan's effects on utilities is uneven across companies. As discussed below, and as shown in Andrews (1992), the degree of conformity of individual company costs with the price cap index presents a source of risk. Moreover, the degree of conformity will vary from company to company.

One risk factor inherent in price cap regulation involves the relative input factor composition in the GNPPI index compared to the company's own input factor composition. For illustration, assume that there are two factors in the economy: labor and capital. Assume that labor cost and capital cost comprise 80% and 20% of GNP, respectively, while the corresponding factors for an individual telco are 60% and 40% of total cost.[7]

The lack of parallel between individual company cost and GNP cost data introduces risk. To illustrate, assume that for the economy as a whole capital cost increases 5% and labor cost is stable. Hence, GNPPI rises by 20% x 5% = 1% while company costs rise by 40% x 5% = 2%. Letting the symbol Δ denote change, the company's own experience differs from the macroeconomy by 1%:

$$\Delta \ GNPPI - \Delta \ company \ costs = 1\% - 2\% = -1\%$$

The effective result is a cost disallowance because of the failure to match the aggregate economy. The Price Cap Index will in effect disallow 1 of 2 percentage points increase in prices. Of course, the converse is also true. Thus, the lack of conformity with the GNP index introduces "index risk" so that year-to-year company profits become statistically more volatile.

A similar source of variance is introduced by the lack of concordance between company experience and inflation-productivity indexes with respect not only to factor composition but also to the skill content of labor, regional versus national labor rates (wages) ratio, and relative productivity gains.

Another source of individual company risk discussed earlier is that the effects of a zone of reasonableness band will vary greatly from company to company. Those companies with low Capital/Net Operating Income C/X ratios are more affected than companies with high C/X ratios for a given zone of reasonableness, and conversely.

Most Price Cap plans contain earnings sharing features. There are several possible variations in the sharing device involving the point at which sharing begins, the number of sharing steps bands, the size of steps, and the amount of the sharing.

---

[7] See Andrews (1992) for a full discussion of the risks inherent in index components.

In conclusion, there are many levers in a price cap regime, and many components of risk, including differentials in factor composition, C/X ratios, and leverage.

Other Forms of Incentive Regulation

Automatic Rate Adjustments: Overview. Under this style of regulation, an automatic adjustment factor is applied to individual cost components that are outside the control of management. This mode is prevalent in electric and gas utility ratemaking, particularly under inflationary conditions. Two examples are fuel adjustment clauses and demand-side management compensatory mechanims for electric utilities and purchased gas costs clauses for local gas distribution utilities.

Generic ROE benchmarks provide additional examples of automatic adjustment mechanisms. The Alabama Rate Stabilization and Equalization plan (RSE) discussed earlier is a noteworthy example.

Automatic Rate Adjustments: Evaluation. The major shortcoming of automatic adjustment mechanisms is that they are not incentive mechanisms per se, but rather tools that usually make it easier for utilities to earn the allowed rate of return.

Industry-wide generic ROE benchmarks whereby rates are adjusted whenever the earned ROE falls outside the allowed ROE band were discarded by both the Federal Energy Regulatory Commission and the Federal Communications Commision because of the inability of any one model or theory to quantify precisely a fair and reasonable rate of return applicable uniformly to all utilities in a given jurisdiction. In any event, generic ROE approaches fail to redress the fundamental limitations of RORR. Although an improvement over RORR in terms of administrative expediency, pricing flexibility, and cost minimization incentives are absent.

Focused Incentives: Overview. A plethora of reward/penalty regulatory programs directed at specific cost categories have been adopted by public utility commissions in several jurisdictions, and plans are under active consideration by several others. These focused incentive programs involve not only specific incentive plans but also a variety of general regulatory oversight activities, including management audits and prudency investigations.

The purpose of most incentive programs is to provide incentives for improved performance and cost reduction. Focused incentive programs are generally comprised of five elements:

1) program *objectives*

2) standards or *targets* used to measure performance

3) development of the *standard*

4) form of the incentive

5) how to *apply* the incentive

Examples of specific incentive program *objectives* include: (a) improving plant productivity or efficiency, (b) reducing operating and maintenance costs, (c) controlling construction costs, (d) reducing regulatory lag, frequency of rate cases, and length of hearing, (e) reducing administrative costs of rate cases, (f) limiting automatic rate adjustments, and (g) improving system reliability.

Examples of performance measures or *targets* include: (a) return on equity (ROE), (b) productivity improvement goals, (c) operating cost increases targets indexed to inflation, (d) construction cost estimates and/or schedule, and (e) aggregate cost of service.

Numerous bases for setting the *standard* are involved. For example, the regulator sets target ROE and formula computation using comparison with other utilities or using historical and projected data through formal hearings or informal consensus. Or, targets are negotiated with intervenors and approved by the regulator.

The incentives can take numerous *forms*. For example, reward/penalty, penalty avoidance only, reward/penalty applied to automatic adjustment, or reward only.

Focused incentive programs are *applied* in numerous modes. For example, charges are adjusted monthly (within limits) to maintain approved ROE; the company absorbs cost savings/overruns; the regulator may disallow some expenses; the ROE is adjusted within limits for cost savings/overruns; rates are adjusted automatically within limits to maintain ROE; the company and customers share cost savings; the regulator may reduce regulatory lag or disallow expenses; or the company receives accelerated cost recovery.

Focused Incentives: Evaluation. The advantage of focused incentive plans is that specific areas of concern are pinpointed that are indeed controllable by management and clear targets are enunciated. The disadvantage is that such plans potentially divert managerial attention from other areas that may be more important. Frequently, such plans create distorted incentives and aberrant managerial behavior. Nor do such plans address the pricing flexibility issue, which is vital in a vibrant competitive environment. Comprehensive company-wide formal incentive regulation plans discussed earlier are far more beneficial than are narrowly-focused incentive mechanisms.

Market-Basket/Yardstick: Overview.   Under market-basket regulation, the utility's overall profit constraint is determined by the profit rate of a sample (basket) of comparable companies. Although the overall aggregate profitability of all services is constrained, there is broad discretion on setting individual service prices and designing rate structure.

A close relative to market basket regulation is "yardstick" regulation, whereby the benchmark becomes the costs of comparable companies rather than their profitability. Rates are set to reflect the average costs of comparable utilities rather than its own costs. The approach simulates competition in that average cost converges to the least cost level and that utility costs are forced to the industry average, and eventually to the minimum cost level.

Market-Basket/Yardstick: Evaluation.   The key to implementing the market-basket approach is of course to define and identify a sample basket of comparable companies. The procedure is reminiscent of the Comparable Earnings approach used in determining a utility's cost of capital.

On the positive side, the approach avoids some of the direct costs of regulation. Rate proceedings are shorter and less complex, since there is no direct price regulation. It is more logical and less arbitrary than RORR. The approach provides ample pricing flexibility, since only aggregate profitability is constrained.

On the negative side, market-basket regulation creates almost as many problems as traditional RORR. It is difficult to find a sample of perfectly comparable firms. Another complication is the ability to distinguish imperfections in the market-basket of companies from imperfections in the return earned by the utility. The increased pricing flexibility inherent in the market-basket approach is not without danger. Only aggregate overall profitability is scrutinized, and not rates on individual services. Rates on certain classes of regulated service could be distorted.

To the extent that a utility has both regulated and unregulated services, the approach is problematic. Since the market-basket index reflects the aggregate performance of the company as a whole, and not the performance of the regulated component, it is difficult to determine if abnormal performance is attributable to unregulated or regulated activities.

The approach contains little incentive to minimize costs. It is difficult to distinguish if above-normal profits stem from excessive rates or from efficiency gains. If from low profits, a rate increase follows, therefore providing an incentive to inflate costs and/or shift costs from unregulated to regulated activities. Finally, the market-basket approach provides little incentive to innovate. In conclusion, market-basket regulation creates almost as many, if not more, problems than traditional RORR.

The chief difficulty with yardstick regulation is that only accounting costs are readily measurable and not economic costs. On the implementation side, the difficulties are prohibitive. The scarcity of homogenous companies with similar market structure, size, asset vintages, and growth patterns renders the approach unrealistic and inoperative.

Split Rate Base Approach: Overview. Under the Split Rate Base (SRB) framework, services are segregated into broad categories depending on the degree of competition prevailing in each category, for example, "competitive," "competitive-transitional," and "utility." Competitive services are deregulated, and competitive-transitional services are subject to expedited tariff approval processes in order to protect competitors and captive customers. For those remaining services requiring regulation, the traditional rate base-rate of return framework is retained. Revenue requirements for the utility segment are determined based on a forward test year using the midpoint in the allowed return range.

For the competitive segment, total flexibility in settting rates and earnings is allowed. Rate of return garantees disappear for both competitive and transitional services. Surpluses and/or shortfalls accrue to shareholders in a symmetrical fashion. Incentives to cross-subsidize the competitive segment with the utility segment are absent after rates are rationalized.

It does not require any radical departure from traditional RORR, since the utility component remains under rate of return-rate base regulation. An incentive mechanism can still be applied to the utility rate base with a ROE zone of reasonableness, although such an incentive is largely academic if service rates are not aligned with costs. Pricing flexibility is attained where it is most needed, that is, in the competitive services markets. Moreover, the SRB can serve as an interim solution until the pricing structure is rationalized.

The SRB approach requires a reliable cost separation system. In the absence of such a regime, the SRB approach is operationally prohibitive. The experience with the SRB is very limited because of the lack of reliable and rational costing data.

Split Rate Base Approach: Evaluation. The SRB approach does raise some additional issues. First, since the linkage between total invested capital and rate base assets is severed, the issue of an appropriate capital structure surfaces. This is really no different than status quo regulation, however, with its long history of dealing with the issue of an appropriate capital structure. Company management is still responsible to its shareholders and is still motivated to maximize stock price, and would therefore select an optimal capital structure consistent with its business risk and an investment grade bond rating.

Second, the approach leaves little incentive for efficiency in the utility segment, relative to the status quo. Granting a zone of reasonableness can provide valid incentives, however. Third, given the segregation of regulated and competitive assets, divisional cost of capital issues are raised, that is, the relative riskiness of the utility and competitive components. Those issues were addressed in Chapter 14.

21.4 Conclusions

It is important to point out that no uniform regulatory model universally applicable to all jurisdictions and to all regulated companies exists. There are advantages and shortcomings in each plan, and tradeoffs must be made. The optimal model for a given company depends on company circumstances and the degree of competition. Any regulatory plan must be adapted to the economic and regulatory context of the industry. The implementation details of various plans may differ across utilities to reflect their unique circumstances.

The dominant objectives of any incentive plan are to: (1) streamline the regulatory process, (2) reduce the size and complexity of rate cases, (3) provide utilities with institutionalized economic incentives to operate efficiently and promote productivity, (4) provide a fair and reasonable return for investors, (5) obtain a faster process and agility for new service introductions and changes to existing services, and maximum flexibility to design, price, and bundle competitive services, and at the same time, (6) provide a workable solution to the local access shortfall, including access to new revenue sources. In other words, the plan must provide tangible benefits to all parties involved, namely regulators, customers, and investors. To facilitate these objectives, the plan must be simple, implementable, use publicly available information, and must be fashioned to supply management with the required incentives to operate efficiently.

ARFs will typically enhance volatility. To illustrate, a typical ARF plan is associated with additional risks, over and beyond the normal business risks associated with the utility's business as usual operations. First, the downside risks related to potential losses resulting from the plan's implementation is often shifted to the shareholders. The plan results in an asymmetrical apportionment of benefits and losses. While the risks of potential losses are borne exclusively by shareholders due to an absence of any return floor and the presence of a limit on the allowable recovery of cost increases, the benefits of added efficiencies and productivity gains achieved over and above the benchmark return are shared equally by ratepayers and shareholders.

Second, because the benchmark return remains in force for a preassigned period, say three to five years, and is typically not subject to review at a time when capital markets are volatile, the company's risks are clearly increased. Third, the impetus of technological change is accelerating the speed at which monopolistic services ("core services") are becoming competitive services ("non-core") in the period covered by the plan. Fourth, the added capital costs over and beyond existing construction plans required by most plans' service modernization requirements impose added financial burdens and risks.

Given these other risk elements, an extra risk premium must be added to the business-as-usual return on equity to compensate for the added risks typically inherent in the ARF. The magnitude of the risk increment is based on the particular risk-enhancing (risk-reduction) features of the plan and on informed judgment. The historical fluctuations in monthly equity costs must be considered in arriving at an appropriate risk premium. The impact of the ARF plan's risks on the company's beta must be considered. It is not unreasonable to assume a beta increase of the order of 0.05 to 0.15 for most plans. The lack of symmetry on investor returns of most plans must be considered, that is, the risk premium must be sufficient to compensate investors for the limited upside returns/unlimited downside returns assymmetry versus comparable risk companies. Assuming some plausible probability distribution of investor equity returns both with and without the ARF plan, an added return premium, 0.50% to 1.00% as a broad order of magnitude, is required to offset a plan's lack of upside potential and to produce the average return that would prevail under orthodox regulation.

Finally, it is worthwhile speculating whether rate of return and cost of capital issues can ever be supplanted altogether by an ARF. Even under a pure price cap regime, which represents the most draconian departure from traditional RORR, the spectre of rate of return remains. This is because the validity of the parameters in a price cap plan can only be assessed by reference to some rate of return benchmark.

References

Andrews, V.L. "Evaluating Financial Repercussions of the FCC's Proposed Price Cap Regulation of Local Exchange Telephone Companies," Center for the Study of Regulated Industry, Reprint No. 4, Georgia State University, 1992.

Brigham, E.F. and Aberwald, D.A. "Recommendations for Setting a Utility's Fair Rate of Return." Public Utility Research Center Working Paper 14-88, University of Florida, 1988.

Canadian Association of Petroleum Producers, "Revitalizing Oil and Gas Pipeline Regulation," Submission to the National Energy Board, Incentive Regulation, Alberta, Canada, 1992.

Larson, A.C. and Monson, C.S. "Public Policy Recommendations for the Flexible Pricing of Telecommunications Services." Revenues and Public Affairs Dept., Southwestern Bell, St. Louis, Missouri, 1987.

Morin, R.A. and Andrews, V. L. *Alternative Regulatory Frameworks,* Public Utilities Reports Inc. and The Management Exchange Inc., Washington DC, 1993.

Morin, R.A. Mississippi Power Company, Prepared Testimony, Mississippi Public Service Commission, Docket No. 93-UA-0302, 1993.

Sikes, A.C. *NTIA Regulatory Alternatives Report,* NTIA Report 87-222. U.S. Department of Commerce. Washington, DC: U.S. Government Printing Office, 1987.

Additional References

Bhattacharyya, S.K. and Laughhunn, D.J. "Price Cap Regulation: Can We Learn From the British Telecom Experience?" *Public Utilities Fortnightly,* Oct. 15, 1987, 22-29.

FREQUENTLY USED EQUATIONS AND FORMULAS

Weighted Average of Capital (overall Return)

$$K = K_d\, D/C + K_e E/C$$

Risk Premium

$$K = R_F + RP$$

Book Return on Equity

$$r = [R + (R - i)\, D/E]\, (1 - T)$$

Holding Period Return

$$R_{it} = \frac{D_t + (P_t - P_{t-1})}{P_t}$$

Market Model

$$R_{it} = \alpha_i + \beta_i R_{Mt} = \varepsilon_{it}$$

Present Value of a Future Sum

$$PV = \frac{f}{(1 + I)^n} = F(1 + i)^{-n}$$

One Year Holding Period Return

$$K_e = D_1/P_0 + (P_1 - P_0)/P_0$$

General Common Stock Valuation Formula

$$P_0 = \sum_{t=1}^{n} \frac{D_t}{(1 + K)^t}$$

Constant Growth Stock Valuation Formula

$$P_0 = \frac{D_1}{K-g}$$

Standard Dcf Model

$$K = D_1/P_0 + g$$

Annual Dcf Model with External Financing

$$K = D_1/P + br + sv$$

Quarterly Dcf Model

$$K = \frac{[D_1(1+k)^{3/4} + D_2(1+K)^{1/2} + D_3(1+K)^{1/4} + D_4]}{P_0} = g$$

Retention Ratio Growth Formula

$$g = br$$

CAPM Model

$$K = R_F + \beta(R_M - R_F)$$

Levered Beta

$$\beta_L = \beta_U[1 = (1-t)\, D/E\,]$$

Arbitrage Pricing Model

$$E(R) = R_F + \beta_1[F_1 - R_F] + \beta_2[F_2 - R_F]$$

Levered Cost of Equity

$$K_e = \rho + (\rho - i)(1-T)\, D/E$$

Weighted Average Cost of Capital

$$K = \rho(1 - T\,D/C)$$

Tax Gain From Debt Financing

$$G = 1 - \frac{(1-T_c)\,(1-T_{ps})}{(1-T_{pb})}$$

INDEX

Accounting beta 75, 361
  earnings beta 361, 364
  fundamental 77, 363
  regression beta 362
Accounting return, *see* Rate of return on equity
Agency costs 423
Allowance for funds used during construction (AFUDC) 79, 83, 241
Allowed rate of return 10
  and cost of capital 23
  on equity 132
  standards 101
Alternative regulatory frameworks 483, 486, 489, 496, 513, 517
Analysts' Forecasts 121
  and historical growth 140, 155
  IBES 61, 134, 146, 155, 205
  of growth rates 153, 205, 209, 217, 218, 221
  Zacks 146, 156
Arbitrage pricing Model (APM) 13, 17, 238, 375
  and utility cost of capital 385
  assumptions 377
  concept 375
  empirical evidence 383
  spanning portfolios 386
  vs CAPM 338, 381, 384, 390
Arithmetic mean 275, 298
Asymmetry, *see* Skewness
Asymmetric information 424, 499

Banded rates 496, 500
Beta
  accounting beta 75, 311, 361
  adjusted beta 67, 68

and capital structure 348
and the CAPM 305, 310, 319, 321, 334
as a measure of risk 45, 52, 63, 71, 283, 302, 337, 349
bias 70
determinants 364, 367, 370
earnings beta 73, 361, 364
estimates 65
fundamental beta 77, 311, 363
historical v. true 69
levered 349
market risk 51
measurement 65
pure-play 74, 348, 351, 361
raw v. adjusted beta 67
regression beta 362
stability 58, 69
thin trading, and 72
unlevered beta 349, 351
Bluefield Water Works v. Public Service Commission of West Virginia 9, 33, 201, 240, 243
Bonds, *see* Debt
Bond rating 80, 82, 226, 332, 414, 463
  optimal 11, 458, 469
Book return, *see* Rate of return on equity
Book value weights v. market value weights 411
British Columbia Electric Railway v. PUC of British Columbia 12
Business Risk 36
  short-term v. long-term 38, 273

Call option, *see* Option